Test Anxiety
The State of the Art

PERSPECTIVES ON INDIVIDUAL DIFFERENCES

CECIL R. REYNOLDS, *Texas A&M University, College Station*
ROBERT T. BROWN, *University of North Carolina, Wilmington*

A Continuation Order Plan is available for this series. A continuation order will bring delivery of each new volume immediately upon publication. Volumes are billed only upon actual shipment. For further information please contact the publisher.

Test Anxiety
The State of the Art

Moshe Zeidner

University of Haifa
Mount Carmel, Israel

Plenum Press • New York and London

Library of Congress Cataloging-in-Publication Data

Zeidner, Moshe.
    Test anxiety : the state of the art / Moshe Zeidner.
        p.   cm. -- (Perspectives on individual differences)
    Includes bibliographical references (p.) and index.
    ISBN 0-306-45729-6
    1. Test anxiety.   2. Stress (Psychology)   3. Test anxiety-
  -Treatment.   4. Test anxiety--Research.   I. Title.   II. Series.
  LB3060.6.Z45 1998
  371.26'01'9--dc21   98-17095
                                                            CIP

ISBN 0-306-45729-6

© 1998 Plenum Press, New York
A Division of Plenum Publishing Corporation
233 Spring Street, New York, N.Y. 10013

http://www.plenum.com

10 9 8 7 6 5 4 3 2 1

Printed in the United States of America

To my dear parents
ARON and REGINA ZEIDNER

and to my close friend and relative
YOSEF AMI

Foreword

Examination stress and test anxiety are pervasive problems in modern society. As the information age continues to evolve, test scores will become even more important than they are today in evaluating applicants for demanding jobs and candidates for admission into highly competitive educational programs. Because test anxiety generally causes decrements in performance and undermines academic achievement, the development of effective therapeutic interventions for reducing its adverse effects will continue to be an important priority for counselors, psychologists, and educators. Alleviating test anxiety will also serve to counteract the diminished access to educational and occupational opportunities that is frequently experienced by test-anxious individuals.

As its title promises, this volume provides a state-of-the-art evaluation of the nature, antecedents, correlates, and consequences of examination stress and test anxiety. Professor Zeidner's cogent and comprehensive analysis of the affective, cognitive, somatic, and behavioral manifestations of test anxiety are grounded in the extensive knowledge he has gained from his own research on the assessment and treatment of test anxiety. This work has also benefitted from the author's long-standing and productive collaboration with leading contributors to test anxiety theory and research, and his active participation in national and international conferences devoted to understanding test anxiety, including those convened by the Society for Test Anxiety Research (STAR).

Recognizing the conceptual complexity of test anxiety as a psychological construct, Zeidner reviews the historical evolution of this construct over the past 50 years, its relation to state and trait anxiety and situational stress, and the critical role of cognitive processes in mediating the effects of examination stress on test performance and achievement. He also recognizes and clearly articulates the importance of distinguishing among the affective, cognitive/worry, and somatic manifestations of anxiety experienced during examinations, and individual differences in the disposition to experience test anxiety as a situation-specific personality trait. Within the context of Lazarus' theory of stress as a transactional process, Zeidner examines and evaluates the environmental antecedents and the impact of personal experiences that contribute to the development of individual differences in test anxiety as a situation-specific trait, and how this trait influences the perception, cognitive appraisal, and emotional reaction to examination stress. The critical role of the perception of threat, the continuing influence of cognitive appraisal and reappraisal, and the importance of test-taking attitudes and methods of coping provide the fundamental elements for a comprehensive theory of test anxiety and its treatment.

The many facets of test anxiety, which are presented in this book in the context of a broad conceptual framework, facilitate an understanding of the basic theoretical and methodological issues that have influenced theory and research on the nature, assessment, and treatment of test anxiety. Detailed information is provided on the construction and validation of measures of test anxiety, the impact of age, gender, and sociocultural factors on test anxiety scores, and the relationship of test anxiety to other motivational and personality constructs. Evidence for the effectiveness of the various cognitive, behavioral, and skills-training programs that have been employed in the treatment of test anxiety is also reviewed, and the major conceptual and methodological issues encountered in intervention studies are carefully considered. The chapters on strategies for coping with examination stress and test anxiety are especially informative.

In summary, this volume makes an invaluable contribution to understanding the nature, assessment, and treatment of test anxiety, and the fundamental theoretical issues and methodological problems that are encountered in this domain of research. Zeidner's consideration of the broad conceptual framework within which test anxiety theory and research has evolved, along with the comprehensive coverage of every facet of this field, serve to enhance the contributions of this volume to psychological science and professional practice. Scholars and researchers concerned with the antecedents, correlates, and consequences of examination stress and test anxiety, and counselors and psychologists involved in interventions that endeavor to alleviate the adverse affects of test anxiety, will find its contents to be extremely helpful in their work.

CHARLES D. SPIELBERGER, PH.D.

Distinguished University Research Professor of Psychology
University of South Florida
Tampa, Florida

Preface

Test anxiety has emerged as one of the most salient constructs in modern-day psychology and by far the most widely studied specific form of anxiety in the literature. Test anxiety is a ubiquitous phenomenon, with some degree of evaluative anxiety being experienced by most people in modern society. The test anxiety construct has matured within a large cocoon of attention ever since its inception in the early 1950s, with researchers making important strides toward understanding its nature, components, origins, determinants, effects, and treatments.

The importance of test anxiety in understanding sources of student stress in evaluative situations and poor test performance is now readily apparent. The topic of test anxiety has prospered, in part, due to the increasing personal importance of test situations for people in modern society, making tests and their long-term consequences significant educational, social, and clinical problems for many. Since test results in most academic and occupational settings have important practical implications for a person's goals and future career, test anxiety is frequently reported to be a meaningful factor impacting upon test scores. In fact, much of the test anxiety research over the past half century has been motivated by the desire to ameliorate the debilitating levels of test anxiety in various settings and populations and to find ways of helping test-anxious persons become more effective in test or testlike situations.

Over the past few decades there has been an upsurge of interest in test anxiety research among psychological and educational researchers. Literally hundreds of researchers have investigated the nature, antecedents, correlates, and consequences of test anxiety, and the literature is prodigious. A wealth of studies relating to various facets of test anxiety has appeared in some of the premiere journals in psychology and education. Test anxiety has become a major topic of research interest in education and various subareas of psychology, including personality and social psychology, educational and developmental psychology, cognitive psychology, health psychology, and counseling and clinical psychology.

The book aims at reflecting the current state of the field of test anxiety and is intended to provide the foundations of knowledge, research, assessment methods, and clinical guidelines upon which more comprehensive understanding can be developed. In view of the burgeoning interest and massive research on various aspects of test anxiety, and the progress achieved by researchers in understanding its nature, components, determinants, and consequences, the time seems ripe for summarizing and assimilating this vast body of literature and integrating it in a well-articulated stress-theoretic framework. Given the upsurge of interest in the topic, the need for a comprehensive text on test anxiety has long been felt by experts in the field. This research-based textbook aims at filling a gap in the literature by providing an up-to-date and comprehensive review and integration of what we know about the major critical facets of test anxiety, including theory, research, assessment, individual differences, and applications. The theoretical and empirical body of research presented in this book is grounded in the work of scores of test anxiety researchers across the globe, and also incorporates and highlights a good number of recent studies on various dimensions of test anxiety conducted by this author.

Structure of the Book and Conceptual Framework

The basic paradigm employed in structuring the material presented herein is based on the assumption that one can most usefully think of test anxiety in terms of its antecedents, phenomenology, concomitants, consequences, and clinical parameters. The organization of the material reflects recent advances in the conceptual, methodological, and empirical research in these areas. This book is divided into six broad but overlapping sections.

Part I surveys *basic and conceptual issues*. Chapter 1 presents a brief historical and conceptual overview of the test anxiety domain of research. Chapter 2 discusses the major cognitive, affective, somatic, and behavioral components of the test anxiety construct. Chapter 3 surveys key perspectives and models of test anxiety.

Part II focuses on key *methodological issues*. Chapter 4 surveys basic research and assessment issues. Chapter 5 walks the reader through the different stages of developing self-report measures of test anxiety.

Part III delineates the *origins, sources, and determinants* of test anxiety, discussing both personal and environmental determinants of test anxiety. Chapter 6 assesses the more distal, yet crucial, developmental antecedents of test anxiety, including constitutional, family, school, and experiential factors. Chapter 7 looks at some more proximal contextual determinants of anxiety reactions in evaluative situations, including both test-related and contextual factors. Chapter 8 assesses a number of personal factors shaping the test anxiety experience, including cognitive structures and processes, self-related cognitions, and belief systems.

Part IV looks at the effects and *consequences of test anxiety for academic performance and achievement*, seeking to assess the complex nature of the test anxiety–performance relationship. Chapter 9 discusses major concepts and issues bearing on the anxiety–performance interface and surveys the evidence for main and interactive effects. Chapter 10 attempts to pinpoint the impact of test anxiety on key phases of the information processing system.

Part V examines the evidence for *individual differences* in test anxiety. Chapter 11 looks at age, gender, sociocultural, and national differences in test anxiety. Chapter 12 maps out the complex pattern of relationships among individual differences in test anxiety and key motivational and personality variables.

Part VI focuses on *coping, interventions, and clinical parameters*. Chapter 13 discusses adaptive and maladaptive strategies in coping with test anxiety. Chapter 14 suggests some optimizing procedures in the test situation to alleviate test anxiety and enhance the performance of test-anxious subjects. Chapters 15 and 16, respectively, present a number of emotion-focused (behavioral) and cognitive-focused interventions aimed at helping examinees cope more efficiently with test situations.

The Epilogue concludes this treatment of test anxiety by pointing to some needed directions for future research.

This book should be of interest to professionals, upper-level undergraduate and graduate students in psychology and education, and students and professionals in the various behavioral, social, and health sciences, especially those who have a serious interest in the study of stress, anxiety, coping, and individual-differences research. It should be suitable for seminars and graduate courses focusing on personality theory and research, stress and adaptation, individual differences, and clinical, counseling, consulting, and developmental psychology. The book may also be useful as a reference work for general readers who wish to gain familiarity with the current status of test anxiety research and applications. Practitioners (psychologists, psychiatrists, counselors, school administrators, and teachers) may find some useful information on etiology, symptomatology, and intervention with respect to test anxiety.

In spite of the tremendous interest and productivity in the area of test anxiety research, a comprehensive, integrative, and widely accepted theory of test anxiety has failed to emerge. Unfortunately, there is currently no general theoretical framework that allows us to integrate the multiple facets of test anxiety and their interrelationships. Thus, I will draw upon several theoretical models in discussing the various issues of phenomenology, antecedents, consequences, and treatment. My penchant is clearly for the type of dynamic perspective offered by transactional cognitive models of stress as discussed in Chapters 1 and 3. Although I have been eclectic in my use of conceptual models and paradigms, I have attempted to examine the material presented, whenever applicable, within the framework of this stress-theoretic dynamic perspective.

The sheer volume of research on test anxiety makes it virtually impossible to survey and do justice to all the significant facets of the construct. Thus, the coverage of various aspects was limited by the space constraints of a one-volume book. There is some overlap among chapters. However, this allows each chapter to stand on its own, and increases the accessibility of each one.

My thanks and appreciation to my family for coping with me over the extended period during which this book was written. I am also grateful to a number of colleagues and friends for their support. I wish to thank Prof. Charles Spielberger, of the University of South Florida, for first kindling my interest in test anxiety research during our talks at the various meetings of the Society for Test Anxiety Research (STAR) and for graciously agreeing to write the Foreword to this book. My thanks go to two dear friends and colleagues, Prof. Norman S. Endler, of York University, and Prof. Ralf Schwarzer, of the Free University of Berlin, who have continuously taken a genuine personal interest in my work in this area and have been exceptionally supportive in many ways over the years. Thanks are due to the following individuals for reading and commenting on earlier versions of various parts of this book's manuscript: Charles S. Carver, University of Miami; Norman S. Endler, York University; Gordon Flett, York University; Heinz Krohne, University of Mainz; Willy Lens, University of Leuven; Gerald Matthews, University of Dundee; Robert Most, Mind Garden; Sharona Meital, University of Haifa; Baruch Nevo, University of Haifa; Jim Parker, Trent University; Paul Pintrich, University of Michigan; Donald Saklofske, University of Saskatchewan; Ralf Schwarzer, Free University of Berlin; and David Share, University of Haifa. I also express my appreciation to Robert Calfee, Stanford University; Steven Hobfoll, Kent State; Bill McKeachie, University of Michigan; and Gabi Salomon, University of Haifa, for their support of my work in this field. Nili Bloch, Idit Dar, Tali Abraham, and Dani Karp provided invaluable technical assistance at various stages of preparing this book. Eliot Werner at Plenum Press has been most supportive, patient, and helpful in all phases required to bring this project to closure. The University of Haifa and the Department of Experimental Psychology, Oxford University, provided congenial academic environments and physical resources necessary to undertake and complete this book. This has been a challenging, thought-provoking, and rewarding experience, and I hope readers will find it to be the same. I hope this volume will help better integrate current test anxiety theory, research, and interventions. I will be rewarded if this book advances our understanding of test anxiety and assists us in enhancing examinees' adaptive coping with evaluative stress.

MOSHE ZEIDNER

Haifa, Israel

Contents

Chapter 3 Models and Theoretical Perspectives 61

II. METHODOLOGY: RESEARCH AND ASSESSMENT METHODS

Chapter 4 Current and Recurrent Issues in Conducting Experimental Test Anxiety Research 95

III. ORIGINS, SOURCES, AND DETERMINANTS OF TEST ANXIETY

IV. CONSEQUENCES OF TEST ANXIETY FOR COGNITIVE PERFORMANCE

VI. COPING, INTERVENTIONS, AND CLINICAL PARAMETERS

Chapter 13   Coping with Test Situations: Resources, Strategies, and Adaptational Outcomes

I

Basic and Conceptual Issues

An Introduction to the Domain
of Test Anxiety

Overview

The second part of the 20th century has been variously designated as the "age of stress," "age of anxiety," or more recently, "age of coping" (Endler, 1996). While stress, anxiety, and coping are universal human experiences, intrinsic to the human condition, the nature of the specific environmental stimuli evoking stress and anxiety emotions has changed remarkably over the years. Whereas in ancient times it may have been wild beasts, natural catastrophes, and the like that served as major sources of apprehension and anxiety, in our modern technological and achievement-oriented society stress and anxiety are evoked largely by social-evaluative and ambiguous environmental situations.

This introductory chapter presents a brief conceptual and historical overview of the domain of test anxiety. I begin by discussing test anxiety as an increasingly pervasive and prevalent phenomenon in modern society, listing the reasons for the upsurge of public and professional interest in the construct over the past half century. I then present a brief historical overview of test anxiety research and zoom in on current conceptions of stress, anxiety, and the test anxiety construct. A number of major conceptual distinctions and differentiations are discussed, with particular focus on the key elements in the test anxiety process.

The Pervasiveness and Prevalence of Test Anxiety in Modern Society

The Widespread Interest in Test Anxiety

Tests and evaluative situations, in particular, have emerged as one potent class of anxiety-evoking stimuli in our society, which bases many important decisions relating to an individual's status in school, college, and work on tests and other assessment devices. In fact, contemporary society is best described as test-oriented and test-consuming (Zeidner & Most, 1992). As one expert put it, "We live in a test-conscious, test-giving culture in which the lives of people are in part determined by their test performance" (S. B. Sarason, 1959, p. 26). Testing is widely used in education and by the industrial, government, and military sectors to help make decisions about people. It is almost impossible to grow up in modern society without encountering some type of test, whether a classroom test in language or math or science, a standardized aptitude or achievement test, a military placement or mechanical aptitude test, a scholastic aptitude test for college application, or an industrial occupational placement test. Test and other assessment data may provide objective and reliable information that directly affects the choices made in the process of vocational guidance and counseling, selection, classification and placement, and screening and diagnosis—all of which help shape an individual's upbringing, school, and career. When one considers the many uses of tests in our culture, and the ways in which they can determine the lives of people who take them, it comes as no surprise that the testing situation may evoke anxiety reactions in many individuals. Very early in life, many children in our culture become test-oriented and test-anxious.

Test anxiety figures prominently in the literature as one of the key villains in the ongoing drama surrounding psychoeducational testing (Zeidner, 1990). Thus, test anxiety is frequently cited among the factors at play in determining a wide array of unfavorable outcomes and contingencies, including poor cognitive performance, scholastic underachievement, and psychological distress and ill health (Gaudry & Spielberger, 1971; Hembree, 1988; Powers, 1986; Zeidner, 1990). Indeed, many students have the ability to do well on exams, but perform poorly because of their debilitating levels of anxiety. Consequently, test anxiety may limit educational or vocational development, as test scores and grades influence entrance to many educational or vocational training programs in modern society.

It is difficult indeed to communicate the pain, suffering, and misery suffered by high-test-anxious subjects before, during, and after major evaluative experiences. The effects of test anxiety may not be noticed by some students until their mind goes blank when encountering a challenging objective test problem or until they freeze up on an important oral exam (Emery & Krumboltz, 1967). Test-anxious students tend to be easily distracted on an exam, experience difficulty in comprehending relatively simple instructions, and also have difficulty organizing or recalling relevant information during the test. High-test-anxious students express concern about the consequences of not performing at a satisfactory level on major exams and embarrassment at probable failure (I. G. Sarason & Sarason, 1990). Also, test-anxious college students, relative to their low-test-anxious counterparts, report suffering from poor mental health and psychosomatic symptoms (Depreeuw & DeNeve, 1992). The foregoing bleak picture is all too representative of the experiences of many test-anxious subjects.

The stresses of academic life are likely to have serious effects upon students who have developed pronounced tendencies to respond to threatening situations with anxiety. Indeed, test anxiety results in crucial real-life consequences for many examinees. The loss to society of the full contribution of potentially capable students through anxiety-related underachievement and/or academic failure constitutes an important mental health problem in education. A number of studies provide concrete illustrations of the toll anxiety takes on student performance and well-being. Hill and Sarason (1966) compared the performance of the 10% most anxious with that of the 10% least anxious elementary school children in one research data base. High-test-anxious students were over 1 year behind national norms in reading and mathematics basic skills performance, whereas the low-test-anxious students were 1 year ahead, with little overlap in achievement test performance observed in these two groups. Furthermore, compared to their low-test-anxious counterparts, high-test-anxious children received lower report card grades and were twice as likely not to be promoted. Another illustration is provided by Spielberger (1966b), who followed up high-trait-anxious students in college for three consecutive years. He found that more than 20% of the high-anxiety students were classified as academic failures, consequently dropping out of college, as compared to fewer than 6% of the low-anxiety students. The importance of test anxiety as a key construct in understanding sources of examinee distress, impaired test performance in evaluative situations, and academic underachievement is now readily apparent. This situation demands that test anxiety be better understood and appropriately dealt with.

In addition to taking its toll in human suffering and impaired test performance, test anxiety may also jeopardize assessment validity in the cognitive domain and constitute a major source of "test bias" (Zeidner, 1990). Thus, affective characteristics such as test anxiety are among the sources of construct-irrelevant variance introducing systematic differences in individual characteristics that affect cognitive test performance, other than the ability or achievement tested. To the extent that anxiety affects performance in some substantial way, some examinees will perform less well than their ability/achievement would otherwise allow. Although the presence of severe anxiety during testing may be recognized in an examinee, the effect cannot be overcome by statistical adjustments. Thus, the measurement of any particular ability or proficiency will be confounded with anxiety (Rocklin & Thompson, 1985).

Concomitant with the increased public concern with evaluative stress and test anxiety, test anxiety research has flourished in recent years. The current widespread interest in helping student populations at all age levels achieve academic excellence, as assessed through high standards of academic and standardized test achievement, has further heightened public concern for reducing test anxiety, or at least its debilitating effects. Furthermore, reducing the effects of anxiety on performance is viewed as one possible avenue to improving the test performance of underachieving examinees. Indeed, much of test anxiety research over the past half century has been conducted to help shed light on the aversive effects of test anxiety on examinee performance, and these concerns have stimulated the development of a variety of therapeutic techniques and intervention programs (see chapters in Spielberger & Vagg, 1995b).

I. G. Sarason (1980a) points out several reasons why interest in test anxiety as a psychological construct has prospered and has persisted over the years. For one, evaluative stress situations are valuable for psychological researchers because they provide a path to the study of stress and a way of understanding how people cope with stress. Thus, test anxiety has been demonstrated to be a convenient vehicle for investigating a wide variety of general problems in the area of stress, anxiety, and coping because it provides a common and easily researched measure of the personal salience of one definable class of situations—one in which people are evaluated. Test anxiety has also proven to be a fruitful and promising area of research for those researchers, clinicians, and educators interested in performance-related emotions and anxieties and how they impact upon individuals' emotional well-being and cognitive performance. Researching stress, anxiety, and coping in evaluative situations is scientifically very convenient in that test situations are experienced by practically everyone in modern societies and their universality makes them significant educational, social, and clinical problems. In addition, research on test anxiety has prospered because testing situations have high salience and face validity for people.

Prevalence of Test Anxiety

According to Hill and Wigfield (1984), the spiraling increase in the usage of test scores to evaluate educational attainments and programs, coupled with greater public pressures for higher levels of school learning and academic achievement, has helped create a more pressure-laden atmosphere in the school and university system. As the consequences and stakes of test performance assume a more important role in school and society, such as determining whether a student is promoted to the next grade, eventually receives a high school diploma, or is admitted to a top university or graduate school, students would be expected to experience greater concern and anxiety about evaluative events. How prevalent, in fact, is test anxiety in modern society?

Partly on account of definitional and methodological problems, data on the prevalence and incidence of test anxiety are surprisingly sparse (King & Ollendick, 1989). Based on a number of estimates of the prevalence rates of test anxiety in school- and college-age populations the phenomenon appears to be reasonably widespread. Hill (1984) projected that two or three children in a typical classroom are highly anxious, with as many as a total of 10 million elementary and secondary school students in the United States performing poorer on tests than they should because anxiety and deficiencies in test-taking strategies impair their performance. Hill (1984) estimated that anywhere from 25% to about 30% of American students suffer the effects of debilitating stress in evaluative situations. This would result in a sizable systematic error in measurement for a good number of students. Furthermore, a study of 1684 Canadian elementary and high school students indicated that in excess of 22% of students were significantly worried about schoolwork and this was the most prevalent stressor by grade 12 (McGuire, Mitic, & Neumann, 1987).

It stands to reason that in an age of ever-increasing technological development, in which specializations and advanced training have become of prime importance for occupational status and success, the specter of academic failures and concerns regarding academic performance are among the most common sources of stress for college students. Indeed, test anxiety appears to be pervasive in college populations (Spielberger, Anton, & Bedell, 1976). Thus, researchers have estimated test anxiety prevalence rates of anywhere between 15% (Hill & Wigfield, 1984) and 20% (H. J. Eysenck & Rachman, 1965) for college student populations. However, it is noted that most studies have attempted to extrapolate prevalence rates from incidental samples that may or may not be representative of their target populations. Large-scale epidemiological surveys of test anxiety in various age groups are lacking and are urgently needed.

Brief Historical Overview of Test Anxiety Research

In this section I briefly survey some of the historical landmarks of test anxiety research. Due to space restrictions I gloss over contributions of a number of early investigators, e.g., Charles Darwin and Sigmund Freud, whose seminal work helped establish anxiety as a subject of scientific study. The following six periods may be distinguished in the relatively brief history of test anxiety research.

Early Studies of Examination Stress and Anxiety: 1900–1950

The attention of early studies of evaluative stress, conducted several decades before the official initiation of test anxiety research in the early 1950s, called attention to the physiological and biochemical changes that accompanied the emotional reactions experienced by examinees during examinations (Spielberger, Gonzalez, Taylor, Algaze, & Anton, 1978). In these studies, test anxiety was basically inferred from physiological reactions that examinees experienced during ego-threatening exams administered under evaluative conditions. Test anxiety was implicitly viewed as equivalent to the physiological arousal associated with the activation of the autonomic nervous system (Spielberger & Vagg, 1995a).

At the beginning of this century, Folin, Demis, and Smillie (1914; as cited by Spielberger & Vagg, 1995a) published what appears to be the first empirical investigation of test anxiety. They observed that approximately 18% of a group of medical students taking an important exam showed evidence of glycosuria (i.e., sugar in the urine) when assessed immediately after the exam; none of these medical students, however, showed any trace of sugar in their urine prior to the exam. Similar findings were reported by the noted physiologist Water B. Cannon (1929) in his early studies of homeostasis and "fight–flight" reactions. Cannon reported that four of nine students passed sugar in their urine after a difficult exam. No evidence of sugar in the urine was found in any of these students prior to the exam. In addition, the noted Russian physiologist Alexander Luria (1932) investigated individual differences among "stable" and "unstable" medical students in expressions of anxiety in test situations.

Just prior to World Word II, a number of American researchers became increasingly concerned with understanding the nature of anxiety surrounding examination situations and how to ameliorate it. In a series of studies of evaluative stress published by C. H. Brown (1938a, 1938b) and his colleagues at the University of Chicago in the 1930s, they called attention to the seriousness of the problem of test anxiety for college students. The suicides of two students at the University of Chicago were attributed to exaggerated concern over approaching exams, which students took in a "deadly" serious manner. The Chicago group developed and validated the first psychometric scale for identifying high-risk test-anxious students.

In the 1930s, psychoanalytic writers in Germany (e.g., Stengel, 1936) were among the first scholars to pay attention to the topic of achievement-related anxiety. Test anxiety was conceptualized in psychoanalytic terms and attributed by these German investigators to traumatic childhood experiences. In passing, I note that the term "anxiety," derived from the Latin *angere* (to strangle), was used to translate Freud's *Angst*. With the publication in America of Freud's (1936) work *The problem of anxiety*, professional interest in anxiety spiraled upward (Phillips, Martin, & Meyers, 1972). Neumann (1933), a German scientist, is credited with publishing the first book on test anxiety, and other German investigators published papers on its etiology and treatment (see Spielberger et al., 1978). Unfortunately, this and other German-based research during this period was never translated into English and subsequently has received little attention in the test anxiety literature.

Initiation of Programmatic Research on the Test Anxiety Construct: 1950s

The study of test anxiety was "officially" launched in the early 1950s by Seymour Sarason and George Mandler at Yale University (S. B. Sarason & Mandler, 1952; Mandler & Sarason, 1952). These researchers are generally credited with being the pioneering researchers in the field and were instrumental in establishing and validating the test anxiety construct. Basically, they and other motivational researchers at the time were interested in testing a number of (neo) behavioristic assumptions relating anxiety, as an indicator of drive, to learning and human performance (Mandler & Sarason, 1952). According to their "interfering response hypothesis," evaluative situations elicit higher levels of the anxiety drive from test-anxious individuals than from non-test-anxious individuals, and, as a result, higher levels of worry and autonomic arousal in the former group. Because anxiety-mediated task-irrelevant responses emitted in test situations were viewed to be incompatible with good performance, individuals high in test anxiety were hypothesized to show decrements on learning and ability task performance relative to their low-test-anxious counterparts. This line of research (S. B. Sarason, Hill, & Zimbardo, 1964; S. B. Sarason, Davidson, Lighthall, Waite, & Ruebush, 1960) opened the way for a systematic examination of the effects of evaluative anxiety on learning and performance in the years to come. S. Sarason and his coworkers made a number of additional seminal contributions to the fledgling field of test anxiety research. Thus, they pioneered the development of the first operational self-report measure of test anxiety for both adult (Test Anxiety Questionnaire) and child (Test Anxiety Scale for Children) populations. In addition, they were the first to conceptualize test anxiety as a multidimensional construct, including a cognitive and affective component. Finally, they conducted the first extensive longitudinal study of anxiety, tracking test anxiety levels of various student cohorts through elementary school years.

Concomitant with S. Sarason's research, Bill McKeachie and his coworkers (McKeachie, 1951; McKeachie, Pollie, & Speisman, 1955) conducted pioneering research in the early 1950s in an effort to find ways to reduce the negative impact of anxiety on students' classroom performance. McKeachie (1951) found that anxious students performed better on multiple-choice exams when given the opportunity to write comments about the questions, and he attributed this improved performance to a reduction in anxiety for students, who could channel some of the tensions evoked by tests.

Conceptual Distinctions and Advances: 1960s

During the 1960s the test anxiety construct was dramatically advanced by a number of important conceptual distinctions, which helped refine thinking and research in the area. First, Spielberger (1966c, 1972a, 1972b, 1972c) applied Cattell and Scheier's (1958) useful distinction of *state* versus *trait* personality traits to the realm of anxiety. Accordingly, Spielberger distinguished between anxiety as a relatively stable disposition or personality trait and anxiety as a more transitory state reaction to specific ego-threatening situations. Based on this distinction, test anxiety was eventually conceptualized as a situation-specific form of trait anxiety (Spielberger et al., 1976).

Alpert and Haber (1960) made a second major conceptual and methodological contribution to the test anxiety literature. They differentiated between *facilitating* and *debilitating* anxiety, claimed to lead to task-related and task-irrelevant behaviors during test situations, respectively. In addition, they developed self-report scales to assess these two independent constructs.

A third conceptual contribution, advanced by Liebert and Morris (1967), was the critical differentiation between worry and emotionality. This distinction proved to be instrumental in shifting test anxiety theory and research toward a more cognitive orientation. According to this conceptualization, anxiety was viewed to be a bidimensional phenomenon, including a cognitive (Worry) and an affective (Emotionality) component. Specifically, Worry was viewed primarily as cognitive concern about the consequences of failure, whereas Emotionality was defined as consisting of perceptions of autonomic reactions evoked by evaluative stress. Liebert and Morris composed scales to measure these two components of test anxiety. In their later work they convincingly demonstrated that the two components are empirically distinct, though correlated, and that Worry relates more strongly to test performance than does Emotionality.

Advances in Model Construction, Research, and Applications: 1970s

In the early 1970s, Wine (1971b) formulated an influential cognitive model, the "cognitive-attentional" or "interference" model, to account for the impact of test anxiety upon performance. This model broke with traditional motivational or arousal explanations and emphasized the role played by cognitive variables on test performance. According to this model, test-anxious persons divide their attention during exams between task-relevant activities, on one hand, and task-irrelevant cognitive activities (preoccupations with worry, self-criticisms, and somatic concern, etc.), on the other. These worry cognitions distract anxious students from the requirements of the task at hand and interfere with the effective use of their time. This model was readily embraced as part of the cognitive *zeitgeist* of the early 1970s, blazing the trail for contemporary cognitive perspectives on anxiety.

A seminal and extensive program of research conducted by Irwin Sarason and his coworkers during the 1960s and 1970s provided convincing support for the cognitive-interference perspective. On the basis of extensive research evidence, Sarason demonstrated that high-test-anxious examinees are indeed more self-centered and self-critical than those who are low in test anxiety and are also more likely to emit personalized, derogatory responses during testing that interfere with their task performance. Furthermore, their programmatic research (e.g., I. G. Sarason, 1972a, 1972b; I. G. Sarason & Ganzer, 1963; I. G. Sarason & Minard, 1962; I. G. Sarason & Stoops, 1978) helped unravel the effects of situational parameters on anxiety and performance in evaluative contexts, as well as determine the combined effects (interactions) between contextual parameters and personality characteristics (high vs. low trait test anxiety). This line of research revealed that when the evaluative nature of the task is stressed (via ego-involving instructions, competitive atmosphere, self-focus, examiner characteristics, etc.), test-anxious individuals perform worse than those low in test anxiety.

Furthermore, applied research in test anxiety burgeoned during the late 1960s and the 1970s. This was largely due to a desire to treat anxiety symptoms and reduce the debilitating effects of test anxiety on student performance (Tobias, 1979). Following Wine's (1971b) call to break with the tradition of only using behavioral techniques (such as systematic desensitization, cue-controlled and applied relaxation, anxiety management training) for the treatment of test anxiety, the rationale and technique of a wide array of cognitive-attentional and cognitive-behavioral techniques were refined and evaluated in the 1970s (attentional training, stress inoculation, systematic cognitive restructuring, studies skills counseling, etc.). Test anxiety reduction programs, whether driven by a behavioral or cognitive orientation, were increasingly implemented and evaluated at a variety of educational institutions in an attempt to reduce the intensity of the emotional reactions experienced by test-anxious persons in evaluative situations.

Toward the end of the 1970s and continuing into the 1980s the basic concepts and assumptions of the cognitive-attentional model came under serious attack, with evidence coming to light favoring a rival "study skills deficit" interpretation. This rival model contended that high-test-anxious students do poorly on academic tasks for two main reasons: (a) because of poorer study habits and test-taking skills, and (b) because of increased arousal and interference evoked by metacognitive awareness on the part of test-anxious individuals regarding their poor encoding, organization, and mastery of the test material (Benjamin, McKeachie, Lin, & Holinger, 1981; Culler & Holahan, 1980; Kirkland & Hollandsworth, 1980).

Research Proliferation, Dissemination, and Integration: 1980s

The 1980s witnessed both the continued proliferation of test anxiety research and its dissemination across the globe, as well as first attempts at institutionalization and integration. The research literature proliferated from the 1960s through the 1980s, with a wealth of studies relating to various facets of test anxiety appearing in some of the premiere journals in psychology, including *Child Development, Cognitive Behavioral Therapy and Research, Journal of Consulting and Clinical Psychology, Journal of Counseling Psychology, Journal of Cross-Cultural Psychology, Journal of Educational Psychology, Journal of Personality, Journal of Personality and Social Psychology, Journal of Research in Personality, Personality and Individual Differences,* and *Anxiety, Stress, and Coping.* In addition, an influential book series edited by C. Spielberger and I. Sarason, *Stress and Anxiety,* contained a number of important research and theoretical studies related to test and evaluative anxiety.

A sizable body of empirical research tested the basic hypotheses of a number of theoretical models of test anxiety (e.g., self-control, attributional self-expectancy). Furthermore, consistent with the cognitive revolution in psychology, a good deal of the research in test anxiety during this period focused on the testing of hypotheses largely derived from information processing models. A major thrust of the research conducted in the 1980s and early 1990s involved uncovering the causal mechanisms through which anxiety impacts upon performance, with the following information processing phases intensively studied during this period: attention, short- and long term memory, levels of processing, retrieval, and decision making. The programmatic research conducted by a number of cognitive psychologists, most notably, R. G. Geen, M. Eysenck, J. H. Mueller, and S. Tobias, applying the notion of limited cognitive resources to anxiety-related decrements in performance, helped elucidate the effects of anxiety on cognitive capacity.

A number of attempts at integrating the prodigious test anxiety literature were made during this period. A major advance in test anxiety research in the early 1980s was the publication of the first comprehensive text on test anxiety, *Test anxiety: Theory, research, and applications*, edited by Irwin G. Sarason (1980b). This compendium consisted of original contributions from some of the key authorities in the field, and assimilated and integrated what was known at the time about the conceptual distinctions, manifestations, measures, correlates, consequences, and treatments of test anxiety. This book continues to serve as a primary reference book on the topic. In addition, a number of reviews published in the 1980s (e.g., Tobias, 1985; Tryon, 1980) sought to integrate and assimilate different aspects of the literature on test anxiety. A major accomplishment in research integration was the publication of the first large-scale meta-analysis of various facets of test anxiety, including its correlates, performance consequences, and treatment effects (Hembree, 1988). This meta-analytic study, restricted mainly to the American literature, allowed the comparison of effect sizes for anxiety treatments, anxiety–performance relationships, and the like, beyond simple vote counting procedures. A second meta-analytic study by Bettina Seipp (1991) on anxiety and academic performance covered the world literature, and the effect sizes reported on the anxiety–performance relationship were about the same as those reported by Hembree.

A notable milestone in the history of test anxiety research was the founding of the Society for Test Anxiety Research (STAR) in June 1980 in Antwerp, Belgium, at the Fourth International Symposium on Educational Testing. The first International STAR conference was held in the Netherlands at the University of Leiden in December 1980, with Charles D. Spielberger, one of the key figures of test anxiety research almost since its inception, elected first president of the organization. The major aim of the society was to stimulate research on test anxiety and to provide a network for facilitating the communication of advances in test anxiety theory, research, assessment, and interventions. Annual meetings have since been held in various sites in Europe and the Middle East (Austria, Belgium, Czechoslovakia, Egypt, Germany, Hungary, Israel, Italy, Norway, Spain, etc.), giving a considerable boost to test anxiety research in those countries whose representatives hosted or participated in the conference. The meetings brought together, in a uniquely congenial and supportive atmosphere, both seasoned and novice researchers, who shared a keen interest in the area of test anxiety. In facilitating the ongoing personal interaction between "first-generation" contributors (e.g., W. McKeachie, B. N. Phillips, I. Sarason, C. Spielberger) and a cohort of second-generation (e.g., C. Carver, M. Covington, K. Hagtvet,

W. Lens, H. Mueller, H. O'Neil Jr., R. Schwarzer, S. Tobias) and third-generation contributors (e.g., M. Boekaerts, D. Hocevar, M. Jerusalem, R. Pekrun, M. Zeidner), these meetings enriched the academic careers of many of today's major contributors to the literature. Furthermore, these meetings were instrumental in launching a number of cross-cultural studies on test anxiety and in initiating the adaptation of standard assessment instruments (e.g., Test Anxiety Inventory, Reactions to Tests) in various national settings. The annual conferences and the seven-volume book series entitled *Advances in Test Anxiety Research* (Volumes 1, 5, and 6 edited by Schwarzer, Van der Ploeg, & Spielberger [1982, 1987, 1989]; Volumes 2–4 edited by Van der Ploeg, Schwarzer, & Spielberger [1983, 1984a, 1984b]; and Volume 7 edited by Hagtvet & Johnsen [1992]) stimulated much research and provided both novice researchers and major contributors to the field with a convenient means for communicating theoretical, empirical, psychometric, and cross-cultural research findings. *Anxiety, Stress, and Coping*, the society's (now renamed Society for Stress and Anxiety Research) journal, appeared in 1988; for the past decade it has become a major source of information about test anxiety.

Recent Advances in Research and Assessment Methodology: 1990–Present

Recent years have witnessed considerable progress in applying sophisticated psychometric and data analytic methods to test anxiety data. Some of the notable advances in measurements issues include the development of new test anxiety scales (e.g., Benson & El-Zahhar, 1994), cross-cultural adaptation and validation of existing scales (Zeidner & Nevo, 1992), testing for cross-cultural scale equivalence at both the item and scale levels (see various papers in the volumes of *Advances in test anxiety research*), and systematic investigation of the psychometric properties and dimensionality of existing scales through sophisticated multivariate statistical procedures (generalizability theory; smallest space analysis; Lisrel; multi-method, multi-trait matrices; see Chapter 5, this book). Great strides were also made in the study of individual and group differences in test anxiety across the globe (see Chapter 11). However, few major conceptual advances or breakthroughs were evidenced during the first half of the 1990s. Interest in the topic of test anxiety peaked in the early 1980s (Figure 1.1) and has shown some signs of a slowdown in growth in terms of research productivity (Figure 1.2).

Stress, Anxiety, and Test Anxiety: Conceptualizations and Important Distinctions

The Domain of Stress and Anxiety Research

Stress, anxiety, and coping is arguably the most widely studied complex of phenomena in psychology today (Hobfoll, Schwarzer & Koo, 1996). Because test

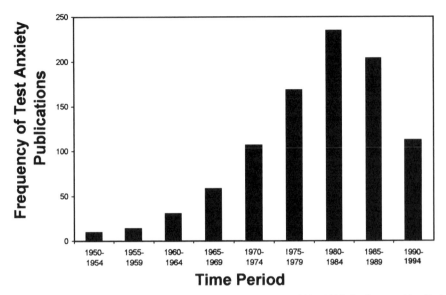

Figure 1.1. Frequency distribution of test anxiety publications from 1950 to 1994. Studies were identified via computer searches of the data bases for *Psychological Abstracts* and the Educational Resources Information Center (ERIC). Additional studies were found by hand, by manually searching major journals, soliciting studies directly from authors, and tracking citations from study to study. Only journal articles and book chapters in English are included.

anxiety may be viewed as a proper subset of the broader domain of stress and anxiety research, I commence this discussion by briefly clarifying these two concepts and their interrelationships in order to place test anxiety research in a broader theoretical framework. (The issue of coping is discussed in Chapter 13.) I then proceed to zoom in on the test anxiety construct.

Psychological Stress

The transactional model of stress and emotion (R. S. Lazarus & Folkman, 1984; R. S. Lazarus, 1991b), the most influential contemporary stress model, conceptualizes stress as a dynamic process or "transaction" between a person and the environment. As R. S. Lazarus and Folkman (1984) put it, psychological stress is "a relationship between the person and the environment that is appraised by the person as taxing or exceeding his or her resources and endangering his or her well-being" (p. 21). The transactional perspective conceptualizes stress as a process that unfolds over time in a sequence of events by which environmental encounters threaten or challenge a person's well-being and by which that person appraises and responds to the impending threat (Gatchel, Baum, & Krantz, 1989). The person generally responds to stress

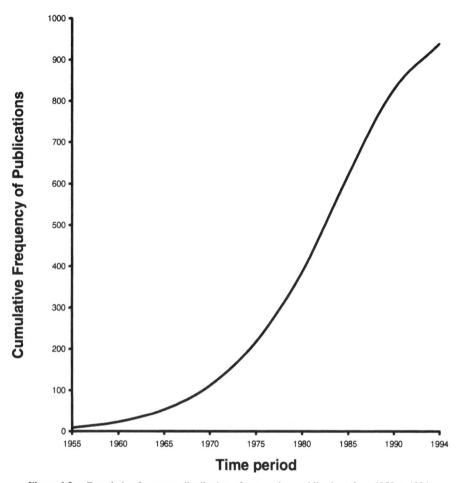

Figure 1.2. Cumulative frequency distribution of test anxiety publications from 1950 to 1994.

and stress emotions by making an effort to return to an equilibrium state, utilizing relevant coping resources and enlisting appropriate coping strategies.

Furthermore, stress involves not only the potentially stressful events themselves, but also interpretations of them and the person's response—which may be cognitive, physiological, affective (e.g., anxiety, anger, or depressive moods), or behavioral. According to the transactional model, perceptions and appraisals of threat intervene between the stressors and emotional states, with a key aim of appraisal being the integration of personal values and agendas with environmental realities (Wells & Matthews, 1994). Thus, the judgment that a particular person–environment relationship is stressful depends largely on cognitive appraisal—the individual's evaluation of the personal significance of ongoing events and his or her capacity to react to them. In fact, the transactional model assumes that some form of appraisal is always involved in the stress process (R. S. Lazarus, 1991a, 1991b, 1991c; R. S. Lazarus & Folkman, 1984). Three categories of appraisal, primary, secondary, and reappraisal, are important in determining emotional experience and influencing subsequent coping efforts. These are discussed in Chapter 8 in greater detail.

Transactional models of stress tend to have at least three basic elements (Deary, Blenkin, Agius, Endler, Zeally, & Wood, 1996): (a) antecedents to stress, (b) mediators of stress, and (c) outcomes of stress. The *antecedents* tend to be divided into personal and environmental variables. Personality variables (e.g., social evaluative trait anxiety, self-efficacy, optimism) are thought to influence a person's perceptions of, or reactions to, stressful events. Aspects of the *environment*, such as the test atmosphere, amount of social support available, or the nature of the cognitive task, are also viewed as antecedent factors. *Mediators* are psychological processes that are thought to influence the stress process between the antecedents and the outcomes. Stress appraisals and threat perceptions as well as coping mechanisms are the variables that tend to appear in this intermediate position. Depending on a particular subject's personal characteristics and coping responses, environmental stressors may have different *outcomes* in terms of physical or psychological disturbances (Endler & Parker, 1990c).

Anxiety

Anxiety, a basic human emotion, signaling uncertainty or threat in the environment, has figured prominently in the literature as one of the most pervasive and important reactions to stress experienced by man (I. G. Sarason, 1986; I. G. Sarason & Sarason, 1990). More than any other emotion, psychological research has centered on how anxiety influences adaptational outcomes such as cognitive and social performance, subjective well-being, and somatic health or illness. As such, it is almost a synonym of psychological stress (R. S. Lazarus, 1991b, 1993b).

A basic metatheoretical assumption in current transactional cognitive-motivational analysis is that both stress and emotions are primarily about person–environment relationships (R. S. Lazarus, 1991a, 1991b, 1991c, 1993b). Thus, the quality or intensity of an emotion is the product of actual or anticipated adaptational encounters with the environment, which are appraised by the individual as having either positive or negative significance for well-being. The cognitive-motivational perspective maintains that there are distinctive core relational themes underlying each emotion. Core relational themes refer to personal meanings attributed to events, which can take the diverse forms of harm or loss, threat, and benefit. Any evoked emotion reflects a high-level synthesis of several appraisals relating to the individual's adaptational status in the current environment. With respect to anxiety, the core theme is danger or threat to ego or self-esteem when a person is facing an uncertain, existential threat. Thus, anxiety appears when an event is appraised as being a threat, this appraisal being largely a cognitive, symbolic process. Emotions, such as anxiety, tell us something of a person's goal hierarchy and belief system and how events were appraised. Thus, the very presence of anxiety in an evaluative encounter is informative because it tells us that an existential threat has not been controlled very well.

I. G. Sarason (1978) theorizes that stress is intrinsic to the interpretation of a specific situation, whereas anxiety is a reaction to a perceived threat and incapacity to cope with the situational challenge in a satisfactory way. An anxious person feels he or she cannot meet the demands of this call (I. G. Sarason, 1978, 1984). Following are some of the major criterial attributes of anxiety enumerated by I. G. Sarason and Sarason (1990):

- The individual appraises a situation as difficult, threatening, or challenging.
- The individual perceives himself or herself as being inefficient or inadequate to the task at hand, lacking coping responses needed to deal forthrightly with a call for action or a situational restraint or opportunity.
- The individual focuses on undesirable consequences of personal inadequacy or on undesirable outcomes.
- The individual is preoccupied with self-deprecatory thoughts about self that compete with cognitive task-related activity.
- The individual expects and anticipates failure and loss of self-esteem or regard by others.

Anxiety is a complex phenomenon and there has been wide disagreement about its definition and criteria. Thus, anxiety has been variously conceptualized as a stimulus condition, as a probability of a harmful future outcome, and as response to a stressful condition (Shechter & Zeidner, 1990). A number of sources of confusion have contributed to the difficulty in reaching agreement on the meaning of anxiety. For one, the lack of distinction between anxiety as a personality trait and anxiety as a transitory emotional state has led to conceptual confusion with respect to anxiety results (Spielberger, 1975). There has also been a lack of agreement concerning whether the term anxiety should refer to observable or recordable events (e.g., accelerated heart and breathing rates, self-reports) or to a hypothetical state (I. G. Sarason, 1978). Part of the confusion grows out of the frequent, almost simultaneous use of anxiety in both of these two senses.

Once anxiety is aroused, the individual reappraises the stressful conditions to try to find a way to deal with them. A variety of coping possibilities are considered, ranging from instrumental activity to alleviate the source of evaluative stress, to defensive and avoidance behavior that enables the person to escape the anxiety-evoking conditions.

Definition of the Test Anxiety Construct

The term "test anxiety," as a scientific construct, refers to the set of phenomenological, physiological, and behavioral responses that accompany concern about possible negative consequences or failure on an exam or similar evaluative situation

(Sieber, O'Neil, & Tobias, 1977). Test-anxious students are characterized by a particularly low response threshold for anxiety in evaluative situations, tending to view evaluative situations, in general, and test situations, in particular, as personally threatening. As a result, they tend to react with threat perceptions, reduced feelings of self-efficacy, self-derogatory cognitions, anticipatory failure attributions, and more intense emotional reactions and arousal at the very first hint of failure (I. G. Sarason, 1986; I. G. Sarason & Sarason, 1990). Test-anxious behavior is typically evoked when a person believes that her or his intellectual, motivational, and social capabilities and capacities are taxed or exceeded by demands stemming from the test situation (I. G. Sarason & Sarason, 1990). However, it is still unclear why the imminence of evaluation is so much more stressful and anxiety arousing for some people than for others.

Test anxiety has been characterized as a special case of a broader "evaluation anxiety" construct (Carver, Peterson, Follansbee, & Scheier, 1983). In fact, test-anxious persons typically interpret a wide range of situations as evaluative and commonly focus on the social-evaluation contingencies in the test situation. In fact, some scholars (Sieber et al., 1977; Wine, 1980) have argued that "test anxiety" is an omnibus term carrying much surplus meaning, which has outlived its usefulness (Wine, 1982). My policy, however, has been to adhere to the traditional label, because the term test anxiety has gained wide currency among both professionals and the general public alike. At least for the time being, it looks like test anxiety is alive and well in public parlance and is the standard term employed in the research literature to denote the phenomenology under consideration.

As is the case for the *anxiety* construct, much of the ambiguity and semantic confusion associated with the status of test anxiety as a psychological construct stems from the fact that different investigators have invested this term with quite divergent meanings. Thus, test anxiety has been used to refer to several related, yet logically very different constructs, including stressful evaluative stimuli and contexts, individual differences in anxiety proneness in evaluative situations (i.e., trait anxiety), and fluctuating anxiety states experienced in a test situation (i.e., state anxiety). Although the question still looms large whether test anxiety is best conceptualized as a relatively stable personality trait (individual difference variable) or an ephemeral emotional state, a widely accepted definition proposed by Spielberger (Spielberger et al., 1976) construes test anxiety as a *situation-specific personality trait*. Accordingly, test anxiety refers to the individual's disposition to react with extensive worry, intrusive thoughts, mental disorganization, tension, and physiological arousal when exposed to evaluative situations (Spielberger et al., 1976; Spielberger & Vagg, 1995a).

Throughout its relatively brief history as a scientific construct, test anxiety has taken on a variety of different meanings as a function of both changes in the *zeitgeist* and variations in the theoretical persuasions of the individual investigators involved in this research arena. Thus, in the early days of test anxiety research the construct was initially defined in *motivational* terms, as drive level (J. T. Spence & Spence,

1966), goal interruption (Mandler & Sarason, 1952), or need to avoid failure (Atkinson & Feather, 1966). Test anxiety was also conceptualized as a relatively stable *personality disposition* that develops when parents hold exaggerated expectations and are overcritical of their children's achievement efforts (e.g., S. B. Sarason et al., 1960; Hill, 1972). In keeping with the cognitive revolution of the late 1960s and early 1970s, test anxiety came to be viewed primarily as a *cognitive-attentional* phenomenon (Wine, 1971b; S. B. Sarason, 1972). Accordingly, the highly anxious person is one who attends, in an exaggerated way, to evaluative cues, to self-generated concern about ability to do well enough, and to feelings of physiological arousal. More recent conceptualizations have viewed test anxiety as part of a cybernetic self-control process, with anxiety reflecting the existence of a conflict between competing reference values (Carver & Scheier, 1991), or as a form of *self-handicapping* employed to preserve one's self-merit in the face of potential failure (Covington, 1992). A number of these traditional and contemporary conceptualizations are presented in some detail in Chapter 3.

Key Elements in the Test Anxiety Process: A Transactional Perspective

Taking the lead from prior discussions of anxiety in the literature from a transactional perspective (Spielberger & Vagg, 1995a; cf. Endler, 1992), Zeidner (1997a) recently proposed an integrative transactional model of test anxiety (Figure

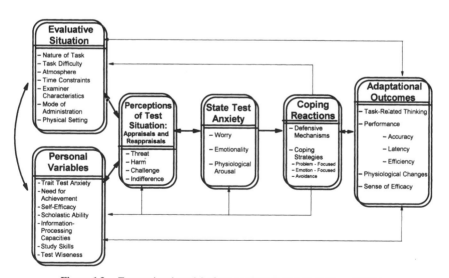

Figure 1.3.   Transactional model of test anxiety. Based on Zeidner (1997a).

1.3). This theoretical framework conceptualizes the phenomenon as a dynamic process involving the reciprocal interaction of a number of distinct elements at play in the stressful encounter between a person and an evaluative situation. Accordingly, the key elements in this process include the evaluative context, individual differences in vulnerability (trait anxiety), threat perceptions, appraisals, and reappraisals, state anxiety, coping patterns, and adaptive outcomes. The relations among the various components in the transactional model are viewed to be dynamic and continuous processes. Thus, not only do individuals react to situations, but they also affect the situations with which they interact, with a constant and continuous interaction between persons and situations. For example, the examiner's behavior during an exam may impact upon the examinee's level of state anxiety in an individual testing situation, yet the examinee's anxiety levels may also have an impact on the examiner's attitudes and behaviors as well. I now discuss a number of the fundamental elements in this model that need to be considered in any explication of the test anxiety process.

Situational Stress

An *evaluative* situation is one in which a person is judged or assessed with respect to some standard of performance. An evaluative situation typically implies chances for either success or failure, and the consequences are in most cases relevant and meaningful to a person's life goals and values (e.g., studies, career, financial status). A *test* is a special case of an evaluative situation. It involves presenting examinees with a series of tasks, circumscribed in time and place, which demand responses that are evaluated against some external criterion of performance. These results generally lead to contingent consequences (Zeidner & Most, 1992). Anxiety may be associated with anticipating a test situation, experiencing it, or recovering from it.

The degree of stress experienced by an individual in a given test situation depends on a variety of contextual factors. One primary factor is represented by the objective properties of the evaluative stressor, including task characteristics (e.g., task content, complexity, ambiguity, difficulty, novelty, interest, fairness, frequency, duration), evaluative atmosphere, nature of feedback cues, time pressures, and physical conditions. Additional factors potentially affecting stress reactions are the individual's perception of the evaluative encounter (i.e., as threat, challenge, harm), perceived personal coping resources, specific strategies used in transacting with evaluative stressors, and the specific evaluative context and period of one's life in which evaluative demands are experienced. Situations in which the person lacks sufficient knowledge about the test context or in which the person is uncertain about the potential cognitive or social demands and affordances (or whether the person has at their disposal the necessary skills to deal with them) tend to be particularly anxiety evoking.

The test anxiety process begins when a person is subjected to a test situation or any situation associated with evaluation. These include immediate events such as a teacher's remark, "Take out your papers and pencils for a short chemistry quiz," or they may be related to the future, such as a career decision that has implications for future challenges and assessments. It is important to remember that test stimuli are conditioned stimuli and their meaning to the individual depends on prior experience. Thus, what is a stimulus of test anxiety for one person may be a neutral event for another.

Current interactional models of anxiety view anxious behavior to be determined by the reciprocal interaction of personal traits and the characteristics of situations. The interaction model posits that state anxiety will be experienced in a social-devaluation situation when there is a congruency or fit between the nature of a person's vulnerability (i.e., high social-evaluation trait anxiety) and the nature of the situation (social-evaluation/ego-threatening). The *differential hypothesis* of the interactional model (Endler, Edwards, & Vitelli, 1991) claims that people high on social-evaluation trait anxiety will show a higher increase in state anxiety than subjects low on social-evaluation anxiety primarily in an evaluative situation (as opposed to, say, a physical threat or daily-routines situation). Furthermore, the same difference in increased anxiety reactions from a neutral to stressful one would not be found between subjects high and low on other forms of trait anxiety (e.g., physical danger; Endler & Magnusson, 1976). The interactionist assumption may be extended to more specialized forms of social-evaluation anxiety such as sports or social performance anxiety. Thus, it may be predicted that anxious-worry and arousal occur when individuals with more-specialized anxiety patterns or traits (e.g., sports anxiety) encounter corresponding stressful situations (e.g., competitive sports situations).

Both transactional and cognitive-social models emphasize the crucial role of situations, but generally view them as informational inputs whose behavioral impact depends on how they are processed by the person (Mischel, 1973). Evaluative situational variables should provide the individual with information which affects behavior insofar as it influences such personality variables as the individual's encoding, expectancies, or subjective value of the stimulus condition. Evaluative situations are powerful to the degree that they lead all persons to construe the particular events the same way, inducing uniform expectancies regarding the most appropriate response pattern. Evaluative situations would be considered to be weak to the degree they are not uniformly encoded, and do not generate uniform expectancies concerning desired behaviors, or fail to provide learning conditions required for successful construction of behavior. Individual differences can determine behavior in a given evaluative situation most strongly when the situation is ambiguously structured so subjects are uncertain how to categorize it and people have no expectations about behaviors most likely to be appropriate.

Trait Anxiety

Aside from the objective properties of the evaluative situation, the response to a given test or test situation is largely determined by the degree to which an event is perceived as threatening, harmful, or challenging (R. S. Lazarus & Folkman, 1984).

However, people differ in the degree in which they are predisposed to view a given evaluative situation as threatening or challenging. In the context of Spielberger's state–trait distinction, test anxiety was conceptualized as a situation-specific form of trait anxiety (Spielberger & Vagg, 1995a). This conception conforms to current thinking emphasizing the need to take situational factors into consideration in assessing trait or dispositional measures (Hodapp, Glanzmann, & Laux, 1995). Accordingly, high-test-anxious persons are viewed as being more likely than their low-test-anxious counterparts to perceive exam situations as more dangerous or threatening, and consequently to experience worry cognitions and intense elevations in state anxiety in situations in which they are evaluated. High levels of state anxiety stimulate test-anxious individuals to plunge inward, thus activating worry cognitions stored in memory that distract the test-anxious student from effective performance.

Trait test anxiety, as a latent construct, is not directly manifested in behavior, but is inferred from the frequency and intensity of an individuals' elevations in state anxiety in evaluative situations over time. Persons who are high in evaluative trait anxiety are disposed to see test or evaluative situations as more dangerous or threatening than low-trait-anxious individuals. Consequently, they are more vulnerable to stress in test situations and tend to experience anxiety state reactions of greater intensity and with greater frequency over time than persons who are low in trait anxiety.

Threat Perceptions, Appraisals, and Reappraisals

Cognitive appraisals are claimed to mediate between persons and situations, so that the meaning or interpretation that an individual assigns to a test situation may be a decisive factor affecting his or her emotions and behaviors. It is not so much evaluative situations per se that evoke anxiety, but rather our appraisals and interpretations of them (R. S. Lazarus & Folkman, 1984). While high-stake testing situations are likely to be perceived as stressful by most persons, whether or not they are in effect regarded as threatening by a particular individual will largely depend upon that person's subjective *appraisal* of the situation as personally threatening. The notion of the "cognitive mediation" of anxiety, a basic principle of transactional theory, implies that situational perceptions do not trigger anxiety directly, but only after the situation has been cognitively appraised (R. S. Lazarus & Folkman, 1984).

Evaluative situations that are personally relevant or meaningful to the individual can be appraised as being challenging, ego-threatening, or harmful. The primary appraisal of the test situation as ego-threatening gives rise to test anxiety, particularly if the person perceives insufficient coping resources or minimal coping ability (R. Schwarzer, 1986). According to Bandura (1988), threat is not a fixed property of situational events or person perception. Rather, it is the match between perceived coping capabilities and potentially hurtful aspects of the environment. Therefore, to understand people's appraisals of evaluative situations and threats and their affective reactions to them it is necessary to analyze their judgments of their coping capabilities, which in large part determine the subjective perilousness of environmental events. Accordingly, individuals who feel they can exercise control over potential threats do not conjure up apprehensive cognitions, and hence are not perturbed by them. But those who believe they cannot manage potential threat experience high levels of anxiety arousal. They tend to dwell on their coping deficiencies and view many aspects of their environment as fraught with danger. That is, the person feels she or he does not have the wherewithal or coping resources or skills to meet the call for action evoked by the stressful encounter. Furthermore, evaluative stress and test anxiety will not result if the individual does not become conscious of a threatening evaluative situation, regardless of the actual threat value of the event. In the same fashion, an evaluative situation that is in reality of little objective threat value might actually create substantial threat if so appraised by the person.

The actual appraisal of a test situation as stressful or threatening will depend on a number of objective and subjective factors including the demands and constraints of the situation, personal experience with similar situations in the past, knowledge of potential consequences, evaluation of its apparent costs, as well as individual differences in aptitudes, skills, and personality dispositions (e.g., trait anxiety, perceived self-efficacy). Thus, according to the interactional analysis presented above, one person may perceive a given test situation (say, matriculation exam in math) as a perfectly innocuous situation, or as a challenge, whereas another person may view the exact same situation as personally threatening or dangerous. Overall, the response to a stressful evaluative situation will be mediated by a cost–rewards analysis, taking into consideration the judged likelihood of the consequences and demand "costs" relative to one's resources.

Threat has been used to describe an individual's subjective appraisal of a situation as threatening or harmful, or dangerous (Spielberger, 1972b; Spielberger et al., 1978). One key ingredient of threat is that it is essentially future-oriented, generally involving the anticipation of potentially harmful events that have not yet happened (failure, need to take makeup exam, social embarrassment and disapproval, etc.). Threat experiences encompass a variety of mental processes, which include perception, thought, memory, and judgments (threat schemata, failure memories). A person who perceives an exam situation as threatening will experience an increase in state anxiety irrespective of the presence of real or objective threat or danger {evaluative stress → perception of threat → increase in state anxiety in test situation}. The intensity of the anxiety state is proportional to the severity of the threat the individual perceives (Spielberger et al., 1978).

Based on M. W. Eysenck's (1992) analysis, the following factors should determine the "threat value" of a potentially threatening exam situation:

- Personal salience of the test ("Its terribly important that I do well on this final exam").
- Subjective probability of negative test outcomes ("I will most certainly flunk my organic chemistry exam").

- Imminence of the event ("The exam is this Tuesday and I haven't even begun studying yet").
- Perceived aversiveness of the event ("I detest taking chemistry exams").
- Perceived unavailability of coping strategies and skills ("I just don't know how to go about studying for this chemistry midterm").

Thus, anxiety in test situations should increase with heightened personal importance of success or failure, greater estimated probability of failure, greater proximity to the test situation, and lowered subjective estimate of competence.

The interactional model (Endler, 1992) proposes a useful conceptual distinction between the attribute of *situation perception* and *situation reaction*. Thus, two persons may be exposed to the exact same objective test situation, yet one may view it as personally threatening, whereas the other may view it in a neutral and nonthreatening manner, as a function of variations in situation perception. Furthermore, two individuals may perceive a given exam situation as being equally ego-threatening, yet one person may react by withdrawing from it (e.g., procrastinating and avoiding studying for the exam), whereas the other may react by exerting maximal effort in "attacking" it (e.g., increasing study time before the exam, planning, gathering information), as a function of differences in situation reaction.

Sieber (1980) stresses that the interpretation of a test situation is based mainly on one's past history. Some individuals have learned to approach test situations as a positive event, whereas others have learned to approach them with great hesitation, trepidation, and fear of failure. The first type of person says, "I will succeed or not and grow from this experience," whereas the latter says, "I most surely will fail and there is no chance I will succeed." Fear of failure and other negative interpretations of test stimuli are based on past experiences. Thus, fear of failure and other negative interpretations of test stimuli are not fear of failing to carry out the operations required at the time, but rather plug into old ideas such as, "If I fail at this exam I am worthless," or, "No one will respect me." Unfortunately, the interpretation of stimuli by test-anxious persons tends to be unexamined and is often accepted as the basic reality of the situation rather than simply one of many possible interpretations.

State Anxiety

Test anxiety, as a transitory emotional state, refers to the emotional reactions that occur in an individual who perceives a particular evaluative situation as personally harmful or threatening (Spielberger et al., 1976). These reactions are characterized by unpleasant feelings of tension and apprehension and perceived arousal, accompanied by heightened activity of the autonomic nervous system (palpitations, sweat, muscle tension, etc.). Such states are typically accompanied by worrisome thoughts about failure, self-ruminative cognitions, and loss of self-merit, often stimulated by increased levels of emotional arousal (Spielberger & Vagg, 1995b).

State anxiety is currently conceptualized as a multidimensional construct, composed of a cognitive and an affective component (Endler & Parker, 1990c). The intensity and duration of a test anxiety state will be determined by a variety of interacting factors, such as the intensity and amount of objective evaluative stress that impinges upon an individual, individual differences in trait test anxiety, and the persistence of the individual's interpretation of the situation as personally threatening (Spielberger et al., 1978). Measures of individual differences in trait anxiety can be assessed by determining the frequency that state anxiety reactions have been manifested in test situations in the past, also providing an estimate of the probability that anxiety states will be experienced in stressful evaluative situations in the future.

Coping Behaviors and Outcomes

Coping, broadly speaking, involves a person's constantly changing cognitive and behavioral efforts to manage (i.e., reduce, minimize, master, tolerate) the internal and external demands of a transaction that is appraised as stressful (R. S. Lazarus & Folkman, 1984; R. S. Lazarus, 1993a). Accordingly, when the demands of an evaluative situation, such as an exam, are perceived as stressful and taxing one's personal resources, efforts are directed at regulating emotional stress and/or dealing with the problem at hand (Folkman & Lazarus, 1986) in order to manage the troubled person–environment transaction (R. S. Lazarus, 1990). By virtue of its effects on appraisal, coping is an important part of the emotion-generating process as well as a reaction to an emotion.

Since elevations in state anxiety surrounding evaluation situations are experienced as unpleasant, an individual will generally engage in cognitive and behavioral operations or responses that serve to reduce or minimize this discomfort. Thus, when faced with a stressful anxiety-evoking evaluative encounter, the individual can employ a wide range of coping responses to regain control of the situation and reinstate equilibrium. This can include instrumental problem-oriented coping, in which the evaluative stressor or threat is directly dealt with, palliative coping, in which the anxiety is ameliorated, and avoidance or defensive behavior. Coping has been claimed to moderate the effects of evaluative stress on critical adaptive outcomes, including stress-related emotions surrounding the exam and test performance (Zeidner & Saklofske, 1996). Chapter 13 provides an in-depth discussion of the role of coping in evaluative stress.

Summary

This introductory chapter aimed at providing a brief overview of the test anxiety domain. Test anxiety, broadly speaking, refers to the set of cognitive, affective, and behavioral reactions that accompany concern over possible negative consequences contingent upon performance in a test or evaluative situation. Test anxiety research has developed dramatically over the past half century, evolving from a novel area of research in the early 1950s to a major field of current psychological and educational interest. Given the technological complexity of modern society and the many ways in which tests and evaluative situations determine the lives of people who take them, it comes as no surprise that the testing situation evokes anxiety reactions in many. Indeed, based on a number of estimates of the prevalence rates of test anxiety in school- and college-age populations, the phenomenon appears to be reasonably widespread. However, large-scale epidemiological studies of test anxiety are sparse and much needed to provide more accurate estimates of the prevalence of test anxiety in various subgroups and settings.

The test anxiety construct has matured within a large cocoon of attention, with researchers making important strides toward understanding its nature, components, origins, determinants, effects, and treatments. The field of test anxiety research has prospered, in part, due to the increasing personal salience of test situations for people in modern society, making tests and their long-term consequences significant educational, social, and clinical problems for many. The importance of test anxiety as a key construct in understanding sources of examinee distress, impaired test performance in evaluative situations, and academic underachievement is now readily apparent. This situation demands that test anxiety be better understood through systematic research and appropriately dealt with. Indeed, much of test anxiety research over the past half century has been conducted to help shed light on the negative effects of test anxiety on examinee performance, and these concerns have stimulated the development of a variety of therapeutic techniques and intervention programs.

Test anxiety is a complex construct and over the years has been vested with a variety of different meanings. Test-anxious behavior is typically evoked when individuals believe that their intellectual, motivational, and social capabilities and capacities are taxed or exceeded by demands stemming from the test situation. Test-anxious students are characterized by a high degree of vulnerability and a particularly low response threshold for anxiety in evaluative situations. Furthermore, test anxiety has been described as a dynamic process constituted by the reciprocal interaction of the evaluative context, individual differences in trait anxiety, appraisals and threat perceptions, state anxiety, and coping patterns and outcomes.

The brief historical survey presented here identified several stages in the history of test anxiety research. Research rapidly accelerated in the 1950s throughout the 1980s, but seems to have reached its plateau in the late 1980s and is experiencing somewhat of a slump in the mid-1990s. Over 25 years ago, S. B. Sarason (1972) mused whether that 20th anniversary of the construct of test anxiety should be a propitious time for a loyal service pin, disengagement, or retirement. As the construct of test anxiety will shortly be celebrating another notable milestone, its "golden anniversary," the time seems ripe to stop and take stock of what we know about test anxiety—where we have been, where we are, and where we might be heading. This, in part, I hope to achieve in the chapters ahead.

A Note to the Reader. Test anxiety has been studied from discrepant conceptual, empirical, and methodological perspectives. In view of the complex and multivariate nature of test anxiety, its many facets, and the prodigious amount of relevant research findings, no single unified model can readily subsume and account for all the data. A number of different perspectives are needed to account adequately for the test anxiety experience. In view of the above, I have been eclectic in the choice of theoretical models in accounting for the diversity of phenomena discussed in this book. However, whenever possible, I have attempted to relate test anxiety research to the broader theoretical domain of stress, anxiety, and coping research, mainly from a process-oriented, cognitive-motivational transactional perspective. My own experience in test anxiety research has taught me that transactional analysis, examining the dynamic interaction between person and evaluative context, seems to be the most useful approach to mapping out the test anxiety domain.

The Nature and Phenomenology of Test Anxiety

> Test anxiety is the interest paid on academic troubles before it is due.
> —Covington and Omelich (1988)

Overview

This chapter sets out to describe the nature, components, and phenomenology of test anxiety, currently viewed as a rather complex multidimensional construct, comprised of a cluster of interacting components and reactions (Covington, 1992; Covington, Omelich, & Schwarzer, 1986; Spielberger et al., 1976; Spielberger & Vagg, 1995a, 1995b). Before discussing test anxiety further, I present two case studies of students who manifest many of the features associated with various levels of test anxiety. These case studies should provide the reader with some insight into the phenomenology of test anxiety. The description is based on the case study data provided by Anton and Lillibridge (1995) for a number of test-anxious college students. Data were gathered through structured interview procedures in conjunction with psychological testing at a university counseling center.

A prototypical case of a moderately anxious student is that of Jane R., a 20-year-old junior majoring in education. Jane was reported to be at the 91st percentile on the Test Anxiety Inventory, a standard measure of test anxiety (i.e., she scored above 91% of a broad student sample on the test anxiety scale). As the deadline for an examination approached, she tended to become progressively more preoccupied with anxious anticipation and worry. While taking a test, she experienced heightened tension and apprehension, but this did not result in "blocking" or affect her recall. After completing an exam, she engaged in self-deprecatory thoughts about her performance until the examination was returned. Although she was successful in maintaining a B average throughout high school and in her first 2 years of college, she regarded test anxiety as a nagging problem and she wanted to do something to change that situation. Psychological testing indicated that she tended to entertain pessimistic thoughts about the future and this pattern appeared to be primarily situational rather than an unstable personality trait. This fits the prevalent conceptions of the typical test-anxious student. Thus, Jane appeared to be bright and capable and highly motivated to do well in an academic setting. She was free from serious psychopathology and even her test anxiety did not prevent her from passing examinations.

However, more severe instances of test anxiety that often require clinical attention are frequently documented. A case in point depicted by the authors, Dale A., was a 23-year-old male junior who described the nature of his subjective experiences in evaluative situations as a feeling of "panic" associated with memory blockage. This occurred primarily in response to test questions that he could not readily answer, and generalized to subsequent questions on the same exam. Sadly, he remembered the answers he had been blocking once the exam was completed. On one of his first exams at the university, this student reported severe blocking in association with worry about failure and not having sufficient time to complete the exam. He failed the exam, although he had adequately prepared for it. After receiving information about his performance, Dale immediately began worrying about subsequent tests. He began to approach tests with feelings of panic and responded to these by rushing through questions. In an effort to escape from the exam situation, he often engaged in random guessing. This pattern generally led to poorer academic performance and is highly prototypical of severe test-anxious students.

Although a number of alternative attempts have been made at determining the dimensionality of the test anxiety construct and in teasing out its key facets, little agreement has been reached among experts on the exact number of facets or components of test anxiety. However, researchers have found it particularly useful to differentiate among *cognitive* facets (worry, irrelevant thinking, etc.), *affective* facets (tension, bodily reaction, perceived arousal), and *behavioral* facets (deficient study skills, procrastination, avoidance behaviors, etc.). Thus, test-anxious individuals may be characterized by their thoughts, somatic reactions, feelings, and observable behaviors in evaluative situations (I. G. Sarason, 1984). In any given test situation, test-anxious subjects may experience all, some, or none of these test anxiety reactions. The specific anxiety response manifested may vary, depending on the constitutional qualities and past experience of the individual, the nature of the problem to be solved, and various situational factors affecting the level of anxiety evoked.

In addition to viewing test anxiety as a set of interrelated and interacting cognitive, affective, and behavioral components, current thinking and research suggests that test anxiety is not a unitary event, but is best conceptualized as a complex dynamic process, consisting of a number of distinct temporal phases (Carver & Scheier, 1994; Covington & Omelich, 1988; Folkman & Lazarus, 1985). Accordingly, threat appraisals, state anxiety levels, and the relationship of appraisal and anxiety to performance outcomes may change as a function of the specific stage of the stressful encounter that is being considered.

Discussions of test anxiety in the literature are commonly guilty of a "uniformity myth," conveying the impression that test anxiety is a rather homogeneous or unidimensional category. However, under the assumption that test anxiety is a multidimensional and multidetermined phenomenon, it stands to reason that a variety of different types of test-anxious examinees may be identified. This simple fact is often overlooked when writers present theory and research relating to the "test-anxious" student—typically treated as a uniform category. Indeed, some examinees may be anxious in test situations because they have poor motivation to succeed on academic tasks; some may have poor study or test-taking skills; some may be anxious because they have low intellectual ability; some tend to be perfectionistic overstrivers and will be dissatisfied with anything less than a perfect score; while others are anxious because they fail to meet social expectations or fear parental punishment.

In this chapter I begin by systematically examining key cognitive, affective, and behavioral components of test anxiety. Each facet is construed as representing a distinct response channel through which test anxiety may be expressed. The reciprocal and dynamic interactions among these diverse components are viewed as underlying the test anxiety experience. I then present the key temporal phases of test anxiety as a dynamic and complex process unfolding over time. I conclude by presenting a tentative typology of test-anxious students and point out a number of differences between test anxiety and related forms of anxiety.

Facets of Test Anxiety

Cognitive Facet

From an information processing perspective, test anxiety is construed mainly as a *cognitive* variable that also has physiological and affective concomitants (Holroyd, Westbrook, Wolf, & Badhorn, 1978; I. G. Sarason & Sarason, 1990). A body of research evidence suggests that certain cognitive expressions of anxiety (self-focused attention and cognitive preoccupation with failure, lack of confidence and feelings of inadequacy in test situations, negative performance expectations, ruminations over potential future consequences of failure, etc.) may be the most salient response characteristic of highly test anxious people to situations in which they are evaluated (Deffenbacher, 1980; Geen, 1987; I. G. Sarason, 1984; I. G. Sarason & Sarason, 1990; Wine, 1982).

T. W. Smith and his coworkers (T. W. Smith, Ingram, & Brehm, 1983) identified two lines of research relating to the cognitive facet of anxiety: (a) *cognitive excesses research*, involving self-preoccupation and self-focused ruminative thoughts (conceptualized as excess cognitive load), and (b) *cognitive deficits research*, involving the reduction in cognitive processes such as attention, memory, and retrieval. Current formulations view cognitive excesses as responsible for cognitive deficits in that attention to negative worrisome thoughts are viewed as being the cause of dysphoric affect and consequently reduced performance in evaluative situations (cognitive excesses → cognitive deficits). Whereas Chapter 10 focuses on "cognitive deficits," this section treats some of the major sources of "cognitive excesses" in test anxiety, such as worry, self-preoccupation, self-referential negative thoughts, and cognitive interference.

The Worry clusters described in the following section are based mainly on a content analysis of the literature bearing on the cognitive components of test anxiety. Rather than view these subcomponents as independent components, they just as readily might be considered subsets of the Worry component or as particular types of Worry clusters. Additional cognitive ingredients of the test anxiety experience, such as threat schemata and dysfunctional thinking patterns, are treated in Chapter 8.

Worry

Worry is currently viewed as the most powerful *cognitive* component of test anxiety (I. G. Sarason, 1988). In the context of test anxiety research, Worry refers to distressing concerns about impending or anticipated evaluative events (Flett & Blankstein, 1994). Liebert and Morris (1967) originally defined Worry as "any cognitive expression of concern about one's own performance" (p. 975). Thus, rather than engage in task-oriented thinking, test-anxious individuals become concerned with the implications and consequences of failure to meet situational challenges (I. G. Sarason, 1986). The Worry component of test anxiety is triggered by external or internal cues that focus upon tests or other forms of threatening evaluative situations, indicating something undesirable, such as task failure, is imminent (Deffenbacher, 1986; M. W. Eysenck, 1992). In particular, worry cognitions are aroused when a person perceives his or her ability to cope with a test as unsatisfactory and is uncertain about the consequences of inadequate coping (I. G. Sarason & Sarason, 1990). Presumably, all students are aroused physiologically under stressful evaluative conditions, but only the test-anxious student is severely preoccupied with self-critical worrisome thoughts. Indeed, a body of research attests that the major differences between high- and low-test-anxious individuals rest not in their level of arousal during tests, but in their cognitive reactions to threatening evaluative situations (Hollandsworth, Glazeski, Kirkland, Jones, & Van Norman, 1979).

"Worry clusters" in long-term memory, which include thoughts and images based on memories of prior confrontations with evaluative threat, have been hypothesized to be a key determinant of the number and duration of worry episodes (M. W. Eysenck, 1984). Thus, individuals high in test anxiety may have more structured and elaborated Worry clusters than their low-test-anxious counterparts, and therefore worry more. These clusters strengthen the relevant associate semantic network and thus fortify both the predisposition to detect threat in the future and the habitual triggering of these internal worry-generating sequences upon the next occurrence of related evaluative threat cues. Self-regulatory tendencies toward worry processes are learned through individual experiences of success and failure, through evaluation and feedback from others, and observation of other's self-statements (L. W. Morris, Davis, & Hutchings, 1981). The strength of the worry response in a test situation is a function of the social learning history of the person and his or her cognitive interpretation resulting from the accumulation of past experience, as well as environmental circumstances capable of eliciting the same type of cognitions largely independent of past learning experiences.

Recent research suggests that worry is quite pervasive in test-anxious students, with high-test-anxious students reported to experience more worry, cognitive interference, and distraction under evaluative stress compared to their less anxious counterparts (Deffenbacher, 1978). Research indicates that test-anxious subjects worry and are self-preoccupied at various stages of the evaluative process (Flett & Blankstein, 1994). When not in an evaluational situation, or anticipating one, the high-test-anxious individual may not worry about possibilities of failure or embarrassment.

Given the prevalence of worry surrounding evaluative situations, one might suspect that some styles of worry actually have an adaptive function, helping the individual deal effectively with test situations (M. W. Eysenck, 1992; Janis, 1958). The conceptual analysis of the different forms that worry may take in both clinical and normal populations (Borkovec, Robinson, Pruzinsky, & DePree, 1983; M. W. Eysenck, 1992) may shed light on the adaptive functions of the Worry component of test anxiety. Although it is unclear to what extent the Worry component of test anxiety differs from worry in a broader sense (Flett & Blankstein, 1994), and care should be taken in generalizing this body of research to the realm of test anxiety until substantiated by empirical research, this literature suggests that worry may play the following roles in test-anxious subjects:

• *Problem-solving function*: Worry, often viewed as a mental form of problem solving, may introduce potential information about evaluative threat into conscious awareness so that problem solving can take place (Borkovec et al., 1983; M. W. Eysenck, 1992). This "preparatory" function of worry may help anticipate the many negative outcomes of evaluative situations, presumably so that solutions might be found. The "work of worry" reduces anxiety by either identifying appropriate coping strategies and making them available, or by helping individuals habituate to the situation and thus increase their tolerance for subsequent threatening evaluative experiences.

• *Motivational function*: On one hand, worry may activate effortful behavior, motivating students to study harder for an upcoming exam so they can maximize their exam performance. On the other hand, worry may serve as a strategic avoidance response, helping to reduce undesired physiological arousal and threatening imagery in the highly test anxious by focusing on the verbal act of worrying (Borkovec et al., 1983).

• *Mastery (control) function*: Test-anxious persons may feel that as long as they worry about negative exam consequences, the less likely they are to happen. These individuals may worry excessively because they believe that it helps them achieve some degree of illusory (superstitious) control over the environment by preventing negative outcomes from happening (Freeston, Rheaume, Letarte, Dugas, & Ladouceur, 1994).

I. G. Sarason (1978) points out that although worry has been viewed as functional and as a step toward dealing effectively with a threatening or challenging reality (Janis, 1958), some persons who describe themselves as characteristically being worriers might not be taking a positive first step in coping with stress when they begin to worry. Rather, they may suffer from obsessive self-preoccupation and the tendency to complicate situations already challenging. Thus, instead of being of help in the coping process, worry may serve to exacerbate or create stress where otherwise it might not exist at all. Indeed, there might be a dysfunctional uncontrollable, form of worry that substantially disqualifies the three functions noted above. In fact, it might be the sense of uncontrollability and low self-efficacy that distinguishes high from low achievers.

Clearly, worry has its costs. For one, worry tends to generate negative affect for an extended duration of time in anticipation of the evaluative encounter (Borkovec et al., 1983). Furthermore, worry may be reinforced and become chronic because most of the threatening events that one is preoccupied with, say total failure on an exam, seldom actually occur. This failure of negative events to materialize may be attributed to the power of worry. Under the common assumption that worrisome thoughts are a reflection of a deep structure schemata or belief system (Meichenbaum & Butler, 1980), worrisome cognitive styles may serve to preserve such schemata from change and may reinforce the deep structure by their very occurrence; this influences how we filter, perceive, interpret, and attend to new information (Borkovec et al., 1983). In addition, the extra cognitive load of worry frequently serve to reduce task performance and efficiency, a notion which is graphically illustrated in Figure 2.1. All these reasons, taken together, reveal why worry may be maladaptive in the long turn.

A strong inverse relationship has been reported in the literature between laboratory task performance and the percentage of time spent worrying during the task (Holroyd et al., 1978). The aversive effects of worry on performance have typically been explained in terms of an interference effect on attention. Accordingly, performance may be hindered as students become preoccupied with their own distractive, negative, and repetitive thoughts and self-evaluation (e.g., "I can't figure out the answer to any of these questions," "Everyone else in this exam hall seems to be doing better than I am") and misdirect attention away from task-relevant information. Furthermore, cognitive theory suggests that the Worry component may absorb some of the limited and valuable processing capacity and attentional resources of working memory, thus reducing attentional capacity for task-related efforts (M. W. Eysenck, 1992). Hamilton's (1975) model of anxiety posits that the processing system of anxious subjects is essentially confronted with two parallel tasks that are competing for cognitive resources. The primary task involves solving an externally presented problem (e.g., test items), whereas the secondary task involves dealing with the intrusion of cognitive material (worry), seeking an end state of anxiety avoidance.

Figure 2.1. Worry: an extra load on the cognitive system.

If the system in its analysis of demand priorities gives precedence to the demands of enduring dispositions, such as anxiety avoidance, then it is likely to allocate more effort and spare capacity to the solution of the anxiety problem, at the expense of solving the primary cognitive task at hand. With primary tasks requiring high levels of information processing, less spare capacity is available, and complex tasks may become severely impaired.

Self-Preoccupation

A growing literature suggests that the tendency to become self-preoccupied and self-focused when confronted with the threat of evaluation may well be at the core of the test anxiety experience (I. G. Sarason, 1980a). Considerable empirical evidence supports the notion that high-test-anxious subjects experience relatively high levels of self-preoccupation and self-devaluing cognitions when confronted with situations that pose testlike challenges (I. G. Sarason, 1980a). Overall, high-test-anxious subjects are reported to be more self-preoccupied with fear of failure and self-blame, tend to emit self-critical and self-depreciating statements, and generally are less content with themselves than low-anxiety subjects (I. G. Sarason & Sarason, 1990; Wine, 1971a, 1982).

There is increasing evidence of the crucial role that self-preoccupation plays in various behavioral outcomes (I. G. Sarason & Sarason, 1990). This includes how anxious examinees feel during an exam, their levels of activation, and how well they perform. Precipitating evaluative events elicit or magnify underlying personal preoccupations (e.g., fear of negative outcomes) and give rise to concern over potential dangers and uncertainty about outcomes. Thus, the anxious person is shown to be prone to high levels of anxious self-preoccupation that interfere with the perception and appraisal of events. This tendency leads to overestimation of the possibility of threats and harmful events in one's environment and the lowered perceived probability of obtaining one's goals. Although all people from time to time question their personal capabilities to perform particular types of cognitive tasks, anxious individuals tend to become overly preoccupied with such thoughts. Thus, saying such things as, "I am a real failure at school," can be self-defeating if the person really has the wherewithal to handle the situation (I. G. Sarason, 1986).

In particular, test-anxious subjects are shown to be preoccupied with *negative self-referential thoughts*, involving negative thoughts and doubts about oneself, one's academic competence, or one's ability to cope with challenging evaluative situations. Thus, high-test-anxious subjects are frequently characterized by the propensity to experience a preponderance of self-derogatory thoughts and by a preoccupation with failure and self-doubt in evaluative situations (Blankstein, Toner, & Flett, 1989). In addition, high-test-anxious individuals are characterized by a set of maladaptive and pessimistic beliefs about themselves and their surroundings (Meichenbaum & Butler, 1980). They overemphasize negative behavioral outcomes, show a tendency to perfectionism, tend to catastrophize, and hold beliefs concerning helplessness and social isolation when under evaluation. The maladaptive quality of high-test-anxious individual's thinking is evident in a variety of manifestations of internal dialogue, including self-oriented rather than task-oriented thinking, deflection of attention from the task at hand, a basic orientation to thinking as negative, and a stereotypic and automatic "run-on character" of thought, having the effect of escalating rather than controlling anxiety (Meichenbaum & Butler, 1980).

A body of research literature reveals a meaningful association between test anxiety and the presence of negative thoughts. Thus, high-test-anxious subjects are reported to describe themselves in more negative terms, endorse a greater number of negative thoughts on cognitive checklists, and make more negative statements about themselves than low-test-anxious subjects (Blankstein, Flett, Boase, & Toner, 1991; Bruch, Pearl, & Giordano, 1986; Galassi, Frierson, & Sharer, 1981a, 1981b; Hunsley, 1987b; I. G. Sarason & Ganzer, 1963; Zatz & Chassin, 1983). Even *imagined* stressful test conditions elicit negative thoughts and self-statements in test-anxious college students (Heimberg, Nyman, & O'Brien, 1987).

Furthermore, high-test-anxious students, compared to their low- and moderate-test-anxious counterparts, are reported to have fewer *positive* self-referential thoughts

(Blankstein & Flett, 1990; Blankstein et al., 1989; Blankstein et al., 1991). Evaluational stressors heavily tip the balance for test-anxious persons in the direction of a higher proportion of negative to positive thoughts. One study found that low-test-anxious subjects report approximately two task-facilitating statements for each task-debilitating response, while for the high-anxious subjects the ratio was one to one (Hollandsworth et al., 1979).

Several examples of studies, briefly discussed below, help illustrate current research on thought content in test-anxious subjects. Galassi, Frierson, and Sharer (1981a) assessed both test anxiety and students' positive and negative thoughts surrounding a History course exam at three different time points (beginning of test, halfway through, and about 10 minutes before exam completion) in a sample of 231 undergraduates. As shown in Figure 2.2, high-test-anxious subjects, compared to their low-test-anxious counterparts, were shown to experience more negative thoughts and fewer positive thoughts during the exam. Negative thoughts (e.g., "escaping from the test situation," "test being too hard," "insufficient time to finish," "the likelihood of obtaining a poor grade") were positively related to test anxiety. Positive thoughts (e.g., "will succeed on the exam" "test is fair," "ability to concentrate on questions," "comprehensibility of the questions," "in control of reactions") were negatively, though modestly, related to test anxiety. Furthermore, the frequency of both positive and negative thoughts during a natural test situation vary with the phase of test taking: The overall number of such cognitions increased as the test progressed, as did the proportion of thoughts with negative content. Table 2.1 presents data on the proportion of positive and negative thoughts reportedly experienced during an exam by students varying in test anxiety levels.

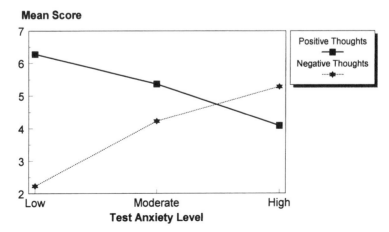

Figure 2.2. Positive and negative thoughts during exam, by test anxiety level. Based on Galassi, Frierson, and Sharer (1981a).

Table 2.1. Percentage of Negative and Positive Exam-Related
Thoughts Endorsed by Low-, Moderate-
and High-Test-Anxious College Subjects

	LTA	MTA	HTA
Negative thoughts			
Test is hard	45.1	53.7	63.8
Not enough time to finish	23.2	43.3	48.8
Wish I could get out or test was over	46.3	71.6	65.0
Work I put into studying won't be shown by my grade	15.9	23.9	43.8
Stuck on a question and it's difficult to answer others	13.4	23.9	33.8
Mind is blank or can't think straight	11.0	28.4	31.3
Going to do poorly on test	11.0	25.4	27.5
Think how awful it will be if I fail or do poorly	11.0	43.3	45.0
Positive thoughts			
Will do all right on test	70.7	53.5	42.5
A fair test	54.9	50.7	50.0
Mind is clear, can concentrate	48.8	32.8	26.3
Understand what questions mean	47.6	47.8	42.5
Feel in control of my actions	46.3	35.8	22.5
Course grade will stay same or increase after this test	40.2	37.3	25.0
Having trouble with some questions, but it's not affecting my performance on the others	35.4	31.3	25.0

Note: HTA, High test anxiety; MTA, moderate test anxiety; LTA, low test anxiety. Selected items from data reported by Galassi, Frierson, and Sharer (1981a). Percentages based on 231 college students assessed via the Checklist of Positive and Negative Thoughts.

Blankstein et al. (1989) provided evidence showing the high-test-anxious students, relative to others, listed a relatively high ratio of statements unfavorable to the self while performing a cognitive task. The proportion of negative self-related thoughts reported by high-test-anxious subjects accounted for about half of their listed thoughts, which was approximately twice that documented for the remaining subjects. Furthermore, about 38% of the negative self-referential thoughts of the high-test-anxious group were classified as "derogatory," as compared to only 22% of the thoughts listed by others. Furthermore, the proportion of task-related thoughts was much greater for low- and moderate-test-anxious groups combined than it was for the high-test-anxious group. The ratio of positive task-facilitative thoughts was positively related with overall test performance ($r = .36$), whereas the ratio of negative self-referential thoughts was negatively related to test performance ($r = -.29$).

Note, however, that the literature on the relationship between test anxiety and negative self-referential thoughts has not yielded entirely consistent results. Some studies (e.g., Galassi, Frierson, & Siegel, 1984; Klinger, 1984) have failed to replicate the frequently reported positive association between test anxiety and negative thoughts elicited during exams. Other studies suggest that it is the failure of test-anxious persons to emit *positive* facilitative thoughts about the task, rather than the high quantity of *negative* task-referential thoughts, that differentiates them from the less-test-anxious persons (Blankstein et al., 1991).

One would expect sleep to be more difficult for test-anxious students before an impending exam, on account of the negative self-preoccupations and evaluative concerns they experience. This notion is supported by one study which reports that test-anxious subjects go to bed in a "very bad mood," have "many worries on their mind," feel "very physically tense," and spend "a long time awake" the night preceding an actual psychology class test (Blankstein, Flett, Watson, & Koledin, 1990).

Cognitive Interference

Cognitive interference refers to thoughts that intrude and pop into one's mind during exams, but have no functional value in solving the cognitive task at hand. It is commonly claimed that when high-test-anxious subjects are confronted with difficult or challenging tasks they are prone to experience interfering cognitive responses, dividing attention between the self and task (I. G. Sarason, 1987). Highly stressed test-anxious subjects have been reported to spend only 60% of their available time on task, with about 40% of the time presumably spent on non-task-related cognitive activities (Deffenbacher, 1978). Field evidence (Deffenbacher & Deitz, 1978) and lab studies (I. G. Sarason & Stoops, 1978) suggest that cognitive interference may be a key factor in reducing the quality or efficiency of exam performance.

Both situational factors as well as individual differences in test anxiety play a crucial role in the likelihood of occurrence of interfering thoughts (I. G. Sarason & Sarason, 1987). Situational effects are evident when interfering thoughts intrude mainly in test situations and rapidly disappear when evaluative stress is removed (I. G. Sarason & Sarason, 1987). High-test-anxious students report elevated levels of cognitive interference under evaluative testing conditions, but cognitive interference tends to be low in test-anxious subjects irrespective of external evaluation (I. G. Sarason & Stoops, 1978; Zatz & Chassin, 1985).

Furthermore, some cognitive intrusions can be thought of as products of personality traits, particularly trait test anxiety, that manifest themselves in particular situations that have evaluational overtones. Thus, highly trait-anxious individuals would be expected to be at particular risk for experiencing debilitating thoughts when confronting challenges posed by particular evaluative situations. According to current thinking, cognitive interference is conceptualized as a joint *interactive* product of threatening evaluative situations, which increase the likelihood of self-oriented cognitions, and individual differences in the vulnerability to such cognitions, namely, trait test anxiety (M. W. Eysenck & Calvo, 1992).

There are several ways of conceptualizing cognitive interference. Recent research has uncovered a number of distinct parameters of cognitive interference, including efforts to dismiss unwanted thoughts, difficulty of dismissal, and the extent to which thoughts are distressing. These parameters were predictive above and beyond actual thought content (Kent & Jambunathan, 1989).

In addition to being distracted by task-irrelevant thoughts, test-anxious students may also be distracted by task-generated thoughts and other irrelevant task-related parameters (e.g., time left to complete exam, inability to leave unsolved problems, etc.; Deffenbacher, 1986). As test-anxious examinees become preoccupied with task irrelevancies, they may employ less efficient strategies with which to solve the task at hand (Bruch, 1978, 1981). There is some research evidence that task-generated interference is positively related to test anxiety scores, with low- and high-test-anxious examinees substantially differentiated by task-generated interference (Deffenbacher & Hazaleus, 1985). Spielberger and Vagg (1985a) argue that task-irrelevant thoughts that are unrelated to worry about test performance or consequences, like poor study habits and negative attitudes toward teachers and courses, would seem to be more meaningfully conceptualized as a correlate, rather than a component, of test anxiety.

Affective Facet

The affective facet consists of both objective somatic symptoms of physiological arousal as well as more subjective manifestations of emotional arousal and tension. Researchers have found it useful to differentiate between actual physiological reactions and one's perception of these reactions. Accordingly, it has been suggested that *Emotionality* be used to designate a person's awareness of physiological changes and bodily arousal under evaluative conditions, and interpretations of one's physiological arousal, as opposed to physiological arousal per se (Deffenbacher, 1980; Holroyd & Appel, 1980; Liebert & Morris, 1967). The differentiation between more objective bodily symptoms and subjective experience is evidenced in some current measures. For example, I. G. Sarason's (1984) Reaction to Tests (RTT) distinguishes between two components of Emotionality, the more objective bodily symptoms and the more subjective feelings of tension.

Physiological Reactions

I begin by discussing heightened autonomic arousal, the most dominant response mode for the expression of anxiety under stressful conditions, and move on to discuss some physiological concomitants of evaluative stress.

Autonomic Arousal.   Autonomic arousal is evidenced during testing in a variety of physiological responses, such as increased heart rate, rate of respiration, gastric sensations, feelings of nausea, sweating, cold and clammy hands, need to pass urine, and shaking and trembling (Suinn, 1984). Symptoms of autonomic arousal (e.g., hands or body perspiring, heart beating fast, stomach tense, dryness in mouth, hands or body trembling) are among the most frequently reported bodily sensations experienced by college examinees (Galassi et al., 1981a, 1981b). Furthermore, to the degree that some examinees experience autonomic changes more diffusely in test situations, they may report subjective feelings of stress. Thus, rather than specifically reporting increased heart rate or identifying muscle spasms, the test-anxious person may talk about "lumps in my throat" or "butterflies in my stomach" while taking an exam.

The *sympathetic* nervous system is responsible for arousing or mobilizing the body for action and preparing various organs to meet an emergency situation quickly and with maximum strength. When under stress, arousal of the sympathetic nervous system and the release of catecholamines prompts a variety of important bodily changes. These include increases in heart rate and heightened blood pressure, heightened contractibility of the heart, constriction of blood vessels and reduced blood flow to the skin (to reduce bleeding), high conversion of stored energy to usable energy, and increasing blood flow to muscles, dilation of pupil of eye, stimulation of sweat glands, scanty secretion of salivary glands, secretion of epinephrine and nor-epinephrine, and inhibition of motility and tone of the gastrointestinal system. It is currently held that physiological responses to test anxiety are mainly sympathetic, with some *parasympathetic* manifestations (e.g., increase of gastrointestinal tract and bowel movement). This readying of the body, described by one of the pioneers of stress research, Walter Cannon, as the "fight–flight" response, is basic to stress (Gatchel et al., 1989). Table 2.2 presents some of the effects of evaluative stress and arousal on autonomic functions.

A body of research supports the claim that evaluative stress is associated with physiological arousal in examinee populations (Hollandsworth et al., 1979; Holroyd et al., 1978). However, as will be documented below, when actual levels of autonomic activity are monitored, high- and low-test-anxious groups cannot be consistently distinguished on the basis of their physiological responses. Furthermore, researchers

**Table 2.2. Effects of Anxiety
on Key Body Functions**

Function	Effect
Respiration	Increased
Contractability of heart	Increased
Blood vessels	Constricted
Pulse	Increased
Heart rate	Increased
Temperature	Raised
Blood sugar	Increased
Sweat gland secretion	Increased
Dilation of eyes	Increased
Gastrointestinal tract activity	Enhanced

have been unable to adduce conclusive evidence of any *specific* pattern of physiological arousal that regularly accompanies the phenomenological components of anxiety (Holroyd et al., 1978; Deffenbacher, 1986).

Although most individuals show increases in physiological activity when exposed to test situations, people may focus on different physiological responses that uniquely define the test anxiety experience for them. Thus, it is not unusual to find reports of increase in heart rate, faster breathing, sweating of the palms, gastrointestinal disturbances, and changes in appetite and digestive processes (or combinations of these) when people report they are experiencing test anxiety. These response patterns are reported to be reliable over time and occur regardless of the type of stress to which the individual is subjected (Hodges, 1976).

Evaluative anxiety, as a special case of general anxiety, may be construed of as a piece of excess evolutionary baggage. The physiological manifestations of anxiety, which helped our ancestors cope with threats in their physical environment through fight-or-flight reactions (increased heart rate, rate of breathing, sweating, muscle tension), may no longer be functional or adaptive in the type of social-evaluative situations we face in modern society. In fact, evidence reviewed in this book suggests they may be quite dysfunctional and debilitating, as anyone experiencing heightened arousal (palpitations, hyperventilation, muscle tension, faintness, etc.) while sitting through a 3-hour aptitude test may attest.

Additional Physiological Concomitants of Evaluative Situations

Endocrine System. It is currently held that psychological stress is mediated by both the nervous system and the endocrine (hormonal) system. The endocrine system is made up of a number of ductless glands (adrenals, pituitary, thyroid, reproduction) which secrete hormones into the bloodstream. The endocrine system interfaces with and complements the activity of the nervous system in controlling bodily activities, using chemical messengers to stimulate, slow, or otherwise govern responses by organ systems (Gatchel et al., 1989). The entire endocrinological system (hypothalamic–pituitary–adrenocortical) controls a variety of neurohormones which are implicated in stress and anxiety. Selye (1956) speculated that the widespread bodily changes that accompany stress and anxiety are mediated by the release of the hormone ACTH (adrenocorticotropic hormone). Thus, when stimulated, the pituitary gland secretes ACTH, which controls secretion of corticosteroids by the cortex. The corticosteroids include glucocorticoids (which help regulate levels of glucose in the blood), cortisol (which accompanies stress and has a number of effects on carbohydrate metabolism), and mineral corticoids (affecting utilization of mineral substances).

Furthermore, arousal of the sympathetic nervous system and the production and release of catecholamines (classical stress hormones) are critically important in an individual's response to stressful test circumstances. Thus, the stimulation of the sympathetic system causes the adrenal medulla to secrete large quantities of adrenaline (epinephrine) and noradrenaline (norepinephrine)—two important stress hormones. Adrenaline is secreted mainly by the adrenal medulla, whereas noradrenaline is primarily released by sympathetic neurons. The stimulation of adrenaline frees stores of glycogen for energy to the muscles and redistributes blood from the viscera to the heart, brain, and extremities. The flow of adrenaline increases systolic blood pressure, and the volume of blood in the muscles leads to an increase in glucose. Noradrenaline supports and extends arousal generated by the nervous system, increasing heart rate and other coronary activity to a limited extent.

A number of empirical studies have reported a meaningful level of hormonal activity in various student populations undergoing major exams. It may come as no surprise that these studies, requiring repeated blood samples taken from examinees at various intervals throughout the exam process, were conducted by and large in medical school settings. Bloch and Brackenridge (1972), for example, obtained blood plasma samples from 78 medical students immediately after they were administered an important oral qualifying medical exam which determined selection for initial residency training at a number of hospitals. A high plasma cholesterol level was positively associated with low self-rating of success on the exam as well as poor exam performance. In addition, a moderate correlation ($r = .35$) was also reported between cortisol and self-reported emotionality, supporting the concept of adrenocortical responsiveness to stress situations. Overall, this study provided evidence that students who are aware of their inadequate performance throughout an exam period react biochemically with raised cholesterol levels. Comparably, Herbert, Moore, de la Riva, and Watts (1986) reported significant hormonal changes in 38 male medical students immediately prior to a major medical school exam. Marked changes in serum cortisol and in urinary catecholamines were reported to occur between 1 and 2 hours before the exam. Both adrenaline and noradrenaline were markedly elevated just before the exam. Furthermore, changes were observed in both cortisol and prolactin, which were both positively, though moderately, associated with debilitating trait test anxiety. However, there were no significant correlations between changes in hormone levels and those in any of the state anxiety scales.

Hudgens, Chatterton, Torre, et al. (1989) obtained profiles of hormonal responses from 25 male medical students the day they took an important 3-hour written exam and on a routine day. Blood samples were obtained at 60, 45, 30, and 15 minutes before the start of the exam and at 90, 120, 180, and 240 minutes after the exam. The analyses show that cortisol was elevated in both the pre- and postexam periods for both exam and self-control conditions relative to an independent nonstudent control. The mean prolactin level for the exam group was significantly elevated over control groups prior to the exam. Both cortisol and prolactin remained elevated in the exam group in the 1.5- to 4-hour postexam period.

Immune System. Recent research has made considerable strides in determining to what extent examination stress may have a detectable influence on the human immune system. Research suggests that evaluative stress factors are capable of altering immunocompetence, presumably because the autonomic activity associated with stress releases peripheral hormones that modulate immunity. Specifically, catecholamines released by sympathetic terminals and the adrenal medulla, as well as hormones released by the adrenal cortex, may participate in the regulation of the immune response (Maier, Watkins, & Fleshner, 1994).

One of the early studies in this field by Kiecolt-Glaser and coworkers (Kiecolt-Glaser, Garner, Speicher, Penn, Holliday, & Glaser, R., 1984; cf. Kiecolt-Glaser, Janice, Speicher, Holliday, & Glaser, R. 1984) reported decreased natural killer cell activity in students dealing with medical school exams, as compared with control levels exhibited 1 month later. Killer cell activity designates the activity of leukocytes that kill cells infected by viruses and other foreign cells or organisms. Furthermore, percentages of T cells were also found to be lower among medical students during exams than had been earlier. T cells, a major component of the immune system, are a particular form of lymphocyte that control other cells and also kill antigen or foreign bodies directly. In addition, the production of interferon, an important lymphokine (i.e., a substance released by lymphocytes that helps signal immune cells) was found to be suppressed among students during the exam. Finally, exams were also associated with decreased proliferative response to challenge by mitogens (Glaser, Kiecolt-Glaser, Speicher, & Holliday, 1985), substances which cause the lymphocytes to multiply and provide evidence of strength of lymphocyte response.

Halvorsen and Vassend (1987) assessed cellular activity in blood samples from students before an important graduate entrance exam in Psychology at three points of time: 6 weeks before the exam, 1 day before the exam, and about 2 weeks after the exam. The results showed that the percentage of monocytes which are circulated in the bloodstream and become effective phagocytes (i.e., have the ability to surround and ingest microorganisms and inert particles) increased at Time 2 of the examination. The proliferative response of T cells to antigens, mitogens, and allogeneic cells decreased from Time 1 to 2. Further evidence for the effects of test situations on immunocompetence come from research on antibody titers. Exam stress is associated with elevated levels of antibody titer to Epstein–Barr virus among medical students (Glaser et al., 1985; Kiecolt-Glaser, Janice, et al., 1984). Antibody titers to latent viruses remain dormant in the body following initial infection. If something happens to weaken the immune system's control of latent viruses and they become active, antibody titers to the virus will increase, thus indicating a decrease in immunocompetence.

In addition to autonomic, endocrine, and immune system reactions to evaluative stressors, the patterning of cortical activity in stressful situations has recently been accorded attention by stress researchers. Thus, it has been suggested that emotional responding may be mediated by the right hemisphere, whereas verbal worry or rumination, a major component of test anxiety, may be mediated by the left hemisphere (Schwartz, Davidson, & Maer, 1975). Recent research by Papsdorf, Ghannam, and Jamieson (1995) suggests that interhemispheric interference results from simultaneous arousal of the right and left cerebral hemispheres. This, in turn, contributes to the difficulty of high-test-anxious students in maintaining attention and hence impairs their performance on cognitive tests.

Emotionality

Although feelings of arousal may occur in both high- and low-test-anxious individuals, they may be interpreted differently. Thus, quite paradoxically, "Emotionality" involves cognitive processes to a substantial degree, i.e., the attention paid to and interpretations of affective/physiological arousal. Indeed, a series of studies showing an inconsistent relationship between self-reported test anxiety and tonic levels of physiological arousal in evaluative situations suggests the need for distinguishing between perceived and actual somatic arousal.

A frequently cited study by Holroyd et al. (1978) continuously monitored the heart rate, heart rate variability, skin conductance level, and skin resistance of 72 female students who exhibited variations in test anxiety in an analog test situation. Although the stress of the test produced clear changes on all four physiological measures, high- and low-test-anxious persons were differentiated only in heart rate variability—which appears to reflect differences in the cognitive and attentional responses of the two groups. Furthermore, although high-test-anxious subjects reported substantially higher levels of state anxiety and worry than their low-test-anxious counterparts, these differences in reported anxiety were generally not accompanied by corresponding differences in autonomic activity. Comparably, Hollandsworth et al. (1979) assessed heart rate and respiration in a small group of high- and low-test-anxious women and found that the three physiological variables assessed during the test period were similar between groups. Interestingly, test-anxious individuals defined their arousal as debilitative, whereas nonanxious subjects viewed their arousal as a cue to exert greater effort toward the test. Note, however, that a number of studies suggest that high- and low-test-anxious subjects may be differentiated in cardiac reactivity under evaluative conditions. Montgomery (1977), for example, reported significant differences in anticipatory cardiac responses between high- and low-test-anxious subjects performing an anagrams task under evaluative stress conditions. Similarly, Deffenbacher (1986) found that high-trait-test-anxious students had higher pulse rates than their low-trait-test-anxious counterparts (79.48 beats/minute vs. 70.40 beats/minute) in a sample of 156 students taking a true-to-life exam. Deffenbacher suggested that since most of the studies reporting nonsignificant findings were conducted under analog test situations, studies carried out in actual test situations may yield a different pattern of results.

In order to elucidate the criterial attributes of the Emotionality component of test anxiety, it is useful to compare it with the Worry component of test anxiety along several key dimensions. These include eliciting temporal patterns, pattern of relationship with academic performance, and intervention implications.

Eliciting Cues. Emotionality has been characterized as a set of autonomic responses that become conditioned to specific testing situations as a function of past experiences (L. W. Morris, Davis, & Hutchings, 1981; Spiegler, Morris, & Liebert, 1968). Current research supports the notion that Emotionality is elicited primarily by external cues (e.g., walking into the exam hall, appearance of examiner, distribution of test booklets) that signal the initiation of evaluation. Worry cognitions, by contrast, are triggered by cues related to negative appraisals of exam performance, perceived as threatening the individual's sense of adequacy and worth (L. W. Morris, Harris, & Rovias, 1981). A study by L. W. Morris and Liebert (1973) in a sample of male undergraduates suggests that the Worry and Emotionality components of anxiety are aroused by different kinds of stress, with Worry scores aroused primarily under failure threat, while Emotionality scores elevated primarily under threat of physical shock.

Temporal Patterns. Emotionality rises sharply immediately before the test and typically wanes as the examinee progresses on the exam (Doctor & Altman, 1969). Worrisome thoughts, in contrast, reach a high level early in the exam process and do not dissipate so rapidly (Liebert & Morris, 1967; Spiegler et al., 1968). This is depicted in Figure 2.3, showing means of Emotionality and Worry scores at pre- and posttest assessment periods in a college exam. In fact, worry has been shown to maintain itself over the entire period of test taking and may be aroused days or even weeks in advance of an exam (Becker, 1982a, 1983; cf. Becker, 1982b).

A recent study by Kim and Rocklin (1994) examined state Worry and Emotionality in a sample of 88 undergraduates taking an exam at three points in time:

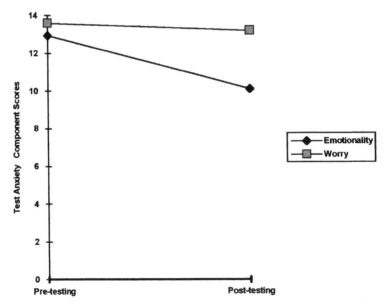

Figure 2.3. Means of Emotionality and Worry scores at pre- and posttest assessment periods in a college exam. Based on data from Spiegler, Morris, and Liebert (1968).

before the exam, after the 7th item, and after the 15th item. Overall, Worry and Emotionality were observed to have substantially different temporal patterns. Students' state Worry was higher during the test than either before or after the test. In contrast, students' state Emotionality peaked at the beginning of the test and then gradually decreased. However, students attempting hard items reported stable levels of Emotionality, perhaps because of their frequent experiences of failure. Thus, under certain conditions, as long as evaluation stress continues, Emotionality remains stable, as does Worry. Doctor and Altman (1969) obtained preexam and postexam ratings of the Worry and Emotionality components of test anxiety for 159 undergraduates surrounding a final psychology course exam. Both Worry and Emotionality scores dropped significantly from pre- to posttest periods, although the absolute change in Worry scores was less than that of Emotionality scores. However, some studies indicate minimal differences in the temporal patterns for Worry and Emotionality scores (Morris & Fulmer, 1976; Holroyd, 1978; C. A. Smith & Morris, 1976; Deffenbacher & Deitz, 1978).

Pattern of Relationship with Academic Performance. As will be discussed in some detail in Chapter 9, current research supports the generalization that Worry is more consistently and strongly related to cognitive performance than is Emotionality. This relationship almost assumes the status of a "truism" in that it has been demonstrated so often (Covington, 1992; M. W. Eysenck, 1982).

Association with Performance Expectancies. A number of studies suggest that the two components of test anxiety are differentiated with respect to their pattern of relationships with performance expectancies. Thus, while Emotionality has been shown to be relatively unrelated to performance expectancy in a test situation, Worry has been shown to vary as an inverse function of one's performance expectancy (Spiegler et al., 1968). Given that worry is conceptualized as negative success expectations, it stands to reason that where persons expect success, considerations of worry should be minimized; where poor performance is expected, they should be maximal.

Intervention Implications. With respect to interventive implications, worry and emotionality may require different methods for their reduction (L. W. Morris & Liebert, 1973). Emotionality, construed to be largely a classically conditioned reaction to specific evaluative stimuli, may be effectively reduced via relaxation and counterconditioning techniques. Debilitatingly high worry, reflecting a lack of self-confidence and low success expectations, may be alleviated through a cognitively oriented approach. Therapeutic approaches aimed at changing expectancies or teaching study-skills training techniques that build confidence in one's ability to perform under threatening evaluative conditions may be particularly effective. Table 2.3 summarizes these criteria for distinguishing the Emotionality and Worry components of test anxiety, and Figure 2.4 graphically presents these two components.

**Table 2.3. Comparison of Cognitive and Affective Components
of Test Anxiety on Key Dimensions**

Dimension	Emotionality	Worry
Eliciting conditions	Test-specific or situational cues	Concern over failure and consequences of evaluation
Temporal relation to exam	Peaks at beginning of exam and dissipates quickly	Relatively stable and elevated before and after exams
Relation to performance	Low and inconsistent	Moderate and consistent
Association with performance expectancies	Minimal	Strong
Useful intervention techniques	Counterconditioning and relaxation techniques	Cognitive-behavioral techniques focusing on modifying expectations

Behavioral Facet

In addition to its cognitive and affective manifestations, test anxiety may also be expressed in a variety of overt behaviors or "behavioral acts." Two key behavioral expressions of test anxiety, study and test-taking deficits and procrastination, are briefly surveyed.

Deficient Study and Test-Taking Skills

Test-anxious students are often said to be characterized by behavioral deficits in a wide variety of academic skills, including utilizing class time, taking and organizing class notes, preparing for exams, integrating the subject matter, and maximizing their use of time on objective exams (Culler & Holahan, 1980; Kirkland & Hollandsworth, 1979, 1980). High-test-anxious students are said to have difficulty encod-

Figure 2.4.   Worry (left) and Emotionality (right) components of test anxiety.

ing information, organizing information into larger patterns of meaning, and effectively employing metacognitive processes such as self-monitoring. In addition, high-test-anxious students are reported to have more problems than low-test-anxious students during both initial learning and review—although retrieval appears to be more of a problem for anxious students than storage and encoding (Benjamin et al., 1981). These deficiencies, in turn, are said to impact upon test performance and achievements—either directly or working through anxiety in the test situation (see Chapter 3 for relevant empirical research).

Procrastination, Avoidance, and Escape Behaviors

Test-anxious persons often evidence a variety of avoidance or escape behaviors at various stages of the exam process. Academic procrastination, a salient form of avoidance behavior characterizing test-anxious subjects at the preparatory stage, involves the tendency to make a habit of putting off academic tasks, and to also experience problematic levels of anxiety associated with this procrastination (Rothblum, Solomon, & Murakami, 1986). A test-anxious student who procrastinates before an important exam is equipped to study, is trying and planning to study, but yet excessively delays studying (Kalechstein, Hocevar, Zimmer, & Kalechstein, 1989). One type of procrastinator disengages from studying for an important test due to the perceived aversiveness of the test material for that person, whereas a second type disengages out of fear of failure on the test (Solomon & Rothblum, 1984).

Consider, for example, the case of a college student majoring in education, who needs to pass a "dreaded" final exam in an educational statistics course as a precondition for college graduation. The student would probably dislike doing class exercises, lack the energy to complete the homework assignments, and perhaps hold irrational beliefs about success in the course (e.g., "only students talented in math have a chance to do well in this course"). Consequently, rather than intensively preparing or studying for an important upcoming exam, the student delays studying until the night before the exam, and instead channels her or his energy in writing up an article for the college gazette. This student may suffer considerable anxiety as a result of procrastination, which serves no rational or reasonable function.

Overall, however, relatively little attention has been paid to procrastination and test avoidance as a component of the response of people high in test anxiety in evaluative situations (Geen, 1985a).

Escape and avoidance behavior may often serve high-test-anxious subjects as a "self-protective" device in reducing their tension and distress during or immediately prior to exam situations. Thus, high-test-anxious subjects frequently attempt to avoid or escape from an impending evaluative situation or show a low degree of task persistency during the evaluative encounter when the constraints against escaping are weak (Geen, 1987). In fact, wishing to escape the test situation is the most frequently reported negative thought that test-anxious subjects experience during an actual exam (Galassi et al., 1981a; cf. Galassi et al., 1981b). Such escape attempts may play a role in the frequently reported performance decrements of highly test-anxious people.

In most real-life or experimental test situations, however, examinees generally do not believe "escape" to be a viable option. Cognitive interference may often be the end result of this inability to escape or disengage physically from the test situation (Carver, 1996). Geen (1985a) hypothesized that when it is not possible to avoid the test per se, anxious subjects often revert to more passive avoidance strategies. At the very least they try to avoid failing by adopting a more cautious strategy to minimize incorrect responding in decision-making tasks (Geen, 1985a, 1987; Hill, 1972; S. B. Sarason, 1966).

Temporal Phases of Test Anxiety

Having discerned the various structural facets or components of test anxiety, I now adopt a more process-oriented approach and will conceptualize anxiety in an evaluative stress situation as a dynamic temporal process unfolding over time. Specifically, I will trace the temporal course of test anxiety through the following four distinct stages of the evaluative stress process: the *anticipatory* stage, involving appraisals of the test situation and preparation for the exam; the *confrontation* phase, involving the actual test-taking experience; the *anticipation* phase, following test taking, but prior to the announcement of grades; and the *outcome* stage, in which the uncertainty is resolved when grades are announced.

(a) *The Anticipatory Stage*, a preparatory phase prior to the exam, constitutes a period of warning regarding the imminence of the impending exam encounter and concomitant preparation for the upcoming exam. Thus, once an individual becomes aware of an upcoming exam, he or she typically becomes concerned with the demands, possibilities, and constraints connected with the future exam. Examinees are typically concerned about how best to prepare for the upcoming exam, and how to regulate feelings and aversive emotions associated with the exam, as well as with the prospects for success on the exam. Since ambiguity is expected to be at its height during the anticipatory stage—because examinees do not know exactly what will be on the exam or what the outcome will be like—the possibilities for both positive and negative outcomes can be seen.

Individuals prepare for upcoming tests largely through task-focused coping, while harboring feelings, expectancies, and cognitions regarding the futility, wisdom, or appropriateness of their study (Covington & Omelich, 1988). High-test-anxious students are characterized by ineffectual study, often indulging in self-protective thoughts involving denial, wishful thinking, and avoidance elements. Although these actions may distance these individuals temporarily from the implications of failure, they will eventually contribute to the very features that students fear by disrupting effective study. By contrast, individuals high in success orientation typically perceive themselves as possessing sufficient effort and ability resources and are less preoccupied with fears of incompetency and negative consequences of performance.

There is some research indicating that students report heightened anxiety in the last several days before a major exam. However, there are marked differences with regard to exactly when anxiety peaks. For some it is the same day as the exam, whereas for others it is as many as 4 days before the exam (Bolger, 1990; Lay, Edwards, Parker, & Endler, 1989).

(b) At the *Confrontation Stage*, examinees actually confront the stressor, i.e., take the exam. It is anticipated that deficiencies in study skills (cognitive), fears about potential failure (motivational), and characteristic anxiety reactions (emotional) will coalesce to elevate interference and discomfort occurring during testing (Covington & Omelich, 1988). Each of these antecedent constructs is expected to trigger various intervening mediators, which in turn impinge upon each other and eventually upon performance. Research by Galassi et al. (1981a) demonstrated that the last 10 minutes of a test represent a critical moment, because negative thoughts and sensations of arousal essentially accumulate as students mount their final efforts to finish the test on time and check the accuracy of their answers. As discussed earlier, the Emotionality component tends to peak during the first few moments of the actual encounter with the exam; Worry, the cognitive component of situational test anxiety, is relatively more stable throughout the exam.

(c) The *Waiting Stage* refers to the postexam stage: examinees have already taken the exam, but grades have yet to be announced. Uncertainty about the specific nature and qualities of the test and test atmosphere has been resolved or meaningfully reduced, and feedback cues from the examination may help examinees predict their exam performance reasonably well (Zeidner, 1991). However, individuals may still feel considerable apprehension about the outcome.

(d) The *Outcome Stage* constitutes the last phase of the stressful encounter. After grades are posted, students finally learn how well they performed on the exam. Any uncertainty about the outcome is resolved at this stage, and the concerns of students turn to the significance of what has already happened and its implications (harm, benefit). The more an encounter unfolds, the more firmly the examinee should be making either a negative or positive appraisal of the outcome. Students who succeed on the exam would be expected to be happy and experience an uplift. By contrast, those who do poorly would be expected to become anxious and moody. In particular, test-anxious subjects should suffer negative self-evaluation and diverse emotions following failure feedback.

During each of the phases described above, anxiety may vary as a function of cognitive appraisals, which, in turn, vary as a function of the objective properties of the specific phase of the test-taking process considered.

Debunking the Uniformity Myth: Different Types of Test-Anxious Students

In order to further refine and enrich the conceptualization, diagnosis, and assessment of test anxiety, thus allowing the tailoring of specific interventions for different types of test-anxious students, some researchers have attempted to identify different types of test-anxious examinees. I briefly sketch some distinct, yet potentially overlapping categories of test-anxious subjects.

Examinees with Deficient Study and Test-Taking Skills

Researchers have differentiated between high-test-anxious students based on differing levels of their study and exam-taking skills (Benjamin et al., 1981; Naveh-Benjamin, McKeachie, & Lin, 1987; Paulman & Kennelly, 1984). One type of test-anxious student is characterized by a major deficiency in study and test-taking skills. Their poor exam performance results from skills deficits that include problems in acquisition (encoding), organization/rehearsal (study skills), and retrieval/application during a test. These students are anxious during testing, and perhaps justifiably so, because they recognize that they possess few organizational strategies to help them perform well on exams and that they are less well prepared owing to their inefficient study skills. In fact, these students tend to do poorly in both nonevaluative as well as in evaluative situations because they do not encode and organize the material well in the first place (Paulman & Kennelly, 1984).

Examinees Experiencing Anxiety Blockage and Retrieval Problems

A second type of test-anxious student includes those who have efficient study skills, but who suffer from anxiety blockage and consequently have problems retrieving information during an exam (Benjamin et al., 1981; Naveh-Benjamin et al., 1987; Paulman & Kennelly, 1984). These anxious students encode material well enough early in study, budget their time during exams, and adopt strategies that maximize success on various types of cognitive exams, including overstudying for an exam. However, they do poorly on exams because they cannot handle the stresses and pressures of evaluative situations. These skilled subjects fail to use their adequate cognitive organization of the subject matter because of task-irrelevant responses in the test situation itself. As the exam approaches, they may experience concentration difficulties in their final stages of study due to anxious arousal (Naveh-Benjamin et al., 1987). During the actual exam, they may be unable to recall, organize, and express what they learned. The excessive effort expended in countering internal cognitive distraction places a limit on processing capability beyond which performance effectiveness falls off rapidly (Paulman & Kennelly, 1984).

Failure-Accepting Examinees

Research by Covington (1992) has identified a particular category of stressed students called "failure acceptors." These students are characterized by poor study skills and are frequently of low academic ability. Because of a personal history of repeated test failures, they come to accept low ability as the primary explanation of their failures, despite early efforts to deflect the personal implications of failure by use of excuses and other subterfuge. Failure acceptors are theorized to have given up the struggle to define their worth in terms of competitive achievement. As a consequence they become accepting of failure, exhibiting apathy, resignation, and a sense of defeat, not unlike those reactions traditionally associated with learned helplessness. These students have given up the struggle to maintain a sense of worth via ability, and because of repeated failures in school have become convinced of their incompetency (Covington, 1992). The relative absence of approach tendencies in this group is associated with incessant self-derogation where ability is concerned and with inferior study skills. Failure-accepting students do not express much pride in their successes nor much shame in their failures.

One important subclass of "failure-accepting" students is made up of low-ability students who become anxious because they simply are not up to doing the academic work required to succeed in school or college (Wigfield & Eccles, 1989). As their failure experiences mount, they tend to become more anxious and worry throughout various stages of the study cycle (Covington & Omelich, 1985). Feelings of incompetency give rise to task-irrelevant worry about ability, which in turn interferes with effective information processing.

Failure-Avoiding Examinees

Failure-avoiding students are those driven to achieve primarily as a means for establishing and maintaining a sense of personal value that involves minimizing the implication of failure in that they lack ability (Covington, 1992; Covington & Omelich, 1987a). This joint demand of maximizing the likelihood of success while discounting failure should it occur places the student in a conflict regarding effort expenditure. For these students, effort is truly a double-edged sword (Covington & Omelich, 1979). On one hand, overstriving and meticulous preparation maximizes one's chance for success, yet failure despite high efforts increases the probability that one's ability will be considered low, thus inducing anxiety reactions. Ironically, the very tension that mobilizes exceptional effort and diligence among these overstrivers during test preparation may also set the stage for subsequent debilitating anxiety during test taking.

Research by Covington and Omelich (1988) suggests that various apprehensions prior to the exam tend to be magnified out of all proportion in these students, especially those worries associated with being revealed as incompetent and of not doing well enough to stay in school. Worries not only linger, but intensify during the test preparation stage—especially as the test grows closer. Worry becomes manifest as defensively oriented thoughts that divert the attention of failure-avoiding students from the study task at hand. Such thoughts are accompanied by emotional tension and occasionally physiological reactions, which in turn add their own unique contributions to the disruption of effective study. As a consequence, failure-avoiding students find themselves largely unprepared even though, on average, they spent as much time studying as did success-oriented students.

Self-Handicappers

For one class of test-anxious students heightened arousal and worry in evaluative situations may simply serve a *self-handicapping function* (Harris, Snyder, Higgens, & Schrag, 1986). Following Jones and Berglas (1978), we may define self-handicapping strategies with respect to test situations as the creation of impediments to performance in evaluative situations so that the individual has a ready excuse for potential failure or other negative self-relevant information. Accordingly, test anxiety might serve as a defensive rationalizing function, providing a convenient and relatively nonperjorative explanation for failure.

One possibly effective way test-anxious students might avoid diagnostic information about intellectual tasks is to reduce effort or avoid the test situation. Such a strategy reduces the self-relevant implications of failure because accurate ability inferences are possible only under conditions of maximal effort or task engagement. Research by T. W. Smith, Snyder, and Handelsman (1982) supports this notion, showing that high-test-anxious persons report lowered effort in a self-handicapping pattern. Furthermore, self-handicappers might exaggerate the amount of anxiety experienced in a test situation so as to provide a ready excuse for anticipated failure. Accordingly, if a low score is obtained the student can rely on the debilitating effects of anxiety as a causal explanation for the failure, leaving the role of intelligence and other dispositional factors ambiguous. This form of causal attribution conforms with the common notion that individuals often use psychological symptoms as a "wooden leg," that is, as an excuse to escape responsibility for actions, thus reducing otherwise burdensome expectations others hold for that person. Experimental research by T. W. Smith et al. (1982) support the hypothesis that highly test-anxious individuals typically use their symptoms in a self-protective fashion, whereas low-test-anxious individuals are not accustomed to strategically employing anxiety symptoms.

Perfectionistic Overstrivers

Overstriving high-test-anxious perfectionists are characterized by high personal standards of academic success, perception of high or even exaggerated expectations, perceived doubt regarding quality of academic performance, and a need for order and organization in their academic work (Blatt, 1995; Covington, 1992). According to Blatt (1995), it is important to differentiate between "adaptive" and "nonadaptive" perfectionists (Blatt, 1995). Accordingly, students who are "adaptive" perfectionists derive a sense of pleasure from their characteristic painstaking efforts and strivings to excel in their academic work, and the success they experience brings them a sense of satisfaction of a "job well done." However, in the case of maladaptive perfectionists, the type believed to be most often associated with test anxiety, deep-seated feelings of inferiority and fear that they will not meet their own self-imposed or externally imposed (parents, teachers, peers) standards force them into an endless cycle of self-defeating overstriving. No effort is ever sufficient as the perfectionistic examinee seeks approval and acceptance and tries to avoid errors and failure.

Because nothing less than a perfect score is considered to be good enough for them, stressful evaluative experiences create intense negative affect and stress for these individuals; each academic task and test situation becomes another threatening challenge or enterprise. For some individuals dominated by irrational thought schemata, anything short of a perfect test score would be considered total failure, resulting in self-criticism and severe upset (Oliver, 1975). These expectations tend to heighten anxiety in evaluative situations, so that these perfectionistic individuals tend to perform less well than they should, even though they are capable of doing the work. On one hand, success is sought after because it reassures them of their own personal value or worth, but on the other hand, it perpetuates anxiety because these individuals know they cannot succeed indefinitely, test after test, since their goal is not merely excellence, but perfection.

Some research suggests that individuals with high levels of self-criticism and perfectionism are vulnerable to experiences of failure—to which they react with increased anxiety and helplessness (Blatt & Zuroff, 1992). These perfectionistic individuals experience considerable negative affect before, during, and after an evaluative task (Frost & Marten, 1990). Furthermore, research by Covington and Omelich (1985) suggests that the defensively driven character of such perfectionistic examinees, characterized by meticulous, excessive study, catches up with them. The presence of anxiety discourages deep-level processing during original learning, and favors instead superficial rote memorization. As tension mounts during the test-taking stage, they suffer a massive failure to recall what they had spent so much time overlearning (Covington & Omelich, 1985).

Hewitt and Flett (1991) differentiated between two types of perfectionists that are particularly relevant to our discussion of test-anxious types. One type, *self-related perfectionists*, are characterized by exceedingly high self-imposed unrealistic standards and intensive self-scrutiny in which there is an inability to accept flaws, faults, or failure within oneself. Often, this form of perfectionism appears to have adaptive potential and is related to resourcefulness and constitutive striving. The second type, *socially prescribed perfectionists*, are characterized by the belief that others maintain unrealistic and exaggerated expectancies that are difficult, if not impossible to meet. Furthermore, they believe that one must meet these standards to win approval and acceptance from significant others. Because these excessive standards are experienced as externally imposed, they can often feel uncontrollable and often result in feelings of failure, anxiety, helplessness, and hopelessness, particularly if the source of these expectations is the examinee's parents, teachers, or peers. Recent research on perfectionism by Gordon Flett and his colleagues suggests that socially prescribed perfectionism is the element most closely tied in with anxiety in evaluative situations (Flett, Hewitt, Endler, & Tassone, 1994/1995). Accordingly, it is the sense of *externally* imposed standards of perfectionism that is most associated with anxiety in evaluative situations, causing high-test-anxious subjects characterized by socially prescribed perfectionism to be especially anxious in test situations.

Related Forms of Social-Evaluation Anxiety

Social situations, by and large, carry the prospect of interpersonal evaluation. The various forms of social-evaluation anxiety differentiated in the literature (e.g., test anxiety, math anxiety, sports anxiety, speech anxiety, audience anxiety, stage fright, communication apprehension, social embarrassment, dating anxiety, etc.) share the prospect or presence of personal evaluation in real or imagined social situations, particularly when a person perceives a low likelihood of obtaining satisfactory evaluations from others (Leitenberg, 1990b). Although the specialized forms of social-evaluative anxiety have important structural similarities, which distinguishes among them are the antecedent conditions and contexts evoking the anxiety and the somewhat different social-evaluation demands and stakes.

Math anxiety, one prevalent form of social-evaluation anxiety, is defined by feelings of tension, helplessness, mental disorganization, and associated bodily symptoms that are evoked in mathematical problem-solving situations (Fennema & Sherman, 1976; Hunsley, 1987a; Richardson & Suinn, 1972; Tobias, 1978; Tobias & Weissbrod, 1980). Math anxiety is claimed to interfere with the manipulation of numbers and the solving of complex mathematical problems in a wide variety of ordinary life and academic situations (Richardson & Suinn, 1972). For the math-anxious person, having to deal with numbers represents a particular form of evaluation stress that is often interpreted as highly threatening to one's self-esteem.

Although math anxiety has traditionally been treated as a particular case of test anxiety, the two constructs should probably best be viewed as being distinct from each other, distinguishable by the stimulus properties of situations that are considered personally threatening. Thus, whereas math-anxious persons are likely to interpret situations involving the *manipulation of numbers* and *mathematics problems* as personally threatening, test-anxious persons are more likely to appraise *examination situations* as personally threatening. In addition, math anxiety includes a reaction to the *content* as well as to the *performance* evaluation. That is, math anxiety focuses not only on the evaluative nature of math tests and problem-solving activities, but also concerns mathematical content, its distinctive features as an intellectual activity, and its meanings for many persons in our society (Richardson & Woolfolk, 1980).

Sports anxiety, another important form of social-evaluative anxiety, has been conceptualized as both a trait and a state, as well as an interactional process (R. E. Smith & Smoll, 1990). Trait sports anxiety is defined as a relatively stable disposition to view sports competition situations as threatening and to respond with cognitive and/or somatic state anxiety (R. E. Smith, Smoll, & Schutz, 1990). State sports anxiety refers to elevations in somatic arousal, increased worry, disruption of concentration, and increased frequency of task-irrelevant thoughts when exposed to a stressful competitive sports condition. Sports Anxiety, as an interactional variable, is construed as the interactive function of social-evaluation and physical danger trait anxiety and stressful situational factors, involving some physical and/or subjectively appraised evaluative threat.

Social anxiety involves feelings of apprehension, self-consciousness, and emotional distress in anticipated or actual social-evaluative situations (Leitenberg, 1990b; cf. with various chapters in Leitenberg, 1990a). Such anxiety occurs when people want to make a favorable impression, but doubt that they will succeed (Schlenker and Leary, 1982). There has to be belief that the situation involves scrutiny or evaluation by others regardless of whether this is actually true or not, that negative evaluation is a possible or even a likely outcome, and that the consequences of such negative evaluation would be harmful. The essence of social anxiety is that the person fears that he or she will be found to be deficient or inadequate by others and therefore will be rejected. Social anxiety may occur in response to immediate, "real" social encounters in which the individual is presently engaged (e.g., oral presentation, performing before an audience, making a date), or to "imagined" encounters in which the individual contemplates an upcoming social interaction or simply thinks about participating in a particular interaction. Social anxiety often hinders the development of personal friendships and sexual relationships, disrupts smooth social performance, and prevents a person from reaching personal goals at school, at college, at work, and in the community. At the extreme end it can develop into a serious personality disorder. Social anxiety has been cited as being more debilitating and distressing than other commonly studied types of anxiety disorders (T. W. Smith et al., 1983), with individuals high in social anxiety at risk for developing more serious disorders (see Endler's [1983a] review of studies on social-evaluation anxiety).

A recent paper by Zeidner (1997b) suggests that notwithstanding the uniqueness of each form of social-evaluation anxiety discussed, these specialized forms share the perceived possibility of failure and resultant disapproval by significant others, who are evaluating the person's performance in relation to some standard (achievement, excellence, normative behavior). Thus, the math-anxious, computer-anxious, sports-anxious, or socially anxious person fears that she or he will not be able to meet accepted performance standards and will be found deficient or inadequate by others, thus resulting in negative social consequences or sanction.

Furthermore, as discussed by Zeidner (1997b), cognitive (worry, task-irrelevant thinking) affective (tension, arousal), and behavioral (avoidant behaviors) facets are evident in the various forms of social-evaluation anxiety discussed. Thus, similar to test-anxious individuals, each of the social-evaluation groups discussed is likely to experience interfering worry cognitions and intense elevation in state anxiety in situations they perceive as dangerous or personally threatening. The various forms of anxiety tend to lead to avoidance behaviors, which, in turn, lead to greater anxiety, thus leading to further avoidance, and so on. In addition, as is the case in test anxiety, anxiety impairs performance in each of the situation-specific anxieties discussed.

Zeidner's (1997b) survey of the research also points to a number of common antecedent correlates of various forms of social-evaluation anxiety (i.e., math, sports, social). Thus, perceptions, appraisals, and expectancies tend to be powerful predictors across various forms of anxiety, with those individuals with lower expectancies of performance and greater perceived importance tending to be more anxious. Furthermore, personal ability, self-efficacy, and self-confidence are among the best personal predictors (negatively) of anxiety in a variety of domains (e.g., math, sports). Also, prior experience and expertise in the task at hand has proven to be a reliable predictor for both math and sports anxiety.

Summary

In contrast to early mechanistic views of test anxiety as a unified construct, test anxiety is currently construed as a complex multidimensional construct embodying a series of interrelated cognitive, affective, and behavioral components and reactions. In any given test situation, test-anxious subjects may experience all, some, or none of these test anxiety reactions. The fact that anxiety is such a complex construct, encompassing as it does both worry and self-preoccupation, physical upset, disruptive feelings, and maladaptive behaviors, makes it particularly difficult for researchers to sort out all these components.

Current research suggests that high- and low-test-anxious examinees are meaningfully differentiated in their cognitive concerns and reactions. These cognitive concerns are manifested in a variety of different ways, including worry, self-preoccupation, and cognitive interference. Overall, the cognitive expression of test anxiety is perhaps best thought of as a joint *interactive* product of threatening evaluative situations that increase the likelihood of worry and self-oriented cognitions, with individual differences in the vulnerability to such cognitions, namely, trait test anxiety.

Current research implicates the major physiological systems (i.e., autonomic, endocrine, and immune systems) in the anxiety response to evaluative stress. Whereas heightened autonomic arousal has been shown to be the dominant response mode for the expression of anxiety in test situations, recent research also suggests that exams may affect both hormonal activity and immunocompetence in examinee populations. Furthermore, researchers have found it useful to differentiate between actual physiological reactions in response to stressful exam situations and Emotionality, designating self-perceptions and interpretations of one's physiological arousal. Indeed, a series of studies has demonstrated that both high-test-anxious and low-test-anxious persons display similar patterns of somatic emotional arousal when either anticipating tests or actually taking them. Overall, the literature fails to report a consistent relationship between self-reported test anxiety, as an individual-differences variable, and physiological activity in test situations.

In addition to its cognitive and affective manifestations, test anxiety may also be expressed in a variety of overt behaviors, such as deficient study skills, procrastination, avoidance behaviors, and cautiousness in responding. Thus, test-anxious students show behavioral deficits in a wide variety of academic skills and frequently procrastinate or attempt to escape from an impending evaluative situation.

Consistent with the notion of reciprocal determinism (Bandura, 1977) and current transactional (interactional) models of stress (R. S. Lazarus & Folkman, 1984; cf. Meichenbaum & Butler, 1980), the cognitive, affective, and behavioral components of test anxiety are predicted to interact in a dynamic fashion over the various phases of the test anxiety process. For example, physiological arousal may prime threat-related thoughts and images, which, in turn, may increase negative emotional reactivity and avoidance behaviors. These reactions, in turn, may serve to heighten physiological responses. Because the different systems of test anxiety may contribute to each other in a spiral of increasing worry, emotional distress, and avoidance, test-anxious individuals often find themselves caught up in a vicious, self-perpetuating cycle. In this framework, test anxiety should not merely be equated with task-irrelevant thinking, emotionality, or poor study skills. Instead, test anxiety should best be construed as a dynamic and complex construct that unfolds over time, with the label "test anxiety" summarizing this entire process.

Based on prior research, I have presented a tentative typology of different types of test-anxious individuals that may be useful for future conceptualization, assessment, and intervention purposes. Note that the specific types of test-anxious students portrayed above are rather loose categories and have not been generated through conventional taxonometric procedures. They probably are not "true categories" in the sense of being mutually exclusive or exhaustive entities. On one hand, additional categories of test-anxious students most certainly exist and need to be identified and carefully researched. On the other hand, it stands to reason that there are hybrid types, with some individuals manifesting the characteristics of one or more types. Additional work is needed in constructing a valid and comprehensive typology of test-anxious students. A better understanding of the nature and etiology of different forms of test anxiety has practical, as well as theoretical, importance. It stands to reason that no single treatment is effective for every type of test-anxious client. Interventions and therapeutic techniques would be most effective if they could be adjusted to suit the needs of different types of test-anxious clients. This differential type of treatment, designed to assure maximum congruence between the test-anxious client and treatment, requires a comprehensive and well-established typology as a starting point.

Test anxiety may be distinguished from the various forms of social-evaluation anxiety mainly by the stimulus properties of situations that are considered personally threatening. Thus, in the case of specialized forms of anxiety, such as math, sports, and social anxiety, in addition to the threat of negative evaluation, the latter also involve anxiety about the specific content under consideration, i.e., manipulation of numbers and mathematics problems, athletic performance, and social interaction, respectively. Thus, most situation-specific forms of anxiety may be a reaction to specific content as well as performance evaluation.

Models and Theoretical Perspectives

Overview

A number of distinctive theoretical models and perspectives have been advanced over the years in order to account for the nature, antecedents, correlates, and consequences of test anxiety. Conceptualizations of test anxiety underlying these models have swayed from drive-oriented and arousal perspectives (J. T. Spence & Spence, 1966; Mandler & Sarason, 1952) to cognitive-attentional formulations (Wine, 1971b), and to those emphasizing skill deficits (Culler & Holahan, 1980; Kirkland & Hollandsworth, 1979, 1980). More recently, self-regulation (Carver & Scheier, 1991; Carver, Scheier, & Klahr, 1987), self-worth (Covington, 1992), and transactional (Spielberger & Vagg, 1987, 1995a, 1995b) perspectives have been applied to test anxiety research and have gained considerable currency.

To account for the multifaceted nature of test anxiety, theoretical models should meet some of the following basic criteria. First, models of test anxiety should detail and account accurately for the phenomenology of test anxiety and sort out its key components and dimensions. Second, models should specify the distal antecedent factors underlying test anxiety as well as specify the more proximal personal and situational antecedent conditions impacting upon anxiety in evaluative situations. Third, models should account for the important correlates and consequences of test anxiety, with particular concern for the processes that cause performance decrements. Finally, models of test anxiety should preferably provide guidelines for modifying test anxiety and propose specific interventions to ameliorate test anxiety and improve test performance.

This chapter surveys key models of test anxiety. Each model's unique contributions to understanding the multivariate and complex nature of the test anxiety construct will be discussed, and the extent to which current models meet the criteria specified above will be assessed. Although a wide array of models applicable to test anxiety research is available, space considerations require that I limit this presentation to some of the broader and more influential models that have significantly advanced the field by providing insights into theory, research, or applications. A number of more specific or restricted models of test anxiety are treated elsewhere in this book (see Chapter 6 for developmental models and Chapter 10 for additional models of the anxiety–performance relationship).

The drive model is presented first. It is included mainly for its historical import, in that the study of anxiety and motivation was essentially the same until the mid 1960s, with both concepts part of the larger drive-theory tradition. I move on to discuss two highly influential test anxiety models, the cognitive-attentional and study-skills deficit model, which gained considerable popularity in the 1970s and the 1980s, respectively. Both models view test anxiety as reflecting some basic form of deficit—attentional deficits in one model, and academic skill deficits in the other. I then present two contemporary motivational models of test anxiety, the self-regulation and the self-merit model. I conclude by presenting a recent version of Spielberger's state-of-the-art transactional model, which stresses the reciprocal determinism relating the person, the nature of the situation, and behavioral outcomes.

Drive Models

The drive perspective assumes that when there is too much drive or arousal in a particular learning or evaluative situation, performance is compromised, particularly if the performance is complex. Although a number of alternative drive models have been put forth (e.g., Mandler & Sarason, 1952; J. T. Spence & Spence, 1966), in this section I briefly present the most extensively researched drive model relevant to test anxiety, the Spence and Spence (K. W. Spence, 1958; J. T. Spence & Spence, 1966; Taylor, 1956) extension of Hullian learning theory (Hull, 1943). This model served as a conceptual framework for the bulk of experimental investigations of anxiety and learning until the mid-1960s. Although very few contemporary studies of test anxiety are based on drive theory, this model remains important for understanding some of the earlier literature focusing on the mechanisms through which arousal may impact upon performance, including a number of classical studies on anxiety and complex performance (e.g., Spielberger, 1966b).

Basic Concepts and Principles

Drive theory, as formulated by J. T. Spence and Spence (1966), is based on Hull's learning theory, which sets out to account for the learning of new responses and the probability that a given response will occur in a given occasion. Although Hull's theory is rather complex, it will suffice to touch briefly upon a number of concepts central to understanding the drive theory as it relates to anxiety. To begin with, the central concept of *drive* (D) refers to the various need states of an individual that combine to determine his or her total level of motivation (activation or arousal) at a particular time. Drive is viewed as a global energizer resulting from motivational states within the person. Another important concept, *habit strength* (H), is defined as the strength of the tendency to make a particular response to a specific stimulus. Habit strength is based on the frequency of past reinforcement of a particular response and is operationalized in terms of the strength of a correct response (e.g., "George Washington") to a stimulus ("Who was the first president of the United States?") relative to all other possible, but incorrect, responses (e.g., "Thomas Jefferson," "John Adams," "Benjamin Franklin"). *Excitatory potential* (E) is defined as the statistical probability that a particular response or set of responses will occur.

Drive theory, as formulated by J. T. Spence and Spence (1966), makes several basic assumptions concerning the learning process. First, in the context of learning a new task, both correct and erroneous response tendencies are evoked; the latter continue to be elicited, even as the correct response is being learned. Second, the strength of both the correct response and competing error tendencies are energized in a multiplicative fashion by drive. Third, the theory postulates that performance is jointly determined by level of drive and the relative strengths of correct and competing response tendencies. More rigorously, drive theory posits that the strength of a given response (R) is dependent upon the excitatory potential (E), which is determined, in turn, by a multiplicative function of total effective drive state (D) and habit strength (H). Mathematically, this may be expressed as follows: $R = f(E) = f(D \times H)$. According to the model, the chance of a correct response occurring in a learning situation depends on the joint influence of habit strength and drive state.

Drive and Anxiety

The Spence–Hull version of drive theory construes anxiety as an index of the individual's level of excitability, thus equating anxiety with Hull's concept of drive. Among the responses aroused by the drive state are not only heightened autonomic reactions, but also task-irrelevant responses and internal self-deprecatory verbalizations. K. W. Spence (1958) postulated that anxious persons are "emotionally responsive," tending to respond more strongly to stressful or aversive stimuli. Furthermore, subjects high in anxiety are described as having a lower threshold for the arousal of anxiety than their low-anxiety counterparts, and tend to react even to mild ego-involving instructions with anxiety and fear of failure. Since this emotional response is akin to the concept of state anxiety in evaluative situations, drive theory proponents (K. W. Spence, 1958; Taylor, 1956) would presumably regard test anxiety as simply a reflection and expression of a high level of general anxiety occurring in an evaluative situation. Presumably, any technique that reduces the general level of arousal should result in decreased anxiety and improved performance in evaluative situations.

Anxiety and Performance

What is the mechanism through which drive impacts upon the performance of anxious subjects in stressful evaluative situations? According to this model, subjects who are anxious will experience response competition, i.e., the activation of various incorrect responses, that will compete with successful performance on the test (J. T. Spence & Spence, 1966). Because anxiety increases the overall drive level, this heightens competition among all possible responses, thereby leading to errors. For example, recalling that the state capital of California is Sacramento depends on whether the response is aroused at all and then, once aroused, how distinctive it is compared to other competing but erroneous responses (e.g., Los Angeles, San Diego).

This model assumes that the effect of anxiety on drive level depends on the relative strength of the correct and competing response tendencies that are evoked by a learning task. Increasing drive energizes all responses, both correct and incorrect. In easy learning situations, in which correct responses are dominant (are stronger than competing responses), the drive properties of anxiety are assumed to strengthen the correct responses and leave weaker responses below the threshold, thus giving rise to facilitative effects. By contrast, for difficult learning tasks, in which competing error tendencies are strong relative to the correct response, high drive will serve to activate or energize already dominant error tendencies, thus debilitating the performance of high-test-anxious subjects. Thus, J. T. Spence and Spence (1966) provided the theoretical underpinnings for one of the key assumptions of the Yerkes–Dodson law (see Chapter 9), namely, that anxiety facilitates performance on easy tasks and debilitates performance on difficult tasks.

Reviews of the experimental literature assessing the predictions of drive theory suggest that although not entirely consistent, the bulk of data are generally in accord with the notion that on difficult tasks anxious subjects perform at a lower level compared to their low-anxiety counterparts (M. W. Eysenck, 1982; Spielberger, 1966b), but often outperform low-anxiety subjects on easy tasks. Overall, however, the facilitative effects of anxiety on easy tasks are found rather infrequently (Heinrich & Spielberger, 1982) and there have been inconsistent results when this model has been applied to complex academic learning materials (O'Neil, Judd, & Hedl, 1977).

This model also suggests that the negative relationship between anxiety and performance will hold at only certain points in the process, i.e., ất the early stages of learning (K. W. Spence, 1958). Accordingly, in the early stages of learning, the response or "habit" to be learned has zero or relatively low strength in relation to the other response tendencies that are aroused by the stimulus. Since drive and habit strength have a multiplicative relation to the tendency to respond in a particular way, an increase in drive at the early stage of learning—without an accompanying increase in the strength of the habit to be learned—results in a relative increase in the probability of evocation of one of the stronger existing "incorrect" responses. An increase in drive will interfere with learning until the correct responses are of sufficient strength to compete successfully with error tendencies, which occurs at a later stage of learning. Research tends to confirm the hypothesis that anxiety hinders performance early in learning, but may even facilitate performance at later stages (e.g., Lekarczyk & Hill, 1969; cf. M. W. Eysenck, 1982). Furthermore, individual variables, such as intelligence, may moderate the effects of arousal and stage of learning on performance (Spielberger, 1966b).

Limitations

The drive model's unique contribution to test anxiety research is in specifying the causal mechanisms through which anxiety may facilitate or debilitate performance in evaluative situations. However, this model is limited in scope by the fact that it best applies to those kinds of learning that are of least interest in academic or practical settings, i.e., relatively simple tasks whose respective habits and strengths and competing response tendencies could be well specified. In fact, this model can only make definite predictions about the effects of anxiety on performance provided there is detailed information available about the relative strengths of all relevant responses and location of response thresholds; such an analysis is difficult, if not impossible, to conduct in meaningful assessment or instructional situations. Furthermore, the model predicts facilitative effects of anxiety on easy tasks, but a review of the test anxiety literature suggests there are relatively few studies showing a facilitative effect of anxiety on any type of task (Tobias, 1985).

Deficit Models

In contrast to the other models included in this chapter, the two models presented in this section were generated from within the domain of test anxiety research. Both models associate test anxiety with some form of deficit—attentional deficit in one model, and academic skill deficit in the other.

Cognitive-Attentional (Interference) Model

Current test anxiety theory, particularly thinking on the anxiety–performance interface, is heavily influenced by a "cognitive-attentional" or "interference" perspective (Culler & Holahan, 1980; Weinstein, Cubberly, & Richardson, 1982; Wine, 1971b; I. G. Sarason, 1980a). This model postulates that performance differences between high- and low-test-anxious students are caused by differences in attentional focus, with these two groups differing in the types of thoughts to which their attention is directed in the face of an evaluative stressor (Meichenbaum & Butler, 1980; I. G. Sarason, 1972a, 1980b, 1984, 1988; Wine, 1971b, 1980).

In contrast to the mechanistic drive perspective presented above, this position maintains that emotional (or physiological) reactivity does not capture the most important or outstanding differences between high- and low-test-anxious individuals (Wine, 1971b). These differences lie more in the nature of cognitive structures and the relative presence of worry, cognitive interference, and self-denigrating thoughts in evaluative situations (I. G. Sarason, 1984). High test anxiety is associated with task-irrelevant thinking, worry, negative self-focus, and the tendency to experience self-devaluing cognitions during stressful tasks (Geen, 1980; Wine, 1980, 1982). By contrast, persons low in test anxiety react to performance evaluation with situational task focus, generating cognitions about the task or situation conducive to task completion or heightened understanding of the situation. Though highly test-anxious individuals often report experiencing higher levels of physiological reactivity than do low-test-anxious persons, these data reflect differences in the phenomenology and contents of consciousness rather than actual tonic reactivity.

Test Anxiety and Cognitive Performance

Cognitive-attentional theory espouses an "interference" explanation to account for the anxiety–performance relationship (Mandler & Sarason, 1952; Wine, 1971b, 1980). Highly test-anxious persons are likely to become extremely self-focused when placed in an evaluative test setting, and self-attention presumably interferes with their performance by distracting them from focusing on the task (Wine, 1971b). High levels of cognitive worry and self-preoccupation cause anxious learners or test takers to divide their attention between task-relevant activities and self-oriented worries about themselves and the quality of their performance, thereby undermining effective performance (Wine, 1971b). The cognitive-attentional hypothesis (Wine, 1971b) is graphically depicted in Figure 3.1.

I. G. Sarason (1980a) views *cognitive interference* as a mediator of the performance deficits associated with test anxiety. Both situational factors as well as individual differences in test anxiety are thought to play a crucial role in the likelihood of occurrence of interfering thoughts (I. G. Sarason & Sarason, 1987). Thus, in test situations, individual differences in test anxiety, in interactions with the stressful evaluative context, determine the tendency in certain individuals to engage in dysfunctional cognitive activity, and this heightened self-preoccupation interferes with task performance (I. G. Sarason, 1980a; I. G. Sarason, Sarason, & Pierce, 1990; I. G. Sarason, Sarason, Keefe, Hayes, & Shearin, 1984). Test anxiety is said to hinder the individual from utilizing task-specific cues and activating relevant knowledge or skills, with test-anxious students becoming preoccupied with their own self-evaluation and with negative consequences (I. G. Sarason, 1972a). Task-irrelevant processing is also claimed to consume working memory capacity in high-test-anxious subjects, which in less anxious individuals remains available for task performance. There is research evidence suggesting that test-anxious subjects worry more and experience more disruptive cognitions under evaluative conditions, which also impair their performance (Kurosawa & Harackiewicz, 1995). This theoretical model, presented in Figure 3.2, is consistent with a wealth of evidence.

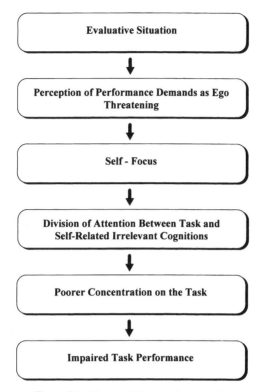

Figure 3.1. The cognitive-attentional model.

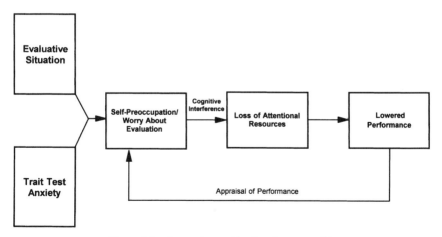

Figure 3.2. Sarason's cognitive-interference model.

What evidence is there in support of the major hypotheses of the cognitive-attention or interference model? At a minimum, evidence needs to be adduced showing that evaluative situations indeed produce an increase in task-irrelevant cognitive activities in high-test-anxious subjects, and that these irrelevant cognitions, in turn, are causally responsible for differential performance decrements in these individuals (evaluative context → cognitive interference → impaired performance). Although a full review of the evidence is beyond the scope of this chapter, I briefly survey some of the empirical research relating to key hypotheses derived from the interference model.

Both experimental and field research provide substantial empirical support for the hypothesis that evaluative situations increase self-preoccupation, task-irrelevant thoughts, and distractibility—particularly among high-test-anxious individuals. Specifically, current research supports the conclusion that under evaluative stress conditions high-test-anxious subjects report higher levels of worry (and emotionality), spend less time on task, and consequently perform more poorly than low-test-anxious subjects (Deffenbacher & Deitz, 1978). Whereas interference is reported to be at a moderately elevated level in high-test-anxious students even under conditions of minimal evaluation, cognitive interference tends to be at a minimum in low-test-anxious subjects irrespective of external evaluation (I. G. Sarason & Stoops, 1978). Thus, under testlike conditions, high-test-anxious scorers report being preoccupied with how poorly they are doing, how other people are doing, what the examiner will think about them, and their overall performance levels. By contrast, under neutral conditions, groups that differ in amount of test anxiety show little or no differences in performance or cognitive interference (see Chapter 9 for a discussion of the interactive effects of test anxiety and test atmosphere on performance).

As discussed in Chapter 2, high-test-anxious individuals are reported to be more self-preoccupied and tend to worry more during an exam than their low-test-anxious counterparts, experiencing a preponderance of self-derogatory thoughts about failure and statements of negative mood (Blankstein et al., 1989). Research by Deffenbacher (1978) indicates that anxious students spend only about 60% of their available time actively engaged in a difficult anagram task (compared to 80% in a nonstress condition). Furthermore, high-test-anxious students, compared to their low-test-anxious counterparts, were reported to have fewer positive self-referential thoughts, along with more negative self-referential thoughts (Blankstein et al., 1989; Blankstein et al., 1991).

Even *imagined* stressful test conditions elicit negative thoughts and self-statements in test-anxious college students. In one study (Heimberg et al., 1987), students were presented with three 60-second visualization levels: low stress—involving a pop quiz in an unimportant class; moderate stress—taking a midterm exam; and high stress—taking a final exam in a "make-it-or-break-it" course. Subjects reported the greatest number of negative self-statements and the smallest number of positive self-statements in response to the most stressful imaginal stimuli. Additional research (Yates, Hannel, & Lippett, 1985) shows that subjects report more mind wandering and cognitive interference following a task presented as a test compared to the practice instructions.

Furthermore, research converges to show that generalized tendencies to have self-deprecatory thoughts and test-related worries are negatively related to intellective tasks, with studies providing a clear link between the general disposition to experience high levels of interfering thoughts and an individual's subpar performance on specific tasks (Bruch, Kaflowitz, & Kuethe, 1986; I. G. Sarason et al., 1995; I. G. Sarason, 1978; Sarason, 1984; I. G. Sarason & Stoops, 1978). Heckhausen (1982), for example, reported that the frequency of retrospectively reported irrelevant thoughts, especially those concerned with self-doubt, was inversely correlated with test performance on an oral exam. Irrelevant thoughts were particularly debilitating for anxious subjects whose fear of failure was greater than their hope for success. Comparably, Prin, Groot, and Hanewald (1994) reported that the more off-task thoughts elementary school students had on an exam, the lower their performance.

As would be predicted from the cognitive-attention model, there is ample evidence that cognitive-attention factors are more central to the debilitating effects of test anxiety on performance outcomes than physiological arousal (Hollandsworth et al., 1979). An impressive body of research evidence, surveyed in Chapters 2 and 9, suggests that the cognitive component of test anxiety is more strongly related to task performance than is emotional arousal. Furthermore, because test anxiety allegedly interferes with attention to tasks given under evaluative conditions, the adverse effects of the Worry component on performance should be greater on complex tasks, requiring more attention, than on less complex tasks. The evidence surveyed in Chapter 9 provides ample evidence in support of the differentially debilitating effects of anxiety on complex versus simple tasks.

In addition, the cognitive-attentional approach implies that the test-anxious person's performance, typically impaired by high arousal and self-related worrisome thoughts, may be markedly improved by systematic training aimed at directing his or her attention to task-relevant variables and away from self-evaluative rumination. A body of research suggests that providing anxious subject with skills which help focus their attention appropriately on task-related thoughts and behaviors, instead of worry, differentially facilitates their performance. Thus, intervention research lends some support to the claim that attentional training is a relatively effective treatment technique for test-anxious students (see Chapter 16).

Skills-Deficit Model

In the early 1980s, the cognitive-attentional model came under heavy fire and was seriously challenged by an alternative paradigm—the study-skills deficit model (Benjamin et al., 1981; Culler & Holahan, 1980; Kirkland & Hollandsworth, 1980; Paulman & Kennelly, 1984). Proponents of this position argued that anxious students were deficient in a wide variety of study and test-taking skills. As the argument goes, since these students typically encode material in inadequate ways during learning, subsequent performance deficits are *not* to be attributed to temporary interference during test taking, but rather to the retrieval of inadequately learned or organized information.

A careful analysis of the various claims made by proponents of the skills-deficit model uncovers several alternative potential causal chains linking deficient skills and test performance. Perhaps the most straightforward and parsimonious claim made by proponents of the skills-deficit hypothesis is that deficient study skills and habits work through poorer intake and organization of study material to reduce test performance in high-test-anxious subjects, without the mediation of state anxiety in the causal process. According to this model, inadequate study habits may develop quite independently of anxiety, with anxiety emerging as a result of repetitive experiences of academic failure due to poor study habits. This process is depicted in Figure 3.3a.

According to a slightly more elaborated version of this hypothesis (Covington & Omelich, 1988), less bright individuals tend to have poorer study habits, which eventually lead to poor test and scholastic performance. These less competent students sense their deficiencies, thus bringing about lower self-esteem at failure and increased test anxiety. Indeed, individuals who suffer from poor skills in acquisition, organization, or retrieval of information tend to have good reason to become anxious, since a lack of skills may provoke both coeffects of anxiety and poor performance. According to this hypothesis, anxiety in the test situation has no causal status, but is simply an epiphenomenon reflecting students' lack of preparation for the test and their metacognitive awareness of their low probability of succeeding on the exam (Covington & Omelich, 1987a). Anxiety, thus viewed, is the end result of this causal chain rather than a major antecedent of poor performance. This process is depicted in Figure 3.3b. However, it is unclear why less bright individuals have poorer study habits. Are bright individuals better able to work out how to study effectively? Do bright individuals study better because they are better motivated to learn? Do good study habits lead to the development of intelligence?

In direct contrast to the claim that the lower test performance of anxious students really has nothing to do with the interference of affective or cognitive components of anxiety, an alternative conceptualization of the skills-deficit position incorporates anxiety as a key mediator variable in accounting for the effects of study skills on performance. Accordingly, students characterized by poor study skills are well aware of their poor preparation for the exam and consequently adopt low self-expectations for success. This, in turn, raises anxiety surrounding the test, which, in turn, impairs performance. Because many high-test-anxious students may never have systematically been taught how to study or how to take exams, and consequently have few effective strategies to call upon to learn and recall information, these students would seem especially likely to focus on negative self-preoccupations and worry about negative outcomes as they struggle through tests (Benjamin et al., 1981; Cubberly, Weinstein & Cubberly, 1986; Culler & Holahan, 1980; Kirkland & Hollandsworth, 1980; Paulman & Kennelly, 1984). This "indirect model" views poor test performance as being causally related to test anxiety, which reflects a student's uncertainty

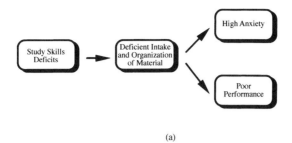

(a)

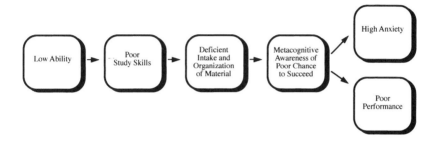

(b)

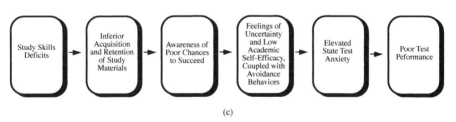

(c)

Figure 3.3. Alternative version of the skills-deficit model (with feedback loop).

caused by inferior learning of materials and poor study habits. This causal chain is depicted in Figure 3.3c.

Empirical Support for the Deficit Position

Evidence in support of the deficit position is forthcoming from a wide body of research attempting to establish empirical links between test anxiety and study skills on one hand, and study skills and poor performance on the other. A body of research is consistent with the basic claim of the skills-deficit position that high-test-anxious students have significantly lower levels of study-skills competence when compared to low-test-anxious students (Culler & Holahan, 1980; Kirkland & Hollandsworth, 1979; Wittmaier, 1972). Furthermore, a number of studies report a significant correlation between dispositional test anxiety and test-taking skills among college students (Bruch, 1981; Paulman & Kennelly, 1984). Bruch (1981) reported a meaningful inverse correlation of $r = -.42$ between test-taking strategies and test anxiety among a sample of college students, with high-test-anxious students scoring about three quarters of a standard deviation below their less anxious counterparts in a measure of study skills. Consistent with the test-taking deficit hypothesis, low-test-anxious students, who reported confidence about classroom testing situations, possessed a repertoire of more effective test-taking strategies than subjects who were moderate or high in test anxiety. However, additional research by Bruch and his coworkers failed to replicate the meaningful association between test anxiety and study skills (Bruch, Juster, & Kaflowitz, 1983).

Culler and Holahan (1980) investigated the relationship between measures of study skills and performance outcomes in a sample of 65 high- and 31 low-test-anxious college students preselected from 800 undergraduates taking psychology courses. The two groups were clearly distinguishable in habits/skills, with high-test-anxious students averaging about one standard deviation below that of their low-test-anxious counterparts on the study habits measure. No major differences were found between high- versus low-test-anxious groups on a number of study habit parameters, such as cramming, missing classes, and late exams. High-test-anxious students reported investing significantly *more* study time than their less anxious counterparts. According to the authors, high-test-anxious students attempt to compensate for lower study competence by increasing the amount of study time. Overall, these findings suggest that at least part of the academic performance decrement in high-test-anxious subjects is a function of differential study skills, thus negating the stereotype of the high-test-anxious student who knows the subject matter, but freezes up at test time.

Research has identified a number of specific study or learning deficits in high-test-anxious students. High-test-anxious students are reported to have difficulty encoding information, organizing information into larger patterns of meaning, and effectively employing metacognitive processes such as self-monitoring (e.g., judging whether or not they understand something well enough to pass a test, or what to do when one learning strategy that worked in the past is no longer appropriate). Furthermore, some data (Topman, Kleijn, Van der Ploeg, & Masset, 1992) suggest that high-test-anxious college students, relative to low-test-anxious students, are deficient in both time management (i.e., developing an optimal balance between time spent on study and other activities) and strategic studying (i.e., monitoring learning processes and active search for learning resources). In addition, high-test-anxious students are reported to have more problems than low-test-anxious students during both initial learning and review—although retrieval appears to be more of a problem for anxious students than storage and encoding (Benjamin et al., 1981).

Furthermore, a number of studies suggest that study skills are reliably related to academic achievement. Thus, data presented by Kirkland and Hollandsworth (1979) suggest that test-taking skills, even when controlling for the effects of scholastic aptitude and debilitative anxiety, are independent predictors of scholastic achievement (i.e., grade point average) in student populations. Additional data on the study-skills–performance association were presented by Culler and Holahan (1980). They found that high-test-anxious, but skilled, undergraduate psychology students who had developed and exercised better study skills did better academically than those with poor study habits. Furthermore, the quality of study habits and amount of study time were reported to be positively related to academic performance, whereas missing classes and delaying exams were inversely related to performance for high-test-anxious students.

A number of studies have sought to determine to what extent study skills bear mainly a direct or indirect effect on test performance. Covington and Omelich (1988) conducted path-analytic research on a sample of 312 Berkeley undergraduates during various stages of the testing process. Their data demonstrate that the mere possession of good study habits bears little *direct* relationship to test performance. Instead, the data attest to the complex nature of the interactions between study skills and both motivational and emotional constructs across various phases of the stressful evaluative encounter (arousal, preparation, and actual test-taking stages). Thus, study skills work through either emotional or motivational mediators across the various examination phases to impact upon test performance. The possession of inadequate study skills was shown to influence indirectly future performance in at least two ways: (a) by encouraging defensive posturing, such as wishful thinking or denial, which often disrupts performance by compromising effective study; (b) by the occurrence of irrelevant and disruptive thoughts, which impair performance. By contrast, causal modeling research by Hodapp and Henneberger (1983) suggests that study skills may bear both a direct impact as well as an indirect impact upon test performance.

Bruch et al. (1983) explored the nexus of relationships between study skills, test anxiety, and test performance. A sample of 72 undergraduate students read a 1300-word passage extracted from an Ecology textbook and then studied it for 20 minutes in preparation for taking two short tests that would follow. Among the three factors assessed, i.e., test anxiety, self-statements during testing, and test-taking strategies, only the latter evidenced a significant and direct relationship to test performance, thus providing support for the test-taking deficit hypothesis. Test-taking skills were shown to affect performance on both essay and multiple-choice tests, but to have a smaller effect on performance tests. Kirkland and Hollandsworth (1979) found that students' knowledge about appropriate test-taking procedures accounted for the second largest amount of explainable variance in grade-point average, after scholastic ability, among a predictor stock of anxiety and study-skills measures.

Paulman and Kennelly (1984) observed that high- and low-test-anxious students with good exam skills report fewer distracting thoughts than their unskilled counterparts. Exam skills were significantly related to dispositional test anxiety on one hand, and to grade point average on the other. The highest state anxiety was experienced by individuals who were unskilled in test taking and who were characterized by high dispositional test anxiety; these individuals also manifested the most cognitive interference and the lowest performance levels on the Raven and Digit Span measures. The data suggest that both poor exam skills and high state test anxiety generated cognitive interference during problem solving that was, in turn, negatively related to performance.

A body of research evidence attests to the importance of study-skills training (Allen, 1971; Mitchell & Ng, 1972) and test-taking training (Kirkland & Hollandsworth, 1980) as useful components in many test-anxiety treatment programs. Accordingly, there is some experimental evidence showing that systematic training in the use of cognitive strategies study skills may be helpful in reducing the debilitating effects of anxiety on the performance of school-aged children (Cubberly et al., 1986). Treatments designed to modify deficient study skills were reported to be more effective than alternative procedures, such as systematic desensitization (Allen, 1971; Holroyd, 1976). Although some work shows that reduction of test anxiety directly leads to better performance, there is also research evidence suggesting that efforts to reduce test anxiety are largely ineffectual unless poor study habits are remediated (Allen, 1971; McCordick, Kaplan, Finn, & Smith, 1979). When level of study habits is ignored, reducing test anxiety is no guarantee that there will be subsequent improvement in academic performance (Mitchell & Ng, 1972).

The major difference between the cognitive-attentional (interference) and skills-deficit model are explicated in Table 3.1.

Although the deficit and interference models have typically been conceptualized as being mutually exclusive, a number of scholars have attempted to reconcile

Table 3.1. A Comparison of the Interference and Skills Deficit Positions along Relevant Dimensions

Dimension	Interference model	Skills-deficit model
Role of test anxiety in exam performance	Anxiety has an important causal role in determining performance outcomes	Anxiety is a correlate of deficient study skills and plays a noncausal role in determining performance
Major loci of deficits in test-anxious persons	Deficits in retrieval of previously learned information	Deficits in encoding and organizing study material due to poor study skills
Test-taking skills in high- and low-test-anxious students	No significant differences among the groups	High-test-anxious subjects are less prepared for tests and less skilled in test taking
Intervention implications	Efforts need to be directed at reducing anxiety in the test situation (particularly the worry component) in order to improve test performance	Efforts need to be directed at improving study and test-taking skills in order to improve performance

between these two positions. Thus, according to the "dual-deficit" hypothesis, originally proposed by Meichenbaum and Butler (1980), the interference and deficit models are best viewed as being complementary, rather than competing, accounts of the depressed performance typically manifested in high-test-anxious subjects. Test anxiety and student skill levels are evaluated as separate components of academic underachievement (Krouse & Krouse, 1981), with high-test-anxious individuals characterized by two primary deficits: (a) a deficit involving poor study and test-taking skills; (b) a deficit involving worry and interference. An alternative conception, the bidirectional model (Benjamin et al., 1981; Covington & Omelich, 1988; Paulman & Kennelly, 1984), suggests that the primary antecedent variable of low self-perception of ability leads to test anxiety, which then results in the shaping of poor study habits. As a result, less material is encoded in the teaching/learning process, eventually leading to poor test performance. This is further aggravated by anxiety-induced retrieval difficulties from worry within the test situation, impacted upon by the recognition that the examinee is ill-prepared for the exam and likely to fail. Furthermore, the accumulation of failure experiences over time leads to increased self-focusing of attention, additional worry and anxiety in the test situation, and consequent self-attention. By the time that the unskilled test-anxious student reaches the exam, he or she is well involved in this self-defeating process. These steps may actually reflect bidirectional interactions at any point in the process.

Limitations

Researchers have recently raised several questions concerning the theory and research base of the skills-deficit model (Tobias, 1986, 1992; Hodapp & Henneberger, 1983). To begin with, the evidence pertaining to the relationship between test anxiety and study skills is contradictory, with a number of studies failing to report a significant correlation between test anxiety and study behaviors. Second, students with good study skills often report experiencing cognitive interference during test situations (Naveh-Benjamin et al., 1987). Since these effective students are assumed to be well-prepared for tests, elevations in their anxiety levels are unlikely caused by insufficient or inadequate study before exams. Proponents of the deficit model would be hard put to explain this finding. Third, test-anxious students frequently describe themselves as being more task-engaged, spending *more*, rather than less, time studying than low-test-anxious students. The deficit hypothesis would predict just the opposite. Fourth, study-skills counseling by itself neither lessens anxiety nor improves academic achievement (Allen, 1971; Mitchell & Ng, 1972). Indeed, the study-skills deficit model would make it difficult to understand why anxiety-reduction programs succeed in reducing arousal or worry without increasing cognitive performance. Because students are still poorly prepared and performance has not improved in most cases, anxious students should continue to be anxious even after exposure to anxiety-reduction treatment programs. In addition, the deficit hypotheses cannot very well explain the finding that anxiety-reduction programs are occasionally effective in improving academic performance of anxious students with good study skills. Since this group possesses effective study skills, the deficit hypothesis would neither predict initial anxiety nor improvement in academic performance when anxiety is reduced.

Contemporary Cognitive-Motivational Models

This section presents two state-of-the-art process models of test anxiety derived from broader motivational perspectives, namely, Carver and Scheier's self-regulation model and Covington's self-worth model. Both models view the dynamics of anxiety in evaluative situations as a specific instantiation of broader motivational principles. The self-regulation model is based on a general cybernetic theory of self-regulation of human behavior which views behavior as a continuous process of bringing to mind goals and intentions and then trying to match behavior to those desired goals (Carver & Scheier, 1991). Anxiety enters the model when there is a major discrepancy between current behaviors and process toward achieving desired goals. The self-worth model is based on a general motivational theory maintaining that self-worth and the protection of one's sense of competence is of highest priority among students in modern society. The model suggests that many achievement-related behaviors, including test anxiety, may be understood as attempts to maintain self-worth and a positive self-image, particularly in the face of academic failure (Covington, 1992).

Self-Regulation Model

Carver and Scheier (1984, 1991) proposed a *self-regulation model* of test anxiety in order to better understand the nature of anxiety in evaluative contexts and its impact on human performance. I begin by briefly sketching the basic concepts and principles of Carver and Scheier's self-regulation theory and then attempt to show its applicability to test anxiety theory and research.

Basic Concepts and Principles of the Self-Regulation Model

This model is based on the assumption that intentional goal-directed behavior in humans displays the functional characteristics of a feedback control system (Carver & Scheier, 1988a, 1988b, 1990; Carver, Scheier, & Klahr, 1987). Accordingly, people establish goals and standards for themselves which they use as reference points in guiding and monitoring their behavior. Present behaviors are continuously sensed and brought to mind and then compared against situationally salient reference values and goals. Any observed discrepancies encountered between present behaviors or states and salient reference values or behavioral standards are handled by adjusting behavior in the direction of the latter.

The basic unit in this suggested cybernetic model is *a feedback loop*. A feedback loop refers to a sensed value ("It's Tuesday, February 10, and I'm only half way through this boring term paper") which is compared to a reference value or standard ("Have the term paper signed, sealed and delivered by Friday, February 13"). Whenever people consistently move toward salient reference values they use to guide behaviors, they manifest the functions of a *negative feedback loop*, which is designed to bridge the gap between intended and actual qualities of behavior. The control system makes adjustments, if necessary, to reduce the discrepancy by shifting the sensed value in the direction of the standard ("Finish up the term paper in 3 days"). However, a great many circumstances exist in which people encounter impediments and are therefore unable to make desired adjustments in their behavior in order to match behavior to goals. These impediments toward reaching the goal, such as skill deficits, serious doubts about self-adequacy or efficacy, and situational constraints, tend to be anxiety-evoking (Carver & Scheier, 1990). Curiously, anxiety states are also viewed as a common obstacle to goal attainment, thus generating further anxiety.

When difficulties are encountered in moving toward whatever goal one has taken up, a second control process kicks in. Accordingly, people remove themselves momentarily from the monitoring of their present behavior and engage in expectancy assessment. The person also becomes more cognizant of her or his present behavior and of how that behavior compares to the present reference value or standard. Furthermore, a person's expectancies of unsuccessful goal attainment come into play at this critical juncture, as she or he assesses the subjective likelihood of being able to execute the desired action. Favorable behavioral expectancies yield behavioral conformity to salient standards, increased on-task effort, and thus performance facilitation (Slapion & Carver, 1981). Unfavorable behavioral expectancies yield mental disengagement, non-task-related rumination, and lowered performance. Self-focus (subsequently) exaggerates whichever tendency follows from the check on expectancies. (See Carver [1996] for some of the subtleties in this useful model.)

Application of the Self-Regulation Model to Test Anxiety

Test anxiety is viewed as a maladaptive coping process, with a number of subjective manifestations of the control process being particularly important for the understanding of test anxiety. These include self-regulation and monitoring, self-focus, outcome expectancies, and the particular quality of affect brought to the situation—hope or confidence versus doubt or despair (Carver et al., 1987).

The model proposes that evaluative pressure makes everyone anxious. The crucial difference is in how different people respond to the arousal and the situation as a whole. Low-test-anxious individuals retain confidence of being able to perform well despite the anxiety, whereas high-test-anxious persons are doubtful of being able to perform (Charles Carver, personal communication, 1996). Furthermore, in highly evaluative circumstances test-anxious persons tend to be focused primarily on avoiding the experience of anxiety, rather than on performing well (Carver et al.,

1983). Test-anxious persons are likely to have strong chronic doubts about either producing adequate performances on exams, being evaluated favorably by significant others, or being able to control their feelings so that they do not feel overwhelmed by them (Carver & Scheier, 1984). Thus, when undergoing evaluation on dimensions that are of critical importance for them, test-anxious persons engage in self-deprecating ruminations and neglect or misinterpret readily available cues.

Following Carver's (1996) recent theorizing, much in line with the self-worth model, a person who is working on a task (e.g., an important midterm exam or paper) often needs to deal with setbacks in the effort to do well on the task. However, a student who is working exceptionally hard studying for an exam as a way of trying to maintain self-esteem, as is often the case in test-anxious subjects, has a bigger job when performance falters. Thus, when self-esteem is on the line, poor test perfor-mance or a continuous series of poor performances in evaluative contexts is more threatening than it is when the test is nothing other than a test. The greater the implications for the overall self-image, the bigger is the potential threat. Following Carver's (1996) line of reasoning, test-anxious persons may tend to generalize from a single bad occurrence of test failure to the broader sense of self-worth. Thus, when they perform poorly on an exam, it means a failure of the self. Generalization in response to bad test outcomes would be reflected in cognitions about broad personal inadequacy, rather than inadequacy pertaining to some particular domain of aca-demic performance. These cognitions by their very nature interfere with further efforts to perform.

Carver and Scheier (1989) further speculated that highly evaluative situations evoke unfavorable outcome expectancies in the test-anxious because it is in similar circumstances that prior failures have occurred. Because of their doubts about their abilities to succeed on cognitive tasks, any interruption from task effort that test-anxious individuals experience during the evaluative situation is likely to lead to the disengagement response. Though this impulse may be restrained from overt expres-sion, the subsequent off-task thinking and the self-deprecatory rumination accom-panying the unfavorable expectancies are likely to lead to impaired performance (Carver et al., 1987).

As postulated by the self-regulation model, interruption of one's efforts toward task engagement (e.g., poor study and test-taking skills interfering with performance on a foreign language exam) automatically leads to self-focus and an assessment of outcome expectancy. If one's expectancy to cope with the impediment is favorable, the result is renewed effort; if the expectancy is unfavorable, the result is an impetus to withdraw mentally from further attempts (Carver & Scheier, 1981). Thus, the test-anxious person, who is characterized by pessimistic attitudes and has serious doubts about being able to cope, tends to have unfavorable outcome expectations, and is not likely to persist in the face of task interruption and anxiety arousal. Furthermore, when the task is to maintain the entire sense of self, as it is in many test-anxious subjects, it is impossible to disengage without in effect renouncing the desired self. As aptly put by Carver (1996), "The more a task matters to the sense of self, the more the person is immersed in the phenomenology of being stuck in a behavioral loop that's not moving forward but can't be let go of" (p. 40).

The self-regulation model of test anxiety draws a number of important links between generalized expectancies, coping, and test performance. Thus, a major claim of the model is that the impact of test anxiety on performance depends on the person's expectancy of being able to cope with the exam and carry out the expectancies and actions associated with the test at hand. Thus, the joint combination or interaction of test anxiety and favorable expectancies leads to *improved* coping. Accordingly, when high-test-anxious individuals expect good outcomes in an evaluative situation, high self-focus will increase their tendency to comply with situational norms and stay in a mode of active engagement with the task, thus facilitating their test performance (Carver et al., 1987; cf. Klinger, 1984). Thus, the test-anxious person with favorable expectancies remains task-engaged, even when highly anxious and self-focused. Favorable expectancies are associated with contrived or repeatedly renewed efforts and ultimately with less performance impairment. By contrast, for those test-anxious persons who expect failure, their attention is focused on perceived deficits of self, salient self-doubts, and the larger ramifications of being unable to proceed toward his or her goal. For these pessimistic individuals high self-focus will lead to mental withdrawal from full engagement in the task and thus adversely effect task performance. Thus, high levels of self-focus should be debilitating only when people have crossed the watershed between confidence to self-doubt. The self-regulation model suggested by Carver and Scheier (1984, p. 12) for the test anxiety process is depicted in Figure 3.4.

Although some experimental data support the hypothesis that test anxiety interacts with self-focus in impacting upon test performance (Carver et al., 1983), there are few studies supporting the crucial hypothesis that the difference in responding to self-focus is mediated by expectancy of performing well. Rich and Woolever (1988) reported that significant performance facilitation occurred during conditions of positive expectancy for test-anxious subjects with induced self-focused attention, whereas significant performance decrements occurred under conditions of negative expectancy. High-test-anxious subjects with a positive expectancy who were made self-aware did not show poorer performance relative to low-test-anxious subjects, but actually performed better. On the other hand, high-test-anxious subjects with a negative expectancy and attentional focus showed the poorest performance.

Limitations

Although this model is one of the premiere models of test anxiety currently available, it does have a number of limitations. For one, advocates of the self-regulation model are somewhat ambiguous about the status of anxiety in the self-regulation process. It is unclear whether heightened anxiety is a factor determining the interruption of the process or an aversive emotional outcome of the interruption of self-regulation, or both. Furthermore, the roles of self-focus and negative self-

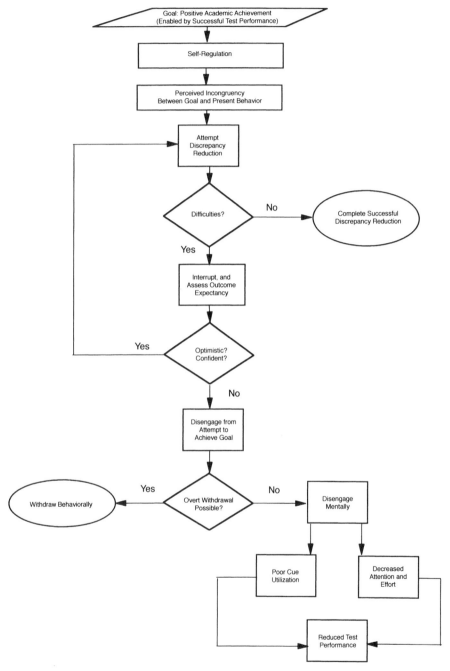

Figure 3.4. Self-regulation model.

expectations in the test anxiety process are somewhat ambiguous. Whereas these factors are sometimes assumed to be essential attributes of test-anxious individuals, at other times they are viewed as external moderating factors which jointly interact to influence test performance. Also, it is somewhat unclear whether the expectancies claimed to moderate the impact of test anxiety upon performance are dispositional expectancies (i.e., optimism as a dispositional tendency or trait) or context-specific expectancy outcomes. Furthermore, there is only scant empirical support in the test anxiety literature for a major hypothesis derived from this model, i.e., that the difference in responding to self-focus in high-test-anxious subjects is mediated by the expectancy of performing well. Finally, the model suggests that because test-anxious persons are prone to engage in expectancy assessments under evaluative situations, teaching them to do otherwise should help reduce their test anxiety and improve their test performance (Carver & Scheier, 1984). Unfortunately, there is little empirical evidence for the effectiveness of this form of intervention among test-anxious subjects and the specific procedures for modifying test anxiety in evaluative situations are not spelled out in sufficient detail.

Self-Worth Model

According to the self-worth model, test anxiety is often best understood in terms of the individual's attempts to maintain self-worth and a positive self-image, particularly when risking academic failure (Covington, 1992). Test anxiety is construed, according to this model, both as a manifestation of perceived intellectual incompetency and as a defensive ploy to ward off low self-evaluation. The various traditions or models accounting for test anxiety (i.e., arousal, skill deficit, cognitive attentional) are claimed to represent different aspects of the same overarching self-worth process.

A major premise of self-worth theory (Covington & Omelich, 1979) is that the search for self-worth and the protection of one's sense of competence is of highest priority among students in modern society. Given Western society's pervasive tendency to equate the ability to achieve with human value, it is not surprising that students' sense of esteem often becomes equated with ability; many students believe that they are only as good as their accomplishments. Thus, whenever possible, individuals will strive to succeed and approach success not only to benefit from the social and personal rewards of high academic achievements, but also to aggrandize their reputations for high ability. Since failure tends to lead to lowered ability estimates by self and others, failure is to be avoided at all costs. The problem with this state of affairs is that if success becomes difficult to come by, as is typically the case when rewards are distributed on a competitive basis, then the first priority is to avoid failure, or at least the implication of failure that one is incompetent (Covington, 1992).

Furthermore, self-worth theory assumes that emotional reactions to failure are mediated in part by attributions to inability, which in turn depend on the conditions of failure. Most high school and college students would prefer to achieve via ability rather than effort. Likewise, they would also prefer to fail via exerting minimal effort than incompetence or low academic ability. In fact, the amount of effort a student expends provides clear information about his or her ability. That is, if a student succeeds on a difficult exam without much effort, the estimates of that student's ability increases. However, should the student try hard and fail on the exam anyway, especially if the exam is easy, attributions to low ability are likely to follow. Presumably, then, shame and dissatisfaction should be greatest when one fails, despite considerable effort, because low ability is implied. Shame would be at a minimum, although guilt should be salient, when little or not effort is expended.

According to the self-worth model, whatever specific form test anxiety may take, it is basically a reaction to failure or the possibility of failure triggered by the implication of low ability (Covington, 1986, 1992). The anxiety aroused in a student following failure experiences on major exams results from the realization on the student's part that he or she is academically incompetent. Thus, anxiety in evaluative situations reflects a fundamental underlying threat to the individual's self-worth (i.e., anticipation of failure or actual failure) leading to self-doubts about one's ability to achieve competitively (Covington, 1986). Because high-test-anxious subjects also perceive themselves as less able (Covington, 1986), perceptions of inability may play a more important role in causing humiliation at failure for these individuals. Test-anxious subjects may place themselves in double jeopardy. Not only may they be less sure of capabilities to begin with, but cognition of inability may exercise greater weight as a causal factor in anxiety reactions.

Covington and Omelich (1979) view effort as a double-edged sword. On one hand, effort is valued by students because teachers and parents reward it, and exerted effort to achieve is a prerequisite for high levels of achievement. On the other hand, effort is also dreaded since a combination of effort and failure invites causal ascriptions of low ability. Thus, while teachers often reward student achievement through effort and punish students for not trying, for many students expending effort when risking failure poses a threat. These students must exert some effort to avoid teacher punishment, but they need to be careful not to exert so much effort as to risk public shame, should they try hard and fail. Covington and Omelich (1979) provide research evidence in a college sample indicating that high effort leads to more negative self-attributions of ability for both male and female students, with students also expecting others to judge them lower in ability when failure is accompanied by high effort.

According to the self-worth model, test anxiety also frequently serves as a defensive tactic used by poor students in their attempt to protect their self-ascriptions of ability and, in the process, to moderate anxiety reactions before, during, and after evaluative situations. Accordingly, high levels of anxiety drive the individual to various defensive ploys in an attempt to avoid exam failure—which further reduces the likelihood of success. Heightened emotionality and intrusive worry, for instance, may provide a student apprehensive about "not making the grade" with a ready-made excuse for failure. Test anxiety as a self-handicapping strategy provides the student with a palatable attribution for poor achievement. However, these self-handicapping strategies, ironically enough, set up the very failures that individuals are attempting to avoid, but at least they are failures "with honor," that is, readily explained, if not always excused.

Limitations

The model is somewhat unclear about the multiple roles assumed by test anxiety in the achievement process. That is, the model fails to specify when test anxiety is to be regarded as a true manifestation of perceived intellectual incompetency and when it serves mainly as a defensive ploy. Furthermore, the model does not explain why some individuals are characterized by a dysfunctional attributional pattern, attributing failure to lack of ability, whereas others are characterized by a more functional pattern, attributing failure to lack of motivation.

Transactional Models

A recent transactional model proposed by Spielberger and Vagg (1995a) provides a cross-sectional analysis of test anxiety as a situation-specific dynamic process. This dynamic process model, which has successfully been applied to the realm of test anxiety, is based on the transactional theoretical framework proposed by R. S. Lazarus (1966; R. S. Lazarus & Folkman, 1984). This model emphasizes the dynamic interaction and reciprocal determinism among the various elements of the stress process: persons, situations, affective reactions, coping behaviors, and adaptive outcomes. This model emphasizes the interaction between personality traits and environmental stressors in determining anxiety states and underscores the crucial role of cognitive appraisals as mediating factors between persons and situations in impacting upon state anxiety. Because this model is based on Spielberger's earlier work on the state–trait theory of anxiety and a "transactional adaptation" of this model to test anxiety research (Spielberger, 1972b), I begin by briefly summarizing some of this earlier work, which provides a basis for the model.

Spielberger's State–Trait Model

Spielberger's state–trait model of anxiety made the useful distinction between anxiety as a personality trait (A-Trait) and anxiety as a personality state (A-State). Thus, trait anxiety refers to a stable disposition to react with anxiety across varying contexts, whereas state anxiety refers to a transitory emotional state of tension and arousal determined by the interaction between a person's trait and present situation (Spielberger, 1972a, 1972b, 1972c; Spielberger et al., 1978).

In the framework of the state–trait distinction, test anxiety is conceptualized as a "situation-specific form of T-Anxiety (Trait anxiety), with worry and emotionality as major components" (Spielberger & Vagg, 1995a, p. 8; cf. Spielberger et al., 1976; Spielberger et al., 1978). Accordingly, "test anxiety" is characterized by the individual's disposition to react with extensive worry, intrusive thoughts, mental disorganization, tension, and physiological arousal across a variety of evaluative conditions (formal tests, interviews, laboratory tasks and exercises, competitive social events, etc.), whereas "state anxiety" refers to the specific level of anxiety experienced in a particular evaluative or test situation, such as an important college examination or athletic competition. Test-anxious students are posited to show higher levels of trait anxiety, tend to perceive exam situations as more dangerous or threatening than those low in trait anxiety, and experience more intense levels of state anxiety when taking tests. High-test-anxious subjects are predicted to respond to the evaluative threat inherent in most exam contexts with greater evaluations in state anxiety, which is essentially equivalent to the Emotionality component of test anxiety, when conceptualized as a situation-specific trait. High levels of state anxiety then stimulate test-anxious individuals to plunge inward, thus activating worry conditions stored in memory that distract the test-anxious student from effective performance.

Transactional Framework

In the context of R. S. Lazarus' (1966) conception of stress as a transactional process, Spielberger (1972b) further distinguished between significant components at play in a temporal sequence of events unfolding in a stressful encounter. Accordingly, the model differentiates among the objective properties of evaluative situations that are potentially stressful (evaluative stressors), the subjective interpretation of a particular situation as more or less threatening for a particular person (threat), the emotional states that are evoked in stressful situations (such as anxiety), the coping reactions and responses to the aversive emotional state (defensive behaviors, palliative and instrumental forms), and adaptive outcomes. The basic components in the anxiety process are depicted in Figure 3.5. Thus, state–trait theory provides a conceptual framework for identifying and classifying the major variables that should be considered in test anxiety research (stress, cognitive appraisal of threat, defenses) and suggests possible interrelationships among these variables.

Transactional Process Model

A recent heuristic transactional process model proposed by Spielberger and Vagg (1987, 1995b), based on a careful analysis of the nature of test anxiety, identified the following key elements of the test anxiety process: (a) personality variables and situational conditions that impact upon students' reactions to evaluative testing situations, (b) the mediating emotional and cognitive processes involved in respond

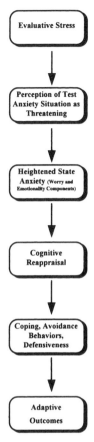

Figure 3.5.   Transactional model of stress and anxiety.

ing to evaluative situations, (c) the correlates and short-term consequences of test anxiety, and (d) various emotion-focused and cognitive-focused intervention strategies designed to help ameliorate the aversive behavioral consequences of test anxiety.

According to this model, when a student enters an exam, the test situation will be initially perceived as more or less personally threatening as a function of individual differences in test anxiety and situational factors. The key situational factors that contribute to the perceptions of a test situation as more or less threatening include the particular domain of subject matter relating to the test questions (history, English, physics, biology, etc.) as well as study and test-taking attitudes and skills that influence how much and how well a student has prepared for an exam and feels he or she can cope with the exam questions. Students with good test-taking skills generally perceive exams as less threatening than students who are less "test wise." Depending on the degree to which an exam is perceived or appraised as threatening, the student will experience an increase in state anxiety and its cognitive manifestations, including self-centered and self-derogatory worry cognitions and other test-irrelevant thoughts. Both the Worry and Emotionality components are predicted to contribute to decrements in test performance. Because test-anxious persons have previously stored more self-derogatory worry cognitions in memory, high state anxiety experienced during an exam will activate a greater number of interfering worry responses, which, in turn, interfere most directly with task performance (Spielberger & Vagg, 1995a).

A central feature of this process-oriented transactional model is the ongoing dynamic interaction and reciprocal influence among distinct elements of the test anxiety process, including study skills and attitudes, perceived threat and appraisals, cognitive processes enlisted before and during the exam, quality of exam performance, and state anxiety experienced during the exam. Accordingly, the affective and cognitive concomitants of test anxiety may provide additional negative feedback that further alters the appraisal of a test situation as more or less threatening. For instance, a person who reacts to an important test situation with heightened degrees of tension, profuse sweating, stomach cramps, and troublesome task-irrelevant thoughts may assess the situation as uncontrollable and even more threatening than at the outset, thus elevating her or his state anxiety levels. Feedback from increased test anxiety, in turn, may lead this test-anxious student to reappraise the exam as more threatening, resulting in a further elevation of state anxiety, with the student caught up in a vicious cycle of negative appraisal and spiraling anxiety reactions.

Cognitive processes, particularly memory and information storage and retrieval, also play an important role in this basically cognitive model. Thus, when students process items presented to them in a test situation, this will stimulate the initiation of a search for relevant task-related information that will enable them to formulate appropriate answers. Feedback from this process may stimulate thoughts and feelings that differ from those occurring earlier in the response chain, which may then contribute to reappraising the test situation as more or less threatening. If the information needed to respond correctly to a test question is not available or cannot be successfully retrieved, the exam will be appraised as more stressful.

Formulating the response to the test question is the final stage of the process model. This stage requires the individual to transform and synthesize the information recovered from memory so that it can be reported in the manner required by the questions. Poor performance at this or any of the previous stages of responding to a test question can lead to emotional reactions and worry cognitions that interfere with attention and contribute to poor performance. Figure 3.6 graphically presents the transactional process model of test anxiety.

A transactional perspective has also been applied successfully to the evaluation of test anxiety intervention programs. Thus, in evaluating test anxiety treatment programs, the model assumes that it is essential to identify both the specific locus of impact and the particular aspects of a therapeutic program that contribute to treatment

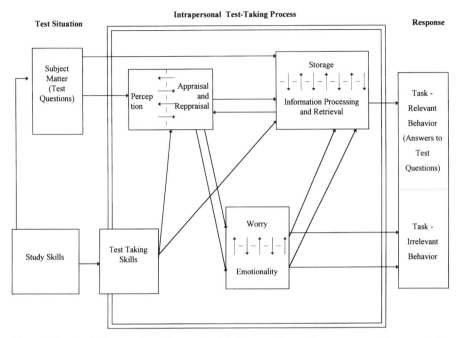

Figure 3.6. Revised transactional process model. The model provides a conceptual framework for analyzing the effects of examination stress on the intrapersonal emotional and cognitive processes that are involved in responding to aptitude, ability, and intelligence tests. The model also encompasses important correlates of test anxiety such as study habits and attitudes (study skills), test-taking skills (test wiseness), and the effects of worry and emotionality on information processing and the retrieval of information from memory storage. Reproduced from Spielberger and Vagg (1995a, p. 12), with permission.

effectiveness (Spielberger & Vagg, 1987; Vagg & Spielberger, 1995). According to the model, some forms of therapy/interventions are directed primarily toward modifying emotional reactions in test situations, whereas others are directed mainly at modifying negative perceptions, appraisals, and reappraisal processes. Given that test anxiety includes both a cognitive and an emotional component, the model posits that the most effective treatment programs for test-anxious students would include both cognitively focused and emotionality focused treatment components. Furthermore, this interactional model posits a reciprocal interaction among the various treatment foci. That is, in modifying irrational appraisals and beliefs, cognitive therapies also indirectly influence emotionality. Likewise, by alleviating aversive emotional reactions in a test situation, one can influence how one copes with worry and irrelevant thoughts (Spielberger & Vagg, 1987). Some of these principles are discussed in greater detail in Chapters 15 and 16.

Limitations

Specific focused hypotheses derived from this transactional model have been put to an empirical test with promising results (see various chapters in Spielberger & Vagg, 1995a). However, most of the studies have tested only specific segments of the model. Research would benefit from the use of sophisticated structural equation modeling procedures to test the validity of the entire nexus of interrelationships among the constructs specified in the model. The model would ideally include dynamic relations (nonrecursive and reciprocal) among the variables. In addition, data collected would be best based on multiple assessment points in a large representative population. The model might also be further enhanced and extended by including postexam stages as well (see Chapter 1), such as the anticipation stage (postexam, but prior to posting of exam grades) and resolution stage (after posting of grades).

Summary

This chapter surveyed key models of test anxiety, both old and new. I now briefly discuss how each of the models has addressed key issues of concern in test anxiety research, including the nature of test anxiety and its key components, distal and proximal antecedents of the phenomenon, cognitive consequences, and forms of effective intervention.

One of the earliest models of test anxiety, the **Drive Model**, emphasizes emotional reactivity and heightened arousal as capturing the nature of test anxiety and in explaining outstanding differences between high- and low-anxious individuals in learning and assessment situations (although acknowledging the importance of disturbing cognitions in anxiety states). Although the noxious or aversive stimuli in the test situation which heighten drive states are emphasized in the model, little is said about the distal factors which may explain why some individuals are more or less aroused in evaluative situations. With respect to the consequences of anxiety, the drive model explicates both the facilitating and debilitating effects of anxiety through the mechanism of response competition, with the effect of anxiety claimed to be dependent on both the stage of learning and task complexity. The drive model has not advocated any specific therapeutic technique, but it would appear that any drive or arousal reduction technique (e.g., relaxation therapy, desensitization) should reduce anxiety and consequently improve performance.

The **Cognitive-Attentional Model** suggests that cognitive interference and self-related deprecative thoughts capture the outstanding differences between high- and low-test-anxious individuals in the face of an evaluative stressor (although acknowledging the importance of arousal and emotionality in stressful exam situations). Test anxiety is presumably construed as a learned behavior that is conditioned over time to assessment situations through repeated negative personal experiences.

Stressful parameters of an evaluative situation (threatening atmosphere, the competitive nature of the situation, task difficulty, severe time constraints, and the like) are important proximal factors evoking elevated levels of test anxiety. Anxiety invariably affects performance by diverting attention from the task to self-depreciating thoughts. It is the cognitive interference of test anxiety in retrieving previously learned and stored material which impacts upon student performance and serves as a trigger for heightened physiological reactivity. This model would advance cognitive-attentional training and modeling to eliminate distracting thoughts and help the test-anxious individual to better control his or her thoughts and focus attention on the task.

According to the **Skills Deficit Model**, the outstanding feature of the test anxiety experience is metacognitive awareness on the part of test-anxious subjects of being unprepared for the task and the resultant feelings of low academic competency and emotional arousal. From an etiological perspective, the deficit model would argue that anxiety and poor performance are due to poor study or test-taking skills resulting from inadequate parental teaching strategies and styles, or poor academic instruction in basic study skills and test-taking strategies. With respect to more proximal factors evoking evaluative stress, the model would underscore the effects of the complex nature of the study material, which enhances the examinee's awareness of inadequate intake of the material due to poor study skills. This model (at least two of three versions) does not attribute a causal relationship to anxiety in affecting performance. Rather, test anxiety is a correlate of the individual's recognition that he or she is ill-prepared for the exam. This model would propose study skills training and counseling to help test-anxious students with deficient study skills enhance their ability to cope with test situations.

The **Self-Regulation Model** claims that the basic difference between high- and low-test-anxious persons is how they respond to test situations and to their arousal under evaluative contexts. Thus, low-test-anxious persons retain confidence of being able to perform well despite anxiety, whereas high-test-anxious persons are doubtful of being able to perform well. This model is silent with respect to the factors accounting for the development of test anxiety, although situational factors enhancing self-focus may exaggerate negative tendencies in test anxious person with low self-expectancies. Behavioral withdrawal and cognitive disengagement are at the roots of performance decrements, leading to poor cue utilization, self-depreciating rumination, and nonattendance to relevant cues. Optimism and outcome expectancies in concert with self-focus are predicted to moderate the anxiety–performance relationship. Although the self-regulation model has not put forth a systematic intervention program, it is implied that manipulating situational factors to raise performance expectancies or shape expectancies (presumably via cognitive modification procedures) may be useful.

The **Self-Merit Model** suggests that high- and low-test-anxious subjects are distinguished by feelings of incompetency combined with attributions of failure to low ability, rather than effort. The self-merit model would attribute the early origins of test anxiety to personal confidence-devaluing experiences in home or school.

Features of the evaluative situations involving demonstration of competency that threaten self-worth are potent sources of evaluative stress and motivational (avoidance and reduced effort), cognitive (poor study skills), and affective factors (heightened arousal) would be operative at various stages of the test anxiety process to produce performance deficits. Although the self-merit model does not directly address intervention, any treatment that would enhance self-confidence and efficacy and reduce threat to competence, including skills training, cognitive behavioral therapy, and the like, should be helpful.

According to the **Transitional Process Model**, it is mainly Worry and Emotionality components that comprise the test anxiety experience. Test anxiety is evoked as a result of the dynamic interaction between a propensity to high evaluative trait anxiety and exposure to a stressful evaluative situation, which elicits perceived threat and resultant high levels of state anxiety. The transactional models would attribute test anxiety, as a situation-specific trait, mainly to constitutional and primary socialization experiences, coupled with personal failure experiences in test situations (or the observation of others' failure experiences). The affective, but primary cognitive, components of test anxiety interact to affect test performance. Both cognitive-focused (including behavioral skills training) and emotion-focused intervention procedures are believed to help the test-anxious individual cope with the multidimensional facets of test anxiety.

The review of test anxiety models in this chapter shows that these models differ with respect to their underlying assumptions and perspectives, degree of empirical validation, coverage of the various facets of the test anxiety construct, and practical utility for designing useful assessment tools and interventions. Yet there appears to be a broad consensus that test anxiety is a complex multidimensional construct, although models differ in the relative emphasis they place on cognitive versus affective components. Furthermore, models are shown to differ in the extent to which they convincingly address the issue of the primary etiological factors underlying test anxiety. In fact, most fall short in adequately accounting for the distal antecedents of test anxiety and in explaining why some persons tend to be more worried and aroused in test situations than others. Most of the models would presumably attribute test anxiety to some form of aversive personal experience in evaluative problem-solving situations either at home or school. With respect to more proximal factors, the various models would agree that stressful parameter of an evaluative situation (threatening atmosphere, the competitive nature of the situation, task difficulty, severe time constraints, and the like) are important proximal factors evoking elevated levels of test anxiety, though for different reasons. Furthermore, the models offer divergent accounts of the causal mechanisms underlying the observed relationship between test anxiety and academic performance. Finally, the models vary considerably in terms of the type of intervention viewed as being most effective in modifying test anxiety.

Few of the existing models discussed in this chapter are genuinely test anxiety models. In fact, it is remarkable that the majority of the models presented in this chapter, representing some of the premiere conceptualizations of test anxiety formulated to date, were not derived from research in the area of test anxiety proper, but rather adapted to the field of test anxiety research from a number of broader domains. Thus, general principles generated from such diverse theoretical areas as Hullian learning theory, self-regulation, self-merit, and self-handicapping, and stress research were applied to test anxiety. These models have been profitably enlisted to shed light on key facets of the phenomenon.

At present, no single theoretical perspective on test anxiety can readily account for the complex and multifaceted nature of test anxiety, including phenomenology, developmental antecedents, correlates and consequences, and therapeutic interventions. Current explanatory models seem capable of subsuming only parts of available research, but no one model is capable of encompassing all of current research. Given the multivariate nature of test anxiety, its various channels of expression, and its myriad causes and consequences, it is reasonable to assume that not one, but several mechanisms are needed to account for test anxiety. Yet there is an urgent need for more comprehensive and integrative models of test anxiety that cover a larger number of facets of the test anxiety domain and synthesize many of the conceptual frameworks presented in this chapter. Some of the best candidates for the key components that should probably be included in more comprehensive models, as they are essential for the test anxiety process, would include trait test anxiety, stressful evaluative situations, state test anxiety, confidence-devaluing experiences in home or school, poor study or test-taking skills, arousal and emotionality, worry, cognitive interference, chronic self-doubts and feelings of incompetency, outcome expectancies, failure and success attributions, poor cue utilization and retrieval, cognitive disengagement, withdrawal of attention, avoidance behaviors, and self-regulatory and coping strategies.

Methodology: Research and Assessment Methods

Current and Recurrent Issues
in Conducting Experimental
Test Anxiety Research

Overview

This chapter provides a basic overview of current and recurrent issues in conducting experimental research in the area of test anxiety. The primary aim of experimental test anxiety research is to test focused predictions derived from existing theory or prior empirical research. The true experiment (Cook & Campbell, 1979) is commonly viewed as the capstone of the scientific method and the ideal paradigm for modern science, providing the strength and rigor that allow one to rule out all or most confounding variables in a research design.

A facet-analytic perspective (Shye, Elizur, & Hoffman, 1994), as applied to stress and anxiety research (McGrath, 1982; Beehr & McGrath, 1996), would suggest that delineating the domain of experimental test anxiety research involves the joint consideration of elements associated with each of the following facets:

1. *Units of observation*, with experimental research always involving one or more observation units (individuals, classrooms, schools, etc.).
2. *Treatments*, involving specific manipulated experimental conditions.
3. *Settings*, with research always involving one or more situations or occasions.
4. *Observations*, with measurement always involving one or more behaviors, properties, or events enacted by observation units in the specific situation(s) under consideration.

When an experimental study in the field of test anxiety is planned, it marks off a domain of possible studies, all of which address the same question (Cronbach, 1982). The research unit(s) of observation, the plan of experimental treatment(s), and research setting(s), together with the specified variable(s) to be observed, constitute the broader domain of investigation. The specific research implemented (i.e., specific sample given the experimental treatment, in a specific time and place, and assessed via specific observation procedures) ultimately produces data from which to make an inference back to the broader original domain.

Because test anxiety research has available to it the same armamentarium of experimental research strategies, data collection methods, and data analytic techniques as does research in any other area within stress, anxiety, and coping research, it falls prey to the same array of seemingly intractable methodological problems that beset research in the stress and coping domain (Beehr & McGrath, 1996). In fact, it is not so much the case that test anxiety research poses new and different methodological problems, as that research in this complex area makes certain methodological problems even more salient and more difficult to manage than they usually are.

I begin by briefly discussing the prevalent units of observation in test anxiety experimental research and move on to discuss treatment plans and the appropriateness of various settings for conducting research. I conclude by discussing observations, i.e., systematic plans for collecting and generating the desired data. I hope that the material presented in this chapter will be useful to the reader in planning experimental test anxiety research, in tackling the experimental test anxiety literature, or in interpreting some of the substantive material presented throughout this book.

Units of Observation

Although a considerable amount of descriptive and correlational test anxiety research has been conducted on school-aged students, the primary subjects or "units of observation" in experimental test anxiety research have been drawn from college student populations, most often undergraduates in psychology and related areas. However, psychology students may not be representative of the general student population, let alone the population at large, thus limiting the generalizability of the results. Moreover, "experimentwise," psychology students often know that ethical considerations limit the degree to which evaluative stress induced in experimental settings would be harmful to them, and consequently may be less reactive to experimental manipulations of evaluative stress than most other students. In addition, many students may accurately guess the purpose of the experiment, thus further affecting the internal validity of the design. Future research would certainly benefit by using more heterogeneous and representative groups as experimental units of observation.

In theory, each experimental and control group constitutes a probability sample (i.e., a random and hence representative sample) of the population. However, because drawing a probability sample involves many practical problems (e.g., high cost, high rate of refusal to cooperate, etc.), probability samples are seldom used in experimental test anxiety research. Although the subject pool seldom constitutes a random sample from some target population, as would ideally be the case, subjects from within a designated pool are randomly *assigned* to various treatment groups. This random assignment procedure appears to be the most economical procedure for canceling out potential artifactual biases that might systematically affect outcomes (Kerlinger, 1973). One possibility of improving on sheer randomization is by matching the subjects in various cells of the experimental design in terms of some variable relevant to the outcome (e.g., trait anxiety, intelligence, defensiveness, social desirability). In choosing sampling units for experimental research, a sensible procedure is to pretest many potential subjects drawn from the target population with respect to trait test anxiety and any other differential characteristics of interest (defensiveness, IQ, etc.), to select those students who would be appropriate subjects (e.g., high-, moderate-, and low-test-anxious subjects), and to assign these persons randomly to treatment and control groups.

A number of approaches have been used in identifying different categories of test-anxious subjects, such as those who are "high test anxious" versus those who are "low test anxious." One common approach is to administer a test anxiety scale to a target group of interest and use the upper quartile (or 30%) of the score distribution in order to define high-test-anxious groups and the lower quartile (or 30%) to define low-test-anxious groups. In some cases, median splits have been used, with those below the median defined as "low anxious" and those above the median defined as "high anxious." Note, however, that using a median split within a student sample of convenience would not accurately locate "high"- or "low"-test-anxious students. Those students above the median in a sample of low-test-anxious students may still be characterized by relatively low absolute levels of test anxiety, whereas those below the mean in a particularly high-test-anxious group might still be highly anxious. Yet another recent approach has been to employ simultaneously both trait and state measures of test anxiety in identifying anxiety groups in experimental research. Thus, Calvo and Carreiras (1993) identified a sample of 36 high-test-anxious students from a larger student population on the basis of two convergent measures of test anxiety: (a) an individual difference trait measure, and (b) a state measure of test anxiety administered under actual stress conditions. Only subjects who scored high or low on *both* measures were identified as high- or low-test-anxious subjects, respectively.

Identification of subjects varying in test anxiety would best be done either by comparing scores with national norms or focusing on students for whom test anxiety is a documented problem (e.g., as evidenced by referral to student counseling or intervention programs, although, here again, referred samples are not always representative of the population, on account of referral bias). Without the availability of standard norms for both state and trait anxiety, subjects identified as high anxious in one study might be classified as low anxious in another. Furthermore, because trait and state anxiety may show quite different distributions, the researcher needs to note carefully whether subjects are to be partitioned on the basis of state or trait distribution of test anxiety scores (Deffenbacher & Hazaleus, 1985).

Treatment Conditions

Stress Induction

When conducting experimental research in the area of test anxiety, it is important to keep in mind the distinction between *evaluation stress*, as an experimentally induced variable, *trait test anxiety*, as an individual difference variable, and *state test anxiety*, as a situation-specific variable. Accordingly, in order to assess the effects of evaluative stress on various criterion variables of interest, experimenters need to contrive ingenious experimental manipulations to evoke stress and resultant state anxiety in experimental subjects. The levels of subjects' state anxiety in response to experimental manipulation should ideally be gauged through direct measurement of state anxiety, although it has often been indirectly inferred from the very nature of the stress manipulations or via trait anxiety scores (Heinrich & Spielberger, 1982).

Seemingly different assumptions underline the procedures of anxiety induction and measurement. If trait test anxiety is measured, it is assumed that in an evaluative setting, those high on trait test anxiety will be in a state of high anxiety, while those who are low on trait test anxiety will be in a state of low anxiety. However, if anxiety is induced in one group by leading them to believe that they are facing a very important exam, it is generally assumed that all members of this group will experience a state of high anxiety. The first assumption implies that only high-trait-anxious people experience a state of high anxiety in evaluative settings; the second implies that everyone is highly anxious when facing an important evaluation. The truth apparently lies close enough to the middle that both procedures seem to be valid for many research purposes.

A variety of techniques have been employed in experimentally inducing evaluative stress and resultant state anxiety in the lab. The most common technique has been provision of *ego-orienting instructions* (e.g., Auerbach, 1973; Deffenbacher & Hazaleus, 1985; I. G. Sarason, 1959; S. B. Sarason, Mandler, & Craighill, 1952). Ego-involving instructions are designed to make assessment conditions as parallel as possible to naturalistic exam procedures and can be broadly classified as inducing "psychologic stress" (Heinrich & Spielberger, 1982). What typically makes these instructions evaluative or ego-threatening are the following characteristics:

- Presenting the test as a measure of intellectual ability (e.g., IQ test).
- Implying that success on the test is reflective of one's overall personality functioning.
- Stressing the importance of the results for prediction of academic or occupational success.
- Stressing the task's time-limited nature.
- Suggesting the possibility of unfavorable comparisons with others.

Negative feedback and failure instructions are another common method of manipulating stress in the lab. Under these conditions, the experimenter typically equates a fictitious norm for subjects, in which subjects are compared with others either favorably (e.g., "You are doing great compared to your classmates") or unfavorably ("You don't seem to have the hang of this like most other kids do"). Difficult, complex, or frustrating tasks have also been employed to arouse stress and anxiety in the lab. McCoy (1965) induced evaluative stress in a group of elementary school children by asking them to make a free drawing of a "poskon"—a nonsense word. Because children were in no way informed that the word is meaningless, it was assumed that the majority of subjects would anticipate failure on this task, thus evoking threat and anxiety, resulting in poor task performance. In order to arouse anxiety, the difficulty level of the test material must be controlled to some extent so that it is not too easy or outlandishly difficult to be taken seriously (Sieber, et al., 1977).

When evaluative stress is manipulated in an experimental setting, it is unclear to what degree the different ways of evoking evaluative stress are comparable, and if so, to what degree we can calibrate these stressor conditions with respect to one another. Is the evaluative stress aroused by negative feedback the same as that aroused by pressured time conditions, or task complexity? Do these stressor conditions converge— in which case they may be regarded as alternative indicators of the same thing—or do they diverge, in which case they must be regarded as indicators of different things?

Nonevaluative or "reassurance" conditions, the other side of the experimental coin, typically include the following features:

- Statements regarding the experimental (rather than evaluative) nature of the test.
- Statements of the experimenter's interest in group performance rather than individual scores.
- Suggestions not to worry if subjects are unable to solve some of the more difficult questions.
- Statements of the unlikeliness of finishing the test or successfully solving all the problems.
- Suggestions not to worry about finishing in the time allotted.
- Suggestions to relax when performing the experimental task.

Figure 4.1 presents an illustration of evaluative and gamelike test environments. Although subjects in the nonevaluative control group(s) do not explicitly receive stress-inducing instructions, it would be wrong to think that they do not experience evaluative stress (Mikulincer, Kedem, & Paz, 1990b). The fact that they are interacting with an adult experimenter in a psychological lab setting, and frequently asked to perform complex cognitive tasks, may have created some form of evaluative stress. It is reasonable, however, to assume that subjects in an evaluative stress condition receive more explicit and stronger situational stress cues than those in the control condition.

Note that trait and state test anxiety have played divergent, but complementary, roles in experimental research. Trait test anxiety has frequently served as a control

Figure 4.1. Evaluative versus game experimental instructions.

variable in studies examining experimental effects on state anxiety, with experimental and control groups often equated with respect to trait anxiety, either through matching designs or by use of covariance techniques. Trait anxiety has also served as an independent "organismic" variable used in partitioning subjects into qualitatively different groups (e.g., high vs. low test anxiety) in experiments designed to probe the interaction between trait test anxiety and a wide array of situational and treatment factors in affecting outcome variables (see Chapters 7 and 9 for examples). State test anxiety, by comparison, has served as a key dependent variable in test anxiety intervention research. As noted by Hill (1972), it has been encouraging indeed that findings for test anxiety, as an individual difference variable, generally parallel those reported for short-term situational manipulations of evaluation anxiety. This leads to greater confidence in the strength and generality of the findings of each type of research (Hill, 1972).

I now point out a number of problems that may occur when inducing evaluative anxiety under experimental conditions. For one, experimental manipulations sometimes fail to achieve the desired results. Researchers have not yet found a satisfactory or failproof way of inducing stress or assuring subjects' ego involvement in test anxiety experiments. By the same token, experimenters have often failed to create truly "neutral" or "nonevaluative" conditions. In fact, a survey of the research suggests that attempts to induce anxiety have been largely unsuccessful (see reviews of the literature by Tobias [1977a, 1977b, 1977c]). Students provided with ego-involving instructions did not have higher levels of state anxiety compared to the nonstress control group—the opposite was often true. Until there is greater reassurance that anxiety is operative in the laboratory situation, it cannot truly be deemed to be a stressful evaluative situation, and all discussion about the effects of anxiety on outcomes may be merely speculative. In order to test the effectiveness of the evaluative threat manipulation, it would appear to be essential to conduct a *manipulation check* to assess subjects' perceptions and state anxiety levels following experimental instructions.

Conventional test cues in these so-called "nonevaluative" situations often override attempts to reassure subjects that they are not being tested. The author experienced this problem several years ago when conducting an experiment designed to assess the effects of test context (game vs. evaluative) on the performance of children from socioculturally different groups. Although test instructions, format, booklet, and atmosphere were all altered in order to create a nonevaluative "game" context, subject feedback during debriefing indicated that a good number of children in the game condition perceived the situation as an evaluative and threatening one, in spite of the multiple manipulations designed to create a nonevaluative "game" context. Given the prior experience of most people in modern society with tests and their general sensitivity to test cues, a test by any other name is still viewed as a test by most. Furthermore, high-test-anxious individuals may fail to discriminate between formal test and nontest situations and tend to respond to all performance situations in which an adult is present as a test situation.

One problem faced by researchers in the area of test anxiety is that of finding ethical ways to induce anxiety in test situations. Clearly, in inducing evaluative anxiety under experimental conditions, some subjects must be made to believe that they are being evaluated and that the outcome of the evaluation will have important stakes or consequences for them. Induction of anxiety through such methods as failure feedback or false threats, particularly when done at a level high enough to achieve ecological validity, presents serious ethical problems (Mueller, 1992). A fake scholastic aptitude or intelligence test would probably arouse state anxiety in most subjects, but might be considered unethical. Current ethical practice requires the investigator to inform the participant of all features of the research that reasonably might be expected to influence willingness to participate, and to explain all other aspects of the research about which the participant inquires.

Design Issues

Experimental design serves to guide the test anxiety researcher in the process of collecting, analyzing, and interpreting observations in order to answer critical questions at the heart of the research as validly and accurately as possible. Whereas the classical experimental design is the two-comparison-group design, including an experimental and control group, experimental test anxiety research has generally employed factorial designs. These more complex designs have been used to test the interactive effects of various environmental factors (atmosphere, examiner behavior, social support, etc.) and test anxiety (either operationalized as a manipulated stress variable or as a situation-specific trait) as they impact upon criterion outcome measures. A major concern in test anxiety research is whether or not the results of the experiment can be generalized to other subjects and conditions. Internal and external validity are two general criteria of research design addressing the concerns of generalizability.

Internal Validity

Internal validity is commonly viewed as being the sine qua non of research design. Internal validity refers to the question of whether the manipulated independent variable (say, test atmosphere) did in fact cause the dependent variable (say, state anxiety). The degree of internal validity of a design determines the degree of confidence one can have about whether a particular set of empirical findings (e.g., "high-test-anxious persons perform better than low-test-anxious persons on easy tasks, but worse on difficult tasks") do reflect a directional casual relation between independent (i.e., task difficulty, test anxiety,) and dependent variables (i.e., task performance). I now briefly point out a number on the more salient threats to the internal validity of experimental designs in test anxiety research (Cook & Campbell, 1979).

History and Maturation.   *History* refers to all events during the time of the study that might affect the individual. Naturally occurring extraneous events that take place in the interval between the onset of the manipulated evaluative stress in an experiment and the measured outcome (affective or cognitive) responses might be responsible for the observed changes in anxiety or performance, rather than the contextual factors manipulated in the experimental hypothesis. *Maturation* could have an effect similar to history. Accordingly, as subjects in the experiment grow, mature, and develop, they might learn how to cope better with evaluative contexts and cope with exams without suffering adverse anxiety consequences. Time and experience alone might have some effect, and this could confound the results of experimental manipulations. A number of biological and psychological processes that produce changes in the experimental subjects studied with the passage of time could affect the dependent variable and thus lead to erroneous inference.

Testing and Instrumentation Effects.   As is well attested in behavioral research. measuring subjects often tends to change them with respect to the very construct being assessed. Subjects may simply remember how they answered items on test anxiety inventories from one administration to the next and try either to show consistency or change. Repeatedly testing subjects on a measure of test anxiety (e.g., before, during, after exam) might sensitize them to the measure itself in a way that would affect their responses to test anxiety scales on later measurements—either lowering or increasing their test anxiety scores. In addition, physical instruments used to test anxiety, such as physiographs, deteriorate with use and over time and need to be recalibrated.

Regression Artifacts. When individuals are selected on the basis of extreme scores on a test anxiety inventory (say "high" vs. "low" test anxious), and the measure is not perfectly reliable, individuals who score well above the average on the pretest will appear to have decreased in their level of test anxiety upon retesting, whereas persons scoring well below the average will appear to have increased in their anxiety level, regardless of the effectiveness of the experimental treatment. A case in point: If the experimental treatment is implemented by teaching coping skills to the particular people who showed high-test-anxiety reactions at pretest time (hence, they appeared to "need" the coping treatment more), then posttest scores on test anxiety are likely to average lower for that experimental group due to random error of measurement alone, without regard to the effectiveness of the intervention techniques. The lower stress reaction score may lead to an erroneous positive conclusion about the effectiveness of the intervention.

Mortality. It is common in test anxiety research, particularly intervention program evaluation assessment, for some subjects to drop out of the study before it has been completed. This mortality effect makes it less likely that the treatment and nontreatment groups will be equivalent at posttest measurement, even if they were equivalent at the start of the study. It is thus difficult to determine whether the attrition was related, either directly or indirectly, to the treatment.

External Validity

Attempts to demonstrate that whatever casual relationships that are postulated between independent and dependent variables are generalizable across people, settings, experimental treatments, and times define the domain of *external* validity (Allen, Elias, & Zlotlow, 1980). Say a lab experiment conducted among elementary school students found that reassuring instructions increased performance when compared to evaluative instructions in high-test-anxious subjects. Whereas these findings may be internally valid and may support a relatively strong inference about whether the independent variable (e.g., examiner instructions) actually led to changes in the dependent variables (e.g., task performance) within the study, those findings say nothing about whether the same thing would happen with other participants (e.g., high school rather than elementary school students), at other times (e.g., in a year from now or during the summer vacation), and in other settings (field rather than the lab). Put another way, the basic issue is whether the relationship found interacts, in the statistical sense, with the experimental population, the nature of the setting, and/ or features of the time period during which the experiment took place.

Of particular concern are selection biases resulting from different recruitment of research participants to experimental and control groups, and reactive arrangements due to the possible artificiality of evaluative stress manipulations in lab settings, that may jeopardize the external validity of experiments in this area. Of course, without actually conducting multiple experiments using different types of subjects, in multiple places, and at multiple times, the test anxiety researcher cannot directly test for such a statistical interaction. Instead, what the researcher must do is examine the selection process by which he or she gained access to the subjects involved and chose the times and places in which to conduct the study, in order to estimate how broad the range of subjects and conditions is over which the findings of that study are likely to hold. One's level of confidence in the external validity of a particular set of findings can only be increased through replications conducted with many different groups of individuals, in many settings, and in many locations. Only after such evidence accumulates and appears to be consistent can we develop confidence in those findings.

Settings

As research always involves carrying out some form of observational procedure in one or more situations (or occasions), a major issue in planning research in the test anxiety domain involves the selection of appropriate *settings* for conducting the test anxiety experiment. In part, this is the familiar "lab versus field" problem. Following McGrath (1982), studies in the test anxiety literature can easily be classified on the basis of whether the research was done in real-life evaluative settings (e.g., oral dissertation exam contexts, SAT college admissions testing, midterm exams) or in an experimentally contrived laboratory setting. The crucial distinction here is not what particular data collection methodology was used (e.g., descriptive, correlational, or experimental), but rather how the situation fits into the ongoing life of the focal person(s) involved (McGrath, 1982). In effect it is the answer to the question: Is the person under examination primarily there in order to be in an experiment or is the exam situation an integral part of his or her ongoing academic or occupational life?

Field Settings

While earlier experimental research in test anxiety commonly employed labora-tory analogues of evaluative situations (I. G. Sarason & Stoops, 1978; Hollandsworth et al., 1979) which have unknown generalizability to real-life situations, contempo-rary research evidences an increased number of studies in true-to-life test situations (e.g., Galassi et al., 1981a; Zeidner & Nevo, 1992). Clearly, both field and laboratory experimental settings bring with them inevitable costs, but also potential benefits; both are needed to further our understanding of the test anxiety phenomenon.

A field experiment carried out in a realistic situation is ideally suited to test anxiety research. In this research setting, one or more independent variables are manipulated by the experimenter under conditions controlled as carefully as the situation will permit. Field experiments are more realistic than lab experiments and therefore usually have a stronger effect than those in the lab (Kerlinger, 1973). Thus, when test anxiety is gauged in naturalistic true-to-life examination contexts, evaluative stress is generally assumed to be operating because students take tests (e.g., IQ tests or course-related exams) that have important consequences for their future. This is especially true when persons are assessed at various points surrounding major exams in school, college, or in the work site that pose a distinct threat to the achievement of important life goals (e.g., Scholastic Aptitude Test, bar exam, career placement exam).

Problems of generalizability from analogue to true exam conditions are good reason for conducting test anxiety research in a natural test setting wherever possible. Despite the technical problems involved in assessing anxiety in true-to-life settings, it is desirable to take advantage of naturalistic variations in anxiety level such as often occurs in the context of classroom or college testing, oral presentations in class, and the like. Experimental manipulations can be judiciously built into natural testing programs (Sieber et al., 1977).

Though employing naturalistic samples in authentic exam settings has the advantage of enhancing the external validity of a study, it simultaneously imposes certain limitations (Kim & Rocklin, 1994). Because state anxiety may fluctuate with the particular phase of the exam process being assessed, it would be important to assess anxiety at several points in time. However, one concern is minimizing the intrusiveness of the study in order not to interfere with exam performance. There has been relatively little research on test anxiety *during* actual tests (positive examples are Galassi et al. [1981a, 1981b, 1984]), presumably because of the ethical questions involved in disrupting student performance during testing. For example, responding to a one-item anxiety rating scale at varying points during the exam may enhance self-awareness of the test situation, enhance examinee's anxiety, and negatively impact upon students' test performance. A further problem is that much of the test anxiety data obtained in naturalistic conditions is assessed after the completion of actual tests (Deffenbacher, 1978; Holroyd et al., 1978). Such data are potentially contaminated by the students' appraisals of their performance and by memory deficits (Galassi et al., 1981b).

Laboratory Settings

A lab experiment is one in which the variance of all (or nearly all) of the possible influential independent variables not pertinent to the immediate problem is kept at a minimum. This is done by isolating the research in a physical setting apart from the routine of ordinary living and manipulating one or more independent variables (e.g., item arrangement or test atmosphere) under controlled conditions. As mentioned earlier, the lab experiment has the virtues of control, precision, and replicability. Its greatest weakness is the artificiality of the situation and consequent lack of strength of the experimental manipulation in evoking stress and anxiety. Because practical as well as ethical considerations make it impossible to generate evaluative stress reactions as intense as found in real life, lab experiments may underestimate both the level of test anxiety and its impact upon performance (R. S. Lazarus & Launier, 1978). This may explain the frequent observation that no behavioral difference among high- and low-anxiety groups follows experimental manipulation.

The experience of test anxiety depends on the individual's interpretation of the situation as a personal social-evaluative threat, taxing the person's coping resources. Therefore experimental realism is even more important in test anxiety research than is usually the case. If the subject perceives the situation as unreal or as nonthreatening, it would be meaningless to speak about the nature and effects of test anxiety in such a situation. Clearly, the ecological validity of such laboratory studies needs to be considered and determined, and results from analogue studies are clearly open to questions of generalizability.

A number of studies in the anxiety literature deal with laboratory tasks in which the stressfulness hinges on the subject being motivated to try to do the task well. If subjects see the task as unimportant or trivial, the idea that they are "aroused" or "stressed" by increasing the difficulty of the task, or by giving failure feedback, is simply not to be taken seriously. Furthermore, when evaluative stress is manipulated in an experimental setting, the resultant anxiety experience may not be truly reflective of the manifold experiences and manifestations of test anxiety in a natural evaluative setting during or prior to an evaluative task (Sieber et al., 1977).

Because there are individual differences in trait test anxiety, or proneness to react with sensitivity to evaluative stress conditions, individuals would be expected to differ in the degree to which a given intensity of an evaluative stressor will evoke state test anxiety. So the question is posed: To what extent is there convergence among high- or low-test-anxious individuals in their stress reactions? Furthermore, do different types of test-anxious persons react to the same stressor with different response patterns? That is, does one type of person react to a given type of stressor condition with a particular stress response pattern, while another type of person reacts to the same or different stress condition with another response pattern, and so on?

It is important to note that test anxiety reactions and coping behaviors in exam contexts are not invariant throughout a testing experience. Rather, there may be critical moments during a test (e.g., the beginning or the end) that cue or heighten test anxiety, and both the level of test anxiety as well as key correlates may vary with the particular phase of anxiety process in which test anxiety is gauged (see Chapters 1 and 2). As a result, it seems important to study students' behaviors at critical junctures in the process.

Observations

As a scientific construct, test anxiety is useful to the extent that it can be measured objectively. The tendency of researchers to endeavor to understand test anxiety through standardized assessment instruments derives largely from the conviction that "science is measurement" (Anderson & Sauser, 1995). Clearly, in order to gain a better understanding of the nomological network in which test anxiety is embedded and be able to formulate reliable generalizations about the nature, antecedents, and consequences of test anxiety, a valid and generalizable measure of the construct is needed. In addition, valid measurements of test anxiety would be highly useful for purposes of diagnosis and treatment assessment. Although a wide variety of observational procedures may be used to assess test anxiety, I focus here on the most prevalent methods of operationalizing the test anxiety construct.

Subjective Self-Reports

Subjective self-report instruments are by far the most popular observational procedures for mapping out the phenomenology of test anxiety. Subjective reports include any direct report by the person regarding his or her test anxiety responses, usually elicited via questionnaires, single-item rating scales, think-aloud procedures, or interviews before, during, or after an important exam.

Self-Report Questionnaires and Inventories

Self-report paper-and-pencil questionnaire measures of *state* anxiety ask individuals to report which of the relevant symptoms of anxiety they are *currently* experiencing in a particular test situation, whereas *trait* measures ask subjects to report symptoms they *typically* or *generally* experience in test situations. The preference for self-report inventories of anxiety implies not only a disillusionment with other types of measures, but also acceptance of the awareness of test anxiety as a conscious process best gauged by subjective self-reports (S. B. Sarason et al., 1960). Unfortunately, many studies use self-report data exclusively, without any attempt to measure salient behavior (e.g., through observational procedures), thus either under- or overestimating the problem.

A wide array of measures have been constructed using conventional psychometric test construction procedures. Such instruments are highly practical: they do not require a great deal of expensive professional time, are relatively inexpensive to produce, and are easily administered and scored (Spielberger & Krasner, 1988). Chapter 5 discusses issues in the development and validation of self-report measures in some detail.

Think-Aloud Procedures

Think-aloud procedures are designed to assess the contents of consciousness in examinees while they are engaged in test taking. These procedures have been claimed to provide a more direct measure of the actual thoughts experienced by students during a test than comparable self-report measures—without imposing the researcher's preconceptions on respondents. Accordingly, subjects are asked to verbalize anything that comes into their minds, no matter what the nature of the thoughts, while working on the cognitive tasks given. Several methods of cognitive assessment have been utilized, including "production methods," which require subjects to generate their own cognitive responses to assessment stimuli, and "endorsement techniques," which simply require subjects to endorse specific thoughts experienced on a checklist (Heimberg et al., 1987).

One production method, the *thought-listing technique*, extensively utilized in the study of test anxiety (Bruch, 1978), asks subjects to provide spoken or written records of their cognitive responses to specific stimuli. Typical instructions are: "Please list as many thoughts and feelings as you can recall having during this test. Every thought and feeling that went through your mind during the time is important (i.e., thoughts and feelings about yourself, the situation, or unrelated to the experiment). Be spontaneous ... it is important that you list all thoughts and feelings *as you experienced them ...*" (Blankstein et al., 1989, p. 273). Subjects are often interrupted in the middle of testing and instructed to write down everything they had thought about while working on the test during the last 3–5 minutes prior to being interrupted. The thoughts are then coded on relevant dimensions, such as their positive valence ("Problems are simple") or negative balance ("Not enough time left") (Cacioppo & Petty, 1981; Bruch, Kaflowitz, & Kuethe, 1986).

Physiological Measures

Test anxiety researchers have occasionally employed physiological measures of arousal in order to gauge changes in somatic activity believed to accompany the phenomenological and behavioral components of test anxiety. Indeed, research data attest that individuals typically show substantial increases in tonic levels of physiological activity when they are exposed to testing situations. Measures of electrodermal responses (Galvanic skin response), respiration (rate/volume), somatic activity (muscle tension), cardiovascular system (pulse rate, heart rate, blood pressure, etc.), and electrical activity of the brain have gained considerable currency in stress and anxiety research over the years (R. J. Morris et al., 1988). Indeed, a variety of peripheral autonomic, neurohormonal, musculoskeletal, and electrocortical measures have been shown to change significantly in response to evaluative stress (Holroyd & Appel, 1980). The use of physiological measures to gauge anxiety in test situations would seem to have a distinct advantage over self-report measures. Because it is difficult to control voluntarily autonomic nervous system responses, these responses should be immune to a number of problems endemic to self-report measures of anxiety, such as faking, defensiveness, and attention to social desirability.

Although physiological measures have been used in numerous analogue lab experiments in test anxiety research, only a handful of studies have assessed physiological functioning in the course of actual true-to-life exam situations (Allen, 1971). Those studies that have used physiological measures typically employed indices that can be obtained in actual examination situations cheaply and with minimal disruption, such as pulse rate and finger sweat prints. Although these measures are typically obtained using a physiograph, less costly measures of electrodermal activity have been used. Representative of these measures is the palmar sweat index, a quantification of the sweat gland activity of the hand, obtained via an impression of the skin.

Despite some important advantages, physiological indices suffer from a number of formidable methodological problems, including questionable construct validity, poor reliability, and low practicality in naturalistic field settings. To begin with, using autonomic reactivity as a measure of test anxiety raises serious concerns relating to the construct validity of these measures. The extent to which static measures of peripheral autonomic reactivity (say pulse rate samples or finger sweat prints) validly reflect central emotional changes that occur as a result of evaluative stressful situations has not been adequately determined (Allen, 1980). Nor has it been demonstrated that individuals with high and low trait anxiety differ in their level of emotional arousal when confronted with evaluative stress. Furthermore, autonomic arousal may not necessarily be synonymous with evaluative anxiety and may be considered a measure of state test anxiety only when the subject cognitively labels arousal as anxiety (Holroyd & Appel, 1980). Clearly, a one-to-one correspondence between state test anxiety and physiological arousal may not be assumed and physiological measures should not be used as an independent criterion for state test anxiety. Other emotional states (e.g., anger) also lead to increased physiological functioning (Hodges, 1976).

Another serious problem related to the construct validity of physiological indices is that one cannot assume that the various measures of physiological arousal used in test anxiety research (heart rate, respiratory rate, skin resistance level) are entirely comparable measures. For example, electrodermal responses and cardiovascular responses may provide very different indices of arousal because each of these indices reflects complex and specific physiological processes sensitive to many internal and external influences. Indeed research suggests that these indices suffer from a lack of convergence with other physiological indices of test anxiety (Lang, Rice, & Sternbach, 1972). Furthermore, discrepancies can sometimes occur when different physiological measures are taken. Thus, for one examinee, heart or respiration rate may be reactive to evaluative stress, but skin conductance will show no changes in this same person; for another, the opposite might be true. Moreover, individual differences can appear among different persons with one showing consistent responsivity under evaluative stress in, say, heart rate reactivity, but just as consistently showing no reactivity in skin conductance.

In addition to the problem of construct validity, virtually all of these physiological measures have serious problems of reliability (McGrath, 1982). Most physiological indices reflect a wide range of differences among individuals, unrelated to specific evaluative stressor conditions. Also, physiological measures reflect an equally wide range of differences within the individual, related to diurnal cycles or other temporal or environmental conditions orthogonal to specific evaluative stressors. These problems require elaborate design controls and counterbalancing, as well as careful calibration of the instruments themselves. In addition, physiological indices evidence low temporal stability, and appear to be sensitive to a variety of situational influences (Allen, 1972, 1980). Some physiological measures (Galvanic skin response, pulse rate, perhaps others) other probably vulnerable to testing or reactivity effects; that is, the measurement procedures themselves may alter the levels of measured state anxiety in evaluative situations.

A related psychometric difficulty involves a lack of normative information against which to judge high levels of emotional arousal in test situations. In contrast to well-developed standardization data reported for a number of test-anxiety questionnaires/inventories (see Chapter 5), we possess little information about how individuals with high and low test anxiety are distributed on physiological indices. To be maximally useful, these data would have to be collected in a variety of situations, ranging from experientially relaxing to highly stressful (Allen, 1980).

Psychometric issues aside, physiological measures also have a number of inherent technical problems when used as measures of test anxiety in a true-to-life naturalistic context. Clearly, locating a complex physiological apparatus (e.g., physiograph) in a classroom or other real-life examination situation is neither cost-efficient nor practical. For example, electrodes need to be attached to examinees, who then need to engage in the long waiting periods needed to obtain steady baseline measures. Aside from possible reactivity of these measures, the cost of using such equipment and of obtaining the necessary technical staff to operate it would be prohibitive, particularly in field settings.

Following McGrath (1982), it is important to distinguish between the observational measures of ongoing physiological processes (e.g., Galvanic skin response, pulse rate) which have been discussed so far, and trace measures of physiological processes. The most commonly used trace measures at the physiological level are biochemical analyses of blood plasma and urine (e.g., accretion levels of eosinophils, corticosteroids, adrenaline products, sugar, cholesterol, CO_2, free fatty acids). Although these trace measures are less likely to be vulnerable to reactivity effects than are observations or subjective reports, they may require sizable portions of time for substantial accretions to occur. Hence they are more useful in studies involving prolonged exposure to evaluative stress (e.g., during the long period of writing a doctoral dissertation). One trace measure of evaluative stress, urinary adrenaline (a catecholamine), may be affected by many factors including diet, steroids, drugs, alcohol, genetic factors, and physical activity and other personality variables (Endler & Parker, 1990c).

Performance Measures

Another approach to the assessment of test anxiety has involved the use of cognitive and behavioral measures of performance. Performance measures of test anxiety (e.g., examination scores, semester grade-point averages, course grades, measures of decrements in cognitive functioning, latency and errors in recall of stress-relevant stimulus materials, etc.) assess a wide array of cognitive and academic skills. Most measures in this category are indices of performance designed to provide data about the types of cognitive disruptions that test-anxious individuals experience in evaluative situations when engaged in particular types of cognitive tasks involving learning, complex problem-solving, and short- and long-term memory.

Performance measures pose a number of difficult conceptual problems. First and foremost, they focus only superficially on the experience of test anxiety. At best, they may be considered to index the effects of test anxiety on cognitive behavior. Second, it is hard to determine what are the psychological functions (e.g., encoding, reasoning, short-term memory, judgment) that, when impaired or otherwise affected, are evidence of test anxiety or of its effects. Third, it is likely that there are vast individual differences in these psychological processes, quite apart from the effects of anxiety on them.

Systematic Observations

Behavioral observations are an extremely valuable additional source of information on test anxiety, permitting great accuracy and more objectivity than self-report or interview procedures. Thus, probably the most direct and least inferential way to assess test-anxious behaviors is to observe relevant behavioral manifestations of the construct in evaluative situations in which they occur (King & Ollendick, 1989). Thus, specific behaviors reflective of test anxiety (distress, tension, apprehension, distraction, avoidance) are operationally defined and recorded. Instead of having examinees rate or rank themselves on a series of items reflecting the test anxiety experience, an alternative approach would be to have a trained observer (experimenter, teacher, therapist) rate the individual's level of test anxiety (Suinn, 1990). Accordingly, the observer utilizes some standard set of observation categories in documenting test-anxious behavior, though sometimes cameras, tape recorders, or other specialized sensing devices are used.

Mandler and Sarason (1952) were the first to employ performance measures involving direct observation of behavioral manifestations of anxiety, such as perspiration, excessive body movement, and inappropriate laughter, when subjects were engaged in exam situations. Individuals with high and low test anxiety scores were discriminable by these criteria. Horne and Matson (1977) conducted observations behind a one-way mirror, with 1-minute time samples of 24 mannerisms related to anxiety (chewing on nails or pencil, hand wringing, "fidgety" trunk movements, etc.) gathered from a group of students who were taking a test. Adequate interobserver reliability of the duration of anxious behavior was reported ($r = .78$). Figure 4.2 graphically depicts systematic observation in a performance situation.

Observations are often touted as the most desirable form of obtaining data and as being more "objective" than alternative methods—presumably not subject to the

Figure 4.2. Systematic observation of test-anxious behavior.

kind of human biases necessarily involved in self-reports. However, the use of observational procedures for measurement of test anxiety is rare and the psychological processes considered to be relevant to test anxiety (or coping with anxiety) are not very amenable to direct observation. To do so requires that someone monitor examinees in evaluative situations continuously, and somehow have access to their ongoing psychological processes. Although early behaviorists tended to accept behavioral observation data on the basis of their surface validity, a variety of problems related to their use have been identified. Among these are the complexity of the observation code, observer bias and reliability, observer drift, the reactive nature of the observation process itself, and the high costs of conducting observational procedures. Test anxiety is inferred from overt behavioral indices, and the accuracy of the observer as to the presence of test anxiety is influenced by the accuracy of the inferential behavioral data (Suinn, 1990). Finally, even a relatively ingenious researcher may be hard put to construct observational procedures or instruments that yield reasonable indirect assessments of all processes related to the test anxiety construct. Furthermore, depending upon how the observations are obtained, this procedure may well introduce some element of artificiality in the setting. The very nature of being observed can introduce an artificial variable, such that the observation process itself can produce changes in the behaviors. Several types of behavioral sampling methods might be considered for use: role playing, simulations, and naturalistic observations.

Unobtrusive Measures

Researchers have seldom used unobtrusive measures (Webb, Campbell, Schwartz, & Sechrest, 1966) to assess test anxiety. One notable exception is a study by Johnson and Sechrest (1968) in which two trace indices of test anxiety were employed. The first was a measure of "paper messiness," under the assumption that anxious and tense subjects would produce messier and more disorganized papers. The second unobtrusive measure consisted of nonessential marks on the margin (letters, symbols, punctuation marks), assumed to be reflective of increased tension and emotional ventilation. The potential of using these measures has not been fully realized in contemporary test anxiety research.

In conclusion, stressful evaluative situations would typically have effects on various response systems (i.e., verbal, physiological, cognitive/performance), and each measurement method possesses unique functions in anxiety assessment and is characterized by specific and unique limitations. Thus, while self-report test anxiety questionnaires provide the most direct assessment of subjective distress, they may be open to a variety of response sets, including deliberate distortion and defensiveness. By contrast, physiological measures are less transparent in terms of being susceptible to conscious distortion, but often suffer from baseline instability and poor reliability and convergent validity. Measures of cognitive performance tend to be relatively stable measures and less susceptible to distortion, but they are somewhat more "remote" indices and tend to be influenced by numerous other factors aside from test anxiety. Because data derived from the various observational domains are relatively independent and frequently exhibit failure of agreement (M. W. Eysenck, 1992), it is desirable to obtain measures from all three systems and "triangulate" any observed effects by means of converging operations (Allen et al., 1980).

Based on work of Beehr and McGrath (1996), Table 4.1 presents an attempt to classify the domain of test anxiety measures using three system levels (psychological, physiological, behavioral) and four operational forms of measurement (self-reports, observations, trace measures, and archival records). As pointed out by Beehr and McGrath (1996), the system levels are to some degree ambiguous and there is not always a clear line between various levels.

Summary

This chapter focused on key issues in conducting experimental research in the area of test anxiety. Each of four major facets of experimental research—population,

**Table 4.1. Classification of Test Anxiety Measures
by System Level and Operational Procedure**

| System level | Operational procedure | | | |
	Subjective report	Observation	Trace measures[a]	Archival records[b]
Psychological	Self-report inventories, rating scales, thought-listing procedures, etc.	Observation of fidgety behavior, nail biting, distressed facial features, lack of concentration, etc.	Smudges left on test paper, grinding of pencils during exam, etc.	Records of counseling sessions describing self-preoccupation, worry, etc.
Physiological	Subjective self-reports of arousal, symptom checklists, etc.	Observation of sweating, muscle tension, etc.	Biochemical analysis of urine or blood samples taken prior to, during, or after test	Medical records of somatic symptoms and illness during test period, etc.
Behavioral	Self-reports of test performance, performance expectancies, etc.	Observations of response quality, speed, nature of errors, etc.	Test protocols	Records of achievement in school or college registrar's office, etc.

Note: Adapted from Beehr and McGrath (1996).
[a]Trace measures refer to the evidence left behind unwittingly by test-anxious examinees, reflective of the behavior of interest.
[b]Archival records are derived from records made for purposes other than the research at hand.

treatments, settings, and observations—were shown to pose special problems to the test anxiety researcher. In discussing the *units of observation* facet, concern was expressed regarding the low degree of representativeness of the specific samples typically studied in test anxiety research (i.e., undergraduates in psychology), as well as the problem of correctly identifying high- and low-test-anxious groups. The self-selected populations with whom experimental studies are typically performed may differ in meaningful ways from the target populations to which results are generalized, so as to partly invalidate the conclusions based on experimental data. Research using highly heterogeneous samples of subjects in a wider array of settings should help reduce this problem (Sieber et al., 1977). Furthermore, individual differences in subjects' sensitivity to evaluative stressors, as well as individual differences in the patterning of state test anxiety responses, need to be controlled for when assessing anxiety responses under evaluative conditions.

A major concern relating to the *treatment* domain bears on the operational validity of various methods of inducing evaluative stress as well as dealing with a host of threats jeopardizing the internal and external validity of common research designs. Also, researchers have generally failed to capture temporal or sequential effects in experimental studies. Anxiety levels change over time, adaptation occurs, defenses develop, coping skills are acquired, and additional sources of anxiety may begin to affect the individual and to have cumulative effects. None of these processes is adequately captured in the "one-shot" experimental studies currently being conducted.

The "lab" versus "field" issue is of major concern when discussing the setting facet. On one hand, there is the problem of low power of stress induction in the lab and the artificiality and lack of generalizability of laboratory results. On the other, there is the problem of the low degree of control over extraneous contaminating variables in the field setting. Clearly, caution needs to be used in generalizing the results of a particular lab study to naturalistic evaluative situations, since what is found in a simulated situation may differ from that found in a true-to-life evaluative context.

In relation to the *observation* domain, a major concern is the low degree of correlation of measures across response channels (cognitive, physiological, behavioral) and the problematic convergent and discriminant validity evidence for current measures. An additional concern is the reactivity effect of obtrusive measures as well as ethical problems involved in interfering with subject's test performance when assessing test anxiety as a state measure over time.

Because replicability is the ultimate test of significance in experimental research, the ideal standard would be to have experimental findings in the area of test anxiety replicated with similar results in different settings, occasions, and populations. Furthermore, test anxiety research should strive to use multimethod approaches and triangulate methods wherever possible. Future research not only needs to be reliable and significant, but meaningful. The field has been dominated by group data that generate significant results, but fail to account for a substantial portion of the variance in test anxiety, and even more so, test performance. Furthermore, researchers pursuing some promising hypothesis (e.g., cognitive-interference or skills-deficit hypothesis) should be aware of potential "confirmatory bias" in their research and not attempt to prove the validity of their hypothesis at all cost (Hollandsworth et al., 1979).

Many researchers have viewed test anxiety as a convenient vehicle for studying broader issues (e.g., stress, coping, aptitude × treatment interaction, situational effects, effects of behavioral therapy). Future experimental research should be driven by an interest in understanding the test anxiety phenomenon per se, as well as shedding additional light on its antecedents and consequences. Furthermore, researchers in the field of test anxiety could benefit by elevating the role of methodology to coequal status with the substantive area being researched.

Developing Self-Report
Test Anxiety Instruments

Overview

Self-report instruments are currently the most widely used measures of test anxiety for both research and practical purposes (Allen, 1980). Self-report instruments, graphically depicted in Figure 5.1, have become popular because they are considered to provide the most direct access to a person's subjective experiential states in evaluative situations, possess good psychometric properties, are relatively inexpensive to produce, and are simple to administer and score. Among the popular early measures, used primarily for research purposes, were the following: (a) Test Anxiety Questionnaire (TAQ; S. B. Sarason & Mandler, 1952), (b) Test Anxiety Scale for Children (TASC; S. B. Sarason et al., 1960); (c) Test Anxiety Scale (TAS; I. G. Sarason & Ganzer, 1963; I. G. Sarason, 1978), (d) Achievement Anxiety Test (AAT; Alpert & Haber, 1960), and (e) Worry/Emotionality Questionnaire (WEQ; Liebert & Morris, 1967). Among the widespread contemporary measures of test anxiety are the following: (a) Test Anxiety Inventory (TAI; Spielberger, 1980); (b) Reactions to Tests (RTT; I. G. Sarason, 1984); (c) Suinn Test Anxiety Behavior Scale (STABS; Suinn, 1969); and (d) Revised Test Anxiety Scale (RTA; Benson, Moulin-Julian, Schwarzer, Seipp, & El-Zahhar, 1992).

This chapter aims at describing methods for developing self-report test anxiety scales. It is quite practical in orientation, discussing the various issues involved in developing test anxiety instruments. Accordingly, I will go through the instrument development process step by step and examine common methods for approaching each step. The goal is for the reader to gain an understanding of how test anxiety scales are developed and what are the practical issues in scale development. Note that much of the material in this chapter is basically *descriptive* in orientation, detailing and exemplifying current scale construction practices in the field of test anxiety. However, on occasion, I shift focus to a *prescriptive* orientation, particularly when discussing areas in which test anxiety scale development is deficient and could be

Figure 5.1.   Illustration of a self-report test anxiety instrument.

meaningfully improved by prescriptive guidelines (e.g., in ways of mapping out and sampling the test anxiety domain).

What to Measure: Defining the Test Anxiety Domain

One needs to start out with an in-depth understanding and determination of the test anxiety domain in order to guide the development of the item pool and facilitate the initial construct validity research. Thus, before operationalization of the test anxiety construct can take place, we need to delineate notions of test anxiety as a psychological construct and have some idea of the kinds of behaviors that would constitute observable and quantifiable instances of anxious behavior in test situations. Furthermore, if a particular characteristic is conceived to be an essential component of test anxiety (e.g., "negative self-concept" or "self-preoccupation"), then its measurement has to be conceptualized accordingly and plans need to be made to assess it as well.

The identification of specific behaviors that represent the construct or define the domain is largely a matter of psychological insight, experience, and the test construc- tor's particular theory, whether implicit or explicit, of the essential nature of test anxiety. As a scientific construct, test anxiety may be operationally defined by specification of procedures for measurement and assessment (or stipulation of experi- mental procedures for evoking the construct under controlled laboratory conditions— which is not our present concern). Since we cannot measure test anxiety directly, as is the case for most personality constructs, we cannot compare a person's score directly with any standard objective index of test anxiety. We may come to know the construct of test anxiety by its exemplars and correlates. Thus, as a hypothetical construct, test anxiety may be inferred by measuring cognitive (e.g., self-focused thoughts and worries, task-irrelevant thoughts), affective (e.g., subjective tension, reports of bodily symptoms), or behavioral (e.g., panicky behavior in test situations, escape behaviors, distractiveness) indices. However, the lack of precision in defining and observing inner constructs such as test anxiety can lead to serious problems in its assessment.

One major obstacle in the way of operationalization of this construct is that attempts at agreeing upon the nature of test anxiety have been largely unsuccessful, with varied and discrepant accounts of test anxiety offered by writers of varying theoretical persuasions (see Chapters 1 and 2). The situation is further complicated by the fact that test anxiety has been variously conceptualized as a trait, a state, or a process variable, and each conception of the construct implies a different set of measurement procedures (Spielberger & Vagg, 1995a). Furthermore, there seems to be little consensus on the component parts, and some of the terms included in multifaceted definitions of test anxiety (e.g., "self-preoccupation" or "task-irrelevant thinking") have low interwriter reliability (I. G. Sarason, 1986).

Facet-Analytic Approach to Domain Definition

Facet theory and analysis (Guttman, 1969; cf. Shye et al., 1994) has proven to be a particularly useful approach for specifying the domain of a wide array of individual difference constructs. In particular, facet theory appears to have considerable potential as a heuristic device for mapping out the domain of test anxiety and specifying its relevant dimensions. Because it has yet to be systematically employed in the construction of test anxiety measures, the following discussion is more of a "prescriptive" than "descriptive" account.

The first and perhaps most crucial step in the facet approach is the specification of a theoretical framework and an *a priori* mapping out of the domain and universe of observations. That is, a definitional system for the universe of content and observations on the test anxiety universe are specified, most typically formalized in the form of a *mapping sentence* (see Figure 5.2). The mapping sentence actually defines the scale to be developed by specifying the key facets and the corresponding elements belonging to each facet. This enables the test constructor to build systematically scales that will contain all the elements contained in these facets or subsets of them. The core of planning a test anxiety scale is the specification of what contents and processes are to be included in the test.

Figure 5.2 presents one possible mapping sentence for the test anxiety domain. It is based on a multidimensional conception of anxiety as a response set to specific kinds of evaluative stimulus situations that are often perceived as stressful and anxiety generating (Hagtvet, 1983b). An additional facet included in the mapping sentence is the specific phase of the stress process during which the person subjectively experiences anxiety. Thus, three major content facets are included in the specified observational domain of test anxiety: (a) *test anxiety response channel* (i.e., worry, task-irrelevant thinking, tension, and bodily symptoms), (b) *assessment period* (i.e., before, during, or after the exam) and (c) *nature of evaluative situation* (i.e.,

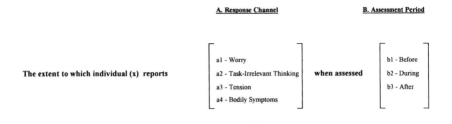

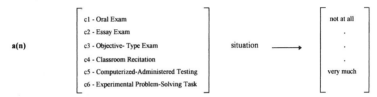

Figure 5.2.   Example of a three-facet mapping sentence for specifying the test anxiety domain.

oral exams, essays, objective-type exams, etc.). The common range involves the extent or degree to which the respondent experiences the various response manifestations of test anxiety (from "not at all" to "very much"). It is important to point out that mapping sentences should probably include additional content facets as well. These might include the following:

- Specific population being assessed (school-age population, college students, elderly).
- Sources of concern over exam failure (lowered self-image, not meeting parental expectations, depreciated classroom status, practical consequences, such as having to repeat the exam or losing financial aid or scholarship).
- Test atmosphere (highly stressful/nonstressful).
- Mode of test administration (individual/group).

Sampling the Domain

A thorough specification of the test anxiety domain is essential in order to guide the development of the initial item pool, and facilitate initial content validation and construct research as well as later interpretation of results. In order for test anxiety test items to exhibit content validity with respect to the test anxiety domain, they should cover all major facets of the content domain, but exclude irrelevant behaviors. The test constructor should begin by providing a clear and detailed statement regarding the general rationale of the operationalizations, specifying the link between the domain and the proposed whole test.

As pointed out by Crocker and Algina (1986), the process by which psychological constructs have been translated into a specific set of items has typically remained private, informal, and insufficiently documented. Typically, the test developer will conceptualize one or more types of behaviors believed to manifest the construct and then simply try to "think up" items that require these behaviors to be demonstrated. Unfortunately, this nonsystematic approach can result in the omission of important areas of behavior or inclusion of areas that are relevant to the construct only in the mind of this particular test developer. Furthermore, current measures often fail to include clear statements of the theoretical rationales influencing the development of many of the measures used in anxiety research. As suspected by I. G. Sarason (1972a), at least some of the investigations have been of the "shotgun variety," with the choice of measures dictated more by expediency than by theoretical considerations.

Elaborated Definition

Thorndike (1982) suggested employing an *elaborated definition* of the construct, which suggests the testing operations by which the attribute under consideration will be assessed. The conception and elaborated definition of test anxiety would emerge from the whole history of the research dealing with the construct. One possible elaborated definition for test anxiety would be: "Test anxiety, as evidenced by perceived arousal, reported worry, negative self-denigrating thoughts, tension, and reports of somatic symptoms in evaluative situations." To broaden, refine, or verify the view of the test anxiety construct, one or all of the following activities could be undertaken:

(a) *Review of research*: Behaviors that have been frequently studied by others are used to define the construct (e.g., worry, arousal, poor self-concept, self-efficacy, low self-expectancies of success, internal failure attributions, etc.).

(b) *Critical incidents*: Behaviors that characterize the extremes of the performance continuum for the test anxiety construct (e.g., relaxation or indifference to evaluative situations, on one extreme; panic and total blackout during exams, on the other).

(c) *Direct observation* of people engaged in behaviors in a variety of evaluative situations (oral tests, written exams, pop quizzes, performance tests, lab experiments, etc.).

(d) *Expert judgment* and input from resource people who have first-hand experience with the test anxiety construct (e.g., consulting with school, counseling, or clinical psychologists about which behaviors to include in test anxiety inventories).

Determining Dimensionality and Broad versus Narrow Mapping of the Domain

The identification of the various dimensions or facets of test anxiety should serve to guide the design of test anxiety scales and the interpretation of their results. Thus, one of the first issues that needs to be addressed relates to the number of dimensions in the domain, as well as the pattern in which the various dimensions are interrelated (Zeidner & Most, 1992). Although most researchers have long rejected the unidimensionality notion underlying some of the earlier measures of test anxiety, they still debate whether two (e.g., Liebert & Morris, 1967; L. W. Morris, Davis, & Hutchings, 1981; Spielberger, 1980) or more (I. G. Sarason, 1984) dimensions best represent the underlying structure of the test anxiety construct.

Clearly, there is a continuous interplay between the test constructor's conception of test anxiety and its dimensionality, at the construct level, and scale development. As a result of these different approaches, the questionnaires developed for measuring test anxiety vary with respect to number of scales. For example, Spielberger's (1972b) conception of test anxiety as a situation-specific personality trait, including Worry and Emotionality as key components, was operationalized by the construction of a 20-item Test Anxiety Inventory comprised of Worry and Emotionality subscales, and a total test anxiety score. By contrast, Sarason's four-factor conceptualization of test anxiety as consisting of Worry, Tension, Task-Irrelevant Thinking, and Bodily Symptoms was operationalized by the construction of a 40-item Reactions to Tests inventory, consisting of four separate component scales and a total score.

A Facet Theory Approach to Domain Sampling

The breadth of the sampling and the relevance to the life-important world of behavior are key concepts for scale development. Sampling of items from the test anxiety domain has generally been conducted in a nonsystematic manner, more often than not based on expertise, intuition, armchair analysis, and trial and error. As mentioned above, facet theory has considerable potential as a heuristic device for systematically mapping out the domain and sampling of items from this domain of discourse. In fact, Guttman (1969) viewed *facets* as an acronym for "facets as assets in the construction of efficient tests systematically." The facet approach to item sampling from the domain is briefly demonstrated below.

Table 5.1. Sample Specification Table for the Test Anxiety Domain

Situation (C)	Response mode (A)			
	Worry (a1)	Task-irrelevant thinking (a2)	Tension (a3)	Bodily symptoms (a4)
Oral exam (c1)	a1c1	a2c1	a3c1	a4c1
Essay exam (c2)	a1c2	a2c2	a3c2	a4c2
Objective exam (c3)	a1c3	a2c3	a3c3	a4c3
Computerized exam (c4)	a1c4	a2c4	a3c4	a4c4
Recitation (c5)	a1c5	a2c5	a3c5	a4c5
Lab experiment (c6)	a1c6	a2c6	a3c6	a4c6

The mapping sentence delineating the test anxiety domain actually defines the scale(s) that can be developed by specifying the key facets and the corresponding elements belonging to each. This enables the test constructor systematically to build scales that will contain all the elements contained in these facets or subsets of them. The mapping sentence supplied in Figure 5.2 implies that three major facets of test anxiety need to be considered and eventually assessed: the person's mode of response to evaluative situations, the time of assessment, and the antecedent stimulus situations arousing anxiety. Assume that we wish to sample items relating to the first and third facets, that is, the response and stimulus situation facets (holding the second facet, time of assessment, constant). Because the response facet consists of 4 elements and the stimulus facet consists of 6 elements, we get a 24-fold classification of scale items by a Cartesian product of facet elements. Table 5.1 is the specification table for construction of items that would cover the specified domain. Thus the core of planning a test anxiety inventory, according to this approach, is the careful specification of what reactions and stimuli conditions are to be included in the scale. Because creating all possible items would be economically and practically unfeasible in most cases, the accepted alternative is to produce a set of item-domain specifications structured so that items written according to these specifications would be interchangeable. The third facet focusing upon time of assessment can be incorporated into the item-writing scheme by asking about each stimulus × response combination with respect to three points in time (before, during, or after testing).

Each of the elements in a facet (e.g., worry, task-irrelevant thinking, tension, bodily symptoms) is termed a *struct*, whereas the facet profile of a given measure is termed a *structuple*. For example, an illustrative item designed to gauge worry responses under oral exam conditions (e.g., "During an oral exam, I frequently worry about not meeting my instructor's expectations") would be designated by the structuple {a1c1}, whereas another item designed to assess a person's bodily symptoms under experimental conditions (e.g., "I feel butterflies in my stomach when solving anagram items during a laboratory experiment") would be designated by the structuple {a4c6}. Thus, any test anxiety item may be classified by the content facets of its structuple or profile. Given this specification table for the scale, the scale constructor can proceed systematically to develop items that tap each of the profiles in the cells, amounting to 24 profiles in all, in this particular example. Coverage of the full test anxiety domain specified in the exemplary mapping sentence presented in Figure 5.2 would require 72 profiles in all to be assessed (4 response elements × 3 time periods × 6 situational stimulus elements).

Item Writing

Once the domain has been mapped, how the questions are then written is important. There are two basic philosophies or approaches to writing items for personality tests, the *rational* and the *empirical*. According to the rational approach, items are written on the basis of a working theory about test anxiety (e.g., Liebert and Morris' two-factor theory), which is supposed to be reflected in the items. According to the empirical approach, items need to show some systematic relation to some internal (e.g., other test items or underlying factors) or external (e.g., school achievement, IQ, study habits, referral for counseling) criteria. The differences between rational and empirical techniques are evident not only in the philosophy guiding the construction of the item pool, but in a wide variety of other aspects of the test construction process (e.g., method of item analyses, dimensionality of tests, validation; see chapters in Zeidner & Most, 1992). However, rather than being two alternatives, the two methods could play complementary roles in the process of test construction, with items generated through rational methods and eventually selected on the basis of the joint consideration of internal consistency and external criterion correlations.

Guidelines for Writing Items

It is commonly agreed that there really is no well-grounded science or even technology of item writing. In spite of some attempts to mechanize and computerize it, skills at writing test anxiety items must be developed through direct experience on a foundation of talent for a particular type of expression. The actual writing and polishing of items to assess test anxiety is a highly skilled undertaking, requiring considerable technical skill, facility of expression, and imagination. Among the many item-writing skills are selection of the most relevant facets and components of test anxiety to be assessed, ingenuity in imbedding these facets and components in a particular situation, incisiveness of phrasing particular evaluative situations, and perceptiveness in designing anchors for test anxiety items. Crocker and Algina (1986) list the following aspects of item construction as important features to keep in mind: (a) accuracy, (b) relevance to test specifications, (c) technical item-construction features, (d) grammar, (e) perceived fairness and unbiased presentation of items, and (f) level of readability.

Some general true and tried principles about writing personality scale items have been found useful by experts, and their application may make writing specific test anxiety items easier. Many authors have provided approximately the same advice on writing items for personality inventories (e.g., Strelau & Angleitner, 1991; Thorndike, 1982; Most & Zeidner, 1995).

Selecting and Piloting Items

The methods for selecting and piloting test anxiety inventory items are essentially the same as for other personality items and have been described in a number of texts (Thorndike, 1982; Nunnally, 1978; Crocker & Algina, 1986; Robertson, 1992). Test anxiety items need to be tried out to determine their level of popularity and their ability to differentiate among criterion groups (Thorndike, 1982). The tryout also serves the purpose of providing data for additional analyses, checking instructions for scale administration, assessing comprehensibility and difficulty of items, assessing scoring procedures, and checking the time limits.

The first tryout should be conducted on a sample of anywhere from 200 to 500 subjects. These subjects should be as similar as possible to the target population with which the test will eventually be used, and should cover the range of age or school grade that characterizes those with whom the test will be used (Thorndike, 1982). Tryout samples of about this size provide stable estimates of item difficulty and discrimination indices (Robertson, 1992).

Because the aim is to separate the "sheep from the goats," one should prepare a larger number of items initially than one expects to need in the final set. In the tryout, one should prepare anywhere from 25% to four times more items than the number of items one wishes to include in the final test (Robertson, 1992; Kline, 1986). For example, in constructing the Hebrew version of the Test Anxiety Inventory, we began with 37 items administered to 209 student candidates taking a college admissions aptitude test battery, and narrowed the number of items down to 20 (there are also 20 items on the original English version). The exact number of items one would prepare would depend on a variety of factors, such as incremental cost of preparing an item, novelty of item format, mode of test administration, etc.

Item Selection Criteria

The item data elicited from the tryout are used for an elaborate set of statistical procedures, known as item analysis, designed to secure the operative soundness of the items in the final test. The most effective items from the initial item pool are chosen and items that do not meet preestablished criteria are eliminated. Robertson (1992) identified two main classes of item analysis techniques employed in current test procedures: classical and modern (or item response theory).

Classical Item Selection

Classical item analysis refers to the standard item statistics used over the past decades, such as item "popularity" (or *difficulty* when aptitude is being assessed) and item discrimination (index of an item's ability to discriminate between those having more and those having less of a particular trait). Item discrimination could be calculated as the correlation between the item score and total score.

Modern Item Selection

Recent advances in the development of latent trait measurement models (Rasch, 1960; Lord, 1980) provide an alternative and perhaps more accurate approach for item selection compared to classical methods. Modern item analysis, known as latent trait or item response theory (IRT), refers to procedures that have evolved over the last 25 years and have become feasible with the availability of high-speed computers. IRT methods express the probability of success on an item as a function of the examinee's standing on the latent attribute, graphically expressed by an item characteristic curve. These probabilistic models allow a population-independent estimate of the relevant parameters of the scale. Although there is a world-wide trend toward increase in usage of latent trait models, only a few recent test anxiety scales or adaptations have been designed to take advantage of the improvements made in test construction by the new latent trait theory methods of scaling (Hodapp et al., 1995; Benson & El-Zahhar, 1992, 1994). These methods appear to have considerable promise for scaling of test anxiety items in the years to come.

It is important to keep in mind that item analysis cannot improve test anxiety scale items and often one needs to pick the least bad from a pretty bad bundle. Item analysis can only analyze the items one enters into the statistics. The key is to have good items to start with, then use item analysis to remove the psychometrically poor ones.

Creating Scales from Items

Assembling Items

A variety of approaches have been used for assembling items for purposes of scale formation, some of which will be briefly mentioned below.

Judgmental Procedures ("Face Validity")

Items on test anxiety instruments are often chosen by a test constructor for a particular scale because they are taken to measure a particular component of the test anxiety construct. Though such items may vary in format and popularity level, they are assumed to measure the same trait. The scale may be based on underlying theory, what test anxiety reactions are expected to be like, or the impressions of test developers and other experts, examinees, and the like.

The Empirical Properties of the Items

Scales may also be identified on the basis of empirical properties of items, particularly as related to the association between the item and an internal or external criterion. Thus, test anxiety items may be chosen for a particular test anxiety scale because as a cluster they have high internal consistency (e.g., as assessed by Cronbach's alpha), because they correlate highly with total test scores, because they discriminate maximally between two divergent groups (high-test-anxious students in a stress inoculation program versus low-test-anxious students not enrolled in an intervention program), or because the items show high correlations with an external representation of the construct (e.g., grade point average).

Factor Analysis

Factor analysis can also be employed along with item-analytic techniques as a heuristic guideline for selecting the best items to put into specific scales. The common procedure is to choose items or tests that show high loading on the target factor. Those items intersecting several factors simultaneously, showing no simple loading on the target factor of interest, but several small or moderate ones, would be dropped. Factor analysis has been the data reduction method of choice among psychometricians constructing test anxiety scales for item scaling purposes, although the results are not always clear-cut. Once one has decided how many dimensions one aims at measuring on the test anxiety scale, factor analysis of the item intercorrelation matrix can help construct scales to measure these dimensions. Accordingly, items within an item pool that correlate most highly with each target dimension uncovered by factor analysis (say the Worry or Emotionality component) can be empirically identified and used for purposes of constructing scales to measure the intended dimensions of interest. By employing some criterion factor loading (often set at greater than .40), sets of items that load on any given factor can be identified as a group of independent scales. For example, in the construction of the Test Anxiety Inventory (Spielberger, 1980), each item included on the final inventory had a salient loading of .40 or higher on one or both factors. Those items that failed to have a salient loading of .40 on either the Worry or Emotionality factors were eliminated. Table 5.2 presents factor loadings of the 20 items on the Hebrew version of the Test Anxiety Inventory. As can be readily seen, all the items loaded over .40 on their target factors, with loadings ranging between .44 and .79.

Confirmatory factor analysis was used early in the 1980s in test anxiety research to test the adequacy of the indicator–factor relationship in the measurement model of

Table 5.2. Factor Matrix for the 20 Items of the Hebrew Version of the Test Anxiety Inventory (TAI/H)

Item number	Emotionality factor	Worry factor
3	.27	.48
4	.06	.74
5	.25	.45
6	.40	.52
15	.19	.71
17	.13	.54
18	.40	.63
20	.11	.75
2	.64	.23
7	.73	.29
8	.76	.09
9	.44	.30
10	.79	.21
14	.71	.22
16	.56	.10
19	.73	.21
1	.60	.28
11	.58	.22
12	.54	.23
13	.37	.51

Note: The table is based on data presented in the Hebrew version of the Test Anxiety Inventory manual (TAH/H; Zeidner, Nevo, & Lipschitz, 1988). The exploratory factor analysis from which these data were generated was based on 594 student candidates who were administered the TAI/H in a college admissions testing context. Worry and Emotionality scores are based on eight items each, with the last four items used for the total score only. The Worry and Emotionality factors accounted for 27% and 19%, respectively, of the total percentage of variance.

test anxiety scales (R. Schwarzer, Jerusalem, & Lange, 1982), and has also recently been employed for purposes of item analysis and selection. For example, in their construction of the Revised Test Anxiety (RTA) Scale, Benson and El-Zahhar (1992) took each subscale on the RTA and ran separate analysis to identify best items for that latent factor.

Although a contentious issue to some test developers, Nunnally (1978) maintains that factor analysis should *not* be used to construct specific scales. Homogeneous scales should be constructed based on the hypotheses regarding the nature of the trait assessed, with item analysis used to select the most appropriate items for the scale. In order to learn how successful one was, one can apply factor-analytic methods to investigate the factor structure of the battery. Regardless of which methodology is employed, the end result of the item-analytic procedures is the identification of three basic classes of items (Robertson, 1992):

(a) Those satisfactory for operational use without further work.
(b) Those with marginal items statistics that might be salvageable after revision.
(c) Those whose item statistics warrants their being discarded.

Sampling and Establishing Scale Norms

Consider a high school student who obtains a total raw score of 53 on the 20-item Test Anxiety Inventory (item range: 1–4). We would be hard put to interpret this score: Does this score indicate high, medium, or low level of test anxiety? For the purpose of anchoring and giving meaning to test scores, we attempt to relate a raw score (or scaled score) to the performance of one or more reference groups. This process is technically called establishing "norms" for the instrument. It is commonly agreed among experts that to obtain appropriate norms, the measure should be administered to a sample from the reference population, once that has been established and defined, that is as similar as possible to the target population.

As Thorndike (1982) pointed out, the normative sample should ideally provide an unbiased and efficient representation of the population, as well as permit an estimate of the precision with which the sample does in fact represent the sample. For example, in norming a test anxiety scale to be used for junior high school students the target groups would ideally consist of all junior high school students in the country. However, it is nearly impossible to list this designated target group completely and accurately and obtain a random sample. As a result, a number of alternative procedures have been used (e.g., stratified cluster random sampling) to overcome this problem and make the sampling more manageable and feasible (see Thorndike [1982] for an informative discussion of sampling procedures). When reviewing a test anxiety inventory, one must carefully review the descriptions of the norms in the manual to confirm the representativeness and adequacy of the sampling.

Validity

Validity is the evidence to prove that the test anxiety scale measures what the author purports it to measure. The mere fact that a scale is called a "Test Anxiety" scale by the test author is not sufficient evidence; one needs empirical evidence to show that the test is indeed valid for the designated purpose. Typically this is done by looking at the items on the scale (face validity evidence), how the scale relates to other measures to which it is similar or dissimilar (convergent and discriminant validity), how it relates to existing samples that relate to the construct (criterion group validity), how well it predicts current behaviors (concurrent validity), or how well it predicts future behaviors (predictive validity).

A test anxiety scale cannot be said to be valid in any abstract sense, but must instead be valid in a particular context, for a specific purpose, and with a specific group of people in mind. The type of validation that is most important depends on the inferences to be drawn from the scale scores. As Anastasi (1986) points out, almost any data collected in the process of developing a scale are relevant to its validity, because they contribute to our understanding of what a test measures. For example, data on internal consistency and retest reliability help to define the homogeneity of the construct and its temporal stability.

Construct Validity

In the broadest sense, validity refers to the number and range of valid inferences a user can make about a person on basis of test scores. Construct validity is a continuous process in which new evidence is assembled bearing on the inferences that we can make about a person based on test scores. The assessment of construct validity in our case involves three general steps: (a) conceptualization and careful analysis of the test anxiety construct, (b) consideration of how the construct is manifested in test anxiety scales and the ways in which the trait does or does not relate to other behaviors in particular situations, and (c) formal testing of whether or not the hypothesized relations actually exist. Thus, what has come to be designated as "construct validity" is actually a comprehensive approach that includes other recognized validation procedures. In fact, test experts have recently come to realize that all questions about test validity actually concern construct validity. This is so because each of the distinct forms of validity helps shed light on the meaning of test scores (Messick, 1989).

Constructs such as test anxiety are ultimately derived from empirically observed behavioral consistencies and are identified and defined through a network of observed relations (Anastasi, 1986). The general logic of construct validity first elaborated by Cronbach and Meehl (1955) stated that in order for a test construct to be scientifically admissible it had to be located in a nomological network. A nomological network consists of statistical and/or deterministic laws that ties observable properties to one another, theoretical constructs to observables, and constructs to one another. The assumption is that in the absence of an infallible criterion measure, one can define a complex psychological phenomenon by showing that its meaning lies in a network of relations among directly observable measures. For example, a measure of test anxiety might be validated by showing that it is related to intelligence, poor study skills, academic self-efficacy, achievement, etc. (see Figure 5.3 for an illustrative nomological network for the test anxiety construct). Each study undertaken to validate the scales is not in itself a "crucial" test of the scale's validity. It merely adds to the total network of studies which constitute evidence for the validity of the test anxiety construct from which the item content of the instrument has been derived.

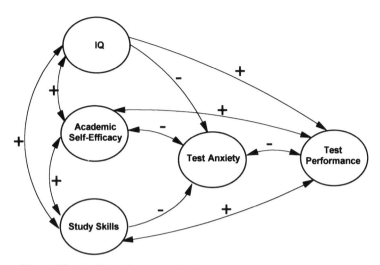

Figure 5.3. An illustrative nomological network for the test anxiety construct.

Internal (Factorial) Evidence

Factor analysis, both exploratory (Spielberger, 1980) and confirmatory (Benson & El-Zahhar, 1992), has been the method of choice in studying the structure and construct validity underlying items on test anxiety inventories (Benson & Bandalos, 1989, 1992; R. Schwarzer, 1984). Most factor-analytic studies of the underlying structure of test anxiety scales have employed the principal factors method to extract factors, with squared multiple correlations as estimates of communality. Orthogonal varimax rotations of the principal factors are then performed in order to spread the variance evenly among the rotated factors. Salient items possessing factor loadings equal to or greater than .40 are then identified. In spite of the many problems inherent in the use of factor analysis for studying the structure of constructs, for well-designed sets of variables, reasonable and replicable solutions can be discerned (Carroll, 1992).

The measurement model used in *confirmatory* factor methods allows one to specify in advance what one believes (on psychological grounds) to be a likely factor structure for the test anxiety scale and then to employ one of the available computer programs (e.g., Lisrel) to establish goodness of fit of the structural model to the observed data (Jöreskog & Sörbom, 1979). Thus, in employing structural equation modeling in developing test anxiety instruments, test constructors and researchers aim to find a model with satisfactory fit to the data that would confirm the separation between the hypothesized underlying latent dimensions. Confirmatory factor-analytic methods allow us to learn about the parameter estimates (i.e., the factor loadings), correlations among the latent variables, and the relationships between the error terms, as well as improve the model's fit to the data utilizing computerized model-fitting techniques.

Recent controversies regarding the dimensionality of test anxiety have been characterized by an increasing number of attempts to cross-validate the factor structure of test anxiety scales by means of confirmatory analyses. The results have been mixed (Benson & Tippets, 1990; Everson, Millsap, & Rodriguez, 1991; Hocevar & El-Zahhar, 1985; Ware, Galassi, & Dew, 1990; Zeidner & Nevo, 1992; Zimmer, Hocevar, Bachelor, & Meinke, 1992). Hagtvet and Sharma (1994) point to the possibility that the Worry items may be more heterogeneous in nature than the Emotionality items, with the former scale tapping different aspect of self-related cognition when faced with threat and uncertainty. However, the consistency of factorial findings is largely restricted to the specific measure used, and Hagtvet (1983a, 1983b) raised the possibility that the factors extracted might be considered method factors rather than substantive personality factors.

Nonmetrical Factor Analysis.   Smallest space analysis (SSA) is a nonmetrical multidimensional scaling technique which has recently been employed in an effort to uncover the dimensionality of test anxiety measures (R. Schwarzer, 1984; Zeidner & Nevo, 1992). This technique represents geometrically, in the smallest dimensionality, pairwise similarities existing within a set of observed variables. The information about the pairwise similarities is treated as nonmetric and the variables are mapped as points in Euclidean space. The correlations are employed as measures of proximity between the variables in order to determine the corresponding interpoint distances. The results are depicted in a map or space diagram which gives information about the distance of each item from the centroid. The distances of each item to all other items within a two-dimensional framework can be determined. The algorithm is such that items that are more highly correlated are closer in multidimensional space. The map containing the configurations of the points in the smallest space (as evaluated by the coefficient of alienation) can be partitioned into regions and subregions to provide information about the structure of the data as a whole, as well as about subsets of variables. Figure 5.4 presents the space diagram of the Worry and Emotionality items of the Hebrew version of the Test Anxiety Inventory. The map shows a neat partitioning of the space into Worry and Emotionality facets or regions. The nonmetrical scaling yielded results that were in line with the two-factor hypothesized structure. Furthermore, Emotionality items are shown to be more homogeneous and clustered together, whereas the Worry items displayed a more heterogeneous pattern (R. Schwarzer, 1984; Zeidner & Nevo, 1992).

External Evidence

Empirical or external criterion validity is determined by comparing test scores with some form of performance or outside measure, whether the measure is taken

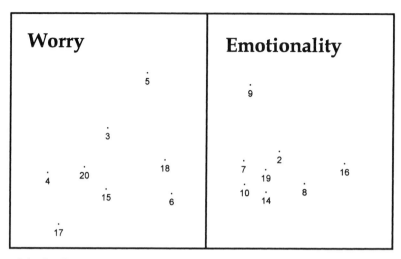

Figure 5.4. Smallest space diagram of Worry and Emotionality items of the Test Anxiety Inventory.

concurrently (approximately same time as the test) or predictively (sometime after test scores were derived). A main problem confronting criterion validity lies in finding an agreed upon or acceptable criterion (P. C. Smith, 1976); at present we have no infallible or perfectly objective criterion against which to validate test anxiety scores. Scores on ability tests, grade point average, observer ratings, behavior in structured evaluative situations, and the like are good candidates for criterion behaviors.

If anxiety is expected to be evoked in the criterion performance, then attempts to minimize anxiety in a selection instrument may in fact reduce its validity as a predictor. The burden on those attempting to assess criterion-related anxiety in the predictor is, of course, to demonstrate that the same level of test anxiety is also triggered in the performance criterion situation.

Convergent and Divergent Validity Evidence

In order to decide if test anxiety deserves construct status, we need to explore not only the variables to which the construct bears a hypothesized relation, but also the variables with which, theoretically, test anxiety should be unrelated (Campbell & Fiske, 1959). One recurring theme has been the importance of establishing convergent and discriminant validity of test anxiety measures. This can be restated as a question: Do different measures of test anxiety, by different operational forms (self-report, observational, etc.), at different system levels (cognitive, physiological, behavioral), all measure the same thing—as indicated by their convergence? Such convergence is an essential condition if we are to be able to separate that part of the variation in the data associated with the particular method of measurement from the part that reflects variation in test anxiety.

To assess the notion of convergence and divergence for the construct of test anxiety, one would need to have at least two different methods for measuring test anxiety (or two different versions of how test anxiety can be measured) and at least two different traits (e.g., test anxiety and sports anxiety). Test anxiety scales are expected to demonstrate *convergent* validity with other test anxiety and evaluative anxiety measures and *divergent* validity with other related measures (e.g., anger, depression, hopelessness).

Threats to Validity in Contemporary Measures

Following are a number of threats to the validity of self-report measures of test anxiety, which may serve as a source of systematic error in the assessment of the construct.

Response Bias

In general terms, response bias is the tendency of a person to favor a particular response, regardless of the stimulus characteristics (Laux & Vossel, 1982). Examples of response bias would be the tendency to agree with or answer "yes" to a questionnaire item (e.g., "I feel calm and relaxed during important exams") regardless of the specific item content. Similarly, giving extreme responses is also a serious threat to test anxiety scales. An important aim in assessing test anxiety is to control the effects of response sets and thus to obtain unbiased measures of emotional states.

Social Desirability

Social desirability, i.e., responding in ways judged socially acceptable to the self, examiner, or others expected to see the results, may influence how an examinee responds to a test anxiety questionnaire, thus undermining confidence in the construct validity of self-report test anxiety measures. People with a social-desirability response set will provide what they consider to be the most socially acceptable answer, irrespective of whether the response accurately describes them (Blankstein & Toner, 1987). There is empirical evidence showing that students higher in social desirability report lower test anxiety scores, although the correlations among the variables is typically modest (e.g., Lunneborg, 1964). Thus, one limiting factor to self-report test anxiety scales is the lack of willingness of the respondent to admit to certain types of symptoms represented on such scales (e.g., palpitations, sweating, blushing, butterflies in stomach) or to ascribe socially undesirable characteristics to himself or herself (tension, ruminative thoughts, etc.).

Defensiveness

Persons who are high in defensiveness may be experiencing test anxiety at some level, but may be repressing conscious feelings about it. In early research on test anxiety with children, it was established that there is a meaningful negative relation between defensiveness and test anxiety (Hill & Sarason, 1966). Although defensiveness or "lie" scales have been devised to measure the extent to which someone denies the occurrence of negative experience common to most persons, these measures are hardly ever used in practice in contemporary test anxiety research.

Fakeability

There is some empirical evidence showing that self-report test anxiety scales are fakeable, with students able to fake bad (high test anxiety levels) or fake good (low test anxiety levels) on these measures (Allen, 1972, 1980; Allen et al., 1980). Thus, test anxiety scales may contain cues for participants who may respond to experimental or clinical demand characteristics with altered scores.

Establishing Scale Reliability

Standard Approaches

Reliability, a major quality desired in any test, is a relative and polymorphous concept. In fact, a scale actually has no single reliability, with reliability referring simultaneously to a test's degree of stability, consistency, predictability, accuracy, or generalizability. The reliability of a test anxiety scale can be assessed from time to time (test–retest), form to form (alternative or equivalent forms), item to item (internal consistency or homogeneity), and scorer to scorer (interobserver or interjudge reliability). See Nunnally (1978) or Crocker and Algina (1986) for specific formulas for calculating reliabilities.

The standard approaches to reliability in personality measurement are as follows:

1. *Internal reliability*: For example, calculate Cronbach alpha coefficients or item–remainder coefficients (the correlation of each item with the sum of the remaining items).
2. *Test–retest reliability*: For example, readminister the same instrument to the same sample and correlate the scores. Various samples would have different time periods (1 month, 3 months, etc.).
3. *Internal or test–retest reliability* for various types of populations (e.g., samples with low reading level would be expected to have lower internal reliabilities, and samples undergoing developmental changes would be expected to have lower test–retest reliabilities.

(d)Provide the *standard error of measurement* (SEM) for all scales and sub-scales, so that confidence bands can be constructed around the test anxiety scale or total score.

How reliable does a test anxiety inventory need to be for purposes of assessment? It is commonly held that the reliability estimates need to be sufficiently high (about .90) for clinical decision making and somewhat lower (about .70) for research. A test anxiety scale that does not have adequate reliability should never be used to make clinical decisions about an individual examinee. According to Kline (1986), the minimum satisfying figure for test reliability is .70. Below that, the test becomes unsatisfactory for use with individuals because the standard error is so large that the interpretation becomes dubious. Fortunately, most popular test anxiety inventories have satisfactory reliability coefficients, typically in the high .70s to low .90s (e.g., Spielberger, 1980; Benson et al., 1992). During longer intervals between assessments, personality traits, such as test anxiety, may change, causing lower stability coefficients. Additional factors influencing reliability are test length, test–retest interval, variability of scores, and variation within test situation (Most & Zeidner, 1995).

Generalizability

In assessing the reliability estimate, one needs to consider the specific sources of error affecting test anxiety scores, the method of reliability estimation, implications of trait stability, and test format, as well as intended usage. Cronbach, Gleser, Rajaratnam, and Nanda (1972), in what is known as generalizability theory, point out that a score may vary not only with the specific scale or occasion of measurement, but also with a variety of other facets (e.g., specific situation, observer, etc.). Thus, if we use a single test anxiety scale score as if it represented the person's test anxiety reactions across time and situations, we are overgeneralizing from the results and we need to test the generalizability of the scores systematically across different test facets. Save for the work of Hagtvet and his co-workers (Hagtvet, 1989), the application of generalizability theory methodology has not gained widespread usage among constructors of test anxiety scales and the power of this method has yet to be sufficiently utilized.

Interpreting Test Scores

To the practitioner using a test anxiety instrument, more important than any of the technical issues is, "What does the scale mean and how can I use it?" Scale meaning can vary from a reading of the items on a test anxiety scale to a rich network of correlations with other instruments, descriptions from expert interpreters, and correlations with behaviors and experimental studies (see the TAI manual [Spielberger, 1980] for concrete illustrations).

The interpretation of test anxiety scores is intrinsically related to the issue of test validity, because validity relates to the appropriateness of meanings and interpretations assigned to test scores rather than to the test scores themselves (Messick, 1989). The following section describes a number of interpretive strategies useful in giving meaning to raw scores obtained on test anxiety scales.

Normative Interpretation Strategy

Scores on a scale indicate an individual's standing relative to the reference population. Thus, all descriptions are relative to a population standard. For example, given that the norm of the Test Anxiety Inventory for male high school students in the United States is 40.87 ($SD = 12.77$), a total score of 60 would be considered to be "high" (92nd percentile), whereas a score of 23 would be considered to be "low" (11th percentile).

The meaning of scores on normative scales are basically more relativistic than acknowledged. Under classical scaling methods, the relative position of a person on a test anxiety scale may change with a different reference population or different set of indicators for the same construct. For example, scaled deviation scores on two test anxiety scales may indicate that the person scores relatively higher on one scale relative to the reference population, but it does not necessarily follow that the individual has more of the component assessed by that scale in any absolute sense.

Few of the existing self-report questionnaires provide adequate large-scale normative data to allow for standardized comparisons to be made across independent investigations. Also, since women tend to report higher than men on test anxiety, it is important that information on gender differences be provided, which is not always the case.

Interpretation in Terms of Reference Factors

The items (scales) entering into a test anxiety scale are best defined in terms of the reference factors which account for its major variables. Accordingly, test constructors will be on safest grounds if they assume that a subject's responses are probably due to higher or lower levels in the major components as defined by the attested factors underlying scale scores. Thus, factor analysis is important not only for the construction of scales, but also for interpretation purposes and for providing meaning to test anxiety scores (Kline, 1986). For example, a high score on a test anxiety measure is best interpreted as due to high test anxiety.

A factor-analytic model tells us how few factors are required to reproduce the original correlation matrix. What it does not yield is information about what it actually means to receive a particular total score. That is, if one student scores higher than another on the Worry scale, what types of situations does that student find anxiety-provoking and what types of reactions are experienced in contrast to the less anxious student? Or, what is the hierarchical structure that defines a continuum of least- to most-anxiety-provoking situations? Or, what is the probability that a particular item will provoke an affirmative anxiety response for any single student?

Assessment within Context

It should be pointed out that test anxiety scale scores need to be understood within the context of a person's life and social milieu. Thus, assessment of scale performance requires appreciation of the possible multiple and interactional influences on anxiety scores (Zeidner & Most, 1992). This includes the subject's past affective and academic history, and current social, emotional, vocational, and economic adjustments, as well as behavior during the exam. When a life history showing, say, no reported test anxiety in the past is in disagreement with the test anxiety scale results, it is best to pause before making a diagnosis or decision on the basis of the test anxiety scale alone, as the former is generally a more reliable criterion. Thus, interpretation should only be made after examining the relevant information beyond test scores. A simple composite test anxiety score should never be used in describing, predicting, or explaining an examinee's behavior. Sound interpretation involves integration of various sources of data and assimilating them into an exposition that describes the examinee's functioning, detailing specific strengths and weaknesses, and predicting the specific behavioral manifestations one could expect to see.

No matter how accurate the interpretation of the data, it will be meaningless unless the results can be communicated effectively. Feedback should be given in terms that are clear and understandable to the receiver. For example, rather than telling Don Most, a first-year college student, that he received a score of 60 on the Test Anxiety Inventory, the counselor may wish to explain that he is currently above 96% of the undergraduate student population in test anxiety level, and therefore relatively high in test anxiety.

Cross-Cultural Adaptations of Test Anxiety Scales

Before cross-cultural comparisons of test anxiety can be undertaken, it is necessary to assure the calibration of the self-report scales employed in different language systems. Recent developments in cross-cultural adaptation of test anxiety scales offer promising strategies for the development of cross-culturally equivalent scales (Hanin, 1988). This work has emphasized the application of a standard strategy of scale adaptation, involving the following phases:

1. *Preparation of the preliminary translation.* After becoming familiar with the rationale and theoretical background of the original scale, a preliminary translation of

the source items into the target language is prepared. Although it would appear to be important to keep the same format and instructions as in the original scale, it is generally agreed that it is more important to convey the meaning and connotation of the original items than blindly adhere to literal translations.

2. *Scale review and revision.* The preliminary form is evaluated by experts experienced in test anxiety theory and test construction procedures, who are asked to review each translated item and compare it with the original item in terms of its content, meaning, form, and clarity of expression. The review team should pay particular attention to the degree to which the translated item conveys the intended meaning of the original items clearly and unambiguously taps the same conceptual aspect of test anxiety in indigenous students as the original version, and adequately relates to the test anxiety experiences of culturally indigenous students. Reviewers can also be asked to offer suggestions for improving the translation. In addition, a cycle of "blind" backtranslations (from the translation back to the original source version) may be employed until an optimal fit is achieved between the source item and target language version.

3. *Scale piloting.* The next step is to carry out a pilot administration of the preliminary form of the scale. The pilot administration aims at determining the psychometric properties of the adapted scale as well as the affective reactions of respondents to the scale items, their format, and instructions. Experimental evaluation of the equivalence of the adapted form of the scale may be assessed by administering the adapted version to male and female samples from the target populations and calculating the psychometric characteristics of the new scale. The cross-language equivalence of the scale may also be tested by administering the scale to bilingual subjects (in counterbalanced order) and relevant statistics calculated. Correlations between original and translated versions in bilingual samples often produce very high correlations. For example, Hocever, El-Zahhar, and Gombos (1989) reported that in a sample of 53 Hungarian bilinguals the correlation between the English and Hungarian forms of the Test Anxiety Inventory was .95.

4. *Scale norming and validation.* The scale is then administered, after careful revision, to a representative sample of the target population, and psychometric properties (means, standard deviations, interitem correlations, test–retest, evaluations, indices of concurrent validity of the scale) and norms are calculated. Internal structure equivalence may be established through item analysis and factor analysis. External validation can be established by demonstrating equivalent nomological networks across cultures. Multigroup confirmatory factor analysis is one technique that is becoming widely used in the cross-cultural validation of personality measures. Accordingly, the factor structure from the sample(s) used to develop the original are compared directly with the factor structure of the new sample. Thus, multigroup confirmatory factor-analytic procedures provide rigorous ways of comparing factor structures across cultures. Further validation research should be conducted and the test manual prepared and disseminated.

Even with high-quality translations, the meaning and interpretation of observed responses remains under question; we can never be sure whether the observed differences in original and translated scale scores are due to real differences in the magnitude of the trait in different cultures, to different meanings of the construct in different cultures, to different manifestations of the construct, or to different operating (culture-specific) response sets. In fact, some cross-cultural data suggest that for items originally developed for one language (say, English) the process of translating them into a second language (say, Arabic) may introduce a larger amount of error due to inherent problems in translation (Hocevar & El-Zahhar, 1988).

Unfortunately, there are no clear-cut rules or independent criteria to judge the quality of translations. Nor are there any objective procedures for establishing identity in the meaning of constructs in different cultures and languages. At the present state of our knowledge in this area, the conclusions about the identity of meanings of a construct measured by a psychological instrument and its translation can only be tentative. Consequently, the interpretation of the scores obtained on translated tests in different cultures (as well as the conclusions derived from the relations of those test scores with other measures) may be imprecise.

Limitations of Current Scales and Needed Areas of Improvement

Despite some of the attractive psychometric and practical strengths of self-report test anxiety scales, these do have their limitations. I briefly present some suggestions for improving test anxiety scale development in light of current drawbacks.

1. *Strive for more complete and systematic domain coverage.* The key content facets represented in current test anxiety scales are rather limited and restricted in scope, with traditional scales ignoring the specificities of individual responses and situations. The response system, with a focus mainly on cognitive and affective parameters, is often the only content facet represented in most current scale items. Seldom do test anxiety scales inform us about the various situational and personal factors eliciting test anxiety (anxiety-proneness, inadequate preparation, over-stimulation), the full range of manifestations of test anxiety (e.g., cognitive, affective, and *behavioral*), coping procedures and strategies, the consequences of test anxiety, or the dynamic fluctuations in test anxiety states across various phases of a stressful evaluative encounter. The restricted content scope can be improved by employing more systematic domain mapping procedures (e.g., through facet theory) and better representation of additional facets in the test specification matrix, and subsequently on the test anxiety inventory.

2. *Refine and differentiate scales.* Current test anxiety measures need to be refined and differentiated. Thus, it might make sense to have one scale in a test anxiety inventory sample a range of potentially anxiety-producing evaluative stimuli (oral test, paper-and-pencil quiz, essay, computerized test); another might deal with the particular response channel or style of reacting to anxiety (worry, arousal,

hopelessness, etc.); another scale might assess the intensity of anxiety elicited; another would tap the styles of coping with evaluative anxiety (defensive reactions, avoidance, palliative coping, instrumental coping, etc.); and yet another would assess perceived consequences (decrements in memory, concentration, retrieval, etc.). A more refined and differentiated test anxiety inventory would allow us to delineate better the profile of test-anxious subjects.

3. *Make scales more relevant for clinical purposes.* When used for clinical purposes, current instruments only allow measurement of the overall level of test

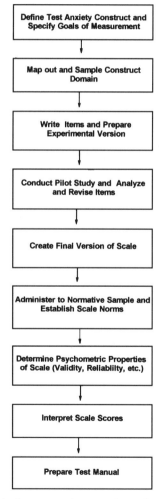

Figure 5.5. Key stages in the process of constructing self-report test anxiety measures.

anxiety or identification of a few of its key components. Prevalent measures are not very informative with respect to how anxiety is expressed in a client and in what situations. Future scales need to be more relevant for planning, execution, and evaluation of clinical or educational intervention through specification of the various antecedent conditions, manifestations, and consequences of test anxiety (Rost & Schermer, 1989b; cf. Rost & Schermer, 1989a).

4. *Separate test anxiety from denial.* Current measures are not sensitive to the problem of various forms of denial of anxiety, including defensiveness and repression (Weinberger, Schwartz, & Davidson, 1979). Lie or defensiveness scales are generally not administered along with test anxiety measures in current practice and there is no practical way to differentiate low test anxiety from denial.

5. *Pay greater attention to the extreme manifestations of test anxiety.* As pointed out by Wine (1980), current instruments are designed to measure the relative presence of test anxiety, but do not inform us enough about the low-test-anxious individual. Thus, future measures need to cover specific manifestations of low anxiety, ranging from a total lack of concern about evaluation and minimal motivation, to supreme self-confidence or high levels of self-efficacy. Similarly, test anxiety measures fail to tell us much about the extremely high test-anxious individual. Therefore, the coverage of items needs to be expanded to reflect the phenomenology of high-test-anxious examinees, including such manifestations as panic attacks, total blackout, and anxiety blockage during important exams.

6. *Differentiate between adaptive and maladaptive manifestations of anxiety.* Current scales do not provide sufficient evidence to separate maladaptive effects of worry or arousal in test situations. Future measures would need to distinguish between facilitating and debilitating arousal, and cognitive processes that are realistic (e.g., worrying about an imminent difficult exam in physics, which is prompted by a genuine threat) and those that are unrealistic (e.g., those prompted by an unlikely exam failure).

Summary

This chapter has surveyed the various stages and considerations in constructing self-report paper-and-pencil measures of test anxiety. Although I have laid out the test construction process in a linear fashion, summarized in Figure 5.5, in reality the actual process is much more dynamic and integrated. Indeed, the process of test anxiety refinement is an endless one. The ultimate test for a test anxiety measure is that it shows practical utility in research and applied settings.

III

Origins, Sources, and Determinants of Test Anxiety

6

The Origins and Development
of Test Anxiety

Overview

When considering the reactions of test-anxious children to evaluative situations, reactions tinged with feelings of worry, apprehension, self-preoccupation, and body tension, one often wonders: How do these individuals come to view the test experience as such an aversive one? How does test anxiety develop? This chapter sets out to shed light on these developmental issues by summarizing what we know about the developmental origins and antecedents of test anxiety.

For the purpose of the exposition, it is useful to distinguish between *distal* and *proximal* antecedents of test anxiety (Phillips et al., 1972). *Distal* factors include organismic and environmental factors (e.g., specific patterns of the parent–child relationship, preschool and early school experiences, cumulative academic failure experiences, etc.), which contribute more indirectly to anxiety reactions as responses to evaluative conditions. They are indirect in the sense that they have their major initial impact as antecedents of anxiety in the early years of life, although their influence continues to be felt throughout life. By contrast, *proximal* antecedents are those factors which are immediately and directly responsible for anxiety reactions in evaluative settings, such as a competitive and evaluative test atmosphere or a difficult and very important exam. As depicted in Figure 6.1 (after Phillips et al., 1972), displaying the role of distal and proximal factors in the development of test anxiety, distal factors are believed to shape test anxiety as a situation-specific trait or disposition, whereas proximal factors are expected to impact upon test anxiety as an emotional state. Both trait and state anxiety interact in contributing to actual manifestations of test anxiety in evaluative situations.

I begin by discussing the role of a number of *distal* factors, mainly biological constitution and primary socialization practices, in the development of test anxiety. I then move on to discuss additional factors shaping the course of test anxiety development in children, such as environmental learning, the school context and atmosphere,

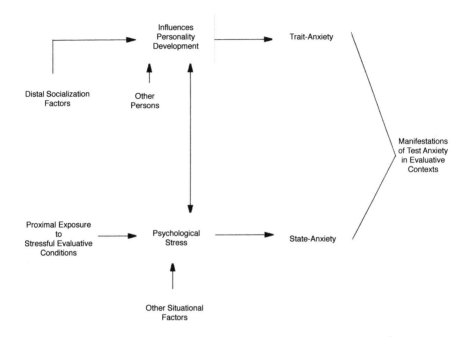

Figure 6.1.   Distal and proximal factors in the development of test anxiety. Adapted from Phillips et al. (1972).

and personal failure experiences. Chapter 7 discusses a number of contextual factors (test atmosphere, task difficulty, etc.) which may be considered to be proximal antecedents of anxiety in evaluative situations.

Biological Makeup

From a biological perspective, anxiety is viewed as being functional with regard to survival and adaptation, facilitating the detection of threat or danger in a potentially hazardous environment (M. W. Eysenck, 1982). Anxiety has considerable survival value because the rapid and early detection of warning signs of danger in the immediate surroundings enables an individual to avoid, prepare for, and cope more effectively with future threatening encounters (M. W. Eysenck, 1982). However, some anxious individuals may have such inborn or highly developed danger detection processes that they may grossly exaggerate the number and severity of threatening or dangerous events in their surroundings.

Research points to a meaningful genetic component underlying the development of trait anxiety, with heredity shown to contribute about half of the variance in explaining individual differences in the major personality factor of neuroticism, or its midlevel trait expression, trait anxiety (H. J. Eysenck & Eysenck, 1985; M. W. Eysenck, 1992). Given that test anxiety is commonly construed as a special case or form of trait anxiety, i.e., social-evaluative trait anxiety (Endler et al., 1991), coupled with the sizable relationship typically reported between trait and test anxiety (Zeidner, 1993), it is not an unlikely hypothesis that individuals are born with a basic "wired-in" propensity to react with increased arousal and elevated worry when confronted with social-evaluative conditions. Accordingly, evaluative anxiety may serve to facilitate the detection of threat in important social contexts in modern society, allowing individuals to prepare for and adequately cope with impending threats of a social-evaluative nature. However, this process may go awry and become maladaptive for persons who are "hypervigilant," i.e., perceive an exaggerated number of evaluative threats in their surroundings or magnify the severity or consequences of such threats.

Furthermore, certain parental child-rearing behaviors often claimed to be important antecedents of test anxiety may largely be an adaptation on the part of parents to biologically determined temperament dispositions or other preexisting characteristics of the child (Hock, 1992). For example, a child's excitable and highly emotional temperament, part and parcel of the child's biological equipment, may try parents' patience and evoke excessive control techniques or punitive child-rearing behaviors on their part; this, in turn, may further strengthen the child's vulnerability to react with heightened excitability and emotionality to stressful social-evaluative situations (i.e., test anxiety). Thus, biological factors may also indirectly impact upon anxiety development in children.

If indeed biological factors are at play in the development of individual differences in test anxiety, they most likely interact with a wide array of environmental experiences and personality factors in determining an individual's manifest level of the construct (Krohne, 1980). Accordingly, the development of test anxiety would best be conceptualized as the joint interaction between an individual's biological vulnerability to respond to social-evaluative threat in the environment and certain environmental experiences which impact upon and further shape, develop, and maintain this propensity. Kagan's work lends additional evidence to the notion that anxiety may have strong biological roots, with enormous stability of autonomic reactivity observed in children from birth to social-evaluative conditions in later life (Kagan & Snidman, 1991). In any case, in view of the paucity of research specifically focusing on the genetic determinants of test anxiety, it is presently difficult to assess the exact role biological factors play in determining individual differences in the manifestation of this construct.

Family Environment and Primary Socialization

Theorists and researchers who have applied the developmental approach to the study of anxiety and test anxiety over the years have emphasized the importance of interpersonal and family influences in understanding the developmental background of a child's disposition to experience anxiety in evaluative situations (Teichman & Ziv, 1994). Family climate and parental socialization practices have been claimed to bear important influences on the development of a child's emotional and social behaviors, including test anxiety (Hill, 1972; Krohne, 1980, 1992). Although more research is clearly desirable, current theory and research provide us with a preliminary and tentative foundation from which to begin sketching the origins and developmental course of test anxiety.

Models of Test Anxiety Development

I now present a number of models conceptualizing the specific role parents play in the etiology and development of test anxiety, primarily during the preschool years. Whereas several generic models attempt to identify family environmental dimensions that are meaningful predictors of child adjustment and general pathology, including manifest anxiety (e.g., Olson, 1979), this section will be concerned only with three theoretical frameworks, i.e., psychodynamic, motivational, and social learning, that have been put forth to account specifically for the etiology and development of *test anxiety*.

S. B. Sarason's Psychodynamic Model

The strong test anxiety reactions in many academically successful students leaves the impression that aside from the conscious meanings and consequences of test success and failure, there are also symbolic and unconscious elements at play in students' reactions to tests and evaluative situations (S. B. Sarason et al., 1960). Taking both symbolic and conscious meanings of evaluative situations into consideration, Sarason and his coworkers put forth an intriguing psychodynamic theory of test anxiety development in children.

According to this dynamic model, the anxiety process begins in early parent–child interactions during the preschool years, at the point when the child's performances and achievements do not live up to their parents' unrealistically high expectations. The discrepancy between the child's level of cognitive performance and high parental expectations typically leads to negative parental judgments of the child's performance in problem-solving situations. As children internalize these negative and derogatory parental reactions and messages, they not only develop a negative view of themselves, but also harbor a hostile attitude and negative feelings toward the rejecting parent. These hostile feelings, in turn, lead to guilt, which results in self-derogations and repression of hostile feelings.

The greater the perceived disparity between parental standards and expectations and the child's manifest performance, the more intense the negative affect aroused in the child. However, children are reluctant to express or even fantasize about the negative emotions and hostility which they feel toward their parents for fear of punishment and guilt. Furthermore, children tend to experience unconscious fantasies about parental retaliation and rejection for any hostile thoughts and feelings they entertain. Because children view potential parental rejection as a serious threat to the fulfillment of their dependency needs, this often leads to feelings of guilt and the further automatic repression of any hostile feelings, as well as initiation of behaviors directed at pleasing their parents. This, in turn, strengthens the child's dependency needs. The child's behavior is judged not in terms of its capabilities or needs, but in terms of standards and values which reflect dependence on the expectations of others. The child's overdependence on parents for approval and support leads to the development of a strong need for achievement and social approval, along with a concomitant strong fear of failure. The child seeks approval, direction, and support from parents and may therefore lose some of the creativity and independent functioning in problem-solving situations in an effort to avoid negative parental evaluations. Figure 6.2 presents schematic representation of the dynamic process described above.

The psychodynamic conception undergirding this model views anxiety as a danger signal associated with threatening unconscious contents and motivations; anxiety activates those processes which have as their major effect repression of dangerous content from consciousness. Furthermore, Sarason's theory is built on the foundation of complex psychodynamic concepts and principles, including the significance of unconscious contents and processes in determining human behavior, the importance of internal conflicts for shaping a child's personality and self-image, the inevitable conflicts between the internal world of the child and external reality, and the psychodynamics of defensive reactions to conflict (S. B. Sarason et al., 1960). According to this psychodynamic perspective, a child's anxiety is evoked in test situations because of the symbolic significance of such contexts in reflecting similar prior evaluative experiences in the home environment and the similarity of roles between teachers and parents (S. B. Sarason et al., 1960). Thus, the child often encounters adults in the school setting who are reminiscent of its parents in that these adults set standards, make stringent cognitive demands, and pass judgments on the child's performance. This similarity may evoke unconscious conflicts and arouse emotions (hostility, anger, anxiety), which are then transferred to authority figures in the child's surroundings—such as the teacher. Teachers who, like parents, set overly high standards and criticize students too harshly, would be especially likely to foster test anxiety in students (Hill & Sarason, 1966).

Since children are likely to regard any adult as an evaluator of their performance, their responses toward their parents as evaluators are likely to generalize to their teachers. I. G. Sarason (1972a) has speculated that among these feelings are hostility toward those whom they believe are passing judgment on them. This hostility is in conflict with their dependency needs; hence it is not expressed, but is turned against the self, taking the form of self-derogation. Consequently, the behavior that teachers are likely to observe in the anxious child are dependence, direction seeking, conformity, and social unresponsiveness.

In sum, anxiety in an evaluative context indicates that something about the exam

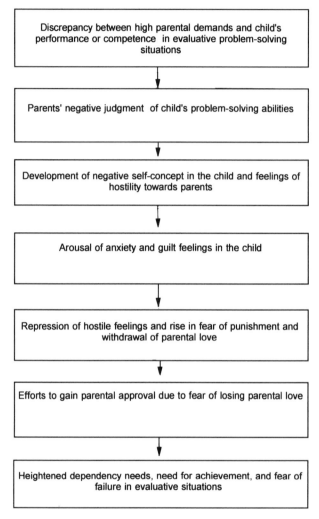

Figure 6.2. Schematic depiction of Sarason's psychodynamic developmental model of test anxiety.

is stirring up waves, and is probably at variance with the child's conscious goals or set of values; this content must therefore be repressed or kept out of awareness. According to Sarason's theory, any in-depth understanding of a child's anxiety responses within an evaluative context requires a close examination of the relationship between the individual's observed reactions in the present evaluative situation and past experiences in social-evaluative or problem-solving situations.

Hill's Dynamic-Motivational Model

Hill's (1972) model of test anxiety rests on the foundations laid by S. B. Sarason and his coworkers, but adds an additional layer to that foundation by attempting to integrate Sarason's psychodynamic perspective with key concepts and principles from Atkinson's theory of achievement motivation (Atkinson & Feather, 1966). Following Sarason's conceptualization, test anxiety is viewed as developing during the preschool years in response to unrealistically high parental standards, coupled with parents' critical reactions to the child's performance in problem-solving situations. Highly anxious children become more responsive to evaluative reactions from adults and they are particularly concerned about both positive and negative adult evaluation.

Hill's model also incorporates key concepts and principles from Atkinson's theory of achievement motivation (Atkinson & Feather, 1966). Accordingly, high parental expectations and standards of performance are believed to underlie the development of two key motivational tendencies in children—to obtain praise and achieve success, on one hand, and avoid criticism and failure, on the other. As children grow older, parental evaluations often become more demanding and critical and children become more sensitive to parental expectations. Thus, children strive harder to obtain parental praise and achieve success, but make an all-out effort to avoid criticism and failure.

Low-anxiety children tend to show a stronger motive to obtain praise than avoid criticism, whereas anxious children show the opposite tendency. Since criticism frequently accompanies failure and praise typically follows success, motives to obtain praise and avoid criticism, respectively, lead to motives to approach success and avoid failure (which is identified with test anxiety in this model). Low-anxiety children show persistence at working on cognitive tasks, a higher level of performance at complex tasks, and a distinct preference for tasks of intermediate difficulty (Hill, 1972). By contrast, in test-anxious children, who are particularly sensitive to adults' negative reactions, the motive to avoid failure becomes more salient and compelling than the motive to achieve success. In fact, both motives, i.e., fear of failure and need to succeed, are stronger in high-test-anxious compared to low-test-anxious children. Accordingly, high-test-anxious children would be expected to persist longer under continued success as well as leave sooner under continued failure compared to less-test-anxious children (Hill, 1972).

As test-anxious children progress through the educational system they become even more strongly motivated to avoid failure than to achieve success. However, the primary locus of evaluative feedback shifts from parents to teachers and eventually to peers. Hill's model predicts that low-test-anxious children should orient to their own internal evaluations of their performance and respond to the informational component of an adult's reactions rather than to social cues or contexts in which the reactions are made. By contrast, test-anxious children tend to avoid situations in which the likelihood of criticism is high and they tend to leave such situations as soon as possible. However, the model predicts that high-test-anxious children would persist longer than low-test-anxious children when an adult is delivering praise in a nonevaluative situation (i.e., one in which the standards of performance and excellence are not applicable).

Despite the similarities, Hill's theory differs from Sarason's theory on two major counts. First, Hill's mode emphasizes social interactions and achievements, and places considerably greater emphasis on the crucial role played by the child's social interactions and achievement histories in the development of test anxiety. Second, Hill's model downplays the dynamic role of children's internal reactions to demanding parental expectations (e.g., hostility or guilt), heavily emphasized in Sarason's model.

Krohne's Social Learning Model of Anxiety Development

Krohne's (1980, 1992) two-process model traces the development of evaluative trait anxiety to a unique configuration of specific parental child-rearing styles and practices. Although the model was originally proposed to account for the development of trait anxiety (and coping) in children, it appears to be readily generalizable to test anxiety development as well, and some of the empirical research substantiating the model has used test anxiety scales as criterion measures.

The model assumes that one's social learning history, primarily the residuals of past experiences and acquired behavioral tendencies, largely determines whether he or she responds to a danger cue with state anxiety or adequate coping strategies. The experiences a child encounters within the family, particularly as determined by parental child-rearing styles, are postulated to shape certain competencies and cognitive structures in children (i.e., perceived competencies and expectancies), which, in turn, are hypothesized to impact upon the development of anxiety (Krohne, 1980).

Following Mischel's (1973) model of cognitive-personal factors in human behavior, specific socialization practices are postulated to shape the child's cognitive structures, which, in turn, are hypothesized to impact upon the development of anxiety in the child (Krohne, 1992). Specifically, parental child-rearing practices are postulated to be associated with the development of specific *competencies* and *expectancies* in the child—two central constructs in the development of individual differences in test anxiety (Krohne, 1980, 1992). Competence expectancies refer to beliefs about one's ability to recognize available courses of appropriate action and to perform successfully certain coping behaviors in problem situations. Essentially, this construct indicates whether the child feels able to tackle challenges and threats in the immediate environment. Consequence expectancies (Bandura, 1977) refer to expectations about the particular type of consequences likely to follow a specific course of action or behavior or the likely outcome of events (e.g., praise or blame following a problem-solving endeavor).

According to this model, a number of socialization and parental child-rearing factors (negative reinforcement and punishment, feedback consistency and parental support vs. restriction) put children at risk for the development of test anxiety. Some of the cardinal factors, to be discussed below, are hypothesized to operate largely through their effects on the construction of competencies and expectancies in the child. Parental styles, such as support and restriction, are of central importance in the development of competencies and competence expectancies. The development of competence expectancies is viewed as being a function mainly of the provision of *parental support*, on one hand, and low degrees of *restriction*, on the other. Parental support refers to parental behavior designed to help the child acquire general problem-solving strategies. Thus, parents who support their children's efforts to solve problems or provide adequate models for effective problem solving tend to foster the development of competency expectations in their children. Frequent manifestations of anxiety are predicted for those children whose parents and immediate environment have failed in helping them develop coping mechanisms for threats in specific areas, such as social-evaluative contexts. Failure by parents to provide sufficient cognitive and affective structure and support in problem-solving situations leads to the dominance of irrelevant response tendencies in the child and consequent poor task performance (Hock, 1992).

Parental restriction designates the parents' tendency to control the child, thus serving to limit the child's ability to use information independently, autonomously, and creatively. Parents who do not encourage their children to try to independently solve problems, who are overcritical or ridicule their children's problem-solving efforts, who restrict their children's actions, or who fail to provide suitable coping models hinder the development of their children's competency expectations. Because dependency on the parent's behavior is maintained, the ability to use information and create new problem-related thoughts and actions is impaired. By contrast, parents who support their children's efforts to solve problems or provide adequate models for effective problem solving tend to foster the development of competency expectations in their children. Further, parents may fail to provide sufficient cognitive and affective structure and support in problem-solving situations, leading to the dominance of irrelevant response tendencies in their children and consequent poor task performance (Hock, 1992).

High-test-anxious children are characterized by the expectation that the social environment responds to their behavior with negative feedback. Their consequence expectancies are accompanied by a high degree of uncertainty, which impedes the establishment of defensive behavior and results in lower coping competencies. The construction of consequence expectancies is predicated to be a function of the frequency and intensity of positive and negative parental feedback, with negative feedback (punishment) crucial for the establishment of threat-related expectancies (Krohne, 1992). Accordingly, the high frequency and intensity of *parental punishment* of a child's undesirable or negative behavior is a major determinant of increased anxiety in the child. Parents who provide frequent positive reward (praise, favorable feedback) tend to instill positive consequence expectancies in their children, whereas parents who provide frequent or intense negative punishment (physical punishment, verbal rebuke, criticism) instill negative consequence expectancies. As a result of the high degree of parental restriction and negative feedback that anxious children often experience in their own socialization, they develop a dispositional expectancy that others in their social environment will respond to their behavior with negative feedback. These children come to expect criticism and failure following problem-solving efforts, thus leading to a strong expectancy of aversive consequences in evaluative situations.

Another key risk factor in parental socialization practice, *inconsistency of parental behavior*, involves praising children for a given behavior on one occasion, but punishing them for the exact same behavior on another. Inconsistent parenting is particularly harmful because this makes it extremely difficult for the child to predict adequately parental reactions and behaviors. Inconsistent parental feedback may evoke feelings of helplessness in children, who come to believe that they are not in control of the consequences of their own reactions. Inconsistency leads to fatalistic external locus of control in children, whereas restriction leads to social external locus of control (powerful others control events). Furthermore, inconsistency in punishment contributes to increased ambiguity of the environment, which in itself is a particularly important risk factor for anxiety development (Krohne, 1980). Under ambiguous threat conditions the child cannot readily identify or implement adaptive behaviors that are potentially available to cope with the danger. Thus, a child who experiences inconsistent parental behavior may develop the belief that his or her reactions and behaviors and the respective environmental consequences are uncorrelated, and over many episodes of inconsistent reaction–consequence relationships may develop a state of learned helplessness (Krohne, 1980). Another risk factor, *response blocking*, is evidenced when the parent does not provide the child with adequate coping models or restricts the degrees of freedom in the child's coping responses. Thus, the highly anxious child is confronted with three aspects of child-rearing that have been identified as anxiety-eliciting conditions for state anxiety: (a) threat perceptions, resulting from frequent and intensive punishment, (b) situational ambiguity, due to inconsistent feedback, and (c) response blocking, relating to inhibition in constructing coping competencies and expectancies (Krohne, 1980).

Note that child-rearing behavior is claimed to determine the construction of two types of cognitive structures in the child (competence and competence expectancies vs. consequence expectancies) via the operation of two different processes (support and restriction via feedback)—hence the term "two-process model." Furthermore, it is interesting to note, in conclusion, that the socialization profile characteristic of test-anxious children (i.e., high negative reinforcement, low feedback consistency, and more restriction than support) is conceptualized as the mirror image of the profile characterizing children who develop adaptive coping dispositions (i.e., low degree of

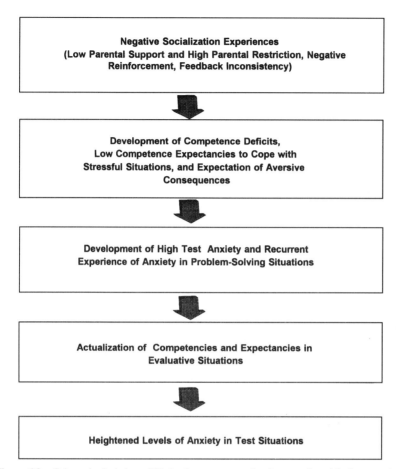

Figure 6.3.   Schematic depiction of Krohne's two-process developmental model of test anxiety.

negative reinforcement, high feedback consistency, and greater support than restriction.) This model is summarized in Figure 6.3.

Empirical Evidence in Support of Developmental Models of Test Anxiety

A number of studies provide empirical support for a cardinal assumption underlying current developmental models of test anxiety, i.e., that this situation-specific trait has its origins in primary socialization practices, primarily the quality and nature of early parent–child interactions. Hermans and his coworkers (Hermans, ter Laak, & Maes, 1972) observed parent–child interactions in a group of children aged 9–10 years while the children were performing several cognitive tasks. Parents of highly anxious children offered their children little constructive help, rejected their children's bid for attention, tended to withhold reinforcement after correct solutions, and produced more negative and fewer positive tension releases. By contrast, parents of low-anxiety children were observed to help their offspring learn task-oriented responses and effective problem-solving strategies, teach their children to rely on their own resources rather than adult supports, and release tension in a more positive way. Hock (1992) confirmed these findings by observing the exchange of aversive communicative behavior between 59 mothers and their 8- to 14-year-old children during a 30-minute simulated "homework period." Aversive communicative behaviors included the expression of annoyance, disappointment, or anger concerning the child's behavior, ignoring the child's seeking of help, blaming the child for task performance, and restriction and control of the child. The mother's aversive acts correlated moderately with the child's Worry ($r = .37$) and Emotionality ($r = .26$), two key components of test anxiety.

Krohne (1992) reported a significant association between children's test anxiety, as criterion variable, and a number of dimensions of familial socialization, including negative parental feedback (blame and punishment), inconsistent child-rearing, and the tendency to control the child. Somewhat higher correlations were found for boys than for girls. Also, higher correlations were observed for the cognitive than the emotional component of test anxiety. However, no support was found for a number of claimed socialization dimensions underlying test anxiety, such as parental support and positive feedback. Kohlmann, Schumacher, and Steit (1988) reported a meaningful relationship between maternal inconsistency and trait anxiety in girls, although father's support tends to moderate this relationship. A review by Krohne (1980) focusing on the developmental antecedents of *trait* anxiety attests to a somewhat different and more complex pattern of relationships between critical socialization dimensions and anxiety in children. M. J. Rosenthal (1990), by contrast, failed to find a significant relation between maternal inconsistency and anxiety in the child in a clinical sample of 450 disturbed children and their mothers.

A number of studies in national settings other than the United States and Europe provide some support for the association between test anxiety and certain variables in the child's early environment. Ahlawat (1989a) explored the association between test anxiety and key dimensions of home environment variables (overdemanding parents, critical/repressive home environment, nurturing parent–child interactions, punishment and control, congenial parent–child relationships, safe/happy home environment, and individual liberty and freedom) in a sample of 720 Jordanian high school students. A multiple regression of test anxiety scores upon the set of family environment scales, by sex, found *punitive control* to be a significant predictor of test anxiety in both male and female students; *negative feedback* was found to be a significant predictor of test anxiety in female students only. Thus, only one of seven family environment dimensions was implicated as a potential predictor of test anxiety in both male and female students. In addition, a correlational study by King-Fun Li (1974) in a sample of 133 Chinese children found stricter parental attitudes among high-test-anxious compared to low-test-anxious *boys*; parents of high-test-anxious children were less in favor of open communication, comradeship, and sharing. These results, however, were not found for girls.

Implications for Test Anxiety Reduction

The research evidence suggesting that it is unrealistically high parental standards and demands for intellectual performance, coupled with punitive child-rearing, that give rise to test anxiety in children have a number of practical implication for parenting practices (Hill, 1972). First, it would seem important that parents set reasonable goals for their children and recognize the child's abilities and level of development. Parents of test-anxious children would often do well to adjust their standards to the child's capabilities, temperament, and level of development, which might paradoxically facilitate their child's school work—assuming that evaluation anxiety has decreased. Parents need to convey the message that failure is a normal and expected part of the learning process, and that a good mixture of success and failure in problem solving is a reflection of optimal learning efforts.

Furthermore, parents should make an all-out effort to encourage success to a greater degree than they react to failure. Thus, parents should consistently encourage effort rather than respond too negatively when a child is failing or doing poorly in school. Parents need to insure that the child obtains feedback concerning how realistic his or her intellectual or academic goals are and information concerning successful performance on the problem at hand. As pointed out by Hill (1972), parents who enjoy their children's successes (rather than suffer from their children's failures) and who communicate these feelings to their children should produce children with minimal evaluation anxiety, who more fully realize their intellectual and achievement potential.

Social Learning and Conditioning

Human learning involves relatively permanent changes in behavior due to environmental experience (Bernstein, Roy, Srull, & Wickmen, 1988). Anxiety is commonly viewed in terms of behavioral response tendencies learned as a result of a person's interactions with the environment and the cumulative effects of various learning processes over time (Hill, 1972; Pekrun, 1985). The scientific principles and models of human learning discussed below may be useful in accounting in part for an individual's acquisition of test-anxious reactions.

Observation and Modeling of Test-Anxious Behavior

Modeling behavior appears to be a particularly promising mechanism for understanding the relationship between an individual's interpersonal relations and behaviors and the development of test-anxiety-proneness and reactions. Research attests to the important role which direct observation and modeling of behaviors of significant human models (e.g., parents, siblings, teachers, peers) may play in the learning of social and affective responses (Bandura, 1965). In fact, much social learning is made possible by exposure to real-life models who perform, intentionally or unwittingly, patterns of behaviors that may be imitated by others (Bandura, 1965). Through observation of both live as well as symbolic models demonstrating specific behaviors in a particular context, people learn and acquire new responses that did not previously exist in their behavioral repertoire. Accordingly, complex emotional response patterns, such as elevated anxiety reactions in evaluative situations, may be acquired observationally by witnessing the arousal, tension, concern, and expressed worry of relevant models undergoing a test or similar evaluative encounter. In addition to modeling of other's behaviors, test anxiety reactions may be further shaped and strengthened by observing one's own anxiety-related reactions in stressful social-evaluation encounters (Pekrun, 1985).

The behaviors manifested by significant role models (e.g., parents, peers, teachers) in reaction to social-evaluative situations and encounters would be expected to influence heavily the learning of test-anxious responses in children. Thus, children who observe significant models in their surroundings exhibiting high anxiety in social-evaluative contexts may learn and adopt similar reactions in evaluative situations by emulating the anxious behaviors of these models. For example, the child who notices that its mother gets upset when she mentions she will have an important aptitude test is being given ample opportunity to learn to be anxious (I. G. Sarason, 1972b). Indeed, a parent or older sibling who is overly upset, preoccupied, tense, and worried in the face of a stressful evaluative encounter would serve as a poor role model for the child to imitate. Exposure to such negative role models over time and in a variety of home (e.g., upcoming visit of supervisor, important colleague, parent-in-laws), work (e.g., supervisor's upcoming evaluation of job performance), or scholastic (e.g., worrying over results of important training program exam) contexts may contribute to the child's development of apprehension of tests and test situations.

Some children may never have the opportunity to learn how to cope with tests due to the absence of appropriate models demonstrating adaptive coping behaviors in evaluative situations. Instead, they learn to cope with test situations in a maladaptive fashion through avoidance behaviors, defensiveness, and palliative coping, which eventually interferes with their performance (see Chapter 13 for a detailed discussion of coping with exams). Further, given that covert learning of anxious reactions is possible even without the observer having a chance to practice the acquired responses, a child may learn test-anxious responses that remain dormant until provided the opportunity to be enacted in an evaluative situation at some later time. Some research evidence (I. G. Sarason, 1978) supports the claim that test-anxious individuals model their behavior after meaningful others in their environment.

Conditioning of Test-Anxious Behaviors

Learning principles and models may account for both the initial acquisition of anxiety reactions to tests and evaluative situations as well as the maintenance of these reactions over time. Although some scholars would disagree (Kimmel, 1975), it is commonly claimed that both *classical* and *operant* conditioning principles (Bernstein et al., 1988) may be enlisted to help explain the learning of test-anxious responses in many test-anxious students.

A good number of specific emotions (e.g., specific fears and phobias) have been successfully accounted for by classical conditioning principles. In the terminology of classical conditioning, an *unconditioned stimulus* is an automatic and unlearned stimulus, which elicits an *unconditioned response* (an automatic response). A *conditioned stimulus* is a neutral stimulus, which is paired with the unconditioned stimulus and eventually comes to elicit a *conditioned response* quite similar in nature to the unconditioned response. With respect to evaluative contexts, an exam may acquire anxiety-evoking properties, i.e., become a conditioned stimulus, on the basis of repeated associations over time between the test stimuli and certain aversive experiences which are intrinsically anxiety-evoking (e.g., failure on an exam). Over time, tests and test contexts may become aversive or negatively valent, and in themselves evoke anxiety reactions. Figure 6.4 provides a schematic diagram of the classical conditioning of anxious reactions to a test situation.

According to classical conditioning theory (Bernstein et al., 1988), as the pairing of conditioned stimuli (e.g., tests and test situations) and unconditioned stimuli (e.g., aversive experience) increases in frequency and intensity, the strength of the conditioned response also increases (i.e., test-anxious reactions). Thus, the classical conditioning model would predict that individuals who are repeatedly exposed to extremely aversive failure experiences surrounding exams would learn to associate evaluative contexts with threat and danger and be readily conditioned to respond to such evaluative situations with elevated levels of anxiety. Also, conditioning theory suggests that as the intensity of the unconditional stimulus increases, so does the strength of the conditioned stimulus and the speed in which it appears. Students who repeatedly experience failure in exam situations, who experience difficulties with specific types of exam contents or procedures, or who are ridiculed and humiliated by teachers, parents, or peers on account of poor exam performance may be conditioned to respond to exam situations with anxiety, dislike, and avoidance behaviors. Furthermore, anxiety responses may be generalized to a variety of other evaluative stimuli, such as specific test content, formats, proctors, or test sites. It is noted in passing that despite the commonly held notion that an individual may become test anxious based on his or her experience with a single aversive event in an evaluative situation,

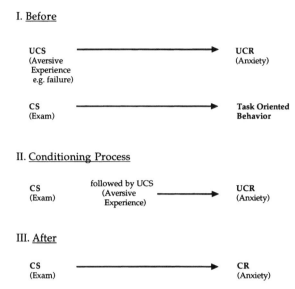

Figure 6.4. Classical conditioning of test anxiety. UCS, Unconditional stimulus; CS, conditioned stimulus; UCR, unconditioned response; CR, conditioned response.

research has not been very successful in documenting or identifying such events in the lives of high-test-anxious children.

Instrumental or *operant learning*, referring to the learning of responses that help produce some rewarding or desired effect, may also help account for the learning and the maintenance of test-anxious reactions over time. Operant learning theory predicts that behaviors that are unrewarded or that are punished become extinguished over time. Accordingly, children who suffer painful consequences despite their efforts to achieve (e.g., receive critical feedback, humiliation, or poor grades) may disengage from studying and resort to avoidance behavior rather than make active attempts to do their best on the task at hand. These avoidance responses, in turn, are often rewarded by anxiety reduction. Furthermore, a child who is continuously or intermittently rewarded when exhibiting heightened anxiety surrounding testing (e.g., by special attention dispensed by teacher, proctors, or parent) may repeat anxious behaviors in order to obtain these environmental reinforcers. Repeated reinforcement of anxious reactions or avoidance responses surrounding evaluative situations may strengthen and maintain these reactions over time, thus enhancing the probability that such responses are made the next time an evaluative situation is encountered. Behavioral interventions are often essential to undo the effects of aversive conditioning before study-skills and attentional training can be effective. Chapter 15 provides a detailed discussion of a number of these behavioral therapeutic techniques.

School Environment

Tests and other evaluative tasks are given in school contexts more frequently and with higher stakes than practically anywhere during childhood and early adolescence. Consequently, the school and classroom climate would be expected to be an important factor in evoking and maintaining students' anxiety in evaluative settings (Pekrun, 1985; Wigfield & Eccles, 1989). In this section I discuss a number of critical dimensions of the school environment which may help shape and maintain test-anxious behaviors in students.

Competitive Climate

A highly competitive and evaluative classroom environment may foster an unhealthy orientation among students, in which trying to outperform other students becomes more important than mastery of the school material. An emphasis on competition and social comparisons in the classroom should make anxious children's self-evaluations even less positive, since many are already performing more poorly than less anxious counterparts. Since anxious children are already apprehensive about failure, an emphasis on outperforming others should make the consequences of failure even more devastating (Wigfield & Eccles, 1990). Students who do not perform well in such competitive environments often come to see themselves as failures and ruminate about their performance deficits rather than focusing on the task at hand. A classroom climate heavily emphasizing competitiveness and social comparison processes may have an especially deleterious effect on the ability perceptions, motivations, and performances of high-test-anxious students. Since teachers are largely responsible for shaping the classroom milieu, the classroom climate may mediate the association between observed teacher characteristics and students' test anxiety (R. Schwarzer, 1984).

Expectancy formulations of test anxiety (Pekrun, 1985) predict that the strength of students' test-anxious reactions to evaluative classroom contexts is a complex function of the perceptions and appraisals of both the objective features of the classroom environment as well as cognitive factors, such as outcome expectancies, subjective value of negative outcomes, and perceived controllability of outcomes. Accordingly, specific classroom variables may enhance students' test anxiety by reducing success expectations for specific academic tasks, by rendering failure outcomes as extremely negative, or by decreasing perceived control over outcomes.

Pekrun (1985) investigated the nexus of relations between failure-related cognitive schemes, classroom atmosphere, and test anxiety in a sizable sample ($n = 798$) of 6th grade German students. Students who view the classroom environment as a competitive and chaotic one, who report receiving more punishment than support from their teachers, and who perceive they are being pressed beyond reasonable limits to do well in school by their teachers tend to show elevated levels of test anxiety. The effects of various classroom climate variables on test anxiety were shown to be mediated by cognitive schemes, i.e., failure-related expectancy and valence beliefs. A study by Harter, Whitesell, and Kowalski (1987) on grades 6–8 showed that students who perceived their school environment as increasingly evaluative and competitive in nature also tended to be more test-anxious. Teachers were reported to foster a competitive environment by frequently contrasting students' performance with that of others, by granting privileges to smart children or awarding prizes for best performance. These behaviors, in turn, tend to increase the importance of ability as a factor in classroom life and heighten the negative affect associated with failure (Blumenfeld, Pintrich, Meece, & Wessels, 1982).

In addition, a series of longitudinal studies by R. Schwarzer and his coworkers (R. Schwarzer, 1984; R. Schwarzer & Jerusalem, 1989) with German elementary school children demonstrated that the higher the perceived achievement pressure and anonymity in the classroom environment, the higher the students' test anxiety level (R. Schwarzer & Jerusalem, 1989). Climate variables were shown to serve as both concurrent and prospective predictors of individual differences in test anxiety at various grade levels (R. Schwarzer & Lange, 1983). A multiple regression analysis indicated that students' perceptions of achievement pressure and competition in the classroom assessed in grade 6 significantly predicted students' test anxiety levels in grade 7. Similarly, perceived competition, achievement pressure, and classroom chaos in grade 9 significantly predicted students' test anxiety levels at grade 10 (R. Schwarzer & Lange, 1983). These results were partially replicated in a large scale (*n* = 2253) longitudinal study of 5th and 6th grade students in Germany (Cherkes-Julkowski, Groebel, & Kuffner, 1982) which identified competition, achievement pressure, and perceived chaos in the classroom as predictors of students' test anxiety.

Evaluative Orientation and Practice

A body of research evidence suggests that the predominant evaluative orientation in the classroom impacts upon children's motivation and self-perception. Thus, children evaluated in terms of individual reference norms (i.e., their own previous performance) showed less fear of failure, more realistic goal setting, and fewer low-ability attributions compared to those evaluated in terms of classroom group reference norms (Boggiano & Ruble, 1986). Also, teachers who, like parents, set overly high standards or criticize their students too harshly should be more likely to foster anxiety in their students than other teachers (Wigfield & Eccles, 1990).

Changes in evaluative practices in the classroom may also be responsible, in part, for increases in students' test anxiety levels (Wigfield & Eccles, 1989, 1990). Hill and Wigfield (1984) convincingly argued that evaluation practices, such as letter grades, can promote a focus on ability perceptions, competition, social comparisons, and negative self-evaluations, which may elicit anxiety in students. As children move through school, the grades they receive become increasingly differentiated, often going from highly undifferentiated to differentiated (from satisfactory–unsatisfactory to A–E letter grades). Parents may also push children to attain higher grades and may be critical if the highest standards are not met. Moreover, evaluations of academic performance become more salient in late elementary and secondary school, and classroom characteristics that increase social comparison become more common. Consequently, grades may take on greater meaning and bear more important consequences for students as high school grade-point average is used for college selection and employment purposes (Wigfield & Eccles, 1990).

Ability Grouping

A review of the literature suggests that ability grouping is an important source of anxiety in students, particularly for those placed in lower tracks or streams (Gaudry & Spielberger, 1971). Children in lower tracks or low-status academic programs would be expected to perceive themselves as inferior compared to their upper-track counterparts and consequently evidence less positive self-concept and higher levels of test anxiety. These predictions were confirmed in a study by Cox (1962), who collected anxiety data for 266 children in grades 4 and 5 who had been placed in superior or inferior streams at the end of grade 3 (based on prior academic achievement). At both grade levels, both boys and girls in the inferior streams were observed to be more test anxious, on average, than those in the upper streams. Interestingly, streaming had no effect on general anxiety scores.

The causal direction in the streaming–anxiety relationship is ambiguous. For one, some studies (e.g., Levy, Gooch, & Kellmer-Prirgle, 1969) suggest that students who are about to be placed in lower tracks are less academically competent and more anxious *before* being streamed. Because the negative relation between ability and test anxiety may underlie the observed streaming effect in some studies, there is no necessary conclusion that streaming raises the anxiety level of lower-stream children. Second, it is commonly held that continued failure experiences, reflected in low school grades, works to increase test anxiety in low achievers. If the school policy is to stream on the basis of past performance, then those placed in the lower streams would tend to have higher test anxiety levels as well as low school grades. Thus, the increased anxiety may not be due to streamlining or tracking, but rather because those streamed have frequently experienced anxiety about past failures (Bradshaw & Gaudry, 1968).

Social Comparison

The social comparison process, in which one's achievements are compared with the norms of a meaningful reference group, allows a quick review of one's relative standing with respect to other target individuals. Social comparison helps shape an individuals' self-perceptions of ability and achievement, which, in turn, may influence test anxiety (R. Schwarzer & Lange, 1983). Social comparison theory would suggest that children who believe they are competent relative to their peers should feel more positive about themselves and less anxious compared to those who believe they are less competent that their peers. Peers may influence test anxiety by setting minimal expected norms of academic performance, by actually passing judgment on peers' performance, or by deriding and humiliating fellow students when these fail to meet set standards. Because a student's classroom typically serves as the most salient reference group for social comparison processes (Cherkes-Julkowski et al., 1982), it stands to reason that students who rank below class norms would perceive test situations as threatening and respond to evaluative situations with elevated worry and arousal. By contrast, students achieving above the norms would be expected to see themselves as competent and therefore more likely to appraise academic demands as challenging rather than threatening.

However, there may be some exceptions to the noted generalization. For instance, the above-average performance of students in low-status contexts, such as low-track inner-city school classes, may not serve to particularly enhance their academic self-concept. Conversely, mediocre or even below-average performance in some very demanding contexts (e.g., elitistic schools or programs) may be associated with positive self-evaluation and low levels of anxiety. Furthermore, some relatively bright students may experience anxiety because they compare themselves with the inordinately high norms of an elitistic group (e.g., gifted students), while some below-average students may feel little anxiety and quite comfortable when comparing themselves with poorer achievers.

Research evidence suggests that social or scholastic experiences that make social comparisons more salient, particularly when lowering one's relative standing in his or her reference group, raises anxiety (Wigfield & Eccles, 1990). Some data show that test anxiety varies with changes in a student's comparison group (R. Schwarzer, 1984; R. Schwarzer & Lange, 1983). Accordingly, the transition between elementary and junior high school itself is often an important source of evaluative threat for students (Wigfield & Eccles, 1989). This is so because school experiences often change at this juncture: students often move from smaller to larger schools, experience ability grouping, have different teachers and more heterogeneous classmates for each subject, and are graded more strictly. These changes tend to make the school environment more impersonal, threatening, and unpleasant for many students at a time when students themselves are going through major psychobiological changes (Wigfield & Eccles, 1989). By the same token, students who enter a high-level track in school may have a hard time and experience greater test anxiety as they will no longer be favored by social comparison processes.

Research evidence is consistent with the notion that students adopt the framework of their current reference group(s) and adjust their perceived ability and test anxiety levels accordingly (R. Schwarzer & Schwarzer, 1982a, 1982b). Furthermore, research suggests that the effects of belonging to or identifying with different reference groups on social comparison processes are mediated through a complex series of variables and processes. These include perceived loss of control, causal attributions of success or failure, and personal learned helplessness (R. Schwarzer & Jerusalem, 1989). Thus, if students attribute their failure to internal and global factors and are uncertain about their ability to control the outcome of their cognitive efforts, and if there is a continued independence between effort and outcome over time, anxiety, followed by resignation and depression, may set in.

Teacher Attributes and Classroom Behaviors

Teachers may bear an important influence on students' test anxiety by conveying differential expectations or responding differently to students high and low in test anxiety. Teachers who set overly high standards and/or criticize students too harshly should be more likely to foster anxiety in their students than other teachers (Hill, 1972). Furthermore, teachers typically form expectations about their students' academic abilities and competencies and these expectations, in turn, tend to influence their behavior toward their students. Hard test data are generally the most important sources of information teachers use to evaluate and form expectations of students (Zeidner, 1992). Students who are highly anxious, and consequently score more poorly on classroom and standardized tests, will be evaluated lower, on average, by their teachers. The low scholastic expectations conveyed to test-anxious children may reinforce their general feelings of inadequacy, thus exacerbating the existing anxiety level. As such, teachers often continue and strengthen trends initiated by parents' interactions with their anxious children, namely, poor problem-solving strategies and high dependence on adults in evaluative problem-solving situations (Dusek, 1980).

Test-anxious students may experience a qualitatively different form of classroom interaction with their teachers compared to their low-test-anxious counterparts. Teachers may employ qualitatively different and less favorable instructional, disciplinary, and social cues in their classroom interactions with test-anxious students, further decreasing these students' ability perceptions and raising their test-anxiety levels. Furthermore, high-test-anxious children may interpret feedback from teachers differently than their low-test-anxious counterparts because of their greater sensitivity to adult reaction (Hill, 1976).

The research data bearing on the impact of the classroom teacher on students' anxiety is mixed. Zimmerman (1970) reported significant associations between selected parameters of teacher–student interactions (e.g., praise–criticism, reinforcement, etc.) and school anxiety levels in a sample of 443 elementary school students. The study suggests that the atmosphere which teacher behavior creates in the classroom relates directly to levels of anxiety in students. There is also some research which lends credence to the intuitive notion that a teachers' level of trait anxiety is related to test anxiety levels in their students. Doyal and Forsyth (1973), for instance, reported a substantial correlation of .65 between the manifest anxiety of ten female third grade classroom teachers and their students' class mean test anxiety scores. Stanton (1974), however, failed to replicate these results on a more sizable sample of 32 teachers and 1047 sixth and seventh grade students.

Wigfield and Eccles (1990) review studies showing that high-test-anxious children do less well when their performance is observed, and this supports the idea that teacher monitoring behavior might affect anxiety arousal. Anxious children may be adversely affected by such practices as the comparison of a failing child to someone who has succeeded, turning attention to someone else who will give a more satisfactory performance, and questioning the child in front of the class in order to find out the nature of his or her difficulties.

Educational Solutions to Test Anxiety

Hill and Wigfield (1984) suggest a number of educational solutions to test anxiety. These include the following:

- Modifying classroom evaluative practices in order to make them less threatening and stressful for students. This may be accomplished by deemphasizing competition and evaluative atmosphere, liberalizing time limits, making tests fairer and less complicated, providing more success experiences on exams, etc.
- Changing the grading system by avoiding letter grading and report cards in the elementary school years. Students should be provided with separate comments relating to their intellectual performance and personal and social behavior and development.
- Preparing children for the pressures inherent in competitive grading at later ages and teaching students to deal with evaluative pressure through test-coping programs.
- Individualizing the learning environment.

History of Failure Experiences in Evaluative Contexts

Current thinking and research points to a person's continued and accumulated failure experiences in evaluative contexts as a key determinant of individual differences in test anxiety (Covington, 1986; Dusek, 1980; R. Schwarzer & Jerusalem, 1989). Accordingly, test anxiety is viewed as the product of certain achievement events, such as failure, that sooner or later befall most learners (Covington, 1986). Test anxiety in children is most likely developed through both direct experiences of failure, in which unreasonable demands, negative feedback, and punishments are imposed on students, as well as through observation of other people's experiences with failures (e.g., parents, siblings, peers, etc.). Through direct or vicarious experience individuals learn to associate the idea of evaluation with lowering of self-esteem and expectation of failure.

Both the *accumulation* as well as *timing* of failure experiences are key concepts to consider in our efforts to understand failure-induced anxiety (Wigfield & Eccles, 1989). Although theoretically one may develop a generalized anxiety reaction to test situations because of some shattering one-time experience, anxiety is generally shaped by *repeated* failure during critical developmental periods, eventually producing a generalizable apprehension of all achievement activities. Whereas a single failure experience represents a challenge to overcome, continued subsequent failures elicit anxiety caused by the implicit implications of low ability. Continual poor performance over time typically evokes self-directed negative affect, causing a person who repeatedly fails in academic settings to experience aversive emotional states such as anxiety, shame, and humiliation (Covington & Omelich, 1979).

Research (Hill & Eaton, 1977) suggests that children who succeed in cognitive tasks learn to approach new problem-solving tasks as challenging and generally cope effectively with test situations. By contrast, children who have experienced continued failure in academic tasks will approach new tasks with considerable anxiety and develop maladaptive coping strategies, and may be more motivated to avoid failure than to approach success—especially when they believe that the task they are engaged in assesses their ability. In fact, test-anxious children have been shown to have a poor history of success in evaluative situations and their problem-solving strategies are often indicative of a generally higher motive to avoid failure and criticism than to approach success (Dusek, 1980).

The timing of failure experiences is also currently held to be of crucial importance. The effects of failure experiences on anxiety appear to be moderated by age. Whereas early failures generally do not have a major effect on children's expectancies for future success and anxiety, as children grow older, failure appears to have a stronger impact on their future expectancies and anxiety experiences (Wigfield & Eccles, 1989). Thus, during elementary school years children with failure experiences and low-ability perceptions would not necessarily be anxious, because they remain optimistic even after failure. This is presumably so because their ability perceptions are relatively undifferentiated and they basically see ability as an unstable rather than enduring underlying characteristic (Nicholls & Miller, 1986). However, by middle elementary school years, when ability perceptions are more differentiated and more closely related to school performance, children who continually fail may think that their poor performance is due to a lack of academic ability, thus lowering their ability perceptions and enhancing their anxiety in test situations (Covington, 1992). A number of studies lend credence to the view that histories of success and failure are important determinants in the development of test anxiety (Bradshaw & Gaudry, 1968; Hill, 1972).

Developmental changes in test anxiety may also be linked to the increasing evaluative pressure that students face as they proceed through school as well as to changes in their level of processing of the evaluative feedback they receive (Wigfield & Eccles, 1990). In contrast to younger children in the lower elementary school grades, the perceptions of upper elementary school children become increasingly differentiated and they learn to process evaluative feedback in more sophisticated ways. By more reliably interpreting evaluative feedback and comparing their performance to that of others, these children develop clearer ideas of their relative standing in the class in terms of ability, and this allows them to alter their expectancies and ability perceptions in response to information about success or failure. Furthermore, research surveyed by Wigfield and Eccles (1990) suggests that during middle elementary school years children become increasingly capable of processing and interpreting evaluative feedback from teachers and comparing their performance to that of other children. They are capable of developing clearer ideas of their standing in class and better understand how their success and failure experiences relate to their future performance possibilities.

In sum, a personal history of failure in cognitive tasks, combined with an unfavorable attributional style and a lack of supportive feedbacks from parents and teachers, may constitute a particularly potent combination in shaping a person's test anxiety. However, as pointed out by Sarason and his coworkers (I. G. Sarason et al., 1990), it usually takes more than simply a history of failure experiences before a full-blown propensity to test-anxiety develops in an individual. In fact, both research and clinical practice attest to a good number of test-anxious persons who are quite competent and rarely experience objective failure. Current phenomenological models of stress and anxiety (Lazarus & Folkman, 1984) would suggest it is not failure per se that causes anxiety. Rather, what counts is how people process their objective successes and failures and how they view the test-taking experience.

Summary

This chapter surveyed theory and research relating to the developmental origins of test anxiety. As shown in Figure 6.5, test anxiety development may be best understood as shaped by a unique configuration of constitutional, familial, social, educational, and experiential factors. These factors interact and mutually impinge upon each other to shape the course of test anxiety development. Among the key dimensions of primary socialization researched in relation to the development of test anxiety are overly high parental standards and expectations, severe parental dominance and control, frequent and intense negative feedback in problem-solving solutions, and low degree of parental support. These socialization practices may interact with a child's biologically determined temperament in determining the child's vulnerability to react with anxiety in evaluative situations.

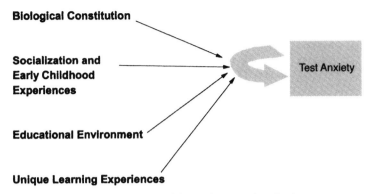

Figure 6.5. Configuration of factors in test anxiety development.

Overall, the empirical evidence in support of the major developmental models of anxiety, which view the origin of test anxiety in parental child-rearing attitudes and practices, is mixed. While research evidence implicates a number of socialization and child-rearing dimensions in the development of test anxiety (e.g., negative feedback and control), there is little consistent evidence in support of other claimed dimensions (e.g., high parental standards and expectations). Furthermore, current models focus on the role the family environment plays in shaping test anxiety, but generally neglect the potential role of a child's biological constitution as a source of evaluative trait anxiety.

Test-anxious behaviors also represent the cumulative effects of various learning processes over time, including observations of the anxiety reactions of self and that of meaningful models in an evaluative context, conditioning of the test situation to aversive events, reinforcement of anxious and avoidance behaviors in evaluative situations, and encoded symbolic information garnered from parents, teachers, and peers. Test anxiety is also fostered by various facets of the teaching/learning process. Students who experience repeated failures in evaluative contexts may begin to believe that their poor performance is due to a lack of ability, thus lowering their ability perceptions and enhancing their state anxiety levels in test situations. Furthermore, certain aspects of the classroom learning experience and environment, particularly the competitive classroom atmosphere, changes in social comparison processes that make evaluation more salient, increased evaluative pressures and emphasis on tests and evaluations, aversive teacher–student interactions, and repeated scholastic difficulty and failure may be important antecedents of test anxiety.

Reviewers of the developmental literature on test anxiety would concur that systematic and well-controlled research on the etiology of test anxiety is rather sparse (Dusek, 1980; Wigfield & Eccles, 1989). The findings and conclusions of much of the current body of data are limited because of the use of nonrepresentative samples, restricted age ranges, and measurement and design constraints. Clearly, future test

anxiety research would benefit from systematic and well-controlled research addressing a wide array of developmental topics and issues, some of which are specified in
subsequent chapters. After close to half a century of research in this area, the
development of test anxiety continues to be a murky area of research which could be
illuminated by systematic and well-controlled studies relating to practically every
one of the etiologic factors claimed to underlie test anxiety development.

Situational Determinants of Anxiety in Evaluative Situations

Overview

According to Lewin's (1951) well-known formulation, behavior (B) is an interactive function of personality (P) and environment (E), as encapsulated in the equation $B = P \times E$. Accordingly, the state anxiety a person manifests in a test situation (B) would be construed as a function of personality variables (P) as well as the anxiety evoked by details of the test or test situation (E). It follows that in order to understand the sources of variation in anxious reactions to test situations, both personality and environmental factors need to be jointly considered. In the previous chapter we examined various developmental factors that may shape and determine the P factor in Lewin's equation, i.e., anxiety-proneness. This chapter looks at the E factor in the equation as it relates to situational determinants of anxiety in evaluative contexts. Indeed, a useful starting point for the analysis of the determinants of test anxiety begins with the objective properties of test situations, as well as the meaning examinees attribute to test situations.

According to the transactional model of stress (R. S. Lazarus & Folkman, 1984), anxiety in an evaluative situation may be viewed as an unpleasant emotional reaction that results from the perception or appraisal of the context as ego-threatening. Accordingly, anxiety is seen as linked to specific situational characteristics of the test and test context by perceptual and cognitive appraisal processes (R. S. Lazarus & Folkman, 1984). If an individual appraises the situational demands of the testing process as potentially dangerous and as exceeding his or her competence and coping resources, the transaction between the person and the test environment will be judged as stressful and anxiety-evoking. It would be reasonable to expect that any facet or aspect of the test (e.g., complexity) or test environment (e.g., ambiguity) that increases the probability or salience of failure and potential loss or aversive consequences will also enhance a person's appraisal of perceived threat in the environment. This, in turn, increases the person's subjective feeling of arousal, apprehension, and worry in the test situation (R. S. Lazarus & Folkman, 1984).

While stress and anxiety researchers have traditionally emphasized the subjective and personality determinants of anxiety in evaluative settings, a wide array of *objective* factors in the test context have recently drawn the attention of anxiety researchers in their effort to understand the sources and determinants of evaluative anxiety. This chapter surveys research on a number of contextual determinants of anxiety reactions in testing, including both test-related (i.e., intrinsic to the test per se) and external variables (i.e., extrinsic to the task). These factors may interact with individual differences in test anxiety and produce a systematic bias in the individual test scores. Particular emphasis will be placed on the possible differential impact of contextual factors on the affective reactions of high- versus low-test-anxious examinees in evaluative contexts. I begin by discussing a number of variables related to the test per se and test administration procedures that may influence anxiety reactions, and then move on to discuss selected factors in the social and physical environment that may determine test-anxious reactions in evaluative situations. The possible *interactive* effects of contextual variables and anxiety as they impact upon test performance are discussed in Chapter 9.

Although the objective and subjective determinants of test anxiety are discussed separately in this book, mainly for analytic purposes, in reality these factors are inextricably intertwined. Thus, a complex and dynamic nexus of relationships exists between individual difference variables, subjective appraisals, and prevailing assessment conditions in impacting upon anxiety in test contexts. On one hand, the objective properties and cues of the test situation determine and shape the individual's appraisals of the situation, with appraisals and subjective judgments generally reflecting and modeling objective or veridical environmental cues. On the other hand, environmental cues and information are subjectively filtered, attended to, and processed, with cognitive and personality factors mediating the effects of objective contextual factors on anxiety in evaluative situations.

Test-Related Variables

Complexity of Cognitive Task

The complexity of the individual items or problems comprising a cognitive task is probably the most salient characteristic of the task per se that examinees find to be anxiety-evoking. For example, O'Neil, Spielberger, and Hansen (1969) reported that systolic blood pressure increased among examinees when engaged in a difficult task, decreased during an easy task period, and showed little change from easy to posttask. It is noted that the complexity may be related to the actual complexity of the material itself or be due to other factors such as the ability of the examinee, amount of preparation, and prior experience with the material under consideration. Since hard test items (and tests) are failed more frequently than easy items (and tests), they can be expected to evoke more anxiety than easier tests. Accordingly, extremely difficult or complex exams would be expected to strengthen failure expectancies in test-anxious subjects and consequently reduce their morale and arouse anxiety, which, in turn, results in performance decrements (Rocklin, 1985; Rocklin & Thompson, 1985). By contrast, when the task at hand is relatively easy and the subjective probability of success is relatively high, the high-test-anxious person should not experience excessive arousal or cognitive interference during task performance. It is normally assumed that students actually perceive psychometrically defined easy or hard items, respectively, as, in fact, easy or hard.

There is a considerable body of research evidence indicating that task complexity in an exam situation is positively associated with state anxiety (see M. W. Eysenck [1982] for an extensive review). Specifically, state anxiety is typically low when the task is easy and high as the task becomes more difficult. Meta-analytic data provided by Hembree (1988) corroborates that students report higher levels of test anxiety when the test material is perceived as being difficult or complex. Further research evidence on the effects of computer-assisted instruction and testing on anxiety suggests that state anxiety increases with difficulty of the material (see chapters in Sieber et al., 1977). It is noted, however, that the relationship between task difficulty and anxiety may not be linear. In fact, comparisons of the effects of specific difficulty levels (e.g., high vs. moderate vs. low) on state anxiety yield some unwieldy findings (Head & Lindsey, 1983).

Task complexity often interacts with test anxiety in determining an individual's level of arousal and consequent performance in an evaluative situation. Thus, high-test-anxious individuals may be optimally aroused when presented with a relatively easy or moderate task, while a difficult task creates an excessive and debilitating level of arousal—resulting in performance decrements. By contrast, since low-test-anxious examinees may not be aroused enough on easy tasks, presenting them with a difficult test should enhance their arousal and motivation, resulting in improved performance. In fact, considerable research (e.g., I. G. Sarason, 1972b; Wine, 1971b) attests that the debilitating effects of test anxiety are most noticeably evidenced in situations in which difficult materials and ego-arousing conditions join forces. The bulk of current research evidence suggests that both stressful test conditions as well as dispositional test anxiety reliably interact with task complexity to impact upon the test anxiety and performance of students.

At present, we do not know how to measure precisely task difficulty or exactly what level of task difficulty is necessary for anxiety to be evoked or for it to exert its debilitating effects. One reasonable measure of task difficulty is the task's demand on a person's general processing resources: the more difficult the task, the greater the demand on resources and vice versa (M. W. Eysenck, 1992). Because difficult tasks make more substantial demands than easy tasks on working memory capacity, this may explain why anxiety has a more detrimental effect on difficult than easy tasks. In addition, difficult tasks are likely to be associated with failure experiences, leading to enhanced state anxiety when a series of difficult items is encountered.

Everson and his coworkers (Everson, Tobias, Hartman, & Gourgey, 1993) contend that it is not task difficulty per se that accounts for increased anxiety in examinees under evaluative conditions. Instead, it is the perception of the exam content as requiring accurate answers and more rigorous understanding for mastery that lowers expectancies and concomitantly increases test anxiety levels. They provided evidence in support of this hypothesis in a sample of 196 college students who indicated the level of anxiety aroused in them by each of four different programs of study (English, mathematics, physical sciences, and social sciences). Physical science courses, typically packaged as difficult and rigorous ones, were reported to elicit the highest levels of evaluative anxiety. Social sciences, by contrast, generally perceived by students to be more popular and less rigorous courses of study, were reported to evoke less test anxiety. Students' perception of the difficulty of course subject matter was correlated with test anxiety, independent of the particular subject and task demands.

Overall, one could argue for individual differences and variability in perceiving a task as difficult or complex. A person who evaluates a math problem as "hard" and something they cannot expect to succeed at, versus another person who sees it as "challenging" and requiring hard work, will not only experience different levels of anxiety, but will moderate anxiety differently. In the first case, anxiety begets anxiety, even to the point of affecting pre- and posttest behaviors. In the second case, it is manageable and motivating, possibly facilitating performance.

Item Arrangement

It is accepted practice for test constructors to arrange test items on standardized tests in order of increasing difficulty, such that easier items are presented first, followed by items of increasing complexity. The major rationale behind this particular item arrangement is that by placing the easier items at the beginning of a test, this increases the examinees' probability of success on early items. This, in turn, enhances examinees' confidence in their ability to handle the more difficult items later on in the test and concomitantly reduces anxiety. Thus, by attaining initial successes, examinees should gain confidence in the quality and sufficiency of their knowledge as they proceed from one success to another throughout the early portions of the test (Covington & Omelich, 1987b).

High-test-anxious individuals may become particularly aroused when they encounter difficult or frustrating items right at the outset. As they proceed through the test they become more and more anxious, which cumulatively affects their ability to answer later items (McKeachie, 1984). Consequently, it has been argued that it would be particularly advantageous for high-test-anxious examinees to be subjected to easier items first, followed by items of increasing difficulty. By the time more difficult items are encountered, the disruptive and inhibitory effects of test anxiety and emotional arousal will have largely dissipated (Covington, 1992). Despite the intuitive appeal of these claims, there are few studies providing solid empirical evidence in support of the anxiety-ameliorating effects of an easy-to-hard item arrangement or evidence showing differential effects of item arrangement on the anxiety of high- versus low-test-anxious examinees.

Test Format

There is some evidence that the particular type of test format used (e.g., essay vs. multiple choice) may affect students' anxiety in a test situation, although the particular nature of the effect may vary by educational level and content assessed. Zeidner (1987a; see also Zeidner, 1987b) reported that school children viewed multiple-choice items as being less anxiety-evoking than essay-type items. Similarly, a study conducted among 100 college students varying in test anxiety (Green, 1981) reported that students high and low in anxiety basically agreed on preference ranks for various test formats, preferring multiple-choice over problem-solving, essay, and interpretive exercises. Shaha (1984) reported that high school students overwhelmingly preferred matching format to multiple-choice format. These students scored equally high on parallel matching and multiple-choice tests and experienced significantly less debilitating anxiety. The authors suggest that because students are accustomed to multiple-choice tests, a different format may not elicit evaluative cues and be less anxiety-evoking. Overall, there is little evidence that particular test formats have a differential impact on the anxiety of high- and low-test-anxious students.

Providing Choice among Items

Theorists have long speculated on the potential effects on state anxiety of providing individuals with varying degrees of choice and decisional control. On one hand, it has been suggested that the constraint of having to choose among competing alternatives may plunge the individual into a conflict situation, thereby heightening subjective stress and often resulting in anxious, panicky behavior. This view is compatible with Janis and Mann's (1977) model of decision making under stressful conditions. It is also consistent with the views of various social philosophers and thinkers (Fromm, Hobbes), who posit a human tendency to submit to outside authority and escape from freedom, which is often construed as threatening (Keinan & Zeidner, 1987). On the other hand, it has been argued that providing individuals with a choice among competing alternatives strengthens their perceived sense of control over a situation, which serves to diminish psychological stress (Averill, 1973). Thus, individuals generally strive in interactions with their environment to enhance their perceived sense of freedom and control (Proshansky, Ittelson, & Rivlin, 1970). Examinee control may help guide persons toward task-oriented choices, thus reducing their anxiety.

In one of the few experimental studies on the effects on anxiety and performance of allowing decisional choice among test items in a true-to-life school testing situation, Keinan and Zeidner (1987) randomly assigned 74 eighth grade students to one of two conditions: (a) *decisional control,* in which students were given a short math quiz consisting of five problems of homogeneous difficulty and instructed to respond to any three of the five, and (b) *no choice,* in which the students were given only the first three problems (out of the five comprising the exam) and instructed to answer all three. The findings show that students tested under perceived decisional control conditions were less state-anxious and attained higher mathematics scores, on average, than those tested under no-choice conditions. The authors suggest that the provision of choice serves to enhance the individual's perceived feeling of control over the source of the threat. This, in turn, allows more favorable psychological adjustments of one's interior milieu to outside stimuli, thereby lowering state anxiety, while concomitantly raising levels of test attainment. It is unclear from this study whether decisional choice works through anxiety to impact upon test performance, and this question warrants further study using causal modeling procedures.

Research in the area of computer-administered testing provides additional evidence indicating that when individuals are allowed some control over materials in computer-assisted instruction, state anxiety is lowered (O'Neil, Judd, & Hedl, 1977). Recent research has looked at the anxiety-reducing properties of various forms of computerized *adaptive testing.* In conventional computerized adaptive tests, items of known difficulty are administered sequentially to an individual by the computer. In computerized *self-adaptive testing,* by contrast, the examinee, not the computer, chooses the next test item from several levels of ability. It has been argued that the increase in examinee's perceived control when choosing the appropriate item difficulty level may serve to lower stress in the exam situation and, as such, may be particularly advantageous to test-anxious subjects. Wise, Plake, Johnson, and Roos (1992) and Rocklin and O'Donnell (1987) provided evidence showing that students taking self-adapted tests not only obtained significantly lower state anxiety scores, but also obtained significantly higher ability scores. However, self-adapted testing was not shown to have a differential beneficial effect on test-anxious students and appears to benefit students at all levels of anxiety equally well.

Situational Variables

Test Environment and Atmosphere

It has frequently been argued that an *evaluative* test atmosphere has special motivational significance and value for high-test-anxious examinees and would therefore be particularly threatening and anxiety-evoking for anxious individuals (I. G. Sarason, Sarason, & Pierce, 1995). Whereas an evaluative test situation is claimed to elicit avoidance motivation and anxiety in highly test-anxious subjects, it is said to represent more of a challenge to the less test-anxious, and evoke approach rather than avoidance behaviors. Deffenbacher (1978) found that high-test-anxious students assessed under evaluative conditions rated both themselves and their abilities more negatively, experienced more task-generated interference, reported greater emotionality and worrisome thoughts, and solved fewer anagrams compared to students who were high in test anxiety, but were assessed under nonevaluative conditions (or students low in test anxiety and assessed under evaluative conditions). Part of their results are presented in Figure 7.1. The data suggest that evaluative stress elicits a tendency for the highly anxious to become preoccupied with worrisome cognitions and task irrelevancies as well as with heightened arousal under evaluative circumstances. A number of studies reviewed by Hill (1972) suggest that high-test-anxious individuals may have difficulty functioning in an evaluative interpersonal situation, whereas low-test-anxious individuals function particularly well in such situations.

Furthermore, some research suggests that the presence of an external observer or audience during testing may negatively impact upon examinees' anxiety in an evaluative situation (Geen, 1977). Observer presence may be particularly anxiety-evoking for high-test-anxious subjects if the observer or examiner is perceived as someone whose function is to evaluate behavior, thus constituting a personal threat to the examinee. Geen (1977) demonstrated that subjects high in test anxiety are not

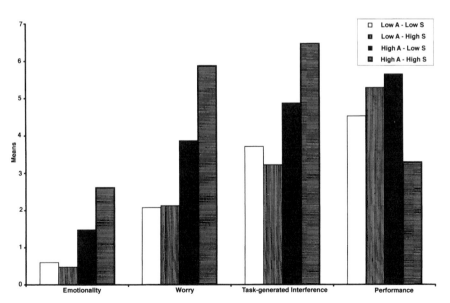

Figure 7.1. Effects of test atmosphere and test anxiety on affective and performance measures. Low A-Low S, Low test anxiety, low evaluative stress; Low A-High S, Low test anxiety, high evaluative stress; High A-Low S, High test anxiety, low evaluative stress; High A-High S, High test anxiety, high evaluative stress. Based on data from Deffenbacher (1978), Table 2, p. 251.

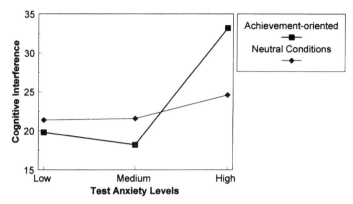

Figure 7.2. Interactive effects of trait test anxiety and test administration conditions upon cognitive interference. Based on I. G. Sarason (1978).

only harmed more than those low in test anxiety by the presence of an examiner during performance, but are also helped more by a reappraisal of the observation that renders it less threatening.

I. G. Sarason (1978) reported a significant interaction between test administration conditions (achievement-oriented vs. neutral) and trait anxiety in impacting upon cognitive interference in an evaluative situation. As shown in Figure 7.2, achievement-oriented instructions, relative to neutral instructions, meaningfully increase cognitive interference primarily among high-test-anxious subjects. Relatively few studies, however, have directly examined the differential effects of the evaluative environment upon anxiety levels of high- versus low-test-anxious individuals. Most studies have simply assumed that the differential decrements in the test performance of high-test-anxious subjects under highly evaluative conditions is accounted for by increased anxiety levels, without conducting necessary manipulation checks and directly assessing test anxiety in the test situation.

Feedback and Success/Failure Experiences

Both informal observations and experimental research suggest that high-test-anxious subjects are characterized by a special sensitivity to situations that might lead to failure and that failure experiences serve to heighten anxiety in high-test-anxious subjects in particular (M. W. Eysenck, 1992; I. G. Sarason, 1959). Research reviewed by Hill and Eaton (1977) suggests that children who have experienced continued failure in evaluative situations learn to approach new tasks with considerable anxiety; these failure-prone students develop maladaptive coping strategies and become more motivated to avoid failure than to approach success—especially when they believe that the task they are engaged in assesses their ability. Indeed, failure feedback would be more likely to produce feelings of anxiety in high-test-anxious subjects who are characterized by fear of failure or who are failure-prone than in low-test-anxious subjects. Furthermore, although seemingly paradoxical, it has been suggested that both success and failure experiences may have similar negative effects on the anxiety and subsequent performance of high-test-anxious students (Phillips, Pitcher, Worsham, & Miller, 1980). The rationale behind this claim is that both success and failure experiences emphasize that the adequacy of performance is being evaluated.

Several studies show that providing examinees with feedback relating to their test performance can have a *positive* effect on their affective state and test scores. Thus, a recent study (Rocklin, 1985; Rocklin & Thompson, 1985) found that immediate item feedback improved test performance, with performance increments attributed to a reduction in student test anxiety (though not directly assessed). L. W. Morris and Fulmer (1976) provided direct evidence for the hypothesis that the Worry component of test anxiety, which is partially dependent on cues and feedback information available to the examinee during testing, decreases as a function of examinee feedback. The hypothesis was supported in a study of 55 students asked to study a journal article, with half given item-by-item feedback and knowledge of the correct response and the remainder no feedback. As hypothesized, Worry decreased for the feedback group only, although Emotionality decreased comparably for both feedback and no-feedback conditions. Overall, however, research examining the effects on state anxiety of providing examinees with item feedback has yielded inconsistent results.

The nature of the feedback (i.e., failure vs. success) appears to be a critical factor in determining the effects of item feedback on examinee anxiety. Thus, a number of studies suggest that providing students with immediate feedback in the testing situation, particularly when negative, can have aversive effects on the examinees' affective state (O'Neil & Richardson, 1977; Strang & Rust, 1973). L. W. Morris and Liebert (1973) found that negative feedback aroused the Worry component of anxiety, but had little effect on the Emotionality component. Strang and Rust (1973) found that providing examinees with item feedback during a college midterm exam increased students' tension and lowered test performance.

Auerbach (1973) investigated the joint effects of orienting instructions (ego vs. task) and type of feedback (Failure, success, no feedback) on state anxiety in a sample of 60 male students. Failure feedback produced significantly greater increases in state anxiety than success feedback conditions or control. Subjects high in trait anxiety who received failure feedback responded with higher state anxiety scores during the test period than did high-test-anxious subjects in the success and control conditions. Further, failure feedback had a differential effect on low-versus high-trait-anxious students: The greatest increase in state anxiety from pre- to posttest conditions was for high-trait-anxious subjects given failure feedback. It may well be that continuous feedback, particularly when negative, may simply provide the anxious students with additional evaluative cues, thus working to trigger worry and self-preoccupation.

Studies have attempted to specify the conditions under which item feedback in computerized testing impacts upon anxiety. Wise and his coworkers examined the effects on posttest anxiety of item feedback (i.e., telling the examinee that the response to the test item is "correct" or "incorrect") under varying item arrangement conditions on a sample of 101 college students (Wise, Plake, Eastman, Boettcher, & Lukin, 1986). Provision of item feedback under random item arrangement conditions actually *increased* anxiety, with lower anxiety found when item feedback was *not* given. Another study by Wise and his coworkers (Wise, Plake, Pozehl, Barnes, & Lukin, 1989) tested the hypothesis that item feedback would increase anxiety in examinees experiencing early failure on a test, but would not affect anxiety outcomes for those experiencing early success. A group of 113 college students were randomly assigned to one of several forms of a computer-based algebra test differing both in the difficulty level of the first five items (i.e., easy vs. difficult) and the type of item feedback provided (i.e., feedback given after each item, running display of number of items correct and incorrect, no feedback). Item feedback was shown to have nonsignificant effects on anxiety for students who received easy initial items, but had a significant effect for students who received difficult initial items. Specifically, students who were administered difficult initial items and given feedback on their performance via a running total score reported levels of posttest state anxiety averaging more than one standard deviation higher than students from the other treatment groups. Additional research is warranted in clarifying the effects of feedback information on test-anxious examinees in both conventional and computer-assisted testing.

Time Pressure

Time pressure and speeded time conditions are frequently considered to be a major source of stress in the test situation (Hill & Wigfield, 1984). Highly timed conditions may elicit heightened emotional arousal and accentuate the debilitating effects of anxiety on test performance (Plass & Hill, 1986). Test-anxious children who had difficulty staying task-focused during the test may be especially affected by the highly speeded conditions of standardized tests that require one to stay task-focused all or most of the time in order to complete test items. Further, extreme time pressures on cognitive tests may increase the chances that high-test-anxious students resort to maladaptive strategies in coping with time pressures. Accordingly, time pressure may elicit opposite strategies in high-test-anxious subjects: slow and overly cautious test behavior on one hand, and rapid, careless responding on the other (Geen, 1987). Whereas an overly cautious style is generally dysfunctional when the premium is on speed, as typical of most traditional forms of testing, a rapid, impulsive style may lead to a higher rate of inaccurate responses and resultant failure. Examinees taking the Graduate Record Examination identified restricted time limits as the most salient anxiety-evoking situational factor (Powers, 1986). Examinees commented that the time limits were far too short and that it was quite easy to "lose your cool" and feel "out of control" (see Figure 7.3).

Figure 7.3.   A source of situational stress in a test situation.

Due to the paucity of current research it is difficult to determine to what extent timing differentially affects anxiety levels under evaluative situations in examinees high and low in test anxiety.

Modes of Test Administration

Computer-administered testing, with its advantages of speed, flexibility, and efficiency, is currently complementing conventional paper-and-pencil testing in a wide variety of educational, industrial, and military contexts. The computerized testing situation is frequently claimed to have a number of anxiety-reducing properties which would be particularly facilitative for high-test-anxious students. These include human–machine testing interactions that may be more objective and affectively neutral than the typical interactions between examiner and examinee, freedom from threatening examiners/proctors, a relatively noncompetitive testing environment, individualization of testing, the opportunity to test examinees at their own pace and whenever they so choose, provision of immediate item feedback, and greater examinee control of the order of item administration (O'Neil & Richardson, 1977). If these methods are found to reduce anxiety, then a clear advantage of computer-administered testing will have been identified. Although empirical research has yielded inconsistent data on the effects of computerized testing as compared to conventional paper-and-pencil testing on state anxiety (see Sieber, O'Neil, & Tobias, 1977, for a review), reviews of the research literature suggest that computerized testing does not generally reduce state anxiety relative to conventional testing (Hedl, O'Neil, & Hansen, 1973; O'Neil & Richardson, 1977; Spielberger, 1977). The amount of anxiety that is induced by computer-presented test materials appears to be more a function of the difficulty of the task and the amount of evaluative threat perceived by the student.

Some evidence suggests that computerized testing may be advantageous, in terms of affective and cognitive outcomes, for *experienced* computer users, but may increase test anxiety and depress performance for *novel* users (Llabre, Clements, Fitzhugh, Lancelotta, Mazzagatti, & Quinones, 1987). Thus, computer-administered testing may lower anxiety in test situations, provided that examinees are "computer literate" (e.g., Llabre et al., 1987).

Summary

This chapter surveyed research on the contextual determinants of anxiety reactions in evaluative situations. Overall, the empirical evidence in support of the effects of specific contextual variables upon test anxiety is not very impressive. A number of contextual variables have been shown to have significant but *modest* effects on examinee test anxiety, including task difficulty, provision of choice among items, test atmosphere and environment, and examiner reassurance and social support. The evidence for the effects of other contextual variables on tension and test anxiety (e.g., test formats, modes of test administration, item feedback, humor, music) is inconsistent. Furthermore, the empirical evidence for the interactive effects of specific contextual variables and trait test anxiety in affecting state test anxiety is sparse, with few variables exhibiting consistent differential effects on the state anxiety of high- versus low-test-anxious examinees. Thus, based on the current body of literature, it is difficult to determine to what extent contextual factors differentially affect anxiety levels in examinees high and low in test anxiety, and additional research on the interactive effects of contextual variables and test anxiety on state anxiety is urgently needed.

As noted at the outset, although objective and subjective determinants of anxiety are presented separately in this book for expository reasons, they are inextricably bound in reality, and almost impossible to disentangle in any given situation. Clearly, objective factors work through appraisals and other cognitive and personality states in impacting upon test anxiety. Although we tend to speak of the objective factors in the test situation (time pressures, task difficulty, etc.) as being anxiety-evoking, it is the *perception* and *cognitive appraisal* of these factors that evoke threat perceptions and resultant anxiety. Thus, a discussion of situational variables cannot really be a sufficient account of anxiety reactions, as any discussion also needs to assess subjective determinants, including appraisals, cognitions, and personality traits and states. I now proceed to discuss some of these important subjective determinants of test anxiety in Chapter 8.

8

Subjective Determinants of Test Anxiety

Men are disturbed not by things, but by the view they take of them.
—Epictetus

Overview

Both the transactional theory of stress and emotion (R. S. Lazarus & Folkman, 1984; R. S. Lazarus, 1991a, 1991b, 1991c) as well as social-cognitive theory (Mischel, 1973) would suggest that regardless of the objective circumstances of evaluative tasks and situations, it is the *subjective* interpretation of the test environment that actually leads to evaluative stress and anxiety reactions. Thus, it is not so much the physical properties of the environment that count in the emotion process, but the subjective meanings individuals attribute to environmental cues and events. Although the various objective properties of tests and test situations addressed in Chapter 7 (evaluative instructions, time pressure, task difficulty, etc.) may be a useful starting point for analyzing anxiety, current thinking would suggest that it is in fact the *perception* and cognitive *appraisal* of these factors that evoke threat perceptions and resultant anxiety. Thus, objective factors are assumed to work through appraisals and other cognitive states in impacting upon test anxiety.

Social-cognitive theory (Mischel, 1973) would support the contention that any meaningful approach to test anxiety must consider the interactions between persons and situations. Situational parameters are viewed as "informational inputs" whose behavioral impact depends on how they are processed by the person (Mischel, 1973). Accordingly, various situational variables provide the examinee with information which influences personality variables, thereby affecting cognitive and affective reactions. Test situations would affect test behavior and affective reactions insofar as they influence such personality variables as the individual's encoding of evaluative information, expectancies about success on the exam, or the subjective value of success/failure.

The present chapter sets out to survey salient subjective determinants shaping test anxiety. This chapter begins by surveying the role of cognitive processes and structures (appraisals, schemata) in test anxiety, moves on to discuss the role of self-related cognitions, and concludes with a discussion of major belief systems (valence, expectancies, attributions) instrumental in shaping test-anxious reactions to evaluative settings. The focus on cognitive factors in this chapter as key determinants of test anxiety reflects the current interest in cognition in personality psychology, in general, and stress and anxiety research, in particular. Thus, I draw heavily from transactional, interactional, and social-cognitive research, which has made considerable strides in uncovering the subjective and personal nature of the test anxiety response. In keeping with current social-cognitive conceptualizations of test anxiety, I view individuals as actively searching for meaning in their environment and attending to events selectively through existing schemata, appraisals, attributions, expectancies, and beliefs.

Cognitive Processes and Structures

Cognitive Appraisals

A major contribution to our understanding of the important role of cognitive variables in stress and emotional reactions comes from the work of Richard Lazarus and his coworkers at Berkeley, who developed the transactional model of stress (R. S. Lazarus & Folkman, 1984). The transactional model views the individual as a participant in an ongoing person–environment relationship. A basic assumption of the model is that a person is an evaluating organism who constantly evaluates the relevance and significance of environmental cues and demands on their well-being. The model further emphasizes the mediating role of appraisals in linking stressful demands to the emotional responses of the individual, with cognitive appraisal posited as an integral feature of all emotional states (R. S. Lazarus, 1991a, 1991b, 1991c, 1993a; R. S. Lazarus & Folkman, 1984). Under the assumption that some cognitive processing of the meaning of an encounter takes place before an emotional reaction is triggered, examinees' anxiety reactions in evaluative settings should be dependent, in part, on the *appraisals* of the test situation as ego-threatening and as taxing one's coping resources.

Lazarus has chosen the term *appraisal* to describe the cognitive process of apprehending and interpreting that mediates between the environment and the individual's emotional reaction. Thus, when encountering an exam situation, such as a final exam in biology, the exam context can be appraised as either challenging or threatening (and possibly harmful). Two major appraisal processes, *primary* and *secondary* appraisal, respectively, converge to determine whether the person–environment transaction is regarded as significant for well-being, and if so, what can be done to cope with the situation.

Primary appraisal is the process of perceiving and evaluating an event or situation as involving threat, challenge, harm, or benefit to oneself. It refers to the judgment that a particular situation is relevant or irrelevant to one's needs and desires or that it will either have a beneficial or a harmful outcome. In the process of primary appraisal, a person assesses and interprets transactions in terms of their importance for well-being, by comparing the model of the situation ("What is at stake") with the model of the subjective self ("What are my coping options?"). Those events classified by the individual as stressful may be further subdivided into the categories of *challenge*, *threat*, or *harm/loss*.

A situation is appraised as *challenging* when it mobilizes activity and involvement that may lead to one's self-improvement, with the person hopeful, eager, and confident to meet the demands of the task. Thus, in appraising an exam situation as challenging, an examinee may see the opportunity for mastery and personal growth in preparing for and succeeding on an exam covering complex subject matter. By contrast, an exam situation is appraised as a *threat* when individuals perceive themselves to be in danger, anticipating failure, harm to self-esteem, or loss. In the case of *harm/loss* appraisals in an evaluative situation, some harm or loss is perceived to already have occurred to the person. The appraised damage can include the injury to important personal goals (e.g., rejection of an important doctoral dissertation research proposal), injury inflicted to one's self-worth (e.g., receiving a lower score than expected on the college admissions Scholastic Aptitude Test), failure (e.g., flunking a major exam or course), or injury to social standing (e.g., not being invited to a departmental social function). When loss appraisals occur, individuals often become overwhelmed by feelings of hopelessness and surrender their pursuit of academic goals.

Secondary appraisal is a judgment about the forms of coping available for mastering anticipated harm or for facilitating potential benefits. It involves the process of bringing to mind a variety of potential responses to those situations appraised to be threatening or challenging. As part of the appraisal process, individuals evaluate their cognitive, social, physical, spiritual, emotional, and material resources in order to readapt to the situation. Thus, secondary appraisals in an exam situation would include context-specific judgments such as how difficult the exam is expected to be, whether or not anything can be done to prevent failure and improve one's prospects for success on the exam, how much control one has over the outcomes, and the like (Folkman & Lazarus, 1985). Further, secondary appraisal involves examinee's evaluation of the particular stakes in the exam situation (R. S. Lazarus & Folkman, 1984). Among the many reasons why students may find an exam to be stressful are failure to achieve the expected grade, appearing incompetent to others, losing the approval of someone important such as parent, friend, or instructor, potential monetary loss (e.g., tuition stipend), and the like.

Reappraisal, an additional form of appraisal identified by the model, involves changed evaluations based on new cues, feedback from one's responses (or the effects of the response), or further reflection about the evidence on which the appraisal was based. For example, an examinee who was very anxious at the beginning of an exam may calm down toward the middle of an exam after reappraising the exam questions as being relatively easy.

Primary and secondary appraisal processes would be expected to operate inter-dependently. For example, if in the course of secondary appraisal a student judges her or his cognitive coping resources to be adequate for dealing with a threatening midterm college exam, the degree of threat, as assessed during primary appraisal, would be diminished. On the other hand, a stressful evaluative encounter that at first might seem nonthreatening can become threatening if coping resources turn out to be inadequate for countering exam demands or overcoming situational and personal constraints.

The transactional model posits that the quality and intensity of most emotions in a potentially stressful situation are generated by the appraisal process. Furthermore, since cognitive appraisal mediates between the situation and the emotional response, most emotions must be understood in terms of a particular kind of cognitive inter-pretation and appraisal. Thus, in a demanding exam situation, a person might experi-ence anxiety, anger, or relief, depending on the nature of the encounter and its appraisal (Folkman & Lazarus, 1985; R. S. Lazarus, 1991b). According to Lazarus' conceptualizations (R. S. Lazarus & Folkman, 1984; R. S. Lazarus, 1991a, 1991b, 1991c), threat and challenge are construed as *anticipatory appraisals*, which evaluate the potential harm or benefit in an upcoming event and elicit anticipatory emotions (e.g., threat, hope). By contrast, harm and benefit appraisals are viewed as *outcome appraisals*, potentially evoking outcome emotions (e.g., shame, gratitude). Note that there is no fixed time for primary and secondary appraisal and they are not strictly linear; rather, they interact and change continuously during the coping process. Furthermore, a person may experience various appraisals and consequent related emotions at the same time. As the person's appraisal of a stressful encounter changes, so, too, will the associated emotions experienced by that person (R. S. Lazarus & Folkman, 1984).

The transactional perspective would predict that individuals high and low in test anxiety would differ considerably in their appraisals of evaluative situations (trait test anxiety → appraisal → state test anxiety). Persons low in test anxiety would tend to view evaluative situations, and the arousal they experience in such situations, more as a challenge than a threat. Consequently, they would be expected to attend to the task rather than to themselves. In contrast, high-test-anxious individuals, being typically preoccupied with self-derogatory thoughts, negatively perceived emotional arousal, anticipation of negative evaluation or failure, and a low sense of efficacy, would experience test situations more as a threat than as a challenge. Differing kinds of appraisals may also lead to a different set of actions and emotions. Accordingly, perceiving an event or situation as challenging tends to evoke instrumental activities designed to handle the problem; appraising an event as a threat tends to evoke anxious arousal; appraising incurred harm or loss tends to evoke anger, sadness, or feelings of helplessness (Folkman & Lazarus, 1985; Carver & Scheier, 1984).

Meichenbaum (1976) proposed that differential styles of appraisal may be evident for high- and low-test-anxious individuals. Consider an exam situation in which some students hand in their exams early. For the high-test-anxious individual this event elicits worrying-type self-statements, namely, "I can't get this problem. I'll never finish. How can that guy have finished already?" resulting in increased anxiety and further task-irrelevant and self-defeating thoughts. In comparison, the low-test-anxious student may readily dismiss the other students' performance by saying to himself, "Those guys who handed in their papers early must know very little. I hope they score this exam on a curve" (Meichenbaum, 1976).

Evaluative Threat Structures and Schemata

According to social-cognitive conceptualizations, cognitive *structures* refer to the assumptions, beliefs, commitments, and meaning systems that influence the way the person construes his or her surroundings. They are the "core organizing principles" that influence what a person attends to, how information is organized and structured, and what meaning is attached to particular informational elements (Meichenbaum, 1976, 1977, 1985; Meichenbaum & Butler, 1980). Cognitive structures function to set behavior in motion, to guide the choice and direction of particular sequences of thought, feeling, and action, and to determine their continuation, interruption, or change of direction. Cognitive structures, in a sense, control the "scripts" for internal dialogue, feelings, and behavior (Meichenbaum & Deffenbacher, 1988). Although cognitive structures are generally adaptive, the structures of individuals suffering from test anxiety tend to focus on one or a few major personal themes such as personal endangerment in evaluative situations, loss of control, or fear of failure and consequent rejection.

Cognitive *processes* refer to the ways individuals process information. This involves the selective attending to, appraisal, interpretation, and retrieval of information. Cognitive processes tend to operate at an automatic "unconscious" level, to shape appraisals in a mood-congruent fashion (Bower, 1981), and to contain a confirmatory bias through which information is selected and processed to be congruent with present and prior experience. People selectively perceive, remember, and interpret experiences so as to filter out information that disconfirms their cognitive set and experience (Meichenbaum & Deffenbacher, 1988). For example, under stressful evaluative circumstances, the test-anxious person is likely to call forth many similar examples of panic and failure from the past and take them as being representative of a class of "test failures due to anxiety," often filtering out more positive experiences and successes (Meichenbaum & Deffenbacher, 1988).

A *schema* may be construed as a rather amorphous cognitive structure representing both knowledge and prior experience. Schemata guide information processing, influencing attentional, perceptual, memory, and comprehension processes. Threat schemata have been claimed to serve a major role in triggering anxiety reactions in stressful contexts. Accordingly, threat schemata influence cognitive functioning in high-test-anxious subjects by directing processing resources to those aspects of the external or internal environment which are congruent with them (i.e., those that present a psychological threat to self-esteem or threat of failure; M. W. Eysenck, 1992).

High levels of test anxiety are claimed to be associated with a mode of processing that serves to increase the intake of threatening information from evaluative environments, with test-anxious individuals attempting to maximize the probability of threat detection by allocating a disproportionate amount of resources to threat stimuli of an evaluative nature (Mathews, 1993; Mueller & Thompson, 1984). Accordingly, high-test-anxious subjects have been hypothesized to exhibit selective attentional bias favoring the processing of information that represents the threat of future failure in evaluative situations, whereas low-test-anxious subjects may not have this tendency (Mathews, 1993). This *interpretive bias* is dependent on the threat schemata or on the most congruent memories that are activated under test-anxious states (M. W. Eysenck, MacLeod, & Mathews, 1987). Due to their negative self-schema, high-test-anxious subjects tend to be biased in processing more self-detrimental than self-enhancing information in test situations and thus constantly perceive ego threat (R. Schwarzer, 1990).

Furthermore, *hypervigilence* has been claimed to be a crucial subjective ingredient in the test anxiety experience. Accordingly, individuals high on test anxiety are inclined to constantly scan the test environment in search of ambiguous stimuli that may serve as potential threats (M. W. Eysenck, 1992). Hypervigilence may be viewed as a type of bias at the level of attention or preattention. Anxious individuals attend vigilantly to anticipated aversive stimuli, scanning ambiguous stimuli in their surroundings in a broad fashion while no danger is identified, but turning to a narrow focus after they have detected a threatening stimulus (M. W. Eysenck, 1992). High-test-anxious subjects are highly distractible because they have to divert their attention to a variety of potential sources of harm. This selective attentional bias is seen as one reason for the performance deficits of anxious individuals (M. W. Eysenck, 1992).

It has further been suggested that test-anxious individuals may encode negative emotional aspects at an early attentional stage, but sometimes avoid additional elaborative processing of a threatening situation, such as a stressful exam, at a later stage. This combination of *vigilant* and *avoidant* processing might serve to maintain a high level of anxiety. Mueller (1992) suggests that the effort at threat detection may be followed by disengagement or by efforts to evade the event tagged as a threat, with the result that less-elaborative encoding occurs. Thus, early attentional bias will ensure that anxiety-prone individuals are constantly being reminded of possible danger, while attempting to avoid elaborations which are counterproductive. The view that test anxiety involves both vigilance and avoidance has received some support from recent experiments showing an interesting discrepancy: anxious subjects do not always show better recall for threatening information, despite their selective attention to it (Mathews, 1993).

Furthermore, memories of threatening events associated with anxiety are presumed to be organized and stored together in long-term memory (M. W. Eysenck,

1992). Accordingly, test-anxious individuals store their previous aversive experiences relating to evaluative situations in long-term memory, thus increasing their vulnerability and susceptibility to anxiety in these situations. For example, if a student fails on a series of important exams in math and physics in the last year of high school, this information is added to long-term memory and is expected to have an impact on the student's susceptibility to experience anxiety in future evaluative situations involving math and quantitative subjects when in college.

Bower's (1981) semantic network model offers a plausible account of the interpretive biases said to characterize high-test-anxious subjects. Accordingly, entering any particular affective state, such as state test anxiety, will tend to activate related or corresponding emotional nodes within the semantic network, most of which contain affect-congruent information. This activation will spread through these associative links to partially activate mood-congruent information (past failures, traumatic exam experiences, worries and concerns of academic competencies, etc.), which will thus be rendered more accessible for a range of subsequent processing operations. The induction of an anxious mood in an evaluative situation would render examples of negative events more accessible and therefore increase their perceived probability. Owing to the increased accessibility of ego-threatening information in high-test-anxious subjects, judgments of future risk across a wide range of evaluative events is also elevated. This would be expected, as risk will spread to other areas by the rich interconnections among threat schemata (Butler & Mathews, 1987). Thus, people high in trait test anxiety can retrieve more unpleasant memories and failure-related experiences surrounding testing. The negative material recalled by high-test-anxious examinees may influence and elevate estimates of the future likelihood of failure and the experience of negative affect across a wide range of evaluative contexts (Mathews, 1993). Individuals low in test anxiety will experience local rather than global elevations in subjective risk, because the spread to other areas is limited by the restricted extent of interconnections among threat schemata in memory.

The notion of threat schemata may help account for the performance decrements among high-test-anxious subjects. The proclivity among test-anxious-subjects to process selectively threatening information, such as those cues indicating personal inadequacies or poor performance, rather than task-relevant information may lead to performance decrements on tasks that require the efficient processing of emotionally neutral information (MacLeod & Mathews, 1988). Furthermore, in a real-life test situation anxious individuals have their attention caught by many inconsequential cues associated with perceived evaluative threat, while the same cues would be neglected by those who are less anxious (Mathews, 1993).

Further, anxious individuals often behave in ways that elicit reactions in others that confirm their expectations and solidify their cognitive structures and schemata. Such anxious individuals point to data that confirm their fears, often without recognizing how they unknowingly contributed to their own difficulties (Meichenbaum & Deffenbacher, 1988).

Empirical Research on Interpretive Bias and Threat Schemata

Although the findings are not entirely consistent, a number of studies have provided experimental support for the notion of negative threat schema in high-test-anxious individuals and for an interpretive bias in the processing of environmental stimuli. Calvo, Eysenck, and Estevez (1994) tested the interpretive bias hypothesis in a sample of 32 college students presented with ego-threat, physical threat, and nonthreat verbal stimuli. Test-anxious subjects were hypothesized to respond more accurately and faster to words representing ego-threat consequences, but slower on words representing nonthreat consequences. The data confirmed that when lexical decisions were primed by ambiguous sentences, test anxiety was associated with quicker decisions on ego-threatening words, thus confirming the predictable ego-threat consequences. Further evidence for interpretive bias in high-test-anxious subjects was provided by Mathews, Mogg, and May (1989). Subjects were asked to write down spellings of auditorily presented words, with some of the lexical stimuli being homophones, having both a threat-related and neutral interpretation (e.g., die–dye; pain–pane). A substantial correlation ($r = .49$) was reported between individual differences in test anxiety and the number of threatening interpretations of ambiguous stimuli. M. W. Eysenck et al. (1987) present additional evidence showing that high-test-anxious subjects show a tendency to interpret ambiguous stimuli in a threatening fashion.

A number of studies have tested the *specificity hypothesis* predicting that high-test-anxious subjects would show encoding and recall benefits for stimuli consistent with their negative self-schema. The rationale behind this hypothesis is that if negative schemata and traits indeed constitute a salient part of a high-test-anxious subject's personality and cognitive structure, the anxious subject should be able to make decisions more quickly about negative self-descriptive information he or she encounters. Overall, the evidence in support of this hypothesis, provided mainly by Mueller and his coworkers, has been mixed. Mueller and Thompson (1984) compiled a set of adjectives that describe subjects as either anxious (*anxious, defensive, emotional, insecure, preoccupied*, etc.) or nonanxious (*alert, bright, capable, versatile*, etc.), and then asked students to judge both lists in terms of self-descriptiveness (i.e., to what extent it is descriptive of themselves) or other descriptiveness (i.e., to what extent it is descriptive of "most students"). While failing to support the notion that high-test-anxious subjects show recall benefits for items consistent with their self-schema, the results do point to an apparent negative bias in the self-concept of anxious students, with the latter accepting more negative adjectives as self-descriptive.

Irrational Thought Patterns

Although the cognitive system is geared to the rapid detection of threat, with anxiety serving an adaptive purpose in this respect, the processes involved in threat detection are often used excessively among test-anxious subjects (M. W. Eysenck, 1992). Indeed, anxious persons, often guided by threat schemata and faulty thinking patterns, tend to exaggerate in their tendency to identify threat signals in their environment (Beck & Clark, 1991). Once schemata containing irrational thoughts become operative they can easily override rational thought processes and result in impaired thinking and decision making.

It should be stressed that individuals are unlikely to tell themselves various irrational things consciously or deliberately when they are confronted with evaluative situations. Rather, because of the habitual nature of one's expectations or beliefs, it is likely that such thinking processes become automatic and seemingly involuntary, like most overlearned sets (Meichenbaum, 1976). Such idiosyncratic cognitions (whether pictorial or verbal) are usually very rapid and often contain an elaborate idea compressed in a few seconds or less. These cognitions are experienced as though they were automatic and involuntary, and they usually possess the quality of appearing plausible (Meichenbaum, 1976).

Researchers (e.g., Beck, 1970) have attempted to identify and sort out the general types of faulty thinking patterns in anxious individuals. The literature on irrational thinking, focusing mainly on clinical populations (Meichenbaum, 1976), has uncovered some of the faulty kinds of thinking often reported in anxious (and depressed) subjects. I now present a number of salient characteristics of irrational thinking documented for clinical populations that may also underlie some of the maladaptive behaviors of high-test-anxious subjects in evaluative situations. The reader should keep in mind that the categories are presented for heuristic purposes and are in need of further empirical substantiation in high-test-anxious populations.

Irrational Thinking Categories

1. *Dichotomous reasoning* refers to the tendency to divide anything into opposites or to think solely in terms of extremes (black or white, good or bad). Thus, the test-anxious person may see things in absolute terms, as either pass or fail. This would be exemplified by remarks such as "Everything in this test situation is working against me," or "I'll never pass an exam in physics." Thus, for a test-anxious subject it is a matter of "passing" or "failing" with little differentiation in between these two extreme poles.

2. *Overgeneralization* is the tendency to make far-reaching conclusions on the basis of little data. Consider, for example, the examinee who makes the unjustified generalization that, "I'll never succeed in any major having to do with math," on the basis of a single failure on a pop quiz in basic college algebra.

3. *Magnification* refers to the tendency to view things as being more important, fearful, or catastrophic than they actually are. Thus, an examinee, for example, may exaggerate the meaning or significance of a particular evaluative encounter, such as interpreting his or her unpleasant sensation or body pain as a sign of a fatal disease. *Minimization*, the other side of the cognitive coin, involves the tendency to belittle

the value of positive experiences and feedback. Thus, the examinee who does really well on a major exam will say, "This really does not count much toward my final grade," or, "Anyone could have done as well on such an easy test."

4. *Arbitrary inference* refers to the process of drawing conclusions when sufficient evidence is lacking or actually contrary to conclusions. For example, an examiner observed staring at the examinee's test paper may be inferred by the examinee as "being out to get me."

Self-Related Thinking

Self-Related Thoughts

Understanding the role of self-related cognitions in test anxiety has been a major research concern since the introduction of the Worry/Emotionality distinction by Liebert and Morris (1967). Current cognitive perspectives view negative self-related cognitions as key precursors (and at the same time components) of the test anxiety experience (R. Schwarzer, 1990). Self-related thoughts surrounding evaluative situations may focus on a wide variety of contents, such as threatening demands and potential dangers in the test situation, personal shortcomings and inadequacies, and coping deficiencies.

A substantial body of empirical evidence suggests that in both actual and analog test situations anxious persons report a greater tendency to focus on negative self-related thoughts than their low-test-anxious counterparts. Thus, test-anxious individuals have been typically described as being negatively "self-focused" or "self-preoccupied," and report a greater incidence of non-task-related thoughts than low-test-anxious persons (I. G. Sarason & Stoops, 1978). In fact, the cognitive component of test anxiety, i.e., Worry, may be viewed as an index of self-preoccupation or self-related thinking (Wine, 1982).

Kendall and Hollon (1981a, 1981b) describe a specific model that can help explain how the same cognitions and self-statements in test-anxious subjects may achieve different emotional and behavioral effects, depending on the examinee's subjective interpretation associated with these thoughts. For example, the statement, "This test problem is very difficult to solve," could increase or decrease persistence on the task depending on whether the subjective meaning associated with the thought reflects the belief that (a) the task is of major importance for the individual and (b) he or she possesses a competence to master the task. An examinee who espouses the latter belief (b) would probably show more persistence than one who does not. This claim is supported by research indicating that differences in competence beliefs are significantly associated with differences in subjects' interpretations of their covert thoughts during testing (Bruch, Kaflowitz, & Kuethe, 1986). Thus, regardless of the proportion of negative thoughts entertained by an examinee, high-competence-belief subjects are less likely to regard their thoughts as having an adverse effect on their test-taking behaviors.

Self-Consciousness and Self-Focus

Evaluative anxiety (or ego-defensive reactions to it) may arise from motives to protect self-esteem, social esteem, or both. Thus, the critical distinction made by A. H. Buss (1980) between *private* versus *public* self-consciousness has important implications for the understanding of the cognitive antecedents of test anxiety. Private self-consciousness refers to inner-directed attention, being present when persons tend to look into themselves, investigate their feelings and attitudes, and ruminate about their identity. Public self-awareness, by contrast, refers to outer-directed attention, i.e., how the individual appears to others. Thus, public self-awareness occurs mainly when persons tend to feel they are being scrutinized or evaluated by others, which, in turn, leads to a preoccupation with one's own public image. Private and public self-consciousness, respectively, are based on the distinction between two different norms of reference—individualistic and social. Whereas individualistic norms are self-determined, personal, and private, social norms are other-determined, social, and public. These two reference norms can play different roles in the self-evaluation process, and have the potential of shaping the content of cognitions in test-anxious persons.

There is growing agreement that both public and private self-processes are involved in anxious behavior in social-evaluative situations (Buss, 1980, 1986). Accordingly, one's public self is sensitive to the evaluation of others and attempts to maintain increased social esteem, whereas the private self monitors the individual's internal standards and attempts to protect self-esteem (Leary, Barnes, Griebel, Mason, & McCormack, 1987). Thus, people may worry about evaluation and test situations either because of the potential impact of these situations on how they see themselves (private self-consciousness) or because it might affect how they believe others view them (public self-consciousness). Private self-consciousness would be reflected in thoughts such as, "If I do poorly I won't be able to face myself," whereas public self-consciousness would be reflected in thoughts such as, "I hope I don't appear stupid to the examiner."

Overall, current research supports the claim that public self-consciousness is meaningfully associated with test anxiety (R. Schwarzer & Jerusalem, 1992). Mueller and Thompson (1984) reported that whereas high- and low-test-anxious groups were not reliably differentiated by private self-consciousness, they were differentiated by public self-consciousness. Furthermore, in their study, test anxiety correlated significantly, though modestly ($r = .20$), with public self-consciousness and with social anxiety ($r = .30$). R. Schwarzer and Jerusalem (1992) report that public self-consciousness correlates strongly (in the .50s) with test anxiety, especially with its cognitive component, Worry. Kurosawa and Harackiewicz (1995) recently demonstrated that situations that are designed to create self-awareness cause test-anxious persons to perform more poorly on a series of word puzzles. In particular, an experimental situation where participants were told they would be observed with a TV camera (thus increasing public self-awareness) was found to be extremely detrimental to the performance of high-test-anxious participants.

Furthermore, the distinction between private and public self-consciousness is based on the assumption that the possibility of receiving negative information about oneself often results in apprehension and anxiety whether or not anyone else is privy to it. Likewise, the possibility of making an unfavorable impression on others produces apprehension even when the individual would never learn the quality of the impression he or she created. An interesting experimental study by Leary et al. (1987) showed that a potential threat to social esteem increased apprehensive cognitions even when there was no self-threat. Similarly, a threat to self-esteem increased apprehensive thoughts even when there was no threat to social esteem. The combined social and self-threats did not increase the number of apprehensive thoughts beyond that. Overall, the impact of conjoint self- and social esteem threats were found to be no greater than the impact of either alone.

Furthermore, it has been claimed that self-consciousness and self-focus may differentially influence the performance of high- and low-test-anxious subjects (Carver et al., 1983). Thus, self-focus may affect high-test-anxious subjects by inducing subjects to withdraw from a task, whereas low-test-anxious subjects are motivated to greater persistence by heightened self-awareness. Figure 8.1, based on experimental data presented by Carver et al. (1983), depicts the performance of high- and low-test-anxious college students on a difficult anagram task under high- and low-self-consciousness conditions. High-test-anxious subjects do considerably worse under high–compared to low-self-consciousness conditions, whereas the performance of low-test-anxious subjects is not reliably differentiated under self-consciousness conditions. Self-focusing may have debilitating effects on performance not only because individuals are unable to devote adequate attention to the task, but because they focus on their own negative character, thus engendering even more anxiety. Furthermore, research suggests that it is not the sheer frequency of negative thoughts which affects performance, but rather the meaning of thoughts (e.g., coping with negative thoughts or being overwhelmed by them), which is reflective of underlying processes.

Self-focusing might be a problem mainly when the material being processed is not relevant to self-attention. However, when self-comparisons are intrinsic to the task, anxious subjects might reap the benefits of integrating input via the self-schema, to at least the same extent, as less anxious students. Thus, the regularly observed retention deficits in test-anxious subjects may be due in part to the nonpersonal content of most memory tasks. Assuming that test-anxious individuals are attending to personal states to a greater extent than are low-test-anxious persons suggests that when the task actually requires self-focusing, spontaneous self-attention might even become an asset (Lang, Mueller, & Nelson, 1983; cf. Mueller & Courtois, 1980). As

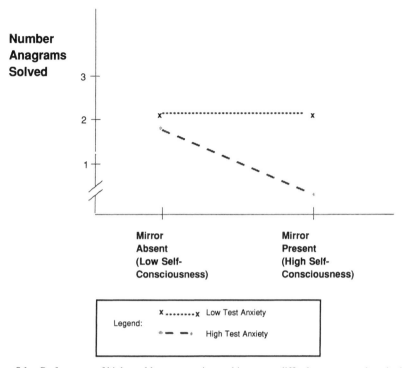

Figure 8.1. Performance of high- and low-test-anxious subjects on a difficult anagram task under high and low self-consciousness conditions. Adapted from Carver et al. (1983).

pointed out by R. Schwarzer (1990), it is clear that self-focusing frequently occurs during evaluating testing situations, but the extent to which it is a separate reaction is still at issue, as is the extent to which it is an antecedent causal agent or a noncausal correlated phenomenon of test anxiety (R. Schwarzer, 1990).

Belief Systems

Task Valence and Expectancy Beliefs

Individual differences in the perceived importance one attaches to success or failure on a cognitive task, along with self-beliefs about one's ability to perform the task, are viewed as critical components of student motivation, potentially affecting student anxiety and performance in achievement situations (Pintrich, 1989). It is commonly held that the threat of a stressful encounter, such as an important test situation, does not reside within the actual situation. Instead, threat would be cognitively mediated by beliefs and expectancies about future harm resulting from inadequate test performance and perceived valences of failure (R. S. Lazarus & Folkman, 1984). Thus, an examinee would be assumed not to react to the concrete test situation, but to a vague, more uncertain, future danger related to the evaluative situation that threatens her or his psychological well-being.

Task Value and Importance

A basic tenet of transactional theory is that stress and anxiety are determined in part by people's goals, values, and belief systems (R. S. Lazarus & Folkman, 1984). Presumably, the greater the subjective importance or value attached to a test, the greater the potential for anxiety in the test situation (Pekrun, 1984, 1985). Value beliefs with respect to test situations would include the examinee's perception of the importance of the test, the utility value of the test for future goals (e.g., career placement, social status, attractiveness to opposite sex), and perhaps also the intrinsic value of the interest in the task. Thus, the perception of the importance of a test has been claimed to serve as a modulating variable: it elevates test anxiety as the perception of the importance of the test increases (Meinke & Zimmer, 1990).

The perceived importance an examinee attaches to a test may vary by goal orientation, with goals conceptualized as cognitive representations of the different purposes people may adopt in different situations (Pintrich & Garcia, 1993). Because the interruption of a behavioral plan or frustration of major personal goals causes stress, the stronger the motive that is endangered by the interruption of personal goals, or the more central the plan is to the individual, the greater is the potential for stress (Phillips et al., 1972). Thus, students may be distinguished by the differing reasons they have for engaging in an evaluative task. This would include different goal orientations, such as intrinsic orientation (e.g., focus on mastery of the material covered by the test, or solving complex test problems) and extrinsic goal orientations (e.g., focus on getting good grades or impressing authority figures).

Performance Expectancy

Current thinking further suggests that anxiety in evaluative contexts is determined in part by expectancies of a negative future event (i.e., test failure) along with the amount of threat implied by the event. In fact, test anxiety has been conceptualized as the expectation of negative consequences following failure (Krohne, Schumacher, & Neumann, 1989). Thus, high-test-anxious subjects are frequently characterized by increased anticipation of not meeting the requirements of the test situation, by expecting negative consequences in the event of failure, and by a low competence expectancy to cope with the evaluative stress of the situation. The expectancy of success has implications for a student's affective reactions, motivation, and performance. If one regards the chances of failure to be very high, as test-anxious subjects often do, this may often lead to a low investment in effort (Covington & Omelich, 1981).

Expectancy models (Magnusson & Stattin, 1981; Pekrun, 1985) postulate that anxiety-inducing expectancy cognitions are influenced by both the objective properties of the external test environment (e.g., task difficulty, time to complete task, adequacy of preparation, etc.) as well as by the subjective characteristics of the individual who experiences the situation. These subjective characteristics would include such individual differences in beliefs and expectancy schemata as probability of failure, level of aspiration, perceived task importance, etc. (Pekrun, 1985). The *strength* of the anxiety response, it is claimed, depends on three major belief factors: (a) the "negative valence" or amount of threat implied by the event (e.g., "If I don't pull an A on this exam I'll never get into the doctoral program in clinical psychology"); (b) the subjective probability of the anticipated event (e.g., "My chances of failing on this biology exam are about 8 out of 10"), and (c) the perceived possibilities to prevent the event (e.g., "Even if I study hard, there is no way I'll pass the exam"). Past contacts with the test situation are transformed into expectancies of subsequent aversive outcomes (e.g., exam failure in the past → high failure expectancies → test anxiety).

Work by Carver and Scheier (1986) suggests that failure expectancies may modulate the effects of anxiety on performance. Accordingly, as tension and frustration mount surrounding the examination, and efforts toward the task are interrupted, test-anxious students self-reflect and assess outcome expectancies. If *failure expectancies* are high, individuals experience an impetus to withdraw and disengage from the task. They also neglect task-relevant cues and increase their self-deprecatory rumination. By contrast, if *success expectancies* are high, this may lead to an increased effort and task engagement. Thus, people who expect good outcomes, even when stressed, keep trying to stay in a mode of active task engagement and attempt to attain their goals. This is true of people high in test anxiety as well, provided they have favorable expectancies.

A number of factors, such as the degree of certainty of the expectancy judgment, the perceived difficulty of the task, and self-judgments of competency, may modulate the effects of performance expectancies on test anxiety. Accordingly, two people may have equally high or low expectancies, but attach different degrees of certainty to their judgments, and thus experience differing amounts of worry about the situation (L. W. Morris & Fulmer, 1976). Furthermore, when confronted with a difficult task, expectations decrease, causing worry to rise. In addition, not only do high-test-anxious subjects have lower expectancies for academic performance, but they also evaluate their academic competence as being low compared to their low-test-anxious counterparts (Arkin, Detchon, & Maruyama, 1982). Because students tend to be well aware of their academic abilities and compare their performance with that of their peers, a person's self-perceptions of ability along with their perceived individual rank in the achievement distribution should be closely related to test anxiety.

Empirical Evidence

A body of data attests to the claim that high- and low-test-anxious subjects differ in their self-expectancies of test performance. Thus, Pekrun (1985) provides data in support of a central assumption of the expectancy value perspective on anxiety, i.e., that anxiety depends on both expectancies and values of negative events. Test anxiety was shown to correlate meaningfully with both future expectancy of failure ($r = .39$) as well as the valence of failure ($r = .48$) in a sample of 798 sixth grade students in Germany. Furthermore, a path analysis showed that both failure-related expectancy and valence beliefs bear a direct and independent effect on anxiety, with both variables evidencing fairly equal effect sizes on state anxiety. These data would suggest that high-test-anxious students have higher failure expectancies and attribute more importance to failure than do their low-test-anxious counterparts. A study by Pekrun (1984) also reported a high correlation ($r = .52$) between test anxiety and the perceived importance (valence) of test failure among college students. Furthermore, a global measure of expectancy belief, indexed by the product of the expectancy of failure and the valence of failure on an exam, correlated even more impressively with test anxiety ($r = .64$). More recently, S. H. Spence, Duric, and Roeder (1996) reported that as a group, test-anxious students expect to perform less well, actually perform at a lower level, and then evaluate themselves less satisfactorily than do their non-test-anxious peers. However, like their nonanxious peers, test-anxious students show overoptimistic expectancies regarding future performance.

Research evidence (Doctor & Altman, 1969; Liebert & Morris, 1967; L. W. Morris & Liebert, 1970; Pekrun, 1984) concurs that the Worry, rather than the Emotionality component varies in test situations as a function of examinee expectations concerning test performance. Furthermore, changes in Worry scores are shown to be dependent on both performance expectancies as well as feedback about one's performance on the test, which, in turn, impacts upon expectancies. Thus, Worry scores have been observed to vary from the preexamination to the postexamination period as an inverse function of performance expectancy (L. W. Morris & Fulmer, 1976). Emotionality scores, by contrast, are reported to decrease gradually and systematically from preexamination to postexamination (C. A. Smith & Morris, 1976) regardless of expectancy changes (Spiegler et al., 1968).

Attributional Styles

Attributional style refers to the nature of causal explanations individuals provide for outcomes, experiences, or events in an attempt to understand their environment (Garcia & Pintrich, 1994). Four causal dimensions underlying attributions have gained wide currency, i.e., locus of causality, stability, globality, and controllability. Locus of causality refers to whether the cause is seen as internal or external to the person. Stability refers to the static nature of the cause, whether it is viewed to be transient or chronic. Globality relates to the omnipresence of the cause, whether it is delimited to a particular situation or pervasive to many situations. Controllability refers to the degree of control one has over the assumed cause of an outcome or event. A well-known attributional model proposed by Weiner and his coworkers (Weiner, Frieze, Kukla, Reed, Rest, & Rosenbaum, 1972) specifies four causal factors, i.e., ability, effort, task difficulty, and luck, defined jointly by the dimensions of locus of causality and stability. Ability and effort are viewed as internal determinants of performance, whereas task difficulty and luck are external determinants. Furthermore, luck and effort are classified as unstable factors, whereas task difficulty and ability are viewed as relatively stable ones.

Research suggests that different types of attributions are related to different affective, cognitive, and motivational effects (Weiner, 1985). Thus, an attribution of lack of effort (internal/unstable) to a failure outcome is shown to be related to a less negative affective response, higher expectations, and increased future levels of persistence than an attribution to low ability (internal/stable), which is related to depressive affect, lower expectancies, and future levels of persistence (Dweck & Elliott, 1983). Furthermore, M. W. Eysenck (1982) reviews studies showing that when failure is attributed to a stable factor, such as lack of ability, there is a much greater decline in the subjective probability of success on the task than when failure is ascribed to a "variable" factor, such as luck or effort. Since internal attributions are relatively unchanging factors, failure is seen as being predictive of subsequent failure. The joint influence of affect and expectancy, shaped by locus of causality and stability attributions, respectively, may affect motivation, which, in turn, determines behavioral outcomes.

Attribution of failure to internal factors, such as ability, are likely to be characterized by stronger affective reactions and a greater loss of self-esteem than attribution of failure to external factors, such as task difficulty. Likewise, attribution of failure to stable factors is expected to produce deficits of greater chronicity than attribution to unstable factors. Finally, deficits attributed to global factors are predicted to generalize further than those attributed to specific factors. Part of the reason why high-test-anxious individuals may show heightened state anxiety relative to low-test-anxious individuals after experiencing failure in evaluative situations is that they are more inclined to feel personally responsible for the failure. Thus, when anxiety is viewed as a threat to self-worth or as a potential failure of self, personal responsibility for one's actions and outcomes is implied. If one does not believe that personal ability and effort might influence outcomes, there is really no threat to self-worth. Furthermore, a generalized unfavorable attributional style will be reflected in a negative self-concept about one's own resources, which might be related to the tendency to perceive oneself as overtaxed. Over time, this may lead to the development of trait test anxiety (Leppin, Schwarzer, Belz, & Jerusalem, 1987).

It has been further suggested that causal attributions are related to the degree of effort an individual is willing to exert in order to succeed on a task, which, in turn, mediates the effects of attributions on test performance (test anxiety $\rightarrow$ causal attributions → motivation → effort → performance). Because low-test-anxious individuals are said to generally ascribe failure to lack of effort—which they believe to be modifiable—they are claimed to marshal greater efforts and also perform better. By contrast, high-test-anxious subjects who believe that their performance is attributable to low ability rather than low effort tend to perform most achievement tasks with relatively little vigor and do not persist in the face of failure. Their effort typically wanes and subsequent performance deteriorates (Boggiano & Ruble, 1986; Arkin & Haugtvedt, 1984). Subjects who attribute failure on academic tasks to global causes can expect the causes of failure to be present in other academic situations and thus expect failure across more dissimilar tasks than do those who attribute failure to specific causes. The transfer of this expectation of failure would, in turn, reduce motivation and reduce performance.

Overall, the attributional style of test-anxious people in case of failure is said to be internal, stable, and global; in case of success it is described as being unstable, external, and situation-specific. For nonanxious people, the opposite attributional style is hypothesized to hold. Although the ideal attributional profiles postulated for low- versus high-test-anxious persons have yet to be confirmed (R. Schwarzer, 1990), there is some convincing evidence in support of differences in specific attributional patterns by level of test anxiety, which I survey below. Table 8.1 summarizes the hypothesized attributional profiles of high- versus low-test-anxious individuals.

Empirical Evidence

I now survey some of the empirical evidence relating to the differential attributional provides of high- versus low-test-anxious individuals.

Internalization of Success in Low-Test-Anxious and Externalization of Success in High-Test-Anxious Subjects. A number of studies provide evidence in support of the notion that low-test-anxious subjects feel "personally responsible" for success (i.e., tend to provide internal attributions), but not for failure, whereas the opposite patterns hold for high-test-anxious subjects (M. W. Eysenck, 1982). Arkin, Detchon, and Maruyama (1981) reported that low-test-anxious students attributed their success

Table 8.1. Attributional Profile of High- versus Low-Test-Anxious Subjects

Attributional facet	Success		Failure	
	HTA	LTA	HTA	LTA
Locus	External	Internal	Internal	External
Stability	Unstable	Stable	Stable	Unstable
Globality	Specific	Global	Global	Specific

Note: HTA, High-test-anxious; LTA, low-test-anxious.

on an exam relatively more to ability and effort and relatively less to task difficulty and luck (and external factors, generally) than did high-test-anxious subjects. Successful students high in test anxiety attributed their performance to external factors (both task and luck), whereas low-test-anxious students attributed their successful performance more to themselves. A later study by Arkin and his coworkers (Arkin et al., 1982) reported that low-test-anxious subjects were far more internal concerning success on an anagram task than were high-test-anxious subjects (see also Arkin, Kolditz, & Kolditz, 1983). Hedl (1990) reported that low-test-anxious students tend to attribute success to positive characterological attributes (and effort) more so than do their high-test-anxious counterparts.

Internalization of Failure in High-Test-Anxious and Externalization of Failure in Low-Test-Anxious Subjects. In addition, a number of studies provide evidence for the hypothesis that high-test-anxious subjects attribute test failure primarily to themselves, whereas low-test-anxious subjects attribute failure to external factors or to internal, unstable, and uncontrollable factors. Early research by Weiner and Potepan (1970) suggested that high-anxiety subjects were more likely than low-anxiety subjects to attribute failure to low ability and less likely to attribute failure to lack of effort. By contrast, low-anxiety subjects were more inclined to ascribe success to ability and effort compared to high-anxiety subjects. Thus, test anxiety correlated positively ($r = .26$) with total internal failure attributions, while correlating inversely with internal ability success attributions ($r = -.31$) in a sample of 173 college students. Overall, success among male college students was found to be associated with self-attributions for success to effort and ability, and the belief that failure was not caused by lack of ability. The noted attributional pattern may make high-test-anxious subjects miserable because they feel responsible for failure, but not successes (M. W. Eysenck, 1982). A study by Leppin et al. (1987) provided further evidence for the internal failure attributions of high-test-anxious subjects. Students received fictitious success or failure feedback on their performance on a series of computer-administered tasks, and were asked to identify which possible factors might explain their achievement. High-test-anxious students tended to see ability as a more important factor when they failed than when they succeeded.

However, the hypothesized attributional profile of high- and low-test-anxious examinees is not consistently borne out by the data. Two studies by Arkin and his coworkers (Arkin et al., 1981, 1982) reported nonreliable differences in the ability attributions of high- and low-test-anxious students under failure conditions. In fact, high-test-anxious students were actually reported to attribute their unsuccessful performance more to task difficulty than were low-test-anxious subjects (Arkin et al., 1981). Similarly, Hedl (1990) found that the predominant *failure* attribution for high-test-anxious subjects was behavioral (i.e., lack of effort) and not characterological.

Globality Attributions. Some current research provides evidence in support of the claim that high-test-anxious subjects tend to generalize their *failures*, but view successes as being more specific. Hedl (1987) reported that test-anxious students made more specific success attributions, whereas the nonanxious tended to generalize their successes, suggesting that high- and low-test-anxious subjects are differentiated on the globality dimension. In a later study, Hedl (1990) administered a sentence memory task to 84 female undergraduates who were asked to assess the probability of success on the task and provide reasons for their performance. Consistent with prior results, high-test-anxious subjects viewed success as being less global. By the same token, Mikulincer and Nizan (1988) reported that students high in anxious worry and irrelevant thinking are characterized by more global attributions. However, the globality dimension has not consistently differentiated more- and less-test-anxious individuals (e.g., Arkin et al., 1983).

External Causal Orientations. Overall, a body of data supports the notion that test-anxious subjects tend to adopt more external locus of causality orientations than their low-test-anxious counterparts. Allen, Giat, and Cherney (1974) reported that external orientation was positively associated with state anxiety both during the first lecture class ($r = .31$) and during oral exam period ($r = .35$) in a sample of 101 psychology students. Hembree's (1988) meta-analytic results, based on 16 different studies, support the notion that high-test-anxious students are inclined to a more external locus of causality or control, with a modest mean correlation of .22 between anxiety and external locus of control.

Overall, current research would suggest that it may be too simple to see test-anxious subjects as endowed with a fixed attributional pattern which is invariably displayed in anxiety-arousing conditions. The anxiety–attribution connection may be conceptualized as a sort of transactional process, such as a feedback loop system developing over time. In an actual performance situation, the self-detrimental attributional style of high-test-anxious subjects, involving externalization of success and internalization of failures, might induce examinees to develop few positive outcome expectancies, to feel generally uncomfortable, and display elevated levels of state anxiety. High levels of anxiety, in turn, may lead to reduced perceptions of situational control and feelings of helplessness, which further strengthen maladaptive attributional styles. The causal attributional approach, while furthering our understanding of the reasons why performance under evaluative conditions increases anxiety, may be rather limited. As M. W. Eysenck (1982) pointed out, the attributional approach ignores some of the major issues, such as: What determines the selection of a particular causal determinant of achievement behavior? Is it being test-anxious or is it the need for self-consistency? Or, how do attributions affect performance?

Summary

The research surveyed in this chapter demonstrates the crucial role of a variety of subjective factors, including cognitive factors, self-related thoughts, and belief systems, in shaping a person's reactions to stressful evaluative situations. Thus, current research implies that how one responds to stressful test situations is in large part influenced by cognitive schemata in long-term memory, primary and secondary appraisals of the specific stressor or evaluative context, and expectancy beliefs and attributions.

Overall, the empirical research reviewed in this chapter confirms that test-anxious individuals differ from their nonanxious counterparts in terms of an interpretive bias in processing ambiguous information in the external environment. Furthermore, high- and low-test-anxious individuals appear to differ considerably in their appraisals of evaluative situations, with high-test-anxious individuals experiencing test situations more as a threat than as a challenge. Research further supports the claim that the greater the subjective importance or value attached to a test, and the higher the estimated expectancy of failure on an exam, the greater the potential for anxiety in the test situation. High-test-anxious subjects are frequently characterized by high failure expectancies in test situations coupled with a low competence expectancy to cope with evaluative stress. Furthermore, the maladaptive attributional patterns of high-test-anxious examinees results in low perceived control over test outcomes and heightened feelings of helplessness. The current data would imply that a critical element in any intervention program aimed at ameliorating test anxiety would be in reshaping those negative schemata, self-perceptions, and maladaptive attributional patterns associated with test anxiety.

Clearly, a wide array of subjective factors shape a person's understanding of the evaluative situation, determining how information about the test and the test environment is attended to, stored, processed, and acted upon. Accordingly, in order to account adequately for the test anxiety experience we need to examine carefully both the parameters of the test and test environment as well as the individual's perceptions, cognitions, beliefs, and attributions surrounding the evaluative context. I underscore once again that personal and contextual variables should be viewed as being interdependent and inextricably intertwined. Any discussion of personal factors needs to consider objective factors in the test situation, whereas a discussion of situational factors also needs to relate to personal characteristics.

IV

Consequences of Test Anxiety for Cognitive Performance

Test Anxiety and Cognitive Performance

Overview

The potentially aversive impact of anxiety on performance is a factor to be reckoned with in virtually any domain in which individuals strive to do well (e.g., academic, social, sports) and when achievement goals are at stake (M. W. Eysenck, 1982; I. G. Sarason, 1980a). Aside from the negative emotional experience associated with test anxiety, high-test-anxious individuals are frequently reported to experience decrements in performance in evaluative situations. Although there may be more to anxiety and performance than interference effects, the presumption that test anxiety interferes with normal cognitive performance has been the cornerstone of many successive advances in our thinking about the dynamics of test anxiety (Covington, 1992). Less interest, however, has focused on possible feedback effects from performance outcomes to test anxiety (Hodapp et al., 1995).

This is the first of two consecutive chapters focusing on the complex pattern of relationship between test anxiety and performance. The present chapter sets out to evaluate current theory and research bearing on the nature of the anxiety–performance relationship, with special emphasis on potential moderating effects. I begin by presenting a number of basic conceptual distinctions crucial to an in-depth appreciation of the major issues at hand. I move on to summarize the major empirical findings and general trends in the research literature bearing on the magnitude and direction of the anxiety–performance relationship. The evidence for a number of commonly claimed moderating variables in the anxiety–performance relationship is then presented and evaluated.

Basic Concepts and Distinctions

I begin by presenting a number of basic conceptual distinctions and differentiations important for understanding some of the issues involved in unraveling the complex nexus of interrelationships between anxiety and performance.

Facilitating versus Debilitating Effects of Anxiety

Whereas research has focused primarily on the *negative* impact of test anxiety on academic performance, one line of research has realized that more is involved than a static correspondence between anxiety and performance. Not only does the relationship between anxiety and performance fail to reach significance on occasion, but it is sometimes reversed, with the presence of anxiety appearing to *stimulate* rather than inhibit performance (Alpert & Haber, 1960).

A useful distinction between the potential *facilitating* and *debilitating* aspects of test anxiety was proposed in the early 1960s by Alpert and Haber (1960). Accordingly, an individual may experience two qualitatively different types of anxiety or arousal states in a test situation. Facilitating anxiety ("Anxiety helps me do better during exams and tests") is claimed to enhance academic performance, whereas debilitating anxiety ("Anxiety interferes with my performance during exams and tests") is claimed to impede performance. According to the bidimensional perspective proposed by Alpert and Haber, facilitating and debilitating anxiety are viewed as being relatively independent anchor points on a continuum, and these two dimensions are assessed independently. Research shows that facilitating and debilitating facets of anxiety are inversely related and almost mirror images in their relation to performance (Hembree, 1988).

According to this bidimensional model, a person may possess a large amount of both types of anxieties; a large amount of one, but not of the other; or practically none of either. There is research evidence showing that students with high debilitating anxiety—at varying grade levels—do poorly in their studies, whereas those with high facilitative anxiety perform relatively well (Alpert & Haber, 1960; Desiderato & Koskinen, 1969; Munz, Costello, & Korabik, 1975). Research presented by Munz et al. (1975) further suggests that college undergraduates classified as "facilitators" obtained higher exam scores than those classified as "debilitators" and "non-effecteds."

A number of explanations have been offered to account for the differential effects (i.e., facilitating vs. debilitating) of anxiety on performance. S. B. Sarason et al. (1952) hypothesized that the arousal evoked in evaluative-situation anxiety will lead to poorer performance in individuals who have dominant task-irrelevant anxiety responses in their repertoire. However, for individuals who do not have such response tendencies, the same stimulus elements will raise their general drive level and motivation, resulting in improved performance. According to an alternative account, it is the interpretation and labeling of the anxious arousal that determines to what extent the effects will be facilitating or debilitating. Accordingly, feelings of arousal may actually occur in both high- and low-test-anxious subjects, but they may be interpreted differentially by different types of individuals or groups; this self-labeling of arousal as motivating or debilitating, respectively, may either facilitate or disturb behavior on cognitive tasks. A third account proposes that defensive reactions, such as cautiousness, mediate the effects of anxiety on performance. In problem-solving situations where such defensive reactions are an asset, anxiety has a facilitating effect on performance. In situations where such defensive situations are a liability, anxiety has an interfering effect upon performance (Ruebush, 1960).

Performance Efficiency versus Effectiveness

In examining the effects of test anxiety on test performance, it is useful to distinguish between a person's performance *effectiveness* and processing *efficiency*. Whereas effectiveness refers to the quality of cognitive performance (e.g., scoring 90 out of 100 points in a final algebra exam), efficiency refers to the amount of effort or processing resources invested (putting in maximal effort vs. moderate effort to reach a predesignated level of mastery or performance on an exam). This is operationalized through quality of performance relative to effort expended. Effort relates to the intensive component of attention, and effective attentional capacity fluctuates continuously as a function of the immediate processing demands. The relationship between these three concepts is represented in the following formula (H. J. Eysenck & Eysenck, 1985; M. W. Eysenck & Calvo, 1992):

$$\text{Efficiency} = \frac{\text{Effectiveness}}{\text{Effort}}$$

As an analogy, consider two identical cars being driven up a hill, only one with a trailer attached to it. Effectiveness is the speed at which each car is traveling, whereas effort corresponds to the extent to which the accelerator is depressed. If the car that has a heavy trailer attached to it (analogous to anxious task-irrelevant processing) proceeds more slowly than the other one with the identical use of the accelerator, the efficiency of that car suffers. However, while progress may be slowed by the trailer, sufficient use of the accelerator will compensate for this; even if traveling at the same speed, this does not mean that these two cars are functioning in the same way. Applied to test anxiety, this suggests that test-anxious individuals may perform as effectively as nonanxious individuals, but only at greater subjective cost to the system (M. W. Eysenck, 1983; H. J. Eysenck & Eysenck, 1985).

Although anxiety does sometimes affect performance effectiveness, its effects on efficiency are claimed to be stronger and more reliable (M. W. Eysenck, 1985). However, in order to compensate for the cognitive interference caused by worry, high-test-anxious subjects increase their efforts or invest extra attentional resources during the task. Indeed, there is research evidence that high-test-anxious subjects exert a greater effort in tasks they are performing than do low-test-anxious subjects (M. W. Eysenck, 1982). As a consequence, high-test-anxious persons may perform more or less at the same level as their low-test-anxious counterparts, but at the cost of greater expenditure in effort. The extent to which anxiety actually impairs performance quality depends largely on the extent to which anxious subjects attempt to compensate for this reduced effectiveness by means of an increase in mental effort. This explains the paradox that while anxiety seems to lead to much task-irrelevant processing, it nevertheless is sometimes associated with minimal impairment of performance or even enhancement of task performance. However, a problem with the processing efficiency notion is that "effort" is a slippery concept, which is quite difficult to operationalize. Thus, the actual evidence for higher effort in anxious subjects is questionable.

Linear versus Curvilinear Anxiety–Performance Relationship

Traditionally, the relationship between test anxiety and cognitive performance has been assumed to be monotonically negative or even linear. That is, as anxiety increases, performance is expected to decrease (L. W. Morris & Liebert, 1970). However, data from a number of laboratory experiments (e.g., Mandler & Sarason, 1952) suggest the possibility of a nonlinear relation between anxiety and performance. Figures 9.1a and 9.1b present graphic plots of linear and nonlinear anxiety–performance relationships, respectively.

The well known *Yerkes–Dodson law* stipulates an inverted U-shaped relationship between arousal and performance in learning situations (Yerkes & Dodson, 1908). Accordingly, the optimal level of motivation for effective performance lies in the middle range, rather than the high or low end of the arousal or stress continuum; drive levels above or below that optimal level will lead to less efficient performance. Furthermore, the peak of this inverted U-function is obtained at lower levels of stimulation for more complex types of learning. This is frequently taken as implying that at low levels of baseline arousal or anxiety, increases in arousal facilitate performance on easy tasks, but hinder performance on more complex tasks; at extremely high levels of arousal, performance on all types of tasks seems to be hindered. The law assumes that there is an optimal level of performance occurring at some moderate level of arousal; as tasks become more and more difficult, the optimal drive level becomes lower and lower.

The Yerkes–Dodson law has been criticized on a number of counts. To begin with, the law simply describes the nature of the anxiety–performance relationship, but fails to provide any explicit account of why arousal, task difficulty, and performance level should be related in the way they are (M. W. Eysenck, 1985). Furthermore, the evidence in favor of this law is contradictory, and few studies in the domain of test anxiety research have confirmed this relationship (Matthews, 1992; Gaudry & Spielberger, 1971). Only on occasion have studies reported curvilinear relationships between test anxiety and performance (M. W. Eysenck, 1982; Rocklin & Thompson, 1985; Mandler & Sarason, 1952). Recent critiques of traditional arousal theory claim to have found little trace of the postulated inverted U-curve relationship in research, and this law is currently rejected as a useful description of the anxiety–performance relationship (Matthews, 1992).

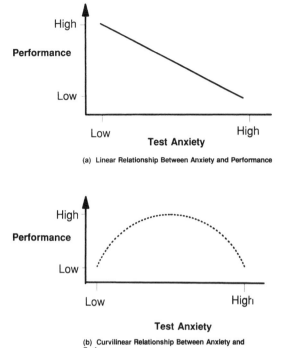

Figure 9.1. Plot of (a) linear and (b) curvilinear relationships between anxiety and test performance.

It is noted, however, that most studies of anxiety and academic performance have been designed in a way that precludes the demonstration of a curvilinear relation. Either these studies have relied on a linear correlation coefficient or they have compared two groups, one scoring above the median on a test anxiety measure and one scoring below. Our usual statistical techniques in examining the anxiety–performance relationship may be inadequate if we expect curvilinear relations (McKeachie, 1977).

Moderating versus Mediating Effects in the Anxiety–Performance Relationship

Aside from attempting to establish the nature of the anxiety–test performance relationship, researchers have addressed two important questions related to this relationship, namely (a) What are the factors that mediate the effects of anxiety on poor performance? (b) What are the personal and contextual factors which may moderate the anxiety–performance relationship? Thus, any discussion of the anxiety–

performance relationship needs to distinguish between two often-confused concepts relating to the functions of third variables in this relationship, namely, mediating versus moderating effects (Baron & Kenny, 1986).

Mediating Effects

The whole process by which anxiety serves to debilitate cognitive performance is highly complex, with a variety of factors possibly mediating the effects of anxiety on performance. These would include such factors as the perception of threat in the test situation, task frustration, expectancies and causal attributions of success and failure, effort, actual and perceived cognitive resources, and coping strategies.

Mediating effects, in our particular case, are typically causal mechanisms through which situational stress or trait anxiety bear an impact upon test performance. A *mediator* variable is a third variable in the relationship (e.g., diversion of attention), which represents the generative mechanism through which the focal independent variable, namely test anxiety, is able to influence the dependent variable of interest, namely task performance (e.g., test anxiety → diversion of attention → poor performance). Indeed, test anxiety may impact upon performance largely on an indirect basis, working through a host of cognitive, motivational, and affective factors. This underscores the limited value of earlier views of a static, "input–output" correspondence between individual differences and test performance. A given variable may be said to function as a mediator in our context to the extent that it accounts for the relation between test anxiety, as predictor, and some performance criterion. The mediating process is graphically presented in Figure 9.2.

A variable would function as a mediator in the anxiety–performance relationship when it meets the following conditions: (a) variations in levels of test anxiety significantly account for variations in the presumed mediator (i.e., path a), (b) variations in the mediator significantly account for variations in the performance variable (i.e., path b), and (c) when paths a and b are controlled, a previously significant relation between test anxiety and cognitive performance is no longer

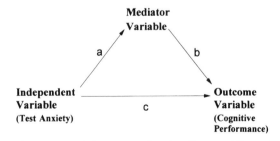

Figure 9.2. The mediating process. Based on Baron and Kenny (1986).

significant. Thus, perfect mediation holds if test anxiety has no effect on performance (path c = 0) when the mediator is controlled.

Moderating Effects

A *moderator* variable, by contrast, is one that differentially influences the magnitude or direction of the relationship between an independent variable (e.g., test anxiety) and a dependent variable (e.g., test performance), as a function of the particular level of the moderator level under consideration. In the context of research on the anxiety–performance relationship, a moderator variable, say test atmosphere, would be one that is observed to strengthen or weaken the association between anxiety and cognitive test performance as a function of the particular level of the moderator variable considered (e.g., *evaluative* vs. *gamelike*). Subjects tested under an evaluative atmosphere might show decrements in test performance due to test anxiety, whereas those tested under neutral conditions may show no similar decrements or even occasionally manifest enhanced performance. Theoretically, the same level of test anxiety can facilitate performance in one situation, but depress performance in another, depending on the particular configuration of personal and contextual variables in the test situation.

Whereas moderator variables specify when certain effects will hold, mediators speak to how or why such effects occur. Furthermore, in the mediator–predictor relation, test anxiety, as predictor variable, is causally antecedent to the mediator. By contrast, moderators and test anxiety, as predictor variable, are at the same level in regard to their role as causal variables antecedent or exogenous to performance effects. Moderator variables always function as independent variables, whereas mediating events shift roles from effects to causes, depending on the focus of the analysis. Figures 9.3A and 9.3B depict the differences between moderating and mediating effects, respectively, in the anxiety–performance association.

The primary test for the moderating effect of a third variable in the anxiety–performance relationship is a significant interaction between test anxiety and the hypothesized moderator variable as they jointly impact upon test performance. If the interaction is significant, it means that the effects of test anxiety on performance are determined to some extent by the experimental factor. If so, then one must inquire further as to its direction and magnitude. The most common statistical procedure used when the performance criterion (say Scholastic Aptitude Test performance) is continuous and both anxiety (e.g., high vs. low state anxiety) and the moderator variable (e.g., difficult vs. easy content) under investigation are dichotomized is a two-way analysis of variance, with test anxiety and the moderator variable as factors in the analysis. When appropriate data are available, the regression analysis is preferred to analysis of variance because it treats the predictor variable as well as the criterion as continuous.

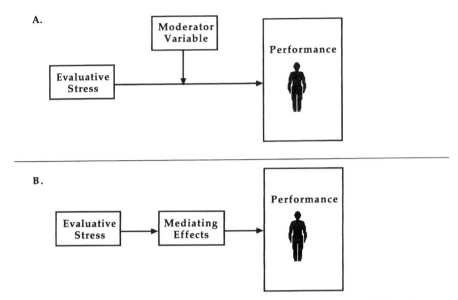

Figure 9.3. Moderating vs. mediating effects in the anxiety–performance relationship.

State versus Trait Anxiety Effects

A major conceptual weakness in the studies of anxiety and cognitive performance is the failure to distinguish between the impact of anxiety as a relatively stable individual difference variable and anxiety as a fluctuating emotional state (Heinrich & Spielberger, 1982). Indeed, there is evidence to suggest that trait-test-anxiety measures may be useful in predicting behavior only when some minimal state level of test anxiety is present in the test situation (Wittmaier, 1974). One methodological weakness evidence in test anxiety research is that arousal is often assessed using a measure of trait anxiety or anxiety-proneness rather than a state anxiety measure (Heinrich & Spielberger, 1982).

As pointed out by Hunsley (1985), in testing for the disrupting effects of test anxiety on performance, researchers have almost exclusively relied on dispositional measures. The explicit assumption is that a dispositional measure of test anxiety accurately reflects a subject's actual level of test anxiety during a particular exam. However, we need to remember that although dispositional variables, such as test anxiety are significantly related to experienced state anxiety (Paulman & Kennelly, 1984), the magnitude of the relation could vary depending on the situational context, thus altering the impact of test anxiety on performance. Furthermore, some of the inconsistency in the reported results in the literature may be due to the fact that different studies have used varying measures of test anxiety (state vs. trait).

Empirical Evidence for the Test Anxiety–Performance Relationship

A veritable flood of studies, beginning at the turn of the century, have demonstrated the existence of a negative relationship between level of anxiety and performance across a variety of testing and assessment conditions. Virtually hundreds of studies have investigated the complex pattern of relations between anxiety and different kinds of performances. Although the findings are sometimes contradictory, it has been repeatedly demonstrated that individuals who are high in test anxiety may experience decrements in performance in evaluative situations (Hembree, 1988; I. G. Sarason, 1980a; Tryon, 1980). Test anxiety has been demonstrated to have a cumulatively adverse effect on school performance throughout elementary school years (Hill & Sarason, 1966) and is often reported to be a major cause of failure in college (Spielberger, 1962; cf. Zeidner & Nevo, 1992).

Test anxiety has been found to interfere with performance both in laboratory settings (e.g., Deffenbacher, 1978; Nottelmann & Hill, 1977) as well as in true-to-life testing situations in school or college (e.g., Alpert & Haber, 1960; Zeidner & Nevo, 1992; Zeidner, Klingman, & Papko, 1988). The higher the reported test anxiety scores, the greater the problems reported in the processing of information (Tobias, 1986). Test and trait anxiety have been empirically linked with impaired performance in simple memory tasks, including digit span (Mueller, 1977), paired-associate learning (J. T. Spence & Spence, 1966), and free recall of word lists (Mueller, 1976). Test anxiety is associated with overall reduced processing on cognitive tasks (Mueller, 1980) and impairs performance on more complex tasks, such as analogical reasoning (Leon & Revelle, 1985). Further, performance decrements have been associated with both situational stress (M. W. Eysenck, 1982) and individual differences in trait anxiety (Mueller, 1977; Zatz & Chassin, 1985). However, despite such empirical demonstrations, there have been sufficient instances of nonconfirmation of predictions to suggest that more is involved than the static correspondence between anxiety, on one hand, and achievement outcomes, on the other.

This chapter will not even attempt to survey this vast body of literature in any detail. Instead, I report general trends in the literature based on meta-analytic research quantifying and summarizing the modal relations found in the empirical research literature. Meta-analysis essentially uses effect sizes (correlations, standardized mean differences, etc.) from primary studies and calculates the weighted means or population effect sizes of the indices garnered from the original studies. When heterogeneity in the effect size indices is detected, as is typically the case in the demonstrated empirical link between anxiety and performance (see below), a search for moderator factors is conducted. They key moderators identified in the literature are discussed later in the chapter.

Meta-Analytic Results

Hembree (1988) collected data dealing with the correlates, causes, effects, and treatments of test anxiety based on 562 North American studies appearing in a series of articles published from 1952 through 1986. The meta-analysis was based on a wide variety of performance measures, including IQ and aptitude test scores, laboratory memory and problem solving tasks, achievement measures, and grade point average. Hembree demonstrated that test anxiety correlated negatively, though modestly, with a wide array of conventional measures of school achievement and ability at both high school and college level. Data collected on students from upper elementary school level through high school show that test anxiety scores are significantly related to grades in mathematics ($r = -.22$), reading and English ($r = -.24$), natural sciences ($r = -.21$), social sciences ($r = -.25$), foreign language ($r = -.12$), and mechanical knowledge ($r = -.12$). Test anxiety correlated more weakly with cognitive test scores assessed in grades 1 and 2 of elementary school than in grades 3 to postsecondary level ($r = -.06$ vs. $-.29$).

Cognitive measures (i.e., aptitude and achievement measures combined) correlated more strongly with the Worry than the Emotionality component of test anxiety ($r = -.31$ vs $-.15$). Similarly, Worry was slightly more strongly correlated with course grades than was Emotionality ($r = -.26$ vs. $-.19$). Higher effects sizes were reported for low- than high-ability students and for tasks perceived as difficult than for those perceived as being easy. Furthermore, test anxiety correlated inversely with performance on laboratory cognitive tasks such as problem solving ($r = -.20$) and memory ($r = -.28$).

Seipp (1991) conducted a second meta-analysis of the literature based on 156 effect sizes appearing in 126 studies published between 1975 and 1988. This study, in contrast to Hembree's meta-analysis, focused on the relationship between anxiety and academic performance exclusive of IQ and elementary cognitive measures. In addition, it included European as well as North American research. The population effect size (i.e., weighted grand mean of all effect sizes) in the meta-analysis was found to be $-.21$, with a 95% credibility interval ranging from $-.36$ to $-.07$ (i.e., after elimination of sampling error, 95% of all effect sizes can be expected to range between $-.36$ and $-.07$). Furthermore, comparable effect sizes were found across gender and cultural groups and for state versus trait measures of anxiety.

Comparable to what was reported by Hembree, Seipp found that the relationship with performance was stronger for the Worry ($r = -.29$) than for the Emotionality ($r = -.15$) component of test anxiety. Thus, one rather firm generalization supported by the literature is that performance is impaired by the Worry component more so than the Emotionality component. Also, the relationship between anxiety and performance was enhanced when measures focused on evaluation threat (i.e., test anxiety measures) compared to general measures of anxiety, and when anxiety was measured after, compared to before, performance. R. Schwarzer (1990) used both Hembree's and Seipp's meta-analytic data bases to estimate the corresponding population effect size of the anxiety–performance relationship to be $r = -.21$. A measured correlation of $-.21$ suggests that anxiety accounts for about 4% of the performance variance in the population. In view of the modest mean correlation between anxiety and performance, researchers must at least entertain the thought that relating anxiety and achievement scores may not be worth the candle (Anderson & Sauser, 1995). However, meta-analytic interpretive procedures would suggest that the practical implications of the effects of anxiety on performance, although rather meager at first glance, are meaningful indeed. Thus, high-test-anxious subjects would be expected to score almost half a standard deviation below their low-test-anxious counterparts on a typical achievement scale. Furthermore, about two-thirds of the students in the low-test-anxious group are expected to score higher than those in the high-test-anxious group. If both anxiety and performance are simplified into dichotomies, only 39% of the low-test-anxious subjects are expected to fail, whereas 61% of the high-test-anxious subjects should fail (Seipp, 1991).

Methodological problems and a number of confounds in current research may lead to faulty estimation of the anxiety–performance relationship, and may also account for some of the reported inconsistency in the findings in this area. As discussed in Chapter 5, cognitive performance is often measured in an analog test situation that evokes only a modest amount of anxiety in the subjects. In artificial test situations anxiety levels may be too low to impair performance. Another confound may be ability. High-test-anxious examinees may simply be low-ability subjects who have learned to be anxious because of their experienced history of repeated failures. According to Rocklin (1985), it may not make much sense to control for intelligence in anxiety research (as a covariate), as it may be impossible to measure mental ability uncontaminated by the examinee's level of anxiety. Thus, independent measures of intelligence may in fact be measures of both anxiety and intelligence.

Furthermore, the effects of test anxiety in educational settings may differ with course content, the conditions of test examination, and the nature of the ability called for on the exam. Thus, the relationship between anxiety and performance may vary for different educational contexts. Further, since the effects of anxiety may differ for objective, multiple-choice exams as opposed to essay exams, and some schools tend to use the former, while others use the latter, the relationship between anxiety and grade point average may vary across different settings (Pervin, 1967). In addition, a wide array of cognitive performance criteria have been used in assessing the relationship between anxiety and performance. Some studies in educational settings use midterm grades, while other use final grades, and others use grade point averages across courses.

Differential Effects of Worry and Emotionality

Current literature strongly supports the generalization that the Worry component is more consistently and strongly related to academic performance than the Emotionality component (L. W. Morris, Davis, & Hutchings, 1981). Thus, there is growing empirical evidence suggesting that test anxiety measures that deal with the cognitions that people entertain while being evaluated are more consistently related to performance than are test anxiety measures that deal with emotional reactions in the same situation (I. G. Sarason, 1984).

Data reported by Zeidner (1990) on a sample of college students sitting for their college admissions tests serve to illustrate the typical pattern of relationship observed between test performance and both the Worry and Emotionality components of test anxiety (see Table 9.1). Although both Worry and Emotionality were correlated significantly with test performance on each section of the Scholastic Aptitude Test, the Worry component ($r = -.30$) was more strongly related to total test performance than was the Emotionality component ($r = -.20$). Further analysis indicated that the Worry component correlated with total exam performance even when the common variance between Worry and Emotionality was partialed out, whereas Emotionality was not found to be related to ability test performance when the common variance between Emotionality and Worry was statistically controlled (Cf. Deffenbacher, 1977a; L. W. Morris & Liebert, 1970).

Hembree (1988) identified over a dozen studies in which Worry and Emotionality have been related to aptitude or scholastic achievement. The population effect size for Worry was reported to be about twice that for Emotionality ($r = -.31$ vs. $-.15$). Similar results were obtained in a meta-analysis focusing on the anxiety–performance relationship conducted by Seipp (1991). Worry ($r = -.22$) was only slightly more strongly correlated with performance than was Emotionality ($r = -.15$). Seipp (1991) concluded that because the Worry–performance relationship is comparable to the overall relationship between test anxiety and performance, anxiety and

Table 9.1. Empirical Relationship between Test Anxiety an Aptitude Test Scores in a Naturalistic College Admissions Testing Situation ($n = 378$)

Aptitude measure	Worry	Emotionality	Test anxiety score
Information	−.18	−.15	−.19
Figural reasoning	−.24	−.15	−.21
Logic	−.28	−.19	−.27
Math	−.28	−.19	−.27
English	−.30	−.15	−.25
Total SAT score	−.30	−.20	−.28

Note: This table is adapted from Zeidner et al. (1988) and Zeidner (1990).

Worry may be regarded as equivalent in terms of their power in predicting cognitive performance.

There is some research suggesting that the effects of Emotionality vary with levels of Worry. Deffenbacher (1977a) administered the Miller Analogies Test at a counseling center to a sample of 82 college students and found that Worry was broadly related to performance, such that high worriers did less well than low worriers. However, the effects of Emotionality varied with Worry level. At low levels of Worry, Emotionality was unrelated to performance, but at high levels of Worry, high Emotionality impaired performance. As can be readily seen from Figure 9.4, while Worry contributed more pervasively to the relationship between anxiety and performance, the negative effects of Emotionality were nested within the upper range of Worry.

A Note on Causality

Although research has attested to a systematic lawfulness in the anxiety–performance relationship, the exact causal direction of this relationship remains uncertain. Because most studies focusing on the anxiety–performance relationship are correlational, they demonstrate associations rather than true dependencies.

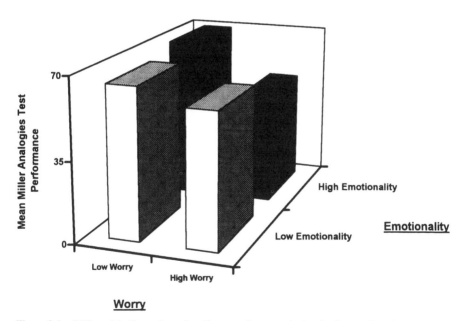

Figure 9.4. Differential effects of emotionality on performance, by levels of worry. Based on data from Deffenbacher (1977a), Table 3, p. 194.

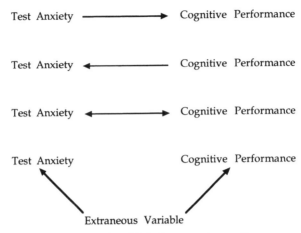

Figure 9.5. Alternative causal models in the test anxiety–performance association.

Strictly speaking, correlational data obtained between test anxiety, as an individual difference variable, and test performance do not definitely establish a causal relationship between these two variables. Thus, it is not entirely clear whether test anxiety really does influence cognitive performance or perhaps should be conceived as resulting from previous performances. Some cross-lagged panel analysis (Hodapp, 1982) assumes that test anxiety can influence performance, but the reciprocal process, how anxiety develops from feedback of performance, is scarcely discussed. Figure 9.5 describes a number of alternative models in conceptualizing the test anxiety–performance relationship. Thus, test anxiety may affect performance; test performance may affect anxiety levels; the causal direction may be bidirectional; or anxiety and test performance may both be affected by some extraneous variable (e.g., IQ).

A number of experts concur that the nature of the anxiety–performance relationship would best be viewed as reciprocal in nature (Dusek, 1980; Phillips et al., 1980). Thus, high levels of test anxiety produce certain aversive patterns of motivation, coping, and task strategies that interfere with learning and performance. The result is that performance suffers, thus leading to further anxiety over time (Phillips et al., 1980). The increasing levels of anxiety, in turn, serve to hinder task performance to a greater degree, which in turn increases anxiety over evaluation. Future research would profit from employing nonrecursive process models in order to better capture the dynamic and cyclical nature of the anxiety–performance relationship.

Moderating Effects

Even a casual glance at the anxiety literature suggests that the nature and strength of the anxiety–performance relationship are not invariant across samples, tasks, and settings, but instead vary as a function of characteristics of the test per se, the test situation, and subjects (Hembree, 1988). To account for the observed variation in the nature of the anxiety–performance relationship, anxiety researchers have devoted considerable efforts in seeking to uncover meaningful *moderating* variables that serve to enhance or weaken the effects of anxiety on performance. I now review the literature on moderating effects in order to identify consistent task, situational, and demographic moderating effects in the anxiety–performance relationship.

Task-Related Variables

Complexity of Cognitive Tasks

A substantial body of research provides empirical support for the claim that the magnitude of the anxiety–performance relationship varies with test difficulty. Hembree's (1988) meta-analytic results support the moderating effects of task complexity. Thus, whereas a substantial mean correlation of −.45 was reported between test anxiety and performance for tests perceived to be difficult, only a trivial correlation of −.07 was reported for tests viewed as being relatively easy. Consistent with these results, M. W. Eysenck and Calvo (1992) summarize the findings of a total of 24 experiments reporting a significant interaction between trait anxiety and task difficulty; in 22 of these the pattern was in the anticipated direction, with anxiety-linked performance deficits more pronounced on relatively difficult than on easy cognitive tasks. Although most of the studies reviewed by Eysenck are based on measures of trait anxiety, rather than test anxiety per se, studies focusing on test anxiety proper are generally consistent with these results (e.g., Harleston, 1962; Rocklin, 1985; Rocklin & Thompson, 1985; I. G. Sarason & Palola, 1960). For example, Rocklin (1985) reported a disordinal interaction between test anxiety and the difficulty level of computer-administered items selected from the Scholastic Aptitude Test. Students with moderate anxiety levels did better on the easy test than on the hard test, while the opposite was true of students low in anxiety.

Accounts of the Anxiety × Task Complexity Interaction. One of the earliest accounts is based on the Yerkes–Dodson (1908) postulated inverted-U-curve relationship between anxiety and performance. Accordingly, the increased stress associated with the high probability of task failure on difficult tasks serves to push test-anxious examinees beyond the optimal anxiety level on the curve and consequently impairs their task performance (Rocklin, 1985). By contrast, examinees who are less than optimally motivated or aroused in the test situation (i.e., low-test-anxious) will typically benefit from a difficult test because the increased arousal evoked by a difficult test, coupled with the greater incentive in succeeding on such a test, will move the low-test-anxious examinees closer to their optimal motivational level. It is noted that the greater the probability of failure on a task, the higher the incentive value of succeeding on the task (Atkinson & Feather, 1966). Additional explanations have been proposed by motivational theorists (J. T. Spence & Spence, 1966).

M. W. Eysenck's (1982, 1983) cognitive model offers an intriguing explanation of the interactive effect. Accordingly, when a task is highly demanding or complex, and subjects have their attentional resources taxed to the limit, the cognitive component of anxiety should have a particularly detrimental effect on test performance by consuming limited attentional resources necessary for task processing. This account rests on the assumption that difficult tasks make greater demands on working memory capacity than do easy tasks, and that the detrimental effects of anxiety on task performance increase directly with the demand that tasks place on the capacity of working memory. Easterbrook's (1959) "narrowing of cue utilization" hypothesis offers yet another cognitive-attentional account of the interactive effect. Because difficult tasks tend to incorporate *more* components than easy tasks, anxious examinees would narrow their attention on complex tasks and thus would be able to attend to fewer task components, thus differentially impairing their performance.

It is important to keep in mind that difficulty has been defined in various ways, not all of which are interchangeable, and researchers are not in complete agreement when it comes to defining the critical attributes of task complexity. M. W. Eysenck and Calvo (1992) argue that task difficulty needs to be defined in terms of the cognitive processes and resources required for task performance. Thus, tasks can be difficult because of their demands on either temporary storage capacity or on processing resources. Difficult tasks also tend to incorporate *more* components than easy tasks. Further, it is important to point out that perceived task difficulty is a function not only of the inherent complexity of the task, but also of a variety of other factors, such as individual differences in intelligence, the examinee's experience with the particular class of problems under consideration, and provision of memory supports (Heinrich & Spielberger, 1982). Thus, the lack of an accepted or uniform definition of task difficulty has been a particularly nagging problem in investigating the differential effects of task difficulty on task performance, making comparisons among different studies problematic (Heinrich & Spielberger, 1982).

As Mueller (1992) has pointed out, when the relationship between anxiety and task difficulty is being studied, it is particularly helpful to identify the components that are involved. There are two advantages in doing this: (a) it helps keep the definition of task difficulty at a more rigorous level, and (b) it makes it possible to determine whether anxiety has the same effects on each component. Mueller (1992) points out that there are other ways to decompose task difficulty (e.g., by using Sternberg's [1985] componential analysis), though relatively little systematic work involving individual differences in anxiety has been done along such lines.

Item Arrangement

The order of presentation of test items, technically termed "item arrangement" or "item difficulty sequence," has been claimed to moderate the effects of anxiety on performance on objective tests. Much of the interest in the moderating effects of item arrangement stems from the prevalent notion that the presence of anxiety will be most disruptive when a test is initially perceived as highly difficult (as would be the case when very difficult items are presented first on a test booklet), and least disruptive when a test is initially perceived as relatively easy, thus guaranteeing initial success (as would be the case when easy items are presented first).

A study by Covington and Omelich (1987b) on a sizable sample of 432 students provided data in support of this "initial success" notion. Subjects were given a psychology exam consisting of an equal number of easy and hard items, with items arranged in one of three different orders: (a) easy/hard, (b) hard/easy, and (c) mixed. Students who combined high evaluative anxiety with a lack of self-confidence were found to be at a distinct disadvantage on hard items, but especially so when difficult items were encountered first. However, the overall pattern of research findings is mixed, with other studies failing to support the moderating effects of item arrangement (Plake, Thompson, & Lowry, 1981; Everson, Shapiro, & Millsap, 1989). It is noted, in passing, that the whole item-arrangement literature ignores the possibility that even if the current items being undertaken are easy, test-anxious subjects may anticipate harder items later on, thus creating apprehension and anxiety about future encounters with difficult items.

Test Format and Administration Procedures

Despite common claims, the empirical evidence for the moderating role of test format and administration procedure is not very impressive or consistent. A case in point is the body of research on the moderating effects of conventional versus computerized testing showing that computer-administered self-adapted testing does not have a particularly beneficial effect for high-test-anxious subjects; instead, it benefits students at all levels of anxiety equally well (Rocklin & O'Donnell, 1987). Other studies even suggest that computerized testing may be disadvantageous for high-test-anxious subjects in that it tends to *increase* students' test anxiety (Hedl et al., 1973) and consequently impairs performance.

Humorous Content

Humorous test content has been claimed to be particularly advantageous for the test performance of high- relative to low-test-anxious subjects. As the argument goes, because humorous test content inhibits anxiety during testing, anxiety fails to exert its typical detrimental effects on the performance of high-test-anxious students (R. E. Smith, Ascough, Ettinger, & Nelson, 1971).

R. E. Smith and his coworkers (R. E. Smith et al., 1971) provided some evidence in support of the moderating effects of humor. A multiple-choice midterm exam was given to a sample of 215 university undergraduates using either a standard exam form or a modified humorous form. As shown in Figure 9.6, the high-trait-test-anxiety

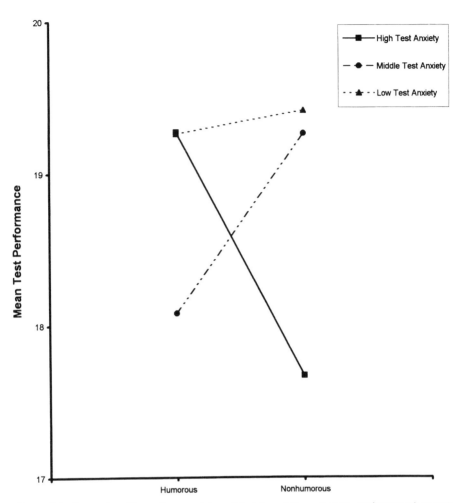

Figure 9.6. Interactive effects of test anxiety and test format (humorous vs. nonhumorous) on test performance. There were 77, 69, and 69 students, respectively, in the low-, moderate-, and high-anxiety groups. Based on data presented in R. E. Smith et al. (1971), Table 1, p. 244.

group receiving the humorous test form scored significantly higher on the test than did the high-test-anxious group who received the nonhumorous form. Furthermore, there was a significant interaction between test anxiety (measured as a trait) and test format, indicating that the effects of humor on performance differed as a function of level of trait anxiety. Whereas in the nonhumorous condition the high-anxiety group performed at a significantly lower level than did either the low- or moderate-test-anxiety groups, in the humorous condition, the high-test-anxious subjects did not differ significantly from the other groups.

However, other studies have failed to replicate this interactive effect (Deffenbacher, Deitz, & Hazaleus, 1981). Paradoxically some data (Hedl, Hedl, & Weaver, 1978) go so far as to suggest that the introduction of humor into a stressful evaluation situation may actually *heighten* the tension and anxiety experienced by highly anxious students and thus negatively impact upon performance. High-test-anxious students may actually find the humorous content distracting and appreciate humor less under achievement-oriented conditions than under nonstressful conditions.

Situational Variables

Test Environment and Atmosphere

Reviews of the anxiety research literature provide sufficient evidence attesting to the significant interactive effects of test anxiety and evaluative atmosphere upon performance outcomes (M. W. Eysenck, 1982; I. G. Sarason, 1972a, 1981; Wine, 1971a, 1979). Specifically, a sizable body of research supports the generalization that achievement-orienting instructions that emphasize the evaluative aspects of a subject's performance increase the performance levels of low-test-anxious subjects, but decrease the performance of those high in test anxiety. The interaction effects for test atmosphere are obtained as tasks are varied along a dimension of testlike versus gamelike (S. B. Sarason et al., 1960; Zweibelson, 1956), and with audience present versus audience absent (Cox, 1964, 1968). It is noted, however, that the moderating effects of evaluative test environment are documented more widely for college- than school-age populations (Hembree, 1988).

The research program carried out by I. G. Sarason and his coworkers has probably been the most comprehensive effort to uncover the nature and causal mechanisms underlying the differential effects of test instructions and environment on the performance of high- and low-test-anxious individuals. An illustrative example presented in Figure 9.7 (based on I. G. Sarason, 1973) reveals the interactive effects of trait test anxiety and test atmosphere (as defined by preliminary achievement-orienting vs. neutral instructions) upon mean anagram solution time. Whereas high-test-anxious subjects performed more poorly (took longer to respond) under the achievement-orienting than under the neutral instructions, the low-test-anxious subjects receiving the two sets of instructions did not differ significantly.

To further provide the reader with the flavor of this genre of research, I briefly describe one exemplary study. I. G. Sarason (1986) administered the Cognitive Interference Questionnaire to a sample of 302 undergraduates who took an untimed 100-item information test (e.g., "What is the capital of Czechoslovakia?" "What is the last name of the author who wrote the Sherlock Holmes stories?") under both evaluative and nonevaluative test conditions. About half of the subjects in the *neutral*

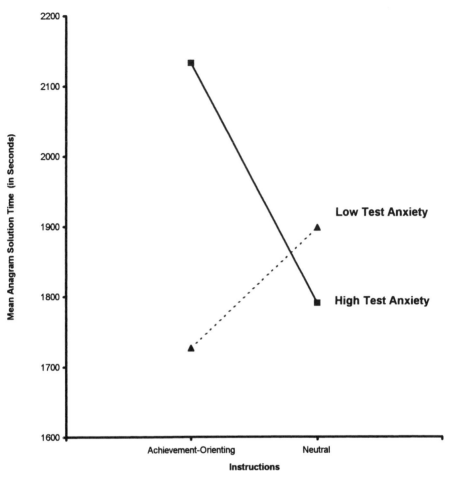

Figure 9.7. Mean anagram solution time (in seconds) for groups differing in test anxiety scores and preliminary instructions (achievement-orienting vs. neutral). Based on data from I. G. Sarason (1973), Table 3, p. 266.

condition were given only the instructions needed to take the information test, whereas the remaining subjects in the *evaluative* condition were told that how much information a person possesses and how the information is used are important aspects of intelligence. High-test-anxious subjects in the neutral condition performed better than high-test-anxious subjects in the evaluative condition. Low and medium test anxiety scorers performed better in the evaluative/ego-involving condition than in the neutral condition. The author suggests that the neutral information instructions functioned to reassure the more anxious subjects. This led to higher performance for the high-test-anxious than for the low and moderately test-anxious subjects, who may have relaxed too much and may therefore not have given the task their full attention.

The most prevalent account of the observed interactive effect, reported in a good number of studies, is that high-test-anxious subjects tend to view most evaluative test situations as a particularly threatening context, thus increasing the strength of task-irrelevant anxiety responses and avoidance behaviors that are debilitating to their test performance (S. B. Sarason et al., 1952). However, the same evaluative test situation may represent a challenge to low-test-anxious individuals, thus facilitating their performance under evaluative conditions. By contrast, under neutral conditions, the nonthreatening instructions would reduce the strength of these anxiety responses (or maintain them at initial level), with high-test-anxious examinees evidencing lower state anxiety and thus performing better than they would under evaluative conditions. Low-test-anxious subjects, however, may lose some of the motivation necessary for good performance, thus depressing their performance compared to evaluative conditions. Further, there is research suggesting that the interaction pattern is often complicated by additional variables, including gender, type of task, or task difficulty (I. G. Sarason & Minard, 1962; Young & Brown, 1973).

Time Pressure and Speeded Conditions

Time pressure has been claimed to show a particularly deleterious effect on the test performance of high-test-anxious compared to low-test-anxious examinees (Hill & Eaton, 1977). This claim has been supported by a substantial body of research conducted since the early 1950s. In the course of their research on the situational determinants of intelligence test scores. Matarazzo and his co-workers (Matarazzo, Ulett, Guze, & Saslow, 1954) reported that whereas trait anxiety was negatively correlated with scores on a timed intelligence test, anxiety was unrelated to scores on an untimed measure of intelligence. These results were replicated shortly thereafter by Siegman (1956).

L. W. Morris and Liebert (1969) provided experimental evidence consistent with the hypothesis that high-test-anxiety examinees do better on untimed tests whereas low-test-anxiety examinees do better on timed tests. Hill and Eaton (1977) provided additional evidence for the interactive effect in school children. A set of basic arithmetic problems was administered to high- and low-test-anxious elementary school students under speed and power testing conditions. They found that under strict *time pressure* conditions, high-test-anxious children performed poorly, as evidenced by taking twice as long and making three times as many errors as low-test-anxious children. When tested under *power* conditions, i.e., with time limits removed, the performance of high-test-anxious children improved markedly, and they did nearly as well as low- and moderately test-anxious children. However, some data suggest that the moderating effects of time may not be consistent across gender groups (Plass & Hill, 1986). It would be desirable to obtain both *rate* and *accuracy* information in future research seeking to clarify the debilitating effects of test anxiety on performance (Galassi et al., 1981a, 1981b, 1984).

External Observer and Audience

The presence of an external observer or audience in the test situation may be particularly debilitating for high-test-anxious subjects, who may be more responsive to the potential evaluation of others and react to such evaluation with increased levels of anxiety (Geen, 1980). Indeed, rather than enhancing positive incentive motivation in the test-anxious, the presence of an observer may lead to greater fear of failure (Geen, 1979) and cautiousness in responding (Geen, 1985a; cf. Geen, 1985b). In contrast, low-test-anxious subjects may be less affected by audience presence because they are more task-oriented and less concerned about external evaluation.

Overall, reviews by Wine (1971b) and Geen (1980) of the empirical research concluded that the presence of external observers tends to degrade the task performance of high-test-anxious subjects, but frequently facilitates the performance of low-test-anxious subjects. Further, Geen (1977) showed that subjects high in test anxiety are not only adversely affected more than those low in test anxiety by the presence of an observer during performance, but are also helped more by an appraisal of the external observer that renders the observation less threatening. The redefinition of the evaluation as potentially helpful (e.g., when the experimenter or examiner explains beforehand that she or he was observing only to give the subject information on how to improve performance) leads to a significantly more effective performance in that condition than found when no explanation of the observation is offered (Geen, 1977).

The effects of test atmosphere may interact with the nature of the examinee's success/failure experiences in the test situation in affecting performance. Evidence presented by Geen (1979) suggests that if an evaluative test session is preceded by a success experience, observer presence is associated with the enhancement, rather than the decrement, of performance. Additional research suggests that audience presence may facilitate the performance of previously acquired behaviors and skills (Ganzer, 1968).

Examiner Characteristics

The personality characteristics (e.g., anxiety) and professional behavior of the examiner in an evaluative situation have been cited as important factors in affecting the state anxiety and consequence performance of test-anxious examinees (S. B. Sarason et al., 1960). Thus, in some ways examiners may be like anxious examinees when it comes to performing in evaluative situations: They may vary in their self-efficacy to form tasks, in their tendency to worry and experience task-irrelevant thinking, and to become autonomically aroused when being evaluated. These concerns and emotions may be communicated to examinees in the test situation, thus increasing examinees' uncertainty and anxiety, and debilitating their performance (I. G. Sarason, 1973). I. G. Sarason (1973) reported that subjects run by low-test-anxious experimenters perform better than those run by high-test-anxious experimenters. Furthermore, there is some research evidence suggesting that the examiner's evaluative behavior may have a differential impact upon the performance of high-test-anxious subjects, although these results were not replicated in a follow-up study (Geen, 1985a).

Additional data presented by DeRosa and Patalano (1991) suggest that examinees' familiarity with the experimenter may also impact upon test performance. They reported a significant relationship between test anxiety and percent change score in the reading scores of 137 elementary school students as a function of the examinees' familiarity with the examiner. Reading scores were more depressed for high- than low-test-anxious subjects when examinees were first tested by familiar and then unfamiliar proctors.

Reassurance and Emotional Social Support

Both anecdotal and experimental evidence suggest that providing examinees with reassurance and emotional support in the test situation may be especially advantageous for the performance of high-test-anxious compared to low-test-anxious individuals. Because high-test-anxious subjects are characterized by certain debilitating response tendencies (excessive worry, self-related cognitions, self-preoccupations, etc.), which interfere with performance in evaluative situations, reassurance and emotional support may reduce the effect of these interfering responses and facilitate exam performance. For low-test-anxious subjects, in contrast, reassurance may function to reduce ego involvement in the task, and may serve as a cue to "take it easy." This, consequently, reduces motivation and subsequent exam performance (I. G. Sarason, 1981). A series of studies by Irwin Sarason and his coworkers provided empirical support for the hypothesis that emotional social support would be relatively more facilitative for highly anxious than for less anxious subjects (I. G. Sarason, 1958a; cf. I. G. Sarason, 1958b).

A study by I. G. Sarason (1981) tested for the moderating effects of social support in a sample of 192 undergraduate students who solved anagram tasks under opportunity for support versus no opportunity for support conditions. Under the *social support* condition students were asked to participate in a prior 20-minute group discussion, in groups of six. Students were told that they were brought together to discuss the problem of anxiety over exams and that they would be given the opportunity for sharing views and joining together socially with fellow students to discuss common problems and consider possible solutions. Among the questions discussed by the group were how students share their worries about tests with others, barriers to this sharing of personal concerns, steps that might be taken to lower tension levels, and the degree to which discussions are felt to be helpful. Two confederates were also present to stimulate discussion, positively reinforce com-

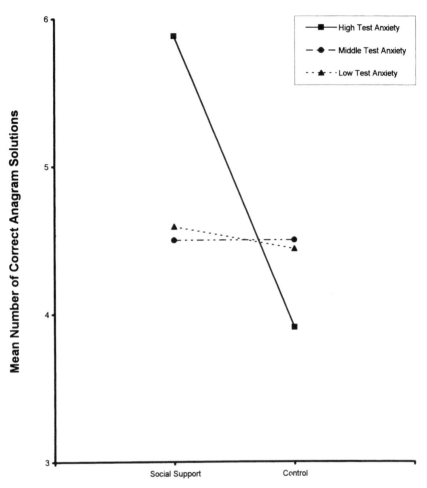

Figure 9.8.   Interactive effects of social support and test anxiety on anagram performance. Based on data from 192 college students reported in I. G. Sarason (1981), Experiment I, Table 2, p. 107.

ments made by participants, and build group solidarity and a sense of sharing. A control group did not engage in a preperformance activity. As shown in Figure 9.8, test anxiety interacted with social support, with the difference in performance between experimental social support and control groups significant for high-test-anxious students only. Thus, whereas high-test-anxious examinees appear to benefit from social support, low-test-anxious examinees seem unaffected by it, implying that high-test-anxious examinees have a particular need for social association. Further research by I. G. Sarason (1981) suggests that social support, defined as association with others and hope of its continuation, may reduce the potency of self-preoccupying thoughts of personal inadequacy and helplessness, thus improving concentration on task, and task performance.

Evaluative Feedback

The type of performance feedback provided in the test situation frequently has been claimed to interact with trait anxiety in affecting test outcomes (M. W. Eysenck, 1982). Accordingly, high-anxiety subjects are predicted to perceive the feedback provided as an additional source of evaluative threat and consequently show elevated levels of state anxiety and consistent impairment of performance as a result of failure feedback. By contrast, low-anxiety subjects are predicted to be either unaffected by negative or failure feedback or to actually *improve* their level of performance. Furthermore, positive feedback and social cues may be particularly reinforcing for anxious individuals who are in need of reassurance that they are performing successfully (Tobias, 1980).

A comprehensive review of the empirical literature (M. W. Eysenck, 1982) supports the claim that high-trait-anxious persons manifest greater adverse effects following failure feedback than do low-anxiety individuals across a wide range of cognitive tasks. By contrast, low-anxiety subjects manifest either no aversive effects or even improve their performance following negative feedback. Although the bulk of the research reviewed by Eysenck was based on measures of trait rather than test anxiety proper, studies focusing specifically on test anxiety attest to the same pattern of results (Hill & Eaton, 1977).

According to Tobias' (1980) information processing model, anxious individuals scan the test environment for cues of evaluative threat and have expectations of receiving negative evaluations in test situations. Failure feedback confirms their worst expectations, making attending to the demands of the task extremely difficult and frequently resulting in a high disruption of performance (Tobias, 1980).

Phase of Testing

A recent study by Zeidner (1991) provides convincing empirical evidence that time of testing (pretest vs. posttest) moderates the relationship between aptitude test anxiety and performance in a natural college admissions test situation. The Test Anxiety Inventory (TAI) was administered to 176 college candidates prior to their being tested on college admissions scholastic aptitude exams, and to 202 students immediately following aptitude testing. Whereas only a negligible relationship was observed between performance and test anxiety under pretest anxiety measurement conditions ($r = -.11$), the latter two variables were observed to be meaningfully related ($r = -.40$) under posttest measurement conditions. Figures 9.9a and 9.9b present the regression plots for the anxiety–performance relationship at pre- and posttesting periods, respectively. These data are consistent with prior meta-analytic research conducted by Hembree (1988) and Seipp (1991) pointing to the moderating

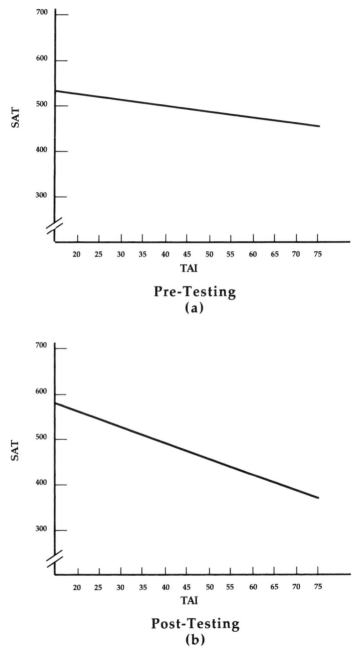

Figure 9.9. Regression plot for the test anxiety–performance relation during (a) pretest versus (b) posttest periods. Plots based on data collected during the course of norming the Hebrew version of the TAI (Zeidner et al., 1988). TAI, Test Anxiety Inventory scores; SAT, college admissions scholastic aptitude test scores (Hebrew version).

effects of time of testing. Seipp (1991) reported average correlations between test anxiety and achievement of $-.21$ compared to $-.28$ when anxiety was assessed prior to and after testing, respectively.

How do we account for the observed moderating effects? Zeidner (1991) theorizes that there is a stronger effect of evaluations of performance on anxiety than there is a direct effect of anxiety on performance. Thus, the emotional and cognitive feedback provided by the exam allows examinees to adjust their interior emotional milieu to the actual level of test performance, leading to higher anxiety–performance relationships following the testing period. Thus, during the highly ambiguous *anticipatory* phase of testing, prior to test administration, the correlation between the emotions associated with threat appraisals (i.e., test anxiety) and test performance would be low because they reflect the high degree of uncertainty about both the emotions and the outcome. However, during the posttest stage, following the test experience, students should have had some important clues as to how they performed (actual or perceived difficulty of items, familiarity with item formats, effectiveness of coping with time pressures, etc.). They would therefore be expected to adjust both their expectations and harm emotions (test anxiety reactions) accordingly.

By contrast, R. Schwarzer (1990) views the moderating effect of time of assessment of anxiety as somewhat of an artifact. He contends that prior to testing, the vast majority of examinees anticipate ego threat, which serves to raise anxiety levels beyond normal levels. The reduction in the consequent variation in state anxiety lowers correlations between anxiety and subsequent performance scores (R. Schwarzer, 1990). Further, according to Covington's (1992) conceptualization, some subjects may intentionally report more anxiety after failure feedback in order to make the impression that their elevated arousal has been the cause of their failure, not incompetence.

Demographic Variables

Gender

Does test anxiety interfere more with the academic achievements of male than female students? The bulk of available research points to similar patterns of the anxiety–performance relationships in male and female students at various educational levels, with little data to suggest that gender moderates the anxiety–performance relationship. For example, Deffenbacher (1977a) found no significant sex group differences in the strength of correlation between test anxiety, as assessed by the Worry–Emotionality scale, and performance in a sample of 53 male and 29 female students who were administered the Miller Analogies Test at a university counseling center. A number of studies report that correlations between Scholastic Aptitude Test scores and total test anxiety scores are comparable for male and female students (Zeidner & Nevo, 1992; Spielberger, 1980).

In one of the few direct tests of gender as a moderating variable in the anxiety–performance relationship, Zeidner (1990) tested for moderating effects among 163 male and 198 female student candidates in Israel sitting for the Scholastic Aptitude Test routinely administered as part of their college admissions test procedures. Regression analysis indicated that sex did not interact with test anxiety in affecting aptitude test performance, i.e., the regression lines for SAT scores as a function of test anxiety were homogeneous for male and female candidates.

Age

Data presented by Hill and Sarason (1966) indicate that the effects of anxiety upon performance increase with grade level during elementary school years. Based on a 5-year longitudinal study of about 700 elementary school children, Hill and Sarason found that the negative relationship between test anxiety (as assessed by TASC scores) and scholastic achievement increased steadily across elementary school years. Thus, in 1st grade the anxiety–performance relationship was negligible; in 3rd and 4th grades it was statistically significant, but modest; by 5th and 6th grades the correlations were moderate and significant. Furthermore, Hill and Wigfield (1984) summarized data showing a stronger anxiety–performance relationship among junior high school and high school students relative to elementary school students. The relationship between anxiety and performance was reported to reach a peak by the 11th grade. Direct tests for moderating effects, however, were not conducted in these studies. Research by Willig, Harnisch, Hill, and Maehr (1983) reported a stronger anxiety–performance negative association in junior high school than in late elementary school in three ethnic groups, i.e., Blacks, Whites, and Hispanics.

Sociocultural Background

Zeidner (1990) conducted one of the few systematic tests for sociocultural bias in test anxiety measures, using the required regression procedures (Jensen, 1980) in a sample of 163 male and 198 female students in Israel sitting for the Scholastic Aptitude Test routinely administered to all student applicants as part of their college admissions procedures. A series of specific tests was conducted for both social class and ethnic group differences, in turn, in the regression parameters of aptitude test scores regressed upon test anxiety. The regressions showed no interaction effects for each of the demographic variables tested. These data support the conclusion that test anxiety does not bear a differential impact upon the performance of students as a function of social class or ethnic group background.

Summary

On the whole, the massive body of empirical research on the anxiety–performance relationship points to a rather modest inverse relationship between test anxiety and cognitive performance. Recent meta-analytic studies, converging at a population correlation at about $-.20$ across various forms of social-evaluative anxiety, suggest that the anxiety effect size is somewhat weaker than commonly thought. Despite the fact that test anxiety-linked performance deficits are extremely common, they are not ubiquitous. In fact, the anxiety spectrum of effects is observed to range from significant degrees of immobilization, through mild discomfort and occasional impaired performance, to enhancing effects. Thus, test anxiety may be usefully viewed as a continuum, with facilitating and debilitating anxiety as anchor points. Why one person or group experiences one kind of test anxiety and others experience another kind is an important question left unanswered by current research.

Furthermore, a common myth which has guided much of the research in this area and that needs to be debunked is that all test-anxious individuals perform poorly (Galassi et al., 1981a). It is important to keep in mind that test anxiety is but one of a host of factors affecting test outcomes, in specific, and student academic performance, in general. Indeed, many individuals who are test-anxious nevertheless perform well on cognitive tests. Any reasonable model of school achievement needs to consider, along with test anxiety, a wide array of cognitive, affective, motivational, somatic, and environmental factors (scholastic abilities, study habits, school attitudes, self-perceptions and self-efficacy, student health, classroom environment, opportunities for enrichment, etc.).

The bulk of available evidence points to task complexity, timing conditions, test atmosphere, phase of testing in which anxiety is assessed, examiner emotional support, and immediate performance feedback as meaningful and relatively consistent moderator variables in the anxiety–performance relationship. The evidence for the remaining variables surveyed is mixed. Overall, these situational effects suggest that the low performance of high-test-anxious students may be due in part to various test-taking factors that differentially debilitate their test performance.

R. Schwarzer (1990) correctly observes that too many dispensable studies have been conducted on the anxiety–performance relationship. It would appear necessary to skip further simplistic correlational and cross-sectional investigations which deal with the mere association between anxiety and performance at one point in time. Instead, longitudinal and experimental studies which aim at more complex cognitive-emotional-behavioral processes should be encouraged to understand better the underlying cause–effect mechanisms.

Furthermore, research in this area has tended to use linear causal models in exploring the link between test anxiety and cognitive performance. Future research would profit from employing process models in order to capture better the dynamic and cyclical nature of the anxiety–performance relationship. Thus, although anxiety appears to be a major cause of performance deficits, there is undoubtedly feedback from perceived and actual performance to anxiety states, which implies a need for a closed-looped modeling of the relationship between anxiety and performance. In addition, longitudinal and process-oriented research on the anxiety–performance relationship is urgently needed. Little research has attempted to track the anxiety–

performance linkages for the same individuals over time, from one test-taking event to another.

From a practical point of view, personality variables such as test anxiety seldom bear such a sizable impact on intellectual performance so as to invalidate assessments of achievement or ability test scores as a whole. The impact of various personality factors affecting performance (e.g., anxiety, motivation, extraversion) may in fact be viewed as key aspects of the individual's global intellectual capacity (Matarazzo, 1972; Wechsler, 1944). Moreover, personality factors may actually *enhance* rather than detract from the validity of cognitive measures. Individuals who do poorly on intelligence or achievement tests because of the debilitating effects of high test anxiety would most likely do poorly on the criterion performance—and for much the same reasons (Zeidner, 1995c).

Text Anxiety and Information Processing

Depend on it, Sir. When a man knows he is to be hanged in a fortnight it concentrates his mind wonderfully.

—*Samuel Johnson*

Overview

Cognitive conceptualizations of test anxiety (Geen, 1980; Hamilton, 1975; M. W. Eysenck, 1982, 1992; Tobias, 1980, 1992) emphasize the importance of various information processing mechanisms as critical intervening factors mediating the effects of anxiety on performance. Recently, considerable work has been directed toward establishing a more refined view of the mechanisms by which anxiety and its components affect performance, and considerable progress has been made toward "unpacking" the global effects of test anxiety on cognitive performance. The information processing model (Neisser, 1967) provides a set of useful concepts and processes for analyzing the specific problems and deficits of high-test-anxious students. According to this model, new information is processed in three main stages: input, processing, and output. Thus, students in a learning situation need to encode the new material to be acquired, store it in memory, bring problem-solving or other processes to bear on cognitive tasks presented, invoke retrieval processes that relate material to previous materials, and finally demonstrate their mastery of the learning material by succeeding on tests and other assessment procedures. High levels of test anxiety may interfere with students' performance and virtually impair cognitive performance at each of the stages involved in processing information (Tobias, 1992). As shown in Figure 10.1, the deficient performance of high-test-anxious subjects may be due in principle to problems in encoding and acquiring the new information, organizing and storing the material, or retrieving it in the test situation itself (Benjamin et al., 1981).

This chapter aims at pinpointing the effects of anxiety on various phases of information processing. I attempt to show how the cognitive representation of anxiety may affect the acquisition of information at the preprocessing stage, the

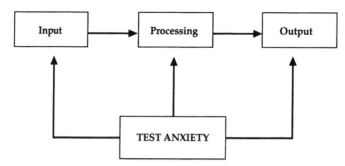

Figure 10.1. Impact of test anxiety at different stages of information processing.

organization and transformation of information in long-term memory, and the retrieval of previously acquired information from memory at the output stage. Although I use a stage model to organize the material presented in this chapter, the
reader is reminded that not all information processing theorists (e.g., connectionists)
are particularly in favor of a stage model.

To provide the reader with a theoretical background for understanding the
material presented, I begin by briefly discussing a number of cognitive models which
have been formulated to account for the effects of test anxiety on performance
deficits.

Causal Models and Mechanisms

Until recently, the well-established relationship between anxious arousal and
achievement outcomes were believed to result from a simple reaction to evaluative
threat, with the mechanisms of disruption caused by the interfering effects of physiological upset that accompany emotional arousal (Covington et al., 1986). However, it
is now widely accepted that it is the cognitive representations of test anxiety, rather
than somatic arousal, which are primary causal factors at play in any account of
performance deficits. I now briefly review a number of cognitive models that have
been proposed to explain some of the anxiety-related performance decrements discussed so far.

Cognitive-Attentional Interference

Task-irrelevant processing is probably the most frequently cited cognitive
mechanism accounting for the association between elevated anxiety and consequent
performance deficits. According to this explanation, evaluative stress may induce a
generalized cognitive-attentional deficit due to the tendency of high-test-anxious

individuals to divert attention away from the task toward self-oriented cognitive concerns and excessive task-irrelevant processing that may interfere with performance. Self-preoccupation can be construed as a handicap that occurs mainly during retrieval, leading to the name of the construct, "test" or "performance" anxiety (Mueller, 1992).

I. G. Sarason and Sarason (1990) suggest two distinct mechanisms that account for the effects of cognitive interference on performance: (a) self-preoccupation and interference of thoughts centering around worry and self-preoccupation (e.g., "I really don't know how to handle this math test"), and (b) distractibility (i.e., wandering off of thoughts). Thus, in evaluative situations distractibility and high levels of intrusive thinking may really be self-defeating and impair performance if the person does not have the wherewithal to handle the situation (see Chapter 3 for a more in-depth treatment of the interference model).

Limited Cognitive Capacity

Recent thinking in the area of attention and memory has conceptualized the human information processing system as a limited-cognitive-capacity system (Baddeley, 1986; Baddeley & Hitch, 1974). Attention and working memory are assumed to work with a single general pool of processing resources that can be allocated flexibly to different concurrent or parallel tasks (M. W. Eysenck, 1982; Kahneman, 1973; Tobias, 1980). Each capacity can be shared by several concurrent processes, thus constituting a *distributable* resource. A number of cognitive theorists (e.g., M. W. Eysenck, 1992; Hamilton, 1975; Tobias, 1980) have posed their explanations of the negative effects of anxiety on performance in terms of "limited cognitive capacity." During the performance of a single task (e.g., a complex verbal reasoning test item) allocation of resources occurs between the cognitive test at hand and worry, conceptualized as a *subject-defined task* (Humphreys & Revelle, 1984). The cognitive component of test anxiety absorbs degrees of freedom available for cognitive processing, with task-irrelevant information, involved mainly in the Worry component of test anxiety, competing with task-relevant information for space in the processing system. The low-test-anxious subject may be viewed as being in a "single-task situation," having to cope mainly with the cognitive task at hand. By contrast, the high-test-anxious subject may be viewed as being in a "dual-task situation," having to cope both with the task at hand and cognitive interference as well.

Consider the analogy of a computer with 8 megabytes of RAM (random access memory) that is running a heavy-duty program requiring 7 megabytes for efficient performance. As long as the memory load is smaller than the system's capacity, the system would be expected to function adequately. However, if there is an in-resident program absorbing about 2 megabytes of RAM in addition to the 7 required by the program we wish to run, the system's resources will be overtaxed. As there would not be enough memory or "cognitive" resources to run both programs at the same time, the system would eventually malfunction or "crash."

Reduced Processing Efficiency

The "processing efficiency" model put forth by M. W. Eysenck (1982, 1997) is complementary to the limited-processing-capacity model. According to this model, high levels of state anxiety reduce processing efficiency, although the effectiveness or quality of performance is not necessarily affected (see Chapter 9 for the distinction between efficiency and effectiveness). It is further claimed that the reduction of attentional resources imposed by the aversive representation of worry and cognitive interference may be partially compensated for by increased effort expended by high-test-anxious subjects.

This model places particular emphasis on the role of *working memory*, contending that the adverse effects of state anxiety on task performance generally become stronger as task demands on working memory capacity increase. Strategic processes (e.g., difficult problem-solving tasks) which require working memory resources will be impaired by anxiety, but only if their resource requirements exceed available working memory capacity. By contrast, performance on automatic processes is not markedly impaired by anxiety because such cognitive operations do not require access to working memory. Performance on easy tasks is often not impaired by anxiety because, despite the functional restriction in available processing resources, sufficient working memory capacity remains for the successful execution of relatively simple tasks (MacLeod & Donnellan, 1993).

The cognitive system is claimed to initiate two types of reactions in order to escape from the state of apprehension associated with worrisome thoughts and to avoid likely aversive consequences of poor performance. First, in an attempt to increase the available capacity of working memory, the system attempts to reduce worry. Second, in order to improve task performance, the system allocates additional processing resources (i.e., effort) and initiates processing activities (e.g., strategies) designed to improve performance. Thus, anxious subjects try to cope with threat and worry by allocating additional resources (i.e., increased efforts) or initiating processing activities. If successful, such attempts increase available working memory capacity.

This model posits the existence of a control or self-regulatory system involved in mediating the effects of anxiety on processing and performance (M. W. Eysenck, 1992). Such a control system is contended to be responsive to indications that the current level of task performance is falling behind that required by the subject. When the system detects the presence of worry or cognitive interference, this typically leads to the allocation of extra processing resources to the task in an attempt to improve the performance. Only when compensatory resources cannot be employed (e.g., limited time, externally paced conditions, concurrent or distracter task) will anxiety be predicted to impair effectiveness as well.

The processing efficiency theory has a number of unique features (M. W. Eysenck & Calvo, 1992). First, there is the important distinction between anxiety effects on efficiency and effectiveness of performance. Second, the cognitive component of test anxiety (i.e., worry) has motivational as well as attentional interference effects, in that it leads to increased effort or compensatory strategies. This conceptualization of the worry component is in direct contrast to other theories of worry (e.g., I. G. Sarason, 1988; Humphreys & Revelle, 1984), in which worry has no similar positive motivational effects. In addition, anxiety is postulated to effect both the storage and processing capacity of the working memory system components which are available for task performance, rather than simply the storage capacity of short-term memory (as in Humphreys & Revelle, 1984) or attentional resources (as in Wine, 1971b). Overall, reviews by M. W. Eysenck (1982, 1992, 1997) identify a body of impressive evidence consistent with the major hypotheses of the model.

Additional models of interest bearing on the anxiety–performance relationship (Hullian drive model, self-control process model, etc.) are presented in Chapter 3.

Anxiety Effects on Various Stages of Information Processing

In this section, I examine the evidence for the effects of test anxiety on the different stages of information processing.

Information Encoding and Acquisition

Current cognitive-attentional models suggest that test anxiety may be particularly disruptive to performance at the acquisition or preprocessing stage, severely reducing the effectiveness by which new information is encoded (Tobias, 1977c, 1980, 1992; Wine, 1980; I. G. Sarason, 1987). Due to the attention-demanding effects of test-anxious worry, a person's ability to attend to and successfully register novel stimuli and new learning material may be reduced, and nominal stimuli often fail to become effective since the student is less able to represent input internally (Tobias, 1992). Meta-analytic research (Hembree, 1988) indicates that test-anxious students report experiencing more encoding difficulties than their low-test-anxious counterparts.

M. W. Eysenck (1992) hypothesizes that the attentional functioning of anxious individuals is such as to maximize the probability of detecting threatening environmental stimuli or events as quickly as possible. Accordingly, test-anxious subjects may frequently scan the environment for potential evaluative threats to their self-esteem or image. There is empirical evidence showing that anxious subjects typically scan the environment more rapidly and thoroughly than nonanxious individuals (M. W. Eysenck, 1992). The processing of additional task-irrelevant environmental information may interrupt the flow of goal-directed thoughts and actions.

Attentional Selectivity and Breadth

Recent theories of test anxiety have interpreted the impaired task performance of high-test-anxious subjects in terms of *selective attention* and narrowing of attention to self (I. G. Sarason, 1972a). Accordingly, under stressful evaluative conditions, high-test-anxious subjects attend to a very limited range of environmental cues and respond with personalized, self-oriented responses which direct attention away from the task (Geen, 1976; I. G. Sarason, 1972a; Wine, 1971b). Much of the research on restricted cue utilization in test-anxious individuals may be traced back to the basic thrust of the *cue-utilization hypothesis* advanced by Easterbrook (1959), emphasizing the effects of anxiety and arousal on selectivity of attention. The fundamental contention of Easterbrook's hypothesis is that states of high emotionality and arousal will produce a restriction in the range of cue utilization and lead to narrowing of attention as a function of physiological activation. As opposed to the attention-dividing effects of worry, emotionality and arousal are claimed to have a narrowing effect on the employment of attention. Thus, the range of cues used, or "breadth of attention," would be predicted to be reduced as anxious arousal increases, with performance suffering as a result.

Starting at relatively low levels of arousal or anxiety, the initial effect of a reduced cue utilization (according to Easterbrook's hypothesis) would be to narrow the focus on the central task and eliminate distracting noncentral stimuli that are unimportant to the task. This would be expected to facilitate performance on the central task at hand (M. W. Eysenck, 1982). However, when all irrelevant cues have been excluded, a further increase in arousal should work to narrow the focus to the point that necessary task-relevant central cues, essential to satisfactory task performance, will be excluded as well. At that point, proficiency on the target task would begin to suffer.

Easterbrook's (1959) hypothesis implies that narrowing of attentional span and utilization of cues under increased anxiety would have a greater adverse effect on difficult tasks, which comprise more cues. Assuming that difficult tasks involve processing and integrating of more relevant features, the point at which a diminished range of attention and cue utilization would start to eliminate relevant cues would occur at lower anxiety levels as difficulty increases. This provides a general theoretical explanation for the Yerkes–Dodson effect (in terms of acquisition or encoding rather than retrieval), postulating a curvilinear relationship between anxiety and performance. In fact, considerable evidence is available for the interaction between anxiety and task difficulty, with high-anxiety subjects performing worse than low-anxiety subjects on hard, but not on easy tasks.

Easterbrook's hypothesis has frequently been tested by using a *dual-task paradigm*, in which a primary task (e.g., reading a narrative passage) and a secondary task (e.g., rehearsing a set of digits) are performed concurrently. The general prediction is that because of attentional narrowing and limited cue utilization, high anxiety should have a more adverse effect on the performance of the secondary than on the primary task. Although the findings are mixed, anxiety in dual-task situations tends to impair performance on subsidiary tasks more than main tasks, thus providing some support for attentional narrowing under high-anxiety conditions (see M. W. Eysenck [1982] for review of evidence).

A number of experimental studies have directly examined the effects of test anxiety on the breadth of the perceptual field. For example, Geen (1976) reported that under evaluative stress conditions high-test-anxious subjects were helped *less* by the addition of relevant information than those who scored low; they were also hindered less in their recall by the insertion of irrelevant and potentially distractive information. Furthermore, Geen (1985b) provided data showing that vigilance interacted with the evaluative nature of the situation in impacting performance. As shown in Figure 10.2, whereas subjects high in test anxiety reported more correct signals in a visual detection task in the no-test than in the test condition, the opposite was true for subjects low in test anxiety.

A number of complementary accounts of the effects of anxiety on encoding and cue utilization have appeared in the literature. Broadbent (1971) considered the observed effects to be due to the influence of arousal on filtering of information. The aroused attentional system is selective in acceptance of inputs, so it devotes a higher proportion of its time to the intake of information from dominant sources and less from relatively minor ones. High arousal restricts the range of cues among which attention may be divided and also disrupts the control of selective attention. Broadbent suggested that a high state of arousal may also impair the process of discrimina-

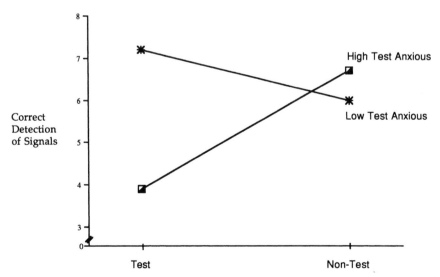

Figure 10.2.   Interaction of trait test anxiety and test conditions (test vs. nontest) on signal detection task performance. Based on data from Geen (1985b), Table 1, p. 967.

tion and ability to focus on relevant stimuli. Hamilton (1975), by contrast, explained the effect under consideration in terms of limited cognitive resources under conditions of cognitive load. Accordingly, anxious arousal works to reduce the amount of spare attentional capacity in the system, i.e., capacity beyond what is required for the primary task (Kahneman, 1973). Whenever a person's piorities in allocation of attention gives precedence to the demands of enduring dispositions, such as the cognitive representations of test anxiety, less space capacity is left over for the demands of the task, particularly under conditions of cognitive load. Thus, a person will often respond to the limited resources by paying less attention to external, task-related inputs, either by narrowing the area of focus for selective attention or by restricting attention to a small number of foci. Alternatively, there may be some automatic mechanism for compensation.

The notion of narrowed cue utilization advanced by Easterbrook's hypothesis has been criticized on a number of counts (M. W. Eysenck, 1982, 1985). To begin with, anxiety has also been found to be associated with a *broadened* range of stimulus perception, rather than a narrowed range (Geen, 1980). Rather than focusing their attention under conditions of high arousal and anxiety, high-test-anxious subjects have sometimes been reported to show diffused attention and greater distractibility in performing the central task, with high-test-anxious subjects attending *less* time to task-relevant information (Deffenbacher, 1978). Furthermore, Easterbrook regarded attentional narrowing as a relatively passive and automatic process under conditions of emotional arousal; it may be more fruitful to regard it as an active coping response when an individual is under informational overload (M. W. Eysenck, 1982). Accordingly, when the environmental demands cannot be handled by the available processing capacity and the total information processing system is in danger of overload, the individual adopts the strategy of restriction of attention to a small number of sources of information.

Recent research and systematic reviews of the evidence suggest that many of the effects of anxiety on performance can be explained in attentional terms and test anxiety may be an antecedent of narrowed cue utilization. However, more research needs to be carried out before firm conclusions can be reached. Overall, Mueller (1992, p. 148) concluded that the evidence "broadly indicates that anxiety affects what the subject attends to, but probably not as uniformly nor so inexorably as proposed by Easterbrook."

Tobias (1977a, 1977c, 1980) suggested that the influence of the effects of test anxiety at the stage of preprocessing and encoding are potentially cumulative, in that information which is not encoded adequately at the preprocessing stage is expected to impose greater difficulty in succeeding information processing. Accordingly, interference and diversion of attention in test-anxious subjects restricts the proportion of input registered, placing a greater burden on processing resources to figure out that proportion of input which has not been successfully registered. Interference at the preprocessing state, according to Tobias (1992), can be considerably reduced by procedures that permit reinspection of the input materials or checking input against a standard. Accordingly, if the input stream in a learning situation has been interfered with by anxiety (e.g. reduced attentiveness), a student could attempt to reinstate it by rereading the text, rewinding an audio- or videotape, going over someone else's notes, and the like.

Distractibility

Test anxiety has been claimed to decrease attentional control and thus increase susceptibility to distraction (Wachtel, 1967). Distractibility refers to the inability to concentrate on the target task in the presence of irrelevant stimulation, whether the stimuli be external (any interfering event) or internal (worries/somatic tension) (R. Schwarzer, 1990). Distractibility, along with attentional capacity and attentional selectivity, have been identified as being among the prime cognitive-attentional factors associated with high trait anxiety (M. W. Eysenck, 1982, 1992).

M. W. Eysenck's (1982, 1992) theory as it relates to hypervigilance would suggest that anxiety should be associated with increased distractibility, as the rapid detection of threatening stimuli in the environment requires diverting processing resources away from the current task to extraneous sources of stimulation, thus increasing distractibility. Further, if test-anxious persons constantly scan the environment to detect evaluative threats, even when tasks are neutral, this could produce extra processing distractions. Thus, the tendency to allocate extra processing resources to threatening stimuli in the test environment would imply the withdrawal of resources from the ongoing test and the subsequent disruption of test performance. Furthermore, given that test-anxious subjects are preoccupied with intrusive thoughts and self-monitoring of performance, it is not surprising that they have difficulty concentrating on the task at hand and are highly distractible. Deffenbacher (1978), in fact, has identified three main forms of potential internal distracters in high-test-anxious subjects: (a) worry, involving a cognitive concern about performance, consequences of failure, and evaluation of one's ability relative to others; (b) emotionality, referring to ones' self-perceived physiological arousal and upset (heart racing, upset stomach, etc.); and (c) task-generated interference, with high-test-anxious subjects more susceptible to task-produced competing responses under high drive conditions. Presumably, external distracters are also important.

The bulk of evidence suggests that persons high in trait test anxiety are more distractible than those low in trait test anxiety, have more trouble concentrating and focusing on the task, and are more susceptible to distraction by external and internal worries and preoccupations (M. W. Eysenck, 1992, 1997; Wine, 1971b). Furthermore, high-anxiety subjects have been reported spending far *less* time than low-anxiety subjects attending to task-relevant information (Deffenbacher, 1978). For example, Nottelman and Hill (1977) found that high-anxiety children were more distractible than low-anxiety children when performing an anagram task, showing substantially more off-task glancing than did low-anxiety children.

Mueller (1980) raised the intriguing possibility that self-preoccupation leads high-test-anxious subjects to encode fewer attributes than low-test-anxious subjects. Consequently, when being tested, anxious subjects would have fewer cues to use spontaneously for retrieval, and would be able to respond to fewer cues task cues. In addition, self-related thoughts and self-monitoring during a test may hinder attending to the relevant cues or executing the retrieval plan. In general, evidence reviewed by Mueller (1980) supports this prediction, showing that anxious subjects should show less recall on a cued test.

Information Storage and Processing

In this section I examine the evidence for the impact of test anxiety on the operations that individuals perform on the input of information, including storage and transformation (deduction).

Memory and Information Storage

Short-Term Memory. Considerable research efforts have recently been devoted in an attempt to localize the effects of test anxiety within specific stages or components of short-term memory. Short-term memory tasks are those which require subjects to maintain information in an available state through rehearsed or other processes, or to retrieve information that has not been attended for a *short* time (Humphreys & Revelle, 1984). For example, presenting a subject with a list of eight consecutive digits and asking the subject to repeat these digits immediately after presentation would involve short-term memory, with minimal processing.

Recent attempts to localize the effects of test anxiety on the information processing system suggest that the *working memory*, the active component of short-term memory, may be the key factor in mediating anxiety-related deficits in cognitive performance (H. J. Eysenck, 1979). The concept of "working memory" proposed by Baddeley and Hitch (1974) is concerned with both active processing and transient storage of information. The working memory system is conceptualized to include the following three separate components: (a) a modality-free *control processor* (executive), an attentional system used extensively in all tasks; (b) an *articulatory loop*, or verbal rehearsal system, which is used for transient storage of verbal material; this component permits storage of a limited amount of information in a phonemic code; and (c) a *visuospatial sketch pad*—specializing in visual and/or spatial information. Since working memory is crucially involved in the temporary holding and processing of information, any anxiety-induced reduction in its capacity would inevitably have wide-ranging effects in the performance of many cognitive tasks (M. W. Eysenck, 1983). It is assumed that the main effects of worry are on the central executive, although the articulatory loop is also implicated (M. W. Eysenck & Calvo, 1992;

Darke, 1988). Furthermore, state, rather than trait, evaluative anxiety appears to underlie deficits in working memory (Matthews, 1986).

A recurring finding in the literature is that state anxiety is negatively related to transient storage capacity, as indexed by digit-span measures (Mueller, 1980). Since digit-span tasks (e.g., "Repeat the following string of digits after me: 9, 3, 7, 4, 2, 8, 1") require maximal utilization of transient storage capacity in working memory, high levels of state anxiety would indeed be predicted to be associated with impaired digit-span task performance. This prediction has been supported repeatedly in the literature. A study by Darke (1988) found that the digit-span performance of high-test-anxious subjects under ego-threatening conditions was approximately 20% lower than that of low-test-anxious subjects. However, a deficit in the short-term component is not always accompanied by a deficit in total recall from memory or organization, suggesting that more is involved in the overall deficit than a structural limit on capacity (Mueller & Overcast, 1976).

A review of the literature by M. W. Eysenck (1992) shows that the vast majority of studies report a significant effect of state anxiety on working memory capacity. In particular, the finding that anxiety-linked performance deficits are particularly reliable on tasks that simultaneously require both processing and storage, i.e., combination of cognitive operations for which the working memory is specialized, adds support to the centrality of working memory in mediating the effects of anxiety on performance. Some recent data provide additional support for these conclusions (MacLeod & Donnellan, 1993; Calvo, Eysenck, Ramos & Jimenez, 1994). While the working memory deficit experienced by high-test-anxious individuals may not seem to be large in absolute terms, it appears to be more substantial when viewed as a proportion of the size of working memory (Mueller, 1980). According to Mueller's calculations, if primary memory capacity is estimated as roughly six or seven items, the difference in one item between high- and low-test-anxious subjects means a loss of about 15%.

In addition to the possible effects of anxiety on the capacity and processing ability of working memory, a number of alternative anxiety effects on short-term memory have been postulated. Tobias (1992) for example, suggested that anxiety may directly interfere in the continual transfer of information between short-term storage and long-term memory. In addition, it has been suggested that high- and low-test-anxious subjects, rather than differing in the size of working memory itself, differ in terms of the *address register*. The register holds information about the contents of short-term storage, but not the events themselves (Broadbent, 1971; Mueller, 1980).

An unsettled but very basic question concerns the extent to which high-test-anxious subjects have a basic and *permanent* working memory capacity lower than their less-test-anxious counterparts, as opposed to simply suffering from a *temporary* reduction under stressful conditions. Whereas some studies (e.g., Darke, 1988) provide experimental data showing that high levels of test anxiety reduce both the basic storage and processing capacity of working memory, others (e.g., Calvo, Ramos, & Estevez, 1992) provide evidence for the hypothesis that basic capacity is not affected in high-test-anxious subjects, as these differences are found only under evaluative contexts and not in neutral nonevaluative testing conditions.

Long-Term Memory.   In addition to the debilitating effects of test anxiety on short-term memory, anxiety has also been claimed to impair retention of information in *long-term memory.* This claim conforms with the hypothesis that heightened arousal, generally accompanying anxious worry, leads to a relative emphasis on processing superficial features of verbal stimuli at the expense of deeper and more semantic processing. Whereas the superficial processing characteristic of test-anxious subjects may be sufficient for succeeding on an immediate test, they may be insufficient for succeeding on delayed tasks. This is based on the assumption that delayed tasks, which require longer term retention, demand more elaborate or in-depth processing of stimuli. Overall, reviews of the literature suggest that high-test-anxious subjects exhibit a greater retention loss over time (H. J. Eysenck & Eysenck, 1985) and perform more poorly than low-test-anxious subjects on both immediate and delayed tasks (Mueller, 1992).

Strategic versus Automatic Task Processing

It has been argued that test anxiety is associated primarily with deficits in the *strategic* rather than the *automatic* processing of information. Accordingly, automatic or highly learned operations will be relatively unaffected by arousal level, whereas operations requiring rehearsal or strategic operations will be hindered by arousal. MacLeod and Donnellan (1993) suggest that the reason why automatic processes are not impaired by anxiety is because such cognitive operations do not require access to working memory. By contrast, strategic processes, which do require working memory resources, will be impaired by anxiety—but only if resource requirements exceed available working memory capacity. More generally, performance on easy tasks often is not predicted to be impaired by anxiety because, despite functional restrictions in available processing resources, sufficient memory capacity remains for the successful execution of relatively simple tasks. By contrast, the solution of cognitively more demanding tasks that require greater attention and processing capacity, would be more seriously interfered with by the presence of distracting worry (Hamilton, 1975). There is some evidence that anxiety seriously disrupts the retrieval of information on more strategic memory tasks (Darke, 1988; MacLeod & Donnellan, 1993).

Depth and Breadth of Processing

Craik and Lockhart's conceptualization of depth of processing analysis (Craik & Lockhart, 1972) stimulated considerable research examining the possible differential effects of test anxiety on superficial versus deep processing. Accordingly, stimulus encodings were seen as varying in terms of the amount of meaningfulness extracted from the stimuli or the "depth of processing." Semantic analysis is generally regarded as involving deep processing, whereas physical/phonemic/acoustic analysis only necessitates shallow processing. Test anxiety has been hypothesized to show a greater negative impact on *deep* than on *superficial* processing of stimuli (Craik & Lockhart, 1972). Thus, compared to their low-test-anxious counterparts, high-test-anxious individuals are predicted either to not process as deeply (or as thoroughly at deep levels), or to not process as deeply with the same speed (Geen, 1980).

The "depth hypothesis" assumes that deep processing results in a stronger memory trace, whereas shallow processing of semantic stimuli results in an unstable memory trace. Indeed, one frequent interpretation of the observed memory deficits of high-test-anxious subjects (who typically recall fewer words on a free-recall test) is that high-test-anxious subjects engage in a more restricted encoding of items, utilizing fewer of the available attributes of stimuli in encoding in memory. Thus, high-test-anxious subjects are less able to utilize vicarious word features to their advantage in organizing material in memory.

Further, the recall of high-test-anxious subjects shows less organization, presumably because they do not encode as broad a range of features, or do not organize them as well (Mueller & Overcast, 1976). As pointed out by Mueller (1976), even if informational content is available in short-term storage, it will dissipate more quickly in high-test-anxious subjects than for less aroused subjects. This is so because low-test-anxious subjects attend more to the deeper features that generally yield more durable memories (Mueller, Elser, & Rollack, 1992; Tobias, 1980). In addition, arousal during information intake will tend to produce a more restricted rehearsal strategy, involving more repetition. By contrast, less aroused subjects are claimed to use more productive rehearsal strategies that elaborate new experiences and connect them with old knowledge (Mueller et al., 1992; Tobias, 1980).

Based on the notion of limited information processing capacity (Hamilton, 1975), it may be reasoned that a task requiring *superficial* processing would not compete as much for processing capacity with the cognitive representation of anxiety, and would therefore disrupt performance less. By contrast, a more complex task, requiring *deeper* processing and elaboration of information, would compete more for processing capacity and disrupt performance to a greater extent. Furthermore, because test-anxious subjects tend to be more self-preoccupied than their less anxious counterparts, they probably would need relatively more time for deep processing. In order to avoid or reduce the more time-consuming endeavors of analyzing deep features or encoding elaborately, high-test-anxious subjects may have adopted an ultimately maladaptive strategy of coping with the competing demands for processing resources by processing information at a superficial level.

The typical paradigm for studying the "anxiety–depth" hypothesis involves free recall of word lists containing both *shallow* and *deep* dimensions for organizations. A list construction with both rhyming (shallow) and word associates (deep) relationships are typically used in the same list. Given the word list {RING, KING, BELL}, with the base word being "RING," subjects might cluster by associate

{BELL}, rhyme {KING}, or both. The "anxiety–depth" hypothesis would suggest that high-test-anxious subjects would show a deficit in terms of associative organization, but no deficit in terms of acoustic organization.

Some research summarized by Mueller (1980) suggests that even when given additional time, anxious subjects persevere on nonsemantic features without processing to deeper levels. Low-anxiety subjects, by contrast, will progress to deeper levels. Furthermore, whereas some research suggests that providing high-test-anxious subjects with orienting instructions to semantically process information is particularly helpful to them (Weinstein et al., 1982), other studies have found no evidence to support this contention (Mueller, 1978).

The notion concerning depth of processing deficit has been criticized on a number of counts (M. W. Eysenck, 1982). First, proponents of this notion are said to have failed to explain adequately why deep encodings should be better remembered than more superficial encodings. Second, because there is a lack of an independent measure of the depth of processing, we cannot be sure whether a procedure which claims to require in-depth or superficial processing (e.g., encoding associates over rhymes on wordlists) in fact does so. Third, there appears to be some serious confounding of depth with "elaboration," or "distinctiveness" of encoding. Fourth, even if increased test anxiety limits processing capacity, subsequent elaborative encoding (which relates features within or across levels) among high-test-anxious subjects may go as deep as in low-test-anxious subjects, but not incorporate as many features (Mueller, 1980). Finally, it is noted that this line of research implies a serial processing model, with shallower levels processed first—which is not necessarily the case.

Overall, however, the results of research relating to the anxiety–depth effect have been rather inconsistent. Whereas some studies show that increased anxiety leads to reduced semantic processing and increased physical processing (e.g., Weinstein et al., 1982) others have not (e.g., Mueller, 1978; Mueller, Carlomusto, & Marler, 1977). A review by Mueller (1992) led him to conclude that relative to their low-test-anxious counterparts, anxious subjects do less processing of deep features of lexical stimuli and also less elaborative rehearsal, thus creating considerable problems for their long-term retention of the material. Furthermore, relative to low-test-anxious subjects, high-test-anxious subjects also do less shallow processing and less maintenance rehearsal as well. This confirms M. W. Eysencks' (1982) conclusion that there is little support for the notion that anxiety impairs semantic processing more than shallow processing.

Language Processing

Recent research has examined the differential influence of test anxiety and emotional reactivity to evaluative stress pressures on various cognitive operations involved in language proficiency. Covington and Omelich (1987b) reported a modest inverse relationship between a proneness to worry under test conditions and general vocabulary scores. Similarly, Calvo, Eysenck, Ramos, and Jimenez (1994) reported a deficit in vocabulary knowledge, as assessed by general vocabulary scores and word knowledge, in high-test-anxious subjects.

Test-anxious subjects are not reported to suffer from slower speed of lexical access. Mueller and Wherry (1982) presented subjects low and high in test anxiety with pairs of words and asked them to make judgments under three conditions: (a) *physical matching* conditions, determining if words such as MEAT and MEET are spelled alike; (b) *acoustic matching* or "homophone conditions," deciding if a word pair, e.g., MEAT–MEET, is pronounced the same, and (c) *taxonomic category membership*, deciding whether or not two words, say INCH–YARD, could be members of the same superordinate grouping. They reasoned that if anxious subjects are characterized by a slower speed of lexical access, greater differences between and high- and low-test-anxious groups would be expected for the taxonomic category member, requiring lexical access, relative to the other conditions. A series of experiments failed to support this prediction, suggesting that anxiety does not slow access to semantic information more than is the case for nonsemantic codes.

A series of experiments by Calvo et al. (1992) among college students demonstrated that high-test-anxious readers were less efficient in their reading comprehension than their low-test-anxious counterparts, employing extra time to acquire an equivalent amount of information. The comprehensive efficiency of readers increased as anxiety decreased, specifically when learning expository texts. The efficiency impairment of test-anxious subjects was associated with a deficit in general vocabulary knowledge, word knowledge on expository texts, reading span, and transitory reduction in working memory capacity. The authors argue that the factor responsible for the negative effects of anxiety is the transient reduction in the processing and storage capacity of working memory (rather than simply performance deficits) under stress conditions. However, the fact that anxiety still impaired reading efficiency after controlling for transitory decrements in working memory capacity suggests that other factors may be producing efficiency impairment (prior knowledge, e.g., vocabulary). It is noted that it is not necessarily the case that word reading reflects working memory resources. It might simply reflect the speed of execution of the various component processes required for reading.

In a recent study by Calvo and Carreiras (1993), a small sample ($n = 36$) of high- and low-test-anxious students read texts word by word with the *moving window technique* (words appearing one at a time on the screen) under "test" conditions. The dependent variable, word-reading time, presumably reflects the amount of working memory resources employed by a reader to perform the cognitive operations leading to comprehension. Multiple regression results indicated that test anxiety did not impair text comprehension, but increased word reading time. Thus, anxious readers need to employ a greater amount of processing resources to obtain a similar comprehension level. Furthermore, interactive effects suggest that anxiety is selectively detrimental to the efficiency of text-level processes, such as those involving integrating information across sentences. In contrast, anxiety was not shown to impair low-level processes, such as encoding and lexical access. Overall, word-level processes, including encoding and lexical access, are not deleteriously affected by test anxiety, with both high- and low-test-anxious subjects having equivalent word-reading times under the different indices. Further, whereas sentence-level processes (proposition, sentence integration) were not significantly impaired by anxiety, text-level processes were detrimentally influenced by test anxiety. The authors suggest that the text-level processes demand an additional amount of working memory compared with word-level and sentence-level processes, and that is why they are the most susceptible to the deleterious effects of anxiety. Because these findings are in contrast with the encoding and lexical access deficits exhibited by poor readers, Calvo and Carreiras (1993) reject the hypothesis that high-test-anxious subjects are poor readers. However, the authors may be guilty of circular reasoning in assuming that whatever task component is anxiety-sensitive must require more working memory.

Conceptual Organization

One of the plausible causes of poor academic performance and learning difficulty in high-test-anxious students may be the poor level of conceptual organization in long-term storage. Accordingly, high levels of test anxiety may have a shallowing effect on the encoding and organization of semantic material by reducing the quality of elaborations and associative paths (Mueller, 1980), with a number of studies consistent with this notion. Naveh-Benjamin et al. (1987) provided data for a small group ($n = 65$) of college students indicating that high-test-anxious students indeed had a more poorly organized structure of major concepts taught in their college course. Mueller (1976) reported that high-test-anxious subjects clustered less on free-recall tasks than those low in test anxiety for the following three categories: taxonomic, acoustic, and associative categories. They also showed less subjective organization of formally unrelated terms and gave less priority in output to previously unrecalled items. Furthermore, research shows that the high-test-anxious subjects make less use of taxonomic group membership in clustering of words and organizing them for memory (Mueller, 1977). Furthermore, there is some research indicating that trait anxiety is related to the breadth of semantic categories in categorization of stimuli (Mikulincer, Kedem, & Paz, 1990a, 1990b). Trait-anxious subjects under evaluative stress are reported to chunk information into *wider* rather than narrower categories.

Judgment and Decision Making

Rational-choice models of decision making assume that decisions are based on the careful weighing of the utilities and probabilities associated with all available courses of action. Thus, in considering whether to buy a Peugeot 306 or Volkswagen Rabbit for the family car, the rational decision maker would be expected to search painstakingly for relevant information (price, size, interior space, safety features, comfort, storage, accessories, driving quality, etc.), weigh each of the alternatives with respect to major criteria of importance, assimilate information in an unbiased manner, and appraise alternatives carefully before making an optimal choice. Research in the area of stress and decision making (Janis & Mann, 1977; Keinan, 1987) suggests that individuals often fail to adhere to a *rational* model of choice and decision making. Furthermore, irrationality might be enhanced by anxiety. Thus, Janis and Mann's (1977) well-known model of decision making posits that under stress, individuals adopt a form of coping termed "hypervigilance" (to be distinguished from M. W. Eysenck's [1992] later use of the term). This mode of coping is manifested by disorganized information processing in a frantic search for a solution: a hasty and incomplete evaluation of information, failure to consider all alternatives, and a rapid shifting among possible solutions, frequently leading to faulty decisions. Hypervigilant behavior would probably characterize the fidgety and panicky behavior of many test-anxious students under severe time pressure when studying for an upcoming exam or when completing the last subtest of a speeded aptitude exam. The model assumes that decisions resulting from processing information and decision making under severe stress are more likely to be faulty than decisions reached after careful appraisal and evaluation of feedback. The optimal form of coping with complex decisions in the Janis and Mann model, termed a "vigilant" coping mode, would require rational behavior, involving the careful consideration and weighing of alternatives and their outcomes, combining utilities and probabilities for each decision option, and choosing the most optimal option.

There is some evidence suggesting that anxious subjects differ from nonanxious subjects in handling information processing prior to making a decision. Thus, Geen (1985b) hypothesized that when searching for information upon which to base a decision, anxious subjects will require more information than will less anxious subjects before they are willing to commit themselves to a decision. As part of this greater tendency for information, anxious subjects may have a greater tendency to reinspect information that they already have observed, since some of the attention was diverted to thoughts about the implications of being evaluated. Green (1985b) provided data showing that high-test-anxious subjects tested under evaluative conditions were more conservative in setting a criterion than high-test-anxious subjects tested under nonevaluative conditions or low-test-anxious persons whether tested under evaluative or nonevaluative conditions.

Research by Keinan (1987) is suggestive that stress may effect the following facets of scanning and consideration of alternatives in the decision-making process:

Nonsystematic scanning: A stressed individual may consider or scan alternatives in a nonsystematic fashion, rapidly shifting back and forth between alternatives. With respect to test situations, a test taker may switch from one test problem to another or one test option to another, thus interfering with the normal smooth flow of test taking.

Premature closure: Because stress may narrow a persons' span of attention, stressed examinees may have trouble assimilating all the information available to them on an exam. Consequently, they focus on a limited number of dimensions and often reach premature closure. Thus, anxious test takers may choose a response on a test item before all the available options have been exhaustively considered or before considering the relevant dimensions on an essay exam question.

Temporal narrowing: The stressed examinee may devote insufficient time to consideration of each alternative, seizing upon a hastily contrived solution that seems to promise immediate relief. Thus, the stressed examinee may seize upon the first idea that comes to mind, or fixate on the first bits of information retrieved from memory in preparing an essay or in solving a complex problem on a multiple-choice exam. For example, a history student writing a mid-term essay exam may fixate on economic factors in explaining Hitler's rise to power in prewar Germany, while failing to consider other dimensions and alternatives, such as historical, social, ideological, military, and geopolitical forces.

While Keinan's (1987) research has provided evidence showing that psychological stress leads to a greater incidence of premature closure and nonsystematic scanning among subjects threatened with threat of shock, the generalizability of these results to evaluative threat conditions has yet to be determined.

Metacognition

Metacognition refers to the knowledge and executive processes a person uses to be cognizant of, to monitor, and to control his or her processing of learning (Everson, Smodlaka, & Tobias, 1992). Everson and coworkers identify two major dimensions of metacognition. The first, *knowing what one knows*, has to do with knowing the necessary information to achieve a task (i.e., declarative or factual information). For example, when taking a course in multivariate statistics, a student may realize that he or she has sufficient background in regression and analysis of variance to handle the course, but needs to brush up on key concepts in linear algebra (e.g., matrices, linear equations, etc.). The second dimension, *executive management*, involves the regulation of cognition, including a dynamic function. Thus, a student studying for a mid-year exam would need to plan her studies to cover and summarize adequately all the material before the exam, monitor her progress, flexibly orchestrate the deployment of different processes (reading, summarizing, rehearsing, elaborating, exercising, etc.), and evaluate the effectiveness of her efforts (e.g., "I need to study twice as hard tomorrow."). Test-anxious students, whose cognitive resources are relatively limited due to incessant worry and preoccupation with the test, thus reducing the remaining intellectual resources that could be utilized for resource-consuming metacognitive processes, may find the division of attention implied by these difficult metacognitive activities especially difficult (Tobias, 1992).

In one of the few empirical studies designed to assess the effects of test anxiety on metacognitive word knowledge on a reading comprehension test, Everson and his coworkers (Everson et al., 1992) had 117 college students complete measures of test anxiety, reading ability, a metacognitive word knowledge task, and measure of reading comprehension. Multiple regression analysis indicated that when controlling for reading ability, anxious worry was negatively related to metacognitive word knowledge. Further, when reading level was statistically controlled for, students' level of anxious worrying and metacognitive word knowledge influenced performance on all measures of reading comprehension subscales.

Information Retrieval and Output

The third juncture at which test anxiety may impact upon cognitive performance is after the storage and processing of information, but either before or while doing the actual "output," namely, test taking or performance (Tobias, 1977a, 1980, 1985). Although interference and task-irrelevant processing could affect almost every stage of processing, research has placed particular emphasis on its effects during information retrieval and output. Interference at the *output* stage represents two distinct subphases: (a) the phase just prior to output, where processing has been completed, but the information has not been reproduced effectively in a test or similar evaluative output situation, (b) cognitive interference experienced in the actual test situation. At the output stage, test anxiety is expected primarily to influence the retrieval of previously acquired information from memory, an effect people probably most closely link to test-anxious deficits. In fact, the well-established finding that anxious students perform more poorly in test situations than their less anxious counterparts is usually attributed to interference by anxiety in the retrieval of prior learning from long-term memory.

Most people, when asked to recall their own personal experiences in test situations, will report having experienced momentary retrieval failures during test performance. Indeed, a common complaint of high-test-anxious persons is, "I knew it cold before the exam" (Covington & Omelich, 1987a). This phenomenon is typically referred to as the "anxiety blockage hypothesis" (Covington & Omelich, 1987a), in which anxiety inhibits test performance by temporarily blocking previously learned information or responses (Covington & Omelich, 1987a). A basic assumption of this hypothesis is that anxiety inhibits not original learning, but performance, and then only temporarily. Further, in order for blockage to occur, it is assumed that the examinee actually acquired those responses which are blocked during the exam. For example, a statistical concept, say, *multicollinearity* (the dependence among predictor variables), may have been learned and understood by a psychology major in an intermediate statistics course, but the concept may have become inaccessible when solving a relevant test item (e.g., "Assess the validity of a regression procedure involving extremely high correlations among the predictors, employing the concept of multicollinearity"). Another example would be the case of the student who has solved a problem involving numerical progressions on an aptitude test (2, 6, 18, 54, —?) and is just about to respond to the test item by filling in the number 162 in the blank space, when anxiety sets in to interfere with the accurate rendering of that response in output. Thus, academic material may be acquired and understood, but then can be lost and become inaccessible in a variety of performance situations, including homework problem solving, reciting the answer before the class, writing an essay, giving an oral report, taking essay exam, and the like.

Test anxiety may impair performance during the actual test-taking process because it leads to task-irrelevant processing (M. W. Eysenck, 1982). Indeed, current research evidence (see Chapters 2 and 8) supports the notion that high-test-anxious individuals engage in more task-irrelevant processing during an exam than their low-test-anxious counterparts. Thus, when attempting to solve a complex problem on an exam, anxious students typically find themselves dividing their attention between the multiple requirements of the complex task (i.e., task-relevant thinking) and various task-irrelevant activities (e.g., ruminative self-preoccupations and criticisms). However, a review of the literature (Mueller, 1980) suggests that anxiety deficits seem to be fairly well established for both recall and recognition types of tests, indicating that the anxiety deficit involves not only retrieval, but also storage processes at least.

In most anxiety research the distinction between acquisition and retrieval is obscured (Tobias, 1985). Because students are tested on what was previously learned, acquisition and retention are confounded. One possible criterion allowing us to differentiate between interference during information processing and interference that occurs just prior to output is that students should have been able to solve the problem during acquisition but *incapable* of doing so during posttest processing.

Summary

This chapter was aimed at mapping out the effects of anxiety on various phases of information processing. Overall, the evidence surveyed in this chapter, although not entirely consistent, suggests that test anxiety may affect cognitive performance, through cognitive processes, at each of the distinct stages of information processing. The key deficits reported for high-test-anxious subjects, notwithstanding mixed results in some cases, are presented and summarized in Table 10.1.

With respect to the *encoding* of information, research suggests that the attention-demanding effects of test-anxious worry may impair a person's ability to attend to and successfully register novel stimuli or new learning material. Test anxiety has also been found to lead subjects to employ less extensive and elaborated encoding strategies and has frequently been reported to be associated with a narrowed perceptual range. However, it is still an unsettled questioned whether anxiety primarily leads to high selectivity and a narrow breadth of attention or whether it leads to increased lability and susceptibility to distraction.

With respect to *memory and processing effects*, there is a convincing body of evidence that test anxiety meaningfully impairs the efficiency of short-term storage, especially hindering performance on tasks requiring considerable amounts of the storage and processing capacity of working memory. Students' long-term memory is also affected by test anxiety. Thus, compared to their low-test-anxious counterparts, high-test-anxious subjects show a greater retention loss over time and perform more poorly on both immediate and delayed tasks. Furthermore, relative to their low-test-

Table 10.1. Information Processing Deficits in High-Test-Anxious Individuals

Deficit area	Brief description
Information encoding	
Encoding difficulties	Test-anxious individuals report experiencing more encoding difficulties than their low-test-anxious counterparts
Interpretive bias	Test-anxious individuals exhibit selective attentional bias favoring threat (see Chapter 8)
Restricted range of cue utilization	Test-anxious individuals attend to fewer environmental features and have a narrow range of cue utilization
Distractibility	Text-anxious subjects have difficulty in concentrating on cognitive tasks; they typically find themselves dividing their attention between the multiple requirements of the complex task and various task-irrelevant activities
Information storage and processing	
Short-term storage	Anxious arousal causes a reduction in cognitive capacity devoted to the task, thus reducing resources for short-term memory tasks in test-anxious persons; working memory is particularly affected
Long-term storage	Test-anxiety impairs retention of information in long-term memory, leading to greater retention loss over time
Depth of processing	Test anxiety leads to a relative emphasis on processing superficial features of verbal stimuli at the expense of deeper semantic processing; test-anxious individuals focus on shallow or physical features rather than deep or semantic features of stimuli
Elaboration and rehearsal	Test-anxious subjects fail to adequately rehearse or elaborate upon information
Conceptual organization	Test anxiety may disrupt the encoding and organization of semantic material by reducing the quality of elaborations and associative paths; test-anxious subjects cluster less on free-recall tasks than those low in test anxiety for taxonomic categories, acoustic categories, and associative categories
Strategic processing	Automatic or highly learned operations are relatively unaffected by test anxiety, whereas complex tasks requiring rehearsal or strategic operations will be hindered by arousal
Language processing	Test-anxious subjects have vocabulary deficits, and are deficient in their comprehension and reading efficiency; anxiety is selectively detrimental to the efficiency of text-level processes, such as those involving integrating information across sentences
Decision making	High-test-anxious subjects have difficulty in absorbing decision-relevant information, tend to have difficulty in scanning alternatives, and adopt more cautious decisional criteria
Metacognition	Test-anxious subjects are deficient in metacognitive knowledge, including knowledge and executive processes used to control learning
Information retrieval	
Interference and anxiety blockage	Anxious subjects suffer from cognitive interference and are self-preoccupied with task-irrelevant information
Information retrieval	Test anxiety impairs retrieval of material and thus lowers performance during the actual test-taking process

anxious counterparts, anxious subjects do less processing of deep features of lexical stimuli and also less elaborative rehearsal, thus creating considerable problems for their long-term retention of the material. Furthermore, there is some evidence indicating that high levels of anxiety may disrupt the encoding and taxonomic organization of semantic material by reducing the quality of elaborations and associative paths. Finally, interference during the *retrieval* or output stage hinders the performance of test-anxious subjects, particularly at higher levels of anxiety and on difficult tasks.

Overall, it appears that test-anxious subjects may suffer from varying degrees of deficits and interference at all three stages of information processing. These deficits are not independent, but may be related in a cumulative fashion. More research is needed detailing how test anxiety influences specific cognitive structures and processes, including scanning behavior, breadth of stimuli utilization, various facets of judgment and decision making, long-term memory, inductive and deductive processes, ideation, and creative behavior. Research is also needed in the area of remediation of specific deficits in encoding, processing, and rehearsal, although some progress had been made in this area (Tobias, 1992). Finally, the various cognitive models discussed here were designed to account for the anxiety-related decrements in performance. These models would best be seen as complementary, rather than conflicting. By and large the models rest on the common assumption of limited cognitive capacity and restricted resources in the human cognitive system. Rather than artificially set one explanation against another in a simplistic manner, it would probably be more productive for researchers to adopt a multistage integrative approach which incorporates the best of several mechanisms considered together. It is important to keep in mind that in many cases, interpretations of anxiety data rest on a particular theory or model of information processing which may be open to challenge. If the theory is wrong, the interpretation is also wrong.

V

Individual Differences

Individual and Group Differences
in Test Anxiety

Overview

Individual and group differences in reactions to tests and evaluative encounters have been the subject of some interest since the inception of evaluative anxiety research. Current research is guided by the assumption that it is important to take individual difference variables into account in explaining the observed variance in test anxiety scores. Accordingly, this chapter surveys the evidence for gender, age, sociocultural, and cross-cultural differences in test anxiety, providing theoretical accounts for group differences when observed.

Gender Group Differences

Gender, as a correlate of many developmental trends, is commonly claimed to impact upon the development and manifestation of anxiety in evaluative situations. Thus, women are said to be more sensitive to evaluative stimuli and consequently show more anxiety in the face of negative evaluation than men. Women are also believed to be more uncomfortable and self-conscious in testing situations than men (Lewis & College, 1987). There is some research data to support the notion that women devalue and underpredict their cognitive performance compared to men (Furst, Tenenbaum, & Weingarten, 1985; Gjesme, 1982; Wine, 1980) and are significantly lower in perceived self-efficacy (Arch, 1987; Benson & Bandalos, 1989). These findings are of special interest in light of research indicating that low levels of self-efficacy are characteristic of persons who are highly test anxious (Hembree, 1988; Hunsley, 1985). Women are also reported to obtain higher scores than men on measures of social anxiety and public self-consciousness administered during actual testing situations (Sowa & LaFleur, 1986). The increased degree of public self-consciousness in women may cause them to become more concerned about their personal inadequacies than men and consequently to feel more apprehensive and uncomfortable in evaluative situations.

Furthermore, men and women have been hypothesized to interpret and respond to evaluative situations in a differential manner (Lewis & College, 1987). Accordingly, men may be more likely than women to perceive a test situation as a personal challenge rather than as a threat, interpreting anxious arousal during a test situation in a positive manner. Because men in test situations exhibit the facilitating responses of low-anxiety individuals (e.g., increased arousal, vigilance, and enthusiasm), their resultant test performance is improved. Women, by contrast, may be prone to perceive the test situation as a threat, and evidence behaviors characteristic of highly anxious individuals (fear, worry, anger, lowering of self-esteem). Thus, evaluative situations may serve to increase efficacy and self-esteem in men, whereas in women they may lead to an increase in arousal, worry, or discomfort, and lowered test performance. There is some empirical data to suggest, in fact, that men show more facilitating anxiety than women, whereas women show more debilitating anxiety than men (Couch, Garber, & Turner, 1983).

Magnitude of Gender Group Differences

Research has consistently pointed to gender group differences in test anxiety, with female students evidencing higher test anxiety levels than male students (Hagtvet, 1985a; Hembree, 1988; Seipp & Schwarzer, 1996; Sowa & Lafleur, 1986; Spielberger, 1980; Zeidner & Nevo, 1992). Gender group differences in test anxiety begin to emerge during the middle years of elementary school, with female students consistently reporting higher levels of test anxiety scores than male students from elementary school through high school and college (Hembree, 1988; Hill & Sarason, 1966).

Meta-analytic findings (Hembree, 1988; Seipp & Schwarzer, 1996) indicate that gender group differences in test anxiety are quite modest, amounting to slightly less than one third of a standard deviation. Furthermore, gender group differences are shown to be of considerably greater magnitude on the Emotionality than on the Worry component of test anxiety. These data support the notion that the affective component of test anxiety is a significant sex-differentiating factor. The results are also concurrent ·with Wine's (1971b) claim that because women show increased responsivity in interpersonal achievement settings compared to men, physiological arousal may be more likely to occur in women in evaluative contexts.

Table 11.1 displays empirical data provided by Zeidner and Nevo (1992), which is illustrative of the general pattern of gender group differences in test anxiety reported in the literature. Test anxiety was assessed among 243 male and 283 female college candidates either prior to or following the administration of scholastic aptitude college entrance exams. Total Test Anxiety Inventory (TAI) scores for female student candidates were observed to be higher than those of their male

**Table 11.1. Test Anxiety Inventory (TAI)
Means and Standard Deviations
for a Sample of Male and Female
College Candidates**

	Male ($n = 245$)		Female ($n = 283$)		
Scale	M	SD	M	SD	D
TAI	38.7	10.2	41.8	9.9	.31
Emotion	17.3	4.9	19.5	5.1	.43
Worry	13.6	4.0	13.7	4.0	.02

Note: D scores represent standardized gender differences (mean TAI total scores for female minus mean TAI total scores for male students, divided by pooled within-group standard deviations).

counterparts by about one third of a standard deviation. When examinees were divided into four groups on the basis of the four quartiles of the TAI score distribution, the majority (66%) of the high-anxiety group (fourth quartile) was comprised of female students, whereas the majority (67%) of the low-anxiety group (first quartile) was comprised of male students. Furthermore, sex differences were negligible on the Worry scale, being manifested mainly on the Emotionality scale. A profile analysis on a subset of the original sample (Zeidner, 1990) revealed significantly divergent sex-group profiles for the two anxiety scales, implying reliable variations in the magnitude of the sex-group differences with the particular component assessed.

Recent research shows a clear trend toward elevated test anxiety in female relative to male students in various national settings across the globe (Seipp & Schwarzer, 1996; see also El-Zahhar & Hocevar, 1991). The higher test anxiety scores in female compared to male students is clearly demonstrated in the cross- cultural data assembled from published research and presented in Tables 11.2 and 11.3. These tables display male and female TAI means and standard deviations for school age and college students, respectively. As shown in Figure 11.1, female students show somewhat higher test anxiety scores across educational groups and national sites. Based on my calculations, the mean effect size for gender in school-age students was .29 (i.e., female students score higher than male students by slightly less than one third of a standard deviation), with the 95% confidence interval ranging from .25 to .34 standard deviation units. The mean gender effect size reported for college students was highly comparable to that reported for school-aged students, i.e., .27 standard deviation units, with the 95% confidence level ranging from .22 to .32.

Seipp and Schwarzer (1996) meta-analyzed the results of over a dozen independent studies based on cross-cultural adaptations of the Test Anxiety Inventory (United States, Netherlands, Germany, Italy, Hungary, Czechoslovakia, Turkey,

Table 11.2. A Cross-Cultural Comparison of Gender Group Differences in Test Anxiety (TAI Total) for School-Age Students

Nation (sample)	Researchers	Year	Male			Female			Gender group difference (D)
			n	M	SD	n	M	SD	
China (Precollege)	Rocklin & Ren-Min	1989	100	37.9	8.8	105	38.6	8.1	.08
Czechoslovakia (ES)	Man, Budejovice, & Hosek	1989	73	37.6	8.9	81	41.9	9.8	.46
Germany (JHS)	C. Schwarzer & Kim	1984	426	37.0	9.3	473	40.6	11.3	.35
Holland (JHS)	Van der Ploeg	1982	57	32.7	10.5	97	37.4	11.2	.43
Hungary (ES)	Sipos, Sipos, & Spielberger	1985	332	38.8	8.4	368	41.2	8.9	.28
India (HS)	Sud & Sharma	1990	359	39.7	10.4	465	42.1	10.8	.22
India (JHS)	Sharma, Parnian, & Spielberger	1983	40	36.9	6.7	40	50.1	8.7	1.68
Iran (JHS)	Sharma, Parnian, & Speilberger	1983	40	46.2	10.7	40	51.8	8.2	.58
Italy (HS)	Comunian	1985	500	38.1	9.6	500	42.4	10.9	.42
Jordan (HS)	Ahlawat	1989b	1014	48.5	11.1	839	50.4	11.2	.17
Korea (JHS)	C. Schwarzer & Kim	1984	367	49.2	13.3	389	51.1	13.7	.14
Turkey (HS)	Oner & Kaymak	1987	197	39.2	9.8	134	44.6	10.2	.54
United States (HS)	Spielberger	1980	527	40.9	12.8	591	45.7	13.6	.36

Note: ES, Elementary school; JHS, junior high school; HS, high school.
D scores (group differences expressed in terms of standard deviation unit scores) represent female–male TAI total score means divided by pooled estimate of the within-group standard deviations. Meta-analysis showed that the mean effect size was .29 ($SE = .022$) for the studies appearing in this table, with the 95% confidence interval from .25 to .34. About 12% of the variance was accounted for by sampling error. Gender group differences were significant in all of the nations save for China.

Table 11.3. A Cross-Cultural Comparison of Gender Group Differences
in Test Anxiety (TAI Total Scores) for College Students

Nation	Researchers	Year	Male			Female			Gender group difference (D)
			n	M	SD	n	M	SD	
China	Rocklin & Ren-Min	1989	167	36.7	9.3	163	38.4	8.8	.19
Holland	Van der Ploeg	1982	116	34.1	10.3	68	36.3	10.6	.21
India (a)	Sharma et al.	1983	40	42.6	7.1	40	44.1	8.3	.19
India (b)	Sud & Sharma	1990	454	38.5	10.3	446	42.5	9.7	.39
Iran	Sharma et al.	1983	40	39.8	9.9	40	46.9	10.6	.69
Israel	Zeidner & Nevo	1992	245	38.7	10.2	283	41.8	9.9	.31
Italy	Comunian	1985	304	36.4	8.9	169	35.4	10.3	−.11
Japan	Araki, Iwawaki, & Spielberger	1992	308	36.3	10.4	451	37.1	9.4	.08
Jordan	Ahlawat	1989b	768	44.6	9.9	951	47.8	10.7	.31
Turkey	Oner & Kaymak	1987	130	34.5	8.2	143	37.5	9.6	.33
United States	Spielberger	1980	654	38.5	12.4	795	42.8	13.7	.33

Note: *D* scores represent the difference between male and female mean TAI total scores, divided by pooled estimates of the within-group standard deviations. A meta-analysis of the difference scores shows that the mean effect size was .27 (*SE* = .025), with the 95% confidence interval from .22 to .32. About 32% of the variance was accounted for by sampling error.

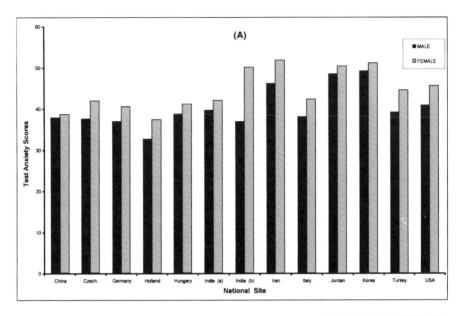

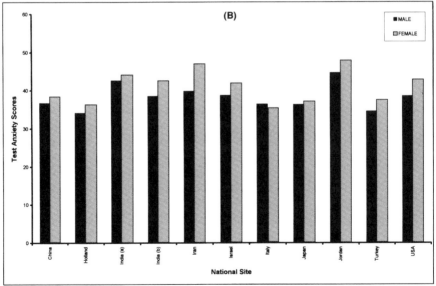

Figure 11.1. Gender differences in test anxiety inventory scores in (A) school-aged and (B) college students in various nations.

Jordan, Egypt, India, China, Korea, Puerto Rico, and Japan). In each of the countries assessed, with the exception of Turkey and China, women scored significantly higher, on average, than their male counterparts. Furthermore, gender differences are higher for the Emotionality than the Worry component in the majority of nations assessed. Because male and female subgroups do not differ to a measurable degree on the Worry component, these data imply that the gender differences in total test anxiety scores are mainly brought about by differences in Emotionality.

Explanations for the Observed Group Differences

Clearly, the bulk of empirical research surveyed above points to the conclusion that women, on average, have higher test anxiety levels than men. On face value, these differences may reflect a greater propensity among women compared to men to react with anxiety under stressful evaluative situations (trait test anxiety) or a stronger arousal of this disposition among women in test or testlike situations (state anxiety). How do we account for these consistent gender group differences in test anxiety?

The most prominent account attributes gender group differences to differential patterns of socialization and styles of child-rearing for boys and girls in our culture (Maccoby & Jacklin, 1974). Accordingly, girls and women may be socialized to express and acknowledge anxiety because anxiety is perceived as a feminine trait (Deaux, 1977). Thus, society's reaction to anxiety in women tends to be more of a supporting and reassuring nature, which allows women to admit rather than to hide their test anxiety. By contrast, anxiety in modern society is regarded as being incongruent with "masculinity," with men expected to repress or deny anxiety. Furthermore, men may be socialized to view test situations as presenting a challenge to be instrumentally coped with and overcome, whereas for women it may present a threat which requires mainly emotion-focused coping or escape behaviors (Deaux, 1977).

In view of the above, some researchers have concluded that the observed gender group differences do not reflect a real difference in actual levels of test anxiety as much as a gender difference in self-presentation and the willingness to openly admit anxiety (Hill & Sarason, 1966). Although both sexes may actually experience test anxiety to a similar degree, the higher level of test anxiety among women may be due to men's greater defensiveness about admitting anxiety. Whereas it is regarded as more "socially acceptable" for women to express anxiety, particularly about academic matters, men may be more defensive because manifestations of anxiety are more ego-alien for them; admission to being test-anxious would be socially disapproved as "unmasculine," particularly during the school years (S. B. Sarason et al., 1960). Hill (1972) cites research in support of the foregoing claim, showing that with increasing age boys in elementary school tend to reveal their anxiety through strong defensiveness. Accordingly, by the middle years of elementary school, boys usually have higher scores on tests of defensiveness (e.g., Hill & Sarason, 1966), suggesting that they may not be revealing their true feelings. This age pattern was not observed among girls in elementary school.

Gender Differences in the Latent Structure of Test Anxiety

Furthermore, it has been claimed that the differences in test anxiety scores for men and women might be explained by differences in the factor structure of the instruments used to measure test anxiety. However, several recent studies examining the underlying structural properties of test anxiety measures for possible gender differences fail to support this claim. Thus, Benson and Tippets (1990) reported gender group invariance in the number of factors, factor loading, and item residuals for TAI items. Gender differences were found primarily in the correlations between Worry and Emotionality, the two latent factors of Spielberger's (1980) Test Anxiety Inventory. Specifically, the relationship among the components for female students was observed to be stronger than that found for their male counterparts. Similarly, Everson et al. (1991) revealed an invariant factor structure for the TAI in a sizable sample (219 men and 282 women) of college students. In both gender groups the theoretical distinction between the Worry and Emotionality components of test anxiety was supported by the latent variable model. However, gender group differences were found in unique factor variances, which suggests that items were not equally reliable in male and female groups. Similar to what was reported by Benson and Tippets (1990), these authors observed gender differences in both the latent means and in the factor covariance structure. The latter finding suggests that the Worry and Emotionality factors may correlate differently for men and women. Rhine and Spaner (1983) also provided evidence suggesting that the factor structure of test anxiety, as assessed by the Test Anxiety Scale for Children (TASC) in a sample of 553 second and third grade children, is highly similar for boys and girls. The four major rotated factors (Test Anxiety, Remote School Concern, Poor Self-Evaluation, and Somatic Signs) accounted for 37.38% and 37.34% of the variance for boys and girls, respectively.

Additional support for the similarity of structural components of test anxiety in men and women came from a smallest space analysis of items on the Test Anxiety Inventory (R. Schwarzer, 1984). The analysis yielded a two-dimensional structure for both boys and girls; coefficients of alienation of .13 and .12 were reported for girls and boys, respectively. In both boys and girls, the Emotionality items were more homogeneous compared to the Worry items, which were less clustered together and displayed a more heterogeneous pattern. A number of additional exploratory and confirmatory factor analyses of items on the TAI have firmly established the discriminant validity of the Worry and Emotionality subscales in both male and female groups (Hedl, 1984; Hocevar & El- Zahhar, 1988; R. Schwarzer, 1984).

In contrast to previous studies, Hagtvet's (1985a; cf. Hagtvet 1985b) research suggests that whereas the Worry–Emotionality distinction is a proper description of boys' anxiety responses in an evaluative interpersonal setting, girls' anxiety responses are most parsimoniously interpreted in terms of a unitary response construct. Thus, Worry and Emotionality components of test anxiety consolidate into a single unified affective-physiological Emotionality component among female students, and this factor is viewed as being the primary sex-differentiating factor.

Overall, research suggests that the factor structure of test anxiety, as operationally assessed mainly by the TAI, is similar for men and women. Therefore, the gender differences noted in the research literature more likely reflect different levels of intensity in responding to test anxiety items, at least for the TAI, than different constructs being measured for men and women.

Age Trends

Although developmental research has not yet sketched a coherent picture of age trends in test anxiety over the life span, a developmental pattern is beginning to emerge, at least for school-age populations, which I briefly sketch below.

Developmental Track of Test Anxiety

Developmental research shows that students' test anxiety scores rise consistently from the early to late elementary school years, stabilizing toward the end of elementary school (S. B. Sarason et al., 1964; Hill & Sarason, 1966). Whereas younger children in the early grades report relatively little test anxiety, the prevalence of test anxiety rises sharply in grades 3–5 (Hembree, 1988). Gender differences also begin to emerge by the middle years of elementary school (3rd–4th grades), with test anxiety scores for girls shown to be higher than for boys (Hill & Sarason, 1966). In general, those who become more defensive over the elementary school years tend to admit to less test anxiety (Hill, 1972).

Test anxiety scores are shown to rise to a high point in junior high school and level off through the rest of high school (Wigfield & Eccles, 1989; see also Manley & Rosemier, 1972). One study reported that high school students are less anxious than their junior high school counterparts (Manley & Rosemier, 1972). Furthermore, there is some evidence to suggest that test anxiety levels decline slightly during the college years (Pekrun & Frese, 1992). A number of the general trends reported above, based mainly on research data collected in the United States, have also been observed in cross-national research. Recent data from Japanese students, for example, indicate that anxiety levels increase from kindergarten to the 4th grade and then remain relatively constant through 12th grade (Araki, Iwawaki, & Spielberger, 1992).

Explanations of Age Increases in Test Anxiety

Reviewers (Dusek, 1980; Hill & Sarason, 1966; Wigfield & Eccles, 1989) have offered a variety of explanations for the developmental trends of test anxiety observed in school-aged children, with particular concern for the reported increases in mean test anxiety levels over the elementary and junior high school years. Among the salient explanations are the following:

- Presumed increase in demands and pressures for academic accomplishments from parents and teachers over the school years.
- Greater complexity of learning materials and tasks over time, thus serving to reduce students' success expectancies and concomitantly enhance anxiety.
- Cumulative failures and detrimental effects of aversive anxiety-evoking experiences.
- Decrease in children's defensiveness and concomitant increase in their willingness to admit to anxiety over the years.
- Increase in the accuracy and reliability of the students' self-reports of test anxiety over the school years.

Elderly subjects have been hypothesized to be more anxious in testing situations than their younger counterparts, with the elderly persons' susceptibility to stress substantially increased when performance on a cognitive task is being evaluated (Ross, 1968). Unfortunately, very few studies speak to this issue. Kooken and Hayslip (1984) claimed that highly anxious older persons may lack the skills with which to cope with tests and task failure, and may account for their low cognitive test performance by external attributions (i.e., task difficulty, luck, unfair assessment procedures, or admission criteria working against the older student). Whitbourne (1976) hypothesized that older adults presumably perceive any test situation in which their cognitive functioning is being evaluated as threatening. These evaluative situations confront the elderly with the recognition that their mental abilities are on the decline and are therefore particularly threatening for them. He provided data showing that when performing a memory task, debilitating anxiety is greater in the elderly (mean age of about 71 years) compared to younger adults (mean age of about 21 years). More recent experimental studies (Mueller, Kausler, Faherty, & Oliveri, 1980), however, suggest that test anxiety may not affect the performance of elderly subjects a great deal more than younger persons.

Overall, it may be premature to make any precise statements about developmental trends in test anxiety over the life course. There is little available information on test anxiety for the adult years and there are lacuna in other time intervals. Furthermore, most of the research is cross-sectional rather than longitudinal, and longitudinal studies tracking the development of test anxiety across childhood and adolescence are urgently needed. Furthermore, the current developmental literature does not allow us to pinpoint precisely the factors underlying the reported developmental trends, which may be accounted for by individuals' exposure to any of a multitude of experiences.

Sociocultural Group Differences

Test anxiety appears to be a major problem for many students in modern society, including those coming from ethnic minority or socioculturally different backgrounds (Hill & Wigfield, 1984). Yet, important sociocultural group differences may exist in the prevalence and magnitude of test anxiety, or in the way test anxiety is experienced, interpreted, and expressed.

Socioeconomic Group Differences

It is commonly held that students from lower-class backgrounds tend to be more test-anxious than their middle-class counterparts, for a variety of reasons (Samuda, 1975). One prominent account focuses on the specific socialization factors inherent to lower-class culture, such as rigid socialization practices, punitive parental attitudes, minimal parental encouragement for achievement, and relatively high expectations of punishment for failure to meet adult demands (Katz, 1967; Zeidner & Safir, 1989). Thus, lower-class students, suffering from a wide array of academic deficits due to inadequate socialization and impoverished home environment, may realize that they are less equipped to cope with school demands and consequently react with increased alarm and evaluative stress. Moreover, lower-class boys are more likely to be in conflict with school demands due to the greater discrepancy between their needs for independence and autonomy and the schools' requirement for conformity and orderliness (Rhine & Spaner, 1983). Due to the conflict between school and lower-class minority home cultures, lower-class students may experience more failure, frustration, and punitive experiences in schools than middle-class children, thus elevating their levels of test anxiety. By contrast, the socialization practices characteristic of middle-class home environments may be more congenial to the development of positive academic skills and attitudes and low evaluative stress (Katz, 1967; Samuda, 1975). Middle-class parents are claimed to be more likely than lower-class parents to provide substantial encouragement and positive reinforcement for academic success, and teach their children impulse control, future time orientation, task persistence, and other attitudes and skills that comprise the "hidden curriculum" which is valued and rewarded by middle-class teachers (Rhine & Spaner, 1983). The congruence of values and goals between middle-class parents and teachers enables children to experience more success and less failure in school than their lower-class counterparts. This reduces the likelihood of developing disturbingly high levels of school or test anxiety. Furthermore, middle-class children are generally perceived more favorably by teachers and make a better adjustment in school (Rhine & Spaner, 1983).

A different line of reasoning (Phillips, 1962) would lead to diametrically opposed predictions regarding the association between social class background and test
anxiety. According to classical developmental models of test anxiety, the difficulty of
children in meeting high parental expectations in problem-solving settings lies at the
core of test anxiety (see Chapter 6). Accordingly, a child can hardly develop such a
negative self-conception in a lower-class family environment in which there is little
concern about the level and rate of intellectual development in the child. In middle-
class family backgrounds, by contrast, high parental expectations would cause school
achievement to become more ego involving for the child, thus increasing the likelihood that children become anxious about achievement and evaluative situations.

Overall, the bulk of the research points to a modest inverse relationship between
test anxiety and family socioeconomic status (Hembree, 1988). Thus, regardless of
ethnic background or culture, subjects from lower socioeconomic levels tend to score
higher on test anxiety measures than their middle-class counterparts. This relationship has been substantiated in a number of cross-cultural studies. Thus, Diaz-
Guerrero (1976) found higher mean test anxiety scores for lower-class students
compared to their middle-class counterparts in both Mexico and the United States.
Zeidner and Safir (1989) reported significant socioeconomic differences in 416 junior
high school students of varying ethnic backgrounds in Israel; social class accounted
for about 6% of the variance in test anxiety scores across ethnic groups. Guida and
Ludlow (1989) compared test anxiety scores (as assessed by the TASC) for a
relatively sizable sample of 1144 Chilean students and several student samples in the
United States (91 inner-city 7th graders; 352 middle-class 7th and 8th graders; and
103 upper class 8th graders). Students from low-social-class backgrounds in both
cultures were significantly higher on test anxiety than those from upper-class backgrounds.

Ethnic Group Differences

A number of studies have compared the pattern of test anxiety in various ethnic
groups in the United States. Research has focused mainly on comparing Black (or
Hispanic) with White students, and Asian-American students with White students.
With respect to African-American student populations, it has been claimed that
minority school children may encounter distinctive developmental experiences in
school and in communities which tend to increase their fear of evaluative situations,
such as repeated academic failures, inordinate number of aversive encounters at
school associated with punishment and criticism, and negative ethnic stereotypes
(Bronzaft, Murgatroyd, Lehman, & McNeilly, 1974; Samuda, 1975). In addition,
Black students may be more generally stressed and anxious on account of low social
status, extensive familial poverty, and fragmented family living conditions (Phillips,
1978). Thus, Black minority students, like many other minority group students in the

United States from "deprived" backgrounds, learn to harbor negative test attitudes and develop high levels of debilitating test anxiety (Samuda, 1975).

Some empirical data are consistent with the foregoing claims. Blacks have been reported to be higher on test anxiety, on average, than majority students at various educational levels (Clawson, Firment, & Trower, 1981; Payne, Smith, & Payne, 1983a,b; Rhine & Spaner, 1983). Meta-analytic findings (Hembree, 1988) help pinpoint the specific grade levels in which these differences are evidenced. Thus, Black students in 2nd–4th grades evidence significantly higher test anxiety scores than their White counterparts; 5th–8th grade Black and White students evidence a marginally significant difference; and Blacks and Whites in high school and college evidence no significant differences.

In addition to the research on Black–White differences in test anxiety, a number of studies have examined the pattern of test anxiety in Asian–American compared to White students. It is noted that American students of Asian ethnic background typically outperform their White peers in attaining academic excellence at high school and university levels. As pointed out by Dion and Toner (1988), the academic success of Asian-American students has been attributed to two aspects of the Confucian ethic that permeates their ethnic heritage: (a) the stress on filial piety and (b) a belief in the efficiency of effort and hard work. Attaining high scholastic achievements is one major way children have of repaying their infinite debt to their parents and of showing filial piety. Relatedly, a strong family orientation in this Confucian ethic means that the students work not only for themselves, but also for their family's honor. The stress on academic excellence in Asian-American families, as manifested in the strong parental pressures on the children in such families to succeed in the academic sphere, may place these students under considerable psychological stress. This constant pressure to succeed in school has been hypothesized to play a role in the development of test anxiety (Dion & Toner, 1988; Pang, 1991).

Dion and Toner (1988) provided data in support of the claim that in North America individuals of Asian descent are more prone to be stressed in evaluative situations than are their counterparts of European descent. They explored test anxiety differences among 312 Canadian undergraduates from diverse ethnic backgrounds (ie., Chinese, Anglo, South European, North European, and Wester European). Chinese students obtained higher test anxiety scores, on average, than the other ethnic groups taken together. Similarly, Pang (1991) reported higher levels of test anxiety in a small sample of Asian-American (n=25) compared to White (n=66) children enrolled in middle school. Students' perception of pleasing parents and parental pressures were significantly related to test anxiety, with Asian-American students aiming more than their White counterparts at pleasing their parents (Pang, 1991).

Some of those who have studied the literature have concluded that the empirical findings bearing upon ethnic group differences in test anxiety are neither consistent nor sufficiently well established (Jensen, 1980). In fact, findings that are statistically significant often confound ethnicity and social class. Jensen (1980) concludes that the bulk of the observed differences, particularly those reported for Blacks versus Whites, are more of a reflection of "Type I errors" in the research literature than of true differences among ethnic groups.

Cross-National Differences

Culture may play an important role in determining the frequency with which anxiety is expressed and the form of its expression (Oner & Kaymak, 1987). A casual glance at the prodigious test anxiety literature highlights the international flavor that characterizes much recent research on the topic (see Volumes 1–7 of *Advances in Test Anxiety Research*). One basic justification and raison d'être of cross-cultural research in the test anxiety domain is that it may provide important insights into the macro-sociocultural antecedents and consequences of test anxiety and its cognitive and affective components. Although there may well be common antecedents of test anxiety across cultures (e.g., importance of evaluative situations for academic success and occupational careers), cultural factors may play a critical role in shaping various parameters of the stress process, including the appraisals, perceptions, and meanings attributed to evaluative situations, the frequency, intensity, and particular forms in which anxiety is manifested in evaluative contexts, the specific modes of coping with evaluative stress, and culture-specific resources and affordances. In fact, current cognitive-motivational models of stress and emotion (e.g., R. S. Lazarus, 1991a, 1991b, 1991c), which view emotions as arising from how a person construes the outcome of a transaction between persons and their environment, beg for the explicit incorporation of cultural factors into conceptualizations of stress, anxiety, and coping processes (Seipp & Schwarzer, 1996). Current models should easily be able to accommodate cross-cultural differences in the diverse goals, values, attitudes, beliefs, commitments, and expectations which the person brings to bear in any encounter with a stressful situation in the environment.

Cross-cultural test anxiety data are by and large based on cultural adaptations of the same instrument, i.e., the Test Anxiety Inventory (TAI), thus allowing valid comparisons across cultures. Descriptive data for the TAI are available for well over a dozen different nations. Some of the data garnered from cross-cultural studies of test anxiety are displayed in Tables 11.4 and 11.5. These tables present descriptive data for Worry and Emotionality component scores for male and female school-aged and college students, respectively, in different nations.

Meta-analytic research was conducted by Seipp and Schwarzer (1996) based on summary TAI data from 14 nations. Although mean test anxiety levels vary across cultures, on the order of over a standard deviation in total TAI scores, overall, test anxiety is shown to be a prevalent and relatively homogeneous cross-cultural phenomenon (Seipp & Schwarzer, 1996). An analysis of published reports suggests that the "average" test anxiety levels across cultures is about 40 points on the TAI (potential range 20–80), with an average standard deviation of about 10 points (Seipp

& Schwarzer, 1996). The highest test anxiety mean values were found in student samples in Egypt, Jordan, and Hungary, followed by Puerto Rico, Korea, and Germany. The lowest anxiety levels were reported for China, Italy, Japan, and the Netherlands. When data were grouped by global geographic regions (i.e., Western Europe, Eastern Europe, Asia, Islamic countries, South America, and North America) the highest mean anxiety was observed in Islamic countries. Comparably high test anxiety levels were also reported in South America and Eastern Europe. Overall, geographic regions were differentiated more on the Emotionality than on the Worry component (Seipp & Schwarzer, 1996).

Despite meaningful average differences in test anxiety across cultures, Seipp and Schwarzer (1996) reported a relatively low degree of cross-national differentiation on total test anxiety scores. Thus, test anxiety appears to be less influenced by culture specificity and indigenous cultural conditions (e.g., prevalent ideology, economic conditions, political situation) than trait anxiety. The authors attribute the relatively homogeneous mean levels of test anxiety across cultures to the low degree of cross-cultural variance in the perceived valence and importance of success on major exams (see Figure 11.2).

Cultural Factors Potentially Influencing Test Anxiety

A number of studies have tested specific hypothesis bearing on the effects of culture-specific factors on the development and manifestation of test anxiety (e.g., Diaz-Guerrero, 1976; El-Zahhar & Hocevar, 1991; Seipp & Schwarzer, 1996). Among the factors that have been hypothesized for cross-national variations in test anxiety are cultural values and norms (particularly as they relate to academic achievement), parental values and socialization practices, the unique features of the educational system and its organization (homework load, emphasis on testing, classroom milieu, testing environment). These variables need to be carefully considered in any effort to understand both test anxiety and student performance. I now give examples of this line of research by presenting research evidence for three separate cultural factors claimed to impact upon the development of test anxiety.

Cultural Values and Orientations

Cultures may be differentiated along a variety of basic value dimensions or syndromes (e.g., individualism vs. collectivism, masculinity vs. femininity, equality vs. inequality, tolerance vs. intolerance of ambiguity, emphasis on long-term vs. short-term gratification of need, emphasis on honor, etc.). Diaz-Guerrero (1976) hypothesized that the basic individualistic orientation of American culture, with its stress on competitive achievement and self-sufficient individualism, is relatively congenial to the development of attitudes, skills, and coping strategies conducive to

Table 11.4. Worry and Emotionality Components
in Different National Settings in School-Age Populations (by Gender)

Nation (sample)	Researchers	Year	Male				Female			
			n	W mean (SD)	E mean (SD)		n	W mean (SD)	E mean (SD)	
China (Precollege)	Rocklin & Ren-Min	1989	100	13.9 (3.5)	13.1 (3.9)		105	14.2 (3.6)	13.4 (3.5)	
Czechoslovakia (ES)	Man, Budejovice, & Hosek	1989	73	13.6 (3.7)	16.4 (4.7)		81	13.9 (4.6)	19.8 (4.6)	
Holland (JHS)	Van der Ploeg	1982	57	12.1 (3.9)	13.3 (5.0)		98	13.3 (4.5)	15.7 (5.3)	
Hungary (ES)	Sipos, Sipos, & Spielberger	1985	332	13.7 (3.5)	16.9 (4.4)		368	13.9 (3.6)	18.3 (4.5)	
India (HS)	Sud & Sharma	1990	359	15.5 (6.4)	16.9 (7.8)		465	18.2 (8.3)	17.4 (8.2)	
Italy (HS)	Comunian	1985	500	14.8 (3.9)	15.6 (5.3)		500	17.3 (5.2)	17.1 (5.8)	
Jordan (HS)	Ahlawat	1989b	1014	18.6 (4.9)	20.3 (5.2)		839	18.8 (5.0)	21.5 (5.3)	
Turkey (HS)	Oner & Kaynak	1987	197	14.9 (4.2)	15.9 (4.7)		134	16.5 (4.8)	18.4 (4.9)	
United States (HS)	Spielberger	1980	527	15.6 (5.3)	16.6 (5.5)		591	17.1 (5.8)	18.9 (5.9)	

Note: W, Worry; E, Emotionality; ES, Elementary school; JHS, junior high school; HS, high school.

**Table 11.5. Worry and Emotionality Components
in Different National Settings in Male and Female College Students**

Nation	Researchers	Year	Male				Female			
			n	W mean (SD)	E mean (SD)		n	W mean (SD)	E mean (SD)
China	Rocklin & Ren-Min	1989	167	13.8 (4.1)	12.5 (4.9)		163	14.0 (3.7)	13.4 (3.8)
Holland	Van de Ploeg	1982	116	11.7 (4.0)	15.1 (5.1)		68	12.2 (3.7)	16.0 (5.3)
India	Sharma et al.	1983	454	15.5 (7.7)	17.6 (6.9)		446	16.5 (6.6)	17.6 (4.2)
Israel	Zeidner & Nevo	1992	245	13.6 (4.0)	17.3 (4.9)		283	13.7 (4.0)	19.5 (5.1)
Italy	Comunian	1985	304	13.9 (3.9)	15.2 (4.5)		169	13.5 (4.1)	14.8 (4.9)
Jordan	Ahlawat	1989b	768	16.9 (4.3)	18.6 (4.8)		951	17.5 (4.7)	20.7 (5.1)
Turkey	Oner & Kaymak	1987	130	13.03 (2.3)	13.9 (4.4)		143	13.3 (3.4)	15.8 (4.9)
United States	Spielberger	1980	654	13.6 (5.0)	16.8 (5.6)		795	14.9 (5.5)	18.9 (6.3)

Note: W, Worry; E, Emotionality.

Figure 11.2.   Test anxiety as a universal phenomenon.

success on standardized exams administered under evaluative conditions. Objective tests, it was claimed, pose a greater threat for Mexican students: Given the greater affiliative obedience toward adult authorities in Mexican culture, Mexican children are much afraid to disappoint their parents and teachers. This hypothesis was substantiated in a cross-cultural longitudinal study in Mexico and the United States in which the TASC was administered to 392 children in the 1st, 4th, or 7th grade when the study began (Diaz-Guerrero, 1976). Mexican students, at all grade levels, reported more test anxiety than their American age equivalents, thus confirming Diaz-Guerrero's cross-cultural hypothesis.

Socialization Practices and Parental Values and Pressures

It has been suggested that culture-specific socialization practices and parental values may be influential in the development of test anxiety. Thus, socialization practices in some Asian cultures (e.g., Korea) may exert considerable pressure on the individual to achieve, while at the same time discouraging individualistic behaviors through the use of guilt and shame. Children are taught to believe that it is a virtue to enhance the family name through scholastic and vocational achievement. Thus, children may develop high levels of public self-consciousness and anxiety. Data presented by C. Schwarzer and Kim (1984) for Korean students tend to support these claims.

Perceived Valence of Exam Success and High-Stake Testing Environments

The perceived importance of test scores for making critical decisions about a student's future, along with a highly selective and competitive educational system, have been hypothesized as being associated with high mean levels of test anxiety at the national level. Although this hypothesis makes intuitive sense, the data in support of this claim are not entirely consistent.

On one hand, this hypothesis has been supported by empirical research indicating that the test anxiety scores of students in some Islamic cultures (e.g., Egypt, Jordan, Saudi Arabia), characterized by highly selective educational systems, are well over one standard deviation above students in other parts of the world (El-Zahhar & Hocevar, 1991; Seipp & Schwarzer, 1996). Islamic countries, such as Egypt and Jordan, frequently attach extremely important consequences to performance on high school examinations, particularly since a single nationwide achievement examination determines both the award of a high school diploma and admission to university (El-Zahhar and Hocevar, 1991). Thus, students' future career and status depend to a large extent on the results of these examinations. Poor results on these achievement exams serve as a barrier in entering a higher status profession. In view of the high stakes involved in achievement testing, with exam failure being an absolute dead end, it is quite understandable why students in these societies tend to view testing situations as especially threatening.

However, some recent research data fail to support the hypothesis that the valence and stakes of testing are meaningfully associated with high modal test anxiety at the national level. Thus, these data show relatively low levels of anxiety among students in Japan, a society which is test-dominated and characterized by exaggerated competitiveness surrounding entrance to the school of choice and college entrance (Araki, Iwawaki, & Spielberger, 1992). Given the importance of school achievement and test outcomes in Japanese culture, one would expect that test anxiety in Japanese students would be well above the normative level of students in other developed countries. However, data reported by O'Neil and Fukumura (1992) fail to bear this hypothesis out. The mean scores obtained for 362 Japanese elementary school children were strikingly low when compared with normative Test Anxiety Inventory data for students in such national sites as Czechoslovoakia, Germany, Hungary, and Korea. Similarly low test anxiety mean scores were observed for Japanese student groups when compared with comparable normative student groups in the United States (Araki, Iwawaki, & Spielberger, 1992).

Problems and Shortcomings in Cross-Cultural Test Anxiety Research

Current cross-cultural investigations of test anxiety have been flawed in a number of respects. One outstanding problem permeating much of the cross-national research in this area is its descriptive and atheoretical nature. Few attempts have been made to generate focused hypotheses for a specific culture based on an in-depth analysis of core cultural values, norms, and expectations, child-rearing practices, culture-based pressure for high achievement, constraints and affordances related to academic achievement, and the like. Instead, researchers have generally simply assessed the magnitude of cross-national differences in test anxiety and provided post hoc, and often forced, attempts to account for observed cross-cultural differences. Since the majority of current cross-cultural studies of test anxiety fail to provide a solid theoretical rationale for generating focused hypotheses and explaining the results, the data generated from these studies are generally difficult to interpret and assimilate.

It is further noted that much of cross-cultural research in this area has been carried out by comparing findings of different researchers across the globe on comparable indices of the test anxiety construct. Comparisons across different nations are often problematic in that studies differ with respect to sampling procedure, time of data collection, demographic characteristics (age, group, educational level, socioeconomic background), ability, and other relevant variables. Due to the lack of comparability of the samples employed in the analyses, the differences found may be artifactual or chance findings (Type I errors). A preferable approach is to collect data in two or more nations simultaneously and compare the results (see, e.g., El-Zahhar & Hocevar, 1991). In this way, steps can be taken to insure that instruments are comparable, procedures are as similar as possible, samples are equivalent on key parameters, and so on. Furthermore, the majority of cross-cultural comparisons were undertaken before normative data for respective cultures were gathered. Thus, cross-cultural research has frequently been based on small and incidental samples of school or college students, and thus may not be representative of their target populations. Finally, whereas most comparisons have looked at mean differences in various nations, few have compared measures of dispersion or other important statistical parameters.

Summary

This chapter examined the research evidence for individual differences in test anxiety. The presentation was guided by the assumption that it is important to take individual difference variables into account in explaining the observed variance in test anxiety scores. Overall, the survey indicates that research on individual difference variables has been rather uneven, with considerable attention paid to some variables (e.g., gender), and relatively little attention to others (e.g., age, ethnicity).

Empirical research has not yet sketched an entirely coherent picture of age trends in test anxiety throughout the life span. The data suggest that test anxiety scores tend to rise consistently from the early to late elementary school years, stabilize toward the end of the elementary school years, rise to a high point in junior high school, and level off through the rest of high school. A small decline in self-reports of test anxiety in college students has been observed. A variety of different explanations have been offered to account for these trends. Overall, it may be premature to make any precise statements about developmental trends and patterns in test anxiety over the entire school period, particularly given the cross-sectional nature of much of this research. Furthermore, the current developmental literature does not allow us to pinpoint precisely the factors underlying the reported developmental trends.

Current research suggests that gender impacts upon the development and manifestation of anxiety in evaluative situations. Specifically, women show consistently higher levels of test anxiety than men, particularly on the Emotionality component. A myriad of different explanations have been offered to explain the existence of gender differences in mean test anxiety levels, including differential patterns of socialization, different coping styles, and differential willingness to admit to anxiety (defensiveness). Although gender appears to make a difference with respect to test anxiety, after so many years of research we still do not know why.

Current research attests that regardless of ethnic background or culture, subjects from lower socioeconomic levels score consistently higher on test anxiety measures than their middle-class counterparts. Lower-class students may realize that they are less equipped to cope with school demands and consequently react with increased alarm and evaluative stress. The empirical findings bearing upon test anxiety differences among ethnic groups in the United States yield inconsistent results, with the findings varying by the specific ethnic categories considered.

Current meta-analytic findings suggest that due to the low degree of cross-cultural variance in the perceived valence and importance of success on major exams in modern society, there appears to be a relatively homogeneous level of test anxiety across cultures. Although research has provided evidence in support of the importance of a number of cultural or nation-specific factors in determining national modal levels of test anxiety, no systematic analysis has been conducted to identify the specific cultural parameters that impact upon test anxiety. Also, there has been little research on the causal mechanisms through which culture may impact upon different phases of the stress and coping process. Such an analysis would appear to be crucial for developing more focused hypotheses for future cross-cultural research. Furthermore, a major problem for cross-cultural research on test anxiety is interpreting the variations observed across national sites. Given the current state of research, it is not clear whether observed differences in mean anxiety scores between two or more cultures should be attributed to population trait anxiety differences, cultural values and socialization practices, different levels of culturally specific evaluative stressors, or assessment artifacts (e.g., lack of comparability of the measures used, possible differences in scale reliabilities or factor structure).

Personal Correlates of Test Anxiety

Overview

Both current thinking in the area of test anxiety research and a casual glance at the literature suggest that test anxiety is meaningfully associated with a wide array of personal variables. Over the past few decades numerous studies in the test anxiety literature have investigated the personal correlates of test anxiety. In addition, a good number of empirical studies in the behavioral sciences have incorporated measures of test anxiety in their design in a variety of capacities (independent, dependent, mediating, or moderating variables). Thus, there is now a wealth of data available for systematically mapping out the nexus of associations between test anxiety and related personal constructs.

This chapter sets out to identify and survey the pattern of relationships between test anxiety and motivational and personality variables. I begin by examining key motivational correlates of test anxiety and move on to assess salient personality and emotional correlates. The chapter concludes with a brief discussion of the relationship between test anxiety and the cognitive facet of personality—intelligence.

Motivational Factors

Current thinking in the area of motivational research would suggest that students' affective reactions to evaluative test situations are shaped by their goals, needs, the values they place on learning outcomes, their success expectations, and motivational beliefs about self-efficacy and attributions for their achievements (Garcia & Pintrich, 1994). In this section I discuss a number of motivational factors that are linked to test anxiety and that together shape a person's affective and cognitive behavior in academic contexts.

Achievement Motivation

Classical achievement motivation theory (Atkinson, 1964; Atkinson & Feather, 1966) posits that all individuals have a basic motive or tendency to seek and approach success, one that instigates and maintains actions directed at achieving success. At the same time, people have an antagonistic motive to avoid failure, which seeks to direct behavior away from the achievement task. Accordingly, achievement striving is conceptualized as the result of an approach–avoidance conflict between these two antagonistic motives, i.e., the tendency to seek success and the tendency to avoid failure, with the stronger of the two tendencies being expressed in action tendencies.

According to Atkinson's theory, when a person's motive to achieve success ("need for achievement") is stronger than his or her motive to avoid failure ("fear of failure") the result of the conflict is to approach the task at hand. However, if the motive to avoid failure is stronger than the motive to achieve success, than the result of the conflict is avoidance behavior. Thus, when the motivation to avoid failure is aroused in individuals surrounding an evaluative situation, which is the case whenever performance is evaluated and failure is a possible outcome, this negative motive will resist or dampen the motivation to undertake activity (Atkinson, 1964). Figure 12.1 depicts the opposite effects of "need for achievement" and "fear of failure" on cognitive tasks; whereas the former leads to approach tendencies, the latter leads to avoidance tendencies.

Fear of failure involves the disposition to be anxious about failure and the consequent desire to avoid situations fraught with possible failure (Atkinson, 1964). Students high on fear of failure generally have an approach–avoidance conflict about academic pursuits in general and test-related contexts in particular. Thus, on one hand, academic achievement is important to these students because self-esteem is often contingent on academic success. On the other hand, learning settings make these persons anxious and they wish to avoid engaging them. The result is heightened state anxiety and the tendency to withdraw from threatening evaluative situations (Hagtvet, 1983a, 1984).

The motive to avoid failure (or "fear of failure") is often cited as a major characteristic of test-anxious students, with fear of failure believed to be at the very heart of test anxiety (I. G. Sarason, 1980a). Furthermore, the cognitive component of test anxiety (i.e., Worry) and the Fear-of-Failure component of achievement motivation are such highly overlapping and conceptually similar constructs that the two terms have often been used interchangeably (Atkinson & Litwin, 1960). Indeed, various test anxiety scales (e.g., Test Anxiety Scale for Children) have traditionally served as proxy measures for the motive to avoid failure (thus making any attempt to assess the magnitude of the correlations between test anxiety and fear of failure quite futile!).

High-test-anxious individuals are predicted to be more motivated to avoid failure than they are to approach success, whereas low-test-anxious individuals are predicted to be more motivated to approach success than avoid failure (Atkinson, 1964). Figure 12.2 depicts the relationship between these two antagonistic motives, i.e., need for achievement and fear of failure, at varying levels of test anxiety (Hill, 1972). Whereas high-test-anxious subjects in an evaluative situation hesitate in performing a response which may lead to failure, low-test-anxious subjects are more strongly motivated to approach success than to avoid failure. When given the

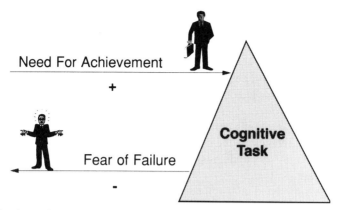

Figure 12.1. Antagonistic effects of need for achievement and fear of failure in a cognitive task situation.

opportunity, high-test-anxious students typically attempt to avoid failure by choosing either very *easy* tasks, in which success is assured, or very *difficult* tasks, in which unsuccessful performance is almost certain, but can be attributed not to the self, but to task difficulty (Weiner et al., 1972). When strength of probability of failure is *intermediate (.50)*, the avoidance motive is most strongly aroused. Based on the

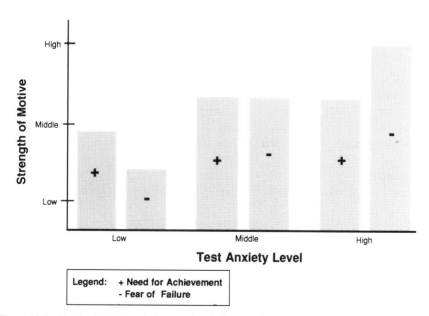

Figure 12.2. Predicted relationship between level of test anxiety and need for achievement at varying levels of test anxiety. After Hill (1972).

assumption that individuals high in fear of failure prefer very low or very high goals, fear of failure has been conceptualized to be a self-motivating system (Heckhausen, 1975). Accordingly, if a person chooses and accomplishes minimal goals, credit goes to task facility—an external factor that does not entitle one to self-reward.. By contrast, if a person chooses high goals, success is typically seen as a lucky event that is attributable to unstable factors—once again not entitling the person to self-reward.

Rand and his colleagues (Rand, Lens, & Decock, 1991) contended that test anxiety research may benefit from combining individual differences in test anxiety with individual differences in the need for achievement when explaining differences in test performance. As is traditionally done in need-for-achievement research, they differentiated among four types of students based on the cross-partitioning of two separate and uncorrelated motivational tendencies, i.e., the motive for success (high vs. low) and the motive to avoid failure (high vs. low). These are: high motive for success, high fear of failure (HH); high motive for success, low fear of failure (HL); low motive for success, high fear of failure (LH); low motive for success, low fear of failure (LL). Individuals high in hope for success and low in fear of failure are defined as *success-oriented* and would be predicted to perform up to par in test situations. Those low in motive for success and high in fear of failure are *failure-oriented* individuals and would be predicted to underachieve in test situations. Furthermore, individuals high in need for achievement and high in test anxiety are predicted to score better on cognitive tasks than individuals with the same level of test anxiety, but with a weak need for achievement. Also, individuals with low test anxiety and low need for achievement will score better than individuals with high anxiety and high need for achievement. A review of the literature supports the notion that not only does achievement behavior vary with test anxiety, but it is differentially affected by level of positive versus negative achievement motivation. Research by Rand, Lens, and Decock (1991) has convincingly demonstrated the usefulness of distinguishing between high-test-anxious individuals who are low in hope for success and those who are high in hope for success, with the latter frequently suffering fewer aversive performance consequences. Furthermore, taking into account both the positive motive of need for achievement and differences in the negative motive of test anxiety has been shown to increase the explained variance on a wide array of cognitive tasks.

Research on the association between test anxiety and the need for achievement has yielded rather inconsistent results. Early research by Atkinson and Litwin (1960) found no significant relationship between test anxiety and the need for achievement. However, meta-analytic data reported by Hembree (1988) indicated that the nature of the relationship among the constructs varies by grade level. Causal modeling conducted by Hagtvet (1983a) suggested that the Worry and Emotionality components of test anxiety are predetermined by fear of failure, with the three constructs interrelated in the following causal sequence:

$$\text{Fear of failure} \rightarrow \text{Worry} \rightarrow \text{Emotionality}$$

Perceived Control and Self-Efficacy

According to R. S. Lazarus and Folkman (1984), situational control appraisals refer to the extent to which the person believes he or she can shape or influence particular person–environment relationships. Perceived threat in a test situation may be conceptualized as a relational property between the dangerous or threatening aspects of the environment, on one hand, and the individual's perceived coping capabilities, on the other (R. S. Lazarus & Folkman, 1984). Thus, people who believe they can exercise control over potential threats do not engage in anxious and apprehensive thinking and are not perturbed by them. Those who believe they cannot manage threatening events that might occur experience stress and anxiety. Situational appraisals of control are products of individual evaluations of the demands of the situation as well as the coping resources and ability to implement coping strategies.

According to current social-cognitive theory, human action is governed not so much by the objective properties of the environment or its level of constraints, as by the perceived level of personal efficacy to bring about changes by productive use of capabilities and enlistment of sustained effort. Thus, people with a firm belief in their self-efficacy figure out ways of exercising some measure of control in environments containing limited opportunities, whereas those who believe themselves to be inefficacious are unlikely to effect major changes even in environments that provide many potential opportunities. When setbacks occur, individuals who believe in their self-efficacy recover more quickly and maintain the commitment to their goals. Social-cognitive theory (Bandura, 1988) posits an interactive, though asymmetric, relation between perceived self-efficacy and anxiety arousal, with coping efficacy exercising the much greater effect. Accordingly, there is a dynamic cycle of decreasing self-efficacy, heightened anxiety, and a further decrease in self-efficacy. Whereas the impact of perceived coping inefficacy on anxiety arousal is well established, the influence of anxiety arousal on self-percepts of efficacy is equivocal.

Both self-efficacy and outcome expectancies have been conceptualized as key precursors of anxiety and test anxiety (R. Schwarzer & Jerusalem, 1992). Whereas efficacy expectancy is the conviction that one can execute behavior required to produce an outcome, outcome expectancy refers to a person's estimate that a given behavior will lead to certain outcomes. Thus, students with low self-efficacy and unfavorable outcome expectancies would be predicted to show higher levels of anxiety. As the level of self-efficacy decreases, anxious arousal is expected to increase. Furthermore, changes in anxiety level indicate that there are changes in the way the person is appraising her or his relationship with the environment. Accordingly, as efficacy expectancies decrease, and resources are judged to be less adequate for satisfying task demands, the relationship is appraised as holding the potential for less control and therefore perceived to be more threatening.

A series of recent studies has provided some consistent evidence for the association between self-efficacy and test anxiety. Data collected in Germany in nine different studies is reported to show correlations ranging from -30 to $-.66$ between self-efficacy and anxiety (R. Schwarzer & Jerusalem, 1992). R. J. Smith, Arnkoff, and Wright (1990) demonstrated that self-efficacy for test success contributes to the prediction of test anxiety, above and beyond the contribution of cognitive interference and poor study skills, in a sample of 178 college students. Topman and her coworkers (Topman et al., 1992) reported that test anxiety was negatively correlated with perceived academic competence ($r = -.29$) as well as test competence ($r = .55$) in a sample of 129 medical science students. Similarly, Pajares and Miller (1994) reported a sizable correlation between math self-efficacy and math anxiety ($r = -.56$) in a sample of 350 undergraduates. These data point to a substantial inverse correlation between perceived self-efficacy and test anxiety.

A recent study by Pintrich, Roeser, and DeGroot (1994) looked at the relationship between test anxiety and self-efficacy at two points in time in a sample of 100 seventh graders. They reported an inverse correlation of $-.40$ between test anxiety and self-efficacy for Time 1 and $-.41$ for Time 2. Furthermore, Pintrich and Garcia (1993) examined the correlations between test anxiety and motivational and cognitive strategies in a sample of 313 students at two points in time, several weeks into the semester and at the end of the semester. Test anxiety was found to be related to self-efficacy for learning and performance both at Time 1 ($r = -.18$) and Time 2 ($r = -.36$).

Optimism

Current thinking and research points to a strong link between the personality dimension of optimism/pessimism and findings related to individual differences in test anxiety (Carver & Scheier, 1989). The dimension of optimism versus pessimism rests on a fundamental difference between people in their generalized expectations of good versus bad outcomes. Whereas optimists are people who generally expect things to work out well, pessimists are people who expect things to go from bad to worse. Test-anxious individuals have been conceptualized as pessimists with respect to test outcomes, that is, those whose expectations for successful test outcomes are not very favorable (Carver & Scheier, 1989). Thus, anxious people often respond to evaluative situations with pessimistic expectancies because of their past experiences with failure in evaluative settings (Carver & Scheier, 1981). Given a stressful situation, test-anxious subjects have been claimed to suffer from a pessimistic mind set, acute lack of confidence, low persistence, and mental disengagement, thus debilitating their test performance.

The self-regulation model of human behavior proposed by Carver and Scheier (see Chapter 3) suggests that the same level of anxiety may be facilitating for one person and debilitating for another, based on the person's expectancy of being able to cope with anxiety and/or successfully executing the behavior at hand. According to this model, anxiety is claimed to have its most debilitating effect on individuals who are relatively pessimistic about their chances of success, such as high-test-anxious subjects, eventually leading to reduced self-confidence and physical or mental disengagement from the cognitive task at hand (Carver & Scheier, 1989).

Test-anxious people normally hold expectations for unfavorable outcomes. The result of these pessimistic expectations is a tendency toward disengagement, particularly mental, when in a stressful situation. Examinees who have unfavorable expectancies typically reconfront bad test situations repeatedly, reexperiencing all of the acute distress and desire to disengage. Individuals who tend to expect bad outcomes do not keep trying, but instead experience the impulse to disengage. In some cases, the impulse is expressed overtly, as withdrawal of effort, or as literally "leaving the field." In other cases, situational constraints prevent this from happening and disengagement is expressed cognitively through off-task thinking, daydreaming, self-distraction, and cognitive interference (Carver, 1996). These cognitive events are hypothesized to cause a deterioration in performance.

The few studies currently available support the notion that pessimism is substantially related to test anxiety. Meta-analytic work by Hembree (1988) suggests that the expectations of high-test-anxious students for success on the exam were more pessimistic, by the order of half a standard deviation, than those of their low-test-anxious counterparts. Comparably, a recent study by Kleijn, Van der Ploeg, and Topman (1994) reported strong inverse correlations between optimism and both the Worry ($r = -.51$) and Emotionality ($r = -.44$) measures of test anxiety in a sample of 129 first-year students in the medical sciences.

Helplessness

Test anxiety and helplessness are closely related motivational constructs. Both test anxiety and helplessness are based on some degree of exposure to stressful environmental events and are largely determined by socialization processes in both the family and school environment. In addition, both constructs are further shaped by self-related cognitions (e.g., perceived coping abilities and competence) as well as situation-related cognitions (e.g., viewing the environment as pressing, competitive, impersonal, and so on; R. Schwarzer, Jerusalem, and Schwarzer, 1983). Helpless students, much like test-anxious students, are likely to consider themselves to be under scrutiny and are overconcerned about performance, will respond to demands as if they were threats, anticipate failure, feel incompetent, and suffer from a maladaptive pattern of attributions.

Under conditions of "learned helplessness" a person comes to believe that his or her responses and outcomes are independent and generalizes this belief to situations in which control is in fact possible (Dweck & Wortman, 1982). When individuals fail to perceive contingencies between their actions and the ensuing consequences, active, goal-oriented responding decreases. The objective noncontingency may be less important than how this noncontingency is experienced or perceived by the individual (Bandura, 1977). If rather than attributing problems or negative outcomes to environmental causes a person attributes negative outcomes to the self, personal helplessness will develop. Accordingly, a student who continuously experiences little or no contingency between his or her study behaviors and outcomes on math exams ("No matter how hard I try on math exams, I always fail") and attributes outcomes to lack of academic ability ("I'm really dumb when it comes to math") may feel considerable anxiety and may eventually develop a feeling of helplessness over time. Furthermore, if a student repeatedly fails on a task, and social comparison processes suggest that the task is not particularly difficult, that student will be inclined to account for the failure via *internal* rather than external attributions. With repeated failure experiences of this sort, the student will eventually attribute failure to ability, and will be convinced of his or her inability. These students may eventually develop a disposition which causes them to view themselves as helpless across a wide range of academic situations.

A recent paper by Pekrun (1995) reported a very strong correlation ($r = .83$) between test anxiety and hopelessness in a sample of 150 students. Hopelessness was also strongly related to anger surrounding a test situation ($r = .53$). Furthermore, in a series of classroom field experiments, McKeachie (1951) and his coworkers showed that a student's sense of helplessness in relation to the instructor's power, along with uncertainty and individual differences in motivation, are key sources of anxiety in test settings. Because students are apprehensive about the consequences of college exam scores for grade assignment, instructors can bar students from attaining some of their most important goals (admission to graduate training, prestige of college graduation, material advantage of good grades in finding a job, etc.) by simply assigning low grades. The degree to which students experience test anxiety is a function of the perception of the instructor's arbitrariness and punitiveness in use of power as well individual differences in motivation, such as fear of failure.

Self-Handicapping

Self-handicapping has been conceptualized as a strategy that enhances the opportunity to externalize or excuse failure (Jones & Berglas, 1978). Although there are variations in the definitions offered for the phenomenon of self-handicapping, it is typically described as the adoption or advocacy of impediments to success in a situation where a person anticipates failure. The theoretical premise is that self-handicapping involves attempts on the part of the individual to adopt a performance impediment (e.g., "I failed because I didn't exert myself" or "I flunked the exam because I was terribly anxious") in anticipation of an esteem-threatening evaluation. Thus, through the process of self-handicapping, a student has a ready-made excuse for impending failure on an exam and may thereby maintain self-esteem and the illusion of competence.

Test anxiety may have a major influence on the self-handicapping process surrounding evaluative conditions (Harris, Snyder, Higgens, & Schrag, 1986). Because failure may dampen one's self-esteem and lower both self- and social evaluation, people high in test anxiety tend to engage in behavior designed to leave ability attributions intact. One possibly effective way of avoiding diagnostic information from intellectual tasks is to reduce effort. Such a strategy reduces the self-relevant implications of failure because accurate ability inferences are possible only under conditions of maximal effort. Accordingly, test anxiety may motivate self-handicapping behaviors and may involve defense maneuvers designed to decrease the likelihood that failures will be attributed to lack of ability (Harris et al., 1986).

A number of studies support the predicted association between test anxiety and self-handicapping. T. W. Smith, Snyder, and Handelsman (1982) found that high-test-anxious persons use reports of lowered effort in a self-handicapping pattern. Harris et al. (1986) examined the differential contributions of selected personality variables, including test anxiety, to self-handicapping in a sample of 104 women within high versus low evaluative stress conditions. Test anxiety was found to be predictive of subjects' anticipated effort, with high-test-anxious subjects anticipating expending less effort. Furthermore, under high-stress conditions, high-test-anxious subjects rated their performance as being less indicative of their true abilities than did low-test-anxious subjects.

Procrastination

Procrastinating or delaying academic tasks, such as delaying the preparation for an important upcoming exam, is documented to be a common practice among college students. Rothblum et al. (1986) reported that nearly one quarter of all college students in their study reported problems with procrastination on various academic tasks, including preparing for exams, writing term papers, and keeping up with weekly readings. A total of 41% of their sample scored high on the procrastination measure, based on the criterion of *nearly always* or *always* procrastinating on the exam and *nearly always* or *always* experiencing anxiety during each procrastination. About 45% of the women and 32% of the men met this criterion. Similarly, a study by Kalechstein et al. (1989) on a small sample of college students reported that 33% of the sample rated themselves as "high" on procrastination.

There is most likely a reciprocal relationship between test anxiety and procrastination. On one hand, test-anxious worry, coupled with self-related failure cognitions, may lead to procrastination in test preparation. Furthermore, the achievement motivation literature has commonly shown that people who have a strong fear of failure and relatively weak achievement motive tend to avoid situations in which the risk of negative evaluation is high. Instead, these individuals seem to prefer either simple tasks, in which the probability of failure is low, or difficult ones, in which failure is expected and therefore brings no loss of evaluation from others. Moreover, Solomon and Rothblum (1984) found that fear of failure accounted for 49% of the variance in a factor analysis of the reasons why students procrastinate, whereas task-aversiveness accounted for 18% of the variance.

On the other hand, habitual procrastination in preparing for tests may enhance test anxiety because it leads to an increase in the potential aversiveness of test taking (Kalechstein et al., 1989). Thus, students who chronically avoid studying for an exam until the very last moment have to cram, frequently receive poorer grades, and often develop a sense of heightened anxiety and helplessness surrounding upcoming test situations. High procrastinators may be motivated to decrease delay only when their anxiety and worry reach peak levels.

Rothblum et al. (1986) assessed procrastination in college students at three points in the term: the week before midterms, the week of midterms, and the week after midterms. High procrastinators were reportedly engaged in lower levels of study behavior during the weeks before exams and were hindered in their studying behaviors by both fear of failure and task-aversiveness. Furthermore, procrastinators were significantly more likely to report heightened test anxiety before an exam, greater weekly state anxiety, and elevated anxiety related to physical symptoms. High and low procrastinators did not differ in their study behaviors or even negative cognitions nearly as much as they did on test anxiety. Procrastination, assessed as a latent factor, has been reported to correlate with the following four dimensions of test anxiety in college students (Kalechstein et al., 1987): Worry ($r = .35$), Irrelevant Thinking ($r = .43$), Tension ($r = .37$), and Bodily Symptoms ($r = .18$).

Time Orientation and Perception

Future time orientation has been conceptualized as a multifacetted construct, composed of the capacity to anticipate, become involved in, and illuminate the future (Gjesme, 1980). Future orientation might be a positive first step toward dealing effectively with a threatening situation, allowing one to prepare for action. However, when the concern and worry about the future are exaggerated and occur repeatedly, as is the case in high-test-anxious subjects, it might not be considered to be a positive preparation for future problem solving and instead may lead to high stress and inability to cope with problems.

Because test anxiety may be construed as a form of future uncertainty in the face of threatening evaluative conditions, test anxiety implies future orientation. Thus, a high-test-anxious individual is expected to anticipate more negative affects in connection with future threatening evaluative situations than individuals low in test anxiety. Gjesme (1980) provided evidence showing that high-test-anxious children are significantly lower on future time orientation and the majority of its critical dimensions. Thus, test anxiety, as assessed by the Test Anxiety Scale for Children, correlated negatively with Future Time Orientation among both 6th grade boys ($r = -.24$) and girls ($r = -.24$). Overall, however, the data relating test anxiety to future time orientation are mixed (Gjesme, 1980).

Furthermore, some research suggests that the passage of time in a test situation is experienced differently by high- and low-test-anxious subjects. I. G. Sarason and Stoop (1978) examined the relationship between test anxiety and time perception under neutral versus achievement-oriented instructions. In the presence of *achievement-oriented* cues, time was shown to pass more slowly for high-test-anxious subjects than for more moderate- and low-test-anxious individuals. Test-anxious subjects overestimated the period of time during which they worked on test materials. Under *neutral instructions*, no differences were found in time perception for high- and low-test-anxious subjects. Under stressful evaluative conditions, high-test-anxious individuals may experience cognitive interference and preoccupation, thus explaining why time goes by so slowly for them.

Although the directionality in the test anxiety–time orientation relationship is inconclusive and open to debate, it is highly plausible that high anxiety, as a defense, might inhibit the development of future time orientation in order to avoid the threatening attributes of future events. In cases where high-test-anxious individuals develop an extended and well-elaborated temporal perspective, the consequence might be constant worry, tension, and stress.

Affective Personality Factors

Trait Anxiety

Current research distinguishes between the individual's actual experiences of anxiety in a specific situation (i.e., state anxiety) and the individual's predisposition to have anxious experiences or engage in anxiety-provoking behaviors in a stressful situation (i.e., trait anxiety). Trait anxiety is a relatively stable condition of the individual, best conceived as a latent disposition or probability to respond with elevated levels of state anxiety under stress (see Chapter 1). Trait anxiety has also recently been shown to be a multidimensional construct which interacts with specific types of situational stress to influence the level of state anxiety experienced (Endler et al., 1991). Thus, test anxiety has been viewed as a particular form of social-evaluative anxiety which predisposes the individual to react with elevated levels of state anxiety in evaluative situations. Accordingly, test anxiety would be expected to be intimately associated with trait anxiety (or neuroticism).

Hocevar and El-Zahhar (1988) reported that both Worry and Emotionality components showed strong positive relationships with trait anxiety in four cross-cultural samples. For Worry the noncorrected Pearson correlation ranged from .45 to .57 in the four samples. Hembree's (1988) meta-analytic data show that test anxiety is in fact strongly related to both trait and state anxiety. In post-secondary school populations test anxiety was reported to be somewhat more highly correlated, on average, with trait anxiety ($r = .53$) than with state anxiety ($r = .45$). This correlation was observed to be stronger in grades 1–12 than in college student populations. L. W.

Morris and Carden (1981) showed that when assessed before an important college exam the higher order factor of Neuroticism correlated .32 with the Worry component of test anxiety and .37 with the Emotionality component. Furthermore, among a series of predictors (locus of control extraversion, etc.), only Neuroticism accurately predicted the degrees of anxiety experienced during the exam.

Anger

While the psychological power structure of the exam situation prohibits a more general expression of anger, hostility, and aggression, the latter may be more widespread in evaluative contexts than commonly thought. Although for most persons test situations are typically associated with anxiety, it is now clear that alternative emotional reactions, including anger and hostility, may frequently be evoked in examinees. Thus, in evaluative academic contexts, characterized by situational frustration and blocking of goal-directed behavior (e.g., obtaining poor marks), it stands to reason that evaluational stress would sometimes result in anger or hostility rather than anxiety.

Whether exam-related stress and arousal will be labeled as anger or anxiety depends on the subtle interaction between the subjective characteristics of the person interpreting his or her arousal and the characteristics of the exam or evaluative situation which may block or thwart goal-directed behavior. Thus, if a person appraising the exam situation concludes that important personal goals have been blocked or frustrated by situational factors, anger may be evoked rather than anxiety or fear. Individual difference variables, particularly trait anger, may play an important role in anger reactions. Thus, individuals more prone to feelings of anger and aggressive behavior will be more likely to attribute anger to a wide array of arousal sources in their environment. Furthermore, a variety of potential test-related and situational factors may arouse angry feelings and a sense of frustration. These include inordinately difficult exam, weak content or face validity, ambiguously worded exam instructions, poor organization of the exam questions, tricky phrasing of test items, inadequate testing facilities, anxious or irritated examiner, lack of time, environmental noise, and poor results. Furthermore, the time at which the anger is experienced surrounding an important exam carries its own implications and consequences. Thus, before the exam, anger may interfere with exam preparation; during the exam, anger may evoke arousal and thus interfere with performance; after the exam, anger may influence how one copes with the outcomes of the exam.

What evidence is there for the association between test anxiety and anger in test situations? A preliminary report of a cross-national study by Tanzer (1995) among secondary school students and university students from Austria, Singapore, and the United States, tested under simulated test situations, suggests that some examinees do experience intense anger in a simulated test situation. Furthermore, anger and anxiety are reported to be distinct, yet correlated, factors. A study by Van der Ploeg (1983a) examined the relationship between test anxiety and anger in a sample of 184 second-year medical students in Holland. Test anxiety was more somewhat more strongly, though modestly, correlated with trait anger ($r = .24$) than with state anger ($r = .12$). The correlations between test anxiety and both trait ($r = .43$) and state anger ($r = .35$) were somewhat higher in a second administration of these scales in a sample of 82 medical students. Similarly, a recent study by Pekrun (1995) reports a strong correlation between test anxiety and anger ($r = .57$) for a sample of 150 students.

Van der Ploeg (1983a) provided evidence of a more qualitative nature in a study of 120 medical students asked to describe a situation or event which made them angry. Surprisingly, only 5% of the responses describing anger-evoking events involved exams. Among the anger-evoking events mentioned were test papers not corrected and returned on time, unfair treatment of students by lecturer or examiner, excessive bureaucracy in registering for the exam, and discrepancies between expected and obtained grades. Similarly, when medical students in a different sample ($n = 155$) were asked to describe what made them angry and why, only about 8–9% of the responses concerned exams. The reasons given for angry responses involved strict time regulations, informal and impatient behaviors of proctors, exam failure, and the like. Further content analyses showed that obstacles in the exam situation, failure, blame, and irritation are major anger-evoking factors.

Depression

Although anxiety and depression are meaningfully related at a conceptual level as key components of negative affectivity, these two constructs are differentiable on a number of salient dimensions (Beck & Clark, 1991). Whereas anxiety stems typically from concerns about future events that may or may not occur, depression typically results from perceived losses in the past (Beck & Emory, 1985). In the case of experienced anxiety, one still sees some prospect for the future, whereas in depression the future is seen as being quite bleak. In the case of anxiety, defects or mistakes are not seen as irrevocable, whereas in depression mistakes are viewed as being irrevocable and the person is seen as being responsible for them and is self-condemning. In the case of anxiety a person anticipates possible damage to goals, with low coping capacity; in depression, the person ruminates about damaged relationship with the surroundings and is consequently preoccupied with failure.

Furthermore, according to M. W. Eysenck (1982), anxious subjects allocate considerable processing resources to threat-related stimuli and actively engage the environment in their coping with threat. This active engagement is manifested in increased effort expenditure, high distractibility, and high attentional selectivity. By contrast, the behavior of depressives is typically characterized by a passive disengagement from the environment, with depressives ruminating and focusing more on past losses, and relatively unresponsive to environmental changes (M. W. Eysenck,

1982). Also, in contrast to anxiety, depression is said to involve low effort expenditure, low distractibility, lack of attentional selectivity, and psychomotor retardation.

Although considerable research has been conducted on the anxiety–depression relationship (Zeidner, Matthews, & Saklofske, in press), the data on the relationship between test anxiety and depression are scant. One study reported that medical students taking an important exam showed higher levels of anxiety and scored higher on a depression scale for the exam period, as measured shortly after the exam, than prior to the exam (Hudgens et al., 1989). Comunian (1989) reported a correlation of .36 between scores on the Test Anxiety Inventory and Children's Depression scale in a sample of 200 Italian high school students. Similarly, Zeidner (1994) recently reported a moderate correlation of .40 between scores on the Beck Depression Inventory and state anxiety in an evaluative situation among 198 Israeli college students taking an important end-of-semester exam. Flett and Blankstein (1994) reported that scores on the Beck Depression Inventory were meaningfully correlated (range .41 to .50) with each of the four subscales of Sarason's Reaction to Tests in a large student sample.

Self-Concept and Self-Regard

Both theory and past research would lend support to the view that a positive self-concept and high self-esteem are related to higher academic ability and attainment, whereas negative beliefs about the self are associated with lower ability, scholastic underachievement, and failure (Covington, 1992). Given prior theory and research showing that high-test-anxious subjects tend to be characterized by self-derogatory thoughts and a low sense of self-merit in evaluative situations, test anxiety would be expected to be inversely related to self-esteem. Furthermore, as pointed out by Dweck and Wortman (1982), high-test-anxious subjects are not only more negative about themselves and their performance, but they also put the two together in a causal fashion and view their poor performance as resulting from their lower competence.

Reviews of the literature point to a meaningful inverse correlation between test anxiety and self-concept. Gaudry and Spielberger's review (1971) points to a strong tendency for high-test-anxious individuals to be self-disparaging and have a low self-image. A meta-analytic study of 36 different studies based on close to 9000 subjects reported a substantial inverse mean population effect size ($r = -.42$) between self-esteem and test anxiety (Hembree, 1988). The meta-analytic data focusing on college populations suggest that high-test-anxious students possess a lower sense of well-being, less self-acceptance, lower capacity for status, less tolerance, and lower intellectual efficiency than low-test-anxious students. A number of studies show similar effects in school-age populations. Krampen (1988) reported that self-concept was strongly correlated with test anxiety both at the beginning of ($r = -.47$) and later on in the school year ($r = .50$). Similarly, Many and Many (1975) reported a moderate inverse mean correlation ($r = -.38$) between scores on the Test Anxiety Scale for

Children and the Coopersmith Self Esteem Inventory in a sample of students in grades 4–8. Lekarczyk and Hill (1969) reported that the inverse correlation observed between self-esteem and test anxiety may be stronger for boys ($r = -.40$) than for girls ($r = -.29$) in a sample of 63 male and 51 female elementary school children. The authors hypothesized that boys with high self-esteem are more likely to have learned the sex-role appropriateness of *not* admitting to anxiety than their low-self-esteem counterparts, thus accounting for the stronger negative correlation. Girls, on the other hand, are less often punished and sometimes are rewarded for admitting to anxiety.

One prevalent view is that causality flows from self-esteem to test anxiety. Test anxiety has been conceptualized as a failure of self, where one's sense of competence has been undermined as a result of experienced failure (Hodapp, 1989). Self-confidence in academic situations implies a sense of self-efficacy and a belief in the competence to master the task at hand. Individuals who feel less confident would be expected to show lower expectations of future success in evaluative situations, which, in turn, would produce higher levels of fear of failure and anxiety, lowered effort and motivation to succeed, and subsequent unfavorable academic performance (Hodapp, 1989). Furthermore, because of low self-esteem and high failure expectancies, a person may be more prone to engage in the characteristic interpretation of upcoming events as portending failure and in the self-handicapping behavior of test anxiety (Many & Many, 1975). Some empirical data lend support to the view that poor self-concept bears a greater influence and prospective association with the development of test anxiety than vice versa. Thus, two longitudinal studies, employing cross-lagged analysis, reported that test anxiety was preceded by a low self-concept or sense of competence in student populations (Krampen, 1988). Hodapp (1989) showed that decreases in self-perceived ability precede the occurrence of test anxiety in school and are causal for its development.

An alternative view is that the causal flow is from test anxiety to self-concept, with a negative self-concept simply reflecting low ability or academic performance and concomitantly high levels of test anxiety. Accordingly, S. B. Sarason et al. (1960) suggested that high-test-anxious children develop self-derogatory attitudes, which, in turn, leads to over concern about personal adequacy. A third and highly probable view is that there is a bidirectional relationship between the two constructs. Thus, anxiety and self-esteem would be expected to be mutually intertwined and reciprocally impact upon each other during the course of development and behavior in evaluative situations.

Type A Personality

Friedman and Rosenman (1974) defined the Type A behavior pattern as "an action–emotion complex that can be observed in a person who is aggressively involved in a chronic, incessant struggle to achieve more and more in less and less time" (p. 67). Type A behavior is basically a style of responding to situations that involve challenge, demands, and threats to a person's sense of control. This behavior pattern has been traditionally characterized by exaggerated competitiveness, striving for achievement, aggression, intense ambition, easily aroused hostility, and a strong sense of time urgency. All of these factors are thought to combine to increase the risk of coronary artery disease. The behavioral pattern elicited is then assumed to lead to physical reactions that have structural effects and that predispose that person to disease (e.g., coronary artery disease, atherosclerosis). The converse, Type B behavioral pattern, is characterized by an absence of these behaviors and consequently of reduced risk of coronary heart disease.

Researchers (Harris et al., 1986) pointed out a number of features that test anxiety and Type A behavior have in common. Thus, both test-anxious and Type A individuals are threatened by evaluative situations, have high achievement needs, have a strong desire to avoid failure, and report using self-handicapping behaviors. Although this suggests that these two variables may be associated and even have a common influence or similar underlying causal mechanisms, empirical research has shown an inconsistent pattern of relationship between them. Whereas Glass (1977) and Feather and Volkmer (1988) failed to report a significant association between test anxiety and Type A behavior pattern, other studies indicated a positive relation between Type A behaviors and test anxiety (Gastorf & Teevan, 1980).

Research by Volkmer and Feather (1991) suggested that it may be useful to examine separately the relationship between test anxiety and different components of Type A behavior. They reasoned that because both test anxiety and the component of *impatience-irritability* are linked to the affective system, this common base would result in a positive correlation between these variables. In contradistinction, because Type A college students are high in achievement strivings, they would be motivated to test themselves in challenging evaluative situations—the same kinds of situations that high-test-anxious subjects would try to avoid. This would suggest an inverse relation between test anxiety and the *achievement-striving* component of Type A behavior. These hypotheses were tested in a sample of 99 high school and 380 college students. A significant positive correlation was reported between test anxiety and the impatience/irritability component of Type A behavior, with correlations of .42 and .23 reported for high school and college students, respectively. However, achievement striving was unrelated to test anxiety.

Emotional States

A wide array of emotional states may impact upon learning and performance in evaluative contexts by influencing cognitive processes, self- and task-related cognitions, motivation, and volition. Emotions are currently conceptualized as systems of closely interrelated cognitive processes, with specific identifiable components (e.g., affective, cognitive, somatic, motivational). Human emotions are geared to enable individuals to react quickly and in a flexible way to situations that are important for adaptation and survival. Given the salience and cardinal importance of a host of tests for social status and economic mobility in modern society, coupled with the notion that emotions function as human reactions to important events, major examinations most likely evoke a variety of different emotions.

To date, however, test anxiety (and to some extent, anger) is the only affective variable which has received widespread scientific attention in relation to evaluative situations. Research would certainly benefit from a systematic mapping out of specific test-related affective states that students experience in negotiating examinations and other evaluative situations (Pekrun & Frese, 1992). As pointed out by Pekrun (1995), we know very little about test-related emotions other than anxiety. Thus, more research attention is clearly warranted focusing both on positive (e.g., enjoyment, hope, joy, relief, pride) and negative (boredom, helplessness, sadness, shame, guilt) emotions at various stages in the examination process (anticipatory, confrontation, postexamination, etc.). Pekrun (1995) has made some advances in this direction, reporting on the test-related emotions of 150 college students. The affective, cognitive, physiological, and motivational facets of a series of positive (joy, hope, relief) as well as negative emotions (anxiety, anger, hopelessness) emotions were measured. Test anxiety was reported to correlate positively with a variety of emotions, including relief ($r = .40$), anger ($r = .57$), and hopelessness ($r = .83$). Test anxiety was not related to hope or joy surrounding test taking.

Intelligence and Scholastic Ability

Intelligence may be construed as a personal resource that can serve as a *buffer* against evaluative stress (Zeidner, 1995c). Thus, highly intelligent individuals, who tend to have a greater adaptive capacity than their less intelligent counterparts, may also be less prone to experience high levels of anxiety and its disruptive effects in evaluative situations. Intelligence may impact upon each of the phases of the evaluative stress process (Zeidner, 1995c). Intelligence can affect the appraisal process by allowing more complex reasoning and consideration of alternatives in a test situation during both primary and secondary appraisal. It stands to reason that individuals with higher intellectual level and problem-solving skills are more likely to diagnose accurately the causes of evaluative stress, collect information bearing on the evaluative situation from a variety of sources, examine the situation from different viewpoints, reason about the causes, and generate options about how to change themselves or the context. Intelligence may also enter into the actual process of coping, affecting both the choice and implementation of particular coping strategies in a stressful test situation. While problem- and emotion-focused strategies will likely be used by people of both high and low intelligence, those lower in intelligence may use emotion-focused coping more frequently because they will assess more situations as ones they can do very little about (Zeidner, Matthews, & Saklofske, in press).

Although a number of studies have failed to report notable differences in intelligence between high- and low-test-anxious subjects (e.g., S. B. Sarason et al., 1960), test anxiety has generally been reported to correlate inversely, though modestly, with intelligence and scholastic ability test performance (Hembree, 1988; Zeidner & Nevo, 1992). Matarazzo (1972) reviewed studies suggesting that the relationship between intelligence and trait anxiety is negligible, with neither pattern nor scatter analysis approaches to the Wechsler intelligence scales showing any relation to a trait measure of anxiety. However, studies utilizing situationally induced anxiety (i.e., state anxiety) did reveal decrements in performance on the same measures of intellectual functioning. He concluded that only when we separate the state anxious from the trait anxious can we detect a decrement in intellectual performance due to anxiety.

I. G. Sarason (1961) obtained scores on 13 intellectual measures for 738 students enrolled in introductory psychology courses at the University of Washington and correlated each of these measures with scores on several different personality scales (i.e., test anxiety, general anxiety, hostility, need for achievement, defensiveness). The results show that test anxiety was the only personality variable which consistently related to the measures of academic aptitude and achievement. Similarly, a review of the literature on the empirical relations between personality and intelligence suggests that anxiety may be the most highly correlated personality variable with intelligence (Zeidner, 1995c).

The nature of the causal flow of direction in the observed relationship between intelligence and test anxiety, however, has been conceptualized and interpreted in a variety of different ways (Zeidner, 1995c). First, test anxiety has been claimed to limit the use of personal wherewithal on intelligence tasks, resulting in lowered test performance. Second, one cannot rule out the possibility that test-anxious individuals are on the average less capable than others, and that at least in some instances, anxiety has developed as a result of failures brought about by low ability. Thus, persons low in intelligence or academic ability may become anxious about the need to confront situations that produce failure, thus leading to increased self-preoccupation, low self-efficacy, feelings of helplessness, and resultant poor test performance. Furthermore, because people of low intelligence are more apt to have experienced the effects of poor academic performance in the past, more of them should be inclined to use test anxiety as a rationalization than would people of high intelligence.

A third interpretation is that individuals with low intelligence are not really smart enough to mask their true feelings and anxieties about exams, as their brighter counterparts do. Thus, the observed negative relations are caused by shortcoming in use of self-report anxiety instruments. A fourth interpretation is that the observed relationship of anxiety to intelligence may be due to the artifactual influences of extraneous variables (e.g., social class, child-rearing practices), which concomitantly influence both test anxiety and intelligence. Finally, intelligence and test anxiety are likely to be related in a bidirectional and reciprocal way, influencing each other in the course of development and day-to-day behavior.

Some data suggest that scholastic ability is not only related to test anxiety, but may also may *mediate* the relationship between anxiety and academic achievement. Lin and McKeachie (1970) found that when ability is controlled for, the differences in academic achievement between high- and low-test-anxious groups tend to become insignificant. Thus, the observed differences in academic achievement of extreme anxiety groups may be largely accounted for by differences in college aptitude. However, matching children for intelligence (i.e., holding ability constant) does not consistently eliminate the negative relationship between anxiety and intellectual performance (Milgram & Milgram, 1977).

Furthermore, there is some evidence suggesting that intelligence may interact with anxiety in *moderating* the effects of anxiety on academic performance. Thus, anxiety is shown to have a more depressing effect on the performance of low- and moderate-ability examinees compared to high-ability examinees (Hembree, 1988; Katahn, 1966; Spielberger, 1962). That is, at low levels of ability, anxiety may lead to performance decrements, except on very easy tasks, whereas at high levels of ability, anxiety often *facilitates* performance on simple and on most tasks of moderate difficulty. Spielberger (1966b) observed that as mean Scholastic Aptitude Test scores increased, the size of the negative correlation between trait anxiety and aptitude test scores *decreased* monotonically (from −.34 to .04). Based on these data, Spielberger predicted that negative correlations between measures of anxiety and intelligence will be observed empirically only for the samples that contain a sizable proportion of subjects with low ability. Data presented by Spielberger and Katzenmeyer (1959) yielded findings consistent with the hypothesis that test anxiety may interact with ability in affecting scholastic performance.

Intelligence may work through perceptions of task difficulty to moderate the impact of anxiety upon task performance. Indeed, the observation that high anxiety facilitates the performance of intelligent or bright subjects and leads to decrements for those who are less intelligent suggests that task difficulty is an "inverse function" of intelligence (Spielberger, 1966a,b,c). It may further be assumed that the higher one's cognitive ability or intelligence, the higher one's subjective probability of success and the lower one's subjective probability of failure. It follows that individuals of high, medium, and low ability, respectively, should have low, medium, and high probabilities of failure. Furthermore, it stands to reason that how easy a task is perceived to be depends on the examinee's intelligence level. According to the Yerkes–Dodson law (1908; see Chapter 9), there is an optimal level of drive for any given task; drive levels above or below that optimal level will lead to less efficient performance. For highly intelligent subjects, cognitive tasks are often perceived to be relatively easy, so that the anxiety level is still in the optimum range, thereby facilitating performance for these highly intelligent students. For examinees of low intelligence, who have fewer cognitive resources upon which to draw, the same task may be perceived (and in fact may actually be) relatively difficult and evoke a larger number of error tendencies. Thus, the low-ability individual often falls into the "debilitating" range of the inverted-U curve, with resultant performance impaired.

Summary

This chapter surveyed some personality and motivational correlates of test anxiety. Some of the variables discussed play a critical role in the development and maintenance of test-anxious reactions in evaluative situations (e.g., self-efficacy), some may be best viewed as critical features of the test anxiety experience (e.g., fear of failure, procrastination), some may play a mediating role in the stress–anxiety or stress–performance association in achievement settings (e.g., attributions), while others may be consequences of test anxiety (e.g., learned helplessness). In fact, it often remains a matter of theory whether a particular personality variable is seen as a constituent of anxiety or as a distinct construct.

This survey of the personal correlates of test anxiety, notwithstanding the mixed nature of some of the data, allows a preliminary sketch of the personal profile of high-test-anxious subjects. Accordingly, high-test-anxious subjects, relative to their low-test-anxious counterparts, tend to evidence higher levels of negative affect (trait anxiety, depression, anger) and lower levels of positive affect (self-concept and self-esteem). High-test-anxious subjects tend to be characterized by a high fear of failure in test situations, but are also reliably differentiated by their differing need for achievement and low hope for success. These subjects tend to have low beliefs in their self-efficacy, show pessimistic attitudes and expectations of success, are less sociable, and tend to be lower in scholastic aptitude. In addition, high-test-anxious subjects tend to procrastinate in studying for exams and use reports of lowered effort in a self-handicapping pattern.

Overall, one would predict a bidirectional relationship between test anxiety and the bulk of the variables discussed, with the constructs impacting upon each either in a transactional process over time. Note, however, that the body of research examining the relationship between test anxiety, as an individual difference variable, and other individual difference variables is basically correlational in nature, with emphasis placed on discovering whether a relationship exists between the variables. Unfortunately, correlational studies do not establish a causal relationship, but merely indicate that two variables are related and this needs to be carefully held in mind. In this case, no casual inference may be clearly made about the relationship between trait test anxiety and the personal variables assessed.

VI

Coping, Interventions, and Clinical Parameters

Coping with Test Situations

Resources, Strategies, and Adaptational Outcomes

> How a man rallies to life's challenges and weathers its storms tells everything of who
> he is and all that he is likely to become.
>
> —*St. Augustine*

Overview

Over the past decade an increasing number of studies have focused on how students cope with stressful examination contexts. As noted in Chapter 1, a wide variety of tests have important consequences for students in modern society, playing an increasingly important role in determining students' academic and occupational careers. To be sure, adaptive coping with exams and evaluative situations is important for a student's psychological well-being and for achieving his or her academic goals and aspirations. While stress researchers have traditionally been more interested in the effects of evaluative stress on anxiety and test attainment than in the role of coping in influencing adaptational outcomes, evaluative conditions such as examinations are currently viewed as a fruitful and promising area of research for understanding how people cope with ego-threatening social encounters (Bolger, 1990; Carver & Scheier, 1994; Folkman & Lazarus, 1985; Zeidner, 1995a,b). Thus, researchers have come to realize that evaluative situations are ideally suited vehicles for examining the coping process during stressful encounters, on several counts. To begin with, an exam embodies many of the criteria of major environmental stressors (preparation for the impending threat or event, confrontation with the stressor, uncertainty about the outcome, and coping with the consequences; Carver & Scheier, 1994; Folkman & Lazarus, 1985). Since the exam process unfolds in a lawful and predictable manner it is relatively easy to control for the temporal aspect of the stressful transaction and thereby zoom in more accurately on coping behaviors during distinct phases of a stressful encounter. Also, inasmuch as exams are ubiquitous events, they are readily accessible situations for purposes of research.

The major aim of this chapter is to attempt to assimilate and integrate this growing literature on coping with tests and evaluative situations. Specifically, this chapter discusses conceptualization, research, and methodological issues bearing on the ways student populations cope with tests, with particular concern for the consequences of examinees' coping efforts for their psychological well-being and test performance. I begin by presenting an overview of the coping process, defining key constructs and discussing a number of major issues in the research literature. I then survey the empirical research literature focusing on students' coping with examination situations and assess the role of coping resources and strategies in impacting upon anxiety and achievement outcomes. I move on to discuss some of the conceptual and methodological problems intrinsic to research on coping adaptiveness, and conclude by providing a number of broad, though tentative, research-based generalizations related to coping with tests and evaluative situations.

The Coping Process

Coping behaviors are commonly viewed as playing a crucial role in mediating between stressful situations and adaptational outcomes. Accordingly, current transactional models of stress (R. S. Lazarus & Folkman, 1984) view stress as a multivariate process involving inputs (i.e., person variables, environmental variables), outputs (i.e., immediate and long-term effects), and the mediation activities of appraisal and coping. Coping processes are of prime importance in that they affect adaptational outcomes (R. S. Lazarus & Folkman, 1984). Given that coping behaviors play a crucial role in mediating between stressful situations and adaptational outcomes, coping would be predicted to help an individual adapt to a stressful situation by reducing distress and improving daily functioning.

Coping, broadly speaking, involves a person's constantly changing cognitive and behavioral efforts to manage (i.e., reduce, minimize, master, tolerate) the internal and external demands of a transaction that is appraised as stressful (R. S. Lazarus & Folkman, 1984; Folkman et al., 1991; Lazarus, 1993a). Accordingly, when the demands of a threatening situation, such as an important classroom test or college exam, are perceived as stressful and taxing one's personal resources, efforts are directed at regulating emotional stress and/or dealing with the problem at hand (Folkman & Lazarus, 1986) in order to manage the troubled person–environment transaction (R. S. Lazarus, 1990).

The coping process is typically described as a linear sequence consisting of three subprocesses, i.e., primary appraisal, secondary appraisal, and specific coping responses. Although I touched upon the topic of cognitive appraisals in Chapters 1 and 8, I briefly reiterate some of the basic concepts at this point for the benefit of the reader. *Primary appraisal* is the process of perceiving and evaluating a situation as involving threat, challenge, harm, or benefit to oneself. *Secondary appraisal* is the process of bringing to mind a variety of potential responses to situations appraised to be threatening or challenging. Primary and secondary appraisals converge to determine whether the person–environment transaction is regarded as significant for well-being and, if so, whether it is primarily *threatening* (containing possibility for harm or loss) or *challenging* (holding possibility of mastery/benefit). Further, the quality and intensity of any emotion in a potentially stressful situation are generated by the appraisal process.

Although researchers have employed various classification schemes in categorizing general coping strategies, there is some consensus surrounding the major categories of coping strategies, namely: (a) problem-focused coping, designed to manage or solve the problem by removing or circumventing the stressor (e.g., carefully planning and spacing one's study schedule in preparing for an exam, studying hard, obtaining good summaries of lecture notes); (b) emotion-focused coping, designed to regulate, reduce, or eliminate the emotional stress associated with the stressful situation (e.g., seeking emotional support from friends, denying the importance of the exam, distancing oneself from the evaluative threat); and (c) avoidance-oriented coping, referring to either the use of person-oriented strategies (e.g., avoidance or seeking of others) or task-oriented strategies (e.g., watching TV, engaging in nonrelevant tasks) designed to circumvent or avoid the stressful situation. Because problem-focused coping would be expected to alter the actual terms of the individual's stressful relationship with the environment, this should lead, in turn, to more favorable cognitive appraisals and a more positive response to the exam situation.

Coping strategies may protect us by eliminating or modifying the conditions that produce stress or by keeping the emotional consequences within manageable bounds (Zeidner & Hammer, 1990). Coping may affect outcomes through its impact on the frequency, intensity, duration, and patterning of physiological stress reactions and the resultant affective and somatic outcomes. Further, coping strategies may impede rather than promote health-related behaviors. For example, a student's health may be negatively affected when coping involves risk taking (high-speed car racing) or substance abuse (alcohol). The *main effects* model suggests that coping has similar effects on well-being regardless of the kind or amount of stress. The *interactive* model suggests that coping moderates the impact of stressful episodes to varying degrees, depending on the type or severity of stress. The possibility for a stress × coping interaction has also led to the view that coping serves a "buffer" effect (Wills, 1986). Thus, if a coping strategy has a buffering effect, it will be of significant value under moderate- to high-stress conditions, but of much less value under low-stress conditions or vice versa. Thus, the buffer hypothesis would suggest that coping should be particularly helpful in a highly stressful evaluative situation relative to a less stressful one. Research results in a variety of contexts provide mixed support for both models (Felton & Revenson, 1984).

Coping Strategies versus Resources

It would be appropriate at this point to distinguish between two related, but distinct concepts that have often been used interchangeably—leading to some confusion in the literature (Menaghan, 1983). These are coping *strategies* and coping *resources*. Coping *resources* are viewed as adaptive capacities that provide immunity against damage from stress (Zeidner & Hammer, 1990). Thus, individuals with high resources have been characterized as resilient and hardy (Kobasa, 1979), while those with low resources have been described as vulnerable and constitutionally fragile. Resources are person characteristics that enable individuals to handle stressors more effectively, experience fewer or less intense symptoms upon exposure to a stressor, such as an impending important exam, or recover faster from exposure. Whereas resources act as "precursors" of behavior (Wheaton, 1983, p. 222) and as "background" factors (Wheaton, 1983, p. 211), strategies refer to behaviors occurring *after* the appearance of the stressor (or in response to chronic stressors). Thus, in agreement with Pearlin and Schooler (1978), *strategies* are understood to be the things that people do or think in reaction to a specific stressor occurring in a particular context.

By affecting a variety of factors in the coping situation (e.g., type of strategy adopted, range of responses considered, interpretation of the event, or effort expended on coping), personal variables may increase an individual's potential for dealing effectively with stress (Wheaton, 1983; Zeidner & Hammer, 1990). According to coping theory (Holahan & Moos, 1990), when stressors are high, personal and social resources should predict stable functioning indirectly through coping efforts, primarily through an association with more frequent attempts at approach coping. Resources may also increase approach coping through the appraisal process by fostering positive beliefs about one's ability to manage successfully a threatening experience. Accordingly, students with rich cognitive, social, or emotional resources are expected to have positive beliefs about their ability to negotiate successfully a stressful examination experience; the positive self-referent thoughts and feelings of self-efficacy may be instrumental in positive exam success.

An example may help to clarify the difference between coping resources and strategies. A student experiencing stress before an important exam may decide to go jogging as a means of reducing tension. Although this strategy may be effective to some extent when resorted to under stressful examination conditions, if overdone, it may lead to negative consequences, such as exercise-related injury. A person with physical resources, however, is someone who has engaged in ongoing physical activity, which, presumably, will better equip him or her to deal with the upcoming exam more effectively than the person who only engages in the strategy under stressful conditions.

Whereas several researchers have viewed seeking "social support" as a coping strategy, it would perhaps best be conceptualized as a resource for coping rather than a specific coping dimension. Thus, social support can be used to facilitate coping and can serve as a resource for various coping behaviors. For example, students facing an important exam situation can use other persons as a source of information (e.g., "Where can I get hold of Psych 1 lecture notes?"), as a source of emotional regulation of social comparison (e.g., "I did better than Tim on the test"), or as a source of escape from one's problems ("Let's go play volleyball and forget about the whole thing").

Coping Styles versus Coping Responses

Furthermore, there is an important distinction in the coping literature between coping *styles* or dispositions and situation-specific coping *responses* (Parker & Endler, 1992). The trait-oriented approach views coping styles as personality dispositions that transcend the influence of situational context or time, thus emphasizing stability in coping rather than change. In contrast, the process or situation-specific approach conceptualizes coping as specific thoughts and behaviors that are performed in response to stressful situations and that change over time. In addition to those researchers who have emphasized the need to study the coping process over the course of a test situation (Folkman & Lazarus, 1985), others have taken an active interest in studying the cross-situation stability of coping behaviors (e.g., Zeidner, 1994). While there is evidence that individuals differ in their stylistic patterns of coping reactions, it is also apparent that situation-specific factors also play a major role in coping reactions (Endler, Kantor, & Parker, 1994). It is further noted that coping strategy and coping style or dispositions are theoretical concepts. What we actually observe when we talk about coping are certain acts (e.g., someone goes to the movies in the evening before an important event). One may assign this behavior to the strategy of attention diversion, but this is a theory-based decision, depending on one's specific theoretical approach.

The *transactional model* of stress and coping (R. S. Lazarus, 1993a, 1993b; R. S. Lazarus & Folkman, 1984), presented in Chapter 3, offers several basic working assumptions impacting on current conceptualizations about adaptive coping. First, coping strategies should not be prejudged as adaptive or maladaptive. Rather, the concern must be for whom and under what circumstances a particular coping mode has adaptive consequences rather than the wholesale categorization of coping as adaptive versus maladaptive. For example, active coping might be adaptive during the earlier phases of an exam, when something can still be done about the situation, whereas wishful thinking or emotional social support might be more adaptive after the exam has been taken. Further, coping is a process embedded in context. Therefore, responses may not only vary across contexts, but also change over time in response to external conditions and as a function of the skill with which they are applied. Thus, coping strategies found to be effective in an exam situation might not be adaptive in the context of family disputes, emotional disorder, occupational stress, or grave traumatic stressors. Another assumption is that coping effectiveness must be empirically demonstrated, with coping strategies not classifiable as being adaptive versus maladaptive on an *a priori* basis (Zeidner & Saklofske, 1996). Finally, coping efforts should not be confounded with coping outcomes (Lennon, Dohrenwend, Zautra & Marbach, 1990).

How Do Students Cope with Examinations?

Over the past decade an increasing number of empirical studies have investi-gated the various ways students cope with stressful social evaluative situations and the impact of coping on adaptational outcomes. Several well-conceived and imple-mented studies have explored students' appraisals, coping behaviors, and emotions across various phases of a stressful examination encounter. I now briefly summarize the major trends in this body of empirical research.

Stages of a Stressful Evaluative Encounter

As indicated in Chapter 2, current research suggests that coping with an evalua-tive encounter is a complex process, with significant changes in the use of various coping strategies across the stages of the evaluative encounter (Folkman & Lazarus, 1985). How do appraisals and coping responses unfold across the various phases of the stressful encounter?

Research by Folkman and Lazarus (1985) suggests that during the *anticipatory stage*, the preparatory phase prior to the exam, an individual becomes aware of an upcoming exam. Examinees are typically concerned about how best to prepare for the upcoming exam, how to regulate feelings and aversive emotions associated with the exam, as well as with the prospects for success on the exam. Since ambiguity is expected to be at its height during the anticipatory stage—because examinees do not know exactly what will be on the exam or what the outcome will be like—the possibilities for both positive and negative outcomes can be seen. This means that examinees can experience both threat and challenge emotions at the early stages of an exam encounter. Problem-focused activities would be considered to be adaptive at this stage since something still can be done to enhance the prospects for success, while at the same time, emotion-focused coping would be needed to help alleviate the tensions and anxieties surrounding performance.

At the *confrontation stage*, examinees actually confront the stressor, i.e., take the exam. Very few studies have assessed objectively how students actually feel and think about the exam at this critical stage, under "*in vivo*" evaluative conditions. Examinees would be expected to employ a variety of coping strategies, including task-oriented and palliative coping techniques to handle the stress evoked during the exam.

During the *waiting stage*, uncertainty about the specific nature and qualities of the test and test atmosphere has been resolved or meaningfully reduced, and feedback cues from the examination may help examinees predict their exam performance reasonably well. However, individuals may still feel apprehension about the outcome. A decrease in instrumental coping would be expected at this stage (as little can be done to improve one's chances of success on the exam), along with a concomitant increase in emotion-focused coping to release built-up tension.

During the *outcome stage*, after grades are posted, students finally learn how well they performed on the exam. Any uncertainty about the outcome is resolved at this stage, and the concerns of students turn to the significance of what has already happened and its implications (harm, benefit). The more an encounter unfolds over time, the more firmly the examinee should be making either a negative or positive appraisal of the outcome. Students who succeed on the exam would be expected to be happy and experience an uplift, and no longer need to cope with the exam. By contrast, those who do poorly would be expected to become increasingly anxious and moody and engage in increased coping.

Appraisals and Emotions in an Evaluative Encounter

Coping theory predicts that as the person's appraisal of a stressful encounter changes, so, too, will the associated emotions (R. S. Lazarus & Folkman, 1984). Recently, a number of studies have corroborated these predictions, showing that anxiety is in flux during various phases of an examination. Bolger (1990) assessed anxiety and coping in a sample of 150 students surrounding an important medical admissions exam. Data were collected at four points in time: 5 weeks before the exam, 10 days before the exam, 2½ weeks after the exam, and 35 days after the exam. Almost all students reported heightened anxiety in the last several days before the exam, though there were marked differences exactly when anxiety peaked. For some it was the same day as the exam, whereas for other it was as many as 4 days before the exam. Similar results were obtained for high school students (Lay et al., 1989).

Figure 13.1 depicts the type of emotions, both positive and negative, expected to be prominent prior to and following an exam. As shown, the anticipatory emotions, threat and challenge, are expected to be prominent prior to the exam, whereas outcome emotions (harm and benefit) are expected to be prominent following the exam. Folkman and Lazarus (1985) reported that the intensity of anticipatory emo-

Emotional Valence	Timing	
	Before Exam	After Exam
Positive	Challenge	Benefit
Negative	Threat	Harm

Figure 13.1. Anticipatory and outcome emotions in an evaluative encounter. After R. S. Lazarus and Folkman (1984).

tions (threat and challenge) decreases significantly from the postexam to the post-grade stage in college students. By contrast, outcome emotions (harm and benefit) increased significantly from the anticipatory to the postexam stage—but did not change after that. Furthermore, practically all the students (94%) reported both threat and challenge emotions prior to the exam, implying that during conditions of maximum ambiguity (i.e., before taking the exam) both types of emotions are likely to be expressed.

These data were replicated, in part, by Carver and Scheier (1994) in their prospective study on coping with exams and adaptational outcomes. Data were gathered on situational coping in a student population along with four classes of appraisal, namely: (a) *threat* ("worried," "fearful," "anxious"), *challenges* ("confident," "hopeful," "eager"), *harm* ("angry," "disappointed," "guilty"), and *benefit* ("pleased," "happy," "relieved"). Appraisals and coping were assessed at the anticipatory, waiting, and postexam stages. Figure 13.2 presents the mean level of appraisals found in this study for the three phases of the exam. It can be seen that threat and challenge emotions were relatively high during the anticipatory stage of the threatening encounter, but fell off after the exam—particularly after grades were posted. By contrast, harm and benefit emotions increased significantly from post-exam to after posting of grades. While threats and challenges were found to concur during the anticipatory or preparation stage, reflecting the anticipation of divergent future outcomes, harm and benefit emotions were inversely related, fitting the idea that these emotions reflect a sense that one or the other outcome has come to pass.

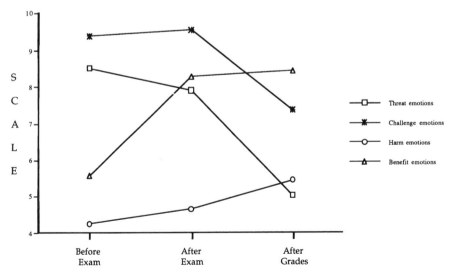

Figure 13.2. Emotions at three stages of the test situation. Based on data presented in Carver and Scheier (1994).

Research conducted by C. A. Smith and Ellsworth (1987) on a sample of 86 Stanford University students sheds additional light on the blend of emotions experienced by examinees during various stages of a stressful examination encounter. Students described their cognitive appraisals and emotions just before taking a college midterm psychology exam and again after receiving grades on the exam. The majority of college students in their study experienced two or more emotions during both stages. A combination of the *anticipatory* emotions of hope, challenge, and fear was the most common blend experienced prior to the exam. After the exam, by contrast, the patterning was more varied: Anger, guilt, and fear combined in a variety of ways, with happiness cooccurring with hope and challenge. Subjects reported feeling considerably more hopeful, challenged, and fearful before taking the exam than they did after receiving their grades. Furthermore, subjects saw the exam as more difficult and important before they took it than they did after seeing their grades. Conversely, subjects reported higher levels of anger, happiness, and guilt after than before the exam. After receiving feedback about their performance (i.e., grades), subjects were more likely to evaluate their situation as both unfair and attributable to someone else. During the anticipatory stage the experience of positive emotions did not preclude that of negative emotions. However, after posting of grades, positive emotions (e.g., happiness) were negatively correlated with negative emotions (i.e., ratings of fear, anger, and anxiety).

Research has evidenced a complex pattern of relations between appraisals and emotions in the test situation, as clearly demonstrated by the work of Carver and Scheier (1994) mentioned earlier. Appraisals and coping were assessed at the anticipatory, waiting, and postexam stage; data on coping styles were obtained at an earlier date. Students' appraisals were significantly related to their coping behaviors: students who perceived the test situation as challenge used more problem-focused coping, whereas those who perceived the situation as a threat used less problem-focused coping. By contrast, harm, an outcome emotion, correlated with a number of palliative tactics. Thus students who felt they were harmed by the test tended to make greater use of alcohol, mental disengagement, and social support. Further, the grades students received on the exam correlated positively with benefit emotions and inversely with harm emotions. Carver and Sheier (1994) found that coping before an exam was a poor prospective predictor of emotions as assessed after the exam. The effects that did emerge reflected maladaptive coping (e.g., mental disengagement before the exam was associated with more threat afterward). Curiously, problem-focused coping predicted *high* levels of threat and challenge later on—possibly because task-focused coping promotes enthusiasm about confronting the next instance of a recurrent stressor (Bolger, 1990).

Personal Variables and Coping

A number of studies have looked at the role of personal variables and resources in the coping process. In Bolger's (1990) study of students' anxiety and coping surrounding an important medical exam, students high on trait anxiety reported more escapist coping methods, and these styles were, in turn, related to state anxiety in the test situation. A path analysis showed that wishful thinking and self-blame are principal responses through which trait anxiety led to higher anxiety. Overall, this study suggests that personality variables such as trait anxiety influence the coping strategies people select and that these strategies, in turn, may influence subsequent outcomes (trait anxiety → coping → state anxiety).

Zeidner (1995b) studied the relationship between coping resources, strategies, and outcomes in a sample of 241 Israeli undergraduates. First-order correlations showed that students with richer coping resources tend to use more problem-focused coping and less avoidance coping under test conditions. Regression analyses showed that when controlling for the effects of other resources, students with richer cognitive resources used *less* emotion-focused coping, whereas students with greater emotional and spiritual resources used *more* emotion-focused coping. However, coping resources were not predictive of problem-focused coping. Furthermore, students with higher cognitive, social, emotional, and physical resources evidenced lower test-anxiety levels in an evaluation situation. Terry (1991) collected data on personality variables, situational appraisals of a stressful college exam situation, and coping strategies used by 138 college students surrounding an exam. Students characterized by low judgments of self-efficacy also used more emotion-focused coping, and those prone to self-denial favored escapist strategies coping. High levels of instrumental action (i.e., problem-oriented coping) predominated when the event was judged as important and when subjects reported high levels of stress.

Specific Ways of Coping with Exams

Folkman and Lazarus (1985) examined the particular coping strategies employed by a sample of 108 college students during the anticipatory, waiting, and outcome stages of a midterm exam. At every stage of the examination, students reported using combinations of most of the available forms of problem-focused and emotion-focused coping, rather than just one form or the other. In fact, practically all the students used problem-focused coping and at least one form of emotion-focused coping during all three phases of the exam in order to cope with their anxieties. Problem-focused coping was at its height during the anticipatory stage, presumably in the service of studying for the exam. Similarly, two forms of emotion-focused coping—emphasizing the positive and seeking social support—were at their height at this stage, steadily decreasing thereafter. Distancing was the most frequently employed strategy during the waiting period, presumably because distancing is useful where there is little to do but wait. While there was a significant decrease in *informational* social support from the anticipatory to waiting period, there was a concomitant increase in *emotional* social support. Thus, subjects who sought informational support during the anticipatory stage, to help them prepare for the exam, shift to emotional support during the waiting period to secure reassurance and comfort afterward. After grades were announced, coping responses were influenced mainly by individual differences in performance.

Carver and Scheier (1994) reported that problem-focused coping behaviors (i.e., "adaptive" responses) were reported to be employed more frequently throughout the exam than those characterized as potentially dysfunctional. Subjects reported relatively high levels of active coping, planning, suppression of competing activities, positive reframing, and acceptance in coping with exam situations. By contrast, subjects reported relatively low levels of denial, mental disengagement, behavioral disengagement, and use of alcohol. Further, coping responses were reported to change from one stage of the adaptational encounter to the other. Problem or task-focused responses (e.g., active coping, planning, suppression, use of instrumental support, acceptance) were high during the period before the exam, but diminished afterward—remaining relatively stable thereafter. Certain palliative reactions (e.g., use of emotional social support and mental disengagement) declined significantly after exam scores were available. Curiously, only denial tended to increase across the transaction: Reports of denial were lowest before the exam, increased afterward, and continued to drift upward to the third measurement. Figure 13.3 presents graphically the three key strategies students use to cope with exams.

Dimensions of Test Coping

What are the dimensions underlying students' coping responses in an evaluative situation? Zeidner (1995b) factor-analyzed a subset of items taken from the COPE scale (Carver, Scheier, & Weintraub, 1989) administered to 241 college students prior to an important midterm exam. The scale consisted of 15 subscales (i.e., active coping, planning, seeking instrumental social support, seeking emotional social support, suppression of competing activities, religion, positive reinterpretation, restraint coping, acceptance, ventilation of emotions, denial, mental disengagement, behavioral disengagement, alcohol/drug use, humor), with respondents indicating the degree to which they actually used each of the coping strategies when preparing for the final examination (0 = not at all, 3 = great extent). A principal factor analysis of the coping scale intercorrelation matrix, followed by varimax rotations, revealed three orthogonal factors, each accounting for an equal percentage of the variance. There were:

1. Problem-focused coping (active coping, planning, suppression of competing activities).
2. Emotion-focused coping (emotional social support, instrumental social support, ventilation, positive reinterpretation, restraint, and humor).
3. Avoidance coping (mental disengagement, behavioral disengagement, religion, denial, alcohol).

Figure 13.3. Three types of coping strategies: (a) problem-focused, (b) emotion-focused, and (c) avoidance.

The dimensions uncovered in this study correspond to those identified by Endler and Parker (1990a; cf. Endler & Parker, 1990b) as being basic dimensions of coping behaviors and styles. These dimensions were found to be differentially predictive of affective outcomes: Whereas emotion-focused and avoidance coping were positively related to test anxiety, problem-focused coping was inversely related to anxiety.

Another attempt to uncover the structure of coping responses in test situations was reported by Rost and Schermer (1989a, 1989b), who factor-analyzed the re-

Figure 13.3. (*Continued*)

sponses of 590 students to 85 coping inventory items pertaining to diverse cognitive, emotional, and behavioral aspects of coping with test anxiety. The following four components of coping with test anxiety were identified:

(a) *Danger control* refers to attempts at controlling the impending threat (e.g., by improving learning and study strategies). Use of these strategies would be expected to increase one's subjectively estimated mastery of the subject matter, and hence reduce the appraised harm and danger associated with the exam. Specific coping behaviors falling under this category would include, "I prepare myself better," "I peruse the material before going to sleep," and "I go to bed early."

(b) *Anxiety repression* refers to the palliative function of repressing the test-related aversive emotions. These strategies are intended to draw attention away from the dangerous environmental cues and divert attention to positive and pleasant cues and bring relief to the examinee—without modifying the cause of the underlying anxiety. Typical items would be, "I stop thinking of the test," "I say to myself that failure is not so serious."

(c) *Anxiety control* refers to all strategies that result in continuous reduction of the cognitive, affective, and somatic anxiety symptoms (e.g., "I try to control breathing," "I try to calm down"), with the intent of relaxing and controlling arousal.

(d) *Situational control* refers to the direct evasion or avoidance of the situational demands (e.g., "I report sick").

Additional research on the structure of coping in evaluative situations is clearly warranted.

Coping, Anxiety, and Test Performance

Coping and Anxiety

Research evidence suggests that emotion-focused coping is reliably associated with anxiety in a stressful evaluative situation and may therefore be indicative of poor adaptation to stress. In a study of coping and anxiety in an Israeli college student sample, Zeidner (1994) assessed 198 students under *daily-routine* versus *evaluative* test conditions. State anxiety scores obtained prior to an important college exam were regressed on trait and situational coping scores, along with personality variables (depressive tendencies, trait anxiety) and academic hassles. Emotion-oriented coping responses, along with academic hassles, social evaluation trait anxiety, and depressive tendencies, were reported to be significant predictors of state anxiety in the regression analysis. It is also noteworthy that coping styles assessed during a neutral period were predictive of congruent coping responses in the evaluative situation (i.e., avoidance coping styles predicted avoidance behavior surrounding the exam, etc.). Blankstein, Flett, and Watson (1992) reported that test anxiety, whether assessed as a trait or a state, was moderately correlated with both avoidance and emotion-focused coping strategies in a sample of college students. The authors reasoned that the elevated levels of tension and worry experienced by test-anxious students surrounding an evaluative situation would capture these students' attention and determine subsequent emotion-focused coping efforts. The authors further contended that since test-anxious students reported avoiding attempts to solve their academic problems, avoidance tendencies are due, in part, to perceived lack of ability and lack of control over outcomes. Bolger (1990) reported that the more students engaged in direct or problem-solving behavior in preparing for a medical exam, the *higher* their anxiety prior to the exam. This suggests that the activities surrounding preparation for an exam, including instrumental ones, may increase unavoidably one's awareness of the threatening event and consequently one's sense of anxiety (Bolger, 1990).

Coping and Examination Performance

Does coping help in improving exam performance? Reports on the nature of the association between coping behaviors and cognitive performance in an evaluative situation have been mixed, with the bulk of studies reporting unimpressive correlations between these two variables. Bolger (1990) reported a nonsignificant relationship between college students' coping responses assessed 10 days prior to an exam and performance on a medical admissions exam. Similarly, Carver and Scheier (1994) found that undergraduate students' coping responses before an exam did not generally predict their exam grades—save for mental disengagement, which was related inversely to the grades obtained. Other studies have also reported nonsignificant predictive effects for coping in relation to exam performance (Edelmann & Hardwick, 1986; Abella & Heslin, 1989).

A number of modest correlations between coping before an exam and exam performance have been reported in the literature. In a study of a small sample ($n = 75$) of undergraduate psychology students, Edwards and Trimble (1992) reported that task-oriented and emotion-oriented *coping responses* are significant predictors of college test performance, even when background variables (sex, trait anxiety, and coping styles) were controlled for in a hierarchical regression analysis; *coping styles* did not have similar predictive effects on exam performance. Furthermore, correlational analysis indicated that whereas task-oriented coping behaviors were positively correlated with test scores, avoidance, whether measured as style or behavior, was inversely related to test performance. Similarly, Klinger (1984) found that instrumental coping behaviors (studying, reading, etc.) prior to the exam were related to test outcomes. These latter findings suggest that certain instrumental coping behaviors conducive to exam performance may enhance the examinee's prospects for doing well on the exam. On the other hand, avoiding an important exam may result in negative cognitive outcomes, as students may not delegate adequate time for exam preparation and may be deficient in their mastery of the skills and information necessary to perform well on the exam. Endler et al. (1994) reported that task-oriented coping related to exam grades, but only among male college students. They concluded that those who focus on the task in preparing for an exam receive better grades than those who do not.

Coping and Adaptational Outcomes

An understanding of the complex relations between coping processes and long-term adaptational outcomes has long been a major concern among stress researchers (Folkman, Lazarus, Dunkell-Schetter, DeLongis, & Gruen, 1986). Evidently, not all responses to a stressful evaluative encounter are adaptive. Some coping behaviors may help alleviate the problem and/or reduce the resulting distress, and therefore may be considered effective. Others may actually exacerbate the problem or become problems in themselves (e.g., alcohol consumption, disruptive anger, hopelessness).

About a decade or so ago most researchers interested in stress and coping would probably not have seriously questioned the assumption that coping is an important determinant of people's emotional well-being during the various phases of a stressful transaction. Today, in contrast, researchers are asking more frequently whether coping helps (Aldwin & Revenson, 1987), whether it is epiphenomenal (McCrae & Costa, 1986a), or whether it may even interfere with outcomes such as emotional adjustment (Aldwin & Revenson, 1987; Carver & Scheier, 1994).

A number of specific techniques have been typically judged by researchers as adaptive, others have been judged as maladaptive, whereas other techniques present dilemmas to researchers (Carver et al., 1989). Theorists have frequently emphasized the positive effects of problem-focused coping and negative effects of emotion-focused coping on psychological outcomes, especially when the threatening situation can be ameliorated by the subject's responses (R. S. Lazarus & Folkman, 1984). While emotion-focused coping or avoidance may help in maintaining emotional balance, an adaptive response to remediable situations still requires problem-solving activities to manage the threat. Active coping is preferred by most persons and is generally more effective in stress reduction (Gal & Lazarus, 1975). Active coping provides a sense of mastery over the stressor, diverts attention from the problem, and discharges energy following exposure to threat. Non-problem-solving strategies are increasingly used when the source of stress is unclear, when there is a lack of knowledge about stress modification, or there is little one can do to eliminate stress (Pearlin & Schooler, 1978). Thus, there is growing evidence that the use of certain strategies, including active coping, logical analysis, purposeful planning, positive reappraisal, suppression of competing activities, acceptance, and use of humor, may be adaptive in a variety of situations (Carver et al., 1989). On the other hand, behavioral or mental disengagement, ventilation of emotions, and tension reduction strategies (e.g., use of alcohol and drugs) are generally candidates for dysfunctional coping tactics. While moderate use of some tactics in coping with exams (e.g., cigarette smoking, overeating) may serve as affect-regulation mechanisms and serve to reduce negative affect, if practiced in excess they may be injurious to health (Wills, 1986).

Researchers often face something of a dilemma in considering how to treat strategies that have multiple functions such as avoidance behaviors, denial, or turning to prayer/religion (Carver et al., 1989). For example, a student might turn to religion in coping with exams as a source of emotional support, as a vehicle for positive reinforcement and growth, or even as a form of active coping. In the face of failure on an important exam, feelings of helplessness and depression may be moderated by the belief that one's fate is in the hands of God, much like in the case of loss or bereavement (see the review of the literature by Stone, Helder, & Schneider [1988]). Similarly, avoidance coping has both its adaptive and maladaptive aspects. On one hand, there is a wealth of data to indicate that avoidance coping, reflecting a temporary disengagement from problem-focused coping, is positively tied to concurrent distress (Billings & Moos, 1984; Holohan & Moos, 1985; Aldwin & Revenson, 1987); this holds true for exam situations as well (Zeidner, 1995b, 1996). On the other hand, avoidance has been argued to be a useful tactic at times because it gives the person a psychological breather and an opportunity to escape from the constant pressures of the stressful situation (Carver, Scheier, & Pozo, 1992).

It is commonly agreed that the major aim of coping with stress in an exam situation is to restore internal equilibrium by either resolving or alleviating the problem causing the stress or by channeling and controlling the emotional strain evoked by the exam. Clearly, deciding on whether particular coping strategies are adaptive or not in any context requires the joint consideration of situational factors (e.g., test difficulty level, test atmosphere) and personality factors (e.g., trait anxiety, beliefs about coping resources and their effectiveness). Further, the selection and efficacy of coping strategies must be viewed in relation to person × situation interactions and a change in any element may affect the process and outcome.

Major Considerations in Assessing Coping Effectiveness

Any evaluation of coping effectiveness in an exam situation requires consideration of a number of factors relating to the specific context, goals of coping, the person under consideration and the like. Some of these factors are briefly described below.

Theoretical Model Underlying Research

Defining effective coping is largely determined by the theoretical model or paradigm guiding research (Folkman, Chesney, McKussick, Ironson, Johnson, & Coastes, 1991). *Psychodynamic* models generally assume a hierarchy of coping and defense in which some processes are seen as superior to others. Coping was once thought of as a generic concept that includes ego defenses, the forerunners of coping, which deal with threats to one's psychological integrity. Earlier, Freud (1933) identified various defense mechanisms (displacement, sublimation, projection, reaction formation, regression, rationalization, repression, etc.) that were unconsciously activated to discharge the stress resulting from id–superego conflicts. Some theorists (Haan, 1977; Vaillant, 1977) differentiated between lower-level defensive behaviors (i.e., rigid, unconscious, automatized, pushed from the past, distorting, process-based, permits impulse gratification through subterfuge coping) and higher-level coping behaviors (i.e., flexible, conscious, purposive, future-oriented, reality-focused, and permits ordered and open impulse gratification). Haan (1977) proposed a tripartite hierarchy with coping as the most healthy process of adaptation, defense as a neurotic process, and ego failure as the most severely regressed process.

These hierarchical developmental approaches spawned trait measures of coping (R. S. Lazarus, 1993a,b). Thus, in the late 1970s, hierarchical views with trait or style emphasis were abandoned in favor of contrasting approaches and treated as a process. One such model, the transactional stress model, focuses on the changing cognitive and behavioral efforts required to manage specific demands appraised as taxing or exceeding the person's resources (Folkman et al., 1991). A contextual definition of coping effectiveness (i.e., what is said, thought, or done in a specific situation) is demanded by interactional models. Thus coping efficacy is determined by its effects and outcomes within a particular situation.

Adaptational Tasks

Coping efforts are centered and structured around certain goals, issues, and patterns of challenges referred to as *coping tasks* (Cohen & Lazarus, 1979). Successful coping depends on the successful resolution of the particular situation-specific coping tasks. With respect to coping with failure on an important exam, adaptive coping would involve a student's need to enhance his or her prospects for success in the future (e.g., studying harder for the next exam, receiving tutorial help, improving study skills), learning to tolerate or adjust to the reality of failure, maintaining a positive self-image, maintaining emotional equilibrium and decreasing emotional stress, and maintaining a satisfying relationship with the environment (e.g., not taking out one's frustration, on account of exam failure, on others in the immediate environment).

Criteria for Assessing Coping Outcome

Appropriate and valid criteria of good or poor adjustment are necessary to evaluate coping effectiveness (R. S. Lazarus, 1969). Ideally, adaptive coping should lead to a permanent problem resolution with no additional conflict or residual outcomes while maintaining a positive emotional state (Pearlin & Schooler, 1978). At present, there are no universal criteria for assessing coping effectiveness—which may further vary across research paradigms, contexts, and even sociocultural settings; a coping response might be judged successful relative to one outcome criterion, but not another. Indeed, the resolution of one coping task might even come at the expense of another (e.g., studying long hours to succeed on an important exam might at the same time contribute to problems at work or marriage breakdown). Coping is a complex process that must be viewed as a multivariate construct and judged according to a number of criteria, including the following:

- Quality of task performance
- Reduction of anxiety and psychological distress
- Reduction of physiological and biochemical reactions (e.g., heart rate, blood rate, pulse, skin conductivity)
- Normative social functioning
- Well-being of self and others affected by the situation (e.g., fellow students, partners, parents)
- Maintenance of positive self-esteem
- Judged effectiveness of a specific strategy on the part of the examinee

Context of Coping

Coping effectiveness must be examined in the context in which problems occur; "without information about the social context we would have half the story" (R. S. Lazarus & Folkman, 1984, p. 299). Also, evaluations of coping effectiveness must be sensitive to broader social (Weidner & Collins, 1993) and cultural factors (Marsella, DeVos, & Hsu, 1985), including social values. Preferred coping methods and perceived effectiveness must be appraised relative to a social or cultural groups' values, norms, world view, symbols, and orientation. Consider the case of a female student who devotes herself to her children or ailing parents at the expense of her academic studies or personal achievement goals. The evaluation of this coping approach is not merely a scientific, but a moral matter, and may differ in traditional versus achievement-oriented societies. Evaluating coping effectiveness must be further addressed relative to a person's normative response to a stressor.

Personal Agendas and Coping Styles

The individual's aspirations and goals are critical in evaluating coping outcomes. General goals and personal meanings and intentions mobilize and direct the choice of the coping strategies employed. Thus, truly to understand coping with exams we need to understand the main threat meanings of a particular examination context. Also, a good match between actual coping behaviors and preferred coping style (e.g., students who have a "monitoring" coping style and receive more information) are important in ensuring positive outcomes (Miller & Mangan, 1983). Personality variables also determine how we interpret and manage stress and judge coping effectiveness. For example, persons with high personal and social resources rely more on active coping and less on avoidance, thus impacting on their coping effectiveness (Holahan & Moos, 1987). Mismatches between actual coping behaviors and preferred coping patterns may be due to a variety of reasons, such as wrong interpretations of the situation, situational contstraints, and the like.

Methodological Problems and Limitations

A number of methodological problems plague research on coping effectiveness, thereby limiting the validity of the generalizations about coping–outcome relations in evaluative situations. These include the following.

Design Issues

Although a good number of coping effectiveness studies in evaluative contexts have been prospective in design, studies have also used cross-sectional designs or examined concurrent relations between coping and outcomes at a particular phase of the stressful encounter (e.g., Folkman & Lazarus, 1985). This provides weak evidence of causality because coping and outcome variables are correlated at any given time (Stone et al., 1988), hampering the pinpointing of direction in the coping–adjustment relationship. Thus, the question remains: Does the association of a particular strategy with fewer symptoms or lower distress mean that coping reduces distress (coping $\rightarrow$ distress) or that people with fewer problems or in better mental health tend to employ a particular strategy (distress $\rightarrow$ coping)? Further, the relationship between coping and outcomes in a test context may arise from some third, unmeasured, preexisting factor such as personality (e.g., Neuroticism; McCrae & Costa, 1986a). Accordingly, coping efforts may be an epiphenomenon, with no real impact on stress and life adaptation.

Difficulty in Measuring the Coping Process

Dispositional tendencies to respond to stressors can best be assessed by analyzing the response patterns of persons at different reaction levels (physiological, behavioral, cognitive) across a multitude of time points as the stressful encounter unfolds over time. To develop such a multilevel process procedure, a theory of the process of evaluative stress reactions and of the dispositions related to this process has to be elaborated. This theory must allow one to predict which special configuration of data across levels and time points should be expected for specific dispositions in a particular stress situation (Heinz Krohne, personal communication, November 1996).

Prevalence of Self-Report Measures in the Assessment of Coping

There is heavy reliance on self-report measures (e.g., questionnaires, checklists) to determine both coping behaviors and outcomes in evaluative situations. Accordingly, respondents are typically presented with an inventory of coping items (e.g., "I tackle the problem step by step," "I pray," "I consume alcohol," etc.) and are asked to indicate how frequently they use each tactic in coping with a particular situation, such as an exam (e.g., "Almost all the time" to "Not at all"). This raises the issue of common method variance that may yield inflated correlations between self-reported coping and outcome responses. Coping items that ask about coping behaviors and frequency of usage of a particular strategy when coping with exams do not provide information about the coping strategy–situation fit, personality of the coper, success in carrying out the coping efforts, outcome, and the like.

Reliance on Potentially Flawed Measures of Coping

There are few methodologically sound instruments to gauge coping styles and behaviors. Many of the most frequently used coping instruments are plagued by a proliferation of diverse coping scales of questionable construct validity, nonreplicability of factor structure, and low scale generalizability and stability (Parker, Endler, & Bagby, 1993; R. Schwarzer & Schwarzer, 1996). The upshot of all this is that the widespread methodological weaknesses of the popular scales used to assess coping in general and coping in test situations, in particular, may have impeded the development of a systematic understanding of the relationship between coping and adaptational outcomes (R. Schwarzer & Schwarzer, 1996). Clearly, if current research is based on measures not well supported by empirical findings, research results may be rendered ambiguous, calling into question the few generalizations that may be culled from the literature. The grave methodological weaknesses with widely used scales may have contributed to the inconsistency in empirical results and lack of consensus in the coping area.

Furthermore, the current practice of constructing coping scales (e.g., avoidance coping) according to the criteria of classical test theory (i.e., according to the idea of achieving a high internal consistency) is problematic. The concept of internal consistency is based on the idea that responses to test items are independent of each other. This is not the case with most actual coping inventories. Take, for example, the stress situation, "the evening before an important exam" and the two avoidance items, "I called a friend" and "I went to a local pub and had a couple of drinks." If an examinee endorses one item, she or he will most likely not endorse the other item, i.e., will not obtain a high avoidance score. Nevertheless, this person exhibited avoidance. As a consequence, it may not be very meaningful to construct subscales made up of different items and to optimize these scales according to the criterion of internal consistency. A single-item approach, with a separate validation of each single item, might be a promising alternative.

Level of Analysis

The tendency in coping research has been to aggregate and combine a number of coping behaviors into one category. Studying global categories (e.g., problem-focused vs. emotion-focused coping) may prevent the more refined and differentiated analysis that might come from examining more specific tactics such as humor, confrontation, information seeking, etc. (Carver et al., 1989; Carver & Scheier, 1994). Indeed, different coping tactics within a general category may have different implications for a person's coping success, so that adaptive coping in an exam situation may be positively associated with one subclass (e.g., emphasizing the positive side of a situation) and inversely related with others (e.g., denial, wishful thinking). It is a gross oversimplification to treat different strategies as one group; we need to clarify the meaning and function of a particular response at a level that permits meaningful generalizations about coping–outcome relations.

Missing Information about the Parameters of Additional Stressors

Coping–outcome relationships are meaningful if the stressful event under consideration represents a significant portion of the designated time period, and similar coping methods are employed with other stressors during that time (McCrae & Costa, 1986a, 1986b). However, it is unreasonable to assume that tests and test situations are the only major stressors and hassles impinging upon the lives of examinees (Zeidner, 1994). Thus, if students who are being compared with respect to their coping strategies are not only simultaneously using different coping responses, but also grappling with different stressors and coping with them differently, we really do not know exactly which factor contributes to outcome variability. A complete model of adaptive coping in an evaluative situation must include all stressful events and coping strategies occurring at a particular time.

Multiple Meanings and Functions of Coping Behaviors

Each coping act may have more than one function, depending on the context in which it occurs. Problem-focused coping, for example, may also regulate emotion, such as would be the case in study-skills training, which may also serve to decrease test anxiety. Thus, the function of a coping strategy may not be fully inferred from a specific coping behavior or act. Similarly, emotion-focused strategies (e.g., humor, relaxation exercises, use of tranquilizers) can have problem-focused functions if they are effective in decreasing anxiety or other aversive emotions which impede functioning. The function of certain coping behaviors or acts can only be determined if one tries to assess the underlying intention. Thus, one really needs to know what the specific function of the coping behavior is rather than the act itself in order to assess the effectiveness of a particular strategy. For example, seeking social support can have the function of trying to avoid thinking about a stressor or of seeking additional information about the aversive situation. The missing information about coping intentions would certainly limit the internal validity and generalizability of coping–outcome relationships.

Multiple Criteria for Assessing Coping Outcomes

Conclusions about coping effectiveness vary depending on the choice of outcome criteria selected (Meneghan, 1983). Thus, a particular coping strategy in an exam situation may have differential effects on different criterion measures. Moreover, the various indices of effective coping may causally influence one another. For example, a student who consumes alcohol or employs avoidance-type behaviors to deal with the pressures of test situations might be judged to cope effectively based on self-report measures of symptom reduction but judged to cope maladaptively based on test results or cognitive functioning in the classroom. Moreover, the various indices of effective coping may causally influence one another. For example, the amount of time spent in studying for an upcoming exam may also impact upon the subject's state of subjective well-being by reducing anxiety and enhancing self-esteem.

Some Tentative Generalizations about Coping and Coping Effectiveness

In spite of recent advances in theory, research, and assessment, the issue of coping effectiveness in general, and in examination contexts in particular, is still open to debate. Deciding which coping behaviors are most effective and for whom poses a conceptual and empirical puzzle (Carver & Scheier, 1994). Although few unequivocal principles have been uncovered in coping research conducted in evaluative situations, a number of generalizations about adaptive coping garnered from the literature will now be put forward.

Adaptive coping in exam situations involves a flexible repertoire and combined use of alternative coping strategies. Stress is best managed when effective methods are used for removing the stressor (or its cause) and coping with affective reactions and emotions. Thus, stress reduction behaviors associated with a difficult university exam might include increased study time, peer assistance, or dropping the course until a later time. In the process, effective strategies for addressing the concurrent anxiety, worry, and depressed mood must be implemented. In instances where the stressor cannot be changed, personal management is critical in determining short- and long-term psychological adjustment to such stress.

The studies surveyed show that examinees use multiple forms of coping in adapting to exam situations, including a wide variety of problem-focused, emotion-focused, and avoidance strategies. Thus, the current research on coping with tests is consistent with research carried out in other settings showing that adults use multiple forms of coping in managing most stressful events (see various chapters in Zeidner & Endler, 1996). This would appear to be functional, for it allows for both the regulation of emotion and management of the stressor (R. S. Lazarus & Folkman, 1984). One may want to try different strategies, in different combinations, to manage stress rather than respond reflexively with the same limited response to varying stressors. One must incorporate relevant problem-solving skills (e.g., study habits, planning) and/or emotion-focused skills (e.g., relaxation) to ensure personal coping efficacy.

Furthermore, the effects of various strategies are rather difficult to disentangle, with emotion-focused and problem-focused strategies impacting upon one another during various stages of a stressful encounter. Accordingly, emotion-focused coping before an important exam can facilitate problem-focused coping by removing some of the anxiety that can hamper problem-focused efforts in preparing for the exam. For example, a student who jogs, prays, drinks, and the like to cope with an upcoming exam may reduce her anxiety to the point where she can "hit the books" and prepare herself intensively for the exam. On the other hand, problem-focused coping can render the threat less forbidding and reduce distress emotions and the need for intensive emotion-focused coping. For example, the student who concentrates in studying for an upcoming exam may find that the exam material is not really that difficult, thus reducing the anxiety surrounding the exam.

It should be pointed out that research in other contexts suggests that while greater flexibility may relate to better emotional adjustment (Mattlin, Wethington, & Kessler, 1990), multiple coping reactions within a given period may reflect ineffective coping (Carver, Scheier, & Weintraub, 1989). This may hold true for exam situations as well. Further, each coping strategy has both its benefits and costs. For example, denying the seriousness of a failing score in a major course may reduce emotional distress, but also negatively affect the amount of effort put into improving the course grade.

Coping with a stressful exam situation is a process; it is a transaction between a person and event that plays out across time and changing circumstances. The studies surveyed converge in painting a rather complex picture of the pattern of appraisals, emotions, and coping that unfold across stressful examination situations. Further, the relevance and effectiveness of a coping reaction appear to vary with the phase of the stressful transaction considered. Before an important exam, examinees' appraisals and emotions are generally reported to be homogeneous and almost all examinees report strong feelings of challenge and fear combined. Thus, positive and negative anticipatory emotions tend to occur simultaneously in the early stages of the exam, but fall off once the uncertainty surrounding the outcome is resolved. As the outcome becomes clearer and less ambiguous, examinees who do well on the exam see the situation as pleasant, whereas those who do not do well see the situation in an aversive light. Inverse relations are observed between outcome emotions (i.e., benefit and harm) after the exam, reflecting the polarization of the subjects' emotions after seeing the grade.

With respect to coping, the studies surveyed tend to converge on the following picture of the coping process in an exam situation: During the anticipatory stages, the initial coping efforts focus on the upcoming exam, with active coping tactics predominating. Problem-focused coping responses at the preexam anticipatory stage are presumably prevalent because something could still be done to influence the outcome. By contrast, a decrease in active coping is evidenced following the exam, presumably because there is very little that can be done to change the results at this stage. Coping right after the exam appears to be an effort to deal with the negative emotions experienced pre-exam. For some, these efforts are channeled primarily into dysfunctional avoidance; for others this means obtaining social support, and emotion-focused coping. After grades are posted, the impetus behind coping now reflects responses to the grades received on the exam, with subjects who had done poorly now reporting higher levels of problem-focused coping than those who succeeded on the exam.

Coping strategies in exam situations are found to work with modest effects, with some people, and some outcomes. Research in evaluative situations concurs that some kinds of coping response to some kinds of test situations and exigencies do make a difference, mainly with respect to *affective* outcomes. Specifically, palliative coping responses are positively related to students' test anxiety levels, whereas problem-focused coping responses tend to be inversely related to anxiety. Thus, in a manageable and controllable exam situation, the type of coping strategy employed may have significant consequences for the outcome. Active studying and planning would be especially important to success, whereas excessive avoidance behavior surrounding final exam period can have potentially disastrous consequences. These conclusions are consistent with a large body of research suggesting that because problem-focused strategies actively confront the problem, they generally have a positive effect on well-being (R. S. Lazarus & Folkman, 1984). High levels of palliative coping are typically associated with poor adaptation to stress (Felton & Revenson, 1984).

Whereas emotion-focused and avoidance coping behaviors appear to be related concurrently to anxiety outcomes, the evidence for coping as a *prospective* predictor of either negative emotions or exam performance is sparse. The associations found in the literature are often concurrent, and thus equivocal about the direction of causal influence. Thus, it is not entirely clear whether coping influences outcomes, whether coping tactics merely covary with adjustment to exam situations, or whether coping and distress are mutually intertwined reflections of something else. The question of the utility of various coping strategies in evaluative situations is without firm answers and more information will be needed before we can feel comfortable contending that coping has a causal influence on well-being. With respect to *cognitive* outcomes, well-designed prospective studies concur that coping has little meaningful influence on exam performance. However, there is some evidence that students who use active coping strategies directly related to exam preparation or skill acquisition will do slightly better on the exam. Thus, students who devote time and energy in preparing for the exam and in planning their work are often better equipped to master the exam compared to those who use avoidance strategies. As pointed out by Carver et al. (1992) in a different context, active coping and continued effort are adaptive in any situation where such effort will produce the desired outcome. Avoidance behavior or giving up prematurely works against the person because by the criterion of successful goal attainment (i.e., maximization of test scores) disengaging in such a situation would be considered dysfunctional. The hypothesis that coping is a significant moderator of stress–outcome relations in an evaluative situation remains to be demonstrated.

Coping patterns should fit both the context and the individual. These is some research suggesting that a good fit between the perceived realities of the situation and coping methods is important, with coping effectiveness related to its appropriateness to the internal/external demands of the situation. This "matching" hypothesis suggests that adaptive coping requires a good fit between the person–environment transaction, the person's appraisal of the transaction, and the consequent coping behavior (R. S. Lazarus & Folkman, 1984; R. S. Lazarus, 1993a).

The data surveyed in this chapter conform with the notion that the nature of the coping efforts used may vary depending on the perceived controllability and manageability of the stressor. In a social-evaluative situation, where one can exert a substantial degree of objective control prior to the evaluative confrontation, students evidence more problem-focused relative to palliative coping responses. This conforms with prior research suggesting that problem-focused coping is more adaptive in situations viewed as changeable, whereas emotion-focused coping or avoidance behaviors are best used in unalterable situations (R. S. Lazarus & Folkman, 1984).

Coping strategies vary between and within individuals. Research attests to individual differences in reacting to an evaluative encounter. Coping is not a direct reflection of the objective evaluative situation; it stems in part from the frame of mind of the person experiencing the event. The sense of threat that triggers the anxiety in a test situation is partly attributable to personal vulnerabilities, which vary from one person to another. In the same way, what coping responses emerge is determined largely by students' knowledge of coping options and partly by their beliefs about the usefulness of these options. Both stress and coping, then, spring from the mental sets brought by the person to the event. Task-focused efforts (e.g., studying) may be activated by certain individuals upon announcement of an exam. Others procrastinate or complain about the course or instructor, yet they may use adaptive coping methods to manage other stressors. Person × situation interactions may also occur; e.g., one student uses problem-focused coping with little skill and is less successful than another who uses emotion-focused coping to alleviate anxiety. Coping strategies may change over time in order to manage both short- and long-term effects of a stressful examination. Yet it is also recognized that the other life stressors aside from examinations themselves may wear down the individual and lead to the use of less effective coping strategies under continued stress (Aldwin & Revenson, 1987; Zeidner, 1994).

Coping responses are not uniformly adaptive. Research has shown that specific coping strategies are more or less effective depending on the type of stress one encounters (Pearlin & Schooler, 1978), and applying the same coping strategies across all situations is not likely to be adaptive. Strategies often viewed as maladaptive (e.g., avoidance, distancing) in an exam situation may be adaptive under some circumstances (e.g., during the intermediary stages of a health crisis) and vice versa (R. S. Lazarus, 1993a). The results of a given coping style are determined by the interaction of personal needs and preferences and the constraints of the specific situation under consideration.

Causal relationships among coping strategies and outcome indices are likely to be multidirectional rather than linear (R. S. Lazarus & Folkman, 1984). It appears that there is a mutually reinforcing causal cycle among stressful examination contexts, poor outcomes on the exam, and maladaptive coping strategies. Coping indices, often seen as dependent variables, might also serve as independent variables in a complex process of reciprocal and unfolding transactions over time.

Summary

There is no consensus about which coping strategies are most effective and adaptive in promoting positive outcomes in exam situations. It is not entirely clear whether coping influences adjustment, whether coping tactics covary with adjustment, or whether coping and distress are mutually intertwined reflections of yet some other human condition or characteristic. Further research is needed to clarify how a coping strategy resolves problems, relieves emotional distress, and prevents future difficulties. Future research should shed light on what outcome measures should serve to validate coping as being adaptive or maladaptive in a test situation; how long a time lag there should be between assessment of coping and outcomes; how coping in test situations differs from coping in other situations; whether it makes sense to talk about coping when students are really responding to challenges as opposed to threats; and what is the ordinary balance of helpful coping to harmful coping with exams.

Furthermore, future research on the effectiveness of coping strategies in examination contexts would benefit from including more precise theoretical statements, continuous and longitudinal data collection, and the inclusion of situational and personal variables, including secondary stressors. Employing multiple assessment points, repeated measures of coping efforts, and various indices of outcomes at regular intervals over meaningful time spans would enhance the exploration of the complex pathways of effects. One may hope that future research will clarify the kind and extent of the effect of coping on adaptational outcomes.

14

Optimizing Procedures

Overview

A common criticism of formal psychoeducational assessment procedures is that the stress of testing leads to such high degrees of evaluative anxiety that many students are unable to perform at a level matching their potential—which would readily be manifested in less stressful situations (Gaudry & Spielberger, 1971). Various characteristics of standardized achievement and ability tests have been claimed to be particularly stressful for test-anxious examinees (Hill & Wigfield, 1984). These include ego-involving test instructions, severe test time limits, difficult test problems, and complicated and unfamiliar test questions and answer formats. If so, factors inherent to the formal test process, structure, and situation may bias the performance of high-test-anxious individuals by causing an underestimation of their cognitive achievements and abilities.

The prevailing attempts to help examinees cope with the effects of evaluative stress typically involve various forms of therapeutic interventions aimed at alleviating debilitating anxiety and/or enhancing study and test-taking skills (see Chapters 15 and 16). That is, most of the current work involves working on the anxiety of the *examinee*. However, test anxiety is commonly construed as being a rather stable personality characteristic, which is relatively resistant to change. Hence, it may be more feasible and promising to modify various parameters of the test and test situation so that the achievement-impairing effects of test anxiety are minimized. Under the assumption that high-test-anxious students might do better if placed in a more congenial learning and testing environment, researchers have recently explored the effectiveness of a number of "optimizing" procedures designed to reduce the interfering effects of state anxiety in high-test-anxious students (Covington, 1992). Optimizing procedures may be helpful in identifying examinees who could benefit most from educational and psychological efforts designed to decrease the effects of anxiety (Hill, 1972). Thus, examinees who show marked gains under optimizing conditions may actually have mastered the test material, but presumably experienced the disruptive effects of test anxiety under formal test conditions.

In this chapter I critically examine a number of suggestions appearing in the literature for optimizing the test or test process in order to create a test environment that is more user-friendly and less anxiety-evoking for test-anxious examinees. I begin by presenting a number of optimizing procedures that relate to the test per se and then move on to discuss procedures for modifying various test situational variables. The optimizing factors to be discussed below were garnered from a variety of sources, including experimental and field research, examinee feedback, expert opinion, and current practice. The focus of this chapter is not on modifying the anxious person, but on modifying the test or test situation.

Modifying Test Item Difficulty and Order

Examinees frequently cite task complexity as a major source of anxiety in standardized aptitude testing and believe that attempts to control task complexity in the test construction process should help in reducing anxiety (Powers, 1986). Further, experimental studies surveyed in Chapter 9 suggest that complex tasks differentially debilitate the test performance of high- versus low-test-anxious students.

Based on current experimental research and examinee feedback it seems safe to conclude that any effort to change testing practice so as to decrease the relative frequency of failure in high-test-anxious students should optimize the performance of students who are particularly vulnerable to the interfering effects of evaluative anxiety. Accordingly, test constructors would do well in assuring that the items comprising the test are not too complex for the target population. It would also help to include a reasonable number of *easier* items on the exam to motivate anxious low-achieving individuals (Kaplan & Saccuzzo, 1989). Clearly, items that are unnecessarily complicated, tricky, or unfair, and may thus artificially increase the level of task difficulty, are unwarranted.

Furthermore, authorities have suggested arranging test items in an order of increasing difficulty (i.e., easier items first) in order to enhance examinees' confidence and minimize anxiety at the initial stages of testing (Gaudry & Spielberger, 1971). When test items are so arranged, students will not encounter items that are too difficult for them to solve early on in an exam. By the time more difficult items are encountered the disruptive effects of test anxiety and emotional arousal will have dissipated (Covington, 1992). Further, this arrangement increases the examinee's perceived probability to succeed on the early items and thereby gain sufficient confidence to negotiate effectively the more difficult items later on in the exam. However, it may be highly impractical to try to optimize test performance by arranging items in a uniform order simply because an arrangement which is best for one student is not necessarily best for another. Preparing multiple test forms to match examinees' preferences would pose considerable practical difficulties— although the possibility exists with the advent of customized testing.

Providing an Opportunity to Comment on Test Items

Research in health psychology has shown that keeping emotions bottled up inside can cause emotional and physical stress (Pennebaker, 1995). Thus, if student examinees actively suppress their anger or anxiety during the exam, these thoughts and emotions may bubble up to form intrusive preoccupying thoughts about the very things they are trying to suppress. Thus, having examinees disclose their feelings and share their emotions about the test may be of critical importance in helping examinees control anxiety.

Early research by McKeachie and his coworkers (McKeachie et al., 1955) indicated that college students experience less tension and threat in the test situation, and also do better, when given the opportunity to comment on difficult or ambiguous test items. Thus, students who were encouraged to write comments about their test questions (i.e., "Feel free to make any comments about the items in the space provided") made higher scores than students with conventional answer sheets (McKeachie et al., 1955). Giving examinees an opportunity to write comments while being tested may have a cathartic effect, helping to dispel some of the tensions as they build up. Thus, allowing students to "blow off some steam" and release pent-up emotions while writing the exam may help reduce the evaluative threat and channel the release of anxiety so that better performance could be expected. Further, commenting on problematic items may give some students more *closure* on the test items, thus improving their test performance. It is interesting to note that allowing students to comment does *not* seem to affect scores on the items about which comments are written, but rather affects performance mainly on succeeding items (McKeachie et al., 1955). This is congruent with the notion that tension is built up throughout the test and that giving individuals the opportunity to comment reduces the increasing tension later on in the test.

The procedure of allowing students to comment on test items can readily be implemented in various examinee populations without much technical difficulty. Accordingly, in order to optimize test performance, exams administered to examinees would include a sizable blank area on the answer sheet for purposes of writing comments or have a separate examinee feedback inventory attached. Examinees would be instructed to make any comments they feel like about the test, and should be told right at the outset that the comments they make are confidential and will in no way affect their grade on the exam. However, before applying this procedure on a large scale to various examinee populations, additional research needs to examine the generalizability of this procedure with school-aged children as well as clarify the mediating factors through which writing comments improves test performance. Unfortunately, this program of research has generally failed to conduct the needed manipulation checks to determine whether or not anxiety is in fact the mediating factor through which comments impact upon performance. Thus, additional research is needed to shed light on the mediating factors through which writing comments influences performance.

Interjecting Humor into the Test Situation

Mechanic (1962) was one of the first researchers to document that college students frequently use humor (e.g., jokes) as a defense mechanism for coping with anxiety engendered by upcoming exams. However, the interest in humor as an anxiety-alleviating factor can be traced back to Freud's psychoanalytic theory (Freud, 1928), which views humor as a basic mechanism in relieving tension and in reducing anxiety. Some research evidence (R. E. Smith et al., 1971) suggests that humor tends to inhibit anxiety in test situations, particularly among high-test-anxious students. Research by Deffenbacher et al. (1981) shows that subjects taking a humorous form of a course exam reported less worry (but curiously scored significantly *lower*!) than their counterparts receiving the regular exam.

The interjection of humor into the test situation has been claimed to enhance task-oriented coping and resultant test performance by reducing examinee tension and evoking positive affective states in examinees (R. E. Smith et al., 1971). It follows that by introducing humor into the testing situation, it should be possible to reduce the interfering effects of anxiety and improve the task performance of many highly anxious subjects. While some recent research has manipulated the actual content of the test items to make it humorous or nonhumorous (e.g., R. E. Smith et al., 1971), in other studies humor is made an adjunct to the test content by adding extraneous humorous elements to the test.

To illustrate the type of humorous modifications of test items employed in research, consider the following experimental test in an abnormal psychology exam, as framed in both a conventional and a humorous format (R. E. Smith et al., 1971, p. 244):

Conventional format: "Over the past six years Tom's behavior has become increasingly more disturbed. He has developed a delusion that somebody is controlling his mind, and he is also having bizarre visual and auditory hallucinations. Which other member of Tom's family is most likely to exhibit bizarre behavior?"

(a) his mother; (b) his sister; (c) his identical twin; (d) it is impossible to make a probability statement.

Humorous format: "Claiming to be a slot machine, Julias has been standing against a wall in a Las Vegas casino for six years making bell-like sounds and occasionally complaining that he is being tilted. Which other member of Julias' family is most likely to exhibit bizarre behavior?"

(a) his mother; (b) his sister; (c) his identical twin; (d) it is impossible to make a probability statement.

Despite the intuitive appeal of employing humor in testing, several recent studies have challenged the popular assumptions concerning the anxiety-relieving properties of humor in the testing process. As one may imagine, a serious problem in attempting to interject humor into the test through modification of test items is that individuals may not find the modified content as being humorous at all. Thus, while some examinees may be "loosened up" by the humor, others may find the modified content embedded in the test as being rather distractive. Furthermore, the scant number of existing studies looking at the effects of humorous content on test anxiety and performance have yielded mixed results. In fact, there is little support for the interactive effect of humor and test anxiety on performance. Overall, current research suggests that interjecting humor in conventional tests can result in differing effects, ranging from significantly reducing anxiety in some individuals to evoking anxiety in others.

Modifications of Test Atmosphere and Environment

In view of the evidence that high-test-anxious students do not respond well to evaluative pressure and competition, any reduction of the ego-threatening characteristics of conventional test situations should reduce evaluative pressures and help create a more congenial testing atmosphere for test-anxious students (Gaudry & Spielberger, 1971). One way of minimizing the testlike atmosphere is by presenting a problem-solving task in a neutral or gamelike manner. Another way would be to tell children that the problems they are about to attempt are difficult for most who try them and they should not worry if they also find the problems challenging or complex (Hill & Wigfield, 1984). Examiners might also consider modifying specific instructions, such as deemphasizing the importance of the task or downplaying the test's competitive nature.

Whereas most individuals are optimally motivated when their attention is focused on task mastery rather than outperforming others, the motivation and performance of high-test-anxious children are especially facilitated by pretask instructions that emphasize task-relevant strategies (Dusek, 1980). Thus, providing test-anxious students with task-oriented instructions (e.g., "Concentrate and keep your mind focused on the problem at hand," "Get absorbed in the task," "Avoid thinking about other things," "Try not to get distracted") rather than evaluative instructions (e.g., "This is an important intelligence test and it is crucial you do well for future success in school") has been shown to reduce intrusive thoughts in student populations and also have a salutary effect on performance (S. B. Sarason, 1972). This is consistent with a body of research conducted from a cognitive-behavioral framework demonstrating that test-anxious individuals can help improve their performance by rehearsing task-oriented instructions during the test (Holroyd, 1976). However, while the performance of test-anxious subjects may be significantly facilitated by attention-directing efforts, people low in test anxiety are not similarly benefited from such efforts.

Note, however, that even when attempts are made to deemphasize the evaluative nature of the task, many examinees still will not be convinced that the situation is indeed a neutral or gamelike one. Even following pretest "neutral" or "gamelike" instructions, many anxious examinees will continue responding to the situation as a threatening, competitive, and evaluative one. Furthermore, instructions which are optimal for high-test-anxious subjects may be disadvantageous or noneffective for low-test-anxious examinees who do their best under different motivating conditions.

Providing Soothing Background Music

Overall, the few studies on the effect of music played during testing (C. A. Smith & Morris, 1976, 1977) converge in showing that soothing, sedative background music may have a relaxing effect on some examinees. Furthermore, Hembree's (1988) meta-analytic research suggests that the presence of unobtrusive music may benefit test performance, especially for high-test-anxious subjects. For example, Stanton (1975) demonstrated that high-test-anxious subjects did better under music than under silence conditions. As the authors observed, "The students in the rooms where music was played as a background seemed more relaxed, less tense and nervous, than did those in the rooms characterized by silence" (p. 82). This was evidenced by students smiling more, nodding pleasantly at other students, and generally displaying fewer facial signs of tension. The data analysis suggests that the background music is necessary only while students are preparing for their task, not while performing the task. Thus, unobstrusive background music may be helpful for some examinees.

Optimizing Test Administration Procedures, Modes, and Formats

Researchers have sought to identify specific testing procedures, administration modes, and formats which may be particularly suited to the characteristics, styles, and test preferences of high-test-anxious individuals in order to minimize their anxiety and optimize their test performance. A number of these suggestions are briefly mentioned below.

The *multiple-choice format*, one of the most commonly used formats in psycho-educational testing, may be particularly advantageous for test-anxious examinees. Because the multiple-choice format requires recognition of the correct response, this format minimizes the need to retrieve information from memory and consequently reduces the perceived complexity of the task and resultant threat and anxiety in test-anxious examinees. A number of recent studies of examinees' test attitudes confirm that multiple-choice formats are viewed as being less anxiety-evoking and less susceptible to the interfering effects of anxiety compared to open-ended items. Green (1981) reported that both high- and low-test-anxious college students preferred multiple-choice to essay and interpretive exercises, although both groups showed highly similar preferences for various item formats. Zeidner (1987a) found that multiple-choice exams were preferred to open-ended exams in a sample of Israeli school-aged children, largely because they were perceived to be less anxiety-evoking. Further, Crocker and Schmitt (1987) report that high-test-anxious students do much better when given a conventional multiple-choice compared to open-ended format, whereas low-test-anxious students do much better with open-ended test formats.

Take-home exams may provide the examinee with greater control over the exam and thus may be particularly suited to the needs of high-test-anxious students on two counts. Examinees who take the exam in the leisure of their home avoid the disruptive and debilitating emotions triggered in most test-anxious examinees by being in an exam room. Also, these examinees may exercise greater degrees of freedom looking up needed information at their own leisure, thus subjecting them to fewer retrieval problems. However, some high-test-anxious students suffering from deficits in study skills (i.e., planning, essay organization, emphasizing essential versus accidental content, etc.) may not profit from take-home exams (Benjamin et al., 1981) and take-home exams raise additional concerns regarding response validity.

Current experimental data support the notion that *providing free choice among items* in an evaluative situation enhances the examinee's perceived feeling of control over the source of threat (Keinan & Zeidner, 1987). This, in turn, serves to lower state anxiety and concomitantly raise levels of test attainment. Based on the evidence, examiners might consider providing examinees with some choice of test items (i.e., offer free-choice exams), whenever appropriate, in order to reduce anxiety and enhance test performance (Keinan & Zeidner, 1987). Testing experts have generally not looked favorably on free-choice exam questions because of psychometric considerations (i.e., lower reliability). However, the considerations relating to examinees' dispositions during testing may be equally important and therefore should be given due weight and consideration by test specialists and teachers when deciding upon test administration policy. Note, however, that there are no data to suggest that providing choice among items is especially advantageous for high-test-anxious individuals.

Corrective testing procedures, in which examinees are allowed to retake tests under less stressful conditions without penalty, have been reported to help reduce anxiety and thus optimize the performance of high-test-anxious examinees (Arkin & Schumann, 1984). It appears that giving anxious students a second attempt at answering questions may reduce their worry and enhance their perceived control and performance (Arkin & Schumann, 1984). High-test-anxious students are reported to experience fewer concentration problems and anxiety, tend to feel more in control of performance, and rate this procedure as less difficult (Arkin & Schumann, 1984). However, one field study using a college sample reported that providing students with a second chance to take a test under nonevaluative conditions may enhance performance on parts of the test in both high- and low-test-anxious groups, but may not be differentially beneficial for high-test-anxious individuals (Covington & Omelich, 1987a).

Relaxing Time Pressures

The bulk of current research suggests that eliminating severe time constraints and allowing more time on speeded tests would be particularly advantageous for the performance of high-test-anxious students (Hill & Eaton, 1977; Hill & Wigfield, 1984; Plass & Hill, 1986). The test environment is more likely to be perceived as nonthreatening and supportive when examinees are encouraged to take their time, thus reducing debilitating anxiety and enhancing performance (S. B. Sarason et al., 1960). Thus, when anxious examinees are under no pressure to hurry, and can consequently review test answers and correct mistakes, the performance of high-test-anxious students should increase dramatically, reaching essentially the same levels as those enjoyed by low-test-anxious students (Hill & Eaton, 1977; S. B. Sarason et al., 1960).

Allowing liberal time limits during testing, where possible, is viewed by some experts to be a particularly helpful optimizing strategy (Covington, 1992). Thus, in view of both experimental data and examinee feedback in true-to-life test situations, test constructors should attempt at eliminating excessive time pressures and allow liberal extensions in time limits so that examinees will not be too hard pressed in reaching and responding to all test items. However, when speed of responding is a key component of the cognitive construct being assessed, as is often the case in tests of general intelligence and special abilities, removing time limits might also reduce the tests' construct validity, and would therefore not be a desirable procedure (Jensen, 1980).

Providing Examiner Support and Reassurance

Examinee feedback data attest that the examiner's disposition, competence, and behavior are key factor underlying anxiety in standardized college selection test situations (Powers, 1986). Some proctors are singled out by these student examinees as contributing to anxiety by the virtue of their demeanor, being viewed as "imperso-nal," "nasty," and "intimidating." Others are criticized because they are "nervous," "disorganized," or "unprepared," and distracting test takers with "endless pacing." A number of students reported that the proctors were too serious throughout the examination and could have made things less tense by adopting a more congenial disposition.

Overall, current research evidence suggests that being exposed to a supportive test environment should decrease evaluative stress and examinee anxiety. Thus, an examinee's anxiety should significantly decrease when the examiner conveys a warm and supportive attitude and shows respect and high regard for those being tested. Examiner reassurance and social support has in fact been shown to counteract the interfering, distracting, and often self-deprecatory thought of high-test-anxious students (I. G. Sarason, 1981). Further, when test-anxious examinees are provided with a supportive and reassuring test climate they will more readily observe and model useful cognitive strategies displayed by the examiner. Aided by these strategies, high-test-anxiety subjects become less self-preoccupied and anxious and more able to manage and guide their own behavior during the test (S. B. Sarason, 1972).

Providing External Aids and Supports

Research evidence supports the claim that the poor test performance of high-test-anxious examinees in evaluative situations is caused in part by anxiety-produced deficits in memory (see Chapter 10). Some test-anxious students are unable to retrieve the information at a time when it is needed for solving test problems on which they are working. These students would well be served by external aids or memory supports that would help them remember and recall previously learned materials (Tobias, 1977a). In a certain sense, providing memory support is similar to being able to review the input again. Memory support may be particularly helpful for high-test-anxious examinees who have problems in their ability to encode, store, or retrieve information from short-term memory, as memory support should minimize the need to perform these operations.

It has been claimed that any provision of memory support which reduces the degree to which students have to rely on their own memory for task solution would increase the achievement of high-test-anxious students (Tobias, 1977a, 1980). Sieber, Kameya, and Paulson (1970) reported an interaction between anxiety and memory support in the performance (mean errors committed) of children on a puzzle and concept formation task. The interaction plot given in Figure 14.1 shows that the performance of low-test-anxious children was superior only under no-memory-support conditions. When memory support was provided, no significant group differences were observed.

Reviews of experimental studies (Hill, 1972; Gaudry & Spielberger, 1971; Tobias, 1977a) provide empirical support for the claim that the provision of memory support differentially facilitates the performance of high-test-anxious students, diminishing the difference in the performance of high- versus low-test-anxious students.

A wide array of memory support procedures have been suggested to help high-test-anxious students perform up to full potential (Phillips et al., 1980; Sieber, 1969). These include detailed systems for organizing ideas and for sorting information, outlining, mnemonic devices, drawing diagrams, and using symbolic logic. Since the results of assessment procedures which place a strong emphasis on memory are more likely to be distorted by anxiety, assessment procedures in which students are allowed to consult notes, textbook passages, and other references (e.g., open-book or take-home exams) may optimize the achievement of anxious students, although creating other psychometric and technical problems. There is some experimental evidence suggesting that high-test-anxious subjects benefit from learning to use a variety of external aids (Tobias, 1977a).

Structuring of the Learning and Test Environment

High-test-anxious individuals typically become distressed when plunged into an unstructured and ambiguous learning or testing situation (Gaudry & Spielberger,

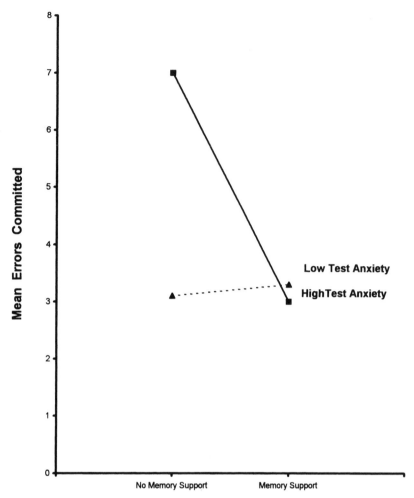

Figure 14.1. Interaction of test anxiety and provision of memory support on mean number of errors committed on a cognitive task. Based on Sieber et al. (1970), Table 1, p. 164.

1971). Thus, when anxious students encounter learning tasks or test problems that are ambiguous or unclear, this works to enhance their perceived probability of failure on the task and thus increases the debilitating effects of cognitive interference (Tobias, 1980). It follows that more structure and organization in the instructional and assessment process may provide test-anxious students with greater channels for control over their anxiety and enhance overall performance. Overall, empirical research supports the notion that the degree to which a cognitive task is well organized and structured may determine in part the effects of anxiety during processing of information (Tobias, 1977a, 1977b, 1977c).

Tobias (1977c) reviewed studies indicating that high-test-anxious students achieve more from organized learning situations and presentations than from less structured ones (e.g., teacher-organized lecture vs. student-centered recitation; well-structured phonic methods of language teaching vs. whole-word method). McKeachie's (1984, 1990) review of the literature provides evidence showing that anxious students do better in courses that are well structured or organized and do rather poorly in classes that are not well organized. In fact, college students have been shown to prefer the autocratic and more rigidly structured teaching method of recitation to discussion and group tutorial (McKeachie's, 1984, 1990).

In view of the above research, it would be reasonable to conclude that teachers or instructors who supply students with sufficient structure and information to reduce situational ambiguity, either during learning or testing, provide them with a potential mechanism for controlling and warding off anxiety in the test situation. Clearly, any modification which assures a tighter and clearer organization of the instructional as well as the test environment would be likely to improve the achievement of test-anxious students. Accordingly, instructors and classroom teachers would do well to pay attention to the following suggestions, culled from the literature, toward achieving an optimal organization and structuring of the academic environment:

- Specify the instructional and testing goals clearly at the outset
- Clarify expectations for student achievements
- Make certain that the material is appropriate to the students' learning level and ability
- Present the material in an organized and structured fashion
- Help dispel some of the uncertainty and ambiguity surrounding testing by providing maximum information about specific evaluative standards and upcoming tests (e.g., specific content to be covered in the test, test format to be used, number of questions)
- Delineate criteria for student grading and make the steps to a good grade explicit
- Use well-structured and clear assessment indices to provide students with indices of their achievement on an ongoing basis

Summary

This chapter surveyed a number of intriguing suggestions in the literature for modifying the conditions of learning and assessment in order to reduce debilitating anxiety and enhance performance of high-test-anxious individuals in evaluative situations. The various optimizing methods discussed hold some promise for slightly reducing the threatening and anxiety-evoking aspects of the study–testing cycle, thus leading to less biased and more accurate assessment of students.

Table 14.1 summarizes a number of practical suggestions extrapolated from the material surveyed in this chapter that may be useful in keeping anxiety in check and

Table 14.1. Some Practical Suggestions for Optimizing Testing Conditions

- Provide examinee with maximum advance information about the test, including content to be assessed, time limits, test format, and mode of administration
- Strive to keep the average item difficulty level under control, incorporate a reasonable number of easy items, place them early on in the exam, and avoid unnecessary use of extremely difficult or complex test material
- Attempt to match the test format and mode of administration with students' preferences for specific test formats (e.g., multiple-choice or essay) and their prior experience (e.g., with computers and computerized testing)
- Assure greater examinee control fo the test situation by allowing choice among items, use of open books, and adaptive testing
- Provide examinees with the opportunity to blow off steam and comment on any facet of the test they so desire during testing
- Create a nonthreatening test atmosphere by providing examinees with task-oriented rather than ego-oriented instructions, avoiding emphasis on competition, eliminating threatening proctors, etc; humor, soothing background music, and snacks may help to ease the tension for some examinees
- Relax time pressures and limits whenever possible
- Provide emotional social support to anxious examinees
- Provide external memory aids and other supports
- Provide appropriate facilities (e.g., recovery room) for anxious examinees who freeze up to regain their composure and continue with the exam

optimizing the test performance of test-anxious examinees. These practical suggestions notwithstanding, Figure 14.2 depicts how one student might imagine "optimal testing conditions."

The reader should keep a number of caveats in mind when evaluating the effectiveness of the various contextual modifications presented in this chapter. First, despite common claims many of the so-called "optimizing" procedures fail to show clear and consistent effects in reducing anxiety and enhancing performance in test-anxious populations, or in differentially impacting upon the anxiety and performance of high- versus low-test-anxious individuals, thus calling into question their value as "optimizing" factors. Also, the effects of particular optimizing conditions (e.g., reassurance, humor, etc.) have not been found to be consistent and uniform across examinees, working to the advantage of some individuals and to the disadvantage of others.

Second, research indicates that low levels of situational stress may be optimal for high-test-anxious individuals, whereas moderate levels of stress and anxiety tend to facilitate the performance of low-trait-test-anxious individuals. Thus, some of the suggested modifications may actually rob low-test-anxious students of their motivation to achieve, as their reasons for success may depend on the presence of a threat to their worth (Covington, 1992). Thus, what may be considered to be optimal for one group of examinees (say, high-test-anxious examinees) may be less than optimal for another (say, low-test-anxious examinees). Clearly, the specific optimizing proce-

Figure 14.2. One student's fantasy of an "ideal" testing situation.

dures should match the population under consideration, with differential procedures provided for low- versus high-test-anxious students.

Third, the long-term aims of the assessment procedures should determine the conditions under which exams are carried out. Keeping the exam situation stressful might help in making it more congruent with criterion performance, thus enhancing the test's validity. Consider an exam designed to select candidates for pilot training. Since the candidates tested will eventually be expected to perform under highly stressful conditions, a pilot selection test would be more valid, from the standpoint of subsequent performance, if it were held under high-stress than under low-stress conditions.

Finally, although this chapter focused on changes in the test and test situation, most work is devoted to changing the examinee. Thus, along with the implementation of optimization procedures modifying specific facets of conventional testing that normally exacerbate the debilitating effects of test anxiety, students cannot escape having to learn how to cope adaptively with existing exam conditions. As formal tests and test procedures are likely to be with us for some time to come, students need to learn how to deal effectively with the conventional aspects of tests and test situations, including difficult test items, a variety of intricate test formats, time pressures, and evaluative instructions.

Emotion-Focused Behavioral Intervention Techniques

> It is not stress that kills us. It is the effective adaptation to stress that permits us to live.
>
> —*Vaillant (1977, p. 374)*

Overview

A bewildering array of test anxiety treatment programs have been developed and evaluated over the past three decades (I. G. Sarason & Sarason, 1990; Zeidner et al., 1988). Test anxiety intervention programs have flowered largely due to the salience of test anxiety in modern society and the general concern for the debilitating effects of test anxiety on the emotional well-being and cognitive performance of many individuals. Treatment fashions and orientations have swayed sharply from the clinical to the behavioral, and more recently to the cognitive perspective—essentially mirroring the evolution of the behavior therapies (Spielberger & Vagg, 1987).

This and the next chapter present a number of salient test anxiety intervention techniques designed to reduce arousal and dysfunctional worry, as well as enhance cognitive performance in test-anxious individuals. The present chapter focuses on key behavioral (emotion-focused) techniques, whereas Chapter 16 describes cognitive-focused, cognitive-behavioral, and skills-focused intervention techniques. I briefly present the theory and underlying rationale for each treatment method presented, the specific techniques employed for reducing anxiety and enhancing performance, and the empirical evidence for the effectiveness of each treatment when applied to the domain of test anxiety.

In presenting ways of changing the *individual's* skills and capacity to cope effectively with conventional test-taking situations, these two chapters jointly complement the material presented in Chapter 14, which focuses on contextual and test-specific modifications and optimizing techniques. Clearly, both changes and modifications in the individual and in the test or evaluative situation are frequently needed to help reduce examinees' anxiety and enhance their coping skills in evaluative situations.

There is no simple organizing principle with which to categorize the plethora of therapeutic techniques and approaches that have proliferated over the past few decades (R. S. Lazarus & Folkman, 1984). According to Spielberger and Vagg (1987; Vagg & Spielberger, 1995), attempts to reduce debilitating levels of test anxiety and enhance test performance have typically focused either on treatments directed toward the *emotional* (affective) or *cognitive* (worry) facets of test anxiety. Thus, treatment programs include both emotion-focused treatments, designed largely to alleviate negative emotional affect experienced by test-anxious persons, and cognitive-focused treatments, designed to help the test-anxious client cope with worry and task-irrelevant thinking and enhance his or her test performance.

Although cognitive-focused approaches view cognitive dysfunction as a major target for test anxiety therapy, it is important to recognize that not all cognitive dysfunction is the same (Kendall, 1993). Following Kendall (1993), it is useful to distinguish between *cognitive distortions* and *cognitive deficiencies* in test-anxious populations, and to distinguish among the treatment techniques that speak to these particular deficiencies. Thus, test-anxious students with cognitive deficiencies lack careful study, test-taking, and information processing skills in evaluative situations— situations in which these skills would be helpful indeed. Targeting cognitive deficiencies or deficits requires developing and deploying study and test-taking skills in thoughtful problem solving. In contrast, cognitive distortions are evident in those who engage in information processing, but do so in a dysfunctional fashion. Thus, performing poorly on an exam because of misguided task-irrelevant thinking is in marked contrast to failure due to poor assimilation of the material in the first place, originating from deficient study skills. Cognitive distortions would require that the faulty thinking first be identified and that the distorted process (e.g., irrational thinking, task-irrelevant preoccupations, negative internal dialogue, etc.) then be corrected.

Figure 15.1 presents the various therapeutic techniques presented in this and the next chapter according to treatment orientation (i.e., affective, cognitive, skills) and method, which, in turn, reflect attempts to pinpoint the client's specific problem, or cluster of problems. Within the emotion-focused and cognitive-focused orientations, techniques may be placed on an emotional–cognitive continuum. The emotionality pole of this continuum is anchored by treatments that consist of anxiety induction and biofeedback training, whereas cognitive restructuring defines the opposite cognitive pole. Multimodal integrative (or technically eclectic) test anxiety treatments that include both cognitive- and emotion-focused therapeutic components (e.g., cognitive behavior modification) may be placed at intermediate points on the continuum, depending on the extent to which a particular treatment component focuses on modifying the cognitive facet or the emotional facet experienced by test-anxious students (Vagg & Spielberger, 1995).

Note, however, that the distinctions among the various treatment orientations are quite fuzzy, and these approaches are becoming increasingly difficult to distin-

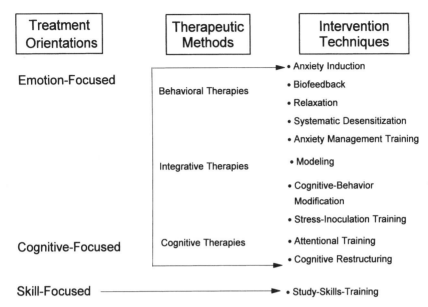

Figure 15.1. Specific therapeutic techniques, structured by therapeutic methods and orientations.

guish (Meichenbaum, 1976). Although there may be highly specific interventions which have an affective (e.g., relaxation therapy), cognitive (e.g., rational emotive therapy), or skills (test-taking counseling) focus, most methods are normally embedded in a multidimensional context. At present, a combination of procedures (whether combined in a truly integrative manner or in the stance of technical eclecticism; Alford & Norcross, 1991) seems to best represent the true nature of the test anxiety intervention process (Meichenbaum, 1976; cf. Deffenbacher, 1977b).

Emotion-Focused Behavioral Techniques

High-test-anxious persons typically report distressingly high levels of arousal in evaluative situations and are frequently preoccupied with their internal physiological processes (as well as with other internally focused cognitions). It may be therefore be beneficial to provide test-anxious students with appropriate coping strategies for managing physiological arousal and reactivity.

The behaviorally oriented therapies presented in this chapter aim primarily at reducing the arousal and heightened emotional reactions of test-anxious persons when faced with stressful evaluative situations. The behavioral treatment literature continues to reflect the assumption that emotional arousal is the major characteristic of test anxiety and to focus on anxiety or arousal reduction. Based on the assumption that anxiety comprises a physiological component, attempts to alleviate anxiety symptoms should prove successful, in part, if they focus on reducing levels of arousal or on altering ways in which people appraise their arousal in evaluative situations.

The basic strategy in the treatments described is directed at teaching the client certain skills (mainly relaxational) so that when confronted by stress-inducing evaluative situations in the future he or she will be able to handle them adequately. The therapies also provide opportunities for application of training either within the therapy setting or in real-life situations. Following are some of the more common intervention strategies employed toward that end.

Anxiety Induction (AI)

Anxiety induction (AI) techniques aim at reducing debilitating test anxiety by presenting the client with highly anxiety-evoking evaluative stimuli until these stimuli are no longer able to evoke anxiety (Dawley & Wenrich, 1973a, 1973c). The underlying behavioristic model posits that acquisition of test anxiety follows a two-stage process: anxiety is first generated through aversive experiences surrounding test situations, and this is then followed by the person learning behaviors aimed at avoiding similar situations now associated with such anxiety. Although classical conditioning principles may account for the initiation of evaluative anxiety, the maintenance of anxiety responses are believed to be due to avoidance behaviors (Suinn, 1984). The use of AI techniques is predicated on the assumption that behavior change is facilitated by conditions producing high arousal. Thus, all that is necessary for successful extinction of test anxiety reactions is to experience anxiety in the absence of primary reinforcement. This negates the assumption of most other behavioral techniques (e.g., desensitization, relaxation therapy—to be discussed below), namely, that test-anxious behavior is best changed under conditions of low arousal.

Therapeutic Techniques

Practically, this approach involves the presentation of conditioned anxiety-evoking evaluative scenes, either imaginally or in real life, in the absence of the original unconditioned stimuli (failure, criticism, humiliation, etc.). In this manner, the client learns that there is nothing to be afraid of in test situations, and the anxiety response is eventually weakened. With repeated presentations of these test-related stimuli, the aversive emotional reaction will be reduced and eventually cease.

Primary examples of AI interventions are *flooding* and *implosion*, which share a common rationale, but differ somewhat in therapeutic procedures. The techniques have in common the principle of confronting the test-anxious client with high-intensity stimulation (King & Ollendick, 1989). However, whereas implosive therapy involves imaginally presenting anxiety-evoking scenes in a hierarchical manner, *flooding* involves exposure (either imaginally or *in vivo*) to scenarios without the hierarchical approach of implosion (Suinn, 1990). A more detailed comparison among these procedures is beyond the scope of this chapter.

Assessment of Effectiveness

Overall, anxiety induction techniques have been used quite infrequently in test anxiety intervention and research, and the relevant research on the effectiveness of these procedures is rather scant. The limited available research suggests that anxiety induction techniques, when applied in simulated test situations among student populations, may effectively reduce anxiety responses (R. E. Smith & Nye, 1973; Prochaska, 1971).

Biofeedback Training (BT)

Biofeedback training (BT) refers to the use of instrumentation (e.g., a physiograph) to provide a person with immediate and continuous information about one or more physiological processes (e.g., skin conductance, temperature, heart rate, blood volume pulse, respiration, electromyograph). Biofeedback training is the product of 20th century biomedical technology, allowing researchers and clinicians to monitor accurately a variety of internal physiological processes. These physiological processes are converted into visual or auditory informational displays that can be consciously perceived and processed, and consequently self-regulated by the brain (Schwartz, 1977). Biofeedback teaches high-test-anxious persons to monitor and modify the physiological processes associated with their emotional reactions. Thus, BT is primarily emotion-focused. However, in some biofeedback treatments, instructions provide information on how to develop and use cognitive cues to facilitate the effects of biofeedback in reducing anxiety.

In the treatment of test anxiety, BT has been used alone and in combination with other treatment approaches to help students become more aware of and sensitive to their internal physiological states of tension and arousal. The long-term effectiveness of biofeedback ultimately depends on the person's motivation and ability to continue using the self-regulation skills in real-life situations (Schwartz, 1977).

Therapeutic Techniques

As mentioned above, in biofeedback-assisted relaxation, the client is given physiological feedback (e.g., muscle or temperature feedback) through either an auditory or visual display. To illustrate how biofeedback training actually works, I briefly describe electromyograph (EMG) training employed in an experimental study by Reed and Saslow (1980). Essentially, the client receives feedback (auditory, visual, or both) on the amount of tension in the monitored muscle group, and the feedback facilitates the relaxation process. Specifically, three electrodes were secured with a rubber headstrap and were placed horizontally on the subject's forehead, attached over the frontalis muscle. Subjects were asked to relax comfortably with eyes closed for approximately 30 seconds to establish baseline audible feedback (i.e., signal heard when relaxed). Subjects then received auditory feedback about the tension of their forehead muscles, with feedback contingent upon increases in muscle tension. Subjects were shown how to adjust the machine when forehead muscle tension fell beyond the relaxation criterion and a signal was no longer heard. Thus, subjects immediately received feedback about their forehead muscle tension, as well as end-of-session information from a dial about overall changes.

Biofeedback training may also be used as an adjunct or aid to other emotion-focused or cognitive-focused treatments, such as desensitization training (discussed below). Thus, the trainee is connected to a physiograph, say EMG channel, and given a series of stressful events related to an upcoming test (a "hierarchy scene"). EMG is adjusted so that if while visualizing the scene the recorded level is beyond the relaxation criterion level, the EMG tone goes off. Subjects try to activate the tone by relaxing. The trainee continues the process of visualizing, relaxing, and visualizing until visualization of the scene occurs with the tone on.

Assessment of Effectiveness

A large body of literature supports the notion of increased physiological control when using physiological feedback and self-regulation (Schwartz, 1977). The list of physiological responses brought under self-control include systolic and diastolic blood pressure, heart rate, blood flow, sweat gland activity, skin temperature, body temperature, respiratory functions, genital responses, stomach motility, fine skeletal muscle control, and various changes in the electrical activity of the brain. There is little question that biofeedback can enhance the self-regulation of muscle activity.

A review of the literature suggests that BT alone is not effective in reducing test anxiety (Reed & Saslow, 1980; Spielberger & Vagg, 1987), nor does the addition of biofeedback training improve the efficacy of other forms of treatment (Vagg & Papsdorf, 1995). Given the potential cost and inconvenience of using biofeedback training, it may not be the treatment of choice for test anxiety intervention.

Relaxation Training (RT)

Relaxation training (RT) is primarily directed toward modifying the emotional reactions of test-anxious students during examinations. Relaxation is a popular and frequently used technique in its own right, as well as in combination with other therapies, largely because it is easy to train and is applicable across most evaluative anxiety-arousing circumstances (Deffenbacher & Suinn, 1988). Given that anxiety in evaluative contexts is frequently characterized by heightened autonomic arousal, RT has been recommended on the premise that maintaining a relaxed state during testing procedures would counteract a person's aroused state. Presumably, if a person knows when and how to apply relaxation, it will be applied directly as a counterresponse to anxiety.

Specific Therapeutic Techniques

I now briefly describe a number of the most prevalent RT techniques employed in test anxiety intervention programs.

Deep Breathing Exercises.   In order to control anxiety in evaluative situations, clients are often given relaxation exercises that emphasize deep breathing and mental relaxation (Meichenbaum & Genest, 1977). The emphasis by some therapists on deep breathing exercises, as opposed to muscular relaxation, derives from several sources: research on the salutary effect of breathing on heart rate and in lowering arousal; positive clinical experience with deep breathing techniques; and the general influence of other (Eastern) exercise procedures indicating the important role of breathing (Meichenbaum & Genest, 1977).

Before an important exam, examinees learn to take a moment to relax by taking several deep breaths and letting the tension out. It is assumed that with practice clients will become increasingly proficient at voluntarily inducing relaxation through slow, deep-breathing exercises. With this greater proficiency should also come the ability to apply relaxation to reduce feelings of anxiety in stressful test situations encountered in naturalistic settings (Denney, 1980).

Progressive Muscle Relaxation Training.   Progressive muscle relaxation (Jacobson, 1938) appears to be the most influential method of relaxation training in test anxiety intervention. Basically, this method of relaxation is a type of isometric training, involving the alternate tensing and relaxing of the major muscle groups, with the gradual elimination of the contractions and the practice of "passive" relaxation. The relaxation exercise moves across muscle groups (for example, hands, biceps, forehead, and shoulders), which are tensed one at a time, with a pause between tension exercises. During the pause, the client is trained to focus upon and increase the sense of relaxation in each particular muscle area. Then, either the muscle group is tensed again or movement to the next muscle group is made (Deffenbacher & Suinn, 1988). Clients are often given homework assignments of practicing relaxation (for about half an hour on a daily basis) at a time when they can be in a comfortable position and relatively free from distractions (Deffenbacher & Suinn, 1988).

Cue-Controlled Relaxation.   Cue-controlled relaxation is designed to enable the client to achieve relaxation and decrease anxiety in response to a self-induced cue word (Paul, 1966). It is accomplished by training the client in relaxation, followed by a pairing of a relaxed state with a cue word such as "calm" or "control." The basic rationale behind this approach is that regular practice of relaxation and cue-word association would lead to the development of a conditioned relaxation response, which could be used to counter anxiety in test-taking settings. The effectiveness of cue-controlled relaxation is claimed not to be limited to target behaviors, but could be used by the subject in any anxiety-eliciting setting. Clients are encouraged to actively employ their ability to relax when confronted with anxiety-provoking situations *in vivo*.

The cue-controlled relaxation procedure consists of several distinct phases. First, clients are trained in progressive relaxation to achieve a deeply relaxed state. After they attain a relaxed state, they are instructed to concentrate on their breathing and to subvocalize a verbal cue such as the word "calm" or "relax" with each exhalation. This second phase serves to pair the verbal cue with the client's relaxation. The association to the cue word is established by having the relaxed subjects focus their attention on their breathing while repeating the cue word silently each time they exhale. According to the classical conditioning paradigm, after a number of these pairings, the cue word alone should elicit relaxation, a feeling of calmness. Typically, several sets of 20 or so cue-word pairings are carried out in treatment sessions and subjects are instructed to practice the procedures on a daily basis. Clients are supposed to self-produce this cue when they felt themselves becoming anxious in naturalistic evaluative situations (Denney, 1980).

Although cue-controlled relaxation training has been claimed to be a valuable procedure for establishing a relaxation response that might readily be evoked in stressful evaluative settings, some subjects report finding cue-controlled relaxation to be too unwieldy to apply during testing situations. Furthermore, cue-controlled relaxation treatment has met with mixed results: Some studies report reductions in test anxiety (Denney, 1980; Russell, Miller, & June, 1975; Russell, Wise, & Stratoudakis, 1976), whereas others do not (Marchetti, McGlynn, & Patterson, 1977).

Relaxation as Self-Control. Relaxation as self-control, a self-management approach, was designed to alleviate anxiety in evaluative situations as well as to develop generalized coping skills (Denney, 1980). Self-control procedures emphasize the attainment of coping skills that the client can effectively apply toward the management and reduction of anxiety, particularly as it arises in real-life situations (Denney, 1980; T. L. Rosenthal, 1980). Proponents of this procedure (e.g., Goldfried, 1971) have long contended that relaxation could be employed as an active coping skill if sufficient attention were paid to teaching clients when and how to relax under anxiety-arousing evaluative conditions.

Clients are informed that the purpose of the treatment is to provide them with effective means for coping with anxiety by relaxation training so that in the future they can bring the relaxation response under voluntary control. Some of the common elements employed in self-control treatment procedures are training in the discrimination of internal anxiety-related cues, training in deep muscle relaxation, means of applying relaxation *in vivo*, and practice of sequence, discrimination, and application of relaxation (Snyder & Deffenbacher, 1977). Individuals are trained to observe and discriminate small changes in anxiety level and identify cues early in the chain of anxiety arousal (Deffenbacher & Snyder, 1976). Clients then receive training in the induction of relaxation and, finally, in the application of relaxation techniques in natural evaluative contexts.

Effectiveness of Relaxation Therapy

A considerable amount of research suggests that when a person learns to relax voluntarily and practices relaxation regularly, subjectively experienced anxiety, as well as tension, lessens (T. L. Rosenthal, 1980). Although it is not clear exactly how relaxation training lowers anxiety, there is little doubt that it generally does. In addition to subjective reports of anxiety-free states from individuals following a relaxation training session, relaxation therapy is claimed to have a number of distinct physiological consequences, including a decrease in pulse rate, blood pressure, and electrodermal activity.

Early studies evaluating the contribution of relaxation to reductions in test anxiety demonstrated that relaxation training alone was ineffective in reducing anxiety (Johnson & Sechrest, 1968). To some this suggested that relaxation was an insufficient treatment for test anxiety. However, Hembree's (1988) more recent meta-analytic research tends to support the effectiveness of relaxation therapy. Accordingly, relaxation therapy is shown to reduce test-anxiety posttreatment scores by about two thirds of a standard deviation relative to control-group test-anxiety scores in high school and postsecondary students. However, the effects on performance, although statistically significant, tend to be negligible. Furthermore, studies examining the effectiveness of specific forms of relaxation training relative to other treatments in test-anxious populations report varying degrees of success (Richter, 1984).

One primary concern in applying relaxation procedures to the test anxiety domain has been the dubious degree of generalization of the relaxation response to actual test-taking situations that occur beyond the confines of the treatment setting itself. Furthermore, despite the popularity of relaxation training in school settings, concern for the age-appropriateness of relaxation training procedures has been raised (King & Ollendick, 1989).

Systematic Desensitization (SD)

Systematic desensitization (SD), originally designed to inhibit excessive physiological responding and anxiety-evoking imagery in the face of aversive stimuli (Wolpe, 1958), is generally considered to be the most popular procedure for the treatment of test anxiety (Tobias, 1979). The "classical" behavior therapy tradition (Wolpe, 1958) views test anxiety as a classically conditioned emotional reaction resulting from a person's aversive experiences in evaluative situations (see Chapter 7). Systematic desensitization proposes that anxiety reactions to test situations may also be unlearned through specific counterconditioning procedures (Sieber et al., 1977).

The test-anxious client is typically trained in a deep muscle relaxation procedure and, while relaxed, instructed to visualize an ordered series of increasingly stressful test-related scenes (an "anxiety hierarchy"). The client imaginally proceeds up the hierarchy until he or she is able to visualize the most stressful scenes on the list without experiencing anxiety (Emery & Krumboltz, 1967). Through repeated pairings of imaginal representations of threatening evaluative situations with deep relaxation, the bond between the threatening evaluative scenes and anxiety is expected to be weakened. In this manner, the anxiety is said to be "counterconditioned" and inhibited by the incompatible relaxation response. Following successful treatment, the client is usually able to approach the previously anxiety-evoking test situations with little or no anxiety (Sieber et al., 1977).

I now briefly describe some of the major phases of SD as applied to test anxiety.

Providing Clients with Rationale for Treatment.   The rationale aims at providing clients with the concept of test anxiety as a learned emotional–cognitive behavioral complex. In addition, desensitization is presented as a process that can be used to unlearn anxiety reactions by replacing the anxiety response with a calm, relaxed state (Deffenbacher & Suinn, 1988). Relaxation training is explained as blocking the anxiety psychologically and physiologically, as one cannot be tensed up and calm and relaxed at the same time.

Relaxation Training.   Although there are many different relaxation training procedures (e.g., biofeedback, meditation, etc.), progressive relaxation is the one most frequently used (Deffenbacher & Suinn, 1988). Prior to beginning progressive relaxation training, a relaxation image is often constructed to be used later in the relaxation process. The relaxation image consists of a specific moment in the person's life that was very relaxing and calming (e.g., hearing some birds chirping gently in the trees, strolling along the beach, feeling a gentle breeze across your face, fishing under the blue skies, reading a favorite novel in the late hours of the night, listening to a favorite piece of classical, jazz, or pop music; Deffenbacher & Suinn, 1988).

Hierarchy Construction.   The goal of hierarchy construction is to develop a list of stressful evaluative situations that can be clearly visualized and elicit increasing amounts of anxiety. Typically, a hierarchy will include anywhere from 8 to 20 items, with an attempt to have the items equally spaced in anxiety-arousing capacity. Generally, the hierarchy begins with nonthreatening or only slightly threatening items (e.g., announcement of an upcoming exam), and proceeds through more and more personally threatening items (e.g., receiving a poor grade on a major exam). When the client is deeply relaxed, the evaluative stimuli are presented in hierarchical order so that he or she imagines the least anxiety-provoking scene first and then progresses to increasingly powerful scenes as rapidly as possible, without disturbing the level of relaxation. As the client moves gradually up the hierarchy, anxiety is deconditioned as relaxation is counterconditioned to the anxiety-arousing stimuli from the hierarchy (see Table 15.1 for typical items appearing on group desensitization hierarchies).

A number of studies (e.g., Ihli & Garlington, 1969) have questioned the necessity of using individually constructed test anxiety hierarchies in order to provide graded exposure to examination anxiety situations. Thus, a composite hierarchy, individually arranged items of the composite, and individually administered SD show the same effects in reducing test anxiety (Allen, 1972; Ihli & Garlington, 1969). The dimensions along which a hierarchy is organized normally include (a) space and time in relationship to an anxiety-arousing situation (e.g., amount of time left before a major test), (b) the nature and importance of the exam situation (e.g., a weekly quiz versus college final exam), and (c) the nature and kind of one's own or others'

Table 15.1. Typical Items Appearing in Systematic Desensitization Hierarchies

- "You hear about someone else who has an upcoming test in a parallel course you are taking"
- "You are in a very rigorous course and the instructor announces a midterm exam that will take place in 10 days"
- "A week has passed and you are studying quite intensively for the exam"
- "You are having difficulty concentrating on the exam material the night before the exam"
- "You are in bed trying to get some sleep the night before the exam and can't help but feel you are not fully prepared"
- "You wake up and realize that this is the day of the final exam that will contribute heavily to your final grade in the course"
- "You leave your room to go to the university to take the exam"
- "On your way to the exam you overhear someone in your class saying he studied very hard for the same exam last semester, yet still failed it"
- "You enter the exam hall"
- "You overhear other students reviewing the material and realize you did not adequately cover the lecture notes"
- "The proctor arrives and you are waiting for exams to be passed out"
- "The exam is being handed out and you receive your copy"
- "You try to concentrate while the instructor is walking around the exam room"
- "You come across an exam item and you are not sure of the answer"
- "While taking a test you come to a question that you are unable to answer; you draw a blank"
- "You see others handing in their exam papers, while you are only about halfway through"
- "You realize you have taken too much time on the first part of the exam and must now hurry, as you have 20 minutes left for the second part"
- "You have only 3 minutes to complete the exam, but have 20 minutes of work to do"
- "You realize you forgot to bring a calculator, and need one to solve some of the more difficult test items"
- "Your mind goes blank and you freeze up during the last 3 minutes of the exam"
- "You receive a notice of failing the exam"

Note: Items were taken from a number of hierarchies reported in the literature (e.g., Garlington & Cotler, 1968; Hudesman, Loveday, & Woods, 1984; Parker, Vagg, & Papsdorf, 1995).

behavior (e.g., a supportive examiner or professor vs. a hostile examiner or professor; Deffenbacher & Suinn, 1988).

Desensitization Proper.   Desensitization proper involves pairing the anxiety-evoking test stimuli with the incompatible response of relaxation. Desensitization procedures are designed to ensure that the previously anxiety-arousing stimuli are now being associated with calmness and relaxation. Thus the first scene presented is the lowest anxiety-arousing scene in the hierarchy because it should have the lowest anxiety-arousing potential and maximize the probability that the relaxation response will be stronger than the anxiety response (Deffenbacher & Suinn, 1988). Generally, the therapist moves to the next scene in the hierarchy after two successive, successful presentations—that is, presentation of the scene without an anxiety signal and with a clear visualization signal. If the scene is presented two times in a row with the examinee signaling anxiety, then the therapist drops back down to the last successfully presented scene, presenting it again successfully two times in a row. For the next treatment session, the first scene presented is the last successful scene from the previous session. A relaxation scene is often useful for clearing the anxiety imagery and for beginning to instill relaxation again. Typically, the scene will be exposed for 20–30 seconds and then terminated by an instruction such as, "OK, now switch that scene from your mind and continue relaxing" (Deffenbacher & Suinn, 1988).

Termination of SD.   Ideally, termination of treatment should be performance based—that is, success in applying treatment in real-life test situations (Deffenbacher & Suinn, 1988).

A number of variants of SD have been advanced in the behavioral literature. *Vicarious desensitization* has been advocated as a treatment for test anxiety that combines the effectiveness of systematic desensitization with the benefits of observational learning. Practically, it amounts to watching people recorded on videotape, in a state of deep muscle relaxation, listening to the therapist tell them to imagine themselves in certain stressful evaluative situations. *In vivo desensitization* parallels imaginal desensitization in procedure, except that the hierarchy is presented in a real-life evaluative context, rather than via imagery. The therapist goes with the client, exposing the client to the graded steps of involvement with the stressful evaluative situation (Deffenbacher & Suinn, 1988). The advantage of *in vivo* desensitization is that transfer to real life is maximized, and self-efficacy may increase more rapidly than in imaginal desensitization. In *massed desensitization* (Dawley & Wenrich, 1973b) clients meet for several hours over 2 or 3 days, as compared to the usual procedure of 1-hour sessions for several days. *Accelerated massed desensitization* carries massed desensitization one step further by presenting participants with the most anxiety-evoking items of an anxiety hierarchy (e.g., top three on hierarchy) in a short-term and intensive (2-hour) marathon desensitization (Suinn, Edie, Nicrolleti, & Spinelli, 1973).

Treatment Effectiveness

How effective is SD in reducing test anxiety? Meta-analytic data provided by Hembree (1988) lend support to the effectiveness of SD in reducing test anxiety. Accordingly, the test anxiety scores of elementary and high school students treated by systematic desensitization were significantly lower, by an order of about half a standard deviation, than the scores of untreated subjects. The test anxiety scores of college students were reduced anywhere from about one half to over a full standard deviation, depending upon the specific method of treatment administration. Furthermore, follow-ups of a year or more have shown that desensitization effects are maintained over extended periods with little evidence of relapse or symptom substitution (Deffenbacher & Suinn, 1988). Systematic desensitization has been shown to be as effective, if not more effective, in reducing test anxiety than a variety of other treatments, including relaxation training (Johnson & Sechrest, 1968), hypnosis (Melnick & Russell, 1976), and study-skills training (Altmaier & Woodward, 1981).

The literature further suggests that various forms of desensitization tend to have similar effects on the reduction of test anxiety. Thus, desensitization may be effectively applied individually and in groups, and using both imagery or *in vivo* procedures (Deffenbacher & Suinn, 1988). Furthermore, standard hierarchies (compiled from individual hierarchies of many clients) are as effective as individual hierarchies tailored to the client (Emery & Krumboltz, 1967), and vicarious desensitization appears to be as effective as standard desensitization (Mann, 1972; Mann & Rosenthal, 1969).

A number of different explanatory principles have been proposed to account for the frequently observed effects of systematic desensitization in reducing maladaptive test anxiety. The effects of SD were originally explained in term of counterconditioning, whereby the deeply relaxed client visualizes evaluative anxiety-evoking situations, thus conditioning relaxation to the evaluative stimuli. The principle of *extinction* has also been enlisted to account for the effects of SD. Accordingly, repeated presentation of a conditioned stimulus (e.g., stressful exam-related stimuli), unaccompanied by an aversive response, will lead to a reduction of the conditioned response. A third conceptualization of the effects of SD is *skill training*, which involves teaching the client general coping skills (deep muscle relaxation) useful in reducing anxiety in a variety of problem situations (Goldfried, 1971; Richardson & Suinn, 1974). Thus, rather than viewing SD as a passive counterconditioning of specific test-related anxieties, SD is construed as directed toward the acquisition of general anxiety-reducing skills when confronted with stressful evaluative circumstances.

However, SD fares less well when cognitive performance is the criterion or outcome variable being assessed. Allen's (1972) review suggests that there is little evidence that SD, in specific, and behavioral treatments, in general, alone can facilitate academic achievement. Hembree's (1988) meta-analysis indicates that systematic desensitization treatments provide a modest mean effect (about one third of a standard deviation) in enhancing grade point average across grade levels. One explanation for the limited results of standard desensitization is that is fails to modify the crucial cognitive components of test anxiety. Thus, although SD does explicitly focus on reducing arousal elicited by an exam, recent formulations suggest that the performance decrements of test-anxious subjects are largely a function of maladaptive cognitive and attentional responses.

Despite the popularity of SD, the procedure does have a number of limitations, aside from its limited effect on cognitive performance. These include the need for the hierarchical arrangement of anxiety-arousing stimuli, which complicates application to groups; presentation and timing of hierarchy items; and instruction in deep muscle relaxation, which is time-consuming and may be problematic for younger children (Kostka & Galassi, 1974). Also, the effects of systematic desensitization are limited, since anxiety reduction generalizes only to anxieties elicited by situations very similar to the desensitized anxiety (Deffenbacher & Shelton, 1978). In addition, recent studies have questioned the active mechanisms and the necessary components of systematic desensitization (King & Ollendick, 1989).

Anxiety Management Training (AMT)

Anxiety management training (AMT) was originally designed as a therapeutic technique suitable for treating any condition where anxiety is a core issue, which is the case in test anxiety (Suinn, 1990). In the context of test anxiety intervention, AMT teaches highly test-anxious subjects to recognize their test-related arousal responses as they are building, and then to use them as cues for initiating the coping response of relaxation in evaluation situations. The theoretical foundation for AMT is based upon the view that clients can be taught first to identify the internal signs, both cognitive and physical, that signal the onset of anxiety and then react to these signs using adaptive coping responses that remove them (Suinn & Deffenbacher, 1988).

Therapeutic Techniques

In practice, each client focuses on a selected few highly stressful anxiety-arousing scenes or episodes, such as a matriculation, graduate admissions, or an oral dissertation exam. Clients are instructed to imagine vividly the stressful evaluative scene and to focus on the anxiety and associated response-produced cues (e.g., racing heart, neck and shoulder tensing, dryness of the mouth, and catastrophic thoughts). The clients are then trained to use these cues to prompt adaptive coping skills to actively relax away tension and reduce anxiety before it mounts too severely. AMT involves a structured set of five basic therapeutic sessions, though the actual number of sessions is individually tailored to the severity of the specific client's problem and rate of progress (Suinn & Deffenbacher, 1988). All sessions take about 60 minutes, with the interval between sessions averaging about 1 week (Suinn & Deffenbacher, 1988). Following is a brief description of the core phases involved in employing AMT (Suinn, 1984).

Rationale and Relaxation Training.   The treatment program begins by presenting clients with the treatment rationale, developing a relaxation scene, introducing relaxation training, and assigning homework (Suinn & Deffenbacher, 1988). Thus, clients are presented with a "self-control" rationale emphasizing the acquisition of coping skills that can be used voluntarily to reduce or eliminate anxiety whenever tension cues are recognized (Denney, 1980). AMT is briefly explained as a means of using relaxation (primarily standard deep muscle relaxation accompanied by breathing exercises) as an active, general coping skill to achieve self-control over anxiety in evaluative situations. Homework exercises are initiated to practice the relaxation method in evaluative situations (e.g., studying for an upcoming exam). In this phase the client also describes a recent example of a heightened anxiety experience in a test situation to form the basis for later guided rehearsal (Suinn, 1984).

Guided Rehearsal for Anxiety Arousal.   The guided rehearsal aims at providing the test-anxious client with practice in anxiety control via relaxation. Thus, once the client has gained some control over the ability to initiate relaxation, the anxiety scene, often involving a real evaluative experience associated with a moderately high level of anxiety, is used to recreate anxiety arousal. The client visualizes the anxiety-evoking evaluative scene, relying upon affective, somatic, or cognitive cues to reelicit the anxiety. The therapist guides the client in recapturing the scene and reexperiencing the anxiety, then guides the client in terminating the scene and regaining a relaxed state. When the client is relaxed, anxiety arousal is initiated once again through the therapist's instruction to switch on the anxiety scene, to use the scene to reexperience the anxiety, and to signal the onset of this anxiety (Suinn & Deffenbacher, 1988). Guided rehearsal aims at helping clients discriminate cues of tension and anxiety, to detect these cues early in their development, and to use these cues as signals to begin actively applying their coping skills (Denney, 1980).

Cue-Discrimination Training.   In the third phase of AMT, the client is instructed to attend to the cues that are indicative of anxiety arousal in evaluative situations, for example, feeling a knot or "butterflies" in the stomach. The idea is to enable the client to perceive quickly early signs of anxiety, and to then introduce relaxation before the anxiety has a chance to build to the point of being out of control (Suinn, 1984).

Graduated Self-Control.   In the self-control training phase of AMT, the client is gradually given more responsibility for regaining relaxation and eliminating the anxiety. Instead of the therapist terminating the anxiety scene and reinitiating the relaxation, the client decides when to end the anxiety scene and takes responsibility for relaxation retrieval (Suinn & Deffenbacher, 1988). At some stage, there is a fading out of therapist control and the completion of client self-control (Suinn & Deffenbacher, 1988).

Transfer to Real-Life Evaluative Situations.   The transfer of self-control over anxiety is the objective of the final phase of AMT. Training involves rehearsal of pairing relaxation with specific anxiety-arousing scenes outside the therapeutic setting. Thus, homework is routinely assigned outside the clinic for the purpose of gradually generalizing coping skills to the external environment, including both test and evaluative nontest situations (Suinn, 1984).

AMT is related to systematic desensitization, but differs from the latter in a number of basic ways (Deffenbacher & Shelton, 1978). First, the rationale for AMT stresses self-management of tension through relaxation, rather than passive counter-conditioning—as is the case in systematic desensitization. Second, in contrast to self-control desensitization, AMT does not require the identification of a hierarchy, nor actual identification of the specific anxiety-evoking stimuli. Instead, there is a much greater emphasis upon purposefully inducing feelings of anxiety and tension by whatever means are most effective. All that is needed, in fact, is for clients to recall an incident in their lives associated with high anxiety and to describe their anxiety reactions and the setting in order to reexperience the anxiety arousal (Suinn, 1990). Third, anxiety is purposely induced and experienced through the visualization of the anxiety-arousing scene, rather than steps being taken to avoid or minimize experienced tension. Fourth, relaxation in AMT is associated with physiological cues of anxiety (profuse sweating, tension, etc.) rather than stimulus events external to the individual, as is the case in systematic desensitization.

Evaluation of Treatment Effectiveness

A body of research supports the effectiveness of AMT in reducing test anxiety. Thus, AMT appears to be as robust and effective, if not more so, than related interventions, such as systematic desensitization (Deffenbacher & Shelton, 1978; Richardson & Suinn, 1973), accelerated mass desensitization (Richardson & Suinn, 1974), active coping self-control (Denney & Rupert, 1977), and self-control desensitization (Deffenbacher, Michaels, Michaels, & Daley, 1980). Furthermore, a review of the literature suggests that whereas clients treated by AMT continued to show reductions in test anxiety during follow-up, desensitization clients actually showed some minor increases (Suinn, 1990). Reductions in debilitating test anxiety were maintained for follow-up periods ranging from several weeks (Deffenbacher et al., 1980), to a year (Deffenbacher & Michaels, 1981a, 1981b). In summary, research indicates that anxiety management training is effective in the reduction of test anxiety, with decreases in levels of anxiety continuing across long periods of follow-up (Suinn, 1990).

Modeling (M)

Modeling, as a test anxiety intervention technique, would involve the live or symbolic (e.g., through videotape) demonstration of desired coping behaviors in a stressful evaluative situation such that they can be subsequently imitated by the test-anxious person (Kendall, 1993). Social-cognitive theory and research suggests that the opportunity to observe a model engaging in adaptive test coping strategies exerts a salutary influence on the observer's coping behaviors in test situations (Bandura, 1976). Furthermore, current thinking and some research would predict that high-test-anxious subjects benefit more from the opportunity to observe a model than do low-test-anxious subjects (I. G. Sarason, 1973). Bandura's (1977) "belief in self-efficacy," the belief that one is capable of performing the actions necessary to achieve desired consequences, has been proposed as a unifying construct for the effects of modeling approaches.

Exposure to models displaying adaptive behavior may play a positive role in facilitating performance. Observational opportunities can provide a person with demonstrations of overt adaptive coping responses and, if the model "thinks through" problems and tactics aloud, it may provide the person with covert coping responses as well. Some research suggests that the learning of high-test-anxious subjects is detrimentally affected by exposure to a model who receives failure feedback on a task, but is positively affected by exposure to a model who receives success feedback on a similar task. The reverse was true for low-test-anxious subjects (I. G. Sarason, 1972b).

Therapeutic Procedures

Practically, the therapist models adaptive through patterns aloud, attempting to teach the client rational thinking styles. The client follows suit by rehearsing and approximating, both overtly, and subsequently covertly, the modeled self-statements or behaviors (Meichenbaum, 1976). Operationally, the treatment proceeds as follows: first, the therapist performs a task while thinking aloud while the client carefully observes the modeled behavior (modeling phase); then the client is asked to perform the same task while the therapist instructs the client aloud; then the client is asked to perform the task again while instructing himself aloud; then the client performs the task while whispering; and finally the client performs the task while instructing himself covertly. In covert modeling procedures the client imagines a model engaged in adaptive coping behavior in stressful evaluative situations, without the use of live or filmed models (Gallagher & Arkowitz, 1978).

Evaluation of Effectiveness

A body of research lends support to the effectiveness of modeling in treating test anxiety. Gallagher and Arkowitz (1978) reported that subjects who underwent covert modeling treatment, imagining a model coping successfully with a test, showed significantly greater reduction in test anxiety compared to no-modeling and delayed-treatment control groups. Research by I. G. Sarason (1986) suggests that modeling of adaptive overt behavior and cognitions may be more generally effective than preperformance reassurance in improving performance. Wine (1982) reviewed a series of studies pointing to the conclusion that exposure to models who are task-oriented and provide attention-directing cognitive structuring clues is beneficial to the performance of test-anxious persons. Of additional benefit is evidence in the behavior of the model that he or she is successfully coping with the worry and tension associated with test anxiety.

Summary

This chapter reviewed some of the major behavioral techniques used at present to treat test anxiety, along with their rationale and empirical basis. The behavioral treatments described in this chapter typically include a number of common components, such as theoretical explanations of test anxiety as a conditioned response and the "deconditioning" rationale for treatment; instructions in specific methods for reducing anxiety, such as relaxation and guided imagery; guided practice in therapeutic methods; and practice (homework, *in vivo* practice). By and large, these emotion-focused treatments rely on key behavioral learning principles (counterconditioning, reciprocal inhibition, extinction, observational and coping skill learning, etc.) and also draw from an arsenal of behavioral techniques, such as deep muscle relaxation, guided imagery, and graduated hierarchies. For example, the use of relaxation and guided imagery is not unique to a particular test anxiety behavioral intervention method, but is common to several methods, including relaxation as self-control, systematic desensitization, and anxiety management training.

The treatment methods, despite common elements, differ on a variety of facets. One dimension along which they differ is the degree of self-control offered the client and the specific training in transfer to situations outside of the treatment context which are built into the program. The methods presented also tend to vary in specific treatment orientation and the use they make of particular behavioral techniques. Some behavioral treatments (e.g., implosion and flooding, anxiety management training) rely on the induction of anxiety, whereas others rely on counterconditioning of anxiety to relaxation responses. Some methods view anxiety as acceptable, and as a stimulus for coping (e.g., relaxation as self-control, anxiety management training), whereas in others, such as systematic desensitization, the presentation of the stimulus is aborted when the subject begins to feel anxious. Some methods (e.g., systematic desensitization) rely on the use of a graduated and stepwise hierarchy in guided rehearsal, whereas others (e.g., anxiety management training) do not. In some methods (e.g., anxiety induction procedures, systematic desensitization) the anxiety-evoking stimuli are test-specific, emphasizing specific test-related stimuli, whereas in others (e.g., anxiety management training) they are not.

A tacit assumption of many behavioral treatments is that the reduction of anxiety would release attentional and cognitive resources, thus enabling test-anxious examinees to devote a higher proportion of their capacity to learning and performing on evaluative tasks. However, procedures designed to reduce emotionality, while clearly useful in modifying subjectively experienced anxiety, by themselves appear to have little effect on cognitive performance. Overall, emotion-focused treatments appear to be relatively ineffective in reducing test anxiety unless these treatments contain cognitive elements. It may therefore be necessary to combine such approaches with therapy modes focusing specifically on cognitive change in order to reliably elicit improvement in cognitive performance. In the following chapter I discuss a number of cognitive- and skill-oriented treatments that may be more likely to effect changes in cognitive performance.

Cognitive-Focused, Cognitive-Behavioral, and Cognitive-Skills Training Intervention Techniques

> You cannot prevent the birds of worry and care from flying over your head. But, you can stop them from building a nest in your head.
>
> —Ancient Chinese proverb

Overview

Recent years have witnessed a proliferation of cognitively oriented intervention programs that emphasize the mediating role of cognitive processes in sustaining or eliminating test anxiety. In part, the documented failure of emotionally oriented behavioral therapies to markedly improve the academic performance of test-anxious students, coupled with the inconsistent relation reported between emotional arousal and test performance, has led to a greater emphasis on cognitive factors in test anxiety intervention (Dendato & Diener, 1986).

"Cognitive therapy" is a generic term that refers to a wide array of therapeutic approaches directed toward modifying the worry and irrational thought patterns of test-anxious clients. Broadly speaking, cognitively oriented approaches to test anxiety intervention are quite similar in assuming that cognitive processes are determining factors in test anxiety, although they differ in terms of actual intervention procedures (Beck & Emory, 1985). A fundamental assumption shared by contemporary cognitive models of test anxiety is that cognitive processes mediate the person's emotional and behavioral responses to stressful evaluative situations. It follows that in order to modify the negative emotional reactions of test-anxious clients to evaluative situations, therapy needs to be directed at reshaping the faulty premises, assumptions, and negative attitudes underlying maladaptive cognitions of test-anxious subjects.

This chapter surveys major test anxiety intervention programs having a cognitive (Beck, 1993), cognitive-behavioral (Meichenbaum, 1993), or cognitive skills orientation. Following the structure of Chapter 15, I first discuss the underlying rationale for each treatment method presented, survey the specific techniques employed for reducing anxiety and enhancing performance, and then examine the empirical evidence for the effectiveness of each treatment method. Note that both emotion-focused and cognitive-focused therapies aim at changing aversive emotions and dysfunctional arousal in test-anxious persons. Whereas the techniques surveyed in Chapter 15 are direct behavioral, emotion-focused interventions, those in this chapter are mostly cognitive-based techniques of changing emotions (i.e., working indirectly through cognition).

I begin by surveying cognitive restructuring and attentional training. I then discuss cognitive-behavior modification and stress inoculation training, premiere multimodal and eclectic interventions that embrace both cognitively and emotionally oriented treatment components. Although these multimodal approaches fall midway on the continuum of emotion-focused–cognitive-focused interventions, they are discussed after cognitive methods since these cognitive-behavioral methods incorporate components of cognitive therapies. I then move on to present study-skills training, an approach with a "cognitive deficiency" orientation. I conclude by presenting a number of basic conceptual and methodological considerations to be kept in mind when implementing test anxiety intervention programs and when conducting program evaluation research.

Cognitive Approaches

I now present two forms of cognitive therapy aimed at correcting cognitive distortions in test anxiety—cognitive attentional training and cognitive restructuring.

Cognitive-Attentional Training (CAT)

A fundamental premise of the cognitive-attentional training (CAT) perspective is that training high-test-anxious subjects to attend to task-relevant stimuli should reduce self-reported worry and tension and consequently enhance their cognitive task performance (Wine, 1980).

Specific Therapeutic Techniques

Attentional training programs traditionally provide clients with instructions to attend fully to the task and to inhibit self-relevant thinking while working on a variety of academic tasks. Thus, clients are typically told to absorb themselves as much as possible in the task at hand and to avoid thinking about other things, including task-irrelevant thoughts and preoccupations (e.g., "Concentrate all your energy on the problem at hand," "Don't let yourself get distracted from the test items"; I. G. Sarason & Turk, 1983).

Explicit attention-directing self-instructions are typically modeled by the therapist and utilized by test-anxious clients to facilitate focusing upon task-relevant variables. When self-focused thoughts surface, subjects are instructed to redirect thoughts to solving the problem at hand. In addition, clients are encouraged to use their developing attentional coping skills to inhibit self-deprecating and ruminative tendencies and to gain practice in ignoring external distracting stimuli under evaluative situations. Both *on-task statements* (e.g., "I will think about that later; now back to the test," "I have plenty of time to complete this exam," "Read the test questions carefully") and *positive self-evaluation* ("I will perform well on this test because I am well prepared," "I can do well if I stick with it") may serve to mediate the direction of attention for the effective test-taker (Kirkland & Hollandsworth, 1980). These cognitive skills and self-statements would ideally be developed in the crucible of the client's personal experience and shaped to fit his or her cognitive and behavioral styles.

Effectiveness of Intervention

A body of experimental research attests to the beneficial effects of attentional instruction on the performance of high-test-anxious students. Research by Mueller (1978) suggests that task-attention-directing procedures that provide specific instructions on appropriate task strategies have beneficial effects on the cognitive performance of test-anxious students, while maintaining the high performance levels of their low-anxious counterparts. I. G. Sarason (1972a) provided evidence that task instructions that provide examinees with information about appropriate problem-solving strategies and away from self-preoccupied worry may be particularly helpful to the test-anxious individual's cognitive functioning. Furthermore, the literature supports the notion that high-test-anxious persons can be trained, through modeling procedures, to be more attentive to task-related stimuli that bear on affective performance (I. G. Sarason, 1973). Wine (1971a, 1971b; cf. Wine, 1980) reported that high-test-anxious students given attentional training to self-instruct in a task-relevant manner by means of modeling and behavioral rehearsal improved significantly on both self-report measures of test anxiety and cognitive performance. Self-instructional procedures also appear to have incremental effects when combined with other methods (Meichenbaum, 1972; Wine, 1971a, 1971b; Wise & Haynes, 1983).

Cognitive Restructuring Therapy (CRT)

"Cognitive restructuring" is a rather fuzzy term which means different things to different people. In fact, it has often been used synonymously with "cognitive therapy." The two most prominent cognitive therapeutic methods in test anxiety intervention are rational emotive therapy (Ellis, 1962, 1977) and systematic rational restructuring (Goldfried, Decenteceo, & Weinberg, 1974). Both forms of treatment are based on the premise that anxiety or emotional disturbance is a result of illogical or "irrational" thinking. Whereas rational emotive therapy gives the rationale for cognitive restructuring, systematic rational restructuring organizes this rationale into a series of more systematic steps and procedures. I begin by presenting rational emotive therapy and move on to present the systematic procedures as implemented in systematic rational restructuring.

Rational Emotive Therapy (RET)

Rational emotive therapy (RET) aims at teaching test-anxious clients to recognize and change their irrational belief systems, presumed to be largely responsible for their anxiety reactions in evaluative situations. Rather than attempting to alleviate directly the worries and emotional reactions of test-anxious individuals, the main therapeutic thrust is to teach clients how to challenge and dispute their own irrational beliefs and faulty assumptions so that they can replace them with more realistic ones (Fletcher & Spielberger, 1995). Thus, test-anxious persons are encouraged to identify the irrational content of their disruptive thoughts, identify the type of evaluative situations in which these thoughts tend to occur, and identify the negative behavioral consequences of these thoughts.

Two key irrational beliefs that maintain test anxiety is that one *must* succeed on major exams at all cost, and that success on these exams is equivalent to self-worth. Furthermore, high-test-anxious individuals are often characterized by a high need of approval, and feel that if they fail, others will not accept them. To top it off, test-anxious individuals are often characterized by perfectionistic beliefs, maintaining that anything less than perfect is failure. Because test-anxious individuals feel they will not meet their high standards of performance and therefore will continue to fail, these predictions become self-fulfilling prophecies.

According to the ABC (Activating events, Beliefs, Consequences) model of RET analysis (Ellis, 1977), a test situation per se does not make one anxious; rather, it is what the person says to oneself that makes one anxious. Accordingly, the test situation, as *activating event* (A = "I am going to be tested next week") is associated with certain irrational *beliefs* (B = "How worthless I will consider myself to be if I flunk this exam"), with aversive emotional *consequences* (C = "I feel terribly anxious about this upcoming exam").

While primarily linked to perceptual, appraisal, and reappraisal processes, RET also indirectly influences emotionality by modifying irrational appraisals (Spielberger & Vagg, 1987). Furthermore, by altering test-anxious students' irrational beliefs, RET might contribute to improved attitudes toward academic work and the strengthening of a person's self-concept (Fletcher & Spielberger, 1995).

Therapeutic Techniques. RET intervention shows test-anxious individuals how to vigorously challenge, question, and dispute their irrational beliefs. The method employed for eliminating irrational beliefs consists in a fairly direct verbal assault upon the thinking patterns and cognitive sets of test-anxious subjects. Thus, test-anxious subjects are shown how to ask themselves some of the following questions: "Why is it so terrible to have failed this exam?" "Who says I must succeed?" "Where is the evidence that I am a worthless person if I fail?" This approach maintains that if test-anxious individuals learn how to dispute persistently and forcefully their irrational ideas, they acquire a new cognitive set. This new cognitive set is composed of beliefs such as: "It is not awful, only very inconvenient, if I fail," "I don't have to succeed, though there are several good reasons why I'd like to," "I am not a worthless person for failing or being rejected. I am merely a person who has done poorly for the present, in certain areas, but who probably can do better later" (Ellis, 1962).

Treatment Effectiveness. A number of studies (Fletcher & Spielberger, 1995; Barabasz & Barabasz, 1981; Wessel & Mersch, 1994) provide evidence showing that RET may be effective in reducing anxiety. However, RET has not been shown to have a meaningful impact upon performance in test situations.

Systematic Rational Restructuring (SRR)

Systematic rational restructuring (SRR) aims at helping test-anxious clients to discover the worrisome task-irrelevant thoughts they entertain during tests, to eclipse such thoughts, and to substitute positive self-statements that redirect their attention to the task at hand (Denney, 1980). The rationale is that test-anxious persons will be able to master their anxiety by learning to control task-irrelevant cognitions that generate their anxiety and direct attention from their task-directed performance.

Specific Therapeutic Procedures. Practically, SRR includes cognitive restructuring along with a self-control rationale. Clients are first introduced to the premise that their beliefs substantially determine the emotions they experience in evaluative settings and are taught that their negative emotions surrounding test situations stem largely from anxiety-engendering thoughts they emit in relation to test-taking situations ("I won't pass," "I'm no good"). They are taught that they need to learn to substitute positive thoughts to counter negative ones ("It is not terrible to fail, only inconvenient").

Imaginal rehearsal is frequently used to help clients gain insight into their faulty thinking. Accordingly, clients are asked to note how anxious they feel when imagining an important test situation, and then to identify what it is that they are saying to themselves that may be creating the upset. Clients are asked to "think aloud" during this process, so that the therapist may prompt them in their attempts at either ferreting out or reevaluating their perception of the event. Following the reevaluation process, they then note the extent to which their anxiety has decreased.

The test-anxious client is taught to produce three types of task-relevant cognitions:

1. *Self instructions* (e.g., "Just tackle one test item at a time").
2. *Coping self-statements* (e.g., "Don't worry about this exam. Worry won't help a bit anyway").
3. *Self-reinforcing statements* (e.g., "It's working. I can control how I feel!").

In addition, students are directed to engage in task-relevant behaviors (e.g., working actively on the test itself) that are incompatible with the generation of negative self-statements (Fletcher & Spielberger, 1995).

Despite the similarity between RET and SRR procedures, both being particular cases of cognitive restructuring, SRR differs somewhat from RET in therapeutic procedure. In SRR, the therapist engages the client more in mutually testing out the rationality of his or her thoughts by authenticating observations, validating assumptions, and taking on an objective perspective (distancing). In RET, by contrast, the therapist challenges the client's false beliefs ("You say it's awful that you failed on the exam. Why is it so awful? Who says you must succeed?") and relies heavily upon formal analysis of the rationality of these believes ("This is another of those common beliefs that you must learn to dispute. Is there any logic to your conclusions from what you've said?"). In addition, SRR places a greater emphasis than RET on replacing negative self-statements with positive self-statements.

Intervention Effectiveness.   Denney's (1980) review of the literature concludes that SRR frequently leads to reductions in self-reports of debilitating test anxiety. However, concomitant improvements in cognitive performance are observed with far less consistency (Denney, 1980). Hembree's (1988) meta-analytic research supports Denney's conclusions with respect to the impact of SRR upon test anxiety. Across studies, cognitive treatment was shown to be effective in reducing test anxiety by the order of about one third of a standard deviation, on average, relative to control groups. Furthermore, a recent review by Vagg and Papsdorf (1995) suggests that there is little evidence that cognitive treatments by themselves help improve performance. When taken together with other, related research in this area, it appears that the *coping emphasis* inherent in rational restructuring may be the effective ingredient in the treatment of test anxiety, rather than the specific nature of the rational restructuring intervention itself (Goldfried, 1988).

Cognitive-Behavioral Approaches

I now discuss cognitive behavioral modification and stress inoculation training, two related cognitive-behavioral approaches to test anxiety treatment and prevention. These approaches are characterized by technical eclecticism (Alford & Norcross, 1991), borrowing or importing techniques from diverse sources without necessarily subscribing to the theories that spawned them. As aptly pointed out by R. S. Lazarus (1992), "remaining theoretically consistent but technically eclectic enables therapists to spell out precisely what procedures they use with various clients and the means by which they select those particular methods" (p. 233).

Cognitive-Behavioral Modification (CBM)

Cognitive-behavioral modification (CBM), as applied to test anxiety intervention, is a multifaceted treatment approach designed to influence the various components of anxiety (Denney, 1980). Given its dual emphasis on modifying both emotional processes and irrational thoughts and cognitions, CBM is linked to both the Worry and Emotionality components of test anxiety. In addition, CBM attempts to modify the perception and appraisal of test situations so as to make them less threatening (Vagg & Spielberger, 1995) as well as provide appropriate problem-solving skills. This results in a powerful approach that merges emotionally oriented and cognitively oriented techniques to alleviate clients' test anxiety and enhance their test performance (Meichenbaum, 1993). CBM is based on the premise that reducing a person's level of test anxiety involves both anxiety reduction training as well as detailed cognitive restructuring of certain faulty beliefs or misconceptions concerning evaluative situations. It is also assumed that some students may require restructuring of their study habits if rewarding and successful academic work is to be ensured.

Therapeutic Phases and Techniques

In the following subsections, I describe the three basic phases of CBM: (a) conceptualization and education, (b) skill training and rehearsal, and (c) application.

Conceptualization and Education.   The first phase of CBM aims at conducting a clinically sensitive assessment of the nature and complexity of the client's test anxiety and in providing clients with a conceptual understanding of both the nature of test anxiety as well as their complex multivariate response to test situations (Meichenbaum & Deffenbacher, 1988). During the educational phase, the therapist conveys the message to clients that anxiety reactions involve a number of behavioral manifestations, such as heightened arousal (e.g., increased heart rate, sweaty palms, body tension) and a set of anxiety-engendering thoughts and images. The therapist then suggests that treatment would be directed at both emotional and cognitive facets of anxiety by (a) helping clients to control their physiological arousal by learning how to relax and (b) eradicating their negative thoughts and self-statements, replacing them with more productive ones. Thus, the two factors of Emotionality and Worry, which characterize the high-test-anxious person's behavior and problems with focusing attention, constitute the basis for the therapy rationale (Meichenbaum & Genest, 1977).

During the educational phase, the client is taught to become more aware of the internal events or cues that trigger anxiety, the components of anxiety, important personal themes that cut across anxiety-arousing evaluative situations, and the potential coping skills the client already possesses. In addition, information is provided to the client about the way distressing emotions are generated, with an emphasis on the cognitive factors or self-statements that are involved. The goal is for clients to come to see their problems as addressable, rather than overwhelming, hopeless, and uncontrollable (Meichenbaum & Deffenbacher, 1988).

Skill Acquisition and Training.   During the second phase of CBM, skill acquisition and training, the client is taught specific coping skills to deal with evaluative stress and anxiety reactions. A variety of alternative skills are considered during this phase, including deep breathing and muscle relaxation, self-instructional training, cognitive restructuring of catastrophic self-statements and coping self-statements for specific phases of the stress process, task-oriented self-instruction, training in problem-solving skills, and self-reinforcement for coping. Acquisition of these skills is developed through the utilization of different strategies, such as self-monitoring, imagery rehearsal, role playing, and homework assignments (Suinn, 1990). I now present some of the basic ingredients and components comprising the second phase of CBM.

• *Insight training.* Test-anxious clients typically undergo an "insight" therapy procedure in which they are made aware of the specific self-oriented and anxiety-engendering thoughts and self-statements they emit prior to, during, and following their test-taking experience. Clients are informed that one of the goals of therapy is for them to become aware of (gain insight into) the self-verbalizations and self-instructions which they emit in evaluative situations and to replace the with incompatible self-instructions and incompatible behaviors. Accordingly, clients are explicitly trained to emit incompatible self-statements ("self-instructions" or "self-talk") which have the effect of avoiding worry and directing attention to the task (e.g., "Just keep cool. Getting riled up over this exam won't help"; Meichenbaum & Deffenbacher, 1988). A basic assumption of this approach is that the private speech of the client may be subjected to the same modification procedures (modeling, reinforcement, aversive consequences, etc.) that are used for modifying overt behaviors.

• *Relaxation skills training.* Relaxation coping skills, aimed at helping the test-anxious client manage his or her anxious arousal and affect, are introduced within a self-management rationale. Clients are trained using a variety of behavioral techniques, including progressive relaxation procedures, relaxation without tension, pleasant imagery, breathing exercises, and cognitively cued relaxation. The use of slow, deep breathing is emphasized during the basic relaxation-training procedure. As these skills are mastered within the session, clients are encouraged to begin to apply them in true-to-life evaluative situations.

• *Coping imagery.* This procedure is basically a modification of systematic desensitization. Thus, clients go through a modified desensitization procedure in which they visualize themselves actively coping with test anxiety in a graded series of test-taking scenes. While the client is visualizing items from a test-related hierarchy, relaxation is employed. Specifically, clients are asked to visualize themselves performing specified test-related behaviors (e.g., studying the night before an exam; taking an exam) and as they become anxious to visualize themselves coping with this anxiety by means of slow deep breaths and self-instructions to "relax" and to be "task-focused." The particular mode of coping imagery employed in CBM is in marked contrast to the mastery-type imagery used in standard desensitization procedures. The standard desensitization treatment procedure has clients signal if the image being visualized elicits anxiety, and then to terminate that image and relax. There is no suggestion within the standard desensitization procedure that a person will in fact realize or experience anxiety in the real-life situation. The *coping imagery* procedure employed in CBM, by contrast, has the person visualize the experienced anxiety and then think of ways in which to cope and reduce such anxiety (Meichenbaum, 1972). Thus, the test-anxious client visualizes beginning to get a little anxious in test situations, but then imagines coping successfully with anxiety by means of slow, deep breaths and appropriate self-instructions and self-talk (Richardson, O'Neil, & Grant, 1977).

• *Self-statements.* The basic premise underlying the particular form of rational restructuring employed in CBM is that the client's anxiety is maintained by the negative test-related self-statements and images in which they engage. It is held that the test-anxious person's negative self-statements become a habitual style of thinking, in many ways similar to the automatization that accompanies the mastery of a motor skill, such as driving a car or skiing. The therapist attempts to "deautomatize" this habitual thinking style, and have clients recognize the incipient signs of their anxiety in order to short-circuit its occurrence at low intensity levels. The positive self-statements typically contain references to test preparation, test taking, and grades, such as, "I know I'm well prepared for this test, so just relax." Several statements designed for reinforcement purposes are also included, such as, "My confidence wasn't even shaken when others turned in their papers before I was finished" (Hussian & Lawrence, 1978). Self-statements which the client rehearses are designed to be representative of the test-anxious individual's private experience. Table 16.1 provides examples of coping self-statements used in CBM test anxiety programs.

• *Self-reward/self-efficacy self-statements.* Self-reward self-statements help the client support his or her coping efforts. They typically provide support for examples of successful coping and reward for the process of trying to cope when anxiety is not managed fully. Examples of self-statements in this category are, "That's it, hang in there. You're doing fine on this test!" and "I'm getting better at this anxiety management procedure day by day" (Meichenbaum & Deffenbacher, 1988).

Table 16.1. Examples of Self-Statements
for Enhancing Coping Ability in Test Situations

Preparing for an exam
- "Don't worry about how you'll do on the exam; worry won't help you make the grade anyway"
- "Just think about what you need to do to get the best possible results on the exam"
- "You can develop a workable, step-by-step, plan in studying for the exam"
- "Think positively and things will go well for you"

Confronting and handling an exam situation
- "Just concentrate on the exam and psych yourself up—you can surely meet this challenge"
- "Don't dwell on your anxiety during the exam, just think about what you have to do and do it, step by step"
- "I don't want to get lost in detail on this essay question; stand back and look at the big picture"
- "Now I feel being in control; back to the exam"
- "Relax; you're in good control of the exam situation; take a slow deep breath; you feel fine"
- "Wonder how many answers I can miss for a B ... I'll figure that out later; just pay attention and finish this up"

Coping with the feeling of being overwhelmed
- "Don't get overanxious; just take off a moment and take a couple of slow, deep breaths ... calm ... and relax ... good"
- "Slow down a little; you have plenty of time to finish the exam, so don't panic"
- "Focus on the test; what is it exactly you have to do?"
- "Don't worry if you begin to feel extremely anxious during the exam; you should expect your anxiety to rise at the outset"
- "This difficult exam will be over in a few minutes, so just keep cool"
- "The two guys seated next to me wizzed through the exam; forget them and concentrate on the task"

Reinforcing self-statements
- "You actually succeeded in solving the exam problem; you did it! fantastic!"
- "The exam was wasn't as difficult as you expected; you did well for yourself"
- "You got more riled up on account of the exam than it was worth"
- "You can really pat yourself on the back the way you handled that challenging test"

Note: Partly adapted from Meichenbaum (1976) and Meichenbaum and Genest (1977).

Two specific requirements for effective skills enhancement are cognitive understanding and practice. Rehearsal is designed to provide the client with the necessary practice to consolidate and strengthen coping skills. Within sessions, skills are rehearsed in role plays, simulations, and imagery. For example, in relaxation coping skills, clients may be asked to imagine such scenes as preparing for an important exam, dealing with moderate test anxiety, handling overwhelming levels of anxiety, and coping with the aftermath.

Application and Followthrough. The third phase of CBM emphasizes the refinement, application, and transferring of learned coping strategies and skills to naturalistic test situations. Thus, as coping skills are mastered and consolidated within sessions, attention is turned to transferring them to the external environment. Typically, this is done through graded homework assignments in which clients practice the acquired skills with either a real or imagined evaluative stressor (Deffen-bacher, 1988). In particular, test-anxious clients work on strengthening cognitive and relaxation coping skills and applying these strategies to real-life test situations. The therapist and test-anxious client discuss the information gathered from such assignments, and application of coping skills is further modified, leading to new, collab-oratively developed assignments (Meichenbaum & Deffenbacher, 1988). Therapist assistance is gradually faded out as clients gain control over their anxiety in true-to-life test situations. The application phase may be affected by a number of factors, such as whether the stress is real or imagined, the amount of exposure to practice, and the use of coping imagery, with some studies showing that *in vivo* procedures may be more effective than imaginal ones (Jaremko, 1979).

CBM typically consists of anywhere from 8 to 20 sessions, although the number of sessions for either individual or group treatments should depend on the needs and progress of the client(s). Future follow-up or "booster" sessions are also part of the procedure and are built into the program (Meichenbaum & Deffenbacher, 1988). The timing of such sessions varies, but in most instances (at least the last sessions) are conducted every 2 weeks, rather than weekly. This gives greater time for coping skill consolidation and a greater sense of self-efficacy as the client is increasingly on his or her own. Further follow-up sessions can take place at 1-, 3-, 6-, and 12-month intervals. Clients often report that knowing they will meet with their therapist or group maintains an awareness of continued efforts to cope (Meichenbaum & Deffen-bacher, 1988).

Treatment Effectiveness

A meta-analytic review of the literature (Hembree, 1988) suggests that CBM procedures are relatively effective in reducing self-reported levels of debilitating test anxiety, and are equally effective, more or less, in reducing both cognitive and affective components of test anxiety (Worry: $d = -.82$; Emotionality: $d = -.73$). Meta-analytic data indicate that CBM raises test performance, on average, by about half a standard deviation ($d = .52$) in school-aged samples, and elevates grade point average by close to three quarters of a standard deviation ($d = .72$) in postsecondary students. CBM treatment techniques may facilitate academic performance by reducing the intensity of worry cognitions, as well as placing a strong emphasis on encouraging and motivating the test-anxious student to cope actively with a variety of stressful situations (Gonzalez, 1995). CBM fares quite well in comparison with other behavioral treatment programs as far as test anxiety is concerned (Leal, Baxter, Martin, & Marx, 1981; Meichenbaum, 1972).

Parametric analysis of the effectiveness of various CBM treatment components suggests that the cognitive component may be more effective than the desensitization component (Kaplan, McCordick, & Twitchell, 1979). Moreover, some research suggests that treatments such as rational restructuring, which directly attack the individual's belief systems and internal dialogue without providing relaxation skills, are as effective as (Goldfried, Linehan, & Smith, 1978) or more effective than (Holroyd,

1976) single or combined cognitive-behavioral approaches. Overall, the component-analytic studies conducted thus far offer no firm conclusion regarding the relative effectiveness of cognitive restructuring and relaxation as coping strategies employed in CBM procedures.

Although CBT has been technically eclectic, successfully combining different therapeutic techniques, it is not a true integrative approach in the sense of developing a true conceptual synthesis among different orientations and procedures (Alford & Norcross, 1991). Huebner (1988) pointed out that CBM model is so broadly inclusive that it raises the question of whether there is indeed a single unifying theoretical rationale that ties together such diverse treatment components as relaxation training, cognitive reframing, expression of affect, and perspective taking. Perhaps, as suggested by Huebner (1988), CBM should be more realistically viewed as an eclectic metaframework that identifies issues or processes that seem to be involved in anxiety-based disorders and attempts to modify them.

Stress Inoculation Training (SIT)

Stress inoculation, a term often used interchangeably with CBM in the literature, is designed mainly to serve as a proactive form of therapy for people high at risk for test anxiety, and applied before test anxiety has emerged as a full-blown problem. In essence, it is a particular approach to CBM when used in a proactive manner. The notion of providing test-anxious clients with a defense they can use against test anxiety for preventive purposes is in some respects analogous to immunization against attitude change or medical inoculation against disease. The underlying principle is that a person's resistance to evaluative stress could be enhanced by exposure to a stimulus that is strong enough to arouse the defenses, but not so powerful as to overcome them (Meichenbaum, 1976). This technique is consistent with the notion that once an unpleasant experience, such as test anxiety, is incorporated as part of one's cognitive plan it becomes less stressful.

Stress inoculation training (SIT) primary prevention programs, designed to inoculate students to test anxiety and enhance coping methods and adjustment, are increasing in popularity and are commonly implemented in schools and university counseling centers in various parts of the world. Primary prevention of stress and anxiety is viewed by many practitioners as cost-effective and believed to reduce the need for future expenditures, which are high in terms of both human suffering and societal or economic consequences.

Zeidner et al. Exemplary SIT Program

I now briefly describe as an example an SIT primary prevention program that my coworkers and I have implemented among 5th and 6th grade elementary school students drawn from 12 classes in northern Israel (Zeidner et al., 1988). The treatment program assessed in this study was based primarily on Meichenbaum's (1977) cognitive modification model, implemented by those teachers whose home-room classes participated in the study. The training program rests on a number of basic assumptions derived from the tenets of psychological health education and primary prevention. First, we assumed that psychological education and provision of test coping skills in the classroom context are preferable to clinically oriented intervention by health professionals implemented only after test anxiety has emerged as a full-blown classroom problem. We further assumed that professional intervention after repeated student failure or acute manifestations of test-anxiety reactions can further heighten students' stress reactions. Therefore, it would be more effective to provide students with relevant coping skills as part of a primary prevention program before acute test-anxiety levels are established.

Following is a brief description of the five major phases of the SIT program implemented and evaluate by our research team.

Educational Presentation

The major aim of the first session was to provide the student with a conceptual framework for understanding the nature of test anxiety by illuminating the nature, origins, and antecedents of test anxiety. It began with self-introductions and the specification of program goals and procedures. The importance of confidentiality, being on time, and member participation was emphasized. A contract was drawn up between the agent of change (i.e., the teacher) and students concerning program duration, student attendance, confidentiality, and so on. Detailed information was given about the behavioral and emotional dynamics of test anxiety, and about a number of strategies for coping with it. Students were asked to generate several examples of anxiety-provoking situations. Through discussion and guided imagery, students were encouraged to reveal how they generally felt under test conditions and how they had typically handled evaluative stress and anxiety reactions in the past. The reported self-statements and preoccupations experienced by students during testing were analyzed, and positive versus negative self-statements were differentiated and discussed. Furthermore, perceptual, cognitive, and behavioral aspects of test anxiety were elaborated on and similarities and differences in student reactions to evaluative situations were pointed out. The legitimacy of feeling anxious during important exams was emphasized, and positive versus negative methods of coping with anxiety were distinguished. Last, students were encouraged to view test anxiety as a natural reaction to evaluative situations, one that they could readily learn to modify and control.

Training in Relaxation Techniques and in the Fundamentals of Rational Thinking

This session was mainly devoted to training students in the use of deep-breathing relaxation exercises as a major tension-reduction technique and as a means of controlling emotional reactions during exams. A relaxation technique of slow, deep breathing and procedures for practicing it were outlined for dealing with physical tension and emotional arousal in evaluative contexts. In addition, students were introduced to the topic of rational thinking and self-analysis. Particular emphasis was placed on "ABC" analysis (activating event, belief system, and emotional consequences) as a tool for countering irrational thoughts and beliefs. Thoughts, feelings, and behaviors that students associated with the examination context were then analyzed according to the ABC scheme. A number of examples of panicky self-instructions and self-talk were provided, as well as a representative list of examples of appropriate self-talk that tends to focus attention on the test rather than on oneself. Furthermore, techniques in self-monitoring of concentration and focusing of attention were demonstrated and practiced. Last, students practiced rational self-analysis of their reported negative thoughts occurring before, during, and after testing. Once each new skill was mastered in the training sessions, attention was devoted toward transferring the application of skills to the external environment.

Coping Imagery and Attentional Focusing Skills

The third session introduced students to coping imagery, which was then practiced in concern with other previously taught techniques (positive self-statements, relaxation exercises, etc.). With the aid of guided imagery technique, students reported their emotional reactions and thoughts under a variety of imagined anxiety-evoking situations (e.g., preparing for an exam, taking an exam, discussing examination results with classmates). Irrational thoughts underlying students' reported emotional reactions were identified and analyzed. In addition, students practiced the use of positive self-statements under imagined stressful test-taking conditions ("You're doing fine; just have to keep calm," "You'll do well on this exam if you take things one step at a time," "You have enough time," "Don't worry, you've done this before," "You're off on a good start, keep cool").

Time Management and Work Schemes

This session focused on the management of time both after and during the exam period. Several general considerations regarding behaving in a manner that fosters a sense of control over the preparation and completion of tests were discussed. Thus students were instructed in how to carefully plan and space their exam study sessions and how to prepare for exams. Students were also introduced to various test-taking strategies (e.g., quick overview of exam items; careful reading of questions and options; tackling easy problems first and leaving more difficult problems for the end; helpful cues in identifying the correct answer). Last, students were provided with further practice in deep-breathing exercises, positive self-thinking, coping imagery, and the implementation of these techniques in various imagined test situations (exceptionally difficult tests, insufficient time to complete exam, etc.).

Rehearsal and Strengthening of Coping Skills

The fifth and final session was aimed at rehearsing and fortifying the coping skills taught in previous sessions, primarily with the aid of guided coping imagery. Students were given instruction in using the coping techniques in future test situations. In conclusion, students summarized what they thought they had learned during the course of the training program.

Treatment Effectiveness

Evaluation of the effects of this proactive SIT program points to its effectiveness in meaningfully enhancing students' cognitive performance in test situations, with student performance meaningfully improving on three cognitive measures. However, the data suggest that the training program was not effective in reducing students' self-reported test anxiety (Zeidner et al., 1988). We suggested that the SIT program taught students some important test-taking skills (e.g., focusing attention and controlling irrelevant thoughts; taking things one step at a time; efficient use of time resources; working schemes) that may have improved performance without having a substantial impact on test anxiety. Thus the cognitive training program may have trained students to become more proficient in organizing, processing, and retrieving information during the exam; performance increments under experimental conditions had little to do with test anxiety.

Cognitive-Skill Deficit Approach: Study-Skills Training (SST)

Recent thinking and research suggests that high-test-anxious students with poor study and test-taking skills would probably benefit most from study-skills training (SST) interventions intended to improve their study and test-taking habits and skills. SST is based on a cognitive-deficit or deficiency model. Whereas SST is directed toward improving a variety of cognitive activities that affect the organization, processing, and retrieval of information (e.g., study habits and test-taking skills), training in study skills does not directly address the specific cognitive concomitants of test anxiety (Spielberger & Vagg, 1987, 1995a; Vagg & Spielberger, 1995). Instead, it is designed to augment other cognitive interventions.

Specific Therapeutic Techniques

The curricular elements of current study-skills training programs typically focus on the following two related treatment components, briefly described below:

(a) *Study-skills training* is designed to teach students how to study, in general, and prepare for tests, in particular. Study-skills training procedures aim at helping students to structure their study time more efficiently and become more proficient in encoding, organizing, processing, and storing information so that it can be retried more effectively and communicated clearly under test conditions. Common elements in study-skills counseling programs include study planning and time management techniques, monitoring study behaviors, enhancing reading and summarizing skills, acquiring techniques useful for studying for the exam, and learning how to use response management techniques (Allen, 1973).

(b) *Test-taking-skills training* is designed to impart techniques that help students comprehend test questions and follow test instructions so that the appropriate information can be retrieved, organized, and clearly communicated (Spielberger & Vagg, 1987). Among the specific techniques for strengthening "test-wiseness" are surveying the length of a test, seeing if certain sections count more or require more time than others, answering only one item at a time, and marking harder items in order to return to them later (Kirkland & Hollandsworth, 1980). Objective and essay items are often dealt with separately (Bajtelsmit, 1977).

Research by Benjamin et al. (1981) suggests that an emphasis on understanding deeper levels of processing of material, rather than rote memorization, should be particularly beneficial for high-test-anxious students. More adequate learning and processing of the material directly enables students to gain better knowledge of the study material and indirectly aborts irrelevant worry responses stemming from their anxiety about the fact they have not yet learned material. Also, by altering the motivational/attitudinal set under which students study, uninspired preparation may give way to more effective strategies of study (Covington, 1992).

To give the reader a flavor of current study-skills training programs, I briefly survey a program implemented by Osterhouse (1972), based on Robinson's (1979) popular SQ3R (= Survey, Question, Read, Recite, Review) method for effective study. The program is designed to help students identify what they are expected to study and assimilate, comprehend these ideas more rapidly, fix these ideas in their memory, and review efficiently for exams. SQ3R was practiced using a chapter from the course text. Practically, the program involves teaching students to:

- *Survey* or skim the study material at hand by reading the titles, headings, charts, illustrations, and any other important introductory or summary materials, in order to develop better expectations of the author's goals and get a general idea of what the reading material is about;
- *Question* themselves by identifying information they want (or are likely to get) from reading the passage, raising pertinent questions while reacting to the materials;
- *Read* the material reflectively, focusing on comprehension of the main ideas of the passage and keeping in mind the author's goals and text structure;
- *Recite* the material, rephrasing the main ideas in their own words;
- *Review* major points and concepts, recalling the linkages among key themes, and concentrating on passages not yet fixed in mind.

In addition, students were taught time management skills involving the modification of proposed time schedules and specific behavioral steps aimed at reducing interruptions and meeting more adequately course-related demands upon their time. Students also practiced prediction of exam questions that might be asked about the kind of material exemplified.

A number of study-skills training programs described in the literature (e.g., Dendato & Diener, 1986; Gonzalez, 1995; Naveh-Benjamin, 1991) also contain study-effectiveness training and time management.

Program Effectiveness

Reviews of the literature suggest that SST, when used alone, is rather ineffective in either reducing anxiety or improving academic performance (e.g., Altmaier & Woodward, 1981; Hembree, 1988; Osterhouse, 1972). However, the combination of study-skills training and behavioral procedures, such as systematic desensitization, has been shown to be effective and superior to either component alone in reducing anxiety (Allen, 1971; Hembree, 1988; Lent & Russell, 1978; Mitchell, Hall, & Piatkowska, 1975; Mitchell & Ng, 1972). Hembree's (1988) integrative review of the literature reported that the highest effect sizes for anxiety reduction were observed when study skills were combined with behavioral therapies. Thus, when SST is combined with behavioral or cognitive-behavioral procedures, test anxiety is reduced anywhere from about .8 to 1.2 standard deviations in high school and precollege student populations, respectively.

With respect to test *performance*, Hembree's meta-analysis shows that SST alone increased test scores by about .39 standard deviations in postsecondary populations; in combination with systematic desensitization, performance was increased by close to twice as much (about three quarters of a standard deviation). Testwiseness training alone increased test scores by only about a quarter of a standard deviation in school-aged and postsecondary populations combined. Furthermore, research suggests that although study counseling alone may be effective in improving the academic performance of students with low to moderate test anxiety, there is little evidence that study counseling alone can improve the grade point average for high-test-anxious students (Gonzalez, 1995).

The synergistic effect of combining study-skills training and behavioral therapies may be due to the superiority of a two-pronged attack on the dual but interrelated problems of deficient preparation and test anxiety. Study-skills training may thus be an important component of any program of treatment for test anxiety (Dendato & Diener, 1986). Noted, however, that while study-skills training can improve study habits, better study habits do not always result in higher grades, because time is required for the improved study skills to influence academic performance. Thus it is unrealistic to expect students to benefit from counseling immediately after such training. Furthermore, such training is likely to add little to anxiety reduction for students with effective study skills (Naveh-Benjamin, 1991).

Evaluation of Cognitive Treatments

Reviews of the literature (Hembree, 1988; Wine, 1980) conclude that cognitively based treatment strategies are more powerful than direct behavioral therapies in effecting test anxiety and performance changes. Hembree's meta-analytic data suggest that the combined effects of cognitive-behavioral treatments (attentional training, cognitive-behavioral modification, stress inoculation training, etc.) in the reduction of test anxiety were about half a standard deviation ($d = -.53$) for elementary and high school students. The mean reduction for college students was close to a standard deviation ($d = -.87$). Cognitive therapies were shown to have a slightly larger effect on the Worry component of test anxiety than behavioral therapies (effects size of $-.82$ vs. $-.65$). Cognitive therapies also had a greater effect on the Emotional component of test anxiety than behavioral therapies (effects size of $-.73$ vs. $-.60$). Similarly, cognitive-behavioral treatments (and study counseling) produced a significant positive effect for grade point average.

Basic Conceptual and Methodological Issues in Test Anxiety Intervention Research

I conclude this chapter by first presenting a number of major considerations in test anxiety intervention, and then move on to present a number of methodological problems in planning and implementing test anxiety interventions.

Major Considerations in Therapeutic Intervention

I now present a number of important considerations that should be held in mind by both researchers and practitioners when developing, implementing, or evaluating test anxiety intervention programs.

Meeting Preconditions for Therapeutic Effectiveness

In order for a test anxiety intervention program to work, a number of preconditions need to be met. First, test-anxious individuals ought to possess certain relevant skills in their behavioral repertoire (e.g., problem-solving, relaxation, study/test-taking skills) to apply under appropriate evaluative circumstances. Second, test-anxious clients must be sufficiently motivated to deal directly with evaluative situations and have the wherewithal to implement efficiently the coping skills they have at their disposal. Third, test-anxious persons must be provided with an adequate amount of practice and experience in applying various coping skills in true-to-life evaluative situations in order to insure transfer of therapy from the treatment environment to the real world.

Performing Careful Diagnosis of Client's Problem

In order to tailor treatment programs to meet the specific needs and problems of the client, a logical first step is a careful diagnostic assessment and analysis of the nature of the test-anxious person's affective and cognitive problem(s). For some test-anxious subjects, provision of skills training may be the treatment of choice, whereas for others it would involve building up of self-confidence in a particular content area (e.g., math), or teaching relaxation skills. Information about the following aspects of the client's problem might be particularly useful (Suinn, 1990):

- Nature of the problem as experienced and defined by the test-anxious client
- Perceived severity and generality of the problem
- Duration and extent of test anxiety
- Perceived origins of test anxiety
- Situation-specific factors which intensify or alleviate anxiety reactions
- Specific consequences of test anxiety for the client
- Suggested changes the client views as potentially helpful

A careful diagnostic assessment may suggest factors other than test anxiety proper that underlie a subject's heightened emotional reactions in test situations. For example, a student may become anxious in test situations because she is resentful of having to pursue a career chosen for her by her parents. In this case, that person needs to be made aware of her own wishes and must first resolve the conflict with her parents. Directly treating that student for test anxiety would not solve the problem (Richardson et al., 1977).

Adjusting Treatment to the Needs of Particular Types of Test-Anxious Person

Interventions and therapeutic techniques would be most effective if they could be adjusted to suit the needs of different types of test-anxious persons (see Chapter 2). Because there are different types of high-test-anxious individuals, each characterized by different problems and concerns (e.g., failure in meeting personal or social expectations, low feelings of self-efficacy and failure acceptance, poor study skills, etc.), no single treatment program would be expected to be equally effective across the board. Thus, for some highly perfectionistic test-anxious individuals therapy may focus on lowering socially prescribed performance expectations, whereas for other "failure-accepting" students therapy may consist of raising performance expectancies and enhancing perceived self-efficacy. Students high in test anxiety with sound study or test-taking skills should profit from treatment focusing on test anxiety reduction. By contrast, students with defective study or test-taking skills and high test anxiety would profit from a combined intervention program to improve their skills as well as decrease test anxiety (Naveh-Benjamin et al., 1987; Naveh-Benjamin, 1991).

Basing Treatment on the Broader Diagnostic Picture and Specific Goals of Therapy

The choice of which therapy to use will be influenced not only by the diagnosis of the specific nature of the client's problem and type of test anxiety, but by the broader diagnostic picture, the immediate and long-term goals of treatment, and the therapeutic orientation adopted. For example, although relaxation may not increase the performance of test-anxious students with study-skill deficits, it may be prescribed by the therapist in order to help the student achieve the immediate goal of achieving control over test anxiety—as a first step toward academic problem-solving (Mitchell & Ng, 1972). Thus, once the anxiety that interferes with learning new study skills is removed, the next step would then be training the student in efficient study skills. Furthermore, there are different ways that a therapist may view a test-anxious client's problem (distorted thinking styles, poor problem-solving skills, etc.) and each of these views may give rise to different treatment procedures (Kendall, 1993; Meichenbaum & Genest, 1977).

Important Role of Self-Efficacy in Affecting Outcomes

According to Bandura's social-cognitive conceptualizations (1986, 1988), it is mastery experienced through personal agency that is the vehicle of change in test anxiety intervention programs. Test-anxious students can be helped to adopt efficient test-taking attitudes and skills by empowering them with the self-regulatory skills and self-beliefs of efficacy for exercising personal control over their motivations. The greatest benefits that psychological treatment can provide the test-anxious client are not specific remedies, but rather tools with which to cope effectively with whatever future evaluative situations might arise. To the extent that treatment equips test-anxious people to exercise control over tests and other evaluative events in their lives, they are less vulnerable to evaluative distress and test anxiety.

Consideration of Individual Differences

Before implementing a particular treatment one needs to determine to what extent the treatment may interact with particular client characteristics. For example, some interventions may reduce anxiety or successfully increase the performance of high-test-anxious individuals, only to have a negative effect on the anxiety performance of others who are low in test anxiety (I. G. Sarason, Sarason, & Pierce, 1995). Another case in point: Whereas some people might considerably benefit from relaxation training, experiencing a substantial decrease in anxiety, some have difficulty in acquiring relaxation skills and benefit little from relaxation training. Some clients may even experience relaxation-induced anxiety during relaxation training (Heide & Borkovec, 1984)!

Interaction among Components of Test Anxiety

A basic consideration is that test anxiety is more than a combination of physiological arousal, negative self-preoccupation, a deficit in stress-related coping skills, and poor study habits. It is the complex interaction among these diverse components that seems to define test anxiety (Meichenbaum & Butler, 1980). Because the cognitive, affective, and behavioral components of test anxiety interweave in contributing to the problem of test anxiety and its treatment, it is predicted that an induced change in one system would generally be followed by a change in the others (Meichenbaum & Butler, 1980). Thus, therapeutic approaches which emphasize cognition often extend to the emotional life, too, and vice versa. For example, it is likely that emotion-focused training (e.g., progressive relaxation) may make the client less anxious and result in a decrease in anxiety-focused, task-irrelevant ideation. By the same token, some forms of cognitive therapy may provide test-anxious subjects with an increased sense of perceived control, which might spill over into the emotional domain and result in lower emotional arousal in a test situation.

Addressing Multiple Modalities and Loci of Therapeutic Impact

One important consideration is that the various components of test anxiety must be dealt with if the anxiety experienced in test situations is to be reduced and improved grades are to occur as a result of treatment (Vagg & Papsdorf, 1995). It is important to have interventions sufficiently complex to deal with the major facets (cognitive, affective, behavioral) of the test anxiety experience. Indeed, a treatment would be expected to be most effective if it impacts upon the entire range of components and chain of events leading to anxious manifestations in evaluative situations (arousal, worry, meaning system, internal dialogue, behavioral acts, etc.), rather than focusing on only one aspect of the process (Meichenbaum & Butler, 1980).

Methodological Problems and Limitations

The general goal of test anxiety intervention program evaluation research is to demonstrate that a particular treatment is effective in reducing test anxiety or improving cognitive performance in target populations. This is achieved in part by demonstrating the efficacy of theoretically relevant treatments to be greater than improvement produced by placebo manipulations or nonspecific pseudotreatments (Allen et al., 1980). In actuality, this proves to be neither a simple nor straightforward task.

A number of desiderata for intervention studies have been enumerated by researchers in the field (Allen, 1971; Allen et al., 1980). Accordingly, well-controlled studies should meet the following basic criteria:

- Precise specification of the rationale, contents, and therapeutic procedures used in each type of intervention program.
- Adequate randomization of subjects to treatment and control groups.
- Use of appropriate nontreated control groups (e.g., placebo, waiting list control, pseudotreatment).
- Specification of the attributes of the therapist as independent factors in promoting change, and complete factorial crossing of therapist and treatment.
- Triangulation of treatment effects through multiple methods of measurement.
- Freedom from confounded format–treatment interactions.
- Appropriate statistical analyses.
- Designation of constant number of sessions.

Many treatment programs fall short in meeting the above criteria.

I now discuss some of the major problems that plague the design, measurement, and analysis of test anxiety intervention studies. These methodological limitations should be held in mind in evaluating current intervention research.

Measurement and Assessment Issues

Assessment of Multivariate Treatment Outcomes.   Traditionally, most test anxiety interventions have determined the effectiveness of treatment programs based on a *single* method of measurement and have failed to use multiple measures or converging methods of measurement (e.g., self-report and performance; Allen et al., 1980). Current thinking suggests that sole reliance on a single method of measurement, even if multiple instruments are used within that method, provides less compelling support for the efficacy of a therapeutic intervention than does the use of multiple methods (Allen et al., 1980). A major justification for the use of multiple methods of measurement is that it permits the documentation of specific treatment effects with greater precision than would otherwise be possible. A case in point: In assessing the effects of systematic desensitization and study counseling, a number of studies employed measures of both anxiety and study skills, thus providing a precise partitioning of the hypothesized roles of treatment effects and permitting the assessment of the effects of both interventions on measures that have different relevance for each (Mitchell & Ng, 1972; Mitchell, Hall, & Piatkowska, 1975).

Follow-up Measurements.   Measurements of the maintenance of treatment effects at various follow-up periods have been rare in the test anxiety literature (Allen et al., 1980). However, in evaluating outcome studies, one needs to determine whether or not treatment had enough time to be reflected in criterion measures. Few of the intervention studies in the test anxiety literature had any kind of long-term follow-up, so it is impossible to judge whether treatment effects lasted once the treatment was completed. Often, long-term effects are more marked and important than short-term effects.

Sampling and Design Issues

Test anxiety intervention research poses a number of serious threats to both the internal and external validity of commonly used designs. Nonspecific treatment changes may powerfully affect therapeutic outcome so that the possibility of reductions in anxiety may be due to nonspecific treatment effects (Holroyd, 1976). Many studies are shown to be deficient in experimental design and in providing safeguards against threats to internal validity (see Chapter 4).

Use of Self-Selected Samples. Some researchers have questioned to what extent typical samples participating in intervention studies are representative of the target population of high-test-anxious individuals. Designs typically use nonclinical groups of college or school-aged students, with no indication of the degree of severity of their test anxiety based on preassessment scores. Few studies, for example, involve subjects who were referred to counseling for clinical services (King & Ollendick, 1989).

A further threat to the external validity of intervention designs relates to the characteristics of the self-selected student volunteer groups composing treatment and control group subjects, who may not be representative of the total population. Volunteers often constitute a small and nonrepresentative percentage of the undergraduate student pool sampled (between 3% and 5%; Allen, 1971), are often reported to be significantly more anxious and motivated than the "average" undergraduate (Allen, 1972; Allen et al., 1980), and are often permitted to choose their own treatment, thus destroying the equivalence of the experimental and control groups. Allen and his coworkers (Allen et al., 1980) reported randomization inadequacies in only about a quarter of the intervention studies they reviewed.

Small Sample Size. Most test anxiety intervention studies have included a small number of participants in both experimental and control groups, with groups often amounting to as few as 8–10 subjects per group (e.g., Meichenbaum, 1972). Clearly, the small sample size limits the generalizability of the results and lowers the power of studies to detect significant effects. Thus, the smaller the number of participants, the greater the likelihood of incorrectly concluding that there are no differences between groups, when in fact there are (Type II error).

Subject Mortality. One problem affecting the internal validity of intervention research is the high *dropout rate* of experimental subjects often observed in these studies. In studies with excessive subject attrition, mean improvement in affective or cognitive outcomes in the experimental relative to the control group could be due to the fact that those students who fail to improve are those most likely to drop out of treatment (Gonzalez, 1995). Allen et al. (1980) reviewed 49 investigations of therapeutic manipulations aimed at alleviating test anxiety in college students. The percentage of dropouts ranged from 0% to 28% with attrition averaging 7.5% (Allen, 1972).

Inadequate Control Group. A review of the literature (Tryon, 1980) suggests that the failure to include a proper control (e.g., wait list, placebo) was the single most frequent threat to internal validity in test anxiety treatment interventions. The importance of including an attention-placebo condition in test anxiety outcome research is highlighted by the repeated observation that mere exposure to therapeutic procedures, even when nonfunctional in nature, often results in symptom reduction. Holroyd (1976) reported that each of the treatment groups and pseudotherapy controls in his study reported lower levels of test anxiety and obtained higher grades than waiting-list control subjects. Thus, "treated" subjects showed substantial improvements regardless of the treatment they received. This may be due to nonspecific treatment elements such as contact with interested therapist and exposure to an impressive treatment ritual. Thus, the inclusion of a placebo procedure is necessary if the efficacy of a treatment procedure is to be demonstrated over nonspecific factors. Failure to include a placebo control group may result in outcome improvement as a result of heightened subject expectancy (Allen, 1971, 1972).

Failure in Crossing Therapists with Treatments. A substantial percentage of investigations that employed multiple therapists was possibly threatened by failure to either factorially cross therapists with treatments or assess possible differences when a factorial crossing is made (Allen et al., 1980). Interpretation of differential between-group outcome is open to any alternative that systematically covaries with treatment (e.g., fatigue, enthusiasm, expectations, etc.) when a single therapist is employed (Allen et al., 1980). Individual therapists may exhibit subtle differences in administering relatively standardized techniques, such as desensitization. Failure to use multiple therapists or to cross treatments and therapists factorially may result in the inappropriate attribution of therapeutic benefits to the treatment(s) under study (Allen, 1972).

Summary

This chapter presented a number of contemporary test anxiety intervention programs with a strong cognitive, cognitive-behavioral, or cognitive-skill orientation. These techniques represent the best in modern cognitive approaches to test anxiety intervention. Each is premised on specific theoretical formulations as well as therapeutic change principles guiding the practitioner's use of the technique (Beck,

1993). Furthermore, each technique has been subjected to systematic research with respect to its effectiveness in the test anxiety domain.

Cognitive attentional training, the first intervention approach presented, provides specific training in the redirection of attention to task-focused thinking and emphasizes the inhibition of task-irrelevant thinking and nonproductive worry. The cognitive attentional approach relates performance decrements to the diversion of attention to self-focused thinking, coupled with the cognitive overload caused by the Worry component of anxiety. By redirecting attention to the task and reducing worry and task-irrelevant thinking, cognitive resources are freed, and when redirected to the task, performance is improved. The beneficial effects of attentional instruction on the anxiety and performance of high-test-anxious students are supported by some empirical research.

Cognitive restructuring intervention, the second cognitive approach discussed, is based on the premise that anxiety emanates from irrational thinking patterns surrounding evaluative situations. Test-anxious individuals are taught how to recognize, vigorously challenge, question, and dispute their irrational beliefs, and replace their maladaptive internal dialogue with more rational structures and beliefs. Both cognitive-attentional training and cognitive restructuring interventions focus their attention on modifying task-irrelevant thoughts and dysfunctional worries of test-anxious subjects, and pay relatively little attention to the direct amelioration of the emotional component of test anxiety. However, in contrast to cognitive-attentional training, cognitive restructuring intervention presumably maintains that anxiety negatively impacts upon performance through the mediation of negative emotional reactions. Presumably, by modifying irrational beliefs and schemata, negative emotional reactions will be reduced and performance improved. However, research indicates that whereas cognitive restructuring reduces anxiety, there is no concomitant improvement in performance.

Cognitive-behavioral modification was presented as a multifaceted program merging both cognitively focused and emotionality focused techniques (as well as skills training in many cases), thus offering the test-anxious client the best of many worlds, so to speak. This multimodal treatment attempts to deal with the multiple manifestations of test anxiety, including negative motivational or affective tendencies, irrational though patterns, and skills deficits, and emphasizes the application and transferring of acquired coping skills to *in vivo* test situations. "Multimodal" treatment packages, such as cognitive-behavior modification, are most likely to be effective by their support for the inclusion of multiple domains related to test anxiety.

Study-skills training, the last approach discussed, focuses on improving students' study and test-taking skills. Study-skills training differs from the other cognitive therapies discussed in that it does not directly focus on modifying the cognitive component of anxiety, but rather centers on improving students' study and test-taking skills. Presumably, improvement of these skills should have a direct impact upon performance though improved mastery of the test material, and also indirectly impact performance through the reduction of worry surrounding inadequate preparation for

the exam. These programs have been successful mainly in enhancing the test performance of high-test-anxious subjects with poor study skills. It is now apparent that
when test-anxious subjects suffer from serious study-skills or test-taking deficits,
alternative forms of treatment would not be expected to lead to performance gains,
inasmuch as the behavioral deficit still exists. At the same time, skills training alone
may lead a person to performance gains, but it may still may leave the person
distressed. Thus, it would take study-skills training together with other forms of
cognitive-behavior therapy for anxiety, in order to achieve the outcome of eliminating distress and increasing test performance.

It is now readily apparent that test anxiety intervention should be based on a
careful theoretical analysis of the nature of test anxiety and its key components and
manifestations (Spielberger & Vagg, 1995a). Traditionally, however, test anxiety
treatment studies have mainly evolved from interest in specific behavioral treatment
techniques rather than from an analysis of the nature and effects of test anxiety
(Spielberger et al., 1976; Wine, 1971a). Indeed, most investigators who have applied
behavioral methodology to the reduction of test anxiety have generally given little
attention to relating the treatment process to important theoretical conceptions. The
current diversity of test anxiety treatments, while supplying the clinician with a rich
variety of treatment options to choose from in rendering services, also reflects a state
of uncertainty marked by the lack of consensus regarding the most effective method
for treating test anxiety.

Epilogue

Overview

This book set out to provide a comprehensive state-of-the-art review of test anxiety theory, research, and applications. As is evident throughout the chapters in this book, contemporary research has made important strides in mapping out the test anxiety domain. Some of the more notable recent advances in test anxiety research include the following:

- More refined conceptualizations of the various elements in the test anxiety process and delineation of the specific stages in the test anxiety process as it unfolds over time.
- Improved differentiation and assessment of distinctive components of test anxiety experience.
- Development of new measurement instruments through state-of-the-art psychometric procedures, and investigation of their psychometric properties and dimensionality via sophisticated multivariate statistical methods.
- Cross-cultural adaptation and validation of existing scales and widespread cross-cultural test anxiety research.
- Explicating the role of cognitive appraisals in the stress and coping process.
- Uncovering the distal developmental antecedents of test anxiety as well as some of the more proximal contextual and subjective determinants of anxiety in evaluative situations.
- Exploration of mediating and moderating effects in the anxiety–performance relationship.
- Identification of coping resources and strategies in coping with test situations.
- Specifying optimal learning and evaluative contexts for test-anxious individuals.
- Evaluating the effectiveness of emotion-focused, cognitive-focused, and skills-focused interventions and treatments, and their specific components.
- Meta-analytic investigations of various facets of the empirical literature.

Directions for Future Research

There is still much uncharted territory in the test anxiety domain that needs to be explored and more extensively mapped out by future research. I conclude by high-lighting a number of these important areas, pointing out needed directions for future research.

Refining Conceptual Models

Although a variety of models and theoretical perspectives have been proposed over the past 50 years or so to cover various facets of test anxiety, no single unifying model is able to account for the multiple phenomena (antecedents, phenomenology, consequences) and the many complex empirical findings. Thus, future test anxiety research would benefit from efforts directed at theory construction. This may be achieved through broader integrative theoretical formulations, amalgamation of exis-ting theoretical perspectives, identification of complementary approaches and com-mon conceptual elements across theories, and so on. A major goal for future research would be to integrate current perspectives into a comprehensive process-oriented transactional model in order to unravel the complex nexus of interdependencies and cause and effect relationships between test anxiety and related cognitive and affective variables.

Developing Useful Taxonomies

Clearly, test anxiety is not a unified phenomenon, and a variety of different types of test-anxious students have been identified. Development of a comprehensive taxonomy of test-anxious students (including the profiles of both high- and low-test-anxious persons) would be useful for theoretical, research, and intervention purposes. Furthermore, despite earnest efforts by practitioners to individualize treatments to the particular needs and problems of test-anxious students, we still do not have clear evidence to indicate which of the various intervention approaches is most effective for particular types of test-anxious students or for treating different manifestations of test anxiety. This stems in part from the absence of an established typology of test-anxious persons.

Furthering Our Understanding of the Test Anxiety Experience and Its Long-Term Outcomes

Further research is needed in order to map out the response systems of test anxiety and how they interact. We also need to find better ways to measure various cognitive, affective, and behavioral expressions of test anxiety. In addition, we need to know more about the specific effects of chronic evaluative stress on the physical and psychological health of student populations. Thus, more research is needed to understand better the effects of evaluative stress on maladaptive types of coping (alcoholic consumption, drug use, etc.), various forms of pathology (suicide, depression, etc.), and somatic illness in high-risk populations.

Uncovering the Developmental Origins of Test Anxiety

We need to know more about the antecedents and developmental origins of test anxiety in our efforts to understand better how children are socialized to different levels of test anxiety. First, future research would benefit from assessing the relative contribution of genetic versus environmental factors in the development of test anxiety. This could be achieved in part through the application of behavioral-genetic research paradigms (e.g., twin and adoption studies) and the use of appropriate statistical techniques in analyzing the data in order to tease out the main and interactive effects of heredity and environment as factors in the development of test anxiety.

Furthermore, researchers need to pay more attention to the delineation, specification, and testing of the causal mechanisms by which posited dimensions of family climate, the dynamics of parent–child interactions (or relations between the child and members of the extended family, including peers and grandparents), or family process risk factors impact upon test anxiety. Since few studies directly assess the validity of specific models of primary socialization practices as they impact upon the development of children's test anxiety, critical tests of competing developmental models are urgently needed. Finally, future research needs to identify both the developmental antecedents of individual vulnerability to evaluative situations as well as the development of resiliency to stress and the ability to cope adaptively with ego-threatening test contexts. We need to understand better why some individuals survive the evaluative atmosphere and aversive personal experience of the home and school setting with aplomb, and why others succumb to it.

Assessing the Effects of School Environment on Test Anxiety

Further research is needed on the specific kinds of school-related encounters that shape children's anxiety reactions and avoidance behaviors in evaluative situations. Research would benefit from more large-scale systematic and controlled studies that would pinpoint the effects of a wide array of classroom and school environmental variables (e.g., group climate and norms, evaluation and grading practices, tracking and streaming, transitional periods, teacher characteristics, teacher–student interactions, peer pressures and expectations, etc.) on the development of test anxiety in general and different anxiety components (e.g., Worry vs. Emotionality), in particular. Additional research is also needed on the relationship between a child's failure-induced anxiety experiences in the preschool and elementary school years and her or his anxiety and cognitive performance later on in life (e.g., high school, college, and on-the-job performance).

Determining the Prevalence of Test Anxiety and Mapping Out Individual Differences in the Test Anxiety Experience

In order to determine the extent and severity of test anxiety in various educational, social, and cultural settings, large-scale epidemiological surveys of test anxiety in the population are urgently needed. Most prior studies attempted to extrapolate prevalence rates of test anxiety from incidental samples that may or may not have been representative of their target populations. Under the assumption that different people may experience test anxiety in different ways, additional research needs to examine individual differences in a variety of areas, such as the experience of test anxiety in various response channels (cognitive, affective, behavioral), the appraisal process (primary and secondary), coping behaviors (defensive systems, instrumental and palliative modes), and adaptational outcomes (cognitive, affective, health, etc.). We also need to understand the different manifestations of test anxiety in various age, gender, and cultural groups. Much of what we know about the nature and prevalence of test anxiety is based on research on college students and school-aged children and youth. We know very little about test anxiety in adults who are in academic or occupational situations requiring testing, the aged, or special groups (the gifted, visually or hearing impaired, etc.).

Although there has been a remarkable increase in cross-cultural research over the years, much of this research is purely descriptive. No systematic analysis has been conducted to identify the specific cultural parameters that impact upon test anxiety, and a cross-cultural theory of test anxiety is yet to be developed. Also, there has been little systematic research on the causal mechanisms through which culture may impact upon different phases of the stress and coping process in evaluative contexts. Such analyses appear to be crucial for developing more focused hypotheses for future cross-cultural research.

Modeling the Test Anxiety–Performance Relationship

Additional work is needed in order to specify more clearly the nature of the test anxiety–performance relationship. More research is needed detailing how test anxiety influences specific cognitive structures and processes, including scanning behavior, breadth of stimulus utilization, various facets of judgment and decision making, long-term memory, inductive and deductive processes, ideation, and creative behavior. We also need to determine who experiences the facilitative effects of anxiety and under what conditions, as well as identify those test-anxious students who respond to high levels of evaluative stress with greater effort and perseverance rather than feelings of helplessness, avoidance, and depressed cognitive performance. Traditionally, research has tended to use linear causal models in exploring the link between test anxiety and cognitive performance. Future research would profit from employing process models in order to capture better the dynamic and cyclical nature of the anxiety–performance relationship. In addition, longitudinal and process-oriented research on the anxiety–performance relationship is urgently needed.

Determining the Relationship between Test Anxiety, Coping, and Adaptive Outcomes

Further research is needed to clarify how coping strategies resolve exam-related problems, relieve emotional distress, and prevent future difficulties in evaluative situations. Future research should shed light on how long a time lag there should be between assessment of coping with tests and adaptive outcomes, how coping in test situations differs from coping in other situations, whether it makes sense to talk about coping when students are really responding to "challenges" as opposed to "threats," and what is the ordinary balance of helpful coping to harmful coping with exams.

Improving Test Anxiety Interventions and Intervention Research

Most available studies of test anxiety intervention programs may be considered "outcome studies." These studies are designed to assess the effectiveness of particular techniques or specific treatment components, but have failed to shed light on the theoretical mechanisms underlying the intervention. More attention needs to be directed in future research toward identifying the specific theoretical mechanisms that mediate the effects of treatment on the emotional, cognitive, and behavioral components of test anxiety. Research needs to assess differential types of treatment designed to assure maximum congruence between the test-anxious client and a particular form of intervention. Thus, future research needs to provide a better answer to the question: What treatment works best, for whom, and under what conditions? Also, we need research to promote the development of interventions that would more reliably reduce test anxiety as well as improve academic performance. Current methods are more successful in modifying the former than the latter.

Improving Research Designs and Analyses

There is a strong need for large-scale and systematic research relating to various facets of test anxiety, based on multiple observations of various target groups, at various time points, and in various contexts and cultural settings. Future research would benefit from application of sophisticated research designs—longitudinal and multivariate experimental designs in particular. Data analysis would also benefit from application of state-of-the-art multivariate procedures, including nonrecursive causal modeling and multidimensional scaling techniques. Future conceptualizations and research should make more allowances for complex associations among variables, including reciprocal relationships and feedback loops as well as nonlinear relationships and interactions. More sophisticated designs would certainly help in assessing the complex interactions between objective characteristics of the evaluative situation, personal variables, the expression of anxiety and related emotions, coping responses, and adaptive outcomes.

Answers to these and related questions may advance our understanding of test anxiety and assist us in enhancing the ability of examinees to cope adaptively with test and evaluative situations.

References

Abella, R., & Heslin, R. (1989). Appraisal processes, coping, and the regulation of stress-related emotions in a college examination. *Basic and Applied Social Psychology, 10,* 311–327.

Ahlawat, K. S. (1989a). Family environmental determinants of test anxiety in Jordanian high school students. In R. Schwarzer, H. M. Van der Ploeg, & C. D. Spielberger (Eds.), *Advances in test anxiety research* (Vol. 6, pp. 203–213). Lisse, The Netherlands: Swets & Zeitlinger.

Ahlawat, K. S. (1989b). Psychometric properties of the Yarmouk Test Anxiety Inventory. In R. Schwarzer, H. M. Van der Ploeg, & C. D. Spielberger (Eds.), *Advances in test anxiety research* (Vol. 6, pp. 263–279). Lisse, The Netherlands: Swets & Zeitlinger.

Aldwin, C. M., & Revenson, T. T. (1987). Does coping help? A reexamination of the relation between coping and mental health. *Journal of Personality and Social Psychology, 53,* 337–348.

Alford, B. A., & Norcross, J. C. (1991). Cognitive therapy as integrative therapy. *Journal of Psychotherapy Integration, 1,* 175–189.

Allen, G. J. (1971). Effectiveness of study counseling and desensitization in alleviating test anxiety in college students. *Journal of Abnormal Psychology, 77,* 282–289.

Allen, G. J. (1972). The behavioral treatment of test anxiety: Recent research and future trends. *Behavior Therapy, 3,* 253–262.

Allen, G. J. (1973). Treatment of test anxiety by group-administered and self-administered relaxation and study counseling. *Behavior Therapy, 4,* 349–360.

Allen, G. J. (1980). The behavioral treatment of test anxiety: Therapeutic innovations and emerging conceptual challenges. In M. Herson, R. Eisler, & P. Miller (Eds.), *Progress in behavior modification* (pp. 81–123). New York: Academic Press.

Allen, G. J., Elias, M. J., & Zlotlow, S. F. (1980). Behavioral interventions for alleviating test anxiety: A methodological overview of current therapeutic practices. In I. G. Sarason (Ed.), *Test anxiety: Theory, research and applications* (pp. 155–185). Hillsdale, NJ: Erlbaum.

Allen, G. J., Giat, L., & Cherney, R. J. (1974). Locus of control, test anxiety, and student performance in a personalized instruction course. *Journal of Educational Psychology, 66,* 968–973.

Alpert, R., & Haber, R. N. (1960). Anxiety in academic achievement situations. *Journal of Abnormal and Social Psychology, 61,* 207–215.

Altmaier, E. M., & Woodward, M. (1981). Group vicarious desensitization of test anxiety. *Journal of Counseling Psychology, 28,* 467–469.

Anastasi, A. (1986). Evolving concepts of test validation. *Annual Review of Psychology, 37,* 1–15.

Anderson, S. B., & Sauser Jr., W. I. (1995). Measurement of test anxiety: An overview. In C. D. Spielberger & P. R. Vagg (Eds.), *Test anxiety: Theory, assessment, and treatment* (pp. 15–34). Washington, DC: Taylor & Francis.

Anton, W. D., & Lillibridge, E. M. (1995). Case studies of test-anxious students. In C. D. Spielberger & P.

R. Vagg (Eds.), *Test anxiety: Theory, assessment, and treatment* (pp. 61–78). Washington, DC: Taylor & Francis.

Araki, N., Iwawaki, S., & Spielberger, C. D. (1992). Construction and validation of a Japanese adaptation of the Test Anxiety Inventory. *Anxiety, Stress, and Coping: An International Journal*, 5, 217–224.

Arch, E. C. (1987). Differential responses of females and males to evaluative stress: Anxiety, self-esteem, efficacy, and willingness to participate. In R. Schwarzer, H. M. Van der Ploeg, & C. D. Spielberger (Eds.), *Advances in test anxiety research* (Vol. 5, pp. 97–106). Lisse, The Netherlands: Swets & Zeitlinger.

Arkin, R. M., Detchon, C. S., & Maruyama, G. M. (1981). Causal attributions of high and low achievement motivation college students for performance on examinations. *Motivation and Emotion*, 5, 139–152.

Arkin, R. M., Detchon, C. S., & Maruyama, G. M. (1982). Roles of attribution, affect, and cognitive interference in test anxiety. *Journal of Personality and Social Psychology*, 43, 1111–1124.

Arkin, R. M., & Haugtvedt, C. (1984). Test anxiety, task difficulty and diagnosticity: The roles of cognitive interference and fear of failure as determinants of choice of task. In H. M. Van der Ploeg, R. Schwarzer, & C. D. Spielberger (Eds.), *Advances in test anxiety research* (Vol. 3, pp. 147–162). Lisse, The Netherlands: Swets & Zeitlinger.

Arkin, R. M., Kolditz, T. A., & Kolditz, K. K. (1983). Attributions of the test anxious student: Self assessments in the classroom. *Personality and Social Psychology Bulletin*, 9, 271–280.

Arkin, R. M., & Schumann, D. W. (1984). Effects of corrective testing: An extension. *Journal of Educational Psychology*, 76, 835–843.

Atkinson, J. W. (1964). *An introduction to motivation*. Princeton, NJ: Van Nostrand.

Atkinson, J. W., & Feather, N. T. (1966). *A theory of achievement motivation*. New York: Wiley.

Atkinson, J. W., & Litwin, G. H. (1960). Achievement motive and test anxiety conceived as motive to approach success and motive to avoid failure. *Journal of Abnormal and Social Psychology*, 60, 52–63.

Auerbach, S. M. (1973). Effects of orienting instructions, feedback information and trait-anxiety level on state-anxiety. *Psychological Reports*, 33, 779–786.

Averill, J. R. (1973). Personal control over aversive stimuli and its relationship to stress. *Psychological Bulletin*, 80, 286–303.

Baddeley, A. D. (1986). *Working memory*. Oxford: Oxford University Press.

Baddeley, A., & Hitch, G. (1974). Working memory. In G. Bower (Ed.), *The psychology of learning and motivation* (Vol. 8, 47–89). Orlando, FL: Academic Press.

Bajtelsmit, J. W. (1977). Test-wiseness and systematic desensitization programs for increasing adult test-taking skills. *Journal of Educational Measurement*, 14, 335–341.

Bandura, A. (1965). Behavioral modification through modeling procedures. In L. Krasner & L. P. Ullmann (Eds.), *Research in behavior modification: New developments and implications* (pp. 310–340). New York: Holt, Rinehart & Winston.

Bandura, A. (1976). Social learning theory. In J. T. Spence, R. C. Carson, & J. W. Thibaut (Eds.), *Behavioral approaches to therapy* (pp. 1–46). Morristown, NJ: General Learning Press.

Bandura, A. (1977). Self-efficacy: Toward a unifying theory of behavioral change. *Psychological Review*, 84, 191–215.

Bandura, A. (1986). *Social foundations of thought and action: A social cognitive theory*. Englewood Cliffs, NJ: Prentice Hall.

Bandura, A. (1988). Self-efficacy conception of anxiety. *Anxiety Research*, 1, 77–98.

Barabasz, A. F., & Barabasz, M. (1981). Effects of rational emotive therapy on psychophysiological and reported measures of test anxiety arousal. *Journal of Clinical Psychology*, 37, 511–514.

Baron, R. M., & Kenny, D. A. (1986). The moderator–mediator variable distinction in social psychological research: Conceptual, strategic, and statistical considerations. *Journal of Personality and Social Psychology*, 51, 1173–1182.

Beck, A. (1970). Cognitive therapy: Nature and relation to behavior therapy. *Behavior Therapy*, 1, 184–200.

Beck, A. T. (1993). Cognitive therapy: Past, present, and future. *Journal of Consulting and Clinical Psychology*, 61, 194–198.

Beck, A. T., & Clark, D. A. (1991). Anxiety and depression: An information processing perspective. In R. Schwarzer & R. A. Wicklund (Eds.), *Anxiety and self-focused attention* (pp. 41–54). London: Harwood.

Beck, A. T., & Emory, G. (1985). *Anxiety disorders and phobias.* New York: Basic Books.

Becker, P. (1982a). Fear reactions and achievement behavior of students approaching an examination. In H. W. Krohne & L. Laux (Eds.), *Achievement, stress and anxiety* (pp. 275–290). London: Hemisphere.

Becker, P. (1982b). Towards a process analysis of test anxiety: Some theoretical and methodological observations. In R. Schwarzer, H. M. Van der Ploeg, & C. D. Spielberger (Eds.), *Advances in test anxiety research* (Vol. 1, pp. 11–17). Lisse, The Netherlands: Swets & Zeitlinger.

Becker, P. (1983). Test anxiety, examination stress, and achievement: Methodological remarks and some results of a longitudinal study. In H. M. Van der Ploeg, R. Schwarzer, & C. D. Spielberger (Eds.), *Advances in test anxiety research* (Vol. 2, pp. 129–146). Lisse, The Netherlands: Swets & Zeitlinger.

Beehr, T. A., & McGrath, J. E. (1996). The methodology of research on coping: Conceptual, strategic, and operational-level issues. In M. Zeidner & N. S. Endler (Eds,), *Handbook of coping: Theory, research, applications* (pp. 65–82). New York: Wiley.

Benjamin, M., McKeachie, W. J., Lin, Y. G., & Holinger, D. P. (1981). Test anxiety: Deficits in information processing. *Journal of Educational Psychology, 73,* 816–824.

Benson, J., & Bandalos, D. (1989). Structural model of statistical test anxiety in adults. In R. Schwarzer, H. M. Van der Ploeg, & C. D. Spielberger (Eds.), *Advances in test anxiety research* (Vol. 6, pp. 137–151). Lisse, The Netherlands: Swets & Zeitlinger.

Benson, J., & Bandalos, D. (1992). Second-order confirmatory factor analysis of the Reactions to Tests Scale with cross-validation. *Multivariate Behavioral Research, 27,* 459–487.

Benson, J., & El-Zahhar, N. (1992, July). *Further validation of the revised test anxiety scale.* Paper presented at the 13th annual conference of the Stress and Anxiety Research conference, Leuven, Belgium.

Benson, J., & El-Zahhar, N. (1994). Further refinement and validation of the revised test anxiety scale. *Structural Equation Modeling, 1,* 203–221.

Benson, J., Moulin-Julian, M., Schwarzer, C., Seipp, B., & El-Zahhar, N. (1992). Cross-validation of a revised test anxiety scale using multi-national samples. In K. A. Hagtvet & B. T. Johnsen (Eds,), *Advances in test anxiety research* (Vol. 7, pp. 62–83). Lisse, The Netherlands: Swets & Zeitlinger.

Benson, J., & Tippets, E. (1990). A confirmatory factor analysis of the Test Anxiety Inventory. In C. D. Spielberger & Diaz-Guerrero (Eds.), *Cross-cultural anxiety* (Vol. 4, pp. 149–156). Washington, DC: Hemisphere.

Bernstein, D. A., Roy, E. J., Srull, T. K., & Wickmen, C. D. (1988). *Psychology.* Dallas, TX: Houghton-Mifflin.

Billings, A. G., & Moos, R. H. (1984). Coping, stress, and social resources among adults with unipolar depression. *Journal of Personality and Social Psychology, 46,* 877–891.

Blankstein, K. R., & Flett, G. L. (1990). Cognitive components of test anxiety: A comparison of assessment and scoring methods. *Journal of Social Behavior and Personality, 5,* 187–202.

Blankstein, K. R., Flett, G. L., Boase, P., & Toner, B. B. (1990). Thought listing and endorsement measures of self-referential thinking in test anxiety. *Anxiety Research, 2,* 103–112.

Blankstein, K. R., Flett, G. L., Boase, P., & Toner, B. B. (1991). Thought listing and endorsement measures of self-referential thinking in test anxiety. In R. Schwarzer & R. A. Wicklund (Eds.), *Achievement, stress, and anxiety* (pp. 133–142). New York: Harwood.

Blankstein, K. R., Flett, G. L., & Watson, M. S. (1992). Coping and academic problem-solving ability in test anxiety. *Journal of Clinical Psychology, 48,* 37–46.

Blankstein, K. R., Flett, G. L., Watson, M. S., & Koledin, S. (1990). Test anxiety, self evaluative worry, and sleep disturbance in college students. *Anxiety Research, 3,* 193–204.

Blankstein, K. R., & Toner, B. B. (1987). Influence of social-desirability responding on the Sarason Test Anxiety Scale: Implications for selection of subjects. *Psychological Reports, 61,* 63–69.

Blankstein, K. R., Toner, B. B., & Flett, G. L. (1989). Test anxiety and the contents of consciousness: Thought-listing and endorsement measures. *Journal of Research in Personality, 23,* 269–286.

Blatt, S. J. (1995). The destructiveness of perfectionism: Implications for the treatment of depression. *American Psychologist, 50,* 1003–1020.

Blatt, S. J., & Zuroff, P. C. (1992). Interpersonal relatedness and self-definition: Two prototypes for depression. *Clinical Psychology Review, 12,* 527–562.

Bloch, S., & Brackenridge, C. J. (1972). Psychological, performance and biochemical factors in medical students under examination stress. *Journal of Psychosomatic Research, 16,* 25–33.

Blumenfeld, P. C., Pintrich, P. R., Meece, J. L., & Wessels, K. (1982). The formation and role of self-perceptions of ability in elementary classrooms. *Elementary School Journal, 82*, 401–420.

Boggiano, A. K., & Ruble, D. N. (1986). Children's responses to evaluative feedback. In R. Schwarzer (Ed.), *Self related cognitions in anxiety and motivation* (pp. 195–227). Hillsdale, NJ: Erlbaum.

Bolger, N. (1990). Coping as a personality process: A prospective study. *Journal of Personality and Social Psychology, 59*, 525–537.

Borkovec, T. D., Robinson, E., Pruzinsky, T., & DePree, J. D. (1983). Preliminary exploration of worry: Some characteristics and processes. *Behaviour Research and Therapy, 21*, 9–16.

Bower, G. H. (1981). Mood and memory. *American Psychologist, 36*, 129–148.

Bradshaw, G. D., & Gaudry, E. (1968). The effect of a single experience of success or failure on test anxiety. *Australian Journal of Psychology, 20*, 219–223.

Broadbent, D. E. (1971). *Decision and stress*. London: Academic Press.

Bronzaft, A, L., Murgatroyd, D., Lehman, H. H., & McNeilly, R. A. (1974). Test anxiety among black college students: A cross-cultural study. *Journal of Negro Education, 43*, 190–193.

Brown, C. H. (1938a). Emotional reactions before examinations. II. Results of a questionnaire. *Journal of Psychology, 5*, 11–26.

Brown, C. H. (1938b). Emotional reactions before examinations. III. Interrelations. *Journal of Psychology, 5*, 27–31.

Bruch, M. A. (1978). Type of cognitive modeling, imitation of modeled tactics, and modification of test anxiety. *Cognitive Therapy and Research, 2*, 147–164.

Bruch, M. A. (1981). Relationship of test-taking strategies to test anxiety and performance: Toward a task analysis of examination behavior. *Cognitive Therapy and Research, 5*, 41–56.

Bruch, M. A., Juster, H. R., & Kaflowitz, N. G. (1983). Relationships of cognitive components of test anxiety to test performance: Implications for assessment and treatment. *Journal of Counseling Psychology, 30*, 527–536.

Bruch, M. A., Kaflowitz, N. G., & Kuethe, M. (1986). Beliefs and the subjective meaning of thoughts: Analysis of the role of self-statements in academic test performance. *Cognitive Therapy and Research, 10*, 51–69.

Bruch, M. A., Pearl, L., & Giordano, S. (1986). Differences in the cognitive processes of academically successful and unsuccessful test-anxious students. *Journal of Counseling Psychology, 33*, 217–219.

Buss, A. H. (1980). *Self-consciousness and social anxiety*. San Francisco: Freeman.

Buss, A. H. (1986). Two kinds of shyness. In R. Schwarzer (Ed.), *Self-related cognitions in anxiety and motivation* (pp. 65–76). Hillsdale, NJ: Erlbaum.

Butler, G., & Mathews, A. (1987). Anticipatory anxiety and risk perception. *Cognitive Therapy and Research, 11*, 551–565.

Cacioppo, J. T., & Petty, R. E. (1981). Social psychological procedures for cognitive response assessment: The thought-listing technique. In T. V. Merluzzi, C. R. Glass, & M. Genest (Eds.), *Cognitive assessment*, (pp. 309–342). New York: Guilford.

Calvo, M. G., & Carreiras, M. (1993). Selective influencing of test anxiety on reading processes. *British Journal of Psychology, 84*, 375–388.

Calvo, M. G., Eysenck, M. W., & Estevez, A. (1994). Ego-threat interpretive bias in test anxiety: On line inferences. *Cognition and Emotion, 8*, 127–146.

Calvo, M. G., Eysenck, M. W., Ramos, P. M., & Jimenez, A. (1994). Compensatory reading strategies in test anxiety. *Anxiety, Stress and Coping, 7*, 99–117.

Calvo, M. G., Ramos, P. M., & Estevez, A. (1992). Test anxiety and comprehension efficiency: The role of prior knowledge and working memory deficits. *Anxiety, Stress and Coping, 5*, 125–138.

Campbell, D., & Fiske, D. (1959). Convergent and divergent validation by the multi-trait multi-method matrix. *Psychological Bulletin, 56*, 81–105.

Cannon, W. B. (1929). *Bodily change in pain, hunger, fear, and rage*. New York: Appleton.

Carroll, J. B. (1992). Cognitive abilities: The state of the art. *Psychological Science, 3*, 266–270.

Carver, C. S. (1996). Cognitive interference and the structure of behavior. In I. G. Sarason, G. R. Pierce, & B. R. Sarason (Eds.), *Cognitive interference: Theories, methods, and findings* (pp. 25–45). Mahwah, NJ: Erlbaum.

Carver, C. S., Peterson, L. M., Follansbee, D. J., & Scheier, M. F. (1983). Effects of self-directed attention on performance and persistence among persons high and low in test anxiety. *Cognitive Therapy and Research, 7,* 333–354.

Carver, C. S., & Scheier, M. F. (1981). Self-consciousness and reactance. *Journal of Research in Personality, 15,* 16–29.

Carver, C. S., & Scheier, M. F. (1984). Self-focused attention in test anxiety: A general theory applied to a specific phenomenon. In H. M. Van der Ploeg, R. Schwarzer, & C. D. Spielberger (Eds.), *Advances in test anxiety research* (Vol. 3, pp. 3–20). Lisse, The Netherlands: Swets & Zeitlinger.

Carver, C. S., & Scheier, M. F. (1986). Functional and dysfunctional responses to anxiety: The interaction between expectancies and self-focused attention. In R. Schwarzer (Ed.), *Self related cognitions in anxiety and motivation* (pp. 111–141). Hillsdale, NJ: Erlbaum.

Carver, C. S., & Scheier, M. F. (1988a). A control-process perspective on anxiety. *Anxiety Research, 1,* 17–22.

Carver, C. S., & Scheier, M. F. (1988b). Performing poorly, performing well: A view of the self regulatory consequences of confidence and doubt. *International Journal of Educational Research, 12,* 325–332.

Carver, C. S., & Scheier, M. F. (1989). Expectancies and coping: From test anxiety to pessimism. In R. Schwarzer, H. M. Van der Ploeg, & C. D. Spielberger (Eds.), *Advances in test anxiety research* (Vol. 6, pp. 3–11). Lisse, The Netherlands: Swets & Zeitlinger.

Carver, C. S., & Scheier, M. F. (1990). Origins and functions of positive and negative affects: A control-process view. *Psychological Review, 97,* 19–35.

Carver, C. S., & Scheier, M. F. (1991). A control-process perspective on anxiety. In R. Schwarzer & R. A. Wicklund (Eds.), *Anxiety and self focused attention* (pp. 3–8). London: Harwood.

Carver, C. S., & Scheier, M. F. (1994). Situational coping and coping dispositions in a stressful transaction. *Journal of Personality and Social Psychology, 66,* 184–195.

Carver, C. S., Scheier, M. F., & Klahr, D. (1987). Further explorations of a control-process model of test anxiety. In R. Schwarzer, H. M. Van der Ploeg, & C. D. Spielberger (Eds.), *Advances in test anxiety research* (Vol. 6, pp. 15–22). Lisse, The Netherlands: Swets & Zeitlinger.

Carver, C. S., Scheier, M. F., & Pozo, C. (1992). Conceptualizing the process of coping with health problems. In H. S. Friedman (Ed.), *Hostility, coping, and health* (pp. 167–199). Washington, DC: American Psychological Association.

Carver, C. S., Scheier, M. F., & Weintraub, J. K. (1989). Assessing coping strategies: A theoretically based approach. *Journal of Personality and Social Psychology, 56,* 267–283.

Cattel, R. B., & Scheier, I. H. (1958). The nature of anxiety: A review of 13 multivariate analyses composing 814 variables. *Psychological Reports Monographs Supplement, 5,* 351–388.

Cherkes-Julkowski, M., Groebel, J., & Kuffner, H. (1982). Social comparison and emotional reactions in the classroom. In R. Schwarzer, H. M. Van der Ploeg, & C. D. Spielberger (Eds.), *Advances in test anxiety research* (Vol. 1, pp. 105–114). Lisse, The Netherlands: Swets & Zeitlinger.

Clawson, T. W., Firment, C. K., & Trower, T. L. (1981). Test anxiety: Another origin for racial bias in standardized testing. *Measurement and Evaluation in Guidance, 13,* 210–215.

Cohen, F., & Lazarus, R. (1979). Coping with the stresses of illness. In G. C. Stone, F. Cohen, & N. E. Adler (Eds.), *Health psychology: A handbook* (pp. 217–254). San Francisco: Jossey-Bass.

Comunian, A. L. (1985). The development and validation of the Italian form of the Test Anxiety Inventory. In H. M. Van der Ploeg, R. Schwarzer, & C. D. Spielberger (Eds.), *Advances in test anxiety research* (Vol. 4, pp. 215–220). Lisse, The Netherlands: Swets & Zeitlinger.

Comunian, A. L. (1989). Some characteristics of relations among depression, anxiety, and self-efficacy. *Perceptual and Motor Skills, 69,* 755–764.

Cook, T. D., & Campbell, D. T. (1979). *Quasi-experimentation: Design and analysis issues for field settings.* Dallas, TX: Houghton-Mifflin.

Couch, J. V., Garber, T. B., & Turner, W. E. (1983). Facilitating and debilitating test anxiety and academic achievement. *Psychological Reports, 33,* 237–244.

Covington, M. V. (1986). Anatomy of failure-induced anxiety: The role of cognitive mediators. In R. Schwarzer (Ed.), *Self-related cognition in anxiety and motivation* (pp. 247–264). Hillsdale, NJ: Erlbaum.

Covington, M. V. (1992). *Making the grade.* Cambridge: Cambridge University Press.

Covington, M. V., & Omelich, C. L. (1979). Effort: The double edged sword in school achievement. *Journal of Educational Psychology, 71,* 169–182.

Covington, M. V., & Omelich, C. L. (1981). As failures mount: Affective and cognitive consequences of ability demotion in the classroom. *Journal of Educational Psychology, 73,* 796–808.

Covington, M. V., & Omelich, C. L. (1985). Ability and effort valuation among failure-avoiding and failure-accepting students. *Journal of Educational Psychology, 77,* 446–459.

Covington, M. V., & Omelich, C. L. (1987a). "I knew it cold before the exam": A test of the anxiety-blockage hypothesis. *Journal of Educational Psychology, 79,* 393–400.

Covington, M. V., & Omelich, C. L. (1987b). Item difficulty and test performance among high-anxious and low-anxious students. In R. Schwarzer, H. M. Van der Ploeg, & C. D. Spielberger (Eds.), *Advances in test anxiety research* (Vol. 5, pp. 127–136). Lisse, The Netherlands: Swets & Zeitlinger.

Covington, M. V., & Omelich, C. L. (1988). Achievement dynamics: The interaction of motives, cognitions, and emotions over time. *Anxiety Research, 1,* 165–183.

Covington, M. V., Omelich, C. L., & Schwarzer, R. (1986). Anxiety, aspirations, and self-concept in the achievement process: A longitudinal model with latent variables. *Motivation and Emotion, 10,* 71–88.

Cox, F. N. (1962). Educational streaming and general and test anxiety. *Child Development, 33,* 381–390.

Cox, F. N. (1964). Test anxiety and the achievement behavior systems related to examination performance in children. *Child Development, 35,* 909–915.

Cox, F. N. (1968). Some relationships between test anxiety, presence or absence of male persons and boy's performance of a repetitive motor task. *Journal of Experimental Child Psychology, 6,* 1–12.

Craik, F. I. M., & Lockhart, R. S. (1972). Levels of processing: A framework for memory research. *Journal of Verbal Learning and Learning Behavior, 11,* 671–684.

Crocker, L., & Algina, J. (1986). *Introduction to classical and modern test theory.* New York: CBS College Publications.

Crocker, L., & Schmitt, A. (1987). Improving multiple-choice test performance for examinees with different levels of test anxiety. *Journal of Experimental Education, 55,* 201–205.

Cronbach, L. J. (1982). *Designing evaluations of educational and social programs.* San Francisco: Jossey-Bass.

Cronbach, L. J., Gleser, G. C., Rajaratnam, N., & Nanda, H. (1972). *The dependability of behavioral measures: Theory of generalizability for scores and profiles.* New York: Wiley.

Cronbach, L. J.. & Meehl, P. E. (1955). Construct validity in psychological tests. *Psychological Bulletin, 52,* 281–303.

Cubberly, W. E., Weinstein, C. E., & Cubberly, R. D. (1986). The interactive effects of cognitive learning strategy training and test anxiety on paired-associate learning. *Journal of Educational Research, 79,* 163–169.

Culler, R. E., & Holahan, C. J. (1980). Test anxiety and academic performance: The effects of study-related behaviors. *Journal of Educational Psychology, 72,* 16–20.

Darke, S. (1988). Anxiety and working memory capacity. *Cognition and Emotion, 2,* 145–154.

Dawley, H. H., & Wenrich, W. W. (1973a). Group implosive therapy in the treatment of test anxiety: A brief report. *Behavior Therapy, 4,* 261–263.

Dawley, H. H., & Wenrich, W. W. (1973b). Massed group desensitization in reduction of test anxiety. *Psychological Reports, 33,* 359–363.

Dawley, H. H., & Wenrich, W. W. (1973c). Treatment of test anxiety by group implosive therapy. *Psychological Reports, 33,* 383–388.

Deary, I. J., Blenkin, H., Agius, R. M., Endler, N. S., Zeally, H., & Wood, R. (1996). Models of job-related stress and personal achievement among consultant doctors. *British Journal of Psychology, 87,* 3–29.

Deaux, K. (1977). Sex differences. In T. Blass (Ed.), *Personality variables in social behavior* (pp. 357–372). Hillsdale, NJ: Erlbaum.

Deffenbacher, J. L. (1977a). Relationship of worry and emotionality to performance on the Miller Analogies Test. *Journal of Educational Psychology, 69,* 191–195.

Deffenbacher, J. L. (1977b). Test anxiety: The problem and possible responses. *Canadian Counsellor, 11,* 59–64.

Deffenbacher, J. L. (1978). Worry, emotionality and task-generated interference in test anxiety. *Journal of Educational Psychology, 70,* 248–254.

Deffenbacher, J. L. (1980). Worry and emotionality in test anxiety. In I. Sarason (Ed.), *Test anxiety: Theory, research and applications* (pp. 111–128). Hillsdale, NJ: Erlbaum.

Deffenbacher, J. L. (1986). Cognitive and physiological components of test anxiety in real life exams. *Cognitive Therapy and Research, 10,* 635–644.

Deffenbacher, J. L. (1988). Introduction: The practice of four cognitive-behavioral approaches to anxiety reduction. *Counseling Psychologist, 16,* 3–7.

Deffenbacher, J. L., & Deitz, S. R. (1978). Effects of test anxiety on performance, worry and emotionality in naturally occurring exams. *Psychology in the Schools, 15,* 446–450.

Deffenbacher, J. L., Deitz, S. R., & Hazaleus, S. L. (1981). Effects of humor and test anxiety on performances, worry, and emotionality in naturally occurring exams. *Cognitive Therapy and Research, 5,* 225–228.

Deffenbacher, J. L., & Hazaleus, S. L. (1985). Cognitive, emotional, and psychological components of test anxiety. *Cognitive Therapy and Research, 9,* 169–180.

Deffenbacher, J. L., & Michaels, A. C. (1981a). A 12-month follow-up of homogeneous and heterogeneous anxiety management training. *Journal of Counseling Psychology, 28,* 463–466.

Deffenbacher, J. L., Michaels, A. C. (1981b). Anxiety management training and self-control desensitization—15 months later. *Journal of Counseling Psychology, 28,* 459–462.

Deffenbacher, J. L., Michaels, A. C., Michaels, T., & Daley, P. C. (1980). Comparison of anxiety management training and self-control desensitization. *Journal of Counseling Psychology, 27,* 232–239.

Deffenbacher, J. L., & Shelton, J. L. (1978). Comparison of anxiety management training and desensitization in reducing test and other anxieties. *Journal of Counseling Psychology, 25,* 277–282.

Deffenbacher, J. L., & Snyder, A. L. (1976). Relaxation as self-control in the treatment of test and other anxieties. *Psychological Reports, 39,* 379–385.

Deffenbacher, J. L., & Suinn, R. M. (1988). Systematic desensitization and the reduction of anxiety. *Counseling Psychologist, 16,* 9–30.

Dendato, K. M., & Diener, D. (1986). Effectiveness of cognitive relaxation therapy and study-skills training in reducing self-reported anxiety and improving the academic performance of test anxious students. *Journal of Counseling Psychology, 33,* 131–135.

Denney, D. R. (1980). Self-control approaches to the treatment of test anxiety. In I. G. Sarason (Ed.), *Test anxiety: Theory, research and applications* (pp. 209–243). Hillsdale, NJ: Erlbaum.

Denney, D. R., & Rupert, P. A. (1977). Desensitization and self-control in the treatment of test anxiety. *Journal of Counseling Psychology, 24,* 272–280.

Depreeuw, E., & De-Neve, H. (1992). Test anxiety can harm your health: Some conclusions based on a student typology. In D. G. Forgays, T. Sosnowski, & K. Wrzesniewski (Eds.), *Anxiety: Recent developments in cognitive, psychophysiological, and health research* (pp. 211–228). Washington: Hemisphere.

DeRosa, A. P., & Patalano, F. (1991). Effects of familiar proctor on fifth and sixth grade students' test anxiety. *Psychological Reports, 68,* 103–113.

Desiderato, O., & Koskinen, P. (1969). Anxiety, study habits and academic achievement. *Journal of Counseling Psychology, 16,* 162–165.

Diaz-Guerrero, R. (1976). Test and general anxiety in Mexican-American school children. In C. D. Spielberger & R. Diaz-Guerrero (Eds.), *Cross-cultural anxiety* (Vol. 1, pp. 135–142). New York: Wiley.

Dion, K. L., & Toner, B. B. (1988). Ethnic differences in test anxiety. *Journal of Social Psychology, 128,* 165–172.

Doctor, R. M., & Altman, F. (1969). Worry and emotionality as components of test anxiety: Replication and further data. *Psychological Reports, 24,* 563–568.

Doyal, G. T., & Forsyth, R. A. (1973). The relationship between teacher and students anxiety levels. *Psychology in the School, 10,* 231–233.

Dusek, J. B. (1980). The development of test anxiety in children. In I. G. Sarason (Ed.), *Test anxiety: Theory, research and applications* (pp. 87–107). Hillsdale, NJ: Erlbaum.

Dweck, C. S., & Elliott, E. S. (1983). Achievement motivation. In P. H. Mussen (Ed.), *Handbook of child psychology* (Vol. 4, pp. 643–692). New York: Wiley.

Dweck, C. S., & Wortman, C. B. (1982). Learned helplessness, anxiety and achievement motivation: Neglected parallels in cognitive, affective and coping responses. In H. W. Krohne & L. Laux (Eds.), *Achievement, stress and anxiety* (pp. 93–125). Washington, DC: Hemisphere.

Easterbrook, J. A. (1959). The effect of emotion on cue utilization and the organization of behavior. *Psychological Review, 66*, 183–201.

Edelmann, R. J., & Hardwick, S. (1986). Test anxiety, past performance and coping strategies. *Personality and Individual Differences, 7*, 255–257.

Edwards, J. M., & Trimble, K. (1992). Anxiety, coping, and academic performance. *Anxiety, Stress and Coping, 5*, 337–350.

Ellis, A. (1962). *Reason and emotion in psychotherapy.* New York: Lyle Stuart.

Ellis, A. (1977). Rational-emotive therapy: Research data that supports the clinical and personality hypotheses of RET and other modes of cognitive-behavior therapy. *Counseling Psychologist, 7*, 2–42.

El-Zahhar, N. E., & Hocevar, D. (1991). Cultural and sexual differences in test anxiety, trait anxiety and arousability: Egypt, Brazil and the USA. *Journal of Cross-Cultural Psychology, 22*, 238–249.

Emery, J. R., & Krumboltz, R. D. (1967). Standard versus individualized hierarchies in desensitization to reduce test anxiety. *Journal of Counseling Psychology, 14*, 204–209.

Endler, N. S. (1983a). Generality of the interaction model of anxiety with respect to two social evaluation field studies. *Canadian Journal of the Behavioral Sciences, 15*, 60–69.

Endler, N. S. (1992). *Personality: An interactional perspective.* Research Report #207. York University. York, Canada.

Endler, N. S. (1996). *Advances in coping research: An interactional perspective.* Paper presented at a symposium on Advances in Coping with Stress: Interactional Perspectives, at the International Congress of Psychology, Montreal, August 1996.

Endler, N. S., Edwards, J. M., & Vitelli, R. (1991). *Endler Multidimensional Anxiety Scales.* Los Angeles: Western Psychological Services.

Endler, N. S., Kantor, L., & Parker, J. D. A. (1994). State-trait coping, state-trait anxiety, and academic performance. *Personality and Individual Differences, 16*, 663–670.

Endler, N. S., & Magnusson, D. (1976). Toward an interactional psychology of personality. *Psychological Bulletin, 83*, 956–974.

Endler, N. S., & Parker, J. D. A. (1990a). *Coping Inventory for Stressful Situations (CISS) Manual.* Toronto: Multi-Health Systems.

Endler, N. S., & Parker, J. D. A. (1990b). Multidimensional assessment of coping: A critical evaluation. *Journal of Personality and Social Psychology, 58*, 844–854.

Endler, N. S., & Parker, J. D. A. (1990c). Stress and anxiety: Conceptual and assessment issues. *Stress Medicine, 6*, 243–248.

Everson, H. T., Millsap, R. E., & Rodriguez, C. M. (1991). Isolating gender differences in test anxiety: A confirmatory factor analysis of the Test Anxiety Inventory. *Educational and Psychological Measurement, 51*, 243–251.

Everson, H. T., Shapiro, L., & Millsap, R. E. (1989, March). *The effects of test anxiety, item difficulty and order, on performance on the Mathematics Achievement Test.* Paper presented at the annual meeting of the American Educational Research Association, San Francisco.

Everson, H. T., Smodlaka, I., & Tobias, S. (1992, August). *Exploring the interaction of test anxiety and metacognitive word knowledge on reading comprehension.* Paper presented at the annual meeting of the American Psychological Association, Washington, DC.

Everson, H. T., Tobias, S., Hartman, H., & Gourgey, A. (1993). Test anxiety and the curriculum: The subject matters. *Anxiety, Stress and Coping, 6*, 1–8.

Eysenck, H. J. (1979). Anxiety, learning, and memory: A reconceptualization. *Journal of Research in Personality, 13*, 363–385.

Eysenck, H. J., & Eysenck, M. W. (1985). *Personality and individual differences.* New York: Plenum Press.

Eysenck, H. J., & Rachman, S. (1965). *The causes and cures of neurosis.* London: Routledge & Kegan.

Eysenck, M. W. (1982). *Attention and arousal: Cognition and performance.* Berlin: Springer-Verlag.

Eysenck, M. W. (1983). Anxiety and individual differences. In G. R. J. Hockey (Ed.), *Stress and fatigue in human performance* (pp. 273–298). New York: Wiley.

Eysenck, M. W. (1984). Anxiety and the worry process. *Bulletin of the Psychonomic Society, 22*, 545–548.

Eysenck, M. W. (1985). Anxiety and cognitive-task performance. *Personality and Individual Differences, 6*, 579–586.

Eysenck, M. W. (1992). *Anxiety: The cognitive perspective.* Hove, UK: Erlbaum.

Eysenck, M. W. (1997). *Anxiety and cognition.* Hove, East Sussex: Psychology Press.

Eysenck, M. W., & Calvo, M. G. (1992). Anxiety and performance: The processing efficiency theory. *Cognition and Emotion, 6,* 409–434.

Eysenck, M. W., MacLeod, C., & Mathews, A. (1987). Cognitive functioning in anxiety. *Psychological Reports, 49,* 189–195.

Feather, N. T., & Volkmer, R. E. (1988). Preference for situations involving effort, time pressure, and feedback in relation to Type A behavior, locus of control, and test anxiety. *Journal of Personality and Social Psychology, 55,* 266–271.

Felton, B. J., & Revenson, T. A. (1984). Coping with chronic illness: A study of illness controllability and the influence of coping strategies on psychological adjustment. *Journal of Consulting and Clinical Psychology, 52,* 343–353.

Fennema, E., & Sherman, J. (1976). Fennema–Sherman Mathematics Attitudes Scales: Instruments designed to measure attitudes toward the learning of mathematics by male and female. *JSAS Catalog of Selected Documents in Psychology, 6,* 31 (MS. No 1225).

Fletcher, T. M., & Spielberger, C. D. (1995). Comparison of cognitive therapy and rational-emotive therapy in the treatment of test anxiety. In C. D. Spielberger & P. R. Vagg (Eds.), *Test anxiety: Theory, assessment, treatment* (pp. 153–169). New York: Taylor & Francis.

Flett, G. L., & Blankstein, K. R. (1994). Worry as a component of test anxiety: A multidimensional analysis. In G. C. L. Davey & F. Tallis (Eds.), *Worrying: Perspectives on theory, assessment and treatment* (pp. 135–181). New York: Wiley.

Flett, G. L., Hewitt, P. L., Endler, N. S., & Tassone, C. (1994/1995). Perfectionism and components of state and trait anxiety. *Current Psychology: Developmental, Learning, Personality, Social, 13,* 326–350.

Folin, O., Demis, W. J., & Smillie, W. G. (1914). Some observations on emotional glycosuria in man. *Journal of Biological Chemistry, 17,* 519–520.

Folkman, S., Chesney, M., McKussick, L., Ironson, G., Johnson, D. S., & Coastes, T. J. (1991). Translating coping theory into an intervention. In J. Eckenrode (Ed.), *The social context of coping* (pp. 239–260). New York: Plenum.

Folkman, S., & Lazarus, R. S. (1985). If it changes it must be a process: Study of emotion and coping during three stages of a college examination. *Journal of Personality and Social Psychology, 48,* 150–170.

Folkman, S., & Lazarus, R. S. (1986). Stress processes and depressive symptomatology. *Journal of Abnormal Psychology, 95,* 103–107.

Folkman, S., & Lazarus, R. S., Dunkel-Schetter, C., DeLongis, A., & Gruen, R. (1986). The dynamics of a stressful encounter: Cognitive appraisal, coping, and encounter outcomes. *Journal of Personality and Social Psychology, 50,* 992–1003.

Freeston, M. H., Rheaume, J., Letarte, H., Dugas, M. J., & Ladouceur, R. (1984). Why do people worry? *Personality and Individual Differences, 17,* 791–802.

Freud, S. (1928). Humor. *International Journal of Psychoanalysis, 9,* 1–6.

Freud, S. (1933). *New introductory lectures on psychoanalyses.* New York: Norton.

Freud, S. (1936). *The problem of anxiety.* New York: Norton.

Friedman, M., & Rosenman, R. (1974). *Type A behavior and your heart.* Greenwich, CT: Fawcett.

Frost, R. O., & Marten, P. A. (1990). Perfectionism and evaluative threat. *Cognitive Therapy and Research, 14,* 559–572.

Furst, D., Tenenbaum, G., & Weingarten, G. (1985). Test anxiety, sex, and exam type. *Psychological Reports, 56,* 663–668.

Gal, R., & Lazarus, R. (1975). The role of activity in anticipation and confronting stressful situations. *Journal of Human Stress, 1,* 4–20.

Galassi, J. P., Frierson Jr., H. T., & Sharer, R. (1981a). Behavior of high, moderate, and low test anxious students during an actual test situation. *Journal of Consulting and Clinical Psychology, 49,* 51–62.

Galassi, J. P., Frierson Jr., H. T., & Sharer, R. (1981b). Concurrent versus retrospective assessment in test anxiety research. *Journal of Consulting and Clinical Psychology, 49,* 614–615.

Galassi, J. P., Frierson Jr., H. T., & Siegel, R. G. (1984). Cognitions, test anxiety, and test performance: A closer look. *Journal of Consulting and Clinical Psychology, 52,* 319 -320.

Gallagher, J. W., & Arkowitz, H. (1978). Weak effects of covert modeling treatment of test anxiety. *Journal of Behavior Therapy and Experimental Psychiatry, 9,* 23–26.

Ganzer, V. J. (1968). The effects of audience presence and test anxiety on learning and retention in a serial learning situation. *Journal of Personality and Social Psychology, 8,* 194–199.

Garcia, T., & Pintrich, P. R. (1994). Regulating motivation and cognition in the classroom: The role of self-schemas and self-regulating strategies. In D. H. Schunk & B. J. Zimmerman (Eds.), *Self-regulation of learning and performance: Issues and educational applications* (pp. 127–153). Hillsdale, NJ: Erlbaum.

Garlington, W. K., & Cotler, S. B. (1968). Systematic desensitization of test anxiety. *Behaviour Research and Therapy, 6,* 247–256.

Gastorf, J. W., & Teevan, R. C. (1980). Type A coronary-prone behavior pattern and fear of failure. *Motivation and Emotion, 4,* 71–76.

Gatchel, R. J., Baum, A., & Krantz, D. S. (1989). *An introduction to health psychology.* New York: Random House.

Gaudry, E., & Spielberger, C. D. (1971). *Anxiety and educational achievement.* New York: Wiley.

Geen, R. G. (1976). Test anxiety, observation, and range of cue utilization. *British Journal of Social and Clinical Psychology, 15,* 253–259.

Geen, R. G. (1977). Effects of anticipation of positive and negative outcomes on audience anxiety. *Journal of Consulting and Clinical Psychology, 45,* 715–716.

Geen, R. G. (1979). The influence of passive audiences on performance. In P. Paulus (Ed.), *The psychology of group influence.* Hillsdale, NJ: Erlbaum.

Geen, R. G. (1980). Test anxiety and cue utilization. In I. G. Sarason (Ed.), *Test anxiety: Theory research and applications* (pp. 43–63). Hillsdale, NJ: Erlbaum.

Geen, R. G. (1985a). Evaluation apprehension and response withholding in solution of anagrams. *Personality and Individual Differences, 6,* 293–298.

Geen, R. G. (1985b). Test anxiety and visual vigilance. *Journal of Personality and Social Psychology, 49,* 963–970.

Geen, R. G. (1987). Test anxiety and behavioral avoidance. *Journal of Research in Personality, 21,* 481–488.

Gjesme, T. (1980). Dimensions of future time orientation in test anxious individuals. *Archiv für Psychologie, 133,* 277–291.

Gjesme, T. (1982). Amount of manifested test anxiety in the heterogeneous classroom. *Journal of Psychology, 110,* 171–189.

Glaser, R. J., Kiecolt-Glaser, J., Speicher, C. E., & Holliday, J. E. (1985). Stress, loneliness, and changes in herpes virus latency. *Journal of Behavioral Medicine, 8,* 249–260.

Glass, D. C. (1977). *Behavior patterns, stress, and coronary disease.* Hillsdale, NJ: Erlbaum.

Goldfried, M. R. (1971). Systematic desensitization as training in self-control. *Journal of Consulting and Clinical Psychology, 37,* 228–234.

Goldfried, M. R. (1988). Application of rational restructuring to anxiety disorders. *Counseling Psychologist, 16,* 50–68.

Goldfried, M. R., Decenteceo, E., & Weinberg, L. (1974). Systematic rational restructuring as a self-control technique. *Behavior Therapy, 5,* 247–254.

Goldfried, M. R., Linehan, M. M., & Smith, J. L. (1978). Reduction of test anxiety through cognitive restructuring. *Journal of Consulting and Clinical Psychology, 46,* 32–39.

Gonzalez, H. P. (1995). Systematic desensitization, study skills counseling, and anxiety-coping training in the treatment of test anxiety. In C. D. Spielberger & P. R. Vagg (Eds.), *Test anxiety: Theory, assessment, and treatment* (pp. 117–132). Washington, DC: Taylor & Francis.

Green, K. E. (1981). Test anxiety level and format preference. *Psychological Reports, 48,* 537–538.

Guida, F. V., & Ludlow, L. H. (1989). A cross-cultural study of test anxiety. *Journal of Cross-Cultural Psychology, 20,* 178–190.

Guttman, L. (1969). Integration of test design and analysis. In *Proceedings of the 1969 invitational conference on testing problems* (pp. 53–65). Princeton, NJ: Educational Testing Service.

Haan, N. (1977). *Coping and defending: Processes of self-environmental organization.* New York: Academic Press.

Hagtvet, K. A. (1983a). A construct validation study of test anxiety: A discriminant validation of fear of failure, worry and emotionality. In H. M. Van der Ploeg, R. Schwarzer, & C. D. Spielberger (Eds.), *Advances in test anxiety research* (Vol. 2, pp. 15–34). Lisse, The Netherlands: Swets & Zeitlinger.

Hagtvet, K. A. (1983b). A measurement study of test anxiety emphasizing its evaluative context. In S. H. Irvine & J. W. Berry (Eds.), *Human assessment and cultural factors* (pp. 393–405). New York: Plenum Press.

Hagtvet, K. A. (1984). Fear of failure, worry and emotionality: Their suggestive causal relationships to mathematical and state anxiety. In H. M. Van der Ploeg, R. Schwarzer, & C. D. Spielberger (Eds.), *Advances in test anxiety research* (Vol. 3, pp. 211–224). Lisse, The Netherlands: Swets & Zeitlinger.

Hagtvet, K. A. (1985a). Sex differences in test anxiety in terms of the worry–emotionality distinction. *School Psychology International, 6,* 195–203.

Hagtvet, K. A. (1985b). A three-dimensional test anxiety construct: Worry and emotionality as mediating factors between negative motivation and test behavior. In J. J. Sanchez-Sosa (Ed.), *Health and clinical psychology* (pp. 109–134). Amsterdam: Elsevier/North-Holland.

Hagtvet, K. A. (1989). *The construct of test anxiety: Conceptual and methodological issues.* Bergen, Norway: Sigma.

Hagtvet, K. A., Johnsen, T. B. (1992). *Advances in test anxiety research,* Vol. 7. Lisse, The Netherlands: Swets & Zeitlinger.

Hagtvet, K. A., & Sharma, S. (1994). The distinction between self- and other-related failure outcome expectancies: An internal domain study of Indian and Norwegian students. In A. Oosterwegel & R. A. Wicklund (Eds.), *The self in European and North American culture.* Boston: Kluwer.

Halvorsen, R., & Vassend, O. (1987). Effects of examination stress on some cellular immunity functions. *Journal of Psychosomatic Research, 31,* 693–701.

Hamilton, V. (1975). Socialization anxiety and information processing: A capacity model of anxiety induced performance deficits. In I. G. Sarason & C. D. Spielberger (Eds.), *Stress and anxiety* (Vol. 2, pp. 45–68). Orlando, FL: Academic Press.

Hanin, Y. L. (1988). Cross-cultural perspectives in the assessment of individual differences: Methodological and conceptual issues. In D. H. Saklofske & S. B. G. Eysenck (Eds.), *Individual differences in children and in adolescents* (pp. 313–320). London: Hodder & Stoughton.

Harleston, B. W. (1962). Test anxiety and performance in problem-solving situations. *Journal of Personality, 30,* 557–573.

Harris, R. N., Snyder, C. R., Higgins, R. L., & Schrag, J. L. (1986). Enhancing the prediction of self-handicapping. *Journal of Personality and Social Psychology, 51,* 1191–1199.

Harter, S., Whitesell, N., & Kowalski, P. (1987). *The effects of educational transitions on childrens perceptions of competence and motivational orientation.* Unpublished manuscript. University of Denver, Denver, Colorado.

Head, L. Q., & Lindsey, J. D. (1983). The effects of trait anxiety and test difficulty on undergraduates' state anxiety. *Journal of Psychology, 113,* 289–293.

Heckhausen, H. (1975). Fear of failure as a self-reinforcing motive system. In I. G. Sarason & C. D. Spielberger (Eds.), *Stress and anxiety* (Vol. 2, pp. 117–128). Washington, DC: Hemisphere.

Heckhausen, H. (1982). Task-irrelevant cognitions during an exam: Incidence and effects. In H. M. Krohne & L. Laux (Eds.), *Achievement, stress and anxiety* (pp. 247–274). Washington, DC: Hemisphere.

Hedl, J. J. (1984). A factor analytic study of the Test Anxiety Inventory. *International Review of Applied Psychology, 33,* 267–283.

Hedl, J. J. (1987). Explorations in test anxiety and attribution theory. In R. Schwarzer, H. M. Van der Ploeg, & C. D. Spielberger (Eds.), *Advances in test anxiety research* (Vol. 5, pp. 55–65). Lisse, The Netherlands: Swets & Zeitlinger.

Hedl, J. J. (1990). Test anxiety and causal attributions: Some evidence toward replication. *Anxiety Research, 3,* 73–84.

Hedl, J. J., Hedl, J. L., & Weaver, D. B. (1978). Paper presented at the meeting of the American Educational Research Association.

Hedl, J. J., O'Neil Jr., H. F., & Hansen, D. N. (1973). Affective reactions toward computer-based intelligence testing. *Journal of Consulting and Clinical Psychology, 40,* 217–222.

Heide, F. J., & Borkovec, T. D. (1984). Relaxation induced anxiety: Mechanisms and theoretical implications. *Behaviour Research and Therapy, 22,* 1–12.

Heimberg, R. G., Nyman, D., & O'Brien, G. D. (1987). Assessing variations of the thought-listing technique: Effects of instructions, stimulus intensity, stimulus modality, and scoring procedures. *Cognitive Therapy and Research, 11*, 13–24.

Heinrich, D. L., & Spielberger, C. D. (1982). Anxiety and complex learning. In H. M. Krohne & L. Laux (Eds.), *Achievement, stress, and anxiety* (pp. 145–165). Washington, DC: Hemisphere.

Hembree, R. (1988). Correlates, causes, effects, and treatment of test anxiety. *Review of Educational Research, 58*, 7–77.

Herbert, J., Moore, G. F., de la Riva, C., & Watts, F. N. (1986). Endocrine responses and examination anxiety. *Biological Psychology, 22*, 215–226.

Hermans, H. J. M., ter Laak, J. J. F., & Maes, P. C. J. M. (1972). Achievement motivation and fear of failure in family and school. *Developmental Psychology, 6*, 520–528.

Hewitt, P. L., & Flett, G. L. (1991). Perfectionism in the self and social context: Conceptualization, assessment, and association with psychopathy. *Journal of Personality and Social Psychology, 60*, 456–470.

Hill, K. T. (1972). Anxiety in the evaluative context. In W. Hartup (Ed.), *The young child* (Vol. 2, pp. 225–263). Washington, DC: National Association for the Education of Young Children.

Hill, K. T. (1976). Individual differences in children's responses to adult response, to adult presence, and evaluative reactions. *Merrill-Palmer Quarterly 22*, 99–104.

Hill, K. T. (1984). Debilitating motivation and testing: A major educational problem, possible solutions, and policy applications. In P. Ames & C. Ames (Eds.), *Research on motivation in education: Student motivation* (pp. 245–274). New York: Academic Press.

Hill, K. T., & Eaton, W. O. (1977). The interaction of test anxiety and success–failure experiences in determining children's arithmetic performance. *Developmental Psychology, 13*, 205–211.

Hill, K. T., & Sarason, S. B. (1966). *The relation of test anxiety and defensiveness to test and school performance over the elementary-school years: A further longitudinal study*. Chicago: University of Chicago Press for the Society for Research in Child Development.

Hill, K. T., & Wigfield, A. (1984). Test anxiety: A major educational problem and what can be done about it. *Elementary School Journal, 85*, 105–126.

Hobfoll, S. E., Schwarzer, R., & Koo, C. K. (1996, August). *Disentangling the stress labyrinth: Interpreting the meaning of the term stress as it is studied*. Position paper prepared for the 1st Meeting of the International Society for Health Psychology Research, Quebec, Canada.

Hocevar, D., & El-Zahhar, N. E. (1985). Test anxiety in the USA and Egypt: A paradigm for investigating psychometric characteristics across cultures. In H. M. Van der Ploeg, R. Schwarzer, & C. D. Spielberger (Eds.), *Advances in test anxiety research* (Vol. 4, pp. 203–213). Lisse, The Netherlands: Swets & Zeitlinger.

Hocevar, D., & El-Zahhar, N. E. (1988). Arousability, trait anxiety and the worry and emotionality components of test anxiety. *Anxiety Research, 1*, 99–113.

Hocevar, D., El-Zahhar, N., & Gombos, A. (1989). Cross-cultural equivalence of anxiety measurements in English-Hungarian bilinguals. In R. Schwarzer, H. M. Van der Ploeg, & C. D. Spielberger (Eds.), *Advances in test anxiety research* (Vol. 6, pp. 223–231). Lisse, The Netherlands: Swets & Zeitlinger.

Hock, M. (1992). Exchange of aversive communicative acts between mother and child as related to perceived child-rearing practices and anxiety of the child. In K. A. Hagtvet & B. T. Johnsen (Eds.), *Advances in test anxiety research* (Vol. 7, pp. 156–174). Lisse, The Netherlands: Swets & Zeitlinger.

Hodapp, V. (1982). Causal inference from nonexperimental research on anxiety and educational achievement. In H. W. Krohne & L. Laux (Eds.), *Achievement, stress and anxiety* (pp. 355–372). Washington, DC: Hemisphere.

Hodapp, V. (1989). Anxiety, fear of failure, and achievement: Two path-analytical models. *Anxiety Research, 1*, 301–312.

Hodapp, V., Glanzmann, P. G., & Laux, L. (1995). Theory and measurement of test anxiety as a situation-specific trait. In C. D. Spielberger & P. R. Vagg (Eds.), *Test anxiety: Theory, assessment, and treatment* (pp. 47–58). Washington, DC: Taylor & Francis.

Hodapp, V., & Henneberger, A. (1983). Test anxiety, study habits, and academic performance. In R. Schwarzer, H. M. Van der Ploeg, & C. D. Spielberger (Eds.), *Advances in test anxiety research* (Vol. 2, pp. 119–227). Lisse, The Netherlands: Swets & Zeitlinger.

Hodges, W. F. (1976). The psychophysiology of anxiety. In M. Zuckerman & C. D. Spielberger (Eds.)

Emotions and anxiety: New concepts, methods, and applications (pp. 175–194). New York: Halsted Press.

Holahan, C. J., & Moos, R. H. (1985). Life stress and health: Personality, coping, and family support in stress resistance. *Journal of Personality and Social Psychology, 49*, 739–747.

Holahan, C. J., & Moos, R. H. (1987). Personal and contextual determinants of coping strategies. *Journal of Personality and Social Psychology, 52*, 946–955.

Holahan, C. J., & Moos, R. H. (1990). Life stressors, resistance factors and psychological health: An extension of the stress-resistance paradigm. *Journal of Personality and Social Psychology, 58*, 909–917.

Hollandsworth Jr., J. G., Glazeski, R. C., Kirkland, K., Jones, G. E., & Van Norman, L. R. (1979). An analysis of the nature and effects of test anxiety: Cognitive, behavioral, and psychological components. *Cognitive Therapy and Research, 3*, 165–180.

Holroyd, K. A. (1976). Cognition and desensitization in a group treatment of test anxiety. *Journal of Consulting and Clinical Psychology, 44*, 991–1001.

Holroyd, K. A. (1978). Effectiveness of an attribution therapy manipulation with test anxiety. *Behavior Therapy, 9*, 526–534.

Holroyd, K. A., & Appel, M. A. (1980). Test anxiety and physiological responding. In I. Sarason (Ed.), *Test anxiety: Theory, research, and applications* (pp. 129–151). Hillsdale, NJ: Erlbaum.

Holroyd, K., Westbrook, T., Wolf, M., & Badhorn, E. (1978). Performance, cognition and physiological responding in test anxiety. *Journal of Abnormal Psychology, 87*, 442–451.

Horne, A. M., & Matson, J. L. (1977). A comparison of modeling, desensitization, flooding, study skills and control groups for reducing test anxiety. *Behavior Therapy, 8*, 1–8.

Hudesman, J., Loveday, C., & Woods, N. (1984). Desensitization of test anxious urban community-college students and resulting changes in grade point average: A replication. *Journal of Clinical Psychology, 40*, 65–67.

Hudgens, G. A., Chatterton Jr., R. T. J., Torre Jr., J. J., Slager, S. E., Fatkin, L. T., Keith, L. G. Rebar, R. W., DeLeon-Jones, F. A., & King, J. M. (1989). Hormonal and psychological profiles in response to a written examination. In S. Breznitz & O. Zinder (Eds.), *Molecular biology of stress* (pp. 265–275). New York: Liss.

Huebner, L. A. (1988). Some thoughts on the application of cognitive-behavioral therapies. *Counseling Psychologist, 16*, 96–101.

Hull, C. (1943). *Principles of behavior*. New York: Appleton.

Humphreys, M. S., & Revelle, W. (1984). Personality, motivation and performance: A theory of the relationship between individual differences and information processing. *Psychological Review, 91*, 153–184.

Hunsley, J. (1985). Test anxiety, academic performance, and cognitive appraisals. *Journal of Educational Psychology, 77*, 678–682.

Hunsley, J. (1987a). Cognitive processes in mathematics anxiety and test anxiety: The role of appraisals, internal dialogue and attributions. *Journal of Educational Psychology, 79*, 388–392.

Hunsley, J. (1987b). Internal dialogue during academic examinations. *Cognitive Therapy and Research, 11*, 653–664.

Hussian, R. A., & Lawrence, P. S. (1978). The reduction of test, state, and trait anxiety by test-specific and generalized stress inoculation training. *Cognitive Therapy and Research, 2*, 25–37.

Ihli, K. L., & Garlington, W. K. A. (1969). A comparison of group vs. individual desensitization of test anxiety. *Behaviour Research and Therapy, 7*, 207–209.

Jacobson, E. (1938). *Progressive relaxation*. Chicago: University of Chicago Press.

Jaffe, P. G., & Carlson, P. M. (1972). Modelling therapy for test anxiety: The role of model affect and consequences. *Behavior Research and Therapy, 10*, 329–339.

Janis, I. L. (1958). *Psychological stress*. New York: Wiley.

Janis, I. L., & Mann, L. (1977). *Decision making: A psychological analysis of conflict, choice, and commitment*. New York: Free Press.

Jaremko, M. E. (1979). A component analysis of stress inoculation: Review and prospectus. *Cognitive Therapy and Research, 3*, 35–38.

Jensen, A. (1980). *Bias in mental testing*. New York: Free Press.

Johnson, S. M., & Sechrest, L. (1968). Comparison of desensitization and progressive relaxation in treating test anxiety. *Journal of Consulting and Clinical Psychology, 32,* 280–286.

Jones, E. E., & Berglas, S. (1978). Control of attributions about the self through self-handicapping strategies: The appeal of alcohol and the role of underachievement. *Personality and Social Psychology Bulletin, 4,* 200–206.

Jöreskog, K. G., & Sörbom, D. (1979). *Advances in factor analysis and structural equation models.* Cambridge, MA: Abt Books.

Kagan, J., & Snidman, N. (1991). Temperamental factors in human development. *American Psychologist, 46,* 856–862.

Kahneman, D. (1973). *Attention and effort.* Englewood Cliffs, NJ: Prentice-Hall.

Kalechstein, P., Hocevar, D., Zimmer, J. W., & Kalechstein, M. (1989). Procrastination over test preparation and test anxiety. In R. Schwarzer, H. M. Van der Ploeg, & C. D. Spielberger (Eds.), *Advances in test anxiety research* (Vol. 6, pp. 63–76). Lisse, The Netherlands: Swets & Zeitlinger.

Kaplan, R. M., McCordick, S. M., & Twitchell, M. (1979). Is it the cognitive or the behavioral component which makes cognitive-behavior modification effective in test anxiety? *Journal of Counseling Psychology, 26,* 371–377.

Kaplan, R. M., & Saccuzzo, D. P. (1989). *Psychological testing: Principles, applications, and issues,* 2nd ed. Pacific Grove, CA: Brooks/Cole.

Katahn, M. (1966). Interactions of anxiety and ability in complex learning situations. *Journal of Personality and Social Psychology, 3,* 475–479.

Katz, I. (1967). The socialization of academic motivation in minority group children. In P. Levine (Ed.), *Nebraska symposium on motivation* (pp. 133–191). Lincoln, NE: University of Nebraska Press.

Keinan, G. (1987). Decision making under stress: Scanning of alternatives under controllable and uncontrollable threats. *Journal of Personality and Social Psychology, 52,* 639–644.

Keinan, G., & Zeidner, M. (1987). Effects of decisional control on test anxiety and achievement. *Personality and Individual Differences, 8,* 973–975.

Kendall, P. C. (1993). Cognitive-behavioral therapies with youth: Guiding theory, current status, and emerging developments. *Journal of Consulting and Clinical Psychology, 61,* 235–247.

Kendall, P. C., & Hollon, S. D. (1981a). Assessing self-referent speech: Methods in the measurement of self-statements. In P. C. Kendall & S. D. Hollon (Eds.), *Assessment strategies for cognitive behavioral interventions.* (pp. 85–118). New York: Academic Press.

Kendall, P. C., & Hollon, S. D. (Eds.). (1981b). *Assessment strategies for cognitive behavioral interventions.* New York: Academic Press.

Kent, G., & Jambunathan, P. (1989). A longitudinal study of the intrusiveness of cognitions in test anxiety. *Behaviour Research and Therapy, 27,* 43–50.

Kerlinger, F. N. (1973). *Foundations of Behavioral Research,* 2nd ed. New York: Holt, Rinehart, & Winston.

Kiecolt-Glaser, J. K., Garner, W. K., Speicher, C., Penn, G. M., Holliday, J., & Glaser, R. (1984). Psychosocial modifiers of immunocompetence in medical students. *Psychosomatic Medicine, 46,* 7–14.

Kiecolt-Glaser, J. K., Janice, K., Speicher, C. E., Holliday, E., & Glaser, R. (1984). Stress and the transformation of lymphocytes by Epstein–Barr virus. *Journal of Behavioral Medicine, 7,* 1–12.

Kim, S. H., & Rocklin, T. (1994). The temporal patterns of worry and emotionality and their differential effects on test performance. *Anxiety, Stress, and Coping: An International Journal, 7,* 117–130.

Kimmel, H. D. (1975). Conditioned fear and anxiety. In C. D. Spielberger & I. Sarason (Eds.), *Stress and anxiety* (Vol. 1, pp. 189–210). Washington, DC: Hemisphere.

King, N. J., & Ollendick, T. H. (1989). Children's anxiety and phobic disorders in school settings: Classification, assessment, and interventions issues. *Review of Educational Research, 4,* 431–470.

King-Fun-Li, A. (1974). Parental attitudes, test anxiety, and achievement motivation: A Hong Kong study. *Journal of Social Psychology, 93,* 3–11.

Kirkland, K, and Hollandsworth Jr., J. G. (1979). Test anxiety, study skills, and academic performance. *Journal of College Student Personnel, 20,* 431–436.

Kirkland, K, and Hollandsworth Jr., J. G. (1980). Effective test taking: Skills acquisition versus anxiety reduction techniques. *Journal of Consulting and Clinical Psychology, 48,* 431–439.

Kleijn, W. C., Van der Ploeg, H., & Topman, R. M. (1994). Cognition, study habits, test anxiety, and academic performance. *Psychological Reports, 75,* 1219–1226.

Kline, P. (1986). *A handbook of test construction.* London: Methuen.

Klinger, E. (1984). A consciousness-sampling analysis of test anxiety and performance. *Journal of Personality and Social Psychology, 47,* 1376–1390.

Kobasa, S. C. (1979). Stressful life events, personality, and health: An inquiry into hardiness. *Journal of Personality and Social Psychology, 37,* 1–11.

Kohlmann, C. W., Schumacher, A., & Steit, R. (1988). Trait anxiety and parental child-rearing behavior: Support as a moderator variable. *Anxiety Research: An International Journal, 1,* 63–77.

Kooken, R. A., & Hayslip, B. (1984). The use of stress inoculation in the treatment of test anxiety in older students. *Educational Gerontology, 10,* 39–58.

Kostka, M. P., & Galassi, J. P. (1974). Group systematic desensitization versus covert positive reinforcement in the reduction of test anxiety. *Journal of Counseling Psychology, 21,* 464–468.

Krampen, G. (1988). Competence and control orientations as predictors of test anxiety in students: Longitudinal results. *Anxiety Research, 1,* 185–197.

Krohne, H. W. (1980). Parental child-rearing behavior and the development of anxiety and coping strategies in children. In I. G. Sarason & C. D. Spielberger (Eds.), *Stress and anxiety* (Vol. 7, pp. 233–245). Washington, DC: Hemisphere.

Krohne, H. W. (1992). Developmental conditions of anxiety and coping: A two-process model of child-rearing effects. In K. A. Hagtvet & B. T. Johnsen (Eds.), *Advances in test anxiety research* (Vol. 7, pp. 143–155). Lisse, The Netherlands: Swets & Zeitlinger.

Krohne, H. W., Schumacher, A., & Neumann, R. (1989). Personality determinants of actual competence expectancies and state anxiety. In R. Schwarzer, H. M. Van der Ploeg, & C. D. Spielberger (Eds.), *Advances in test anxiety research* (Vol. 5, pp. 27–36). Lisse, The Netherlands: Swets & Zeitlinger.

Krouse, J. H., & Krouse, H. J. (1981). Toward a multimodal theory of academic underachievement. *Educational Psychologist, 16,* 151–164.

Kurosawa, K., & Harackiewicz, J. M. (1995). Test anxiety, self-awareness, and cognitive interference: A process analysis. *Journal of Personality, 63,* 931–951.

Lang, K. A., Mueller, J. H., & Nelson, R. E. (1983). Test anxiety and self-schemas. *Motivation and Emotion, 7,* 169–178.

Lang, P. J., Rice, D. G., & Sternbach, R. A. (1972). The psychophysiology of emotion. In N. S. Greenfield & R. A. Sterbach (Eds.), *Handbook of psychophysiology.* New York: Holt, Rinehart, & Winston.

Laux, L., & Vossel, G. (1982). Theoretical and methodological issues in achievement-related stress and anxiety research. In H. W. Krohne & L. Laux (Eds.), *Achievement, stress and anxiety* (pp. 3–18). Washington, DC: Hemisphere.

Lay, C. H., Edwards, J. M., Parker, J. D. A., & Endler, N. S. (1989). An assessment of appraisal, anxiety, coping, and procrastination during an examination period. *European Journal of Personality, 3,* 195–208.

Lazarus, R. S. (1992). Multimodal therapy: Technical eclecticism with minimal integration. In J. C. Norcross & C. F. Newman (Eds.), *Handbook of psychotherapy intervention* (pp. 231–263). New York: Basic books.

Lazarus, R. S. (1966). *Psychological stress and the coping process.* New York: McGraw-Hill.

Lazarus, R. S. (1969). *Patterns of adjustment and human effectiveness.* New York: McGraw-Hill.

Lazarus, R. S. (1990). Theory-based stress measurement. *Psychological Inquiry, 1,* 3–13.

Lazarus, R. S. (1991a). Cognition and motivation in emotion. *American Psychologist, 46,* 352–367.

Lazarus, R. S. (1991b). *Emotion and adaptation.* Oxford: Oxford University Press.

Lazarus, R. S. (1991c). Progress on a cognitive-motivational-relational theory of emotion. *American Psychologist, 46,* 819–834.

Lazarus, R. S. (1993a). Coping theory and research: Past, present and future. *Psychosomatic Medicine, 55,* 237–247.

Lazarus, R. (1993b). Why we should think of stress as a subset of emotion. In L. Goldberger & S. Breznitz (Eds.), *Stress: Theoretical and clinical aspects.* (pp. 21–39). New York: Free Press.

Lazarus, R. S., & Folkman, S. (1984). *Stress, appraisal, and coping.* New York: Springer.

Lazarus, R. S., & Launier, R. (1978). Stress related transactions between person and environment. In L. A.

Pervin & M. Lewis (Eds.), *Perspectives in interactional psychology* (pp. 287–327). New York: Plenum Press.

Leal, L. L., Baxter, E. G., Martin, J., & Marx, R. W. (1981). Cognitive modification and systematic desensitization with test anxious high school students. *Journal of Counseling Psychology, 28,* 525–528.

Leary, M. R., Barnes, B. D., Griebel, C., Mason, E., & McCormack, J. (1987). The impact of conjoint threats to social- and self-esteem on evaluation apprehension. *Social Psychology Quarterly, 50,* 304–311.

Leitenberg, H. (Ed.). (1990a). *Handbook of social and evaluation anxiety.* New York: Plenum Press.

Leitenberg, H. (1990b). Introduction. In H. Leitenberg (Ed.), *Handbook of social and evaluation anxiety* (pp. 1–6). New York: Plenum Press.

Lekarczyk, D. T., & Hill, K. T. (1969). Self-esteem, test anxiety, stress, and verbal learning. *Developmental Psychology, 1,* 147–154.

Lennon, M. C., Dohrenwend, B. P., Zautra, A. J., & Marbach, J. J. (1990). Coping and adaptation to facial pain in contrast to other stressful life events. *Journal of Personality and Social Psychology, 59,* 1040–1050.

Lent, R. W., & Russell, R. K. (1978). Treatment of test anxiety by cue-controlled desensitization and study-skills training. *Journal of Counseling Psychology, 25,* 217–224.

Leon, M. R., & Revelle, W. (1985). Effects of anxiety on analogical reasoning: A test of three theoretical models. *Journal of Personality and Social Psychology, 49,* 1302–1315.

Leppin, A., Schwarzer, R., Belz, D., & Jerusalem, M. (1987). Causal attribution patterns of high and low test-anxious students. In R. Schwarzer, H. M. Van der Ploeg, & C. D. Spielberger (Eds.), *Advances in test anxiety research* (Vol. 5, pp. 67–86). Lisse, The Netherlands: Swets & Zeitlinger.

Levy, P., Gooch, S., & Kellmer-Prirgle, M. L. (1969). A longitudinal study of the relationship between anxiety and streaming in a progressive and a traditional junior school. *British Journal of Educational Psychology, 39,* 166–173.

Lewin, K. (1951). *Field theory in social science.* New York: Harper.

Lewis, E. C., & College, C. (1987). Differential responses of females and males to evaluative stress: Anxiety, self-esteem, efficacy, and willingness to participate. In R. Schwarzer, H. M. Van der Ploeg, & C. D. Spielberger (Eds.), *Advances in test anxiety research* (Vol. 5, pp. 97–106). Lisse, The Netherlands: Swets & Zeitlinger.

Liebert, R. M., & Morris, L. W. (1967). Cognitive and emotional components of test anxiety: A distinction and some initial data. *Psychological Reports, 20,* 975–978.

Lin, Y. G., & McKeachie, W. J. (1970). Aptitude, anxiety, study habits and academic achievement. *Journal of Counseling Psychology, 17,* 306–309.

Llabre, M. M., Clements, N. E., Fitzhugh, K. B., Lancelotta, G., Mazzagatti, R. D., & Quinones, N. (1987). The effect of computer-administered testing on test anxiety and performance. *Journal of Educational Computing Research, 3,* 429–433.

Lord, F. M. (1980). *Applications of item response theory to practical testing problems.* Hillsdale, NJ: Erlbaum.

Lunneborg, P. W. (1964). Relations among social desirability, achievement and anxiety measures in children. *Child Development, 35,* 169–182.

Luria, A. R. (1932). *The nature of human conflict.* New York: Liveright.

Maccoby, E. E., & Jacklin, C. N. (1974). *The psychology of sex differences.* Stanford, CA: Stanford University Press.

MacLeod, C., & Donnellan, A. M. (1993). Individual differences in anxiety and the restriction of working memory capacity. *Personality and Individual Differences, 15,* 163–173.

MacLeod, C., & Mathews, A. (1988). Anxiety and allocation of attention to threat. *Quarterly Journal of Experimental Psychology, 38,* 653–670.

Magnusson, D., & Stattin, H. (1981). *Situation-outcome contingencies: A conceptual and empirical analysis of threatening situations.* Report from the Department of Psychology, University of Stockholm, Stockholm, Sweden.

Maier, S. F., Watkins, L. R., & Fleshner, M. (1994). Psychoneuroimmunology: The interface between behavior, brain and immunity. *American Psychologist, 49,* 1004–1017.

Man, F., Budejovice, C., & Hosek, V. (1989). The development and validation of the Czech form of the Test Anxiety Inventory. In R. Schwarzer, H. M. Van der Ploeg, & C. D. Spielberger (Eds.), *Advances in test anxiety research* (Vol. 6, pp. 233–243). Lisse, The Netherlands: Swets & Zeitlinger.

Mandler, G., & Sarason, S. B. (1952). A study of anxiety and learning. *Journal of Abnormal and Social Psychology, 47,* 166–173.

Manley, M. J., & Rosemier, R. A. (1972). Developmental trends in general and test anxiety among junior and senior high school students. *Journal of Genetic Psychology, 120,* 219–226.

Mann, J. (1972). Vicarious desensitization of test anxiety through observation of videotape treatment. *Journal of Counseling Psychology, 9,* 1–7.

Mann, J., & Rosenthal, T. L. (1969). Vicarious and direct counterconditioning of test anxiety through individual and group desensitization. *Behaviour Research and Therapy, 7,* 359–367.

Many, M. A., & Many, W. A. (1975). The relationship between self-esteem and anxiety in grades four through eight. *Educational and Psychological Measurement, 35,* 1017–1021.

Marchetti, A., McGlynn, F. D., & Patterson, A. S. (1977). Effects of cue-controlled relaxation, a placebo treatment, and no treatment on changes in self reported and psychophysiological indices of test anxiety among college students. *Behavior Modification, 1,* 47–72.

Marsella, A. J., DeVos, G., & Hsu, F. (Eds.). (1985). *Culture and self: Asian and Western perspectives.* New York: Tavistock.

Matarazzo, J. D. (1972). *Measurement and appraisal of adult intelligence,* 5th ed. Baltimore, MD: Williams and Wilkins.

Matarazzo, J. D., Ulett, G. A., Guze, S. B., & Saslow, G. (1954). The relationship between anxiety level and several measures of intelligence. *Journal of Consulting Psychology, 18,* 201–205.

Mathews, A. (1993). Attention and memory for threat in anxiety. In R. Krohne (Ed.), *Attention and avoidance* (pp. 119–135). Toronto: Hogrefe & Huber.

Mathews, A., Mogg, K., & May, J. (1989). Implicit and explicit memory bias in anxiety. *Journal of Abnormal Psychology, 98,* 236–240.

Matthews, G. (1986). The effects of anxiety on intellectual performance: When and why are they found? *Journal of Research in Personality, 20,* 385–401.

Matthews, G. (1992). Mood. In A. P. Smith & D. M. Jones (Eds.), *Handbook of human performance* (pp. 161–193). London: Academic Press.

Mattlin, J. A., Wethington, E., & Kessler, C. (1990). Situational determinants of coping and coping effectiveness. *Journal of Health and Social Behavior, 31,* 103–122.

McCordick, S. M., Kaplan, R. M., Finn, M. E., & Smith, S. H. (1979). Cognitive behavior modification and modeling for test anxiety. *Journal of Consulting and Clinical Psychology, 47,* 419–420.

McCoy, N. (1965). Effects of test anxiety on children's performance as a function of instructions and type of task. *Journal of Personality and Social Psychology, 2,* 634–641.

McCrae, R., & Costa, P. T. (1986a). Situational determinants of coping responses: Loss, threat, and challenge. *Journal of Personality and Social Psychology, 46,* 919–928.

McCrae, R., & Costa, P. T. (1986b). Personality, coping, and coping effectiveness in an adult sample. *Journal of Personality, 54,* 383–405.

McGrath, J. E. (1982). Methodological problems in research in stress. In H. W. Krohne & L. Laux (Eds.). *Achievement, stress and anxiety* (pp. 19–47). Washington, DC: Hemisphere.

McGuire, D. P., Mitic, W., & Neumann, J. (1987). Perceived stress in adolescents: What normal teenagers worry about. *Candada's Mental Health, 1987* (June), 2–5.

McKeachie, W. J. (1951). Anxiety in the college classroom. *Journal of Educational Research, 45,* 153–160.

McKeachie, W. J. (1977). Overview and critique. In J. E. Sieber, H. F. O'Neil, & S. Tobias (Eds.), *Anxiety, learning and instruction* (pp. 1–11). Hillsdale, NJ: Erlbaum.

McKeachie, W. J. (1984). Does anxiety disrupt information processing or does poor information processing lead to anxiety? *International Review of Applied Psychology, 33,* 187–203.

McKeachie, W. J. (1990). Learning, thinking and Thorndike. *Educational Psychologist, 25,* 127–141.

McKeachie, W. J., Pollie, D., & Speisman, J. (1955). Relieving anxiety in the classroom examinations. *Journal of Abnormal and Social Psychology, 50,* 93–98.

Mechanic, D. (1962). *Students under stress: A study in the social psychology of adaptation.* New York: Free Press.

Meichenbaum, D. (1972). Cognitive modification of test anxious college students. *Journal of Consulting and Clinical Psychology, 39,* 370–380.

Meichenbaum, D. (1976). Cognitive-behavior modification. In J. T. Spence, R. C. Carson, & J. W. Thibaut (Eds.), *Behavioral approaches to therapy.* Morristown, NJ: General Learning Press.

Meichenbaum, D. (1977). *Cognitive-behavior modification. An integrative approach.* New York: Plenum Press.

Meichenbaum, D. (1985). *Stress inoculation training.* New York: Pergamon Press.

Meichenbaum, D. (1993). Changing conceptions of cognitive behavior modification: Retrospect and prospect. *Journal of Consulting and Clinical Psychology, 61,* 202–204.

Meichenbaum, D., & Butler, L. (1980). Toward a conceptual model for the treatment of test anxiety: Implications for research and treatment. In I. G. Sarason (Ed.), *Test Anxiety: Theory, research and applications* (pp. 187–208). Hillsdale, NJ: Erlbaum.

Meichenbaum, D., & Deffenbacher, J. L. (1988). Stress inoculation training. *Counseling Psychologist, 16,* 69–90.

Meichenbaum, D., & Genest, M. (1977). Treatment of anxiety. In G. Harris (Ed.), *The group treatment of human problems* (pp. 3–15). New York: Grune & Stratton.

Meinke, D. L., & Zimmer, J. W. (1990, July). *Levels of test anxiety and test performance on differentiated examinations.* Paper presented at the annual meeting of the Society for Stress and Anxiety Research, Berlin.

Melnick, J., & Russell, R. W. (1976). Hypnosis versus systematic desensitization in the treatment of test anxiety. *Journal of Counseling Psychology, 23,* 291–295.

Meneghan, E. G. (1983). Individual coping efforts and family studies: Conceptual and methodological issues. In H. I. McCubbin, M. S. Sussman, & J. M. Patterson (Eds.), *Social stress and the family* (pp. 113–135). New York: Haworth Press.

Messick, S. (1989). Validity. In R. L. Linn (Ed.), *Educational measurement,* 3rd ed. (pp. 13–103). New York: Collier Macmillan.

Mikulincer, M., Kedem, P., & Paz, D. (1990a). Anxiety and categorization: 1. The structure and boundaries of mental categories. *Personality and Individual Differences, 8,* 805–814.

Mikulincer, M., Kedem, P., & Paz, D. (1990b). The impact of trait anxiety and situational stress on the categorization of natural objects. *Anxiety Research, 2,* 85–101.

Mikulincer, M., & Nizan, B. (1988). Causal attribution, cognitive interference, and the generalization of learned helplessness. *Journal of Personality and Social Psychology, 55,* 470–478.

Milgram, R. M., & Milgram, N. A. (1977). The effect of test content and context on the anxiety–intelligence relationship. *Journal of Genetic Psychology, 130,* 121–127.

Miller, S. M., & Mangan, C. E. (1983). Interacting effects of information and coping style in adapting to gynecologic stress: Should the doctor tell all? *Journal of Personality and Social Psychology, 45,* 223–236.

Mischel, W. (1973). Toward a cognitive social learning reconceptualization of personality. *Psychological Review, 80,* 252–283.

Mitchell, K., R., Hall, R. F., & Piatkowska, O. E. (1975). A group program for the treatment of failing college students. *Behavior Therapy, 6,* 324–336.

Mitchell, K, R., & Ng, K. T. (1972). Effects of group counseling and behavior therapy on the academic achievement of test anxious students. *Journal of Counseling Psychology, 19,* 491–497.

Montgomery, G. K. (1977). Effects of performance evaluation and anxiety on cardiac response in anticipation of difficult problem solving. *Psychophysiology, 14,* 251–257.

Morris, L. W., & Carden, R. L. (1981). Relationship between locus of control and extraversion–introversion in predicting academic behavior. *Psychological Reports, 48,* 799–806.

Morris, L. W., Davis, M. A., & Hutchings, C. H. (1981). Cognitive and emotional components of anxiety: Literature review and a revised Worry–Emotionality Scale. *Journal of Educational Psychology, 73,* 541–555.

Morris, L. W., & Fulmer, R. S. (1976). Test anxiety (Worry and Emotionality) changes during academic testing as a function of feedback and test importance. *Journal of Educational Psychology, 68,* 817–824.

Morris, L. W., Harris, E. W., & Rovias, D. S. (1981). Interactive effects of generalized and situational expectancies on the arousal of cognitive and emotional components of social anxiety. *Journal of Research in Personality, 15,* 302–311.

Morris, L. W., & Liebert, R. M. (1969). Effects of anxiety on timed and untimed intelligence tests: Another look. *Journal of Consulting and Clinical Psychology, 33,* 240–244.

Morris, L. W., & Liebert, R. M. (1970). Relationship of cognitive and emotional components of test anxiety to physiological arousal and academic performance. *Journal of Consulting and Clinical Psychology, 35,* 332–337.

Morris, L. W., & Liebert, R. M. (1973). Effects of negative feedback, threat of shock, and level of trait anxiety on the arousal of two components of anxiety. *Journal of Counseling Psychology, 20,* 321–326.

Morris, R. J., Kratochwill, T. R., & Aldridge, K. (1988). Fears and phobias. In J. C. Witt, S. N. Elliot, & F. M. Greshem (Eds.), *Handbook of behavior therapy in education* (pp. 679–717). New York: Plenum Press.

Most, R. B., & Zeidner, M. (1995). Constructing personality and intelligence instruments: Methods and issues. In. D. H. Saklofske & M. Zeidner (Eds.), *International Handbook of Personality and Intelligence* (pp. 475–503). New York: Plenum Press.

Mueller, J. H. (1976). Anxiety and cue utilization in human learning and memory. In M. Zuckerman & C. D. Spielberger (Eds.), *Emotion and anxiety: New concepts methods and applications* (pp. 197–231). Hillsdale, NJ: Erlbaum.

Mueller, J. H. (1977). Test anxiety, input modality, and levels of organization in free recall. *Bulletin of the Psychonomic Society, 9,* 67–69.

Mueller, J. H. (1978). The effects of individual differences in test anxiety and type of orienting task on levels of organization in free recall. *Journal of Research in Personality, 12,* 100–116.

Mueller, J. H. (1980). Test anxiety and the encoding and retrieval of information. In I. G. Sarason (Ed.), *Test Anxiety: Theory, research and applications* (pp. 63–86). Hillsdale, NJ: Erlbaum.

Mueller, J. H. (1992). Anxiety and performance. In A. P. Smith & D. M. Jones (Eds.), *Handbook of human performance,* 3rd ed. (pp. 127–160). London: Academic Press.

Mueller, J. H., Carlomusto, M., & Marler, M. (1977). Recall as a function of method of presentation and individual differences in test anxiety. *Bulletin of the Psychonomic Society, 10,* 447–450.

Mueller, J. H.. & Courtois, M. R. (1980). Retention of self-descriptive and nondescriptive words as a function of test anxiety level. *Motivation and Emotion, 4,* 229–237.

Mueller, J. H., Elser, M. J., & Rollack, D. N. (1992, July). *Test anxiety and implicit memory.* Paper presented at the 25th International Congress of Psychology, Brussels, Belgium.

Mueller, J. H., Kausler, D. H., Faherty, A., & Oliveri, M. (1980). Reaction time as a function of age, anxiety, and typicality. *Bulletin of the Psychonomic Society, 16,* 473–476.

Mueller, J. H., & Overcast, T. D. (1976). Free recall as a function of test anxiety, concreteness, and instructions. *Bulletin of the Psychonomic Society, 8,* 194–196.

Mueller, J. H., & Thompson, W. B. (1984). Test anxiety and distinctiveness of personal information. In H. M. Van der Ploeg, R. Schwarzer, & C. D. Spielberger (Eds.), *Advances in test anxiety research* (Vol. 3, pp. 21–38). Lisse, The Netherlands: Swets & Zeitlinger.

Mueller, J. H., & Wherry, K. L. (1982). Test anxiety and reaction time for matching decisions. *Journal of Research in Personality, 16,* 281–289.

Munz, D. C., Costello, C. T., & Korabik, K. (1975). A further test of the inverted-U hypothesis relating achievement anxiety and academic test performance. *Journal of Psychology, 89,* 39–47.

Naveh-Benjamin, M. (1991). A comparison of training programs intended for different types of test anxious students: Further support for an information processing model. *Journal of Educational Psychology, 83,* 134–139.

Naveh-Benjamin, M., McKeachie, W. J., & Lin, Y. (1987). Two types of test-anxious students: Support for an information processing model. *Journal of Experimental Psychology, 79,* 131–136.

Neisser, U. (1967). *Cognitive psychology.* Englewood Cliffs, NJ: Prentice-Hall.

Neumann, J. (1933). *Anxiety and illness before examination.* Gütersloh, Germany: Bertels.

Nicholls, J. G., & Miller, A. T. (1986). Conception of ability in children and adults. In R. Schwarzer (Ed.), *Self related cognitions in anxiety and motivation* (pp. 265–284). Hillsdale, NJ: Erlbaum.

Nottelmann, E. D., & Hill, K. T. (1977). Test anxiety and off-task behavior in evaluative situations. *Child Development, 48,* 225–231.

Nunnally, J. C. (1978). *Psychometric theory.* New York: McGraw-Hill.

Oliver, R. (1975). Overcoming test anxiety. *Rational Living, 10*, 6–12.

Olson, D. H. (1979). Circumplex model of marital and family systems: Cohesion and adaptability dimensions. *Family Process, 18*, 3–28.

O'Neil Jr., H. F., & Fukumura, T. (1992). Relationship of worry and emotionality to test performance in a Juku environment. *Anxiety, Stress and Coping, 5*, 241–251.

O'Neil Jr., H. F., Judd, W. A., & Hedl, J. J. (1977). State anxiety and performance in computer-based learning environments. In H. F. Sieber, H. F. O'Neil Jr., & S. Tobias, (Eds.), *Anxiety, Learning and Instuction* (pp. 201–220). Hillsdale, NJ: Erlbaum.

O'Neil Jr., H. F., & Richardson, F. C. (1977). Anxiety and learning in computer-based learning environment. In J. E. Sieber, H. F. O'Neil Jr., & S. Tobias, (Eds.), *Anxiety, learning and instuction* (pp. 133–147). Hillsdale, NJ: Erlbaum.

O'Neil Jr., H. F., Spielberger, C. D., & Hansen, D. N. (1969). Effects of state anxiety and task difficulty on computer-assisted learning. *Journal of Educational Psychology, 60*, 343–350.

Oner, N., & Kaymak, D. A. (1987). The transliteral equivalence and the reliability of the Turkish TAI. In R. Schwarzer, H. M. Van der Ploeg, & C. D. Spielberger (Eds.), *Advances in test anxiety research* (Vol. 5, pp. 227–239). Lisse, The Netherlands: Swets & Zeitlinger.

Osterhouse, R. A. (1972). Desensitization and study-skills training as treatment for two types of test anxious students. *Journal of Counseling Psychology, 19*, 301–307.

Pajares, F., & Miller, M. D. (1994). Role of self-efficacy and self-concept beliefs in mathematical problem solving: A path analysis. *Journal of Educational Psychology, 86*, 193–203.

Pang, V. O. (1991). The relationship of test anxiety and math achievement to parental values in Asian-American and European-American middle school students. *Journal of Research and Development in Education, 24*, 1–10.

Papsdorf, J. D., Ghannam, J. H., & Jamieson, J. (1995). Test anxiety, hemispheric lateralization, and information processing. In C. D. Spielberger & P. R. Vagg (Eds.), *Test anxiety: Theory, assessment, and treatment* (pp. 79–92). Washington, DC: Taylor & Francis.

Parker IV, J. C., Vagg, P. R., & Papsdorf, J. D. (1995). Systematic desensitization, cognitive coping, and biofeedback in the reduction of test anxiety. In C. D. Spielberger & P. R. Vagg (Eds.), *Test anxiety: Theory, assessment, and treatment* (pp. 171–182). Washington, DC: Taylor & Francis.

Parker, J. D. A., & Endler, N. S. (1992). Coping with coping assessment: A critical review. *European Journal of Personality, 6*, 321–344.

Parker, J. D. A., Endler, N. S., & Bagby, R. (1993). If it changes, it might be unstable: Examining the factor structure of the Ways of Coping Questionnaire. *Psychological Assessment, 4*, 361–368.

Paul, G. L. (1966). *Insight vs. desensitization in psychotherapy.* Stanford, CA: Stanford University Press.

Paulman, R. G., & Kennelly, K. J. (1984). Test anxiety and ineffective test taking: Different names, same construct? *Journal of Educational Psychology, 76*, 279–288.

Payne, B. D., Smith, J. E., & Payne, D. A. (1983a). Grade, sex, and race differences in test anxiety. *Psychological Reports, 53*, 291–294.

Payne, B. D., Smith, J. E., & Payne, D. A. (1983b). Sex and ethnic differences in relationships of test anxiety to performance in science examinations by fourth and eighth grade students: Implications for valid interpretations of achievement test scores. *Educational and Psychological Measurement, 43*, 267–270.

Pearlin, L. I., & Schooler, C. (1978). The structure of coping. *Journal of Health and Social Behavior, 19*, 2–21.

Pekrun, R. (1984). An expectancy-value model of anxiety. In H. M. Van der Ploeg, R. Schwarzer, & C. D. Spielberger (Eds.), *Advances in test anxiety research* (Vol. 3, pp. 53–72). Lisse, The Netherlands: Swets & Zeitlinger.

Pekrun, R. (1985). Classroom climate and test anxiety: Developmental validity of expectancy value theory of anxiety. In H. M. Van der Ploeg, R. Schwarzer, C. D. Spielberger (Eds.), *Advances in test anxiety research* (Vol.4, pp. 147–158). Lisse, The Netherlands: Swets & Zeitlinger.

Pekrun, R. (1995, July). *Emotions in achievement settings: Two studies on learning-related and test-related academic emotions.* Paper presented at the 4th European Congress of Psychology, Athens, Greece.

Pekrun, R., & Frese, M. (1992). Emotions in work and achievement. *International Review of Industrial and Organizational Psychology, 7*, 153–200.

Pennebaker, J. W. (1995). *Emotion, disclosure, and health.* Washington, DC: APA.

Pervin, L. (1967). Aptitude, anxiety and academic performance: A moderator variable analysis. *Psychological Reports, 20,* 215–221.

Phillips, B. N. (1962). Sex, social class, and anxiety as sources of variation in school achievement. *Journal of Educational Psychology, 53,* 316–322.

Phillips, B. N. (1978). *School stress and anxiety: Theory, research and intervention.* New York: Human Sciences Press.

Phillips, B. N., Martin, R. P., & Meyers, J. (1972). Interventions in relation to anxiety in school. In C. D. Spielberger (Ed.), *Anxiety: Current trends in theory and research* (Vol. 2, pp. 410–464). New York: Academic Press.

Phillips, B. N., Pitcher, G. D., Worsham, M. E., & Miller, S. C. (1980). Test anxiety: Theory research and application (pp. 327–346). Hillsdale, NJ: Erlbaum.

Pintrich, P. R. (1989). The dynamic interplay of student motivation and cognition in the college classroom. *Advances in motivation and achievement, 6,* 117–160.

Pintrich, P. R., & Garcia, T. (1993). Intraindividual differences in students' motivation and self-regulated learning. *German Journal of Educational Psychology, 7,* 99–107.

Pintrich, P. R., Roeser, R. W., & DeGroot, E. A. M. (1994). Classroom and individual differences in early adolescents' motivation and self-regulated learning. *Journal of Early Adolescence, 14,* 139–161.

Plake, B. S., Thompson, P. A., & Lowry, S. (1981). Effect of item arrangement, knowledge of arrangement, and test anxiety on two scoring methods. *Journal of Experimental Education, 49,* 214–219.

Plass, J. A., & Hill, K. T. (1986). Children's achievement strategies and test performance: The role of time pressure, evaluation anxiety, and sex. *Developmental Psychology, 22,* 31–36.

Powers, D. E. (1986). *Test anxiety and the GRE general test.* Report No. 86-45. Princeton, NJ: Educational Testing Service.

Prochaska, J. O. (1971). Symptom and dynamic cues in the implosive treatment of test anxiety. *Journal of Abnormal Psychology, 77,* 135–142.

Prin, P. J. M., Groot, M. J. M., & Hanewald, G. J. F. P. (1994). Cognition in test-anxious children: The role of on-task and coping cognition reconsidered. *Journal of Consulting and Clinical Psychology, 62,* 404–409.

Proshansky, H. M., Ittelson, W. H., & Rivlin, L. G. (1970). Freedom of choice and behavior in a physical setting. In H. M. Proshansky, W. H. Ittelson, & L. Rivlin (Eds.). *Environmental psychology: Man and his physical settings.* New York: Holt, Rinehart, & Winston.

Rand, P., Lens, W., & Decock, B. (1991). Negative motivation is half the story: Achievement motivation combines positive and negative motivation. *Scandinavian Journal of Educational Research, 35,* 13–30.

Rasch, G. (1960). *Probabilistic models for some intelligence and attainment tests.* Copenhagen: Danish Institute for Educational Research.

Reed, M., & Saslow, C. A. (1980). The effects of relaxation instructions and EMG biofeedback on test anxiety, general anxiety, and locus of control. *Journal of Clinical Psychology, 36,* 683–690.

Rhine, W. R., & Spaner, S. D. (1983). The structure of evaluative anxiety among children differing in socioeconomic status, ethnicity, and sex. *Journal of Psychology, 115,* 145–158.

Rich, A. R., & Woolever, D. K. (1988). Expectancy and self-focused attention: Experimental support for the self-regulation model of test anxiety. *Journal of Social and Clinical Psychology, 7,* 246–259.

Richardson, F. C., O'Neil Jr., H. F., & Grant, R. D. (1977). Development and evaluation of an automated test-anxiety reduction program for computer-based learning environment. In J. E. Sieber, H. F. O'Neil Jr., & S. Tobias (Eds.), *Anxiety, learning, and instruction* (pp. 173–201). Hillsdale, NJ: Erlbaum.

Richardson, F., & Suinn, R. M. (1972). The Mathematics Anxiety Rating Scale: Psychometric data. *Journal of Counseling Psychology, 19,* 551–554.

Richardson, F. C., & Suinn, R. M. (1973). A comparison of traditional systematic desensitization, accelerated massed desensitization, and anxiety management training in the treatment of mathematics anxiety. *Behavior Therapy, 4,* 212–218.

Richardson, F. C., & Suinn, R. (1974). Effects of two short-term desensitization methods in the treatment of test anxiety. *Journal of Counseling Psychology, 21,* 457–458.

Richardson, F. C., & Woolfolk, R. L. (1980). Mathematics anxiety. In I. G. Sarason (Ed.), *Test Anxiety: Theory, research and applications* (pp. 271–287). Hillsdale, NJ: Erlbaum.

Richter, N. C. (1984). The efficacy of relaxation training with children. *Journal of Abnormal Child Psychology, 12*, 319–344.

Robertson, G. J. (1992). Psychological tests: Development, publication, and distribution. In M. Zeidner & R. Most (Eds.), *Psychological testing: An inside view* (pp. 159–214). Palo Alto, CA: Consulting Psychologists Press.

Robinson, F. (1979). *Effective study*, 4th ed. New York: Harper & Row.

Rocklin, T. (1985). Interactive effects of test anxiety, test difficulty and feedback: Implications for ability testing. In H. M. Van der Ploeg, R. Schwarzer, & C. D. Spielberger (Eds.), *Advances in test anxiety research* (Vol. 4, pp. 79–87). Lisse, The Netherlands: Swets & Zeitlinger.

Rocklin, T., & O'Donnell, A. M. (1987). Self-adapted testing: A performance-improving variant of computerized adaptive testing. *Journal of Educational Psychology, 79*, 315–319.

Rocklin, T., & Ren-Min, Y. (1989). Development and adaptation of the Chinese Test Anxiety Inventory: A research note. In R. Schwarzer, H. M. Van der Ploeg, & C. D. Spielberger (Eds.), *Advances in test anxiety research* (Vol. 6, pp. 245–251). Lisse, The Netherlands: Swets & Zeitlinger.

Rocklin, T., & Thompson, J. M. (1985). Interactive effects of test anxiety, test difficulty, and feedback. *Journal of Experimental Psychology, 77*, 368–372.

Rosenthal, M. J. (1990). Inconsistent parenting and anxiety in the child. *Anxiety Research, 3*, 61–63.

Rosenthal, T. L. (1980). Modeling approaches to test anxiety and related performance problems. In I. G. Sarason (Ed.), *Test Anxiety: Theory, research and applications* (pp. 245–270). Hillsdale, NJ: Erlbaum.

Ross, E. (1968). Effects of challenging and supportive instructions on verbal learning in older persons. *Journal of Educational Psychology, 59*, 261–266.

Rost, D. H., & Schermer, F. J. (1989a). The assessment of coping with test anxiety. In R. Schwarzer, H. M. Van der Ploeg, & C. D. Spielberger (Eds.), *Advances in test anxiety research* (Vol. 6, pp. 179–191). Lisse, The Netherlands: Swets & Zeitlinger.

Rost, D. H., & Schermer, F. J. (1989b). The various facets of test anxiety: A subcomponent model of test anxiety measurement. In R. Schwarzer, H. M. Van der Ploeg, & C. D. Spielberger (Eds.), *Advances in test anxiety research* (Vol. 6, pp. 37–52). Lisse, The Netherlands: Swets & Zeitlinger.

Rothblum, E. D., Solomon, L. J., & Murakami, J. (1986). Affective, cognitive, and behavioral differences between high and low procrastinators. *Journal of Counseling Psychology, 33*, 387–394.

Ruebush, B. K. (1960). Interference and facilitating effects of test anxiety. *Journal of Abnormal and Social Psychology, 60*, 205–212.

Russell, R. K., Miller, D. E., & June, L. N. (1975). A comparison between group systematic desensitization and cue-controlled relaxation in the treatment of test anxiety. *Behavior Therapy, 6*, 172–177.

Russell, R. K., Wise, F., & Stratoudakis, J. P. (1976). Treatment of test anxiety by cue-controlled relaxation and systematic desensitization. *Journal of Counseling Psychology, 23*, 563–566.

Samuda, R. J. (1975). *Psychological testing of American minorities*. New York: Harper & Row.

Sarason, I. G. (1958a). Effect on verbal learning of anxiety, reassurance, and meaningfulness of material. *Journal of Experimental Psychology, 56*, 472–477.

Sarason, I. G. (1958b). Interrelationships among individual difference variables, behavior in psychotherapy, and verbal conditioning. *Journal of Abnormal and Social Psychology, 56*, 339–344.

Sarason, I. G. (1959). Intellectual and personality correlates of test anxiety. *Journal of Abnormal and Social Psychology, 59*, 272–275.

Sarason, I. G. (1961). A note on anxiety, instructions and word association performance. *Journal of Abnormal and Social Psychology, 62*, 153–154.

Sarason, I. G. (1972a). Experimental approaches to test anxiety: Attention and the uses of information. In C. D. Spielberger (Ed.), *Anxiety: Current trends in theory and research* (Vol. 2, pp. 383–403). New York: Academic Press.

Sarason, I. G. (1972b). Test anxiety and the model who fails. *Journal of Personality and Social Psychology, 28*, 410–413.

Sarason, I. G. (1973). Test anxiety and social influence. *Journal of Personality, 41*, 261–271.

Sarason, I. G. (1978). The Test Anxiety Scale: Concept and research. In C. D. Spielberger & I. G. Sarason (Eds.), *Stress and anxiety* (Vol. 5, pp. 193–216). Washington, DC: Hemisphere.

Sarason, I. G. (1980a). Introduction to the study of test anxiety. In I. G. Sarason (Ed.), *Test Anxiety: Theory, research and applications* (pp. 3–14). Hillsdale, NJ: Erlbaum.

Sarason, I. G. (Ed.). (1980b). *Test Anxiety: Theory, research and applications.* Hillsdale, NJ: Erlbaum.

Sarason, I. G. (1981). Test anxiety, stress, and social support. *Journal of Personality, 49,* 101–114.

Sarason, I. G. (1984). Stress, anxiety, and cognitive interference: Reactions to tests. *Journal of Personality and Social Psychology, 46,* 929–938.

Sarason, I. G. (1986). Test anxiety, worry, and cognitive interference. In R. Schwarzer (Ed.), *Self-related cognitions in anxiety and motivation* (pp. 19–35). Hillsdale, NJ: Erlbaum.

Sarason, I. G. (1987). Test anxiety, cognitive interference, and performance. In R. E. Snow & M. J. Farr (Eds.), *Aptitude, learning and instruction: Cognitive and affective process analyses* (Vol. 3, pp. 131–142). Hillsdale, NJ: Erlbaum.

Sarason, I. G. (1988). Anxiety, self-preoccupation and attention. *Anxiety Research, 1,* 3–7.

Sarason, I. G., & Ganzer, V. J. (1963). Effects of test anxiety and reinforcement history on verbal behavior. *Journal of Abnormal and Social Psychology, 67,* 513–519.

Sarason, I. G., Minard, J. (1962). Test anxiety, experimental instructions, and the Wechsler Adult Intelligence Scale. *Journal of Educational Psychology, 53,* 299–302.

Sarason, I. G., & Palola, E. G. (1960). The relationship of test and general anxiety, difficulty of task, and experimental instructions to performance. *Journal of Experimental Psychology, 59,* 185–191.

Sarason, I. G., & Sarason, B. R. (1987). Cognitive interference as a component of anxiety: Measurement of its state and trait aspects. In R. Schwarzer, H. M. Van der Ploeg, & C. D. Spielberger (Eds.), *Advances in test anxiety research* (Vol. 5, pp. 3–14). Lisse, The Netherlands: Swets & Zeitlinger.

Sarason, I. G., & Sarason, B. R. (1990). Test anxiety. In H. Leitenberg (Ed.), *Handbook of social and evaluative anxiety* (pp. 475–496). New York: Plenum Press.

Sarason, I. G., Sarason, B. R., Keefe, D. E., Hayes, B. E., & Shearin, E. N. (1984). Cognitive interference: Situational determinants and trait-like characteristics. *Journal of Personality and Social Psychology, 51,* 215–226.

Sarason, I. G., Sarason, B. R., & Pierce, G. R. (1990). Anxiety, cognitive interference, and performance. *Journal of Social Behavior and Personality, 5,* 1–18.

Sarason, I. G., Sarason, B. R., & Pierce, G. R. (1995). Cognitive interference: At the intelligence–personality crossroads. In D. Saklofske & M. Zeidner (Eds.), *International handbook of personality and intelligence* (pp. 285–296). New York: Plenum Press.

Sarason, I. G., & Stoops, R. (1978). Test anxiety and the passage of time. *Journal of Consulting and Clinical Psychology, 1,* 102–109.

Sarason, I. G., & Turk, S. (1983). *Test anxiety and the direction of attention.* Unpublished manuscript, University of Washington, Seattle, Washington.

Sarason, S. B. (1959). What research says about test anxiety in elementary school children. *NEA Journal, 48,* 26–27.

Sarason, S. B. (1966). The measurement of anxiety in children: Some questions and problems. In C. D. Spielberger (Ed.), *Anxiety and behavior* (pp. 63–79). New York: Academic Press.

Sarason, S. B. (1972). Anxiety, intervention, and the culture of the school. In C. D. Spielberger (Ed.), *Anxiety and behavior: Current trends in theory and research* (Vol. 2, pp. 381–403). New York: Academic Press.

Sarason, S. B., Davidson, K. S., Lighthall, F. F., Waite, R., & Ruebush, B. K. (1960). *Anxiety in elementary school children.* New York: Wiley.

Sarason, S. B., Hill, K. T., & Zimbardo, P. G. (1964). A longitudinal study of the relation of test anxiety to performance on intelligence and achievement tests. *Monographs of the Society for Research in Child Development,* No. 29.

Sarason, S. B., & Mandler, G. (1952). Some correlates of test anxiety. *Journal of Consulting and Clinical Psychology, 46,* 102–109.

Sarason, S. B., Mandler, G., & Craighill, P. G. (1952). The effect of differential instructions on anxiety and learning. *Journal of Abnormal and Social Psychology, 47,* 561–565.

Shechter, M., & Zeidner, M. (1990). Anxiety: Towards a decision theoretic perspective. *Journal of Mathematical and Statistical Psychology, 43,* 15–28.

Schlenker, B. R., & Leary, M. R. (1982). Social anxiety and self-presentation: A conceptualization and model. *Psychological Bulletin, 92,* 641–669.

Schwartz, G. E. (1977). Biofeedback and the self-management of disregulation disorders. In R. B. Stuart

(Ed.), *Behavioral self-management: Strategies, techniques, and outcomes* (pp. 49–70). New York: Brunner/Mazel.

Schwartz, G. E., Davidson, R. J., & Maer, F. (1975). Right hemisphere lateralization for emotion in the human brain: Interactions with cognition. *Science, 190,* 286–288.

Schwarzer, C., & Kim, M. J. (1984). Adaptation of the Korean form of the Test Anxiety Inventory: A research note. In H. M. Van der Ploeg, R. Schwarzer, & C. D. Spielberger (Eds.), *Advances in test anxiety research* (Vol. 3, pp. 227–285). Lisse, The Netherlands: Swets & Zeitlinger.

Schwarzer, R. (1984). Worry and emotionality as separate components in test anxiety. *International Review of Applied Psychology, 33,* 205–220.

Schwarzer, R. (1986). Self-related cognitions in anxiety and motivation: An introduction. In R. Schwarzer (Ed.), *Self-related cognitions in anxiety and motivation* (pp. 1–17). Hillsdale, NJ: Erlbaum.

Schwarzer, R. (1990). Current trends in anxiety research. In P. J. D. Drenth, J. A. Sergeant, & R. J. Takens (Eds.), *European perspectives in psychology* (Vol. 2, pp. 225–244). Chichester: Wiley.

Schwarzer, R., & Jerusalem, M. (1989). Development of test anxiety in high school students. In C. D. Spielberger, I. G. Sarason, & J. Strelau (Eds.), *Stress and anxiety* (Vol. 12, pp. 65–79). New York: Hemisphere.

Schwarzer, R., & Jerusalem, M. (1992). Advances in anxiety theory: A cognitive process approach. In K. A. Hagtvet & B. T. Johnsen (Eds.), *Advances in test anxiety research* (Vol. 7, pp. 2–17). Lisse, The Netherlands: Swets & Zeitlinger.

Schwarzer, R., Jerusalem, M., & Lange, B. (1982). A longitudinal study of worry and emotionality in German secondary school children. In R. Schwarzer, H. M. Van der Ploeg, & C. D. Spielberger (Eds.), *Advances in test anxiety research* (Vol. 1, pp. 67–81). Lisse, The Netherlands: Swets & Zeitlinger.

Schwarzer, R., Jerusalem, M., & Schwarzer, C. (1983). Self-related and situation-related cognitions in test anxiety and helplessness: A longitudinal analysis with structural equations. In H. M. Van der Ploeg, R. Schwarzer, & C. D. Spielberger (Eds.), *Advances in test anxiety research* (Vol. 2, pp. 35–44). Lisse, The Netherlands: Swets & Zeitlinger.

Schwarzer, R., & Lange, B. (1983). Test anxiety development from grade 5 to grade 10: A structural equation approach. In H. M. Van der Ploeg, R. Schwarzer, & C. D. Spielberger (Eds.), *Advances in test anxiety research* (Vol. 2, pp. 147–157). Lisse, The Netherlands: Swets & Zeitlinger.

Schwarzer, R., & Schwarzer, C. (1982a). Achievement anxiety with respect to reference groups in school. *Journal of Educational Research, 75,* 305–308.

Schwarzer, R., & Schwarzer, C. (1982b). Test anxiety with respect to school reference groups. In R. Schwarzer, H. M. Van der Ploeg, & C. D. Spielberger (Eds.), *Advances in test anxiety research* (Vol. 1, pp. 95–104). Lisse, The Netherlands: Swets & Zeitlinger.

Schwarzer, R., & Schwarzer, C. (1996). A critical survey of coping instruments. In M. Zeidner & N. S. Endler (Eds.), *Handbook of coping: Theory, research, applications* (pp. 107–132). New York: Wiley.

Schwarzer, R., Van der Ploeg, H. M., & Spielberger, C. D. (Eds.). (1982), *Advances in test anxiety research,* Vol. 1. Lisse, The Netherlands: Swets & Zeitlinger.

Schwarzer, R., Van der Ploeg, H. M., & Spielberger, C. D. (Eds.). (1987). *Advances in test anxiety research* Vol. 5. Lisse, The Netherlands: Swets & Zeitlinger.

Schwarzer, R., Van der Ploeg, H. M., & Spielberger, C. D. (Eds.). (1989). *Advances in test anxiety research* Vol. 6. Lisse, The Netherlands: Swets & Zeitlinger.

Seipp, B. (1991). Anxiety and academic performance: A meta-analysis of findings. *Anxiety Research, 4,* 27–41.

Seipp, B., & Schwarzer, C. (1996). Cross-cultural anxiety research: A review. In C. Schwarzer & M. Zeidner (Eds.), *Stress, anxiety, and coping in academic settings* (pp. 13–68). Tubingen, Germany: Francke-Verlag.

Selye, H. (1956). *The stress of life.* New York: McGraw-Hill.

Shaha, S. H. (1984). Matching-tests: Reduced anxiety and increased test effectiveness. *Educational and Psychological Measurement, 44,* 869–881.

Sharma, S., Parnian, S., & Spielberger, C. D. (1983). A cross-cultural study of test anxiety levels in Iranian and Indian students. *Personality and Individual Differences, 4,* 117–120.

Shye, S., Elizur, D., & Hoffman, M. (1994). *Introduction to facet theory: Content design and intrinsic data analysis in behavioral research.* Thousand Oaks, CA: Sage.

Sieber, J. E. (1969). A paradigm for experimental modification of the effects of test anxiety on cognitive processes. *American Educational Research Journal, 6,* 46–61.

Sieber, J. E. (1980). Defining test anxiety: Problems and approaches. In I. G. Sarason (Ed.), *Test Anxiety: Theory, research and applications* (pp. 15–40). Hillsdale, NJ: Erlbaum.

Sieber, J. E., Kameya, L. I., & Paulson, F. L. (1970). Effect of memory support on the problem solving abilities of test anxious children. *Journal of Educational Psychology, 61,* 159–168.

Sieber, J. E., O'Neil Jr., H. F., & Tobias, S. (1977). *Anxiety, learning and instruction.* Hillsdale, NJ: Erlbaum.

Siegman, A. W. (1956). The effect of manifest anxiety on a concept formation task, a nondirected learning task, and on timed and untimed intelligence tests. *Journal of Consulting Psychology, 20,* 176–178.

Sipos, K., Sipos, M., & Spielberger, C. D. (1985). The development and validation of the Hungarian form of the Test Anxiety Inventory. In H. M. Van der Ploeg, R. Schwarzer, & C. D. Spielberger (Eds.), *Advances in test anxiety research* (Vol. 4, pp. 221–229). Lisse, The Netherlands: Swets & Zeitlinger.

Slapion, M. J., & Carver, C. S. (1981). Self-directed attention and facilitation of intellectual performance among persons high in test anxiety. *Cognitive Therapy and Research, 5,* 115–121.

Smith, C. A., & Ellsworth, P. C. (1987). Patterns of appraisal and emotion related to taking an exam. *Journal of Personality and Social Psychology, 52,* 475–488.

Smith, C. A., & Morris, L. W. (1976). Effects of stimulative and sedative music on cognitive and emotional components of anxiety. *Psychological Reports, 38,* 1187–1193.

Smith, C. A., & Morris, L. W. (1977). Differential effects of stimulative and sedative music on anxiety, concentration, and performance. *Psychological Reports, 41,* 1047–1053.

Smith, P. C. (1976). Behaviors, results, and organizational effectiveness: The problem of criteria. In M. D. Dunnette (Ed.), *Handbook of industrial and organizational psychology* (pp. 745–775). Chicago: Rand McNally.

Smith, R. E., Ascough, J. E., Ettinger, R. F., & Nelson, D. A. (1971). Humor, anxiety and task performance. *Journal of Personality and Social Psychology, 19,* 243–246.

Smith, R. E., & Nye, S. L. (1973). A comparison of implosive therapy and systematic desensitization in the treatment of test anxiety. *Journal of Consulting and Clinical Psychology, 41,* 37–42.

Smith, R. E., & Smoll, F. L. (1990). Sport performance anxiety. In H. Leitenberg (Ed.), *Handbook of social and evaluative anxiety* (pp. 417–453). New York: Plenum Press.

Smith, R. E., Smoll, F. L., & Schutz, R. W. (1990). Measurement and correlates of sport-specific cognitive and somatic trait anxiety: The Sport Anxiety Scale. *Anxiety Research, 2,* 263–280.

Smith, R. J., Arnkoff, D. B., & Wright, T. L. (1990). Test anxiety and academic competence: A comparison of alternative models. *Journal of Counseling Psychology, 37,* 313–321.

Smith, T. W., Ingram, R. E., & Brehm, S. S. (1983). Social anxiety, anxious preoccupation and recall of self-relevant information. *Journal of Personality and Social Psychology, 44,* 1276–1283.

Smith, T. W., Snyder, C. R., & Handelsman, M. M. (1982). On the self-serving function of an academic wooden leg: Test anxiety as a self-handicapping strategy. *Journal of Personality and Social Psychology, 42,* 314–321.

Snyder, A. L., & Deffenbacher, J. L. (1977). Comparison of relaxation as self-control and systematic desensitization in the treatment of test anxiety. *Journal of Consulting and Clinical Psychology, 45,* 1202–1203.

Solomon, L. J., & Rothblum, E. P. (1984). Academic procrastination: Frequency and cognitive-behavioral correlates. *Journal of Counseling Psychology, 31,* 503–509.

Sowa, C. J., & LaFleur, N. K. (1986). Gender differences within test anxiety. *Journal of Instructional Psychology, 13,* 75–80.

Spence, J. T., & Spence, K. W. (1966). The motivational components of manifest anxiety: Drive and drive stimuli. In C. D. Spielberger (Ed.), *Anxiety and behavior* (pp. 291–326). New York: Academic Press.

Spence, K. W. (1958). A theory of emotionally based drive (D) and its relation to performance in simple learning situations. *American Psychologist, 13,* 131–141.

Spence, S. H., Duric, V., & Roeder, U. (1996). Performance realism in test-anxious students. *Anxiety, Stress and Coping, 9,* 339–355.

Spiegler, M. O., Morris, L. W., & Liebert, R. M. (1968). Cognitive and emotional components of test anxiety: Temporal factors. *Psychological Reports, 22,* 451–456.

Spielberger, C. D. (1962). The effects of manifest anxiety on the academic achievement of college students. *Mental Hygiene, 46,* 420–426.

Spielberger, C. D. (Ed.). (1966a). *Anxiety and Behavior.* New York: Academic Press.

Spielberger, C. D. (1966b). The effects of anxiety on complex learning and academic achievement. In C. D. Spielberger (Ed.), *Anxiety and behavior* (pp. 361–398). New York: Academic Press.

Spielberger, C. D. (1966c). Theory and research in anxiety. In C. D. Spielberger (Ed.), *Anxiety and behavior* (pp. 3–20). New York: Academic Press.

Spielberger, C. D. (1972a). *Anxiety: Current trends in theory and research.* New York: Academic Press.

Spielberger, C. D. (1972b). Conceptual and methodological issues in anxiety research. In C. D. Spielberger (Ed.), *Anxiety* (Vol. 2, pp. 481–493). New York: Academic Press.

Spielberger, C. D. (1972c). Current trends in theory and research on anxiety. In C. D. Spielberger (Ed.), *Anxiety—Current trends in theory and research* (Vol. 1, pp. 3–19). New York: Academic Press.

Spielberger, C. D. (1975). The measurement of state and trait anxiety: Conceptual and methodological issues. In L. Levi (Ed.), *Emotions—Their parameters and measurement* (pp. 713–725). New York: Raven Press.

Spielberger, C. D. (1977). Computer-based research on anxiety and learning: An overview and critique. In J. E. Sieber, H. F. O'Neil Jr., & S. Tobias (Eds.), *Anxiety, learning and instruction* (pp. 117–133). Hillsdale, NJ: Erlbaum.

Spielberger, C. D. (1980). *Test Anxiety Inventory: Preliminary professional manual.* Palo Alto, CA: Consulting Psychologists Press.

Spielberger, C. D., Anton, W. D., & Bedell, J. (1976). The nature and treatment of test anxiety. In M. Zuckerman & C. D. Spielberger (Eds.), *Emotions and anxiety: New concepts, methods, and applications* (pp. 317–344). Hillsdale, NJ: Erlbaum.

Spielberger, C. D.. Gonzales, H. P., Taylor, C. J., Algaze, B., & Anton, W. D. (1978). Examination stress and test anxiety. In C. D. Spielberger & I. G. Sarason (Eds.), *Stress and anxiety* (Vol. 5, pp. 167–191). New York: Wiley.

Spielberger, C. D., & Katzenmeyer, W. G. (1959). Manifest anxiety, intelligence and college grades. *Journal of Consulting Psychology, 23,* 278.

Spielberger, C. D., & Krasner, S. S. (1988). The assessment of state and trait anxiety. In R. Noyes Jr., M. Roth, & G. D. Burrows (Eds.), *Handbook of anxiety* (Vol. 2, pp. 31–51). Amsterdam: Elsevier.

Spielberger, C. D., & Vagg, P. R. (1987). The treatment of test anxiety; A transactional process model. In R. Schwarzer, H. M. Van der Ploeg, & C. D. Spielberger (Eds.), *Advances in test anxiety research* (Vol. 5, pp. 179–186). Lisse, The Netherlands: Swets & Zeitlinger.

Spielberger, C. D., & Vagg, P. R. (1995a). Test anxiety: A transactional process. In C. D. Spielberger & P. R. Vagg (Eds.), *Test anxiety: Theory, assessment, and treatment* (pp. 3–14). Washington, DC: Taylor & Francis.

Spielberger, C. D., & Vagg, P. R. (Eds.). (1995b). *Test anxiety: Theory, assessment, and treatment.* Washington, DC: Taylor & Francis.

Stanton, H. E. (1974). The relationship between teachers' anxiety level and the test anxiety level of their students. *Psychology in the Schools, 11,* 360–363.

Stanton, H. E. (1975). Music and test anxiety: Further evidence for an interaction. *British Journal of Educational Psychology, 45,* 80–82.

Stengel, E. (1936). Prüfungsangst und prüfungsneurose. *Zeitschrift für psychoanalytische Padagogik, 10,* 300–320.

Sternberg, R. J. (1985). *Beyond IQ: A triarchic theory of human intelligence.* Cambridge: Cambridge University Press.

Stone, A. A., Helder, L., & Schneider, M. M. (1988). Coping with stressful events: Coping dimensions and issues. In L. H. Cohen (Ed.), *Life events and psychological functioning: Theoretical and methodological issues* (pp. 182–210). Newbury Park, CA: Sage.

Strang, H. R., & Rust, J. O. (1973). The effects of immediate knowledge of results and task definition on multiple-choice answering. *Journal of Experimental Education, 42,* 77–80.

Strelau, J., & Angleitner, A. (1991). *Explorations in temperament: International perspectives on theory and measurement.* New York: Plenum Press.

Sud, A., & Sharma, S. (1990). Test anxiety in two cultures: A comparative study. In P. J. Drenth, J. A.

Sergeant, & R. J. Takens (Eds.), *European perspectives in psychology* (Vol. 3, pp. 377–388). New York: Wiley.

Suinn, R. M. (1969). The STABS, a measure of test anxiety for behavior therapy: Normative data. *Behaviour Research and Therapy*, 7, 335–339.

Suinn, R. M. (1984). Generalized anxiety disorder. In S. Turner (Ed.), *Behavioral theories and treatment of anxiety* (pp. 279–320). New York: Plenum Press.

Suinn, R. M. (1990). *Anxiety management training*. New York: Plenum Press.

Suinn, R. M., & Deffenbacher, J. L. (1988). Anxiety management training. *Counseling Psychologist*, 16, 31–49.

Suinn, R. M., Edie, C., Nicoletti, J., & Spinelli, R. R. (1973). Automated short-term desensitization. *Journal of College Student Personnel*, 14, 471–476.

Tanzer, N. K. (1995). *Experience of anger and anxiety emotions during examinations: Cross-cultural evidence*. Research Report 1995/1. Department of Psychology, University of Graz, Graz, Austria.

Taylor, J. A. (1956). Drive theory and manifest anxiety. *Psychological Bulletin*, 53, 303–328.

Teichman, Y., & Ziv, R. (1994). Characteristics of extended family and children's trait anxiety. *Anxiety, Stress, and Coping: An International Journal*, 7, 291–303.

Terry, D. J. (1991). Coping resources and situational appraisals as predictors of coping behavior. *Personality and Individual Differences*, 12, 1031–1047.

Thorndike, R. L. (1982). *Applied psychometrics*. Boston: Houghton-Mifflin.

Tobias, S. (1977a). Anxiety and instructional methods: An introduction. In J. E. Sieber, H. F. O'Neil Jr., & S. Tobias (Eds.), *Anxiety, learning and instruction* (pp. 73–86). Hillsdale, NJ: Erlbaum.

Tobias, S. (1977b). Anxiety-treatment interactions: A review of research. In J. E. Sieber, H. F. O'Neil Jr., & S. Tobias (Eds.), *Anxiety, learning and instruction* (pp. 86–117). Hillsdale, NJ: Erlbaum.

Tobias, S. (1977c). A model for research on the effect of anxiety on instruction. In J. E. Sieber, H. F. O'Neil Jr., & S. Tobias (Eds.), *Anxiety, learning and instruction* (pp. 223–240). Hillsdale, NJ: Erlbaum.

Tobias, S. (1978). Who's afraid of math, and why? *Atlantic Monthly*, 242, 63–65.

Tobias, S. (1979). A research in educational psychology. *Journal of Educational Psychology*, 71, 573–582.

Tobias, S. (1980). Anxiety and instruction. In I. G. Sarason (Ed.), *Test Anxiety: Theory, research and application* (pp. 289–310). Hillsdale, NJ: Erlbaum.

Tobias, S. (1985). Test anxiety: Interference, defective skills and cognitive capacity. *Educational Psychologist*, 3, 135–142.

Tobias, S. (1986). Anxiety and cognitive processing of instruction. In R. Schwarzer (Ed.), *Self-related cognitions in anxiety and motivation* (pp. 35–54). Hillsdale, NJ: Erlbaum.

Tobias, S. (1992). The impact of test anxiety on cognition in school learning. In K. A. Hagtvet & B. T. Johnsen (Eds,), *Advances in test anxiety research* (Vol. 7, pp. 18–31). Lisse, The Netherlands: Swets & Zeitlinger.

Tobias, S., & Weissbrod, C. (1980). Anxiety and mathematics: An update. *Harvard Educational Review*, 50, 63–70.

Topman, R. M., Kleijn, W. C., Van der Ploeg, H. M., & Masset, E. A. (1992). Test anxiety, cognitions, study habits and academic performance: A prospective study. In K. A. Hagtvet & B. T. Johnsen (Eds,), *Advances in test anxiety research* (Vol. 7, pp. 239–259). Lisse, The Netherlands: Swets & Zeitlinger.

Tryon, G. S. (1980). The measurement and treatment of test anxiety. *Review of Educational Research*, 50, 343–372.

Vagg, P. R., & Papsdorf, J. D. (1995). Cognitive therapy, study skills training, and biofeedback in the treatment of test anxiety. In C. D. Spielberger & P. R. Vagg (Eds.), *Test anxiety: Theory, assessment, and treatment* (pp. 183–194). Washington, DC: Taylor & Francis.

Vagg, P. R., & Spielberger, C. D. (1995). Treatment of test anxiety: Application of the transactional process model. In C. D. Spielberger & P. R. Vagg (Eds.), *Test anxiety: Theory, assessment, and treatment* (pp. 195–215). Washington, DC: Taylor & Francis.

Vaillant, G. E. (1977). *Adaptation to life*. Boston: Little & Brown.

Van der Ploeg, H. M. (1982). The relationship of worry and emotionality to performance in Dutch school children. In R. Schwarzer, H. M. Van der Ploeg, & C. D. Spielberger (Eds.), *Advances in test anxiety research* (Vol. 1, pp. 55–56). Lisse, The Netherlands: Swets & Zeitlinger.

Van der Ploeg, H. M. (1983a). Test anxiety and anger: Some empirical considerations. In H. M. Van der

Ploeg, R. Schwarzer, & C. D. Spielberger (Eds.), *Advances in test anxiety research* (Vol. 2, pp. 67–80). Lisse, The Netherlands: Swets & Zeitlinger.

Van der Ploeg, H. M. (1983b). The validation of the Dutch form of the Test Anxiety Inventory. In H. M. Van der Ploeg, R. Schwarzer, & C. D. Spielberger (Eds.), *Advances in test anxiety research* (Vol. 2, pp. 191–202). Lisse, The Netherlands: Swets & Zeitlinger.

Van der Ploeg, H. M., Schwarzer, R., & Spielberger, C. D. (Eds.) (1983), *Advances in test anxiety research*, Vol. 2. Lisse, The Netherlands: Swets & Zeitlinger.

Van der Ploeg, H. M., Schwarzer, R., & Spielberger, C. D. (Eds.) (1984a), *Advances in test anxiety research*, Vol. 3. Lisse, The Netherlands: Swets & Zeitlinger.

Van der Ploeg, H. M., Schwarzer, R., & Spielberger, C. D. (Eds.) (1984b), *Advances in test anxiety research*, Vol. 4. Lisse, The Netherlands: Swets & Zeitlinger.

Volkmer, R. E., & Feather, N. T. (1991). Relation between Type A scores, internal locus of control and test anxiety. *Personality and Individual Differences*, *12*, 205–209.

Wachtel, P. L. (1967). Conceptions of broad and narrow attention. *Psychological Bulletin*, *68*, 417–429.

Ware, B. W., Galassi, J. P., & Dew, K. M. H. (1990). The Test Anxiety Inventory: A confirmatory factor analysis. *Anxiety Research*, *3*, 205–212.

Webb, E. J., Campbell, D. T., Schwartz, R. D., & Sechrest, L. (1966). *Unobtrusive measures: A survey of nonreactive research in social science*. Skokie, IL: Rand McNally.

Wechsler, D. (1944). *The measurement of adult intelligence*, 3rd ed. Baltimore, MD: Williams & Wilkins.

Weidner, G., & Collins, R. L. (1993). Gender, coping, and health. In H. W. Krohne (Ed.), *Attention and avoidance: Strategies in coping with aversiveness* (pp. 241–265). Gottingen, Germany: Hogrefe & Huber.

Weinberger, D. A., Schwartz, G. E., & Davidson, R. J. (1979). Low anxious, high anxious, and repressive coping styles: Psychometric patterns and behavioral and physiological responses to stress. *Journal of Abnormal Psychology*, *88*, 369–380.

Weiner, B. (1985). An attributional theory of achievement motivation. *Psychological Review*, *92*, 548–573.

Weiner, B., Frieze, I., Kukla A., Reed, L., Rest, S., & Rosenbaum, R. M. (Eds.). (1972). *Perceiving the causes of success and failure*. Morristown, NJ: General Learning Press.

Weiner, B., & Potepan, P. A. (1970). Personality characteristics and affective reactions towards exams of superior and failing college students. *Journal of Educational Psychology*, *61*, 144–151.

Weinstein, C. E., Cubberly, W. E., & Richardson, F. C. (1982). The effects of test anxiety on learning at superficial and deep levels of processing. *Contemporary Educational Psychology*, *7*, 107–112.

Wells, A., & Matthews, G. (1994). *Attention and emotion: A clinical perspective*. Hillsdale, NJ: Erlbaum.

Wessel, I., & Mersch, P. A. (1994). A cognitive behavioural group treatment for test anxious adolescents. *Anxiety, Stress and Coping*, *7*, 149–161.

Wheaton, B. (1983). Stress, personal coping resources, and psychiatric symptoms: An investigation of interactive models. *Journal of Health and Social Behavior*, *24*, 208–229.

Whitbourne, S. K. (1976). Test anxiety in elderly and young adults. *International Journal of Aging and Human Development*, *7*, 201–210.

Wigfield, A., & Eccles, J. S. (1989). Test anxiety in elementary and secondary school students. *Educational Psychologist*, *24*, 159–183.

Wigfield, A., & Eccles, J. S. (1990). Test anxiety in the school setting. In M. Lewis & S. M. Miller (Eds.), *Handbook of developmental psychopathology: Perspectives in developmental psychology* (pp. 237–250). New York: Plenum Press.

Willig, A. C., Harnisch, D. L., Hill, K. T., & Maehr, M. L. (1983). Sociocultural and educational correlates of success–failure attributions and evaluation anxiety in the school setting for black, Hispanic, and Anglo children. *American Educational Research Journal*, *20*, 385–410.

Wills, T. A. (1986). Stress and coping in early adolescence: Relationships to substance use in urban high schools. *Health Psychology*, *5*, 503–529.

Wine, J. D. (1971a). *An attentional approach to the treatment of test anxiety*. Unpublished manuscript. Counseling Services Report. University of Waterloo, Waterloo, Ontario, Canada.

Wine, J. D. (1971b). Test anxiety and the direction of attention. *Psychological Bulletin*, *76*, 92–104.

Wine, J. D. (1979). Test anxiety and evaluation threat: Children's behavior in the classroom. *Journal of Abnormal Child Psychology*, *7*, 45–59.

Wine, J. D. (1980). Cognitive–attentional theory of test-anxiety. In I. G. Sarason (Ed.), *Test Anxiety: Theory, research and applications* (pp. 349–385). Hillsdale, NJ: Erlbaum.

Wine, J. D. (1982). Evaluation anxiety: A cognitive–attentional construct. In H. W. Krohne & L. Laux (Eds.), *Achievement, stress and anxiety* (pp. 207–219). Washington, DC: Hemisphere.

Wise, E. H., & Haynes, S. N. (1983). Cognitive treatment of test anxiety: Rational restructuring versus attentional training. *Cognitive Therapy and Research, 7,* 69–78.

Wise, S. L., Plake, B. S., Eastman, L. A., Boettcher, L. L., & Lukin, M. E. (1986). The effects of item feedback and examinee control on test performance and anxiety in a computer-administered test. *Computers in Human Behavior, 2,* 21–29.

Wise, S. L., Plake, B. S., Johnson, P. L., & Roos, L. L. (1992). A comparison of self-adapted and computerized adaptive tests. *Journal of Educational Measurement, 29,* 329–339.

Wise, S. L., Plake, B. S., Pozehl, B. J., Barnes, L. B., & Lukin, M. E. (1989). Providing item feedback in computer-based tests: Effects of initial success and failure. *Educational and Psychological Measurement, 49,* 479–486.

Wittmaier, B. (1972). Test anxiety and study habits. *Journal of Educational Research, 65,* 852–854.

Wittmaier, B. C. (1974). Test anxiety, mood, and performance. *Journal of Personality and Social Psychology, 29,* 664–669.

Wolpe, J. (1958). *Psychotherapy by reciprocal inhibition.* Stanford, CA: Stanford University Press.

Yates, G. C. R., Hannel, G., & Lippett, R. M. (1985). Cognitive slippage, test anxiety, and responses in a group testing situation. *British Journal of Educational Psychology, 55,* 28–33.

Yerkes, R. M., & Dodson, J. D. (1908). The relation of strength of stimulus to rapidity of habit-formation. *Journal of Comparative and Neurological Psychology, 18,* 459–482.

Young, F. A., & Brown, M. (1973). Effects of test anxiety and testing conditions on intelligence test scores of elementary school boys and girls. *Psychological Reports, 32,* 643–649.

Zatz, S., & Chassin, L. (1983). Cognitions of test-anxious children. *Journal of Consulting and Clinical Psychology, 51,* 526–534.

Zatz, S., & Chassin, L. (1985). Cognitions of test-anxious children under naturalistic test-taking conditions. *Journal of Consulting and Clinical Psychology, 53,* 393–401.

Zeidner, M. (1987a). Essay versus multiple choice type classroom exams: The students' perspective. *Journal of Educational Research, 80,* 352–358.

Zeidner, M. (1987b). Sociocultural differences in test attitudes and motivations: The Israeli scene. In R. Schwarzer, H. M. Van der Ploeg, & C. D. Spielberger (Eds.), *Advances in test anxiety research* (Vol. 5, pp. 241–250). Lisse, The Netherlands: Swets & Zeitlinger.

Zeidner, M. (1990). Does test anxiety bias scholastic aptitude test performance by gender and sociocultural group? *Journal of Personality Assessment, 55,* 145–160.

Zeidner, M. (1991). Test anxiety and aptitude test performance in an actual college admission testing situation: Temporal considerations. *Personality and Individual Differences, 12,* 101–109.

Zeidner, M. (1992). Key facets of classroom grading: A comparison of teacher and student perspectives. *Contemporary Educational Psychology, 17,* 224–243.

Zeidner, M. (1993). Coping with disaster: The case of Israeli adolescents under threat of missile attack. *Journal of Youth and Adolescence, 22,* 89–108.

Zeidner, M. (1994). Personal and contextual determinants of coping and anxiety in an evaluative situation: A prospective study. *Personality and Individual Differences, 16,* 899–918.

Zeidner, M. (1995a). Adaptive coping with test situations: A review of the literature. *Educational Psychologist, 30,* 123–133.

Zeidner, M. (1995b). Coping with examination stress: Resources, strategies, and outcomes. *Anxiety, Stress and Coping, 8,* 279–298.

Zeidner, M. (1995c). Personality trait correlates of intelligence. In D. H. Saklofske & M. Zeidner (Eds.), *International handbook of personality and intelligence* (pp. 299–319). New York: Plenum Press.

Zeidner, M. (1996). How do high school and college students cope with test situations? *British Journal of Educational Psychology, 66,* 115–128.

Zeidner, M. (1997a). *Test anxiety: A transactional perspective.* Occasional Paper. Laboratory for Cross-Cultural Research in Personality and Individual Differences, University of Haifa, Haifa, Israel.

Zeidner, M. (1997b). *Social evaluation anxieties: Theory and current research.* Occasional Paper #A297.

Laboratory for Cross-Cultural Research in Personality and Individual Differences, University of Haifa, Haifa, Israel.

Zeidner, M. (in press). Cross-cultural and individual differences in test anxiety. *World Psychology.*

Zeidner, M., & Endler, N. (Eds.). (1996). *Handbook of coping: Theory, research, applications.* New York: Wiley.

Zeidner, M., & Hammer, A. (1990). Life events and coping resources as predictors of stress symptoms in adolescents. *Personality and Individual Differences, 11,* 693–703.

Zeidner, M., Klingman, A., & Papko, O. (1988). Enhancing students' test coping skills: Report of a psychological health education program. *Journal of Educational Psychology, 80,* 95–101.

Zeidner, M., Matthews, G., & Saklofske, D. H. (in press). Intelligence and mental health. In *Encyclopaedia of mental health.* New York: Academic Press.

Zeidner, M., & Most, R. (1992). An introduction to psychological testing. In M. Zeidner & R. Most (Eds.), *Psychological testing: An inside view* (pp. 2–47). Palo Alto, CA: Consulting Psychologists Press.

Zeidner, M., & Nevo, B. (1992). Test anxiety in examinees in a college admission testing situation: Incidence, dimensionality, and cognitive correlates. In K. A. Hagtvet & B. T. Johnsen (Eds,), *Advances in test anxiety research* (Vol. 7, pp. 288–303). Lisse, The Netherlands: Swets & Zeitlinger.

Zeidner, M., Nevo, B., & Lipschitz, H. (1988). *The Hebrew version of the Test Anxiety Inventory.* Haifa: University of Haifa.

Zeidner, M., & Safir, M. (1989). Sex, ethnic, and social differences in test anxiety among Israeli adolescents. *Journal of Genetic Psychology, 150,* 175–185.

Zeidner, M., & Saklofske, D. (1996). Adaptive and maladaptive coping. In M. Zeidner & N. S. Endler (Eds.), *Handbook of coping: Theory, research, applications* (pp. 505–531). New York: Wiley.

Zimmer, J., Hocevar, D., Bachelor, P., & Meinke, L. D. (1992). An analysis of the Sarason (1984) four-factor conceptualization of test anxiety. In K. A. Hagtvet & B. T. Johnsen (Eds,), *Advances in test anxiety research* (Vol. 7, pp. 103–113). Lisse, The Netherlands: Swets & Zeitlinger.

Zimmerman, B. J. (1970). The relationship between teacher class behavior and student school anxiety levels. *Psychology in the Schools., 7,* 89–93.

Zweibelson, I. (1956). Test anxiety and intelligence test performance. *Journal of Consulting Psychology, 20,* 479–481.

Index

An "*f*" or "*t*" suffix following a page number indicates that the listing may be found in a figure or table, respectively, on the page.